MAGILL BOOKS INDEX

"MAGILL BOOKS INDEX"

ALL AUTHORIZED EDITIONS
1949-1980
BY TITLE AND BY AUTHOR

Compiled by

The Salem Press Staff

SALEM PRESS
Englewood Cliffs

LIBRARY OF CONGRESS CATALOG CARD NO. 80-53597

ISBN 0-89356-200-9

First Printing

PRINTED IN THE UNITED STATES OF AMERICA

PUBLISHER'S NOTE

MAGILL BOOKS INDEX provides a single source for the retrieval of more than twenty million words of original literary criticism and commentary scattered throughout more than one hundred volumes and covering the fields of fiction, drama, poetry, nonfiction, history, biography, literary criticism, philosophy, religion, science fiction, cinema, and several other related fields.

This comprehensive data base specifies the edition, volume, and page number where Magill reference material—pertaining to more than ten thousand titles representing works of more than five thousand authors—appears. Prompt retrieval is assured if the Magill book cited is available in the library's stacks. The individual listings, incidentally, form a highly selective checklist of ten thousand important works in the Humanities, developed through consultations with hundreds of professors and scholars throughout the United States and abroad over the past thirty years.

Occasionally a given title will appear in several separate Magill volumes. For example, articles on THE DIVINE COMEDY may be found in MASTERPLOTS, MASTERPIECES OF CATHOLIC LITERATURE, and the Ancient and Medieval Series of GREAT EVENTS FROM HISTORY, providing three different approaches to this towering work: (1) literary, (2) religious, and (3) historical. Such "duplications," spelled out in MAGILL BOOKS INDEX, provide individualized approaches to a particular title, a feature that many librarians may find of value.

Another useful feature of the Index is a listing of more than two thousand individual titles covering scholarly literature dealing with the twelve hundred Events appearing in GREAT EVENTS FROM HISTORY. A reader interested in information on medieval universities, for example, will find an Event article on "The Founding of the University of Paris"; but in addition, the Index also lists THE UNIVERSITIES OF EUROPE IN THE MIDDLE AGES, and THE MEDIEVAL UNIVERSITY, two major scholarly works on the subject for which reviews appear along with the major article on the Event itself. Thus the presence of internal scholarly literature accompanying the main article is made known through the Index.

Magill reference sets applicable to this Index are listed in the Code System section in the order of their chronological publication. Whether your library has the original editions or a revised version, MAGILL BOOKS INDEX will guide you immediately to any of the ten thousand titles you seek—by title *and* by author.

Not included in this Index are the following Magill references, which are not applicable to the purposes of this work.

CYCLOPEDIA OF WORLD AUTHORS, 2v.
CYCLOPEDIA OF WORLD AUTHORS, Revised Edition, 3v.
CYCLOPEDIA OF LITERARY CHARACTERS, 2v.
MAGILL'S QUOTATIONS IN CONTEXT, First Series 2v.
MAGILL'S QUOTATIONS IN CONTEXT, Second Series 2v.
MAGILL'S BIBLIOGRAPHY OF LITERARY CRITICISM, 4v.
CONTEMPORARY LITERARY SCENE 1973, THE, 1v.
CONTEMPORARY LITERARY SCENE II, 1v.

CODE SYSTEM

MP1   MASTERPLOTS, First Series. 2 vols. Salem Press, New York. 1949. 510 digests from world literature.

MPv3   MASTERPLOTS, Volume Three. Salem Press, New York. 1952. 250 additional digests from world literature.

MPv4   MASTERPLOTS, Volume Four. Salem Press, New York. 1953. 250 additional digests from world literature.

MP2   MASTERPLOTS, Second Series. 2 vols. Salem Press, New York. 1955. Reprints of the 500 digests originally published in MASTERPLOTS, Volumes Three and Four, alphabetically collated.

MP3   MASTERPLOTS, Third Series. 2 vols. Salem Press, New York. 1960. 500 additional digests and essay-reviews from world literature.

MP4   MASTERPLOTS, Fourth Series. 2 vols. Salem Press, New York. 1968. 500 additional digests and essay-reviews from world literature.

MWL1   MASTERPIECES OF WORLD LITERATURE IN SUMMARY FORM, First Series. Harper and Brothers, New York. 1952. This one-volume edition corresponds exactly to MASTERPLOTS, First Series. This edition was also published by Hamish Hamilton, London, 1959.

MWL2   MASTERPIECES OF WORLD LITERATURE IN SUMMARY FORM, Second Series. Harper and Brothers, New York. 1955. This one-volume edition corresponds exactly to MASTERPLOTS, Second Series. This edition was also published by Hamish Hamilton, London, 1961.

MWL3   MASTERPIECES OF WORLD LITERATURE IN SUMMARY FORM, Third Series. Harper and Brothers, New York. 1960. This one-volume edition corresponds exactly to MASTERPLOTS, Third Series.

MWL4   MASTERPIECES OF WORLD LITERATURE IN SUMMARY FORM, Fourth Series. Harper & Row Publishers, New York. 1969. This one-volume edition corresponds exactly to MASTERPLOTS, Fourth Series.

MP6   MASTERPLOTS: COMBINED EDITION. 6 vols. Salem Press, New York. 1960. Reprints of the 1,510 digests and essay-reviews published in the First, Second, and Third Series of MASTERPLOTS, alphabetically collated.

MP8   MASTERPLOTS: COMPREHENSIVE EDITION. 8 vols. Salem Press, New York. 1968. Reprints of the 2,010 digests and essay-reviews originally published in the First, Second, Third, and Fourth Series of MASTERPLOTS, alphabetically collated.

MP12   MASTERPLOTS: REVISED EDITION. 12 vols. Salem Press, Englewood Cliffs. 1976. Reprints of the 2,010 digests and essay-reviews originally published in the First, Second, Third, and Fourth Series of MASTERPLOTS, alphabetically collated, plus new critical evaluations of 1,300 of the titles in MASTERPLOTS.

MPCE   1,300 CRITICAL EVALUATIONS OF SELECTED NOVELS AND PLAYS. Salem Press, Englewood Cliffs. 1976. Reprints of the 1,300 critical evaluations first published in MASTERPLOTS: REVISED EDITION.

MPAm   MASTERPLOTS: AMERICAN FICTION SERIES. Salem Press, New York. 1964. A collection of the American fiction digests originally published in the First, Second, and Third Series of MASTERPLOTS.

MPEng   MASTERPLOTS: ENGLISH FICTION SERIES. Salem Press, New York. 1964. A collection of the English fiction digests originally published in the First, Second, and Third Series of MASTERPLOTS.

MPEur   MASTERPLOTS: EUROPEAN FICTION SERIES. Salem Press, New York. 1964. A collection of the European fiction digests originally published in the First, Second, and Third Series of MASTERPLOTS.

MPDr   MASTERPLOTS: DRAMA SERIES. Salem Press, New York. 1964. A collection of the drama digests originally published in the First, Second, and Third Series of MASTERPLOTS.

MPPo   MASTERPLOTS: POETRY SERIES. Salem Press, New York. 1964. A collection of the poetry essay-reviews originally published in the First, Second, and Third Series of MASTERPLOTS.

MPNf   MASTERPLOTS: NONFICTION SERIES. Salem Press, New York. 1964. A collection of the nonfiction essay-reviews originally published in the First, Second, and Third Series of MASTERPLOTS.

A54-
A76   MASTERPLOTS ANNUAL. Salem Press, New York (A54-A71); Salem Press, Englewood Cliffs (A72-A76). Each of these volumes, published yearly between 1954 and 1976, inclusive, contains essay-reviews of 100 outstanding books published in the United States during the preceding year.

BMA   BEST MASTERPLOTS. Salem Press, New York. 1963. Reprints of 175 essay-reviews selected from the 1954-1962 MASTERPLOTS Annuals.

SCL7   SURVEY OF CONTEMPORARY LITERATURE. 7 vols. Salem Press, New York. 1971. A collection of the 1,500 essay-reviews originally published in the MASTERPLOTS Annuals between 1954 and 1969, inclusive, alphabetically collated.

SCLs   SURVEY OF CONTEMPORARY LITERATURE SUPPLEMENT. Salem Press, Englewood Cliffs. 1972. 100 additional essay-reviews of newly selected outstanding books published in the United States between 1954 and 1972, inclusive.

SCL12 SURVEY OF CONTEMPORARY LITERATURE: REVISED AND ENLARGED EDITION. Salem Press, Englewood Cliffs. 1972. A collection of the 2,300 essay-reviews originally published in SCLs and the MASTERPLOTS Annuals between 1954 and 1976, inclusive, alphabetically collated.

LA77- MAGILL'S LITERARY ANNUAL. Salem Press, Englewood Cliffs. A
LA80   two-volume set, published yearly beginning in 1977, containing essay-reviews of 200 outstanding books published in the United States during the preceding year.

Ph   MASTERPIECES OF WORLD PHILOSOPHY. 2 vols. Salem Press, New York. 1961. 200 essay-reviews of philosophical works. This two-volume set was published in a one-volume edition by Harper & Row Publishers, New York, 1961, and by Allen & Unwin Ltd., London, 1962.

RCh   MASTERPIECES OF CHRISTIAN LITERATURE. 2 vols. Salem Press, New York. 1963. 300 essay-reviews of important works of Protestant literature. This two-volume set was published in a one-volume edition by Harper & Row Publishers, New York, 1963.

RCa   MASTERPIECES OF CATHOLIC LITERATURE. 2 vols. Salem Press, New York. 1965. 300 essay-reviews of important works of Roman Catholic literature. This two volume set was published in a one-volume edition by Harper & Row Publishers, New York, 1965.

HAnc   GREAT EVENTS FROM HISTORY: ANCIENT AND MEDIEVAL SERIES. 3 vols. Salem Press, Englewood Cliffs. 1972. Summaries of 336 events from ancient and medieval history, including critical analyses of more than six hundred scholarly works dealing with the events.

HEur   GREAT EVENTS FROM HISTORY: MODERN EUROPEAN SERIES. 3 vols. Salem Press, Englewood Cliffs. 1973. Summaries of 336 events from modern European history, including critical analyses of more than six hundred scholarly works dealing with the events.

HAmer   GREAT EVENTS FROM HISTORY: AMERICAN SERIES. 3 vols. Salem Press, Englewood Cliffs. 1975. Summaries of 338 events from American history, including critical analyses of more than six hundred scholarly works dealing with the events.

HWor   GREAT EVENTS FROM HISTORY: WORLDWIDE TWENTIETH CENTURY SERIES. 3 vols. Salem Press, Englewood Cliffs. 1980. Summaries of 190 events from the twentieth century, including more than three hundred critical analyses of scholarly works dealing with the events.

SF   SURVEY OF SCIENCE FICTION LITERATURE. 5 vols. Salem Press, Englewood Cliffs. 1979. 513 essay-reviews of American and European science fiction novels and short story collections.

Cine   MAGILL'S SURVEY OF CINEMA, First Series. 4 vols. Salem Press, Englewood Cliffs. 1980. 515 essay-reviews of English-language films, with complete cross-indexes of directors, screenwriters, cinematographers, editors, and performers.

Title Index

An asterisk appearing by a title indicates that extensive bibliographical sources for the work may be found in *Magill's Bibliography of Literary Criticism*. 4 vols. Salem Press, Englewood Cliffs. 1979.

"A". *Louis Zukofsky*. LA80(I-1).
A 1-12. *Louis Zukofsky*. SCL12(I-1), SCL7(I-1), A68(1).
Aaron Burr Conspiracy, The. *Walter F. McCaleb*. HAmer(I-464).
Aaron Burr: The Years from Princeton to Vice President, 1756-1805. *Milton Lomack*. LA80(I-6).
Abadon. *Janez Mencinger*. SF(I-1).
Abba Eben: An Autobiography. *Abba Eben*. LA78(I-1).
Abbé Constantin, The. *Ludovic Halévy*. MP12(I-1), MPCE(I-1), MP8(I-1), MP6(I-1), MPEur(1), MP1(I-1), MWL1(1).
Abdication of Charles V (Event). HEur(I-153).
Abdication of Edward VIII (Event). HEur(III-1420).
Abe Lincoln in Illinois. Cine(I-1).
*Abe Lincoln in Illinois. *Robert Sherwood*. MP12(I-4), MPCE(I-2), MP8(I-4), MP6(I-3), MPDr(1), MP1(I-3), MWL1(3).
Abélard and St. Bernard: A Study in 12th Century Modernism. *A. Victor Murray*. HAnc(III-1316).
Abélard Writes *Sic et Non* (Event). HAnc(III-1313).
Abolition of Slavery in the British Colonies (Event). HEur(II-715).
Abortion: Law, Choice and Morality. *Daniel Callahan*. HWor(III-1158).
Abortion in the Seventies: Proceedings of the Western Regional Conference on Abortion. *Bonnie Andrikopoulos* and *Warren M. Hearn*, eds. HWor(III-1156).
About the House. *W. H. Auden*. SCL12(I-5), SCL7(I-5), A66(1).
Above the Battle. *Thomas C. Leonard*. LA79(I-1).
Abraham and Isaac. *Unknown*. MP12(I-8), MPCE(I-4), MP8(I-7), MP6(I-5), MPDr(4), MP3(I-1), MWL3(1).
Abraham Lincoln. *Carl Sandburg*. MP12(I-11), MP8(I-9), MP6(I-7),

Literary Supplement. HWor(I-28).

Acts of King Arthur and His Noble Knights, The. *John Steinbeck.* LA77(I-7).

*Ada or Ardor: A Family Chronicle. *Vladimir Nabokov.* SCL12(I-43), A70(1), SF(I-16).

Adam. *David Bolt.* SCL12(I-47), SCL7(I-38), A62(1).

*Adam Bede. *George Eliot.* MP12(I-29), MPCE(I-11), MP8(I-23), MP6(I-19), MPEng(5), MP1(I-8), MWL1(8).

Adam Link—Robot. *Eando Binder.* SF(I-22).

Adam Smith and the Scotland of His Day. *C. R. Fay.* HEur(I-487).

Adam Smith Publishes *The Wealth of Nations* (Event). HEur(I-485). *See also* Wealth of Nations, The.

Adam's Dream. *Julia Randall.* SCL12(I-51), A70(4).

Adams Papers, The. *Lyman H. Butterfield,* ed. SCL12(I-55), SCL7(I-42), A62(4), BMA(8).

Adam's Rib. Cine(I-6).

Address of Tatian to the Greeks. *Tatian.* RCh(I-26).

Addresses. *Abraham Lincoln.* MP12(I-32), MP8(I-25), MP6(I-21), MPNf(4), MP3(I-9), MWL3(9).

Addresses to the German Nation. *Johann Gottlieb Fichte.* HAnc(II-587).

Adlai Stevenson and the World. *John Bartlow Martin.* LA78(I-6).

Adlai Stevenson of Illinois. *John Bartlow Martin.* LA77(I-12).

*Admirable Crichton, The. *James M. Barrie.* MP12(I-35), MPCE(I-13), MP8(I-28), MP6(I-24), MPDr(8), MP1(I-10), MWL1(10).

Admiral of the Ocean Sea. *Samuel Eliot Morison.* Different analyses on this title appear in: HAnc(III-1758), HEur(I-18), HAmer(I-19).

Admission of Alaska and Hawaii into the Union (Event). HWor(II-790).

Admission of the People's Republic of China to the United Nations (Event). HWor(III-1110).

Adolf Hitler. *John Toland.* LA77(I-17).

Adolf Hitler Publishes *Mein Kampf* (Event). HWor(I-188).

*Adolphe. *Benjamin Constant.* MP12(I-39), MPCE(I-15), MP8(I-30), MP6(I-26), MPEur(4), MP3(I-12), MWL3(12).

Adoption of the Articles of Confederation (Event). HAmer(I-288).

Adoption of the Constitution (Event). HAmer(I-330).

Adoption of the Heavy Plow (Event). HAnc(II-1099).

Adoption of the Ordinance of 1785 (Event). HAmer(I-306).

Adoption of the Weimar Constitution (Event). HEur(III-1295).

Adoption of Virginia Statute of Religious Liberty (Event). HAmer(I-318).

Adornment of the Spiritual Marriage, The. *John of Ruysbroeck.* RCh(I-272).

Adrienne. *André Maurois.* SCL12(I-58), SCL7(I-45), A62(8).

Advancement of Learning, The. *Francis Bacon.* Ph(I-369).

Advances in Hellenistic Astronomy (Event). HAnc(I-398).

Advantage of Lyric: Essays on Feeling in Poetry, The. *Barbara Hardy*.
    LA78(I-11).
Advent of the Labour Government in Great Britain (Event).
    HEur(III-1517).
Adventurer, The. *Paul Zweig*. SCL12(I-63), A75(1).
*Adventures in the Skin Trade. *Dylan Thomas*. SCL12(I-66),
    SCL7(I-50), A55(4).
*Adventures of Augie March, The. *Saul Bellow*. MP12(I-43),
    MP8(I-33), MP4(I-1), MWL4(1).
Adventures of Conan Doyle, The. *Charles Higham*. LA77(I-22).
Adventures of Robin Hood, The. Cine(I-9).
Adventures of Tom Sawyer, The. Cine(I-15).
*Advice to a Prophet. *Richard Wilbur*. SCL12(I-69), SCL7(I-53),
    A62(12).
Advise and Consent. Cine(I-18).
Advise and Consent. *Allen Drury*. SCL12(I-72), SCL7(I-56), A60(3).
Advisors, The. *Herbert F. York*. LA77(I-27).
Aelita. *Alexei Tolstoi*. SF(I-28).
*Aeneid, The. *Vergil (Publius Vergilius Maro)*. MP12(I-46),
    MPCE(I-17), MP8(I-36), MP6(I-29), MPPo(3), MP1(I-11),
    MWL1(11).
Aeronauts: A History of Ballooning, 1783-1903, The. *L. T. C. Rolt*.
    HEur(I-498).
Aeschylus Writes the *Oresteia* (Event). HAnc(I-248).
*Aesop's Fables. *Aesop*. MP12(I-51), MP8(I-39), MP6(I-31),
    MPEur(7), MP3(I-15), MWL3(15).
Aesthetic. *Benedetto Croce*. MP12(I-53), MP8(I-41), MP4(I-3),
    MWL4(3). A different analysis on this title appears in: Ph(II-745).
Aeterni Patris. *Pope Leo XIII*. RCa(II-691).
A. F. of L. from the Death of Gompers to the Merger, The. *Philip Taft*.
    HAmer(III-1657).
A. F. of L. in the Time of Gompers, The. *Philip Taft*. HAmer(II-1155).
*Affair, The. *C. P. Snow*. MP12(I-56), MP8(I-44), MP4(I-6),
    MWL4(6). A different analysis on this title appears in: SCL12 (I-76),
    SCL7(I-59), A61(1), BMA(11).
Affinities. *Vernon Watkins*. SCL12(I-80), SCL7(I-62), A64(1).
Affirmative Discrimination: Ethnic Inequality and Public Policy. *Nathan
    Glazer*. Different analyses on this title appear in: HWor(II-897;
    II-970).
Affluent Society, The. *John Kenneth Galbraith*. SCL12(I-83),
    SCL7(I-65), A59(1).
AFL-CIO: Labor United. *Arthur J. Goldberg*. HWor(II-732).
Africa and the Victorians. *Ronald Robinson* and *John Gallagher* with *Alice
    Denny*. HEur(II-1051).
African Patriots: The Story of the African National Congress of South Africa,

*Age of Reason, The. *Thomas Paine.* MP12(I-70),   MP8(I-56),
    MP4(I-11),   MWL4(11).
Age of Reason Begins, The. *Will Durant* and *Ariel Durant.*
    SCL12(I-140),   SCL7(I-96),   A62(15),   BMA(14).
Age of Reconnaissance: Discovery, Exploration, and Settlement, 1450-1650,
    The History of Civilization *series. J. H. Parry.* HAmer(I-20).
Age of Reform, The. *Richard Hofstadter.* SCL12(I-144),   SCLs(1). A
    different analysis on this title appears in: HAmer(II-1228).
Age of Revolution, The. *Winston S. Churchill.* SCL12(I-149),
    SCL7(I-100),   A58(4),   BMA(18).
Age of Roosevelt, The. Vol. I. *Arthur M. Schlesinger, Jr.* SCL12(I-153),
    SCL7(I-104),   A58(7).
Age of Roosevelt, The. Vol. II. *Arthur M. Schlesinger, Jr.* SCL12(I-157),
    SCL7(I-107),   A60(7). A different analysis on this title appears in:
    HAmer(III-1619).
Age of Roosevelt, The. Vol. III. *Arthur M. Schlesinger, Jr.*
    SCL12(I-161),   SCL7(I-111),   A61(4).
Age of the Chartists. *John L. Hammond* and *Barbara Hammond.*
    HEur(II-735).
Age of Uncertainty, The. *John Kenneth Galbraith.* LA78(I-23).
Age of Voltaire, The. *Will Durant* and *Ariel Durant.* SCL12(I-165),
    SCL7(I-115),   A66(5).
*Agnes Grey. *Anne Brontë.* MP12(I-73),   MPCE(I-24),   MP8(I-59),
    MP6(I-38),   MPEng(7),   MP3(I-16),   MWL3(16).
Ah, Wilderness! Cine(I-26).
Aids to Reflection. *Samuel Taylor Coleridge.* RCh(II-663).
*Aiglon, L'. *Edmond Rostand.* MP12(VI-3222),   MPCE(II-1194),
    MP8(IV-2509),   MP6(III-1606),   MPDr(438),   MPv4(271),
    MP2(I-551),   MWL2(551).
Airships. *Barry Hannah.* LA79(I-5).
*Ajax. *Sophocles.* MP12(I-77),   MPCE(I-25),   MP8(I-62),
    MP6(I-40),   MPDr(10),   MPv3(1),   MP2(I-6),   MWL2(6).
Akenfield. *Ronald Blythe.* SCL12(I-169),   A70(7).
Aku-Aku. *Thor Heyerdahl.* SCL12(I-172),   SCL7(I-119),   A59(6).
Al filo del agua. *Agustin Yáñez.* MP12(I-81),   MP8(I-64),
    MP6(I-42),   MPAm(7),   MP3(I-19),   MWL3(19).
Alamein. *C. E. Lucas Philips.* HEur(III-1468).
Alamein, El. *General Michael Carver.* HEur(III-1468).
Alas, Babylon. *Pat Frank.* SF(I-38).
Alaska Pipeline: The Politics of Oil and Native Land Claims, The. *Mary Clay
    Berry.* HWor(II-1024).
Alaskan Oil: Alternative Routes and Markets. *Charles J. Cicchetti.*
    HWor(II-1025).
Albert Camus: A Biography. *Herbert R. Lottman.* LA80(I-15).
Albert Einstein. *Banesh Hoffman.* SCL12(I-176),   A73(7).

Albert Einstein: The Human Side, New Glimpses from His Archives. *Albert Einstein*. LA80(I-19).
Albert Gallatin. *Raymond Walters, Jr.* SCL12(I-180), SCL7(I-122), A58(10).
Albigensian Crusade, The. *Jacques Madaule*. HAnc(III-1443).
*Alcestis. *Euripides*. MP12(I-84), MPCE(I-28), MP8(I-67), MP6(I-45), MPDr(12), MP1(I-16), MWL1(16).
*Alchemist, The. *Ben Jonson*. MP12(I-88), MPCE(I-31), MP8(I-69), MP6(I-46), MPDr(14), MPv3(3), MP2(I-8), MWL2(8).
*Aleck Maury, Sportsman. *Caroline Gordon*. MP12(I-93), MPCE(I-34), MP8(I-72), MP6(I-49), MPAm(10), MP1(I-17), MWL1(17).
*Aleph and Other Stories: 1933-1969, The. *Jorge Luis Borges*. SCL12(I-183), A71(10).
Alexander Graham Bell Invents the Telephone (Event). HAmer(II-1089).
Alexander Hamilton, Vol. I: Youth to Maturity, 1755-1788. *Broadus Mitchell*. SCL12(I-187), SCL7(I-125), A58(14).
Alexander Hamilton, Vol. I: Youth to Maturity, 1755-1788 *and* Vol. II: The National Adventure, 1788-1804. *Broadus Mitchell*. HAmer(I-359).
Alexander Hamilton: A Biography. *Forrest McDonald*. LA80(I-23).
Alexander Hamilton and the Constitution. *Clinton Rossiter*. SCL12(I-191), SCL7(I-128), A65(5).
Alexander Pope. *Peter Quennell*. SCL12(I-194), A70(10).
Alexander the Great. *Sir William W. Tarn*. HAnc(I-361).
Alexander's Victory at Gaugamela (Event). HAnc(I-358).
Alexandria Quartet, The. *Lawrence Durrell*. MP12(I-96), MP8(I-75), MP4(I-14), MWL4(14).
Alexandrian Library: Glory of the Hellenic World, The. *Edward Alexander Parsons*. HAnc(II-925).
Alexis de Tocqueville's Visit to America (Event). HAmer(II-673).
Alfie. Cine(I-31).
Alfonso X of Castile, Patron of Literature and Learning. *Evelyn S. Procter*. HAnc(III-1525).
Alfred Hugenberg: The Radical Nationalist Campaign Against the Weimar Republic. *John A. Leopold*. LA78(I-28).
Alger Hiss. *John Chabot Smith*. LA77(I-38).
Algeria Wins Its Independence (Event). HEur(III-1628).
Algerian Insurrection, 1954-1962, The. *Edgar O'Ballance*. HEur(III-1630).
Algiers Motel Incident, The. *John Hersey*. SCL12(I-199), SCL7(I-131), A69(1).
Algonquin Indians Sell Manhattan Island for Twenty-Four Dollars (Event). HAmer(I-80).
Alice Adams. Cine(I-33).
*Alice Adams. *Booth Tarkington*. MP12(I-104), MPCE(I-35),

MP8(I-83), MP6(I-51), MPAm(13), MP1(I-20), MWL1(20).

*Alice's Adventures in Wonderland. *Lewis Carroll.* MP12(I-107), MPCE(I-36), MP8(I-85), MP6(I-53), MPEng(10), MP1(I-21), MWL1(21).

Alien. Cine(I-37).

All About Eve. Cine(I-40).

All Fall Down. *James Leo Herlihy.* MP12(I-112), MP8(I-88), MP4(I-21), MWL4(21), SCL12(I-203), SCL7(I-135), A61(7).

*All Fools. *George Chapman.* MP12(I-114), MPCE(I-39), MP8(I-90), MP6(I-55), MPDr(17), MP3(I-22), MWL3(22).

*All for Love. *John Dryden.* MP12(I-117), MPCE(I-40), MP8(I-92), MP6(I-57), MPDr(19), MPv3(5), MP2(I-11), MWL2(11).

All God's Dangers: The Life of Nate Shaw. *Theodore Rosengarten.* SCL12(I-206), A75(6).

*All Green Shall Perish. *Eduardo Mallea.* SCL12(I-211), SCL7(I-138), A67(8).

All Hallows Eve. *Charles Williams.* MP12(I-122), MP8(I-95), MP4(I-23), MWL4(23).

All Men Are Brothers. *Shih Nai-an.* MP12(I-125), MPCE(I-43), MP8(I-98), MP6(I-60), MPEur(12), MP3(I-24), MWL3(24).

*All My Friends Are Going to Be Strangers. *Larry McMurtry.* SCL12(I-216), A73(12).

All Over. *Edward Albee.* SCL12(I-221), A72(1).

All Quiet on the Western Front. Cine(I-43).

*All Quiet on the Western Front. *Erich Maria Remarque.* MP12(I-130), MPCE(I-45), MP8(I-102), MP6(I-63), MPEur(16), MPv4(6), MP2(I-13), MWL2(13).

*All Said and Done. *Simone de Beauvoir.* SCL12(I-225), A75(11).

All That Jazz. Cine(I-46).

*All the King's Men. *Robert Penn Warren.* MP12(I-133), MPCE(I-46), MP8(I-104), MP6(I-65), MPAm(15), MPv3(8), MP2(I-15), MWL2(15).

All the Little Live Things. *Wallace Stegner.* SCL12(I-229), SCL7(I-143), A68(11).

All the President's Men. Cine(I-51).

All the President's Men. *Carl Bernstein* and *Bob Woodward.* SCL12(I-233), A75(15).

All the Years of American Popular Music. *David Ewen.* LA78(I-30).

Allegory of Love, The. *C. S. Lewis.* MP12(I-138), MP8(I-107), MP4(I-26), MWL4(26). A different analysis on this title appears in: HAnc(III-1300).

Allied Invasion of France (Event). HEur(III-1491).

Allies of a Kind: The United States, Britain and the War Against Japan, 1941-1945. *Christopher Thorne.* LA79(I-9).

Alligator Bride, The. *Donald Hall.* SCL12(I-237), SCLs(5).

*All's Well That Ends Well. *William Shakespeare.* MP12(I-143), MPCE(I-49), MP8(I-112), MP6(I-68), MPDr(22), MPv3(10), MP2(I-18), MWL2(18).

Almanac for Moderns, An. *Donald Culross Peattie.* MP12(I-146), MP8(I-115), MP4(I-30), MWL4(30).

*Almayer's Folly. *Joseph Conrad.* MP12(I-149), MPCE(I-50), MP8(I-118), MP6(I-70), MPEng(13), MPv4(8), MP2(I-20), MWL2(20).

Alp. *William Hjortsberg.* SCL12(I-241), A70(14).

Alpha Omega. *Winfield Townley Scott.* SCL12(I-245), A72(4).

Alphabet, The. *David Diringer.* HAnc(I-82).

Alteration, The. *Kingsley Amis.* SF(I-43).

*Amadis de Gaul. *Vasco de Lobeira.* MP12(I-152), MPCE(I-51), MP8(I-121), MP6(I-72), MPEur(18), MP3(I-27), MWL3(27).

Amateurs. *Donald Barthelme.* LA78(I-37).

Amazing Universe, The. *Herbert Friedman.* HWor(II-1013).

Ambassador Prepares for War, The. *Herbert H. Rowen.* HEur(I-346).

*Ambassadors, The. *Henry James.* MP12(I-156), MPCE(I-53), MP8(I-124), MP6(I-75), MPAm(18), MPv3(12), MP2(I-22), MWL2(22).

Ambassador's Journal. *John Kenneth Galbraith.* SCL12(I-248), A70(18).

Amber to Amperes. *Ernest Greenwood.* HEur(II-562).

*Amelia. *Henry Fielding.* MP12(I-161), MPCE(I-56), MP8(I-127), MP6(I-77), MPEng(16), MP1(I-24), MWL1(24).

Amen. *Yehuda Amichai.* LA78(I-42).

America as a Civilization. *Max Lerner.* SCL12(I-252), SCL7(I-147), A58(17).

America by Design: Science, Technology, and the Rise of Corporate Capitalism. *David F. Noble.* HWor(II-614).

America in the Sixties: An Intellectual History. *Ronald Berman.* HAmer(III-1864).

America in Vietnam. *Guenter Lewy.* LA79(I-14).

America, Russia, and the Cold War, 1945-1971. *Walter La Feber.* Different analyses on this title appear in: HAmer(III-1808), HWor(II-1052).

*American, The. *Henry James.* MP12(I-166), MPCE(I-58), MP8(I-130), MP6(I-80), MPAm(21), MP1(I-27), MWL1(27).

American Art Since 1900: A Critical History. *Barbara Rose.* HAmer(III-1414).

American Buffalo. *David Mamet.* LA78(I-46).

American Caesar: Douglas MacArthur, 1880-1964. *William Manchester.* LA79(I-20).

American Catholic Crossroads. *Walter J. Ong, S. J.* RCa(II-1076).

American Catholic Dilemma. *Thomas O'Dea.* RCa(II-1066).

American Challenge, The. *Jean-Jacques Servan-Schreiber.* SCL12(I-255), SCL7(I-150), A69(5).

American College and University: A History, The. *Frederick Rudolph.*
  HAmer(I-314).
American Colonies in the Seventeenth Century, The. *Herbert L. Osgood.*
  HAmer(I-113).
American Common School: An Historic Conception, The. *Lawrence A.*
  Cremin. HAmer(I-578).
American Commonwealth, The. *James Bryce.* MP12(I-169),
  MP8(I-132),   MP4(I-32),   MWL4(32).
American Conservatism in the Age of Enterprise, 1865-1910. A Study of
  William Graham Sumner, Stephen J. Field, and Andrew
  Carnegie. *Robert G. McCloskey.* HAmer(II-1170).
American Crisis: Congress and Reconstruction, 1865-1867, An. *William R.*
  Brock. HAmer(II-1007).
American Diplomacy in the Great Depression: Hoover-Stimson Foreign
  Policy, 1929-1933. *Robert H. Ferrell.* HAmer(III-1601).
American Diplomacy, 1900-1950. *George F. Kennan.* HAmer(II-1298).
American Elegies. *Robert Hazel.* SCL12(I-259),   A70(21).
American Graffiti. Cine(I-56).
American Immigration. Chicago History of American Civilization
  series. *Maldwyn Allen Jones.* HAmer(II-1222).
American in Paris, An. Cine(I-60).
American in Vietnam. *Guenter Lewy.* HWor(III-1232).
American Intervention Short of War, 1939-1941 (Event). HAmer(III-1686).
American Labor from Defense to Reconversion. *Joel Seidman.*
  HWor(II-574).
American League Story, The. *Lee Allen.* HAmer(III-1500).
American Leonardo: A Life of Samuel F. B. Morse, The. *Carleton Mabee.*
  HAmer(II-745).
American Maritime Industries and Public Policy, 1789-1914, The. *John G.*
  Hutchins. HAmer(II-810).
American Negro Revolution from Nonviolence to Black Power,
  The. *Benjamin Muse.* HWor(II-808).
American Negro Slave Revolts. *Herbert Aptheker.* HAmer(II-688).
*American Notebooks, The. *Nathaniel Hawthorne.* MP12(I-172),
  MP8(I-135),   MP4(I-35),   MWL4(35).
American Occupation of Germany: Politics and the Military, 1945-1949,
  The. *John Gimbel.* HWor(II-650).
American Painting of the Nineteenth Century: Realism, Idealism, and the
  American Experience. *Barbara Novak.* HAmer(I-616).
American Petroleum Industry: The Age of Illumination, 1859-1899,
  The. *Harold F. Williamson* and *Arnold R. Daum.* HAmer(II-915).
American Prisons: A History of Good Intentions. *Blake McKelvey.*
  HWor(II-888).
American Railroads. *John F. Stover.* HAmer(I-628).
American Renaissance, The (Event). HAmer(II-848).

American Renaissance: Art and Expression in the Age of Emerson and
Whitman. *Francis O. Matthiessen.* HAmer (II-850).
American Republic, The. *Orestes Augustus Brownson.* RCa(II-667).
American Revolution, 1775-1783, The. *John R. Alden.* HAmer(I-259).
American Science and Invention, a Pictorial History. *Mitchell Wilson.*
HAmer(II-840).
American Secretaries of State and Their Diplomacy, Vol. XVII: John Foster
Dulles, The. *Louis L. Gerson.* HWor(II-694).
American Sexual Behavior and the Kinsey Report. *Morris Leopold Ernst* and
David Loth. HWor(II-622).
American Slavery, American Freedom: The Ordeal of Colonial
Virginia. *Edmund S. Morgan.* SCL12(I-262), A76(11).
American Tariff Controversies in the Nineteenth Century. *Edward
Stanwood.* HAmer(II-1276).
American Tory, The. *William H. Nelson.* HAmer(I-249).
*American Tragedy, An. *Theodore Dreiser.* MP12(I-175),
MPCE(I-59), MP8(I-138), MP6(I-82), MPAm(23), MP1(I-29),
MWL1(29).
American Verdict, An. *Michael J. Arlen.* SCL12(I-265), A74(1).
*American Visitor, An. *Joyce Cary.* SCL12(I-269), SCL7(I-154),
A62(19).
Americanization of Emily, The. Cine(I-64).
Americans: The Democratic Experience, The. *Daniel J. Boorstin.*
SCL12(I-272), A74(5).
Americans: The National Experience, The. *Daniel J. Boorstin.*
SCL12(I-277), SCL7(I-157), A66(8).
America's Changing Population. *Oliver Bell,* ed. HWor(II-1081).
America's Colonial Experiment: How the United States Gained, Governed,
and in Part Gave Away a Colonial Empire. *Julius W. Pratt.* Different
analyses on this title appear in: HAmer(II-1294; II-1321).
America's Coming-of-Age. *Van Wyck Brooks.* MP12(I-179),
MP8(I-140), MP4(I-38), MWL4(38).
America's Frontier Heritage. *Ray Allen Billington.* HAmer(II-1216).
America's Retreat from Victory: The Story of George Catlett
Marshall. *Joseph R. McCarthy.* HAmer(III-1767).
America's Western Frontiers. *John A. Hawgood.* SCL12(I-281),
SCLs(9).
Among the Dangs. *George P. Elliott.* SCL12(I-284), SCL7(I-161),
A62(22).
*Amores. *Ovid (Publius Ovidius Naso).* MP12(I-183), MP8(I-144),
MP4(I-41), MWL4(41).
*Amorosa Fiammetta, L'. *Giovanni Boccaccio.* MP12(VI-3240),
MPCE(II-1198), MP8(IV-2525), MP6(III-1611), MPEur(424),
MP3(I-550), MWL3(550).
Amos Studies. *Julian Morgenstern.* HAnc(I-127).

Amphibious Campaign for West Florida and Louisiana, 1814-1815: A Critical
   Review of Strategy and Tactics at New Orleans, The. *Wilburt S.
   Brown.* HAmer(I-536).
*Amphitryon. *Plautus (Titus Maccius Plautus).* MP12(I-185),
   MPCE(I-62), MP8(I-146), MP6(I-84), MPDr(25), MPv3(15),
   MP2(I-24), MWL2(24).
*Amphitryon 38. *Jean Giraudoux.* MP12(I-189), MP8(I-149),
   MP6(I-86), MPDr(28), MP3(I-30), MWL3(30).
Amrita. *R. Prawer Jhabvala.* SCL12(I-287), SCL7(I-164), A57(4).
Amulet. *Carl Rakosi.* SCL12(I-290), SCL7(I-167), A69(8).
*Anabasis. *St.-John Perse.* MP12(I-192), MP8(I-152), MP6(I-88),
   MPPo(6), MP3(I-32), MWL3(32).
Anabasis, The. *Xenophon.* MP12(I-196), MP8(I-156), MP6(I-92),
   MPNf(7), MP3(I-36), MWL3(36).
Analects of Confucius, The (Lun Yü). *Confucius.* Ph(I-5).
Analogue Men. *Damon Knight.* SF(I-48).
Analogy of Religion, The. *Joseph Butler.* RCh(II-573).
Analysis of Knowledge and Valuation, An. *Clarence Irving Lewis.*
   Ph(II-1096).
Analysis of the Sensations, The. *Ernst Mach.* Ph(II-691).
Anarchists' Convention, The. *John Sayles.* LA80(I-28).
Anatomy of a Murder. *Robert Traver.* SCL12(I-293), SCL7(I-170),
   A59(9).
Anatomy of British Sea Power: A History of British Naval Policy in the
   Pre-Dreadnought Era, 1880-1905, The. *Arthur J. Marder.*
   HEur(II-1059).
Anatomy of Melancholy, The. *Robert Burton.* MP12(I-200),
   MP8(I-160), MP6(I-95), MPNf(11), MP3(I-39), MWL3(39).
Anaxagoras: Fragments. *Anaxagoras of Clazomenae.* Ph(I-22).
Anaximander: Fragments. *Anaximander of Miletus.* Ph(I-1).
Ancient Egyptian Religion: An Interpretation. *H. Frankfort.* HAnc(I-54).
Ancient Egyptians: A Sourcebook of Their Writings, The. *Adolf Erman.*
   HAnc(I-36).
Ancient Italy. *Ettore Pais.* HAnc(I-255).
Ancient Mesopotamia: Portrait of a Dead Civilization. *A. Leo Oppenheim.*
   HAnc(I-43).
And Chaos Died. *Joanna Russ.* SF(I-53).
—And I Worked at the Writer's Trade: Chapters of Literary History,
   1918-1978. *Malcolm Cowley.* LA79(I-24).
And Never Said a Word. *Heinrich Böll.* LA79(I-29).
And Other Stories. *John O'Hara.* SCL12(I-296), SCL7(I-173),
   A69(10).
*And Quiet Flows the Don. *Mikhail Sholokhov.* MP12(I-202),
   MPCE(I-64), MP8(I-162), MP6(I-97), MPEur(21), MP1(I-30),
   MWL1(30).

And Then There Were None. Cine(I-68).

Andersen's Fairy Tales (Selections). *Hans Christian Andersen.* MP12(I-205), MPCE(I-65), MP8(I-164), MP6(I-98), MPEur(23), MPv4(11), MP2(I-27), MWL2(27).

*Andersonville. *MacKinlay Kantor.* SCL12(I-300), SCL7(I-177), A55(7).

André Malraux. *Jean Lacouture.* LA77(I-43).

"Andrea Barbarigo Merchant of Venice 1418-1449" *in* Johns Hopkins University Studies in Historical and Political Science. *Frederic C. Lane.* HAnc(III-1355).

Andreas Vesalius of Brussels, 1514-1564. *C. D. O'Malley.* HEur(I-134).

Andrew Jackson: The Border Captain. *Marquis James.* HAmer(I-561).

Andrew Jackson and the Course of American Empire, 1767-1821. *Robert V. Remini.* LA78(I-50).

Andrew Jackson's Battle with the Second Bank of the United States (Event). HAmer(II-696).

Andrew Johnson and Reconstruction. *Eric L. McKitrick.* Different analyses on this title appear in: HAmer(II-1029; II-1052).

Andria. *Terence (Publius Terentius Afer).* MP12(I-212), MPCE(I-68), MP8(I-169), MP6(I-102), MPDr(31), MPv3(17), MP2(I-31), MWL2(31).

*Andromache. *Euripides.* MP12(I-216), MPCE(I-71), MP8(I-171), MP6(I-105), MPDr(33), MP3(I-40), MWL3(40).

*Andromache. *Jean Baptiste Racine.* MP12(I-219), MPCE(I-73), MP8(I-173), MP6(I-106), MPDr(35), MPv3(19), MP2(I-33), MWL2(33).

Andromeda. *Ivan Yefremov.* SF(I-58).

Andromeda Strain, The. *Michael Crichton.* SCL12(I-304), A70(24). A different analysis on this title appears in: SF(I-63).

*Anecdotes of Destiny. *Isak Dinesen.* SCL12(I-308), SCL7(I-181), A59(11).

Angel and the Serpent: The Story of New Harmony. *William E. Wilson.* HAmer(I-514).

*Ángel Guerra. *Benito Pérez Galdós.* MP12(I-223), MPCE(I-76), MP8(I-175), MP6(I-108), MPEur(28), MP3(I-42), MWL3(42).

Angel of the Revolution, The. *George Griffith.* SF(I-67).

Angels with Dirty Faces. Cine(I-72).

Angle of Ascent. *Robert Hayden.* LA77(I-48).

*Angle of Repose. *Wallace Stegner.* SCL12(I-311), A72(7).

Anglo-American Union: Joseph Galloway's Plans to Preserve the British Empire, 1774-1788. *Julian P. Boyd.* HAmer(I-248).

*Anglo-Saxon Attitudes. *Angus Wilson.* SCL12(I-314), SCL7(I-184), A57(7).

Anglo-Saxon England. *F. M. Stenton.* HAnc(III-1250).

Aniara. *Harry E. Martinson.* SF(I-72).

Animal Crackers.   Cine(I-75).

Animals in That Country, The.   *Margaret Atwood.*   SCL12(I-318),
     A70(28).

Anna and the King of Siam.   Cine(I-78).

*Anna Christie.   *Eugene O'Neill.*   MP12(I-226),   MPCE(I-78),
     MP8(I-177),   MP6(I-110),   MPDr(37),   MPv3(21),   MP2(I-35),
     MWL2(35).

Anna Karenina.   Cine(I-82).

*Anna Karénina.   *Count Leo Tolstoy.*   MP12(I-229),   MPCE(I-79),
     MP8(I-179),   MP6(I-112),   MPEur(30),   MP1(I-32),   MWL1(32).

*Anna of the Five Towns.   *Arnold Bennett.*   MP12(I-233),   MPCE(I-82),
     MP8(I-181),   MP6(I-114),   MPEng(19),   MPv4(15),   MP2(I-37),
     MWL2(37).

Annals of Tacitus, The.   *Tacitus (Cornelius Tacitus).*   MP12(I-236),
     MP8(I-184),   MP6(I-116),   MPNf(13),   MP3(I-44),   MWL3(44).

Annals of the Parish.   *John Galt.*   MP12(I-240),   MPCE(I-83),
     MP8(I-188),   MP6(I-120),   MPEng(22),   MPv4(17),   MP2(I-39),
     MWL2(39).

Annals of the Roman People.   *Livy (Titus Livius).*   MP12(I-243),
     MP8(I-191),   MP6(I-122),   MPNf(17),   MP3(I-47),   MWL3(47).

Anne Sexton: A Self-Portrait in Letters.   *Anne Sexton.*   LA78(I-54).

Annexation of Bosnia, 1908-1909, The.   *Bernadotte E. Schmitt.*
     HEur(III-1204).

Annexation of Russian America to the United States, The.   *Victor J.*
     Farrar.   HAmer(II-1039).

Annie Hall.   Cine(I-86).

Anniversaries: From the Life of Gesine Cresspahl.   *Uwe Johnson.*
     SCL12(I-321),   A76(14).

Anonymous Sins and Other Poems.   *Joyce Carol Oates.*   SCL12(I-325),
     A70(31).

Another I, Another You.   *Richard Schickel.*   LA79(I-34).

"Another Interpretation of *Enneads,*" *in* Modern Schoolman.   *Leo*
     Sweeney.   HAnc(II-825).

Another World, 1897-1917.   *Anthony Eden.*   LA78(I-59).

Anpao: An American Indian Odyssey.   *Jamake Highwater.*   LA78(I-63).

Anschluss, The (Event).   HEur(III-1425).

Anschluss: The Rape of Austria.   *Gordon Brook-Shepherd.*   HEur(III-1426).

Anselm Writes the *Cur Deus Homo* (Event).   HAnc(III-1291). *See also* Cur
     Deus homo.

*Answer from Limbo, An.   *Brian Moore.*   SCL12(I-328),   SCL7(I-188),
     A63(7).

Antarctic Treaty, The. Hearings Before the Committee on Foreign
     Relations.   HWor(II-803).

Anthony Adverse.   *Hervey Allen.*   MP12(I-246),   MPCE(I-84),
     MP8(I-194),   MP6(I-125),   MPAm(25),   MP1(I-34),   MWL1(34).

Anthracite Coal Strike (Event). HAmer(II-1329).

Anthracite Coal Strike of 1902, The. *Robert J. Cornell.* HAmer(II-1331).

"Anthracite Strike of 1902: A Record of Confusion, The" *in* Mississippi Valley Historical Review. *Robert H. Wiebe.* HAmer(II-1332).

Anti-Corn Law League, 1838-1846, The. *Norman McCord.* HEur(II-767).

*Antigone. *Sophocles.* MP12(I-250), MPCE(I-86), MP8(I-197), MP6(I-127), MPDr(39), MP1(I-37), MWL1(37).

Anti-Intellectualism in American Life. *Richard Hofstadter.* SCL12(I-330), SCLs(11). A different analysis on this title appears in: HAmer(II-1304).

Anti-Memoirs. *André Malraux.* SCL12(I-333), SCL7(I-190), A69(14).

Antiquary, The. *Sir Walter Scott.* MP12(I-254), MPCE(I-89), MP8(I-199), MP6(I-128), MPEng(25), MPv3(23), MP2(I-41), MWL2(41).

Anti-Slavery Movement in England: A Study in English Humanitarianism, The. *Frank J. Klingberg.* HEur(II-718).

Antitotalitarian Literature of the 1930's and Early 1940's (Event). HWor(I-241).

Antiworlds. *Andrei Voznesensky.* SCL12(I-337), SCL7(I-194), A67(12).

Antonin Artaud. *Antonin Artaud.* LA77(I-52).

Antonin Artaud. *Martin Esslin.* LA78(I-68).

*Antony and Cleopatra. *William Shakespeare.* MP12(I-258), MPCE(I-91), MP8(I-202), MP6(I-131), MPDr(41), MPv3(25), MP2(I-43), MWL2(43).

Anxiety and the Christian. *Hans Urs von Balthasar.* RCa(II-969).

Anxiety of Influence, The. *Harold Bloom.* SCL12(I-342), A74(10).

Apartment, The. Cine(I-90).

Ape and Essence. *Aldous Huxley.* SF(I-78).

Apes, Angels, and Victorians. *William Irvine.* SCL12(I-346), SCL7(I-199), A55(11), BMA(22).

Apocalypse Now. Cine(I-94).

Apollo 11 Lands on the Moon (Event). HAmer(III-1940).

Apollo's Revelations at Delphi (Event). HAnc(I-120).

Apologia pro Vita Sua. *John Henry Cardinal Newman.* MP12(I-263), MP8(I-205), MP6(I-133), MPNf(20), MP3(I-49), MWL3(49). Different analyses on this title appear in: RCh(II-743), RCa(II-661).

Apology. *Plato.* Ph(I-42).

Apology for Raimond Sebond. *Michel Eyquem de Montaigne.* Ph(I-359).

*Apology for the Life of Colley Cibber, Comedian, An. *Colley Cibber.* MP12(I-266), MP8(I-208), MP6(I-135), MPNf(23), MP3(I-52), MWL3(52).

Apology for the True Christian Divinity, An. *Robert Barclay.* RCh(I-526).

Apology of Aristides, The. *Aristides.* Different analyses on this title appear in: RCh(I-9), RCa(I-10).

Apology of Athenagoras, The. *Athenagoras.* RCh(I-29).

Apology of Origen in Reply to Celsus, The. *John Patrick*. HAnc(II-733).

Apology of Tertullian, The. *Tertullian*. Different analyses on this title
    appear in: RCh(I-39), RCa(I-41).

Apostle, The. *Sholem Asch*. MP12(I-269), MPCE(I-94), MP8(I-211),
    MP6(I-138), MPAm(28), MP1(I-38), MWL1(38).

Apostolic Preaching and Its Developments, The. *Charles Harold Dodd*.
    HAnc(II-609).

Apostolic Succession in the First Two Centuries of the Church, The. *Arnold
    Ehrhardt*. HAnc(II-744).

Apostolic Tradition, The. *Saint Hippolytus*. RCh(I-54).

Appearance and Reality. *Francis Herbert Bradley*. Ph(II-706).

Appearance of the "False Dimitry" (Event). HEur(I-231).

Appearance of the Gilgamesh Epic (Event). HAnc(I-40). *See also* Epic of
    Gilgamesh, The.

Appearance of the Intertestamental Jewish Apocrypha (Event).
    HAnc(I-443).

Appearance of the Knickerbocker School (Event). HAmer(I-481).

Appearance of the Sibylline Books (Event). HAnc(I-200).

Appearance of the Waldensians (Event). HAnc(III-1381).

Appearance of the *Zohar* (Event). HAnc(III-1559).

Appearance of Zoroastrian Ditheism (Event). HAnc(I-163).

Apple of the Eye, The. *Glenway Wescott*. MP12(I-273), MPCE(I-96),
    MP8(I-214), MP6(I-140), MPAm(31), MP1(I-40), MWL1(40).

*Appointment in Samarra. *John O'Hara*. MP12(I-276), MPCE(I-97),
    MP8(I-216), MP6(I-142), MPAm(33), MPv3(27), MP2(I-46),
    MWL2(46).

Apprenticeship of Duddy Kravitz, The. Cine(I-98).

Arab Oil Embargo and the Energy Crisis (Event). HWor(III-1137).

Arabesque and Honeycomb. *Sacheverell Sitwell*. SCL12(I-349),
    SCL7(I-202), A59(14).

Arabian Nights' Entertainments, The (Selections). *Unknown*.
    MP12(I-281), MPCE(I-100), MP8(I-219), MP6(I-144),
    MPEur(32), MPv4(19), MP2(I-48), MWL2(48).

Arabian Sands. *Wilfred Thesiger*. SCL12(I-352), SCL7(I-205),
    A60(10).

"Arabic Historiography as Related to the Health Professions in Medieval
    Islam," *in* Medical History. *Sami K. Hamarneh*. HAnc(III-1228).

Arab-Israeli War (Event). HEur(III-1654).

Arabs, Israelis, and Kissinger, The. *Edward R. F. Sheehan*. LA77(I-57).

Arbitration, The. *Menander*. MP12(I-288), MPCE(I-103),
    MP8(I-224), MP6(I-149), MPDr(44), MP3(I-54), MWL3(54).

*Arcadia. *Sir Philip Sidney*. MP12(I-293), MPCE(I-106),
    MP8(I-227), MP6(I-151), MPEng(28), MP3(I-56), MWL3(56).

Archaeologist of Morning. *Charles Olson*. SCL12(I-355), A72(9).

Archimedes. *Sir Thomas L. Heath*. HAnc(I-424).

Architecture of America: A Social and Cultural History, The. *John Burchard* and *Albert Bush-Brown*. HAmer(II-1233).

*Areopagitica. *John Milton*. MP12(I-299), MP8(I-230), MP4(I-42), MWL4(42).

Argenis. *John Barclay*. MP12(I-302), MPCE(I-110), MP8(I-233), MP6(I-154), MPEng(31), MP3(I-59), MWL3(59).

*Ariel. *Sylvia Plath*. SCL12(I-358), SCL7(I-208), A67(17).

Aristarchus of Samos: The Ancient Copernicus. *Sir Thomas L. Heath*. HAnc(I-399).

"Aristocracy: Conflict and Transformation, The," *in* Paideia. *Werner W. Jaeger*. HAnc(I-116).

Aristocrat, The. *Conrad Richter*. SCL12(I-363), SCL7(I-213), A69(18).

Aristotle. *John Herman Randall*. HAnc(I-365).

Aristotle, Fundamentals of the History of His Development. *Werner W. Jaeger*. HAnc(I-330).

Aristotle Writes the *Politics* (Event). HAnc(I-343). *See also* Politics.

Aristotle's Ethical Theory. *W. F. R. Hardie*. HAnc(I-331).

Aristotle's Isolation of Science as a Discipline (Event). HAnc(I-363).

Aristotle's Syllogistic. *Lynn C. Rose*. HAnc(I-350).

Armada, The. *Garrett Mattingly*. SCL12(I-367), SCL7(I-217), A60(13), BMA(25). A different analysis on this title appears in: HEur(I-195).

Armada Guns: A Comparative Study of English and Spanish Armaments. *Michael Lewis*. HEur(I-196).

Armageddon in the Middle East. *Dana Adams Schmidt*. SCL12(I-371), A75(19).

Armageddon 2419 A.D. *Philip Francis Nowlan*. SF(I-84).

Arme Heinrich, Der. *Hartmann von Aue*. MP12(I-307), MPCE(I-111), MP8(I-237), MP6(I-158), MPPo(10), MP3(I-63), MWL3(63).

*Armies of the Night, The. *Norman Mailer*. SCL12(I-374), SCL7(I-220), A69(21).

Armory Show, The (Event). HAmer(III-1411).

Arms and Men. *Walter Millis*. SCL12(I-380), SCL7(I-225), A57(10).

Army Air Forces in World War II, Vol. V: The Pacific: Matterhorn to Nagasaki, June 1944 to August 1945, The. *Wesley Frank Croven* and *James Lea Cate*, eds. HWor(I-489).

Arne. *Björnstjerne Björnson*. MP12(I-310), MPCE(I-112), MP8(I-239), MP6(I-160), MPEur(37), MP1(I-42), MWL1(42).

Arnold Bennett: A Biography. *Margaret Drabble*. SCL12(I-385), A75(22).

Arnold Toynbee Publishes *A Study of History* (Event). HWor(I-329). *See also* Study of History, A.

Around the World in 80 Days. Cine(I-101).

Arrest Sitting Bull. *Douglas C. Jones*. LA78(I-72).

Arrival of the First Negroes and the Origins of Slavery in British North

*Ash Wednesday. *T. S. Eliot.* MP12(I-339), MP8(I-259),
MP6(I-175), MPPo(12), MP3(I-72), MWL3(72).
Ashes. *Stefan Zeromski.* MP12(I-341), MPCE(I-126), MP8(I-261),
MP6(I-177), MPEur(45), MPv4(24), MP2(I-54), MWL2(54).
Ashes: Poems New & Old. *Philip Levine.* LA80(I-35).
Ask at the Unicorn. *Norman Thomas.* SCL12(I-407), SCL7(I-232),
A64(10).
Asquith. *Roy Jenkins.* SCL12(I-410), SCL7(I-235), A66(12).
Assassination of John F. Kennedy: The Reasons Why, The. *Alfred H.
Newman.* HAmer(III-1903).
Assassination of Lincoln and the End of the Civil War (Event).
HAmer(II-1014).
Assassination of President Kennedy (Event). HAmer(III-1899).
Assassinations of Martin Luther King and Robert F. Kennedy (Event).
HAmer(III-1927).
*Assassins, The. *Joyce Carol Oates.* SCL12(I-413), A76(18).
Assault on the Unknown: The International Geophysical Year. *Walter
Sullivan.* HWor(II-766).
*Assistant, The. *Bernard Malamud.* SCL12(I-416), SCL7(I-238),
A58(19).
Astronomer and Other Stories, The. *Doris Betts.* SCL12(I-418),
SCL7(I-240), A67(22).
*At Lady Molly's. *Anthony Powell.* SCL12(I-424), SCL7(I-246),
A59(17), BMA(28).
At Midnight on the 31st of March. *Josephine Young Case.* SF(I-89).
At Play in the Fields of the Lord. *Peter Matthiessen.* SCL12(I-428),
SCL7(I-249), A66(15).
At the Crossroads. *Evan S. Connell, Jr.* SCL12(I-432), SCL7(I-253),
A66(19).
At the Earth's Core. *Edgar Rice Burroughs.* SF(I-93).
At the Mountains of Madness. *H. P. Lovecraft.* SF(I-97).
*At the Sign of the Reine Pédauque. *Anatole France.* MP12(I-345),
MPCE(I-128), MP8(I-264), MP6(I-179), MPEur(48),
MPv4(26), MP2(I-57), MWL2(57).
Atala. *François René de Chateaubriand.* MP12(I-349), MPCE(I-129),
MP8(I-267), MP6(I-182), MPEur(51), MPv4(29), MP2(I-59),
MWL2(59).
*Atalanta in Calydon. *Algernon Charles Swinburne.* MP12(I-353),
MPCE(I-131), MP8(I-270), MP6(I-184), MPPo(14), MPv3(31),
MP2(I-61), MWL2(61).
Ataturk. *Patrick Balfour Lord Kinross.* SCL12(I-434), SCL7(I-255),
A66(21).
Atheism in Pagan Antiquity. *A. B. Drachmann.* HAnc(I-381).
Atheistic Communism. *Pope Pius XI.* RCa(II-858).
Athenian Democracy. *A. H. M. Jones.* HAnc(I-208).

"Athenian Expedition to Sicily, The," *in* Vol. V *of* The Cambridge Ancient
　　History. *W. S. Ferguson.* HAnc(I-310).
Athenian Invasion of Sicily (Event). HAnc(I-308).
Athenian Tribute Lists, The. *Benjamin D. Merrit, H. T. Wade-Gery* and
　　M. F. McGregor. HAnc(I-245).
Atlantic Migration, 1607-1860: A History of the Continuing Settlement of the
　　United States, The. *Marcus L. Hansen.* HAmer(II-756).
Atomic Bomb and the End of World War II, The. *Herbert Feis.*
　　HAmer(III-1755).
Atomic Diplomacy: Hiroshima and Potsdam. *Gar Alperovitz.* Different
　　analyses on this title appear in: HEur(III-1515), HAmer(III-1756).
Atomic Energy for Military Purposes. *Henry DeWolf Smyth.* Different
　　analyses on this title appear in: HWor(I-250; I-393).
Atomic Energy in the Soviet Union. *Arnold Kramish.* HEur(III-1563).
Atomic Quest. *Arthur Holly Compton.* SCL12(I-437), SCL7(I-258),
　　A57(14).
Atomic Research (Event). HWor(I-246).
Atomists (1805-1933), The. *Sir Basil Schonland.* HWor(I-285).
Attachments. *Judith Rossner.* LA78(I-77).
Attack on Christendom. *Søren Kierkegaard.* RCh(II-728).
Attalids of Pergamon, The. *Esther V. Hansen.* HAnc(I-488).
Attempts to Contact Intelligent Beings in Space (Event). HWor(II-827).
Aubrey's Brief Lives. *Oliver Lawson Dick,* ed. SCL12(I-441),
　　SCL7(I-262), A58(22).
*Aucassin and Nicolette. *Unknown.* MP12(I-356), MPCE(I-132),
　　MP8(I-273), MP6(I-186), MPEur(54), MP1(I-48), MWL1(48).
Audubon: A Vision. *Robert Penn Warren.* SCL12(I-445), A70(39).
*August 1914. *Aleksandr I. Solzhenitsyn.* SCL12(I-450), A73(17).
Augustan Principate in Theory and Practice During the Julio-Claudian Period,
　　The. *Mason Hammond.* HAnc(I-564).
Auguste Comte and Positivism. *John Stuart Mill.* HEur(II-805).
Augustine of Hippo: A Biography. *Peter Brown.* HAnc(II-948).
Augustine Writes the *City of God* (Event). HAnc(II-940). *See also* City of
　　God, The.
Augustine Writes the *Contra Julianum* (Event). HAnc(II-946).
Augustus. *J. Buchan.* HAnc(I-549).
Augustus. *John Williams.* SCL12(I-455), A73(21).
Auntie Mame. *Patrick Dennis.* SCL12(I-460), SCL7(I-266), A55(14).
Austerlitz: The Story of a Battle. *Claude Manceron.* HEur(II-570).
Austria Annexes Bosnia and Hercegovina (Event). HEur(III-1202).
Austria, Germany, and the *Anschluss*, 1931-1938. *Jürgen Gehl.* Different
　　analyses on this title appear in: HEur(III-1399; III-1427).
Austrian *Ausgleich*, The (Event). HEur(II-939).
"Authority and Law in Mesopotamia," *in* Journal of the American Oriental
　　Society. *E. A. Speiser.* HAnc(I-49).

Autobiography, An. *Anthony Trollope.* MP12(I-359), MP8(I-275), MP4(I-46), MWL4(46).

Autobiography of a Hunted Priest, The. *John Gerard.* RCa(I-571).

Autobiography of an Ex-Coloured Man, The. *James Weldon Johnson.* SCL12(I-463), SCLs(14).

*Autobiography of Benjamin Franklin, The. *Benjamin Franklin.* MP12(I-362), MP8(I-278), MP6(I-188), MPNf(29), MP3(I-74), MWL3(74). A different analysis on this title appears in: HAmer(I-238).

Autobiography of Benjamin Robert Haydon, The. *Benjamin Robert Haydon.* MP12(I-365), MP8(I-281), MP4(I-48), MWL4(48).

Autobiography of Benvenuto Cellini, The. *Benvenuto Cellini.* MP12(I-368), MPCE(I-133), MP8(I-284), MP6(I-190), MPNf(32), MPv3(34), MP2(I-64), MWL2(64).

Autobiography of Bertrand Russell: 1872-1914, The. *Bertrand Russell.* SCL12(I-466), SCL7(I-269), A68(15).

Autobiography of Bertrand Russell: 1914-1944, The. *Bertrand Russell.* SCL12(I-471), SCL7(I-273), A69(26).

Autobiography of Bertrand Russell: 1944-1969, The. *Bertrand Russell.* SCL12(I-476), A70(45).

Autobiography of Johannes Jörgensen, The. *Johannes Jörgensen.* RCa(II-801).

Autobiography of Leigh Hunt, The. *Leigh Hunt.* MP12(I-373), MP8(I-287), MP4(I-51), MWL4(51).

Autobiography of Malcolm X, The. *Malcolm X.* SCL12(I-481), SCLs(17).

Autobiography of Mark Twain, The. *Samuel Langhorne Clemens.* SCL12(I-485), SCL7(I-278), A60(19).

*Autobiography of Miss Jane Pittman, The. *Ernest J. Gaines.* SCL12(I-489), A72(15).

Autobiography of My Mother, The. *Rosellen Brown.* LA77(I-72).

Autobiography of Saint Margaret Mary Alacoque, The. *Saint Margaret Mary.* RCa(II-615).

Autobiography of Upton Sinclair, The. *Upton Sinclair.* HAmer(III-1355).

Autobiography of Values. *Charles Augustus Lindbergh.* LA79(I-43).

Autobiography of William Butler Yeats, The. *William Butler Yeats.* MP12(I-376), MP8(I-290), MP4(I-54), MWL4(54).

Autocrat of the Breakfast Table, The. *Oliver Wendell Holmes.* MP12(I-379), MP8(I-293), MP6(I-193), MPNf(35), MP3(I-76), MWL3(76).

Autocrisi. *Piero Prosperi.* SF(I-102).

autre monde, Un. *J. J. Grandville* and *Taxile Delord.* SF(I-105).

Autumn Across America. *Edwin Way Teale.* SCL12(I-493), SCL7(I-282), A57(17).

Autumn of the Patriarch, The. *Gabriel García Márquez.* LA77(I-77).

Available Man: The Life Behind the Masks of Warren Gamaliel Harding,

Backwoods Utopias: The Sectarian and Owenite Phases of Communitarian Socialism in America, 1663-1829. *Arthur E. Bestor.* HAmer(I-515).
Bacon's Rebellion (Event). HAmer(I-151).
Bad and the Beautiful, The. Cine(I-112).
Bad Day at Black Rock. Cine(I-116).
Bad Lands, The. *Oakley Hall.* LA79(I-47).
Bad Man, A. *Stanley Elkin.* SCL12(I-521), SCL7(I-299), A68(19).
Bad Mouth: Fugitive Papers on the Dark Side. *Robert M. Adams.* LA78(I-81).
Bad Seed, The. *William March.* SCL12(I-524), SCL7(I-302), A54(10).
Baghdad Railway Concession (Event). HEur(II-1133).
Bakke Case: The Politics of Inequality, The. *Joel Dreyfuss* and *Charles Lawrence III.* LA80(I-45).
Balance of Power in the Interwar Years, 1919-1939, The. *William J. Newman.* HWor(I-200).
Baldur's Gate. *Eleanor Clark.* SCL12(I-527), A71(14).
Balkan Wars, The (Event). HEur(III-1240).
Balkans Since 1453, The. *L. S. Stavrianos.* Different analyses on this title appear in: HAnc(III-1661), HEur(I-89; I-370; I-476).
Ball of Fire. Cine(I-119).
*Ballad of Peckham Rye, The. *Muriel Spark.* SCL12(I-530), SCL7(I-305), A61(10).
*Ballad of the Sad Café, The. *Edward Albee.* SCL12(I-534), SCL7(I-309), A64(12).
*Balthazar. *Lawrence Durrell.* SCL12(I-538), SCL7(I-313), A59(20), BMA(31).
Baltimore and Ohio Railroad Begins Operations (Event). HAmer(I-624).
Bambi. *Felix Salten.* MP12(I-415), MPCE(I-143), MP8(I-324), MP6(I-208), MPEur(59), MP1(I-52), MWL1(52).
Bamboo Bed, The. *William Eastlake.* SCL12(I-542), A70(49).
Bancroft Publishes *History of the United States from the Discovery of the American Continent* (Event). HAmer(II-730). *See also* History of the United States from the Discovery of the American Continent.
*Band of Angels. *Robert Penn Warren.* SCL12(I-546), SCL7(I-317), A55(17).
Band Wagon, The. Cine(I-123).
Bank Dick, The. Cine(I-129).
Banks and Politics in America, from the Revolution to the Civil War. *Bray Hammond.* Different analyses on this title appear in: HAmer(I-568; II-699).
*Barabbas. *Pär Lagerkvist.* MP12(I-419), MPCE(I-145), MP8(I-327), MP6(I-211), MPEur(62), MP3(I-85), MWL3(85).
Barbarian West, 400-1000, The. *J. M. Wallace-Hadrill.* HAnc(II-1138).
Barbarossa; The Russian-German Conflict, 1941-1945. *Alan Clark.* HEur(III-1474).

Barbary Coast: Algiers Under the Turks, 1500-1830, The. *John B. Wolf.*
    LA80(I-49).
Barber of Seville, The. *Pierre A. Caron de Beaumarchais.* MP12(I-423),
    MPCE(I-147),   MP8(I-330),   MP6(I-213),   MPDr(58),
    MPv3(40),   MP2(I-70),   MWL2(70).
*Barchester Towers. *Anthony Trollope.* MP12(I-426),   MPCE(I-149),
    MP8(I-332),   MP6(I-215),   MPEng(35),   MP1(I-55),   MWL1(55).
Barefoot in the Head. *Brian W. Aldiss.* SF(I-125).
Bargaining for Supremacy: Anglo-American Naval Collaboration,
    1937-1941. *James R. Leutze.* LA78(I-85).
*Barnaby Rudge. *Charles Dickens.* MP12(I-431),   MPCE(I-152),
    MP8(I-335),   MP6(I-218),   MPEng(38),   MPv3(42),   MP2(I-72),
    MWL2(72).
Barnum. *M. R. Werner.* HAmer (II-1068).
Baron Münchausen's Narrative. *Rudolph Erich Raspe.* MP12(I-435),
    MPCE(I-153),   MP8(I-339),   MP6(I-221),   MPEur(65),
    MPv3(46),   MP2(I-76),   MWL2(76).
*Barren Ground. *Ellen Glasgow.* MP12(I-438),   MPCE(I-154),
    MP8(I-342),   MP6(I-223),   MPAm(44),   MP1(I-57),   MWL1(57).
Barry Lyndon. Cine(I-132).
*Barry Lyndon. *William Makepeace Thackeray.* MP12(I-443),
    MPCE(I-156),   MP8(I-345),   MP6(I-226),   MPEng(42),
    MPv3(48),   MP2(I-78),   MWL2(78).
*Bartholomew Fair. *Ben Jonson.* MP12(I-446),   MPCE(I-157),
    MP8(I-348),   MP6(I-228),   MPDr(60),   MPv4(31),   MP2(I-80),
    MWL2(80).
Baruch: The Public Years. *Bernard M. Baruch.* SCL12(I-550),
    SCL7(I-320),   A61(13).
Basic Christian Ethics. *Paul Ramsey.* RCh(II-1117).
Basic Verities. *Charles Péguy.* RCa(II-879).
"Basilius of Caesareia," *in* A Dictionary of Christian Biography. *Edmund
    Venables.* HAnc(II-895).
Bass Saxophone, The. *Josef Škvorecký.* LA80(I-54).
Batouala. *René Maran.* MP12(I-451),   MP8(I-351),   MP6(I-231),
    MPEur(68),   MP3(I-87),   MWL3(87).
Battle: The Story of the Bulge. *John Toland.* SCL12(I-553),
    SCL7(I-323),   A60(22). A different analysis on this title appears in:
    HEur(III-1498).
Battle for Alaska Statehood, The. *Ernest Gruening.* HWor(II-795).
Battle for Italy, The. *W. G. F. Jackson.* HEur(III-1488).
Battle for Leyte Gulf (Event). HAmer(III-1731).
Battle for Leyte Gulf, The. *C. Vann Woodward.* HAmer (III-1734).
Battle of Aboukir Bay (Event). HEur(I-538).
Battle of Actium (Event). HAnc(I-551).
"Battle of Actium, The," *in* The Journal of Roman Studies. *Sir William W.*

Battle of Zama (Event).   HAnc(I-437).
Battle Stalin Lost: Memoirs of Yugoslavia, 1948-1953, The.   *Vladimir Dedijer.*   HWor(II-642).
Battles of Gettysburg, Vicksburg, and Chattanooga (Event).   HAmer(II-997).
Battles of Saratoga (Event).   HAmer (I-277).
Bay of Noon, The.   *Shirley Hazzard.*   SCL12(I-562),   A71(17).
Bay of Pigs: The Leaders' Story of Brigade 2506, The.   *Haynes Johnson.*   HWor(II-929).
Bay of Pigs: The Untold Story.   *Peter Wyden.*   LA80(I-59).
Bay of Pigs Invasion Repulsed, The (Event).   HWor(II-926).
*Bay of Silence, The.   *Eduardo Mallea.*   MP12(I-454),   MP8(I-354),   MP6(I-233),   MPAm(47),   MP3(I-89), MWL3(89).
Bazaar of Heraclides, The.   *Nestorius.*   RCh(I-162).
*Beach of Falesá, The.   *Robert Louis Stevenson.*   MP12(I-456),   MPCE(I-160),   MP8(I-356),   MP6(I-235),   MPEng(45),   MP3(I-91),   MWL3(91).
Beard Publishes *An Economic Interpretation of the Constitution* (Event).   HAmer(III-1426).
Beard's Roman Women.   *Anthony Burgess.*   LA77(I-81).
Beardsley.   *Stanley Weintraub.*   SCL12(I-566),   SCL7(I-333),   A68(22).
*Beastly Beatitudes of Balthazar B, The.   *J. P. Donleavy.*   SCL12(I-573),   SCL7(I-340),   A69(30).
Beasts.   *John Crowley.*   SF(I-133).
Beasts and Men.   *Pierre Gascar.*   SCL12(I-576),   SCL7(I-343),   A57(20).
Beasts of the Southern Wild and Other Stories.   *Doris Betts.*   SCL12(I-579),   A74(17).
Beau Geste.   Cine(I-135).
*Beauchamp's Career.   *George Meredith.*   MP12(I-460),   MPCE(I-161),   MP8(I-359),   MP6(I-238),   MPEng(48),   MPv3(50),   MP2(I-83),   MWL2(83).
Beauty and Sadness.   *Yasunari Kawabata.*   SCL12(I-584),   A76(21).
Beautyful Ones Are Not Yet Born, The.   *Ayi Kwei Armah.*   SCL12(I-588),   SCL7(I-346),   A69(33).
*Beaux' Stratagem, The.   *George Farquhar.*   MP12(I-464),   MPCE(I-163),   MP8(I-362),   MP6(I-240),   MPDr(63),   MPv3(53),   MP2(I-86),   MWL2(86).
Beaver Coat, The.   *Gerhart Hauptmann.*   MP12(I-469),   MPCE(I-166),   MP8(I-365),   MP6(I-242),   MPDr(66),   MP3(I-94),   MWL3(94).
Beaverbrook.   *A. J. P. Taylor.*   SCL12(I-591),   A73(25).
Beccaria Publishes *On Crimes and Punishments* (Event).   HEur(I-456). *See also* On Crimes and Punishments.
*Bech: A Book.   *John Updike.*   SCL12(I-598),   A71(21).
Becket.   Cine(I-138).
Bedbug, The.   *Vladimir Mayakovsky.*   SF(I-138).

Bedford Forrest and His Critter Company. *Andrew Lytle.* SCL12(I-602), SCL7(I-349), A61(16).

Been in the Storm So Long: The Aftermath of Slavery. *Leon F. Litwack.* LA80(I-65).

Before Adam. *Jack London.* SF(I-144).

Before My Time. *Maureen Howard.* SCL12(I-605), A76(25).

Before My Time. *Niccoló Tucci.* SCL12(I-609), SCL7(I-352), A63(9).

Before *Silent Spring*: Pesticides and Public Health in Pre-DDT America. *James Whorton.* HWor(II-944).

Before the Dawn. *John Taine.* SF(I-149).

Before the War. *G. P. Gooch.* HEur(II-1115).

*Beggars' Bush, The. *John Fletcher* and *Philip Massinger.* MP12(I-472), MPCE(I-167), MP8(I-368), MP6(I-245), MPDr(69), MP3(I-96), MWL3(96).

*Beggar's Opera, The. *John Gay.* MP12(I-476), MPCE(I-169), MP8(I-371), MP6(I-247), MPDr(72), MP1(I-59), MWL1(59).

Beginners, The. *Dan Jacobson.* SCL12(I-612), SCL7(I-355), A67(28).

Beginning Again. *Leonard Woolf.* SCL12(I-616), SCL7(I-359), A65(8).

Beginning of Extensive Submarine Warfare (Event). HEur(III-1254).

Beginning of Modern Submarine Warfare. *Henry L. Abbot.* HAmer(I-269).

Beginning of the Chartist Movement (Event). HEur(II-741).

Beginning of the *Fronde* (Event). HEur(I-324).

Beginning of the Penny Press (Event). HAmer(II-713).

Beginning of the Rome-Constantinople Schism (Event). HAnc(III-1237).

Beginning of the Third Republic in France: A History of the National Assembly (February-September 1871), The. *Frank H. Brabant.* HEur(II-976).

Beginning with O. *Olga Broumas.* LA78(I-91).

Beginnings of Commercial Television Broadcasting (Event). HAmer(III-1674).

Beginnings of Metaphysics (Event). HAnc(I-231).

Beginnings of Organized Labor (*Commonwealth* v. *Hunt*) (Event). HAmer(II-785).

Beginnings of Renaissance Sculpture (Event). HAnc(III-1665).

Beginnings of State Universities (Event). HAmer(I-312).

Beginnings of Telephony. *Frederick L. Rhodes.* HAmer(II-1091).

Beginnings of the American Rectangular Land Survey System, 1784-1800. *William D. Pattison.* HAmer(I-310).

Beginnings of Trigonometry (Event). HAnc(II-716).

Beginnings of Unitarianism in America, The. *Conrad Wright.* HAmer(I-572).

Beguiled, The. Cine(I-141).

Begum's Fortune, The. *Jules Verne.* SF(I-153).

Behind the Screen: The History and Techniques of the Motion
    Picture. *Kenneth Macgowan.* HAmer(II-1335).
Behold the Man. *Michael Moorcock.* SF(I-157).
Being and Having. *Gabriel Marcel.* RCh(II-1003).
Being and Nothingness. *Jean-Paul Sartre.* Ph(II-1079).
Being and Time. *Martin Heidegger.* Ph(II-886).
Being There. Cine(I-145).
*Being There. *Jerzy Kosinski.* SCL12(I-619), A72(21).
Being with Children. *Phillip Lopate.* SCL12(I-624), A76(29).
*Bel-Ami. *Guy de Maupassant.* MP12(I-481), MPCE(I-172),
    MP8(I-374), MP6(I-249), MPEur(71), MP1(I-62), MWL1(62).
Belgian Revolution (Event). HEur(II-686).
Belgium and Poland in International Relations, 1830-1831. *J. A. Betley.*
    HEur(II-693).
Belief and Faith. *Josef Pieper.* RCa(II-1121).
*Bell, The. *Iris Murdoch.* MP12(I-485), MP8(I-377), MP4(I-67),
    MWL4(67), SCL12(I-628), SCL7(I-362), A59(23), BMA(35).
*Bell for Adano, A. *John Hersey.* MP12(I-488), MPCE(I-174),
    MP8(I-380), MP6(I-252), MPAm(49), MP1(I-64), MWL1(64).
*Bell Jar, The. *Sylvia Plath.* SCL12(I-632), A72(25).
Bells in Winter. *Czeslaw Milosz.* LA79(I-51).
Bend in the River, A. *V. S. Naipaul.* LA80(I-69).
Benedictine Monachism. *Dom Edward Cuthbert Butler.* HAnc(II-1032).
*Benefactor, The. *Susan Sontag.* SCL12(I-637), SCL7(I-365), A64(16).
Ben-Hur. Cine(I-149).
Ben-Hur: A Tale of the Christ. *Lewis (Lew) Wallace.* MP12(I-491),
    MPCE(I-175), MP8(I-382), MP6(I-254), MPAm(51),
    MP1(I-66), MWL1(66).
*Benito Cereno. *Herman Melville.* MP12(I-495), MPCE(I-177),
    MP8(I-385), MP6(I-256), MPAm(54), MP3(I-98), MWL3(98).
Benjamin Franklin: A Biography in His Own Words. *Benjamin Franklin.*
    SCL12(I-643), A73(32).
Benjamin Franklin: An American Man of Letters. *Bruce I. Granger.*
    HAmer(I-239).
Benjamin Franklin and American Foreign Policy. *Gerald Stourzh.*
    HAmer(I-303).
Benjamin Franklin Writes His *Autobiography* (Event). HAmer(I-236). *See
    also* Autobiography of Benjamin Franklin, The.
Benjamin Lundy and the Struggle for Negro Freedom. *Merton L. Dillon.*
    HAmer(II-721).
Benjamin minor. *Richard of St. Victor.* RCh(I-220).
Benjamin minor *and* Benjamin major. *Richard of St. Victor.* RCa(I-339).
*Beowulf. *Unknown.* MP12(I-500), MPCE(I-181), MP8(I-388),
    MP6(I-258), MPPo(17), MP1(I-68), MWL1(68).
*Bérænice. *Jean Baptiste Racine.* MP12(I-504), MPCE(I-184),

MP8(I-390), MP6(I-260), MPDr(75), MP3(I-101), MWL3(101).
Berge, Meere und Giganten. *Alfred Döblin.* SF(I-163).
Bergson Publishes *Creative Evolution* (Event). HEur(III-1183). *See also*
 Creative Evolution.
Bergsonian Philosophy and Thomism. *Jacques Maritain.* HEur(III-1185).
Berkeley Student Revolt, The (Event). HAmer(III-1912).
Berlin. *Theodor Plevier.* SCL12(I-648), SCL7(I-371), A58(33).
Berlin Airlift (Event). HEur(III-1543).
Berlin Airlift, The (Event). HAmer(III-1794).
Berlin Blockade: A Study in Cold War Politics, The. *Walter Phillips*
 Davidson. Different analyses on this title appear in: HEur(III-1546),
 HAmer(III-1798).
Berlin Conference on African Affairs (Event). HEur(II-1048).
*Berlin Stories, The. *Christopher Isherwood.* SCL12(I-651),
 SCL7(I-374), A54(13).
Bernard Berenson: The Making of a Connoisseur. *Ernest Samuels.*
 LA80(I-73).
Bernard Shaw: Collected Letters, 1874-1897. *George Bernard Shaw.*
 SCL12(I-655), SCL7(I-377), A66(27).
Bernard Shaw: Collected Letters, 1898-1910. *George Bernard Shaw.*
 SCL12(I-661), A73(37).
*Berryman's Sonnets. *John Berryman.* SCL12(I-666), SCL7(I-383),
 A68(28).
Berserker. *Fred Saberhagen.* SF(I-168).
Bertolt Brecht: Collected Plays, Volume I. *Bertolt Brecht.* SCL12(I-669),
 A72(30).
Bertrand Russell and Alfred North Whitehead Publish *Principia Mathematica*
 (Event). HWor(I-79).
Best and the Brightest, The. *David Halberstam.* SCL12(I-673), A73(42).
*Best Man, The. *Gore Vidal.* SCL12(I-679), SCL7(I-386), A61(19).
Best of C. L. Moore, The. *Catherine L. Moore.* SF(I-173).
Best of C. M. Kornbluth, The. *Cyril M. Kornbluth.* SF(I-178).
Best of Cordwainer Smith, The. *Cordwainer Smith.* SF(I-186).
Best of Henry Kuttner, The. *Henry Kuttner.* SF(I-191).
Best of Philip K. Dick, The. *Philip K. Dick.* SF(I-196).
Best of Sholom Aleichem, The. *Sholom Aleichem.* LA80(I-77).
Best Years of Our Lives, The. Cine(I-155).
*Betrothed, The. *Alessandro Manzoni.* MP12(I-507), MPCE(I-185),
 MP8(I-392), MP6(I-262), MPEur(74), MPv3(55), MP2(I-88),
 MWL2(88).
Better Half, The. *Andrew Sinclair.* HAmer(III-1515).
*Between the Acts. *Virginia Woolf.* MP12(I-512), MPCE(I-188),
 MP8(I-395), MP6(I-264), MPEng(51), MP3(I-102), MWL3(102).
Between Two Empires. *Theodore Friend.* SCL12(I-682), SCLs(28).
Between War and Peace: The Potsdam Conference. *Herbert Feis.*

HEur(III-1514).

*Bevis of Hampton. *Unknown.* MP12(I-516), MPCE(I-189),
MP8(I-398), MP6(I-267), MPPo(19), MP3(I-105), MWL3(105).

Beyond Apollo. *Barry N. Malzberg.* SF(I-202).

*Beyond Good and Evil. *Friedrich Wilhelm Nietzsche.* MP12(I-520),
MP8(I-401), MP6(I-269), MPNf(39), MP3(I-108), MWL3(108).
A different analysis on this title appears in: Ph(II-696).

*Beyond Human Power, II. *Björnstjerne Björnson.* MP12(I-523),
MPCE(I-191), MP8(I-404), MP6(I-272), MPDr(77),
MPv4(34), MP2(I-90), MWL2(90).

Beyond the Aegean. *Ilias Venezis.* SCL12(I-685), SCL7(I-389),
A57(23).

Beyond the Bedroom Wall. *Larry Woiwode.* SCL12(II-689), A76(33).

Beyond the Bridge. *Jack Matthews.* SCL12(II-693), A71(24).

Beyond the Hundredth Meridian: John Wesley Powell and the Second
Opening of the West. *Wallace Stegner.* HAmer(II-1107).

Beyond This Horizon. *Robert A. Heinlein.* SF(I-207).

Bhowani Junction. *John Masters.* SCL12(II-696), SCL7(I-393),
A54(16).

Bible in Spain, The. *George Henry Borrow.* MP12(I-528),
MP8(I-407), MP4(I-69), MWL4(69).

Bible, Religion, and the Public Schools, The. *Donald E. Boles.*
HWor(II-951).

Biblical Theology of Saint Irenaeus, The. *John Lawson.* HAnc(II-749).

Bicentennial Almanac, The. *Calvin D. Linton,* ed. HWor(III-1291).

Bicentennial Celebration, The (Event). HWor(III-1287).

Bicentennial USA: Pathways to Celebration. *Robert G. Hartje.*
HWor(III-1290).

Bid Me to Live. *H. D.* SCL12(II-699), SCL7(I-396), A61(21).

Big Ball of Wax. *Shepherd Mead.* SF(I-213).

Big Knife, The. Cine(I-159).

*Big Sky, The. *A. B. Guthrie, Jr.* MP12(I-531), MPCE(I-193),
MP8(I-410), MP6((I-275), MPAm(57), MP1(I-70), MWL1(70).

Big Sleep, The. Cine(I-162).

Big Steel and the Wilson Administration: A Study in Business Government
Relations. *Melvin I. Urofsky.* HAmer(III-1463).

Big Story: How the American Press and Television Reported and Interpreted
the Crisis of Tet 1968 in Vietnam and Washington. *Peter Braestrup.*
HWor(II-1040).

Big Time, The. *Fritz Leiber, Jr.* SF(I-218).

Big Woods. *William Faulkner.* SCL12(II-702), SCL7(I-399), A55(20).

*Biglow Papers, The. *James Russell Lowell.* MP12(I-535),
MP8(I-413), MP6(I-277), MPPo(22), MP3(I-111), MWL3(111).

Bijou. *David Madden.* SCL12(II-705), A75(28).

Bill, the Galactic Hero. *Harry Harrison.* SF(I-223).

*Billiards at Half Past Nine. *Heinrich Böll.* SCL12(II-709), SCLs(31).

Billy Budd. Cine(I-165).

*Billy Budd, Foretopman. *Herman Melville.* MP12(I-538),
MPCE(I-195), MP8(I-416), MP6(I-280), MPAm(60),
MPv4(36), MP2(I-92), MWL2(92).

Billy Liar. *Keith Waterhouse.* SCL12(II-713), SCL7(I-402), A61(24).

*Biographia Literaria. *Samuel Taylor Coleridge.* MP12(I-544),
MP8(I-419), MP4(I-72), MWL4(72).

Biography of the Constitution of the United States: Its Origin, Formation,
Adoption, Interpretation, A. *Broadus Mitchell* and *Louise P. Mitchell.*
Different analyses on this title appear in: HAmer(I-332; I-369).

Birch Interval. *Joanna Crawford.* SCL12(II-716), SCL7(I-405),
A65(11).

Birdman of Alcatraz. Cine(I-169).

*Birds, The. *Aristophanes.* MP12(I-547), MPCE(I-199),
MP8(I-422), MP6(I-282), MPDr(80), MPv3(57), MP2(I-94),
MWL2(94).

Birds, Beasts, and Relatives. *Gerald M. Durrell.* SCL12(II-719),
A70(53).

*Birds Fall Down, The. *Rebecca West.* SCL12(II-722), SCL7(I-408),
A67(31).

*Birds of America. *Mary McCarthy.* SCL12(II-726), A72(33).

Birdy. *William Wharton.* LA80(I-79).

Birth and Rebirth of Pictorial Space, The. *John White.* HAnc(III-1694).

Birth of Britain, The. *Winston S. Churchill.* SCL12(II-729),
SCL7(I-412), A57(26), BMA(38).

Birth of Islam (Event). HAnc(II-1075).

Birth of Jesus (Event). HAnc(I-567).

Birth of the Bill of Rights, 1776-1791. *Robert A. Rutland.* HAmer(I-369).

Birth of the First Human Conceived *in Vitro* (Event). HWor(III-1324).

Birth of the Oil Industry, The. *Paul H. Giddens.* HAmer(II-914).

Birthday King, The. *Gabriel Fielding.* SCL12(II-732), SCL7(I-415),
A64(22).

Bishop Fulbert and Education at the School of Chartres. *Loren C.
MacKinney.* HAnc(III-1234).

Bishop's Bonfire, The. *Sean O'Casey.* SCL12(II-735), SCL7(I-418),
A55(23).

"Bishop's Maiden, The," *in* The Myth of Christian Beginnings. *Robert L.
Wilken.* HAnc(II-842).

Bismarck. *Werner Richter.* SCL12(II-739), SCL7(I-422), A66(32).

Bismarck: The Man and the Statesman. *A. J. P. Taylor.* Different analyses
on this title appear in: HEur(II-967; II-971).

Bismarck and Modern Germany. *W. N. Medlicott.* HEur(II-920).

Bismarck and the Development of Germany. *Otto Pflanze.* HEur(II-921).

Bismarck and the German Empire. *Erich Eyck.* HEur(II-966).

Bismarck Becomes Minister-President of Prussia (Event).   HEur(II-880).
Bismarck, the Hohenzollern Candidacy, and the Origins of the Franco-German
    War of 1870.   *Lawrence D. Steefel.*   Different analyses on this title
    appear in: HEur(II-952; II-956).
Bitter Heritage: Vietnam and American Democracy, 1941-1966, The.   *Arthur
    M. Schlesinger, Jr.*   HAmer(III-1910).
Bitter Honeymoon.   *Alberto Moravia.*   SCL12(II-742),   SCL7(I-425),
    A57(29).
*Bitter Lemons.   *Lawrence Durrell.*   SCL12(II-745),   SCL7(I-428),
    A59(26).
Bitter Tea of General Yen, The.   Cine(I-172).
Black Arrow, The.   *Robert Louis Stevenson.*   MP12(I-552),
    MPCE(I-202),   MP8(I-425),   MP6(I-284),   MPEng(54),
    MP1(I-72),   MWL1(72).
Black Cloud, The.   *Fred Hoyle.*   SF(I-228).
Black Cloud, White Cloud.   *Ellen Douglas.*   SCL12(II-747),
    SCL7(I-430),   A64(25).
Black Death, The.   *George G. Coulton.*   HAnc(III-1628).
Black Death and Men of Learning, The.   *Anna M. Campbell.*
    HAnc(III-1629).
Black Easter.   *James Blish.*   SF(I-233).
Black English.   *Joey Lee Dillard.*   SCL12(II-750),   A73(48).
Black Family in Slavery and Freedom, 1750-1925, The.   *Herbert G.
    Gutman.*   LA77(I-87).
Black Flame, The.   *Stanley G. Weinbaum.*   SF(I-238).
"Black Hole" Investigations (Event).   HWor(II-835).
Black Insurgency Movements in Zimbabwe/Rhodesia (Event).
    HWor(II-981).
Black Jack: The Life and Times of John J. Pershing.   *Frank E. Vandiver.*
    LA78(I-96).
*Black Lamb and Grey Falcon.   *Rebecca West.*   MP12(I-556),
    MPCE(I-204),   MP8(I-428),   MP6(I-287),   MPNf(42),
    MP1(I-75),   MWL1(75).
Black Like Me.   *John Howard Griffin.*   SCL12(II-754),   SCLs(34).
Black Moses: The Story of Marcus Garvey and the Universal Negro
    Improvement Association.   *E. David Cronon.*   HAmer(III-1447).
Black Narcissus.   Cine(I-177).
Black Nationalist Movement in South Africa (Event).   HWor(III-1272).
Black Obelisk, The.   *Erich Maria Remarque.*   SCL12(II-758),
    SCL7(I-433),   A58(36).
Black Orchid.   *Nicholas Meyer* and *Barry Jay Kaplan.*   LA78(I-100).
Black Prince, The.   *Shirley Ann Grau.*   SCL12(II-761),   SCL7(I-436),
    A55(26).
*Black Prince, The.   *Iris Murdoch.*   SCL12(II-764),   A74(22).
Black Ships Off Japan: The Story of Commander Perry's Expedition.   *Arthur*

C. Walworth. HAmer(II-886).

Black Sox Scandal and the Rise of Spectator Sports (Event). HAmer(III-1497).

Black Sun. *Geoffrey Wolff.* LA77(I-91).

Black Swan, The. *Thomas Mann.* MP12(I-559), MP8(I-431), MP4(I-74), MWL4(74), SCL12(II-767), SCL7(I-439), A54(19).

Black Ulysses. *Jef Geeraerts.* LA79(I-55).

Black Valley. *Hugo Wast.* MP12(I-562), MPCE(I-205), MP8(I-434), MP6(I-289), MPAm(63), MP3(I-113), MWL3(113).

Blackberry Winter. *Margaret Mead.* SCL12(II-771), A73(52).

Blackmail. Cine(I-181).

Blanco. *Allen Wier.* LA80(I-83).

Blancs, Les. *Lorraine Hansberry.* SCL12(VI-4187), A73(219).

Blast of War, The. *Harold Macmillan.* SCL12(II-775), SCL7(I-442), A69(36).

Blazing Saddles. Cine(I-184).

*Bleak House. *Charles Dickens.* MP12(I-566), MPCE(I-207), MP8(I-437), MP6(I-292), MPEng(57), MP1(I-77), MWL1(77).

Bleeding Kansas (Event). HAmer(II-889).

Bless the Beasts and Children. *Glendon Swarthout.* SCL12(II-781), SCLs(37).

Bless This House. *Norah Lofts.* SCL12(II-785), SCL7(I-448), A54(22).

Blind Ambition. *John W. Dean III.* LA77(I-96).

Blind Date. *Jerzy Kosinski.* LA78(I-104).

Blithe Spirit. Cine(I-188).

*Blithedale Romance, The. *Nathaniel Hawthorne.* MP12(I-571), MPCE(I-210), MP8(I-440), MP6(I-294), MPAm(66), MPv3(59), MP2(I-97), MWL2(97).

Blockade Busters. *Ralph Barker.* LA78(I-108).

Blood, Hook & Eye. *Dara Wier.* LA78(I-112).

Blood in My Eye. *George L. Jackson.* SCL12(II-789), A73(55).

Blood Mountain. *John Engels.* LA78(I-117).

Blood Oranges, The. *John Hawkes.* SCL12(II-793), A72(36).

*Blood Wedding. *Federico García Lorca.* MP12(I-574), MPCE(I-211), MP8(I-443), MP6(I-297), MPDr(83), MPv4(38), MP2(I-99), MWL2(99).

Bloodfire. *Fred Chappell.* LA79(I-60).

*Bloodline. *Ernest J. Gaines.* SCL12(II-797), SCL7(I-452), A69(41).

Bloodshed and Three Novellas. *Cynthia Ozick.* LA77(I-101).

Bloody Mary. *Carolly Erickson.* LA79(I-64).

Bloody Sunday (Event). HEur(III-1156).

"Bloody Sunday" in Ulster (Event). HWor(III-1117).

Bloody Tenent of Persecution, The. *Roger Williams.* RCh(I-454).

Bloomsbury: A House of Lions. *Leon Edel.* LA80(I-88).

Blot in the 'Scutcheon, A. *Robert Browning.* MP12(I-578),

MPCE(I-213),   MP8(I-446),   MP6(I-299),   MPDr(86),
MPv3(62),   MP2(I-102),   MWL2(102).

Blow-Up.   Cine(I-191).

Blue Denim.   *James Leo Herlihy* and *William Noble* .   SCL12(II-802),
SCLs(41).

Blue Estuaries, The.   *Louise Bogan.*   SCL12(II-807),   SCL7(I-457),
A69(45).

Blue Garden, The.   *Barbara Howes.*   SCL12(II-810),   A73(59).

Blue Hammer, The.   *Ross Macdonald.*   LA77(I-105).

*Blue Juniata.   *Malcolm Cowley.*   SCL12(II-813),   SCL7(I-461),
A69(48).

Blue Nile, The.   *Alan Moorehead.*   SCL12(II-816),   SCL7(I-464),
A63(12).

Blue Skies, Brown Studies.   *William Sansom.*   SCL12(II-819),
SCL7(I-467),   A62(30).

Blue Wine and Other Poems.   *John Hollander.*   LA80(I-94).

Body and Soul.   Cine(I-195).

Body Rags.   *Galway Kinnell.*   SCL12(II-822),   SCL7(I-470),   A68(31).

Body Snatcher, The.   Cine(I-198).

Boer War, The (Event).   HEur(II-1128).

Boer War, The.   *Edgar Holt.*   HEur(II-1130).

Boer War, The.   *Thomas Pakenham.*   LA80(I-97).

Boethius: Some Aspects of His Times and Work.   *Helen M. Barrett.*
HAnc(II-1020).

Boethius Writes the *Consolation of Philosophy* (Event).   HAnc(II-1018).
See also Consolation of Philosophy.

Bohemians of the Latin Quarter, The.   *Henri Murger.*   MP12(I-581),
MPCE(I-214),   MP8(I-449),   MP6(I-301),   MPEur(77),
MPv4(41),   MP2(I-104),   MWL2(104).

Bolivia: The Uncompleted Revolution.   *James M. Malloy.*   HWor(I-291).

Bolsheviks: The Intellectual and Political History of the Triumph of
Communism in Russia, The.   *Adam B. Ulam.*   Different analyses on
this title appear in: HEur(II-1107; III-1276).

Bolsheviks Come to Power, The.   *Alexander Rabinowitch.*   LA77(I-109).

Bombing of Pearl Harbor (Event).   HAmer(III-1697).

Bombshell.   Cine(I-202).

Bonaparte in Egypt.   *J. Christopher Herold.*   HEur(II-539).

Bondage of the Will, The.   *Martin Luther.*   RCh(I-347).

*Bondman, The.   *Philip Massinger.*   MP12(I-585),   MPCE(I-215),
MP8(I-452),   MP6(I-304),   MPDr(89),   MP3(I-116),   MWL3(116).

*Bonds of Interest, The.   *Jacinto Benavente.*   MP12(I-589),
MPCE(I-217),   MP8(I-455),   MP6(I-307),   MPDr(92),
MPv3(64),   MP2(I-107),   MWL2(107).

Boniface VIII.   *Thomas Sherer Boase.*   HAnc(III-1594).

Bonjour Tristesse.   *François Sagan.*   SCL12(II-825),   SCL7(I-473),

A55(29).

Bonnie and Clyde. Cine(I-205).

Book of Changes, The. *R. H. W. Dillard.* SCL12(II-828), A75(32).

Book of Common Prayer, A. *Joan Didion.* LA78(I-121).

Book of Daniel, The. *E. L. Doctorow.* SCL12(II-831), A72(39).

Book of Merlyn, The Unpublished Conclusion to *The Once and Future King*, The. *T. H. White.* LA78(I-126).

Book of Proverbs. *Otloh of St. Emmeram.* RCa(I-276).

Book of Salvation, The. *Avicenna.* Ph(I-278).

Book of Sand, The. *Jorge Luis Borges.* LA78(I-131).

Book of Sentences, The. *Peter Lombard.* RCa(I-328).

Book of Songs. *Heinrich Heine.* MP12(I-593), MP8(I-458), MP6(I-309), MPPo(25), MP3(I-118), MWL3(118).

Book of the Body, The. *Frank Bidart.* LA78(I-136).

*Book of the Courtier, The. *Baldassare Castiglione.* MP12(I-596), MP8(I-461), MP4(I-77), MWL4(77).

Booker T. Washington: The Making of a Black Leader, 1856-1901. *Louis R. Harlan.* HAmer(II-1252).

Booker T. Washington Delivers His "Atlanta Compromise" Speech (Event). HAmer(II-1249).

*Books Do Furnish a Room. *Anthony Powell.* SCL12(II-837), A72(44).

Boon Island. *Kenneth Roberts.* SCL12(II-841), SCL7(I-476), A57(32).

Borgia Pope: Alexander the Sixth, The. *Orestes Ferrara.* HEur(I-28).

*Boris Godunov. *Alexander Pushkin.* MP12(I-599), MPCE(I-218), MP8(I-464), MP6(I-312), MPDr(95), MPv4(44), MP2(I-109), MWL2(109).

Born Free. *Joy Adamson.* SCL12(II-845), SCL7(I-480), A61(26).

Born on the Fourth of July. *Ron Kovic.* LA77(I-115).

Born Yesterday. Cine(I-209).

Borough: A Poem in Twenty-Four Letters, The. *George Crabbe.* MP12(I-602), MP8(I-467), MP4(I-79), MWL4(79).

*Borstal Boy. *Brendan Behan.* SCL12(II-849), SCL7(I-483), A60(25).

*Bosnian Chronicle. *Ivo Andrić.* SCL12(II-852), SCL7(I-486), A64(27).

Boston Massacre (Event). HAmer(I-231).

Boston Tea Party (Event). HAmer(I-241).

Boston Tea Party, The. *Benjamin W. Labaree.* HAmer(I-243).

*Bostonians, The. *Henry James.* MP12(I-605), MP8(I-470), MP4(I-82), MWL4(82).

Boswell. *Stanley Elkin.* SCL12(II-856), SCL7(I-490), A65(13).

Boswell: Laird of Auchinleck, 1778-1782. *James Boswell.* LA78(I-140).

Boswell: The Ominous Years. *James Boswell.* SCL12(II-870), SCL7(I-503), A64(31).

Boswell for the Defence, 1769-1774. *James Boswell.* SCL12(II-859), SCL7(I-493), A60(27), BMA(41).

Boswell in Search of a Wife, 1766-1769. *James Boswell.*   SCL12(II-862),
 SCL7(I-496),   A57(36),   BMA(44).
Boswell on the Grand Tour. *James Boswell.*   SCL12(II-866),
 SCL7(I-499),   A55(32),   BMA(47).
Boswell's London Journal: 1762-1763. *James Boswell.*   MP12(I-608),
 MP8(I-473),   MP4(I-85),   MWL4(85).
Boulanger Crisis, The (Event).   HEur(II-1053).
Bourbon Restoration, The. *Guillaume De Bertier De Sauvigny.*   Different
 analyses on this title appear in: HEur(II-599; II-684).
Bourbons of Naples, 1734-1825, The. *Harold Acton.*   HEur(II-643).
*Bourgeois Gentleman, The. *Molière (Jean Baptiste Poquelin).*
 MP12(II-611),   MPCE(I-219),   MP8(I-476),   MP6(I-314),
 MPDr(98),   MPv4(46),   MP2(I-111),   MWL2(111).
*Bouvard and Pécuchet. *Gustave Flaubert.*   MP12(II-615),
 MPCE(I-222),   MP8(I-478),   MP6(I-316),   MPEur(80),
 MP3(I-121),   MWL3(121).
Boy with Green Hair, The.   Cine(I-212).
Boys in the Band, The. *Mart Crowley.*   SCL12(II-876),   SCL7(I-509),
 A69(51).
Bracknels, The. *Forrest Reid.*   MP12(II-619),   MPCE(I-223),
 MP8(I-481),   MP6(I-319),   MPEng(60),   MPv4(48),   MP2(I-113),
 MWL2(113).
Bradford of Plymouth. *Bradford Smith.*   HAmer(I-76).
Braggart Soldier, The. *Plautus (Titus Maccius Plautus).*   MP12(II-623),
 MPCE(I-224),   MP8(I-484),   MP6(I-321),   MPDr(100),
 MP3(I-123),   MWL3(123).
Brain Wave. *Poul Anderson.*   SF(I-242).
Brains Trust, The. *Rexford Guy Tugwell.*   HAmer(III-1612).
Braintree Mission, The. *Nicholas E. Wyckoff.*   SCL12(II-880),
 SCL7(I-513),   A58(39).
*Brand. *Henrik Ibsen.*   MP12(II-627),   MPCE(I-227),   MP8(I-487),
 MP6(I-323),   MPDr(103),   MP3(I-126),   MWL3(126).
Brandeis: A Free Man's Life. *Alpheus Thomas Mason.*   HAmer(III-1371).
Brandt Wins West German Elections (Event).   HEur(III-1690).
Brautigan's. *Richard Brautigan.*   SCL12(II-883),   A70(56).
Brave African Huntress, The. *Amos Tutuola.*   SCL12(II-890),   SCLs(46).
*Brave New World. *Aldous Huxley.*   MP12(II-631),   MPCE(I-229),
 MP8(I-490),   MP6(I-325),   MPEng(63),   MP1(I-79),   MWL1(79).
 A different analysis on this title appears in: SF(I-247).
Braving the Elements. *James Merrill.*   SCL12(II-894),   A73(62).
Breach of Faith: The Fall of Richard Nixon. *Theodore H. White.*   Different
 analyses on this title appear in: HWor(III-1135; III-1202).
*Bread and Wine. *Ignazio Silone.*   MP12(II-636),   MPCE(I-233),
 MP8(I-492),   MP6(I-327),   MPEur(83),   MP1(I-81),   MWL1(81).
Bread of Those Early Years, The. *Heinrich Böll.*   LA77(I-119).

Breakfast at Tiffany's. Cine(I-215).
*Breakfast at Tiffany's. *Truman Capote.* SCL12(II-898), SCLs(49).
*Breakfast of Champions. *Kurt Vonnegut, Jr.* SCL12(II-902), A74(25).
Breaking Away. Cine(I-218).
Breaking Open. *Muriel Rukeyser.* SCL12(II-906), A74(29).
Breaking Ranks: A Political Memoir. *Norman Podhoretz.* LA80(I-101).
Break-Up of the Habsburg Empire, 1914-1918: A Study in National and Social
    Revolution, The. *Z. A. B. Zeman.* HWor(I-163).
Brethren: Inside the Supreme Court, The. *Bob Woodward* and *Scott*
    Armstrong. LA80(I-104).
Bride of Frankenstein, The. Cine(I-222).
*Bride of Lammermoor, The. *Sir Walter Scott.* MP12(II-640),
    MPCE(I-236), MP8(I-495), MP6(I-330), MPEng(65),
    MP3(I-128), MWL3(128).
Bride of the Innisfallen, The. *Eudora Welty.* SCL12(II-911),
    SCL7(I-516), A55(35).
*Brideshead Revisited. *Evelyn Waugh.* MP12(II-645), MPCE(I-238),
    MP8(I-498), MP6(I-333), MPEng(68), MP1(I-83), MWL1(83).
*Bridge, The. *Hart Crane.* MP12(II-649), MP8(I-501), MP6(I-335),
    MPPo(28), MP3(I-131), MWL3(131).
Bridge at Andau, The. *James A. Michener.* SCL12(II-914),
    SCL7(I-519), A58(42).
*Bridge of San Luis Rey, The. *Thornton Wilder.* MP12(II-651),
    MPCE(I-239), MP8(I-503), MP6(I-337), MPAm(69),
    MP1(I-86), MWL1(86).
*Bridge on the Drina, The. *Ivo Andrić.* MP12(II-656), MP8(I-506),
    MP4(I-87), MNL4(87). A different analysis on this title appears in:
    SCL12(II-917), SCL7(I-522), A60(30).
Bridge on the River Kwai, The. Cine(I-225).
Bridge Over the River Kwai, The. *Pierre Boulle.* SCL12(II-920),
    SCL7(I-525), A54(25).
Bridge Too Far, A. *Cornelius Ryan.* SCL12(II-923), A75(35).
Brief Encounter. Cine(I-230).
Brief Lives. *John Aubrey.* MP12(II-659), MP8(I-509), MP4(I-89),
    MWL4(89).
Brief Narrative of the Case and Trial of John Peter Zenger, Printer of the *New*
    York Weekly Journal, A. *James Alexander.* HAmer(I-191).
*Briefing for a Descent into Hell. *Doris Lessing.* SF(I-254).
Brigadier and the Golf Widow, The. *John Cheever.* SCL12(II-929),
    SCL7(I-528), A65(16).
Bright Victory. Cine(I-234).
*Brill Among the Ruins. *Vance Bourjaily.* SCL12(II-931), A72(48).
Bring the Jubilee. *Ward Moore.* SF(I-260).
Bringing Up Baby. Cine(I-237).
Brink: Cuban Missile Crisis, 1962, The. *David Detzer.* LA80(I-110).

Britain and France Between Two Wars. *Arnold Wolfers*. HEur(III-1361).
Britain and the European Community, 1955-1963. *Miriam Camps*. HWor(III-1149).
Britain Between the Wars, 1918-1940. *Charles Loch Mowat*. Different analyses on this title appear in: HEur(III-1318; III-1327).
Britain, Her Peoples, and the Commonwealth. *Robert B. Eckles* and *Richard W. Hale, Jr*. HEur(III-1375).
Britannia: A History of Roman Britain. *Sheppard Frere*. HAnc(II-618).
*Britannicus. *Jean Baptiste Racine*. MP12(II-662), MPCE(I-242), MP8(I-512), MP6(I-340), MPDr(106), MP3(I-133), MWL3(133).
British Battleships. *Oscar Parkes*. HEur(III-1190).
British Common People, 1746-1946, The. *G. D. H. Cole* and *Raymond Postgate*. HEur(II-739).
British Conquest of New Netherland (Event). HAmer(I-140).
British Empire Before the American Revolution, Vol. III: The Victorious Years, 1758-1760: The Great War for the Empire, The. *Lawrence H. Gipson*. HAmer(I-204).
British Empire Before the American Revolution, Vol. VI: The Years of Defeat, 1754-1757: The Great War for the Empire, The. *Lawrence H. Gipson*. HAmer(I-204).
British Evacuation from Dunkirk (Event). HEur(III-1456).
"British Foreign Policy and Colonial Questions, 1895-1904," *in* The Cambridge History of the British Empire. *F. H. Hinsley*. HEur(III-1154).
British Revolution, 1880-1939, The. *Robert Rhodes James*. LA78(I-145).
British Scientists of the Nineteenth Century. *James G. Crowther*. HEur(II-561).
British Supremacy in South Africa, 1899-1907. *G. H. L. Le May*. HEur(II-1131).
*Broad and Alien Is the World. *Ciro Alegría*. MP12(II-666), MPCE(I-244), MP8(I-515), MP6(I-342), MPAm(72), MPv4(50), MP2(I-116), MWL2(116).
Broadway Melody, The. Cine(I-243).
Broadway Melody of 1940. Cine(I-245).
Broca's Brain: Reflections on the Romance of Science. *Carl Sagan*. LA80(I-116).
Broken Arrow. Cine(I-248).
Broken Ground, The. *Wendell Berry*. SCL12(II-935), SCL7(I-530), A65(18).
Broken Jug, The. *Heinrich von Kleist*. MP12(II-671), MPCE(I-247), MP8(I-518), MP6(I-345), MPDr(109), MP3(I-135), MWL3(135).
Broken Seal: "Operation Magic" and the Secret Road to Pearl Harbor, The. *Ladislas Farago*. HAmer(III-1701).
Broken Wing: A Study in the British Exercise of Air Power, The. *David Divine*. HEur(III-1464).
*Bronze Horseman: A Petersburg Tale, The. *Alexander Pushkin*.

MP12(II-674),   MP8(I-521),   MP4(I-91),   MWL4(91).

Brooklyn Bridge: Fact and Symbol. *Alan Trachtenberg.* SCL12(II-939), SCL7(I-534),   A66(35). A different analysis on this title appears in: HAmer(II-1062).

Brooklyn Bridge Erected (Event). HAmer(II-1060).

Brother Ass. *Eduardo Barrios.* MP12(II-677),   MP8(I-524), MP4(I-94),   MWL4(94).

Brotherly Love. *Gabriel Fielding.* SCL12(II-943),   SCL7(I-538), A62(33).

Brothers, The. *Terence (Publius Terentius Afer).* MP12(II-681), MPCE(I-248),   MP8(I-528),   MP6(I-347),   MPDr(112), MP3(I-138),   MWL3(138).

*Brothers Ashkenazi, The. *Israel Joshua Singer.* MP12(II-684), MPCE(I-249),   MP8(I-531),   MP6(I-349),   MPEur(86), MPv4(53),   MP2(I-118),   MWL2(118).

*Brothers Karamazov, The. *Fyodor Mikhailovich Dostoevski.* MP12(II-688),   MPCE(I-251),   MP8(I-534),   MP6(I-351), MPEur(89),   MP1(I-88),   MWL1(88).

Brothers Mann: The Lives of Heinrich and Thomas Mann, 1871-1950 and 1875-1955, The. *Nigel Hamilton.* LA80(I-119).

Brothers Reuther, The. *Victor G. Reuther.* LA77(I-124).

Brothers' War, Biafra & Nigeria, The. *John De St. Jorre.* HWor(II-1005).

Brown Decades, The. *Lewis Mumford.* MP12(II-693),   MP8(I-537), MP4(I-97),   MWL4(97).

*Brushwood Boy, The. *Rudyard Kipling.* MP12(II-696), MPCE(I-254),   MP8(I-540),   MP6(I-354),   MPEng(71), MPv4(55),   MP2(I-120),   MWL2(120).

*Brut, The. *Layamon.* MP12(II-699),   MP8(I-542),   MP6(I-356), MPPo(30),   MP3(I-140),   MWL3(140).

Brutal Friendship, The. *Frederick W. Deakin.* SCL12(II-946), SCL7(I-541),   A64(37). A different analysis on this title appears in: HEur(III-1489).

Buck Privates. Cine(I-252).

*Buckdancer's Choice. *James Dickey.* SCL12(II-949),   SCL7(I-544), A66(38).

Bucky. *Hugh Kenner.* SCL12(II-955),   A74(34).

*Buddenbrooks. *Thomas Mann.* MP12(II-702),   MPCE(I-256), MP8(I-545),   MP6(I-359),   MPEur(92),   MP1(I-91),   MWL1(91).

Buenos Aires Affair, The. *Manuel Puig.* LA77(I-129).

Bug Jack Barron. *Norman Spinrad.* SF(I-265).

Building of Santa Sophia (Event). HAnc(II-1040).

Building of the Alaska Pipeline (Event). HWor(II-1022).

Building of the Appian Way (Event). HAnc(I-373).

Building of the Berlin Wall (Event). HEur(III-1624).

Building of the Great Pyramid (Event). HAnc(I-25).

Building of the Maginot Line (Event).   HEur(III-1359).
Building of the Parthenon (Event).   HAnc(I-276).
Building of the Roman Aqueducts (Event).   HAnc(II-626).
Building of the Slavic Alphabet (Event).   HAnc(II-1173).
Building of the Suez Canal (Event).   HEur(II-818).
Building of the Temple (Event).   HAnc(I-101).
Bulgaria During the Second World War. *Marshall Lee Miller*.
    HWor(I-447).
Bull from the Sea, The. *Mary Renault*.   SCL12(II-959),   SCL7(I-549),
    A63(14).
Bullet Park. *John Cheever*.   SCL12(II-964),   A70(63).
Bullitt.   Cine(I-255).
*Bulwark, The. *Theodore Dreiser*.   MP12(II-707),   MPCE(I-259),
    MP8(I-548),   MP6(I-362),   MPAm(75),   MP3(I-142),   MWL3(142).
Burger's Daughter. *Nadine Gordimer*.   LA80(I-123).
Buried Alive: The Biography of Janis Joplin. *Myra Friedman*.
    SCL12(II-968),   A74(39).
Buried Land, A. *Madison Jones*.   SCL12(II-973),   SCL7(I-554),
    A64(39).
Burn, Baby, Burn: The Los Angeles Race Riots, August, 1965. *Jerry Cohen
    and William S. Murphy*.   HAmer(III-1925).
Burned-Over District: The Social and Intellectual History of Enthusiastic
    Religion in Western New York, 1800-1850, The. *Whitney R. Cross*.
    Different analyses on this title appear in: HAmer(I-423; I-644).
Burning Glass, The. *S. N. Behrman*.   SCL12(II-977),   SCL7(I-558),
    A69(54).
Burning Glass, The. *Charles Morgan*.   SCL12(II-981),   SCL7(I-562),
    A54(28).
Burnt Ones, The. *Patrick White*.   SCL12(II-994),   SCL7(I-565),
    A65(22).
*Burnt-Out Case, A. *Graham Greene*.   MP12(II-711),   MP8(I-551),
    MP4(I-99),   MWL4(99),   SCL12(II-987),   SCL7(I-568),   A62(36).
*Burr: A Novel. *Gore Vidal*.   SCL12(II-991),   A74(44).
Burr Conspiracy, The. *Thomas P. Abernethy*.   HAmer(I-465).
Burr's Conspiracy (Event).   HAmer(I-461).
*Bury My Heart at Wounded Knee. *Dee Alexander Brown*.
    SCL12(II-994),   A72(52).
Bus Stop.   Cine(I-259).
*Bus Stop. *William Inge*.   SCL12(II-998),   SCLs(52).
*Bussy D'Ambois. *George Chapman*.   MP12(II-714),   MPCE(I-261),
    MP8(I-554),   MP6(I-364),   MPDr(115),   MPv4(57),   MP2(I-122),
    MWL2(122).
But Not in Shame. *John Toland*.   SCL12(II-1002),   SCL7(I-572),
    A62(39),   BMA(51).
Butch Cassidy and the Sundance Kid.   Cine(I-264).

Butterflies of the Province, The. *Honor Tracy.* SCL12(II-1007), A71(27).
By Daylight and in Dream. *John Hall Wheelock.* SCL12(II-1010), A71(29).
*By Love Possessed. *James Gould Cozzens.* SCL12(II-1014), SCL7(I-577), A58(44).
By the North Gate. *Joyce Carol Oates.* SCL12(II-1018), SCL7(I-580), A64(43).
Byron. *Leslie A. Marchand.* SCL12(II-1021), SCL7(I-583), A58(47), BMA(56).
Byzantine Missions Among the Slavs. *Francis Dvornik.* HAnc(II-1176).
Byzantium: Its Triumphs and Tragedy. *René Guérdan.* HAnc(III-1720).
Byzantium: The Imperial Centuries, A.D. 610-1071. *Romilly Jenkins.* HAnc(III-1217).
Byzantium and the Roman Primacy. *Francis Dvornik.* HAnc(III-1239).

Cab at the Door, A. *V. S. Pritchett.* SCL12(II-1025), SCL7(I-587), A69(57).
*Cabala, The. *Thornton Wilder.* MP12(II-719), MPCE(I-264), MP8(I-557), MP6(I-367), MPAm(78), MP1(I-94), MWL1(94).
Cabaret. Cine(I-267).
Cabin, The. *Vicente Blasco Ibáñez.* MP12(II-722), MPCE(I-265), MP8(I-559), MP6(I-369), MPEur(95), MPv4(59), MP2(I-125), MWL2(125).
Cabin in the Sky. Cine(I-271).
Cabin Road. *John Faulkner.* SCL12(II-1029), A70(66).
Cabot Voyages and Bristol Discovery Under Henry VII, with the Cartography of the Voyages by R. A. Skelton, The. *James A. Williamson.* HAmer(I-26).
Cabot Wright Begins. *James Purdy.* SCL12(II-1033), SCL7(I-591), A65(25).
Cadmus. *Unknown.* MP12(II-725), MPCE(I-266), MP8(I-562), MP6(I-371), MPEur(98), MP1(I-96), MWL1(96).
*Caesar and Cleopatra. *George Bernard Shaw.* MP12(II-728), MP8(I-564), MP6(I-373), MPDr(118), MP3(I-145), MWL3(145).
*Caesar or Nothing. *Pío Baroja.* MP12(II-731), MPCE(I-268), MP8(I-567), MP6(I-375), MPEur(100), MP1(I-97), MWL1(97).
Caesar's Column. *Ignatius Donnelly.* SF(I-272).
Caesar's Conquest of Gaul (Event). HAnc(I-516).
Caesar's Conquest of Gaul. *Thomas Rice Holmes.* HAnc(I-518).
Caetano Becomes Premier of Portugal (Event). HEur(III-1673).
Cage for Loulou, A. *Rudolph von Abele.* LA79(I-70).
Caged Panther, The. *Harry Meacham.* SCL12(II-1037), SCL7(I-595), A68(34).
*Cain. *George Gordon, Lord Byron.* MP12(II-734), MPCE(I-269), MP8(I-570), MP6(I-378), MPDr(121), MPv3(66), MP2(I-127),

MWL2(127).

Caine Mutiny, The.   Cine(I-275).

*Cakes and Ale.   W. Somerset Maugham.   MP12(II-737),   MPCE(I-270),
      MP8(I-573),   MP6(I-380),   MPEng(73),   MP1(I-99),   MWL1(99).

Cale.   Sylvia Wilkinson.   SCL12(II-1041),   A71(32).

Caleb Williams.   William Godwin.   MP12(II-740),   MPCE(I-272),
      MP8(I-575),   MP6(I-382),   MPEng(75),   MP1(I-101),   MWL1(101).

Calendar of the Roman Republic, The.   A. K. Michels.   HAnc(I-539).

California Gold: The Beginning of Mining in the Far West.   Rodman W.
      Paul.   HAmer(II-845).

California Gold Rush (Event).   HAmer(II-843).

California Progressives, The.   George E. Mowry.   HAmer(II-1310).

*Call It Sleep.   Henry Roth.   MP12(II-744),   MP8(I-577),   MP4(I-102),
      MWL4(102),   SCL12(II-1045),   SCL7(I-599),   A65(28).

Call Northside 777.   Cine(I-280).

Call of All Nations, The.   Saint Prosper of Aquitaine.   RCa(I-204).

*Call of the Wild, The.   Jack London.   MP12(II-748),   MPCE(I-274),
      MP8(I-581),   MP6(I-384),   MPAm(80),   MP1(I-103),   MWL1(103).

Call to Honour, The.   Charles de Gaulle.   SCL12(II-1050),   SCL7(I-604),
      A55(38).

Calling of the Albigensian Crusade (Event).   HAnc(III-1441).

Calling of the First General Assembly of Virginia (Event).   HAmer(I-65).

Calling of the States-General by Louis XVI (Event).   HEur(I-502).

Calling of the Council of Constance (Event).   HAnc(III-1680).

Calvin: The Origins and Development of His Religious Thought.   François
      Wendel.   HEur(I-119).

Calvin Publishes Institutes of the Christian Religion (Event).   HEur(I-116).
      See also Institutes of the Christian Religion, The.

Camberwell Beauty and Other Stories, The.   V. S. Pritchett.
      SCL12(II-1053),   A75(41).

"Cambodia: The Verdict Is Guilty on Nixon and Kissinger," in Far Eastern
      Economic Review.   William Shawcross.   HWor(II-1088).

"Cambodia: When the Bombing Finally Stopped," in Far Eastern Economic
      Review.   William Shawcross.   HWor (II-1088).

Cambodia: Year Zero.   François Ponchaud.   HWor(III-1216).

Cambridge Ancient History, Vol. V: Athens, 478-401 B.C., The.   Marcus N.
      Todd, E. M. Walker and F. E. Adcock.   HAnc(I-244).

Cambridge Ancient History, Vol. VII: The Primitive Institutions of Rome,
      The.   H. Stuart Jones.   HAnc(I-284).

Cambridge Economic History, The.   E. E. Rich.   HAnc(III-1517).

Cambridge Economic History, Vol. I: The Agrarian Life of the Middle Ages,
      The.   M. M. Postan.   HAnc(III-1325).

Cambridge Economic History, Vol. II: Trade and Industry in the Middle Ages,
      The.   M. Postan and E. E. Rich, eds.   HAnc(III-1517)

Cambridge History of Poland, Vol. II: From Augustus to Pilsudski, 1697-1935,

The. *W. F. Reddaway.* Different analyses on this title appear in: HEur(I-471; II-889).

Cambridge Medieval History, Vol. I: The Christian Roman Empire and the Foundation of the Teutonic Kingdoms, The. *Henry Melvill Gwatkin and J. P. Whitney, eds.*

Cambridge Medieval History, Vol. VII: The Swiss Confederation in the Middle Ages, The. *Paul E. Martin.* HAnc(III-1605).

Camel: Its Uses and Management, The. *A. G. Leonard.* HAnc(I-31).

Camels to California. *H. D. Fowler.* HAnc(I-32).

Camille. Cine(I-285).

*Camille. *Alexandre Dumas (fils).* MP12(II-751), MPCE(I-276), MP8(I-584), MP6(I-386), MPDr(124), MP1(I-105), MWL1(105).

Camp Concentration. *Thomas M. Disch.* SF(I-277).

Campaign in Norway, The. *T. K. Derry.* HEur(III-1448).

Campaigns of Napoleon: The Mind and Method of History's Greatest Soldier, The. *David Chandler.* HEur(II-621).

*Campaspe. *John Lyly.* MP12(II-754), MPCE(I-277), MP8(I-586), MP6(I-388), MPDr(126), MP3(I-148), MWL3(148).

Can Such Things Be? *Ambrose Bierce.* SF(I-283).

Canaris: Hitler's Master Spy. *Heinz Höhne.* LA80(I-125).

*Cancer Ward, The. *Aleksandr I. Solzhenitsyn.* SCL12(II-1056), SCL7(I-608), A69(61).

*Candida. *George Bernard Shaw.* MP12(II-757), MP8(I-588), MP6(I-390), MPDr(128), MP3(I-150), MWL3(150).

*Candide. *François Marie Arouet de Voltaire.* MP12(II-759), MPCE(I-278), MP8(I-590), MP6(I-392), MPEur(103), MP1(I-107), MWL1(107).

Candido: Or, A Dream Dreamed in Sicily. *Leonardo Sciascia.* LA80(I-129).

Cane. *Jean Toomer.* SCL12(II-1061), SCLs(55).

Cannibal, The. *John Hawkes.* MP12(II-763), MP8(I-592), MP4(I-105), MWL4(105).

Cannibals All: Or, Slaves Without Masters. *George Fitzhugh.* HAmer(I-651).

Cannibals and Missionaries. *Mary McCarthy.* LA80(I-133).

Canons of the Council of Sardica, The. *Hamilton Hess.* HAnc(II-874).

Canons of the First Council of Arles, 324 A.D., The. *Joseph M. O'Donnell.* HAnc(II-859).

"Canossa: A Revision," *in* Traditio. *Karl Frederick Morrison.* HAnc(III-1271).

*Canterbury Tales, The (Selections). *Geoffrey Chaucer.* MP12(II-769), MPCE(I-281), MP8(I-598), MP6(I-393), MPPo(33), MPv4(62), MP2(I-129), MWL2(129).

Canticle for Leibowitz, A. *Walter M. Miller, Jr.* SF(I-288).

Cántico. *Jorge Guillén.* SCL12(II-1064), SCL7(I-612), A66(43).

*Cantos. *Ezra Pound.* MP12(II-776), MP8(I-603), MP6(I-398),
    MPPo(38), MP3(I-151), MWL3(151).
Capable of Honor. *Allen Drury.* SCL12(II-1067), SCL7(I-615),
    A67(35).
Cape Cod Lighter, The. *John O'Hara.* SCL12(II-1071), SCL7(I-619),
    A63(18).
Capetian Kings of France: Monarchy and Nation (987-1328), The. *Robert
    Fawtier.* HAnc(III-1202).
Capital Punishment. *Charles L. Black, Jr.* SCL12(II-1073), A75(44). A
    different analysis on this title appears in: HWor(III-1284).
Capitalism and Slavery. *Eric Williams.* HEur(II-720).
Capitalism and the Reformation. *M. J. Kitch.* HAnc(III-1522).
Captain Blackman. *John A. Williams.* SCL12(II-1076), A73(65).
Captain Cook and the South Pacific. *John Gwyther.* SCL12(II-1080),
    SCL7(I-621), A55(41).
Captain Dreyfus: The Story of a Mass Hysteria. *Nicholas Halasz.*
    HEur(II-1078).
Captain Horatio Hornblower. *C. S. Forester.* MP12(II-779),
    MPCE(I-284), MP8(I-606), MP6(I-400), MPEng(77),
    MP1(I-109), MWL1(109).
Captain Pantoja and the Special Service. *Mario Vargas Llosa.* LA79(I-75).
*Captain Singleton. *Daniel Defoe.* MP12(I-783), MPCE(I-286),
    MP8(I-609), MP6(I-402), MPEng(80), MP3(I-154), MWL3(154).
Captain Steele. *Calhoun Winton.* SCL12(II-1083), SCL7(I-624),
    A65(32).
Captains Courageous. Cine(I-289).
*Captains Courageous. *Rudyard Kipling.* MP12(II-787), MPCE(I-288),
    MP8(I-612), MP6(I-405), MPEng(83), MP1(I-111), MWL1(111).
*Captain's Daughter, The. *Alexander Pushkin.* MP12(II-792),
    MPCE(I-291), MP8(I-615), MP6(I-407), MPEur(105),
    MP1(I-113), MWL1(113).
Captive and the Free, The. *Joyce Cary.* SCL12(II-1085), SCL7(I-626),
    A60(33).
Captives, The. *Plautus (Titus Maccius Plautus).* MP12(II-797),
    MPCE(I-294), MP8(I-618), MP6(I-410), MPDr(130),
    MPv4(66), MP2(I-134), MWL2(134).
Capture of Constantinople by the Crusaders (Event). HAnc(III-1436).
Car Thief, The. *Theodore Weesner.* SCL12(II-1088), A73(69).
Caravan Merchants and the Fairs of Champagne, The. *Richard D. Face.*
    HAnc(III-1424).
"Cardinal," *in* The Catholic Encyclopedia. *Johannes Baptist Sägmüller.*
    HAnc(III-1246).
Cardinal Jiménes and the Making of Spain. *Reginald Merton.*
    HAnc(III-1730).
"Cardinalis: The History of a Canonical Concept," *in* Traditio. *Stephen*

Kuttner. HAnc(III-1245).
Cards of Identity. *Nigel Dennis.* SCL12(II-1092), SCL7(I-629), A55(44).
Carefree. Cine(I-292).
*Caretaker, The. *Harold Pinter.* MP12(I-800), MP8(I-620), MP4(I-110), MWL4(110).
Carlist Wars in Spain (Event). HEur(II-726).
Carlos: The King Who Would Not Die. *John Langdon-Davies.* HEur(I-374).
Carlos Finlay and Yellow Fever. *Carlos E. Finlay.* HAmer(II-1315).
Carmen. *Prosper Mérimée.* MP12(II-803), MPCE(I-295), MP8(I-623), MP6(I-411), MPEur(108), MP1(I-116), MWL1(116).
Carmen Deo nostro. *Richard Crashaw.* RCa(II-600).
*Carmina. *Catullus (Gaius Valerius Catullus).* MP12(II-806), MP8(I-625), MP6(I-413), MPPo(41), MP3(I-156), MWL3(156).
Carnal Knowledge. Cine(I-295).
Carnegie Publishes *The Gospel of Wealth* (Event). HAmer(II-1167).
Carnival: Entertainments and Posthumous Tales. *Isak Dinesen.* LA78(I-150).
Carolina Regulator Movements (Event). HAmer(I-213).
Caroline, O Caroline. *Paul van Herck.* SF(I-294).
"Carolingian Coup d'Etat and the Volte-Face of the Papacy, The," *in* Mohammed and Charlemagne. *Henri Pirenne.* HAnc(II-1133).
Carolingian Empire, The. *Heinrich Fichtenau.* HAnc(II-1149).
Carousel. Cine(I-298).
Carrier of Ladders, The. *W. S. Merwin.* SCL12(II-1095), A72(55).
Carry on Nurse. Cine(I-301).
Carrying the Fire: An Astronaut's Journeys. *Michael Collins.* SCL12(II-1098), A75(47).
Carson of Venus. *Edgar Rice Burroughs.* SF(I-298).
Cartier and Roberval Search for a Northwest Passage (Event). HAmer(I-28).
Casablanca. Cine(I-305).
Casablanca Conference, The (Event). HEur(III-1477).
*Casanova's Chinese Restaurant. *Anthony Powell.* SCL12(II-1101), SCL7(I-632), A61(30), BMA(60).
Case of Conscience, A. *James Blish.* SF(I-303).
Case of Sergeant Grischa, The. *Arnold Zweig.* MP12(II-809), MPCE(I-296), MP8(I-628), MP6(I-415), MPEur(110), MP1(I-118), MWL1(118).
"Case of the Louisiana Traveler: *Plessy* vs. *Ferguson*, The" *in John A. Garraty's* Quarrels That Have Shaped the Constitution. *C. Vann Woodward.* HAmer(II-1266).
Casebook on Existentialism, A. *William V. Spanos,* ed. HWor(I-255).
Casebook on *The Grapes of Wrath*, A. *Agnes McNeill Donohue,* ed.

HWor(I-421).

Casey Agonistes and Other Science Fiction and Fantasy Stories. *Richard McKenna*. SF(I-308).

*Cass Timberlane. *Sinclair Lewis*. MP12(II-813), MPCE(I-298), MP8(I-631), MP6(I-418), MPAm(83), MP1(I-120), MWL1(120).

Cassandra Singing. *David Madden*. SCL12(II-1104), A70(69).

Caste. *Thomas William Robertson*. MP12(II-816), MPCE(I-299), MP8(I-633), MP6(I-420), MPDr(132), MPv4(68), MP2(I-135), MWL2(135).

Casti connubii. *Pope Pius XI*. RCa(II-808).

*Castle, The. *Franz Kafka*. MP12(II-820), MPCE(I-301), MP8(I-636), MP6(I-422), MPEur(113), MP1(I-122), MWL1(122).

Castle Keep. *William Eastlake*. SCL12(II-1107), SCL7(I-635), A66(46).

*Castle of Fratta, The. *Ippolito Nievo*. MP12(II-883), MPCE(I-302), MP8(I-638), MP6(I-424), MPEur(115), MP3(I-158), MWL3(158). A different analysis on this title appears in: SCL12(II-1110), SCL7(I-638), A59(28).

*Castle of Otranto, The. *Horace Walpole*. MP12(II-829), MPCE(I-305), MP8(I-641), MP6(I-427), MPEng(86), MP1(I-124), MWL1(124).

*Castle Rackrent. *Maria Edgeworth*. MP12(II-834), MPCE(I-308), MP8(I-643), MP6(I-429), MPEng(88), MP1(I-126), MWL1(126).

Castlereagh and Adams: England and the United States, 1812-1823. *Bradford Perkins*. HAmer(I-524).

Castles and the Crown, The. *Townsend Miller*. Different analyses on this title appear in: HAnc(III-1749), HEur(I-41).

Castro Seizes Power in Cuba (Event). HWor(II-743).

Casuals of the Sea. *William McFee*. MP12(II-839), MPCE(I-312), MP8(I-645), MP6(I-430), MPEng(90), MP1(I-128), MWL1(128).

*Cat and Mouse. *Günter Grass*. MP12(II-842), MP8(I-647), MP4(I-113), MWL4(113), SCL12(II-1114), SCL7(I-641), A64(46).

Cat on a Hot Tin Roof. Cine(I-308).

*Cat on a Hot Tin Roof. *Tennessee Williams*. MP12(II-845), MP8(I-650), MP4(I-115), MWL4(I-115), SCL12(II-1117), SCL7(I-644), A55(47), BMA(63).

Cat People. Cine(I-312).

*Catcher in the Rye, The. *J. D. Salinger*. SCL12(II-1121), SCLs(58).

*Catch-22. *Joseph Heller*. MP12(II-848), MP8(I-653), MP4(I-117), MWL4(117), SCL12(II-1125), SCL7(I-647), A62(44).

Catechetical Lectures, The. *Saint Cyril, Bishop of Jerusalem*. Different analyses on this title appear in: RCh(I-92), RCa(I-90).

Catherine Carmier. *Ernest J. Gaines*. SCL12(II-1130), SCLs(61).

Catherine de' Médici. *Jean Hertier.* HEur(I-160).

Catherine, Empress of All the Russias. *Vincent Cronin.* LA79(I-80).

Catherine the Great. *Joan Haslip.* LA78(I-155).

Catherine the Great and the Russian Nobility. *Paul Duke.* HEur(I-467).

Catherine the Great's *Instruction* for Radical Social Reform (Event). HEur(I-464).

Catholic Question in English Politics, 1820-1830, The. *G. I. T. Machin.* HEur(II-673).

Catholic Runs for President: The Campaign of 1928, A. *Edmund A. Moore.* HAmer(III-1568).

Catholicism. *Henri de Lubac, S. J.* RCa(II-856).

*Catiline. *Ben Jonson.* MP12(II-852), MPCE(I-313), MP8(I-657), MP6(I-432), MPDr(135), MP3(I-161), MWL3(161).

Cato Writes the *De Agri Cultura* (Event). HAnc(I-465).

*Cat's Cradle. *Kurt Vonnegut, Jr.* SCL12(II-1134), SCLs(65). A different analysis on this title appears in: SF(I-313).

Caught in That Music. *Seymour Epstein.* SCL12(II-1138), SCL7(I-651), A68(37).

Caught in the Web of Words. *K. M. Elisabeth Murray.* LA78(I-160).

Cause for Wonder. *Wright Morris.* SCL12(II-1142), SCL7(I-655), A64(49).

"Cause of Refraction in Medieval Optics, The," *in* The British Journal for the History of Science. *David C. Lindberg.* HAnc(III-1556).

Cavalcade. Cine(I-316).

Cavalleria Rusticana. *Giovanni Verga.* MP12(II-855), MPCE(I-314), MP8(I-660), MP6(I-435), MPEur(118), MPv3(68), MP2(I-137), MWL2(137).

*Cave, The. *Robert Penn Warren.* SCL12(II-1145), SCL7(I-658), A60(35).

Caves of Steel, The. *Isaac Asimov.* SF(I-318).

Cavour and Garibaldi. *Denis Mack Smith.* HEur(II-873).

Cawdor. *Robinson Jeffers.* MP12(II-858), MPCE(I-316), MP8(I-662), MP6(I-437), MPPo(44), MP1(I-130), MWL1(130).

Ce Monde est nôtre. *Francis Carsac.* SF(III-1435).

*Cecilia. *Fanny Burney.* MP12(II-861), MPCE(I-318), MP8(I-664), MP6(I-438), MPEng(92), MP3(I-163), MWL3(163).

Celebration. *Harvey Swados.* SCL12(II-1149), A76(37).

Celebration of the Eleusinian Mysteries (Event). HAnc(I-158).

Celebration of the Last Supper (Event). HAnc(II-595).

Celebrations and Attacks: Thirty Years of Literary and Cultural Commentary. *Irving Howe.* LA80(I-136).

Celestina. *Fernando de Rojas.* MP12(II-865), MPCE(I-320), MP8(I-667), MP6(I-441), MPEur(120), MPv4(70), MP2(I-139), MWL2(139).

Céline. *Patrick McCarthy.* LA77(I-134).

Cell, The.   *Carl P. Swanson* and *Peter L. Webster*.   HWor(I-504).
Cellular Research (Event).   HWor(I-501).
Celts: The People Who Came out of the Darkness, The.   *Gerhard Herm*.
    LA78(I-164).
*Cenci, The.   *Percy Bysshe Shelley*.   MP12(II-869),   MPCE(I-321),
    MP8(I-670),   MP6(I-444),   MPDr(138),   MP1(I-131),   MWL1(131).
*Centaur, The.   *John Updike*.   SCL12(II-1153),   SCL7(I-662),   A64(52).
Centennial.   *James A. Michener*.   SCL12(II-1157),   A75(50).
Central Ideas in Amos.   *A. S. Kapelrud*.   HAnc(I-126).
Centuries of Santa Fe, The.   *Paul Horgan*.   SCL12(II-1161),
    SCL7(I-666),   A57(39).
C'era una volta un planeta.   *L. R. Johannis*.   SF(I-322).
*Ceremonies in Dark Old Men.   *Lonne Elder III*.   SCL12(II-1165),
    A70(72).
*Ceremony in Lone Tree.   *Wright Morris*.   MP12(II-872),   MP8(I-672),
    MP4(I-121),   MWL4(121). A different analysis on this title appears in:
    SCL12(II-1168),   SCL7(I-670),   A61(33),   BMA(66).
Certain Smile, A.   *Françoise Sagan*.   SCL12(II-1172),   SCL7(I-673),
    A57(42).
Cervantes: A Biography.   *William Byron*.   LA79(I-84).
*César Birotteau.   *Honoré de Balzac*.   MP12(II-876),   MPCE(I-322),
    MP8(I-676),   MP6(I-446),   MPEur(123),   MPv3(70),
    MP2(I-142),   MWL2(142).
César Chávez Organizes the Farm Workers (Event).   HWor(II-842).
C. G. Jung.   *E. A. Bennet*.   HEur(III-1312).
Chaco War, The (Event).   HWor(I-289).
Chadwick Discovers the Neutron (Event).   HWor(I-283).
*Chainbearer, The.   *James Fenimore Cooper*.   MP12(II-880),
    MPCE(I-323),   MP8(I-679),   MP6(I-448),   MPAm(85),
    MP3(I-166),   MWL3(166).
Champagne for Caesar.   Cine(I-320).
Chance and Circumstance: The Draft, the War and the Vietnam
    Generation.   *Lawrence M. Baskir* and *William A. Strauss*.
    LA79(I-88).
Chance Meetings.   *William Saroyan*.   LA79(I-92).
*Change of Skin, A.   *Carlos Fuentes*.   SCL12(II-1175),   SCL7(I-676),
    A69(65).
Change of Weather.   *Winfield Townley Scott*.   SCL12(II-1180),
    SCL7(I-680),   A65(34).
*Changeling, The.   *Thomas Middleton* and *William Rowley*.
    MP12(II-885),   MPCE(I-325),   MP8(I-683),   MP6(I-451),
    MPDr(140),   MP3(I-169),   MWL3(169).
Changing Attitudes Toward Religion in America (Event).   HWor(I-507).
Changing Patterns in Education (Event).   HWor(I-513).
Changing Room, The.   *David Storey*.   SCL12(II-1183),   A74(47).

Changing Social Contract, The (Event). HWor(II-848).

"Changing Strategic Balance in Asia, The," *in* Sino-American Détente and Its Policy Implications. *A. Doak Barnett*. HWor(III-1126).

Character of Man, The. *Emmanuel Mounier*. RCa(II-902).

Characteristics. *Anthony Ashley Cooper, Earl of Shaftesbury*. Ph(I-459).

Charade. Cine(I-323).

Charles A. Beard: An Appraisal. *Howard K. Beale*. HAmer(III-1430).

Charles de Bourbon: High Constable of France. *Christopher Hare*. HEur(I-84).

Charles Demailly. *Jules de Goncourt* and *Edmond de Goncourt*. MP12(II-888), MPCE(I-326), MP8(I-686), MP6(I-454), MPEur(126), MP3(I-171), MWL3(171).

Charles Evans Hughes and the Illusions of Innocence: A Study in American Diplomacy. *Betty Glad*. HAmer(III-1535).

Charles Francis Adams, 1807-1886. *Martin B. Duberman*. SCL12(II-1187), SCL7(I-683), A62(48). A different analysis on this title appears in: HAmer(II-1075).

Charles Ives and His America. *Frank R. Rossiter*. SCL12(II-1191), A76(41).

Charles Lyell. *Edward Bailey*. HEur(II-679).

Charles O'Malley. *Charles Lever*. MP12(II-892), MPCE(I-327), MP8(I-689), MP6(I-456), MPEng(95), MP1(I-133), MWL1(133).

Charles Stewart Parnell. *F. S. L. Lyons*. LA78(I-169).

Charles Sumner and the Coming of the Civil War. *David Donald*. SCL12(II-1195), SCL7(I-687), A61(36), BMA(69).

Charles VIII of France Invades Italy (Event). HEur(I-21).

Charles I Ascends the Throne of Spain (Event). HEur(I-40).

Charles XII and the Collapse of the Swedish Empire, 1682-1719. *R. Nisbet Bain*. HEur(I-377).

Charles Townshend. *Lewis B. Namier* and *John Brooke*. HAmer(I-229).

*Charley Is My Darling. *Joyce Cary*. SCL12(II-1198), SCL7(I-690), A61(38).

Charly. Cine(I-326).

*Charmed Life, A. *Mary McCarthy*. SCL12(II-1201), SCL7(I-693), A55(50).

Charmed Lives: A Family Romance. *Michael Korda*. LA80(I-141).

Charter of the Economic Rights and Duties of States (Event). HWor(III-1206).

*Charterhouse of Parma, The. *Stendhal (Marie-Henri Beyle)*. MP12(II-895), MPCE(I-328), MP8(I-692), MP6(I-459), MPEur(129), MP1(I-135), MWL1(135).

Chartering of the American Fur Company (Event). HAmer(I-476).

Chartering of the Second Bank of the United States (Event). HAmer(I-539).

Chartist Movement, The. *Mark Hovell*. HEur(II-743).

Chartist Studies. *Asa Briggs*. HEur(II-744).
Chartres' Preservation of Classical Learning (Event). HAnc(III-1231).
*Chaste Maid in Cheapside, A. *Thomas Middleton*. MP12(II-900),
    MPCE(I-331), MP8(I-694), MP6(I-460), MPDr(143),
    MP3(I-174), MWL3(174).
Château, The. *William Maxwell*. SCL12(II-1204), SCL7(I-696),
    A62(51).
Chateaubriand: A Biography, Vol. I (1768-93): The Longed-for
    Tempests. *George D. Painter*. LA79(I-95).
Chaucer and the French Tradition. *Charles Muscatine*. HAnc(III-1658).
Chaucer Writes the *Canterbury Tales* (Event). HAnc(III-1655). *See also*
    Canterbury Tales, The.
Chávez and the Farm Workers. *Ronald B. Taylor*. HWor(II-846).
Chekhov. *Ernest J. Simmons*. SCL12(II-1208), SCL7(I-700), A63(20).
*Chéri. *Sidonie Gabrielle Claudine Colette*. MP12(II-905),
    MPCE(I-334), MP8(I-697), MP6(I-463), MPEur(131),
    MP3(I-176), MWL3(176).
Cherish the Sea. *Jean de la Varende*. HAnc(III-1506).
*Cherry Orchard, The. *Anton Chekhov*. MP12(II-908), MPCE(I-335),
    MP8(I-700), MP6(I-465), MPDr(146), MPv3(73), MP2(I-144),
    MWL2(144).
Chesapeake. *James A. Michener*. LA79(I-99).
*Chevalier of the Maison Rouge, The. *Alexandre Dumas (père)*.
    MP12(II-912), MPCE(I-338), MP8(I-702), MP6(I-467),
    MPEur(134), MP3(I-179), MWL3(179).
*Chicago Poems. *Carl Sandburg*. MP12(II-918), MP8(I-706),
    MP4(I-124), MWL4(124).
Chicago School of Architecture: A History of Commercial and Public Building
    in the Chicago Area, The. *Carl W. Condit*. HAmer(II-1235).
Chicago Sociology, 1920-1932. *Robert E. Faris*. HAmer(III-1361).
Chickamauga. *Glenn Tucker*. SCL12(II-1212), SCLs(68).
Chieko's Sky. *Kotaro Takamura*. LA79(I-105).
*Child Buyer, The. *John Hersey*. SCL12(II-1216), SCL7(I-703),
    A61(41). A different analysis on this title appears in: SF(I-325).
Child of Montmartre, The. *Paul Léautaud*. SCL12(II-1219),
    SCL7(I-706), A60(39).
Child of Our Time. *Michel del Castillo*. SCL12(II-1222), SCL7(I-709),
    A59(31).
Childe Cycle, The. *Gordon R. Dickson*. SF(I-330).
*Childe Harold's Pilgrimage. *George Gordon, Lord Byron*.
    MP12(II-921), MP8(I-709), MP4(I-127), MWL4(127).
*Childhood, Boyhood, Youth. *Count Leo Tolstoy*. MP12(II-924),
    MP8(I-712), MP4(I-129), MWL4(129).
Childhood's End. *Arthur C. Clarke*. SF(I-337).
Children at the Gate, The. *Edward Lewis Wallant*. SCL12(II-1225),

SCL7(I-712), A65(37).

Children Is All. *James Purdy.* SCL12(II-1228), SCL7(I-715), A63(23).

Children of Dune. *Frank Herbert.* Different analyses on this title appear in: LA77(I-139), SF(I-343).

*Children of God. *Vardis Fisher.* MP12(II-927), MPCE(I-341), MP8(I-715), MP6(I-470), MPAm(89), MP1(I-137), MWL1(137).

*Children of Herakles, The. *Euripides.* MP12(II-930), MPCE(I-342), MP8(I-718), MP6(I-473), MPDr(148), MP3(I-182), MWL3(182).

Children of Pride, The. *Robert Manson Meyers.* SCL12(II-1231), A73(72).

*Children of Sánchez, The. *Oscar Lewis.* SCL12(II-1236), SCL7(I-718), A62(55), BMA(72).

Children of the Atom. *Wilmar H. Shiras.* SF(I-349).

Children of the Ghetto. *Israel Zangwill.* MP12(II-933), MPCE(I-343), MP8(I-720), MP6(I-474), MPEng(98), MPv4(73), MP2(I-146), MWL2(146).

Children of the Sun. *Martin Green.* LA77(I-144).

*Children of Violence: Vols. I and II. *Doris Lessing.* SCL12(II-1240), SCL7(II-723), A65(40).

Children of Violence: Vols. III and IV. *Doris Lessing.* SCL12(II-1245), SCL7(II-728), A67(38).

Children's Hour, The. Cine(I-329).

Child's Play. *David R. Slavitt.* SCL12(II-1248), A73(77).

Childwold. *Joyce Carol Oates.* LA77(I-149).

Chilly Scenes of Winter. *Ann Beattie.* LA77(I-154).

Chimera. *John Barth.* SCL12(II-1252), A73(80).

China Diplomacy, 1914-1918. *Madeleine Chi.* HWor(I-126).

China Market: America's Quest for Informal Empire, 1893-1901. *Thomas J. McCormick.* HAmer(II-1299).

China's Economy and the Maoist Strategy. *John G. Gurley.* HWor(II-561).

China's Republican Revolution: The Case of Kwangtung, 1895-1913. *Edward J. M. Rhoads.* HWor(I-95).

Chinatown. Cine(I-332).

Chinese and the Americans, The. *Jules Archer.* HWor(III-1128).

Chinese Communist Party in Power, 1949-1976, The. *Jacques Guillermaz.* LA78(I-174).

Chinese Foreign Policy After the Cultural Revolution, 1966-1977. *Robert G. Sutter.* LA79(I-108).

Chinese Immigration. *Mary Roberts Coolidge.* HAmer(II-1125).

Chinese Revolution of 1911, The (Event). HWor(I-92).

Chips with Everything. *Arnold Wesker.* MP12(II-937), MP8(I-723), MP4(I-132), MWL4(132).

Chisholm Trail, The. *Wayne Gard.* HAmer(II-1022).

*Chita. *Lafcadio Hearn.* MP12(II-940), MPCE(I-345), MP8(II-727), MP6(I-477), MPAm(92), MPv3(75), MP2(I-149), MWL2(149).

Chord of Steel, The. *Thomas B. Costain.* HAmer(II-1090).

Chosen, The. *Chaim Potok.* SCL12(II-1254), SCL7(II-731), A68(41).

Chou En-lai: China's Gray Eminence. *Kai-yu Hsu.* HWor(III-1268).

*Chouans, The. *Honoré de Balzac.* MP12(II-943), MPCE(I-346),
    MP8(II-730), MP6(I-478), MPEur(138), MPv3(76),
    MP2(I-151), MWL2(151).

Christ and Culture. *H. Richard Niebuhr.* RCh(II-1121).

Christ and Society. *Charles Gore.* RCh(II-942).

Christ and Time. *Oscar Cullmann.* RCh(II-1072).

Christ in Christian Tradition: From the Apostolic Age to Chalcedon. *Aloys
    Grillmeier, S. J.* HAnc(II-965).

Christ of Faith, The. *Karl Adam.* RCa(II-1000).

Christian Directory, A. *Richard Baxter.* RCh(I-501).

Christian Discourses. *Søren Kierkegaard.* RCh(II-709).

Christian Doctrine. *J. S. Whale.* RCh(II-1051).

Christian Doctrine of Justification and Reconciliation, The. *Albrecht
    Ritschl.* RCh(II-758).

Christian Dogmatics. *Hans Lassen Martensen.* RCh(II-712).

Christian Education of Youth, The. *Pope Pius XI.* RCa(II-801).

Christian Faith, The. *Friedrich Schleiermacher.* RCh(II-657).

Christian Faith and the Interpretation of History. *G. L. Keyes.*
    HAnc(II-944).

"Christian Festivals (Christmas and Epiphany), The," *in* Christian Worship, Its
    Origin and Evolution. *Louis Duchesne.* HAnc(II-886).

Christian Humanism. *Louis Bouyer.* RCa(II-1058).

Christian Message in a Non-Christian World, The. *Hendrik Kraemer.*
    RCh(II-1038).

"Christian Ministry, The," *in* Saint Paul's Epistle to the Philippians. *J. B.
    Lightfoot.* HAnc(II-683).

Christian Mysticism. *William Ralph Inge.* RCh(II-816).

Christian Nurture. *Horace Bushnell.* RCh(II-736).

Christian Pastor, The. *Washington Gladden.* RCh(II-812).

Christian Philosophy of St. Thomas Aquinas, The. *Étienne Gilson.*
    HAnc(III-1547).

Christian Platonists of Alexandria, The. *Charles Bigg.* HAnc(II-735).

Christian Realism in Contemporary American Theology. *George Hammar.*
    HAmer(III-1606).

Christian Spirituality. *Rev. Pierre Pourrat.* HAnc(II-932).

Christian System, The. *Alexander Campbell.* RCh(II-672).

Christian Theology: An Ecumenical Approach. *Walter Marshall Horton.*
    RCh(II-1148).

Christian Theology in Outline. *William Adams Brown.* RCh(II-840).

Christian Understanding of God, The. *Nels Ferré.* RCh(II-1124).

Christianity Among the Religions of the World. *Arnold Toynbee.*
    SCL12(II-1258), SCL7(II-735), A58(50).

Churchill Revised: A Critical Assessment. *A. J. P. Taylor.* HEur(III-1530).

Churchill, Roosevelt, Stalin. *Herbert Feis.* Different analyses on this title
appear in: HEur(III-1480; III-1503).

Churchills, The. *A. L. Rowse.* SCL12(II-1268), SCL7(II-745),
A59(34).

Churchill's "Iron Curtain" Speech (Event). HEur(III-1526).

CIA and the Cult of Intelligence, The. *Victor Marchetti* and *John D.
Marks.* SCL12(II-1271), A75(54).

Cicero, De Oratore. *E. W. Sutton* and *H. Rackham,* eds. HAnc(I-522).

Cicero Writes the *De Officiis* (Event). HAnc(I-541).

Cicero Writes the *De Oratore* (Event). HAnc(I-521). *See also* Cicero's
Orations.

Cicero Writes the *De Republica* (Event). HAnc(I-526).

"Cicero's *de Officiis* in Christian Thought: 300-1300," *in* University of
Michigan Essays and Studies in English and Comparative
Literature. *N. E. Nelson.* HAnc(I-544).

"Cicero's Ideal in His De Republica," *in* Journal of Roman Studies. *W. W.
How.* HAnc(I-529).

Cicero's Orations. *Cicero (Marcus Tullius Cicero).* MP12(II-959),
MP8(II-745), MP6(I-488), MPNf(51), MP3(I-188), MWL3(188).

*Cid, The. *Pierre Corneille.* MP12(II-961), MPCE(I-349),
MP8(II-747), MP6(I-490), MPDr(150), MP1(I-142),
MWL1(142).

Cimarron. Cine(I-339).

*Cinna. *Pierre Corneille.* MP12(II-966), MPCE(I-352), MP8(II-749),
MP6(I-492), MPDr(152), MP3(I-190), MWL3(190).

Cinq-Mars. *Alfred Victor de Vigny.* MP12(II-969), MPCE(I-353),
MP8(II-752), MP6(I-494), MPEur(141), MPv4(75),
MP2(I-153), MWL2(153).

CIO Challenge to the AFL: A History of the American Labor Movement,
1935-1941, The. *Walter Galenson.* HAmer(III-1658).

Circle of Chalk, The. *Unknown.* MP12(II-973), MPCE(I-354),
MP8(II-755), MP6(I-497), MPDr(155), MP3(I-193),
MWL3(193).

Circles: A Washington Story. *Abigail McCarthy.* LA78(I-179).

Circus: From Rome to Ringling. *Marian Murray.* HAmer(II-1070).

Citadel, The. Cine(I-343).

Citadel of Learning, The. *James Bryant Conant.* SCL12(II-1275),
SCL7(II-748), A57(45).

Cities in Flight. *James Blish.* SF(I-358).

Citizen Hearst. *W. A. Swanberg.* SCL12(II-1279), SCL7(II-752),
A62(61). A different analysis on this title appears in: HAmer(II-1245).

Citizen Kane. Cine(I-346).

Citizen Kane Book, The. *Pauline Kael, Herman J. Mankiewicz* and *Orson
Welles.* SCL12(II-1283), A72(59).

Citizen of the Galaxy. *Robert A. Heinlein.* SF(I-363).
Citizen Thomas More and His Utopia. *Russell Ames.* HEur(I-51).
City. *Clifford D. Simak.* SF(I-369).
City and the Stars, The. *Arthur C. Clarke.* SF(I-374).
City in History, The. *Lewis Mumford.* SCL12(II-1289), SCL7(II-756), A62(64).
*City Life. *Donald Barthelme.* SCL12(II-1293), A71(36).
City Lights. Cine(I-352).
*City of God, The. *Saint Augustine.* Different analyses on this title appear in: Ph(I-258), RCh(I-140), RCa(I-188).
City of Truth, The. *Lev Lunts.* SF(I-378).
City Without Walls and Other Poems. *W. H. Auden.* SCL12(II-1296), A71(38).
City-State and World State. *Mason Hammond.* HAnc(I-509).
Ciudad, La. *Mario Levrero.* SF(I-383).
Civil Constitution of the Clergy (Event). HEur(I-516).
Civil Rights Act of 1964, The (Event). HWor(II-965).
Civil Rights Acts of the 1960's, The (Event). HWor(II-806).
Civil War: Fort Sumter to Perryville, 1861-1862, The. *Shelby Foote.* SCL12(II-1299), SCL7(II-759), A59(37).
Civil War: Fredericksburg to Meridian, 1862-1864, The. *Shelby Foote.* SCL12(II-1303), SCL7(II-763), A64(55).
Civil War: Red River to Appomattox, 1864-1865, The. *Shelby Foote.* SCL12(II-1305), A75(58).
Civil War in Angola and the Intervention of Cuba, The (Event). HWor(III-1219).
Civil War in China, The (Event). HWor(I-211).
Civil War in China: The Political Struggle, 1945-1949. *Suzanne Pepper.* HWor(I-215).
*Clarissa. *Samuel Richardson.* MP12(II-976), MPCE(I-355), MP8(II-758), MP6(I-499), MPEng(104), MP1(I-143), MWL1(143).
Class and American Sociology: From Ward to Ross. *Charles Hunt Page.* HAmer(III-1359).
*Claudius the God. *Robert Graves.* MP12(II-981), MPCE(I-358), MP8(II-761), MP6(I-502), MPEng(107), MP1(I-146), MWL1(146).
*Clayhanger Trilogy, The. *Arnold Bennett.* MP12(II-984), MPCE(I-359), MP8(II-763), MP6(I-504), MPEng(109), MP1(I-148), MWL1(148).
*Clea. *Lawrence Durrell.* SCL12(II-1308), SCL7(II-765), A61(44), BMA(83).
Cleaning Up America. *John Quarles.* HWor(II-878).
Cleared for Landing. *Ann Darr.* LA79(I-113).
Clement of Rome Addresses the Corinthians (Event). HAnc(II-667).

Cleopatra.   Cine(I-356).

Cligés.   *Chrétien de Troyes*.   MP12(II-989),   MPCE(I-362),
    MP8(II-766),   MP6(I-506),   MPPo(46),   MP3(I-195),   MWL3(195).

"Climax of Chemical Therapy in the 10th Century Arabic Medicine, The," *in*
    Der Islam.   *Sami K. Hamarneh*.   HAnc(II-1181).

"Climax of Medieval Arabic Professional Pharmacy, The," *in* Bulletin of the
    History of Medicine.   *Sami K. Hamarneh*.   Different analyses on this
    title appear in: HAnc(II-1181; III-1228).

Climax of Populism: The Election of 1896, The.   *Robert F. Durden*.
    HAmer(II-1271).

Climbing into the Roots.   *Reg Saner*.   LA77(I-164).

Clipper of the Clouds *and* The Master of the World.   *Jules Verne*.
    SF(I-386).

Clipper Ship Era, The.   *Arthur H. Clark*.   HAmer(II-809).

*Clock Without Hands.   *Carson McCullers*.   SCL12(II-1314),
    SCL7(II-771),   A62(67).

Clockwork Man, The.   *E. V. Odle*.   SF(I-392).

*Clockwork Orange, A.   *Anthony Burgess*.   SF(I-396).

*Cloister and the Hearth, The.   *Charles Reade*.   MP12(II-993),
    MPCE(I-363),   MP8(II-770),   MP6(I-509),   MPEng(112),
    MP1(I-150),   MWL1(150).

Cloned Lives.   *Pamela Sargent*.   SF(I-402).

Close Encounters of the Third Kind.   Cine(I-362).

*Closed Garden, The.   *Julian Green*.   MP12(II-998),   MPCE(I-366),
    MP8(II-773),   MP6(I-511),   MPEur(144),   MPv3(79),
    MP2(I-155),   MWL2(155).

Closing Circle: Nature, Men and Technology, The.   *Barry Commoner*.
    HWor(II-545).

Closing of the Frontier (Event).   HAmer(II-1213).

Cloud Forest, The.   *Peter Matthiessen*.   MP12(II-1003),   MP8(II-776),
    MP4(I-136),   MWL4(136),   SCL12(II-1319),   SCL7(II-775),
    A62(71),   BMA(89).

Cloud of Danger: Current Realities of American Foreign Policy, The.   *George
    F. Kennan*.   LA78(I-183).

Cloud of Unknowing, The.   *Unknown*.   Different analyses on this title
    appear in: RCh(I-288),   RCa(I-466).

*Clouds, The.   *Aristophanes*.   MP12(II-1006),   MPCE(I-369),
    MP8(II-779),   MP6(I-514),   MPDr(158),   MP1(I-152),
    MWL1(152).

*Clown, The.   *Heinrich Böll*.   SCL12(II-1323),   SCL7(II-779),   A66(49).

Clown on Fire.   *Aaron Judah*.   SCL12(II-1326),   SCL7(II-782),   A68(45).

Coal Miner's Daughter.   Cine(I-365).

Cockatoos, The.   *Patrick White*.   SCL12(II-1329),   A76(45).

*Cockpit.   *Jerzy Kosinski*.   SCL12(II-1334),   A76(50).

*Cocktail Party, The.   *T. S. Eliot*.   MP12(II-1010),   MPCE(I-372),

MP8(II-781), MP6(I-515), MPDr(160), MPv3(81),
MP2(I-158), MWL2(158).

Cocteau: A Biography. *Francis Steegmuller.* SCL12(II-1338), A71(42).

Codeword Barbarossa. *Barton Whaley.* HWor(I-454).

Codification of the Canon Law (Event). HAnc(III-1491).

Coffin for King Charles, A. *C. V. Wedgwood.* SCL12(II-1342),
SCL7(II-785), A65(45).

Cold Comfort Farm. *Stella Gibbons.* MP12(II-1016), MP8(II-784),
MP4(I-139), MWL4(139).

Cold Dawn: The Story of SALT. *John Newhouse.* HWor(II-1059).

Cold Ground Was My Bed Last Night. *George Garrett.* SCL12(II-1345),
SCL7(II-788), A65(47).

Cold War and Its Origins, Vol. I: 1917-1950, The. *D. F. Fleming.* Different
analyses on this title appear in: HEur(III-1558), HAmer(III-1780).

Cold War and Its Origins, Vol. II: 1950-1960, The. *D. F. Fleming.*
HEur(III-1558).

Cold War as History, The. *Louis J. Halle.* HEur(III-1536).

Collapse of France (Event). HEur(III-1451).

Collapse of the Fourth French Republic (Event). HEur(III-1607).

Collapse of the Nixon Administration (Event). HWor(III-1200).

Collapse of the Third Republic, The. *William L. Shirer.* SCL12(II-1348),
A70(75).

Collapsing Universe: The Story of Black Holes, The. *Isaac Asimov.*
HWor(II-838).

Collected Essays. *Thomas Henry Huxley.* Ph(II-712).

Collected Letters of D. H. Lawrence, The. *D. H. Lawrence.*
MP12(II-1019), MP8(II-787), MP4(I-141), MWL4(141). A different
analysis on this title appears in: SCL12(II-1352), SCL7(II-791),
A63(26).

Collected Papers. *Charles Sanders Peirce.* Ph(II-952).

Collected Plays, The. *Lillian Hellman.* SCL12(II-1355), A73(83).

Collected Poems. *John Betjeman.* SCL12(II-1361), SCL7(II-794),
A60(41), BMA(93).

Collected Poems. *Basil Bunting.* LA79(I-119).

Collected Poems. *Walter de la Mare.* MP12(II-1022), MP8(II-790),
MP6(I-518), MPPo(50), MP3(I-198), MWL3(198).

Collected Poems. *Lawrence Durrell.* SCL12(II-1365), SCL7(II-798),
A61(49).

Collected Poems. *Horace Gregory.* SCL12(II-1368), SCL7(II-801),
A65(50).

Collected Poems. *Kathleen Raine.* SCL12(II-1370), SCL7(II-803),
A58(53).

Collected Poems. *Edith Sitwell.* SCL12(II-1373), SCL7(II-806),
A55(59), BMA(97).

Collected Poems. *Wallace Stevens.* SCL12(II-1377), SCL7(II-820),

A54(31),   BMA(100).

Collected Poems. *James Wright.* SCL12(II-1380),   A72(64).

Collected Poems, The. *Muriel Rukeyser.* LA80(I-148).

Collected Poems: 1955. *Robert Graves.* SCL12(II-1383),   SCL7(II-809),
A55(56).

Collected Poems: 1961. *Robert Graves.* SCL12(II-1387),   SCL7(II-813),
A62(74).

Collected Poems: 1951-1971. *A. R. Ammons.* SCL12(II-1391),   A73(88).

Collected Poems: I. *Muriel Spark.* SCL12(II-1401),   SCL7(II-823),
A69(69).

Collected Poems and Epigrams of J. V. Cunningham, The. *J. V.
Cunningham.* SCL12(II-1394),   A72(67).

Collected Poems, 1919-1976. *Allen Tate.* LA78(I-188).

Collected Poems 1940-1978. *Karl Shapiro.* LA79(I-124).

Collected Poems, 1948-1976. *Dannie Abse.* LA78(I-192).

Collected Poems 1956-1976. *David Wagoner.* LA78(I-197).

Collected Poems, 1934-1952. *Dylan Thomas.* MP12(II-1025),
MP8(II-793),   MP6(I-520),   MPPo(53),   MP3(I-201),   MWL3(201).

Collected Poems of Howard Nemerov, The. *Howard Nemerov.*
LA78(I-200).

Collected Poems of James Agee, The. *James Agee.* SCL12(II-1398),
SCL7(II-817),   A69(72).

Collected Poems of Stevie Smith, The. *Stevie Smith.* LA77(I-168).

Collected Short Prose of James Agee, The. *James Agee.* SCL12(II-1405),
SCL7(II-827),   A69(74).

Collected Stories, The. *Isaac Babel.* SCL12(II-1408),   SCL7(II-830),
A55(62).

Collected Stories, 1939-1976. *Paul Bowles.* LA80(I-151).

Collected Stories of Ellen Glasgow, The. *Ellen Glasgow.*
SCL12(II-1411),   SCL7(II-833),   A64(57).

Collected Stories of Hortense Calisher, The. *Hortense Calisher.*
SCL12(III-1413),   A76(54).

Collected Stories of Jean Stafford, The. *Jean Stafford.* SCL12(III-1416),
SCLs(72).

Collected Stories of Katherine Anne Porter, The. *Katherine Anne Porter.*
SCL12(III-1419),   SCL7(II-835),   A66(51).

*Collected Stories of Peter Taylor, The. *Peter Taylor.* SCL12(III-1425),
A71(46).

Collected Works of Jane Bowles, The. *Jane Bowles.* SCL12(III-1431),
SCL7(II-841),   A67(41).

*Collector, The. *John Fowles.* SCL12(III-1436),   SCL7(II-846),
A64(59).

Collegians, The. *Gerald Griffin.* MP12(II-1028),   MPCE(I-376),
MP8(II-796),   MP6(I-523),   MPEng(115),   MPv4(77),
MP2(I-160),   MWL2(160).

Colloquia Peripatetica. *John Duncan.* RCh(II-762).

Colomba. *Prosper Mérimée.* MP12(II-1031), MPCE(I-377), MP8(II-799), MP6(I-526), MPEur(147), MPv4(80), MP2(I-162), MWL2(162).

Colonia Felice, La. *Carlo Dossi.* SF(I-406).

Colonial Merchants and the American Revolution, 1763-1776, The. *Arthur M. Schlesinger, Sr.* HAmer(I-244).

Colonial Period of American History, Vol. II: The Settlements, The. *Charles M. Andrews.* Different analyses on this title appear in: HAmer(I-94; I-99; I-118).

Colonial Period of American History, Vol. IV: England's Commercial and Colonial Policy, The. *Charles M. Andrews.* HAmer(I-123).

Colonial South Carolina: A Political History, 1663-1763. *M. Eugene Sirmans.* HAmer(I-137).

Colonial Virginia. *Richard L. Morton.* HAmer(I-63).

Colony and Mother City in Ancient Greece. *A. J. Graham.* HAnc(I-132).

Color of Darkness. *James Purdy.* MP12(II-1034), MP8(II-802), MP4(I-144), MWL4(144). A different analysis on this title appears in: SCL12(III-1439), SCLs(74).

Colossus. *D. F. Jones.* SF(I-409).

*Colossus and Other Poems, The. *Sylvia Plath.* SCL12(III-1443), SCLs(77).

Columban Church, The. *John A. Duke.* HAnc(II-1084).

Columbus Lands in America (Event). HEur(I-16).

Columbus Lands in the New World (Event). HAmer(I-17).

Column and the Arch, The. *W. P. P. Longfellow.* HAnc(I-502).

Combat in the Erogenous Zone. *Ingrid Bengis.* SCL12(III-1447), A73(92).

Come Back, Little Sheba. Cine(I-370).

Come Back to the Farm. *Jesse Stuart.* SCL12(III-1452), A72(70).

Come Gentle Spring. *Jesse Stuart.* SCL12(III-1457), A70(78).

Come ladro di notte. *Mauro Antonio Miglieruolo.* SF(I-415).

Come, Let Us Worship. *Godfrey Diekmann, O. S. B.* RCa(II-1103).

Come Out into the Sun. *Robert Francis.* SCL12(III-1461), SCL7(II-849), A67(45).

Comedians. *Trevor Griffiths.* LA77(I-174).

*Comedians, The. *Graham Greene.* SCL12(III-1465), SCL7(II-853), A67(49).

*Comedy of Errors, The. *William Shakespeare.* MP12(II-1037), MPCE(I-378), MP8(II-805), MP6(I-528), MPDr(163), MPv3(83), MP2(I-164), MWL2(164).

Coming Fury, The. *Bruce Catton.* SCL12(III-1470), SCL7(II-858), A62(78).

Coming Home. Cine(I-374).

*Coming of Age, The. *Simon de Beauvoir.* SCL12(III-1475), A73(96).

Coming of Rain, The.   *Richard Marius*.   SCL12(III-1479),   A70(82).
Coming of the French Revolution, The.   *Georges Lefebvre*.   Different
     analyses on this title appear in: HEur(I-508; I-513).
Coming of the Italian-Ethiopian War, The.   *George W. Baer*.
     HEur(III-1403).
Coming of the War, 1914, The.   *Bernadotte E. Schmitt*.   Different analyses
     on this title appear in: HEur(III-1246; III-1344).
Coming Race, The.   *Edward Bulwer-Lytton*.   SF(I-418).
Command Decisions.   *Kent Roberts Greenfield*.   HAmer(III-1723).
Command of the Howe Brothers During the American Revolution,
     The.   *Troyer S. Anderson*.   HAmer(I-279).
Commentaries.   *Caesar (Gaius Julius Caesar)*.   MP12(II-1040),
     MP8(II-808),   MP6(I-530),   MPNf(53),   MP3(I-204),   MWL3(204).
Commentary on Aristotle's *De anima*.   *Saint Albert the Great*.   RCa(I-360).
Commentary on Galatians.   *Ragnar Bring*.   RCh(II-1180).
Commentary on the Apostles' Creed, A.   *Rufinus of Aquileia*.   RCa(I-169).
Commentary on the *Summa theologica* of Saint Thomas.   *Saint Cajetan*.
     RCa(I-516).
Commerce of the Prairies, The.   *Josiah Gregg*.   HAmer(I-590).
"Commissioning" of the Septuagint (Event).   HAnc(I-418).
Commissioning of the Vulgate (Event).   HAnc(II-909).
Commodity Conflict.   *L. N. Rangarajan*.   HWor(III-1208).
Commodore Perry Opens Japan to American Trade (Event).
     HAmer(II-884).
Common Market, The.   *Jean François Deniau*.   HEur(III-1603).
Common Market, The.   *Nancy L. Hoepli*, ed.   HWor(III-1151).
Common Market: The European Community in Action, The.   *J. Warren
     Nystrom* and *Peter Malof*.   HEur(III-1604).
Common Market Formed by Western European Nations (Event).
     HEur(III-1601).
Common People of Pompeii: A Study of the Graffiti, The.   *Helen H.
     Tanzer*.   HAnc(II-662).
Commonitory, The.   *Saint Vincent of Lérins*.   Different analyses on this title
     appear in: RCh(I-153),   RCa(I-198).
"Commonwealth v. Hunt," *in* Columbia Law Review.   *Walker Nelles*.
     HAmer(II-787).
Communications and Meteorological Satellites (Event).   HWor(II-751).
Communism and the Conscience of the West.   *Fulton J. Sheen*.
     RCa(II-944).
Communist *Coup* in Czechoslovakia, The (Event).   HWor(II-626).
Communist Party of the Soviet Union, The.   *Leonard Schapiro*.   Different
     analyses on this title appear in: HEur(II-1106; III-1158; III-1350).
Communist Strategy and Tactics in Czechoslovakia, 1918-1948.   *Paul
     Zinner*.   HWor(II-629).
Communist World and Ours, The.   *Walter Lippmann*.   SCL12(III-1484),

SCL7(II-863), A60(45).

Communists Lose Italian Elections (Event). HEur(III-1538).

Community of Oil Exporting Countries, The. *Zuhayr Mikdashi.*
HWor(II-914).

Compass Flower, The. *W. S. Merwin.* LA78(I-205).

Compilation of the Muratorian Canon (Event). HAnc(II-767).

Compilation of the *Summa Theologiae* (Event). HAnc(III-1544). *See also*
Summa Theologica.

Compilation of the Talmud (Event). HAnc(II-985).

Complaint: Or, Night Thoughts, The. *Edward Young.* MP12(II-1042),
MP8(II-810), MP4(I-146), MWL4(146).

Complaisant Lover, The. *Graham Greene.* SCL12(III-1487),
SCL7(II-866), A62(82).

Compleat Angler, The. *Izaak Walton.* MP12(II-1044), MP8(II-812),
MP6(I-532), MPNf(55), MP3(I-206), MWL3(206).

Complete Poems. *Elizabeth Bishop.* SCL12(III-1490), A70(86).

Complete Poems. *Marianne Moore.* SCL12(III-1494), SCL7(II-869),
A68(47).

Complete Poems of Cavafy, The. *Constantine P. Cavafy.*
SCL12(III-1499), SCL7(II-874), A62(84).

Complete Ronald Firbank, The. *Arthur Annesley Ronald Firbank.*
SCL12(III-1502), SCL7(II-877), A62(87).

Complete Stories of Flannery O'Connor, The. *Flannery O'Connor.*
SCL12(III-1506), A72(75).

Complete Works of Nathanael West, The. *Nathanael West.*
SCL12(III-1509), SCL7(II-881), A58(55), BMA(103).

Completion of the Augustan Settlement (Event). HAnc(I-562).

Completion of the H.M.S. *Dreadnought* (Event). HEur(III-1187).

Completion of the Transcontinental Telegraph (Event). HAmer(II-930).

Composition of Egyptian Wisdom Literature (Event). HAnc(I-35).

Composition of *Four Quartets*, The. *Helen Gardner.* LA79(I-128).

Composition of the Book of Genesis (Event). HAnc(I-96).

Composition of the *Defensor Pacis* (Event). HAnc(III-1608).

Composition of the Nibelungenlied (Event). HAnc(III-1405). *See also*
Nibelungenlied, The.

Composition of the *Romance of the Rose* (Event). HAnc(III-1467).

Composition of the *Song of Roland* (Event). HAnc(III-1308). *See also* Song
of Roland, The.

Compromise of 1850, The (Event). HAmer(II-854).

Compulsion. Cine(I-380).

Comrades. *August Strindberg.* MP12(II-1047), MPCE(I-379),
MP8(II-815), MP6(I-535), MPDr(166), MP3(I-208),
MWL3(208).

Comte Publishes *Positive Philosophy* (Event). HEur(II-803).

*Comus. *John Milton.* MP12(II-1051), MPCE(I-381), MP8(II-817),

MP6(I-537),   MPDr(168),   MP3(I-210),   MWL3(210).
Concept of Mind, The. *Gilbert Ryle.* Ph(II-1109).
Conception of Mechanistic Atomism (Event). HAnc(I-264).
Conception of the Apostolic Succession, The (Event). HAnc(II-742).
Concerning Illustrious Men. *Suetonius (Gaius Suetonius Tranquillus).*
    MP12(II-1054),   MP8(II-820),   MP4(I-148),   MWL4(148).
Concerning Rhetoric and Virtue. *Alcuin.* RCa(I-261).
Concluding Unscientific Postscript. *Søren Kierkegaard.* Different analyses
    on this title appear in: Ph(II-626),   RCh(II-704).
Conclusion of Franco-American Treaties (Event). HAmer(I-282).
Concordat of Bologna (Event). HEur(I-44).
Condemnation of Christian Averroism (Event). HAnc(III-1564).
Condemnation of Jesus (Event). HAnc(II-601).
Condemnation of Wycliffe (Event). HAnc(III-1640).
Conditionally Human. *Walter M. Miller, Jr.* SF(I-423).
Condor Passes, The. *Shirley Ann Grau.* SCL12(III-1513),   A72(78).
Conduct of the Chaco War, The. *David Hantzler Zook, Jr.* HWor(I-293).
Conduct of the Ministry of Jesus (Event). HAnc(II-589).
Confederacy, The. *Charles P. Roland.* HAmer(II-943).
Confederate Nation: 1861-1865, The. *Emory M. Thomas.* LA80(I-156).
Confederation of the United Colonies of New England (Event).
    HAmer(I-109).
*Confessions. *Saint Augustine.* MP12(II-1057),   MP8(II-823),
    MP6(I-539),   MPNf(58),   MP3(I-213),   MWL3(213). Different
    analyses on this title appear in: Ph(I-252),   RCh(I-128),   RCa(I-165).
*Confessions. *Jean Jacques Rousseau.* MP12(II-1060),   MP8(II-826),
    MP6(I-542),   MPNf(61),   MP3(I-215),   MWL3(215).
Confessions of a Disloyal European. *Jan Myrdal.* SCL12(III-1517),
    SCL7(II-885),   A69(76).
*Confessions of an English Opium Eater. *Thomas De Quincey.*
    MP12(II-1063),   MPCE(I-383),   MP8(II-829),   MP6(I-545),
    MPNf(64),   MPv4(82),   MP2(I-167),   MWL2(167).
Confessions of Edward Dahlberg, The. *Edward Dahlberg.*
    SCL12(III-1521),   A72(82).
*Confessions of Felix Krull, Confidence Man. *Thomas Mann.*
    MP12(II-1067),   MPCE(I-385),   MP8(II-832),   MP6(I-548),
    MPEur(150),   MP3(I-218),   MWL3(218). A different analysis on this
    title appears in: SCL12(III-1524),   SCL7(II-889),   A55(65),
    BMA(107).
*Confessions of Nat Turner, The. *William Styron.* SCL12(III-1528),
    SCL7(II-893),   A68(53). A different analysis on this title appears in:
    HAmer (II-686).
*Confidence Man, The. *Herman Melville.* MP12(II-1071),
    MPCE(I-386),   MP8(II-835),   MP6(I-551),   MPAm(94),
    MP3(I-221),   MWL3(221).

*Conquistador. *Archibald MacLeish.* MP12(II-1088), MP8(II-850),
　　MP6(I-560), MPPo(56), MP3(I-223), MWL3(223).
*Conscience of the Rich, The. *C. P. Snow.* MP12(II-1091),
　　MP8(II-853), MP4(I-152), MWL4(152). A different analysis on this
　　title appears in: SCL12(III-1549), SCL7(II-903), A59(40).
*Conscious Lovers, The. *Sir Richard Steele.* MP12(II-1094),
　　MPCE(I-392), MP8(II-856), MP6(I-562), MPDr(171),
　　MPv4(85), MP2(I-174), MWL2(174).
Consciousness in Concord. *Henry David Thoreau.* SCL12(III-1552),
　　SCL7(II-906), A59(43).
Conservation and the Gospel of Efficiency: The Progressive Conservation
　　Movement, 1890-1920. *Samuel P. Hays.* HAmer(III-1376).
Conservationist, The. *Nadine Gordimer.* SCL12(III-1555), A76(57).
Considerations on the Principal Events of the French Revolution. *Madame de
　　Staël.* MP12(II-1100), MP8(II-859), MP4(I-155), MWL4(155).
*Consolation of Philosophy, The. *Saint Anicius Manlius Severinus
　　Boethius.* MP12(II-1104), MP8(II-863), MP6(I-564),
　　MPNf(67), MP3(I-225), MWL3(225). Different analyses on this title
　　appear in: Ph(I-264), RCa(I-229).
Consolidation of France (Event). HAnc(III-1733).
Conspiracy at Mukden: The Rise of Japanese Military. *Takehiko
　　Yoshihashi.* HWor(I-273).
Constant Circle, The. *Sara Mayfield.* SCL12(III-1558), SCL7(II-909),
　　A68(57).
Constantine and the Conversion of Europe. *A. H. M. Jones.*
　　HAnc(II-849).
Constitution of the Athenians, The. *Hartvig Frisch.* HAnc(I-228).
Constitutional and Legal History of Medieval England, A. *Bryce Lyon.*
　　Different analyses on this title appear in: HAnc(III-1531; III-1572).
Constitutional History of England, The. *Frederick William Maitland.*
　　HAnc(III-1570).
Constitutionalism: Ancient and Modern. *Charles Howard McIlwain.*
　　Different analyses on this title appear in: HAnc(II-787; III-1387).
Construction of the Erie Canal (Event). HAmer(I-546).
Construction of the First Transcontinental Railroad (Event).
　　HAmer(II-969).
Construction of the National Road (Event). HAmer(I-491).
*Consuelo. *George Sand.* MP12(II-1106), MPCE(I-396),
　　MP8(II-865), MP6(I-566), MPEur(153), MP1(I-156),
　　MWL1(156).
Consul's File, The. *Paul Theroux.* LA78(I-215).
Consumer Movement, The. *James S. Haskins.* HWor(II-860).
Contemplative Life, The. *Julianus Pomerius.* RCa(I-220).
Contemporary European Thought and Christian Faith. *Albert Dondeyne.*
　　RCa(II-1061).

Contemporary Writers. *Virginia Woolf.* SCL12(III-1562), SCL7(II-913), A67(53).

*Contenders, The. *John Wain.* SCL12(III-1565), SCL7(II-916), A59(45).

Continental Congress, The. *Edmund C. Burnett.* HAmer(I-258).

Continuing Search for Peace in the Middle East, The (Event). HWor(I-145).

Contour in Time. *Travis Bogard.* SCL12(III-1568), A73(100).

Contours of American History, The. *William Appleman Williams.* HWor(II-667).

Contra Celsum. *Origen.* Different analyses on this title appear in: RCh(I-66), RCa(I-71), HAnc(II-734).

Contraception: A History of Its Treatment by the Catholic Theologians and Canonists. *John T. Noonan, Jr.* HEur(III-1662).

Contraception: Authority and Dissent. *Charles E. Curran.* HEur(III-1663).

Contributors and Contributions to the Southern Literary Messenger, 1834-1864, The. *David K. Jackson.* HAmer(II-727).

Convening of the First Continental Congress (Event). HAmer(I-246).

Convening of the Second Continental Congress (Event). HAmer(I-256).

Conversations of Goethe with Eckermann and Soret. *Johann Peter Eckermann.* MP12(II-1109), MP8(II-868), MP4(I-158), MWL4(158).

Conversion of Clovis (Event). HAnc(II-995).

Conversion of Constantine (Event). HAnc(II-846).

Conversion of Hungary (Event). HAnc(III-1210).

Conversion of Ireland (Event). HAnc(II-969).

Conversion of Lithuania (Event). HAnc(III-1650).

Conversion of Northumbria (Event). HAnc(II-1081).

Conversion of Russia (Event). HAnc(III-1205).

Cool Fire, The. *Bob Shanks.* LA77(I-180).

Cool Hand Luke. Cine(I-384).

Cooper's Creek. *Alan Moorehead.* SCL12(III-1572), SCL7(II-919), A65(52).

Coorinna. *Erle Wilson.* SCL12(III-1576), SCL7(II-923), A54(40).

Copernican Revolution, The. *Thomas S. Kuhn.* Different analyses on this title appear in: HEur(I-141; I-239).

Copernicus Publishes *De Revolutionibus Orbium Coelestium* (Event). HEur(I-138).

Copperhead, The. *Harold Frederic.* MP12(II-1113), MPCE(I-397), MP8(II-872), MP6(I-569), MPAm(103), MP3(I-227), MWL3(227).

*Coriolanus. *William Shakespeare.* MP12(II-1116), MPCE(I-398), MP8(II-875), MP6(I-571), MPDr(174), MPv3(90), MP2(I-176), MWL2(176).

Corn Is Green, The. Cine(I-387).

Cornelius Chronicles, The. *Michael Moorcock.* SF(I-433).

Cornerstone, The. *Zoé Oldenbourg.* MP12(II-1121), MP8(II-878),
    MP4(I-162), MWL4(162), SCL12(III-1579), SCL7(II-926),
    A55(68).
Coronado: Knight of Pueblos and Plains. *Herbert E. Bolton.* HAmer(I-43).
Coronado's Expedition and the Founding of Santa Fe (Event).
    HAmer(I-40).
Coronation of Napoleon as Emperor (Event). HEur(II-564).
Coronation of Pepin (Event). HAnc(II-1131).
Correspondence of Pope Gregory VII: Selected Letters from the Registrum,
    The. *Ephraim Emerton.* HAnc(III-1265).
Corrida at San Feliu, The. *Paul Scott.* SCL12(III-1582), SCL7(II-929),
    A65(56).
Corridors of Power. *C. P. Snow.* SCL12(III-1586), SCL7(II-933),
    A65(59).
*Corsican Brothers, The. *Alexandre Dumas (père).* MP12(II-1124),
    MPCE(I-401), MP8(II-881), MP6(I-574), MPEur(156),
    MPv3(93), MP2(I-179), MWL2(179).
Cosmicomics. *Italo Calvino.* SF(I-438).
*Cossacks, The. *Count Leo Tolstoy.* MP12(II-1128), MPCE(I-403),
    MP8(II-884), MP6(I-576), MPEur(159), MPv3(95),
    MP2(I-181), MWL2(181).
Cost of Discipleship, The. *Dietrich Bonhoeffer.* RCh(II-1028).
Cotton Trade and Industrial Lancashire, 1600-1780, The. *Alfred P.
    Wadsworth* and *Julia De Lacy Mann.* HEur(I-407).
Council Fires on the Upper Ohio: A Narrative of Indian Affairs in the Upper
    Ohio Valley Until 1795. *Randolph C. Downes.* HAmer(I-385).
Council of Chalcedon, The. *R. V. Sellers.* HAnc(II-954).
Council of Chalcedon and the Armenian Church, The. *Karekin Sarkissian.*
    HAnc(II-966).
Council of Trent (Event). HEur(I-143).
Council, Reform and Reunion, The. *Hans Küng.* RCa(II-1110).
Count Frontenac and New France Under Louis XIV. *Francis Parkman.*
    MP12(II-1133), MP8(II-886), MP4(I-164), MWL4(164).
*Count of Monte-Cristo, The. *Alexandre Dumas, (père).* MP12(II-1136),
    MPCE(I-406), MP8(II-889), MP6(I-578), MPEur(161),
    MP1(I-158), MWL1(158).
*Counterfeiters, The. *André Gide.* MP12(II-1140), MPCE(I-409),
    MP8(II-892), MP6(I-580), MPEur(164), MP1(I-160),
    MWL1(160).
Counter-Reformation, 1550-1600, The. *B. J. Kidd.* HEur(I-146).
*Countess de Charny, The. *Alexandre Dumas (père).* MP12(II-1146),
    MPCE(I-413), MP8(II-895), MP6(I-583), MPEur(167),
    MP3(I-230), MWL3(230).
Country and the City, The. *Raymond Williams.* SCL12(III-1590),
    A74(52).

MP2(I-192),   MWL2(192).

Craig's Wife.   Cine(I-397).

Cranford.   *Mrs. Elizabeth Gaskell.*   MP12(II-1191),   MPCE(I-437),
    MP8(II-925),   MP6(II-609),   MPEng(123),   MPv3(106),
    MP2(I-194),   MWL2(194).

Crazy in Berlin.   *Thomas Berger.*   SCL12(III-1605),   SCLs(81).

Crazy Salad.   *Nora Ephron.*   SCL12(III-1609),   A76(60).

*Cream of the Jest, The.   *James Branch Cabell.*   MP12(II-1194),
    MPCE(I-438),   MP8(II-927),   MP6(II-611),   MPAm(110),
    MP1(I-168),   MWL1(168).

Creation of the Athenian Empire (Event).   HAnc(I-242).

Creation of the Confederate States of America (Event).   HAmer(II-941).

Creation of thee Federal Republic of Germany and the German Democratic
    Republic, The (Event).   HWor(II-647).

Creation of the "Holy Roman Empire" (Event).   HAnc(III-1195).

Creation of the Imperial Bureaucracy (Event).   HAnc(II-621).

Creation of the New Comedy (Event).   HAnc(I-368).

Creation of the Office of Commissioner of Education (Event).
    HAmer(II-1031).

Creation of the Office of Scientific Research and Development (Event).
    HAmer(III-1692).

Creation of the Sexagesimal System (Event).   HAnc(I-21).

Creation of the Tennessee Valley Authority (Event).   HAmer(III-1621).

Creative Evolution.   *Henri Bergson.*   Ph(II-767).

Creed of a Savoyard Priest, The.   *Jean Jacques Rousseau.*   RCh(II-605).

Cress Delehanty.   *Jessamyn West.*   SCL12(III-1612),   SCL7(II-944),
    A54(43).

Crest Jewel of Wisdom.   *S'aṅkara.*   Ph(I-268).

*Crime and Punishment.   *Fyodor Mikhailovich Dostoevski.*
    MP12(II-1197),   MPCE(I-440),   MP8(II-929),   MP6(II-613),
    MPEur(179),   MP1(I-170),   MWL1(170).

"Crime of 1873," The (Event).   HAmer(II-1083).

Crime of Galileo, The.   *Giorgio de Santillana.*   SCL12(III-1615),
    SCL7(II-947),   A55(71). A different analysis on this title appears in:
    HEur(I-287).

*Crime of Sylvestre Bonnard, The.   *Anatole France.*   MP12(II-1202),
    MPCE(I-443),   MP8(II-932),   MP6(II-615),   MPEur(182),
    MPv3(108),   MP2(I-196),   MWL2(196).

Crimean War, The (Event).   HEur(II-813).

Criminal Justice in Our Time.   *A. Dick Howard.*   HAmer(III-1896).

*Crisis, The.   *Winston S. Churchill.*   MP12(II-1207),   MPCE(I-446),
    MP8(II-935),   MP6(II-618),   MPAm(112),   MP1(I-172),
    MWL1(172).

*Crisis, The.   *Thomas Paine.*   MP12(II-1211),   MP8(II-938),
    MP6(II-620),   MPNf(69),   MP3(I-238),   MWL3(238).

Crisis: The Inside Story of the Suez Conspiracy. *Terence Robertson.*
    HEur(III-1591).
Crisis and Compromise: Politics in the Fourth Republic. *Philip M.*
    Williams. HEur(III-1611).
Crisis in Freedom: The Alien and Sedition Acts. *John C. Miller.*
    HAmer(I-416).
Crisis in Lebanon. *Fahim I. Qubain.* HWor(II-760).
Crisis of 1830-1842 in Canadian-American Relations, The. *Albert B. Corey.*
    HAmer(II-803).
Crisis of Railroad Transportation, The (Event). HWor(I-520).
Crisis of the Constitution, The. *Margaret A. Judson.* HEur(I-267).
Crisis of the House Divided: An Interpretation of the Issues in the
    Lincoln-Douglas Debates. *Harry V. Jaffa.* HAmer(II-909).
Crisis on the Left: Cold War Politics and American Liberals,
    1947-1954. *Mary Sperling McAuliffe.* LA79(I-138).
*Critic, The. *Richard Brinsley Sheridan.* MP12(II-1214),
    MPCE(I-448), MP8(II-941), MP6(II-622), MPDr(187),
    MPv3(110), MP2(I-199), MWL2(199).
Critical Essays. *Roland Barthes.* SCL12(III-1619), A73(104).
Critical Essays of William Hazlitt. *William Hazlitt.* MP12(II-1217),
    MP8(II-943), MP4(I-166), MWL4(166).
Critical Point, The. *Irving Howe.* SCL12(III-1623), A74(56).
Critique of Judgment. *Immanuel Kant.* Ph(I-556).
Critique of Practical Reason. *Immanuel Kant.* Ph(I-545).
Critique of Pure Reason. *Immanuel Kant.* MP12(II-1220),
    MP8(II-946), MP6(II-624), MPNf(72), MP3(I-240), MWL3(240).
    A different analysis on this title appears in: Ph(I-531).
Critique of the Gotha Program. *Karl Marx.* HEur(II-995).
Crito. *Plato.* Ph(I-54).
Crock of Gold, The. *James Stephens.* MP12(III-1223), MPCE(I-449),
    MP8(II-949), MP6(II-627), MPEng(125), MP1(I-175),
    MWL1(175).
Crocodile Fever. *Lawrence Earl.* SCL12(III-1627), SCL7(II-951),
    A54(46).
*Crome Yellow. *Aldous Huxley.* MP12(III-1226), MPCE(I-450),
    MP8(II-951), MP6(II-629), MPEng(127), MP1(I-177),
    MWL1(177).
Cromwell. *Roger Howell, Jr.* LA78(I-219).
Cross and the Fasces: Christian Democracy and Fascism in Italy,
    The. *Richard A. Webster.* HEur(III-1357).
Cross of Iron, The. *Willi Heinrich.* SCL12(III-1630), SCL7(II-954),
    A57(48).
Crossbowman's Story, A. *George Millar.* SCL12(III-1634),
    SCL7(II-958), A55(74).
Crossroads. *James McConkey.* SCL12(III-1638), SCL7(II-962),

A68(60).

Crossroads of Death: The Story of the Malmédy Massacre and Trial. *James J. Weingartner.* LA80(I-162).

Crossroads to Civil War: Lebanon, 1958-1976. *Kamel Suleiman Salibi.* HWor(III-1239).

Crotchet Castle. *Thomas Love Peacock.* MP12(III-1229), MPCE(I-451), MP8(II-953), MP6(II-631), MPEng(129), MPv4(90), MP2(I-201), MWL2(201).

Crow. *Ted Hughes.* SCL12(III-1641), A72(89).

Crown of Feathers and Other Stories, A. *Isaac Bashevis Singer.* SCL12(III-1645), A74(60).

Crucial Conversations. *May Sarton.* SCL12(III-1651), A76(63).

Crucial Decade, The. *Eric G. Goldman.* SCL12(III-1654), SCL7(II-965), A57(51).

Cruise of the Cachalot, The. *Frank T. Bullen.* MP12(III-1232), MPCE(I-452), MP8(II-955), MP6(II-632), MPEng(131), MP1(I-178), MWL1(178).

"Crusader States, 1243-1291, The," *in* The Later Crusades 1189-1311. Vol. II *of Setton's* A History of the Crusades. *Steven Runciman.* HAnc(III-1576).

Crusaders for American Liberalism. *Louis Filler.* HAmer(III-1355).

Crusades, The. *Zoé Oldenbourg.* SCL12(III-1658), SCL7(II-969), A67(59).

*Cry, the Beloved Country. *Alan Paton.* MP12(III-1235), MPCE(I-454), MP8(II-957), MP6(II-634), MPEur(185), MPv4(91), MP2(I-202), MWL2(202).

*Crying of Lot 49, The. *Thomas Pynchon.* SCL12(III-1662), SCL7(II-973), A67(63).

Cryptozoic! *Brian W. Aldiss.* SF(I-443).

Crystal Age, A. *William Henry Hudson.* SF(I-449).

Crystal Palace Exhibition (Event). HEur(II-799).

Crystal World, The. *J. G. Ballard.* SF(I-453).

Crystallization of the *Code of Barcelona* (Event). HAnc(III-1514).

Crystallization of the New Testament (Event). HAnc(II-779).

C. S. Lewis: A Biography. *Roger Lancelyn Green* and *Walter Hooper.* SCL12(III-1666), A74(66).

Cuba: Island of Paradox. *R. Hart Phillips.* SCL12(III-1669), SCL7(II-976), A60(48).

Cuba: The Making of a Revolution. *Ramón Eduardo Ruiz.* HWor(II-746).

"Cuba: Time for a Change," *in* Foreign Policy. *Abraham F. Lowenthal.* HWor(III-1253).

Cuba Under Castro: The Limits of Charisma. *Edward Gonzalez.* HWor(II-747).

Cuban Crises as Reflected in the New York Press, 1895-1898, The. *Joseph E. Wisan.* HAmer(II-1246).

Cuban Invasion: The Chronicle of a Disaster, The. *Karl E. Meyer* and *Tad Szulc.* HWor(II-931).

Cuban Missile Crisis, The (Event). HAmer(III-1888).

"Cubans in Africa, The," *in* Newsweek. *Angus Deming,* et al. HWor(III-1321).

Cubs and Other Stories, The. *Mario Vargas Llosa.* LA80(I-165).

Cudjo's Cave. *John Townsend Trowbridge.* MP12(III-1238), MPCE(I-455), MP8(II-959), MP6(II-636), MPAm(115), MPv4(94), MP2(205), MWL2(205).

Culmination of the Synthesis of Islamic and Greek Thought (Event). HAnc(III-1395).

Cultivation of Polyphony (Event). HAnc(III-1409).

Cultural Contradictions of Capitalism, The. *Daniel Bell.* LA77(I-184).

Cultural Development at the Court of Harun al-Rashid (Event). HAnc(II-1142).

Cultural Materialism: The Struggle for a Science of Culture. *Marvin Harris.* LA80(I-170).

*Culture and Anarchy. *Matthew Arnold.* MP12(III-1242), MP8(II-962), MP4(I-169), MWL4(169).

Culture of Narcissism: American Life in an Age of Diminishing Expectations, The. *Christopher Lasch.* LA80(I-175).

Cunning of the Dove, The. *Alfred Duggan.* SCL12(III-1672), SCL7(II-979), A61(51).

Cupid and Psyche. *Unknown.* MP12(III-1245), MPCE(I-456), MP8(II-965), MP6(II-639), MPEur(187), MP1(I-180), MWL1(180).

Cur Deus homo. *Saint Anselm of Canterbury.* Different analyses on this title appear in: RCh(I-202), RCa(I-286).

Cursus theologicus. *John of St. Thomas.* RCa(II-605).

Custer and the Great Controversy: The Origin and Development of a Legend. *Robert M. Utley.* HAmer(II-1096).

Custer's Luck. *Edgar I. Stewart.* HAmer(II-1097).

*Custom of the Country, The. *Edith Wharton.* MP12(III-1249), MPCE(I-459), MP8(II-967), MP6(II-641), MPAm(118), MP3(I-243), MWL3(243).

Cybele's Introduction into Rome (Event). HAnc(I-432).

Cyberiad, The. *Stanislaw Lem.* SF(I-457).

*Cyclops, The. *Euripides.* MP12(III-1252), MPCE(I-461), MP8(II-969), MP6(II-643), MPDr(189), MP3(I-245), MWL3(245).

*Cymbeline. *William Shakespeare.* MP12(III-1255), MPCE(I-462), MP8(II-971), MP6(II-645), MPDr(191), MPv3(112), MP2(I-207), MWL2(207).

*Cypresses Believe in God, The. *José María Gironella.* MP12(III-1259), MP8(II-974), MP4(I-172), MWL4(172), SCL12(III-1676),

SCL7(II-983),   A55(78).

Cyprus Crisis, The (Event).   HWor(III-1193).

Cyrano de Bergerac.   Cine(I-400).

*Cyrano de Bergerac. *Edmond Rostand.* MP12(III-1262),
    MPCE(I-464),   MP8(II-977),   MP6(II-647),   MPDr(194),
    MPv3(115),   MP2(I-210),   MWL2(210).

Cyropaedia. *Xenophon.* MP12(III-1267),   MP8(II-979),   MP4(I-174),
    MWL4(I-174).

Cyrus Field: Man of Two Worlds. *Samuel Carter III.* HEur(II-835).

Cyrus Hall McCormick. *William T. Hutchinson.* HAmer(II-681).

Czechoslovakia Invaded by Russians (Event).   HEur(III-1666).

Czechoslovakia Since World War II. *Tad Szulc.* HEur(III-1671).

Daddy Long Legs.   Cine(I-404).

Dagon. *Fred Chappell.* SCL12(III-1680),   SCL7(II-986),   A69(82).

Daguerre Develops the First Permanent Photograph (Event).   HEur(II-747).

Daguerreotypes and Other Essays. *Isak Dinesen.* LA80(I-180).

Daily Telegraph Episode (Event).   HEur(III-1207).

Daimler Develops the Gasoline Internal Combustion Engine (Event).
    HEur(II-1033).

Daimon. *Gianni Montanari.* SF(I-462).

*Daisy Miller. *Henry James.* MP12(III-1270),   MPCE(I-467),
    MP8(II-982),   MP6(II-649),   MPAm(120),   MP1(I-182),
    MWL1(182).

Dalla Terra alle stelle. *Ulisse Grifoni.* SF(I-465).

Damaged Souls. *Gamaliel Bradford.* MP12(III-1273),   MP8(II-984),
    MP4(I-176),   MWL4(176).

Dame Care. *Hermann Sudermann.* MP12(III-1275),   MPCE(I-468),
    MP8(II-986),   MP6(II-651),   MPEur(189),   MPv4(96),
    MP2(I-212),   MWL2(212).

Damnable Question, The. *George Dangerfield.* LA77(I-188).

*Damnation of Theron Ware, The. *Harold Frederic.* MP12(III-1279),
    MPCE(I-470),   MP8(II-989),   MP6(II-653),   MPAm(122),
    MPv4(99),   MP2(I-214),   MWL2(214).

Dance in the Sun, A. *Dan Jacobson.* SCL12(III-1684),   SCL7(II-990),
    A57(55).

Dance of Death, The. *August Strindberg.* MP12(III-1283),
    MPCE(I-472),   MP8(II-992),   MP6(II-656),   MPDr(196),
    MPv4(101),   MP2(I-217),   MWL2(217).

Dance the Eagle to Sleep. *Marge Piercy.* SCL12(III-1687),   A71(55).

*Dance to the Music of Time, A. *Anthony Powell.* MP12(III-1288),
    MP8(II-995),   MP4(I-178),   MWL4(178). A different analysis on this
    title appears in: SCL12(III-1690),   SCL7(II-993),   A63(28).

Dance to the Music of Time: Second Movement, A. *Anthony Powell.*
    MP12(III-1293),   MP8(II-1000),   MP4(I-183),   MWL4(183).

Dancer in Darkness, A. *David Stacton*. SCL12(III-1695), SCL7(II-997), A63(32).
Dancers at the End of Time. *Michael Moorcock*. SF(I-468).
Dangerous Acquaintances. *Pierre Choderlos de Laclos*. MP12(III-1299), MPCE(I-475), MP8(II-1006), MP6(II-658), MPEur(192), MP3(I-246), MWL3(246).
Daniel Coit Gilman: Creator of the American Type of University. *Abraham Flexner*. HAmer(II-1080).
*Daniel Deronda. *George Eliot*. MP12(III-1304), MPCE(I-477), MP8(II-1009), MP6(II-660), MPEng(133), MP3(I-249), MWL3(249).
Daniel Martin. *John Fowles*. LA78(I-225).
Daniel O'Connell, the Irish Liberator. *Denis Gwynn*. HEur(II-672).
Daniel Webster. *Irving H. Bartlett*. LA79(I-143).
Daniel Webster. *Claude M. Fuess*. HAmer(I-662).
Daniel Webster and the Rise of National Conservatism. *Richard N. Current*. HAmer(II-805).
Dante. *Thomas G. Bergin*. SCL12(III-1699), SCL7(II-1001), A66(56). A different analysis on this title appears in: HAnc(III-1601).
Dante. *T. S. Eliot*. MP12(III-1308), MP8(II-1012), MP4(I-188), MWL4(188).
Dante Writes the *Divine Comedy* (Event). HAnc(III-1598). *See also* Divine Comedy.
*Daphnis and Chloë. *Longus*. MP12(III-1310), MPCE(I-479), MP8(II-1014), MP6(II-663), MPEur(195), MP1(I-183), MWL1(183).
Dark and the Light, The. *Elio Vittorini*. SCL12(III-1703), SCL7(II-1005), A62(90).
*Dark as the Grave Wherein My Friend Is Laid. *Malcolm Lowry*. SCL12(III-1706), SCL7(II-1008), A69(86).
*Dark at the Top of the Stairs, The. *William Inge*. SCL12(III-1710), SCL7(II-1011), A59(48).
Dark Is Light Enough, The. *Christopher Fry*. SCL12(III-1713), SCL7(II-1014), A54(150).
Dark Journey, The. *Julian Green*. MP12(III-1313), MPCE(I-480), MP8(II-1016), MP6(II-665), MPEur(197), MPv3(117), MP2(I-219), MWL2(219).
*Dark Labyrinth, The. *Lawrence Durrell*. SCL12(III-1716), SCL7(II-1017), A63(35).
Dark Lady, The. *Louis Auchincloss*. LA78(I-229).
*Dark Laughter. *Sherwood Anderson*. MP12(III-1317), MPCE(I-482), MP8(II-1019), MP6(II-667), MPAm(125), MP1(I-185), MWL1(185).
Dark Night of the Soul, The. *Saint John of the Cross*. RCh(I-406).
Dark Universe. *Daniel F. Galouye*. SF(I-474).

Dark Victory. Cine(I-409).

Darkening Island. *Christopher Priest.* SF(I-480).

Darkness and Dawn. *George A. England.* SF(I-484).

*Darkness at Noon. *Arthur Koestler.* MP12(III-1321), MPCE(I-485), MP8(II-1021), MP6(II-669), MPEur(200), MP1(I-187), MWL1(187).

Darkness Visible. *William Golding.* LA80(I-184).

Darkover. *Marion Zimmer Bradley.* SF(I-488).

Darling. Cine(I-412).

Darrow: A Biography. *Kevin Tierney.* LA80(I-188).

Darwin and the Darwinian Revolution. *Gertrude Himmelfarb.* SCL12(III-1719), SCL7(II-1020), A60(51).

Darwin and the Modern World View. *John C. Greene.* HEur(II-858).

Darwin Publishes *On the Origin of Species* (Event). HEur(II-855). *See also* On the Origin of Species.

Darwin's Century. *Loren Eiseley.* HEur(II-856).

Das Nibelungenlied: Entstehung und Gestalt. *Friedrich Panzer. See* Nibelungenlied: Entstehung und Gestalt, Das.

Daughter of France. *V. Sackville-West.* SCL12(III-1723), SCL7(II-1023), A60(54).

Daughter of Silence. *Morris L. West.* SCL12(III-1727), SCL7(II-1027), A62(93).

Daughter of the Legend. *Jesse Stuart.* SCL12(III-1731), SCL7(II-1031), A66(60).

Daughter to Napoleon. *Constance Wright.* SCL12(III-1734), SCL7(II-1034), A62(96).

Daumier: Man of His Time. *Oliver W. Larkin.* SCL12(III-1738), SCL7(II-1038), A67(66).

*David Copperfield. *Charles Dickens.* MP12(III-1324), MPCE(I-486), MP8(II-1023), MP6(II-671), MPEng(136), MP1(I-189), MWL1(189).

David Harum. *Edward Noyes Westcott.* MP12(III-1331), MPCE(I-490), MP8(II-1027), MP6(II-674), MPAm(127), MP1(I-192), MWL1(192).

Da Vinci's Bicycle. *Guy Davenport.* LA80(I-195).

Davy. *Edgar Pangborn.* SF(I-493).

Davy Invents the Arc Lamp (Event). HEur(II-560).

Dawn of a New Era, 1250-1453, The. *Edward P. Cheyney.* HAnc(III-1516).

Dawn Patrol. Cine(I-416).

Day After Judgment, The. *James Blish.* SF(I-497).

Day After Sunday, The. *Hollis Summers.* SCL12(III-1742), SCL7(II-1042), A69(89).

Day America Crashed, The. *Tom Shachtman.* LA80(I-200).

Day by Day. *Robert Lowell.* LA78(I-233).

Day I Stopped Dreaming About Barbara Steele and Other Poems,

The. *R. H. W. Dillard.* SCL12(III-1747), SCL7(II-1047), A67(69).

Day in Late September, A. *Merle Miller.* SCL12(III-1750), SCL7(II-1050), A64(61).

Day Is Dark *and* Three Travelers, The. *Marie-Claire Blais.* SCL12(III-1754), SCL7(II-1054), A68(63).

Day Lincoln Was Shot, The. *Jim Bishop.* SCL12(III-1758), SCL7(II-1058), A55(81). A different analysis on this title appears in: HAmer (II-1017).

Day of Concord and Lexington: Nineteenth of April, 1775, The. *Allen French.* HAmer(I-254).

"Day of Dupes," The (Event). HEur(I-278).

Day of Infamy. *Walter Lord.* SCL12(III-1761), SCL7(II-1061), A58(60), BMA(114).

Day of the Leopards. *W. K. Wimsatt.* LA77(I-194).

Day of the Lion, The. *Giose Rimanelli.* SCL12(III-1765), SCL7(II-1064), A54(49).

Day of the Triffids, The. *John Wyndham.* SF(I-502).

Day of Trinity. *Lansing Lamont.* HAmer(III-1695).

Day Sailing. *David R. Slavitt.* SCL12(III-1768), A70(90).

Day the Money Stopped, The. *Brendan Gill.* SCL12(III-1773), SCL7(II-1067), A58(63).

Day the Perfect Speakers Left, The. *Leonard Nathan.* SCL12(III-1776), A70(94).

Days in the Yellow Leaf. *William Hoffman.* SCL12(III-1780), SCL7(II-1070), A59(50).

Days of Henry Thoreau, The. *Walter Harding.* SCL12(III-1783), SCL7(II-1073), A66(63).

Days of the Phoenix. *Van Wyck Brooks.* SCL12(III-1786), SCL7(II-1076), A58(66).

Days of Wine and Roses. Cine(I-418).

DDT: And Newer Persistent Insecticides. *T. F. West* and *G. A. Campbell.* HWor(I-427).

De contemptu mundi. *Pope Innocent III.* RCa(I-342).

De Corpore. *Thomas Hobbes.* Ph(I-399).

De corpore Christi. *William of Ockham.* RCh(I-267).

De magistro. *Saint Augustine.* RCa(I-140).

De monarchia. *Dante Alighieri.* Different analyses on this title appear in: RCh(I-255), RCa(I-438).

De potestate regia et papali. *John of Paris.* RCa(I-432).

De primo principio. *John Duns Scotus.* RCa(I-423).

De Principiis. *Origen.* Ph(I-240).

*De Profundis. *Oscar Wilde.* MP12(III-1334), MP8(II-1031), MP4(I-190), MWL4(190).

De regno Christi. *Martin Bucer.* RCh(I-396).

De religione laici. *Edward Herbert, First Lord of Cherbury.* RCh(I-467).
*De Rerum Natura. *Lucretius (Titus Lucretius Carus).* MP12(III-1337),
   MP8(II-1033), MP6(II-676), MPNf(75), MP3(I-252),
   MWL3(252). A different analysis on this title appears in: Ph(I-218).
De sacro altaris mysterio. *Pope Innocent III.* RCa(I-345).
De trinitate. *Saint Augustine.* RCa(I-173).
De trinitate. *Saint Anicius Manlius Severinus Boethius.* RCa(I-223).
De veritate. *Saint Thomas Aquinas.* RCa(I-379).
De viris illustribus. *Saint Jerome.* RCa(I-148).
Dead Father, The. *Donald Barthelme.* SCL12(III-1789), A76(66).
Dead Fires. *José Lins do Rêgo.* MP12(III-1339), MP8(II-1035),
   MP6(II-678), MPAm(130), MP3(I-254), MWL3(254).
Dead Sea Scrolls, The. *Millar Burrows.* HWor(II-601).
Dead Sea Scrolls, 1947-1969, The. *Edmund Wilson.* HWor(II-602).
*Dead Souls. *Nikolai V. Gogol.* MP12(III-1342), MPCE(I-491),
   MP8(II-1038), MP6(II-681), MPEur(202), MP1(I-194),
   MWL1(194).
Dead Zone, The. *Stephen King.* LA80(I-205).
Dean Acheson. *David S. McLellan.* LA77(I-197).
*Dear Brutus. *James M. Barrie.* MP12(III-1345), MPCE(I-493),
   MP8(II-1041), MP6(II-683), MPDr(199), MP1(I-196),
   MWL1(196).
Death and Immortality. *Michele Federico Sciacca.* RCa(II-1078).
Death at an Early Age. *Jonathan Kozol.* SCL12(III-1792),
   SCL7(II-1079), A68(67).
*Death Comes for the Archbishop. *Willa Cather.* MP12(III-1349),
   MPCE(I-495), MP8(II-1043), MP6(II-685), MPAm(133),
   MP1(I-199), MWL1(199).
Death Dance. *Angus Wilson.* SCL12(III-1797), A70(98).
Death in Life: Survivors of Hiroshima. *Robert Jay Lifton.*
   SCL12(III-1801), SCLs(84).
Death in Midsummer and Other Stories. *Yukio Mishima.*
   SCL12(III-1804), SCL7(II-1084), A67(71).
*Death in the Family, A. *James Agee.* MP12(III-1354), MP8(II-1046),
   MP4(I-192), MWL4(192), SCL12(III-1808), SCL7(II-1088),
   A58(69), BMA(117).
Death in Sanchez Family, A. *Oscar Lewis.* SCL12(III-1813), A70(101).
*Death in Venice. *Thomas Mann.* MP12(III-1357), MPCE(I-498),
   MP8(II-1049), MP6(II-688), MPEur(205), MPv4(103),
   MP2(I-221), MWL2(221).
*Death Kit. *Susan Sontag.* SCL12(III-1817), SCL7(II-1092), A68(72).
Death of a Hero. *Richard Aldington.* MP12(III-1362), MPCE(I-501),
   MP8(II-1052), MP6(II-690), MPEng(140), MPv4(105),
   MP2(I-223), MWL2(223).
Death of a President, The. *William Manchester.* HAmer(III-1902).

Death of a Salesman. Cine(I-421).
*Death of a Salesman. *Arthur Miller.* MP12(III-1365), MPCE(I-502), MP8(II-1054), MP6(II-692), MPDr(201), MPv4(107), MP2(I-225), MWL2(225).
*Death of Artemio Cruz, The. *Carlos Fuentes.* MP12(III-1369), MP8(II-1057), MP4(I-195), MWL4(195), SCL12(III-1821), SCL7(1096), A65(63).
Death of Charles II of Spain (Event). HEur(I-372).
Death of Franco and the Restoration of the Monarchy (Event). HWor(II-1043).
*Death of Ivan Ilyich, The. *Count Leo Tolstoy.* MP12(III-1373), MPCE(I-504), MP8(II-1061), MP6(II-694), MPEur(208), MP3(I-256), MWL3(256).
Death of Lorca, The. *Ian Gibson.* SCL12(III-1827), A74(69).
Death of Socrates (Event). HAnc(I-318).
Death of Stalin (Event). HEur(III-1566).
Death of the Detective, The. *Mark Smith.* LA77(I-202).
Death of the Dragon, The. *Sakyo Komatsu.* SF(I-508).
Death of the Earth, The. *J. H. Rosny (the Elder).* SF(II-513).
Death of the Fox. *George Garrett.* SCL12(III-1831), A72(92).
Death of the Gods, The. *Dmitri Merejkowski.* MP12(III-1377), MPCE(I-507), MP8(II-1063), MP6(II-696), MPEur(210), MP1(I-201), MWL1(201).
*Death of the Heart, The. *Elizabeth Bowen.* MP12(III-1381), MPCE(I-509), MP8(II-1066), MP6(II-699), MPEng(142), MPv4(110), MP2(I-228), MWL2(228).
Death of the King's Canary, The. *Dylan Thomas* and *John Davenport.* LA78(I-238).
Death of the Roman Republic. *John James Stewart Perowne.* HAnc(I-497).
Death of Virgil, The. *Hermann Broch.* MP12(III-1385), MPCE(I-511), MP8(II-1069), MP6(II-701), MPEur(213), MP3(I-258), MWL3(258).
Death Ship, The. *B. Traven.* MP12(III-1388), MP8(II-1072), MP4(I-199), MWL4(199).
Death, Sleep & the Traveler. *John Hawkes.* SCL12(III-1836), A75(65).
Death Takes a Holiday. Cine(I-424).
Death's Duell. *John Donne.* MP12(III-1391), MP8(II-1075), MP4(I-202), MWL4(202).
Deaths of Mao Tse-tung and Chou En-lai (Event). HWor(III-1264).
Deathworld Trilogy, The. *Harry Harrison.* SF(II-519).
Debates with Historians. *Pieter Geyl.* HWor(I-331).
Debit and Credit. *Gustav Freytag.* MP12(III-1393), MPCE(I-512), MP8(II-1077), MP6(II-703), MPEur(216), MP3(I-261), MWL3(261).
Decade of Decisions: American Policy Toward the Arab-Israeli Conflict,

1967-1977. *William B. Quandt.* LA78(I-243).

Decadence: The Strange Life of an Epithet. *Richard Gilman.* LA80(I-210).

Decades, The. *Johann Heinrich Bullinger.* RCh(I-381).

*Decameron, The (Selections). *Giovanni Boccaccio.* MP12(III-1397), MPCE(I-514), MP8(II-1080), MP6(II-706), MPEur(219), MPv4(112), MP2(I-230), MWL2(230).

*Decay of the Angel, The. *Yukio Mishima.* SCL12(III-1839), A75(68).

Decembrist Revolt, The (Event). HEur(II-665).

Decembrists, The. *Mikhail Zetlin.* HEur(II-668).

Decent Interval. *Frank Snepp.* HWor(III-1230).

Decision at Trafalgar. *Dudley Pope.* SCL12(III-1843), SCL7(II-1102), A61(55), BMA(121).

Decision by the United States to Construct an Atomic Bomb (Event). HWor(I-389).

Decision in Germany. *Lucius D. Clay.* HEur(III-1548).

Decision in Korea. *Rutherford Poats.* HWor(II-680).

Decision to Aid Russia, 1941: Foreign Policy and Domestic Politics, The. *Raymond H. Dawson.* HAmer(III-1690).

"Decision to Halt at the Elbe, The," *in* Command Decisions. *Forrest C. Pogue.* HWor(II-582).

Decision to Intervene, The. *George F. Kennan.* SCL12(III-1847), SCL7(II-1106), A59(54), BMA(125).

Decisive Battles of World War II: The German View. *H. A. Rohwer* and *J. Jacobsen,* eds. Different analyses on this title appear in: HEur(III-1469; III-1475; III-1494).

Declaration of Faith (and Other Writings), A. *Gregory Thaumaturges.* RCh(I-64).

Declaration of Independence (Event). HAmer(I-261).

Declaration of Independence: A Study in the History of Political Ideas, The. *Carl L. Becker.* HAmer(I-263).

Declaration of Sentiments, The. *Jacobus Arminius.* RCh(I-424).

Declaration of the First Punic War (Event). HAnc(I-408).

Declaration of the Pragmatic Sanction of Bourges (Event). HAnc(III-1703).

*Decline and Fall. *Evelyn Waugh.* MP12(III-1404), MPCE(I-517), MP8(II-1085), MP6(II-711), MPEng(145), MPv4(117), MP2(I-235), MWL2(235).

Decline of Bismarck's European Order: Franco-Russian Relations, 1875-1890, The. *George F. Kennan.* LA80(I-215).

Decline of Imperial Russia, 1855-1914, The. *Hugh Seton-Watson.* HEur(III-1181).

Decline of the Medieval Church, The. *Alexander C. Flick.* HAnc(III-1646).

Decline of the West, The. *Oswald Spengler.* SCL12(III-1851), SCL7(II-1110), A63(38).

Decolonization. HWor(II-985).

Decretum Gratiani. *Johannes Gratian.* RCa(I-324).

Dedication of Aelia Capitolina (Event).   HAnc(II-702).

Deep Waters. *William Hope Hodgson.*   SF(II-524).

Deeper into Movies. *Pauline Kael.*   SCL12(III-1855),   A74(73).

*Deephaven. *Sarah Orne Jewett.*   MP12(III-1409),   MPCE(I-520),
    MP8(II-1088),   MP6(II-714),   MPAm(136),   MPv4(120),
    MP2(I-238),   MWL2(238).

Deer Hunter, The.   Cine(I-427).

*Deerslayer, The. *James Fenimore Cooper.*   MP12(III-1413),
    MPCE(I-521),   MP8(II-1091),   MP6(II-716),   MPAm(139),
    MP1(I-203),   MWL1(203).

Defeat in Teutoburger Forest (Event).   HAnc(II-578).

Defeat of the Spanish Armada (Event).   HEur(I-193).

Defence of Guenevere and Other Poems, The. *William Morris.*
    MP12(III-1417),   MP8(II-1094),   MP4(I-204),   MWL4(204).

*Defence of Poesie. *Sir Philip Sidney.*   MP12(III-1420),   MP8(II-1097),
    MP4(I-206),   MWL4(206).

*Defence of Poetry, A. *Percy Bysshe Shelley.*   MP12(III-1423),
    MP8(II-1100),   MP4(I-208),   MWL4(208).

"Defence of Rhyme, A," *in* Elizabethan and Jacobean Quartos. *Samuel
    Daniel.*   HAnc(III-1352).

Defenestration of Prague (Event).   HEur(I-250).

*Defense, The. *Vladimir Nabokov.*   SCL12(III-1859),   SCL7(II-1114),
    A65(69).

Defense of Berlin, The. *Jean Edward Smith.*   HEur(III-1626).

Defense of the Constitutions of Government of the United States of America,
    A. *John Adams.*   MP12(III-1426),   MP8(II-1103),   MP6(II-719),
    MPNf(77),   MP3(I-263),   MWL3(263).

Defense of the True and Catholic Doctrine of the Sacrament, A. *Thomas
    Cranmer.*   RCh(I-385).

Defenses of Spanish Florida, 1565-1763, The. *Verne E. Chatelain.*
    HAmer(I-37).

Defensor Pacis of Marsiglio of Padua: A Critical Study, The. *Ephraim
    Emerton.*   HAnc(III-1610).

Defiance in Manchuria: The Making of Japanese Foreign Policy,
    1931-1932. *Sadako N. Ogata.*   HWor(I-274).

De Gaulle. *François Mauriac.*   HEur(III-1686).

De Gaulle: A Political Biography. *Alexander Werth.*   HEur(III-1685).

De Gaulle Revolution, The. *Alexander Werth.*   HEur(III-1609).

De Gaulle Steps Down (Event).   HEur(III-1683).

Degrees of Knowledge. *Jacques Maritain.*   Different analyses on this title
    appear in: Ph(II-963),   RCa(II-828).

Deification of Ptolemy Philadelphus (Event).   HAnc(I-403).

Deirdre. *James Stephens.*   MP12(III-1428),   MPCE(I-523),
    MP8(II-1105),   MP6(II-721),   MPEng(148),   MPv4(122),
    MP2(I-240),   MWL2(240).

*Deirdre of the Sorrows. *John Millington Synge.* MP12(III-1432),
    MPCE(I-525), MP8(II-1108), MP6(II-723), MPDr(204),
    MP3(I-265), MWL3(265).
*Delicate Balance, A. *Edward Albee.* SCL12(III-1862), SCL7(II-1117),
    A67(75).
Delineation of the Seven Sacraments (Event). HAnc(III-1338).
Deliverance. Cine(I-432).
*Deliverance. *James Dickey.* SCL12(III-1866), A71(58).
Delmore Schwartz: The Life of an American Poet. *James Atlas.*
    LA78(I-249).
Delphic Oracle, The. *H. W. Parke* and *D. E. W. Wormell.* HAnc(I-123).
Delphine. *Madame de Staël.* MP12(III-1436), MPCE(I-527),
    MP8(II-1110), MP6(II-725), MPEur(224), MPv4(125),
    MP2(I-243), MWL2(243).
*Delta Wedding. *Eudora Welty.* MP12(III-1439), MPCE(I-529),
    MP8(II-1113), MP6(II-727), MPAm(142), MPv4(127),
    MP2(I-245), MWL2(245).
*Delusions, Etc., of John Berryman. *John Berryman.* SCL12(III-1870),
    A73(108).
*Demian. *Hermann Hesse.* SCL12(III-1874), SCL7(II-1121), A66(66).
Demise of the Puritan Ethic in America, The (Event). HWor(I-526).
Demobilization after World War I (Event). HAmer(III-1478).
Demobilization and Reconversion after World War II (Event).
    HAmer(III-1759).
Democracy in America. *Alexis de Tocqueville.* MP12(III-1443),
    MP8(II-1116), MP4(I-211), MWL4(211).
Democracy in France Since 1870. *David Thomson.* HEur(III-1413).
Democracy's College: The Land-Grant Movement in the Formative
    Stage. *Earle D. Ross.* HAmer(II-977).
Democratic Representation: Reapportionment in Law and Politics. *Robert A.
    Dixon, Jr.* HAmer(III-1886).
Democratic Revolution of 1928 (Event). HAmer(III-1566).
*Democratic Vistas. *Walt Whitman.* MP12(III-1446), MP8(II-1119),
    MP4(I-213), MWL4(213).
Democratic-Republican Societies, 1790-1800. *Eugene P. Link.*
    HAmer(I-379).
Democritus: Fragments. *Democritus of Abdera.* Ph(I-37).
Demolished Man, The. *Alfred Bester.* SF(II-529).
*Demon: An Eastern Tale, The. *Mikhail Yurievich Lermontov.*
    MP12(III-1449), MP8(II-1122), MP4(I-216), MWL4(216).
Demons, The. *Heimito von Doderer.* SCL12(III-1877), SCL7(II-1124),
    A62(100).
Demonstration of Apostolic Teaching, The. *Saint Irenaeus.* RCa(I-47).
Departures. *Donald Justice.* SCL12(II-1880), A74(77).
Depression Decade: From New Era Through New Deal, 1929-1941. *Broadus*

Mitchell. HAmer(III-1596).

Deputy, The. *Rolf Hochhuth.* SCL12(III-1883), SCL7(II-1127), A65(71).

Der Grüne Heinrich. *Gottfried Keller.* *See* Grüne Heinrich, Der.

Descartes. *S. V. Keeling.* HEur(I-296).

Descartes Publishes *Discourse on Method* (Event). HEur(I-294). *See also* Discourse on Method.

Descent into Hell. *Charles Williams.* MP12(III-1452), MP8(II-1125), MP4(I-218), MWL4(218).

Descent of Man, and Selection to Relation to Sex. *Charles Darwin.* MP12(III-1455), MP8(II-1128), MP4(I-221), MWL4(221).

Descent of Woman, The. *Elaine Morgan.* SCL12(III-1887), A73(111).

Desegregation and the Law: The Meaning and Effect of the School Segregation Cases. *Albert P. Blaustein* and *Clarence C. Ferguson, Jr.* HAmer(III-1852).

*Desert Music and Other Poems, The. *William Carlos Williams.* SCL12(III-1891), SCL7(II-1131), A54(52).

Desert Solitaire. *Edward Abbey.* SCL12(III-1894), SCL7(II-1134), A69(93).

Deserted House, The. *Lydia Chukovskaya.* SCL12(III-1897), SCL7(II-1137), A68(75).

Desire Under the Elms. *Eugene O'Neill.* MP12(III-1458), MPCE(I-531), MP8(II-1131), MP6(II-730), MPDr(206), MPv3(119), MP2(I-247), MWL2(247).

De Soto and the Conquistadores. *Theodore Maynard.* HAmer(I-36).

DeSoto's Expedition and the Founding of St. Augustine (Event). HAmer(I-33).

Despair. *Vladimir Nabokov.* SCL12(III-1901), SCL7(II-1141), A67(78).

Destinies of Darcy Dancer, Gentleman, The. *J. P. Donleavy.* LA78(I-254).

Destiny Bay. *Donn Byrne.* MP12(III-1463), MPCE(I-534), MP8(II-1133), MP6(II-732), MPEng(151), MPv4(129), MP2(I-249), MWL2(249).

Destiny of Man, The. *Nikolai Berdyaev.* Different analyses on this title appear in: Ph(II-940), RCh(II-960).

Destruction of Pompeii (Event). HAnc(II-659).

Destruction of the European Jews, The. *Raul Hilberg.* HWor(I-399).

Destruction of the Golden Horde (Event). HAnc(III-1742).

Destruction of the Greek Empire and the Story of the Capture of Constantinople by the Turks, The. *Edwin Pears.* HAnc(III-1720).

Destruction of the Serapeum (Event). HAnc(II-924).

Destry Rides Again. Cine(I-436).

Details of a Sunset and Other Stories. *Vladimir Nabokov.* LA77(I-206).

Détente and the Democratic Movement in the U.S.S.R. *Frederick C. Barghoorn.* HWor(II-995).

Détente with the Soviet Union (Event). HWor(II-1050).

Devaluation of the Dollar (Event).   HWor(III-1097).
Development of Direct Democracy (Event).   HAmer(II-1307).
Development of Gothic Architecture (Event).   HAnc(III-1416).
Development of Inhalation Anaesthesia with Special Reference to the Years,
    1846-1900, The. *Barbara M. Duncum.* HAmer(II-793).
Development of Lenses (Event).   HAnc(III-1555).
Development of Modern Italy, The. *Cecil Jackson Squire Sprigge.*
    HWor(I-140).
Development of Radar (Event).   HWor(I-324).
Development of Religion and Thought in Ancient Egypt. *James Henry
    Breasted.*   HAnc(I-55).
Development of Scientific Cattle Breeding (Event).   HAnc(III-1426).
Development of the Antiochene Episcopacy (Event).   HAnc(II-681).
Development of the Christian Calendar (Event).   HAnc(II-877).
Development of the Ford Assembly Line and Adoption of the
    Five-Dollar-a-Day Minimum Wage (Event).   HAmer(III-1421).
Development of the German Public Mind: A Social History of German
    Political Sentiments, Aspirations, and Ideas, Vol. I: The Middle Ages
    and Reformation, The. *Frederick Hertz.*   HEur(I-252).
Development of the German Public Mind: A Social History of German
    Political Sentiments, Aspirations, and Ideas, Vol. II: The Age of the
    Enlightenment, The. *Frederick Hertz.*   Different analyses on this title
    appear in: HEur(I-89; I-370).
Development of the Guilds of Florence (Event).   HAnc(III-1303).
Development of the Miracle Play (Event).   HAnc(III-1221).
Development of the Penitential System (Event).   HAnc(II-762).
Development of the Salk Vaccine (Event).   HAmer(III-1835).
Development of the Teletype (Event).   HWor(I-1).
Devil and John Foster Dulles, The. *Townsend Walter Hoopes.*
    SCL12(III-1905),   A74(80). A different analysis on this title appears in:
    HWor(II-693).
Devil Drives, The. *Fawn M. Brodie.*   SCL12(III-1908),   SCL7(II-1145),
    A68(79).
Devil in Massachusetts: A Modern Enquiry into the Salem Witch Trials,
    The. *Marion L. Starkey.*   HAmer(I-172).
Devil Rides Outside, The. *John Howard Griffin.*   SCL12(III-1913),
    SCLs(88).
Devil to Pay in the Backlands, The. *Joao Guimaraes Rosa.*
    SCL12(III-1917),   SCL7(II-1150),   A64(65).
Devil's Advocate, The. *Morris L. West.*   SCL12(III-1920),
    SCL7(II-1153),   A60(57).
Devil's Elixir, The. *Ernst Theodor Amadeus Hoffmann.*   MP12(III-1467),
    MPCE(I-536),   MP8(II-1136),   MP6(II-734),   MPEur(227),
    MP3(I-267),   MWL3(267).
Devil's Horsemen: The Mongol Invasion of Europe, The. *James Chambers.*

LA80(I-220).

Devil's Yard. *Ivo Andrić.* SCL12(III-1923), SCL7(II-1156), A63(42).

*Devotion of the Cross, The. *Pedro Calderón de la Barca.*
MP12(III-1471), MPCE(I-537), MP8(II-1139), MP6(II-736),
MPDr(208), MP3(I-270), MWL3(270).

Devotions Upon Emergent Occasions. *John Donne.* RCh(I-441).

Dewey Publishes *The School and Society* (Event). HAmer(II-1301).

D. H. Lawrence: A Composite Biography. *Edward Nehls,* ed.
SCL12(III-1926), SCL7(II-1159), A60(60), BMA(129).

D. H. Lawrence's Nightmare: The Writer and His Circle in the Years of the
Great War. *Paul Delany.* LA80(I-223).

Dhalgren. *Samuel R. Delany.* SF(II-533).

Diable boiteux, Le. *Alain René Le Sage.* MP12(III-1474),
MPCE(I-538), MP8(II-1141), MP6(II-738), MPEur(230),
MP3(I-271), MWL3(271).

Dial M for Murder. Cine(I-440).

"Dialectic Without the Forms," *in* Aristotle on Dialectic. *Friedrich
Solmsen.* HAnc(I-351).

Dialogue Between the Soul and the Body, The. *Saint Catherine of Genoa.*
RCa(I-530).

Dialogue Concerning the Two Chief World Systems. *Galileo Galilei.*
RCa(II-593).

Dialogue des héros de roman. *Nicolas Boileau-Despréaux.*
MP12(III-1479), MP8(II-1145), MP6(II-741), MPNf(79),
MP3(I-275), MWL3(275).

Dialogue of Comfort Against Tribulation, A. *Saint Thomas More.*
RCh(I-354).

Dialogue of Saint Catherine of Siena, The. *Saint Catherine of Siena.*
Different analyses on this title appear in: RCh(I-280), RCa(I-473).

Dialogues. *Saint Gregory the Great.* RCa(I-241).

Dialogues, The. *Theodoret of Cyrus.* RCh(I-156).

Dialogues Concerning Cause, Principle, and One. *Giordano Bruno.*
Ph(I-365).

*Dialogues Concerning Natural Religion. *David Hume.* Different analyses
on this title appear in: Ph(I-525), RCh(II-615).

Dialogues of Plato, The. *Plato.* MP12(III-1482), MP8(II-1148),
MP6(II-744), MPNf(82), MP3(I-277), MWL3(277).

Dialogues of Sulpicius Severus, The. *Sulpicius Severus.* RCa(I-157).

Dialogues on Metaphysics and on Religion. *Nicolas de Malebranche.*
Ph(I-422).

*Diana of the Crossways. *George Meredith.* MP12(III-1486),
MPCE(I-540), MP8(II-1152), MP6(II-748), MPEng(154),
MP1(I-206), MWL1(206).

Diaries of a Cabinet Minister, The. *Richard Crossman.* LA77(I-211).

Diaries of Evelyn Waugh, The. *Evelyn Waugh.* LA78(I-258).

Diaries of Kafka: 1910-1923, The. *Franz Kafka.* MP12(III-1491), MP8(II-1155), MP4(I-224), MWL4(224).
Diary. *John Evelyn.* MP12(III-1494), MP8(II-1158), MP6(II-750), MPNf(86), MP3(I-281), MWL3(281).
*Diary. *Samuel Pepys.* MP12(III-1497), MP8(II-1161), MP6(II-753), MPNf(89), MP3(I-283), MWL3(283).
Diary and Letters of Mme. D'Arblay, The. *Fanny Burney.* MP12(III-1499), MP8(II-1163), MP4(I-226), MWL4(226).
Diary of a Country Priest, The. *Georges Bernanos.* MP12(III-1503), MPCE(I-543), MP8(II-1167), MP6(II-755), MPEur(234), MPv3(121), MP2(I-251), MWL2(251).
Diary of a Rapist, The. *Evan S. Connell, Jr.* SCL12(III-1930), SCL7(II-1163), A67(82).
Diary of a Writer. *Fyodor Mikhailovich Dostoevski.* MP12(III-1506), MP8(II-1170), MP4(I-230), MWL4(230).
*Diary of Anaïs Nin, The. *Anaïs Nin.* LA77(I-217).
Diary of Anaïs Nin: 1931-1934, The. *Anaïs Nin.* SCL12(III-1933), SCL7(II-1166), A67(84).
Diary of Anaïs Nin: 1934-1939, The. *Anaïs Nin.* SCL12(III-1937), SCL7(II-1170), A68(83).
Diary of David Brainerd, The. *David Brainerd.* RCh(II-594).
Diary of Henry Crabb Robinson, The. *Henry Crabb Robinson.* MP12(III-1509), MP8(II-1173), MP4(I-232), MWL4(232).
Diary of Virginia Woolf, Vol. I: 1915-1919, The. *Virginia Woolf.* LA78(I-264).
Diary of Virginia Woolf, Vol. II: 1920-1924, The. *Virginia Woolf.* LA79(I-147).
Dias Rounds the Cape of Good Hope (Event). HEur(I-11).
(Diblos) Notebook, The. *James Merrill.* SCL12(III-1940), SCL7(II-1173), A66(69).
Dick, The. *Bruce Jay Friedman.* SCL12(III-1943), A71(61).
Dick Gibson Show, The. *Stanley Elkin.* SCL12(III-1946), A72(97).
Didache *or* The Teaching of the Twelve Apostles, The. *Unknown.*
    Different analyses on this title appear in: RCh(I-23), RCa(I-1.)
Didactica magna. *Johannes Amos Comenius.* RCh(I-489).
Diderot. *Arthur M. Wilson.* SCL12(III-1951), A73(116).
Diderot: The Testing Years, 1713-1759. *Arthur M. Wilson.* HEur(I-429).
Diderot Pictorial Encyclopedia of Trades and Industry, A. *Charles Coulston Gillispie.* HEur(I-430).
Different Woman, A. *Jane Howard.* SCL12(III-1954), A74(84).
Digby Grand. *George J. Whyte-Melville.* MP12(III-1512), MPCE(I-545), MP8(II-1176), MP6(II-757), MPEng(157), MPv3(123), MP2(I-253), MWL2(253).
Digital Computers and the Information Revolution (Event). HWor(II-535).
Dignity of Man, The. *Russell W. Davenport.* SCL12(III-1958),

SCL7(II-1176), A55(83).

Dimension of Miracles. *Robert Sheckley.* SF(II-539).

Dimitry, Called the Pretender, Tsar and Great Prince of All Russia, 1605-1606. *Philip L. Barbour.* HEur(I-233).

Dingley Tariff, The (Event). HAmer(II-1273).

Dinner at Eight. Cine(I-444).

*Dinner Party, The. *Claude Mauriac.* MP12(III-1516), MP8(II-1179), MP4(I-235), MWL4(235), SCL12(III-1961), SCL7(II-1179), A61(58).

Dionysius the Areopagite on the Divine Names and the Mystical Theology. *C. E. Rolt.* HAnc(II-1013).

Dionysius the Pseudo-Areopagite: The Ecclesiastical Hierarchy. *Thomas L. Campbell.* HAnc(II-1014).

Diplomacy and Dogmatism: Bernardino de Mendoza and the French Catholic League. *De Lamar Jensen.* HEur(I-221).

Diplomacy of Imperialism, 1890-1902, The. *William L. Langer.* HEur(II-1116).

Diplomacy of the American Revolution, The. *Samuel Flagg Bemis.* HAmer(I-284).

Diplomacy of the Balkan Wars, 1912-1913, The. *Ernst C. Helmreich.* HEur(III-1242).

Diplomacy of the Russo-Japanese War, The. *John A. White.* HEur(III-1150).

Diplomatic Relations Established Between East and West Germany (Event). HWor(III-1167).

Diplomatic Revolution, The (Event). HEur(I-437).

"Diplomatic Revolution, The" *in* The New Cambridge Modern History. *David Bayne Horn.* HEur(I-440).

Dirty Dozen, The. Cine(I-448).

Dirty Harry. Cine(I-451).

Dirty Linen *and* New-Found-Land. *Tom Stoppard.* LA78(I-268).

Disappearance, The. *Philip Wylie.* SF(II-543).

Disarmament Deadlock, The. *John W. Wheeler-Bennett.* HWor(I-278).

Disciple, The. *Paul Bourget.* MP12(III-1519), MPCE(I-547), MP8(II-1182), MP6(II-759), MPEur(237), MP1(I-209), MWL1(209).

Discourse Against the Greeks, The. *Tatian.* RCa(I-23).

Discourse Concerning the Holy Spirit. *John Owen.* RCh(I-518).

Discourse on Method. *René Descartes.* Ph(I-380).

Discourse on the Origin of Inequality. *Jean Jacques Rousseau.* MP12(III-1522), MP8(II-1185), MP4(I-237), MWL4(237).

Discourse on the Priesthood. *Saint John Chrysostom.* RCa(I-123).

Discourse on Universal History. *Jacques Bénigne Bossuet.* RCa(II-608).

Discourses. *Pietro Aretino.* MP12(III-1524), MP8(II-1187), MP4(I-239), MWL4(239).

Discourses Against the Arians. *Saint Athanasius*. RCa(I-94).

Discourses and Manual. *Epictetus*. Ph(I-224).

Discourses Upon the Existence and Attributes of God. *Stephen Charnock*.
RCh(I-539).

Discoveries of Archimedes (Event). HAnc(I-422).

Discovery and Conquest of Mexico, The. *Bernal Díaz del Castillo*.
HEur(I-62).

Discovery and Demonstration of an Effective Anesthetic (Event).
HAmer(II-791).

Discovery of America (Event). HAnc(III-1756).

Discovery of God, The. *Henri de Lubac, S. J.* RCa(II-1025).

"Discovery" of Iron (Event). HAnc(I-58).

Discovery of Pulsars (Event). HWor(II-1009).

Discovery of Quasars (Event). HWor(II-899).

Discovery of the Dead Sea Scrolls (Event). HWor(II-598).

Discovery of the Great West: La Salle, The. *Francis Parkman*.
HAmer(I-147).

Discovery of the Mind: The Greek Origins of European Thought,
The. *Bruno Snell*. HAnc(I-176).

Discovery of the Neanderthal Man (Event). HEur(II-822).

Discovery of the Structure of DNA (Event). HEur(III-1572).

Discovery That Yellow Fever Is Spread by a Mosquito (Event).
HAmer(II-1313).

Discrepancies and Apparitions. *Diane Wakoski*. SCL12(III-1965),
SCL7(II-1183), A66(72).

Discussion of the Date of Easter (Event). HAnc(II-857).

Dispatches. *Michael Herr*. LA78(I-272).

Dispossessed, The. *Ursula K. Le Guin*. SF(II-548).

Disputation of the Sacrament of the Eucharist, A. *Peter Martyr Vermigli*.
RCh(I-376).

Disraeli. *Robert Blake*. HEur(II-1000).

Disruption of American Democracy, The. *Roy Franklin Nichols*.
HAmer(II-891).

Dissemination of the *Book of the Dead* (Event). HAnc(I-52).

Dissent Among Soviet Intellectuals (Event). HWor(II-988).

Dissent on Development. *Peter T. Bauer*. HWor(III-1209).

Dissolution of the Habsburg Monarchy, The (Event). HWor(I-158).

Dissolution of the Virginia Company: The Failure of a Colonial Experiment,
The. *Wesley F. Craven*. HAmer(I-67).

Distaff Diplomacy: The Empress Eugénie and the Foreign Policy of the
Second Empire. *Nancy Nichols Barker*. HEur(II-852).

Distant Mirror: The Calamitous 14th Century, A. *Barbara W. Tuchman*.
LA79(I-151).

Distant Music, The. *H. L. Davis*. SCL12(III-1968), SCL7(II-1186),
A58(73).

Divan, The. *Hāfiz.* MP12(III-1527), MP8(II-1190), MP6(II-761), MPPo(61), MP3(I-285), MWL3(285).

Divided Left: American Radicalism, 1900-1975, The. *Milton Cantor.* LA79(I-157).

Divided Soul: The Life of Gogol. *Henri Troyat.* SCL12(III-1972), A74(89).

Divine Comedies. *James Merrill.* LA77(I-222).

*Divine Comedy, The. *Dante Alighieri.* MP12(III-1529), MPCE(I-548), MP8(II-1192), MP6(II-763), MPPo(63), MP1(I-211), MWL1(211). Different analyses on this title appear in: RCh(I-259), RCa(I-443), HAnc(III-1600).

Divine Fire, The. *May Sinclair.* MP12(III-1534), MPCE(I-551), MP8(II-1195), MP6(II-766), MPEng(160), MPv4(131), MP2(I-256), MWL2(256).

Divine Imperative, The. *Emil Brunner.* RCh(II-986).

Divine Institutes, The. *Lucius Caecilius Firmianus Lactantius.* Different analyses on this title appear in: RCh(I-79), RCa(I-81).

Divine Love and Wisdom. *Emanuel Swedenborg.* MP12(III-1537), MP8(II-1197), MP6(II-768), MPNf(91), MP3(I-287), MWL3(287).

Divine Milieu, The. *Pierre Teilhard de Chardin, S. J.* Different analyses on this title appear in: RCh(II-1152), RCa(II-1054).

Divine Names, The. *Dionysius, the Pseudo-Areopagite.* RCh(I-165).

Divine Relativity, The. *Charles Hartshorne.* RCh(II-1088).

Diving into the Wreck. *Adrienne Rich.* SCL12(III-1977), A74(94).

Divinity School Address, The. *Ralph Waldo Emerson.* RCh(II-684).

Divino afflante Spiritu. *Pope Pius XII.* RCa(II-883).

Do Androids Dream of Electric Sheep? *Philip K. Dick.* SF(II-554).

Do, Lord, Remember Me. *George Garrett.* SCL12(III-1981), SCL7(II-1190), A66(74).

*Do with Me What You Will. *Joyce Carol Oates.* SCL12(III-1985), A74(98).

Docteur Lerne, Le. *Maurice Renard.* SF(II-560).

Dr. Bloodmoney, or How We Got Along After the Bomb. *Philip K. Dick.* SF(II-564).

*Doctor Brodie's Report. *Jorge Luis Borges.* SCL12(III-1990), A73(118).

Dr. Ehrlich's Magic Bullet. Cine(I-454).

*Doctor Faustus. *Thomas Mann.* MP12(III-1539), MPCE(I-553), MP8(II-1199), MP6(II-770), MPEur(240), MPv4(133), MP2(I-258), MWL2(258).

*Doctor Faustus. *Christopher Marlowe.* MP12(III-1543), MPCE(I-555), MP8(II-1202), MP6(II-773), MPDr(210), MPv3(125), MP2(I-261), MWL2(261).

Doctor in Spite of Himself, The. *Molière (Jean Baptiste Poquelin).* MP12(III-1546), MPCE(I-557), MP8(II-1205), MP6(II-775),

MPDr(213),   MP3(I-289),   MWL3(289).

Dr. Jekyll and Mr. Hyde.   Cine(I-457).

Dr. Jekyll and Mr. Hyde.   Cine(I-461).

Dr. Jekyll and Mr. Hyde.   *Robert Louis Stevenson.*   MP12(III-1550),
    MPCE(I-559),   MP8(II-1208),   MP6(II-778),   MPEng(162),
    MP1(I-214),   MWL1(214).

Doctor Mirabilis.   *James Blish.*   SF(II-569).

*Doctor Pascal.   *Émile Zola.*   MP12(III-1553),   MPCE(I-561),
    MP8(II-1210),   MP6(II-780),   MPEur(243),   MP3(I-291),
    MWL3(291).

Dr. Strangelove.   Cine(I-465).

*Doctor Thorne.   *Anthony Trollope.*   MP12(III-1558),   MPCE(I-564),
    MP8(II-1213),   MP6(II-782),   MPEng(164),   MPv3(128),
    MP2(I-263),   MWL2(263).

Dr. Zhivago.   Cine(I-468).

*Doctor Zhivago.   *Boris Pasternak.*   MP12(III-1561),   MP8(II-1216),
    MP4(I-241),   MWL4(241),   SCL12(III-1994),   SCL7(II-1194),
    A59(57),   BMA(133).

Doctors Mayo, The.   *Helen Clapesattle.*   HAmer(II-1181).

Doctor's Wife, The.   *Brian Moore.*   LA77(I-226).

Doctrine of Judicial Review: Its Legal and Historical Basis and Other Essays,
    The.   *Edward S. Corwin.*   HAmer(I-439).

Dodsworth.   Cine(I-471).

*Dodsworth.   *Sinclair Lewis.*   MP12(III-1565),   MPCE(I-565),
    MP8(II-1220),   MP6(II-785),   MPAm(145),   MPv3(130),
    MP2(I-265),   MWL2(265).

Does Anyone Else Have Something Further to Add?   *R. A. Lafferty.*
    SF(II-574).

Dog Day Afternoon.   Cine(I-474).

Dog Soldiers.   *Robert Stone.*   SCL12(III-1999),   A75(72).

Dog Who Wouldn't Be, The.   *Farley Mowat.*   SCL12(III-2002),
    SCL7(II-1199),   A58(76).

Dog Years.   *Günter Grass.*   SCL12(III-2005),   SCL7(II-1202),   A66(78).

Dogmatics.   *Emil Brunner.*   RCh(II-1076).

Dollar Diplomacy (Event).   HAmer(III-1379).

Dollmaker, The.   *Harriette Simpson Arnow.*   SCL12(III-2009),
    SCL7(II-1206),   A54(55).

*Doll's House, A.   *Henrik Ibsen.*   MP12(III-1570),   MPCE(I-568),
    MP8(II-1223),   MP6(II-787),   MPDr(216),   MP1(I-216),
    MWL1(216).

Dolphin For Lizzie and Harriet, and History, The.   *Robert Lowell.*
    SCL12(III-2013),   A74(103).

Domains.   *James Whitehead.*   SCL12(III-2019),   SCL7(II-1210),   A69(96).

*Dombey and Son.   *Charles Dickens.*   MP12(III-1574),   MPCE(I-571),
    MP8(II-1225),   MP6(II-789),   MPEng(167),   MPv3(132),

MP2(I-267), MWL2(267).
Domestic Relations. *Frank O'Connor.* SCL12(III-2022), SCL7(II-1213), A58(78).
Domestication of the Camel (Event). HAnc(I-30).
Domestication of the Horse (Event). HAnc(I-1).
Dominion of New England: A Study in British Colonial Policy, The. *Viola F. Barnes.* HAmer(I-165).
Dominique. *Eugène Fromentin.* MP12(III-1579), MPCE(I-574), MP8(II-1228), MP6(II-791), MPEur(246), MP3(I-294), MWL3(294).
*Don Carlos. *Johann Christoph Friedrich von Schiller.* MP12(III-1582), MPCE(I-576), MP8(II-1231), MP6(II-793), MPDr(218), MPv4(136), MP2(I-270), MWL2(270).
Don Flows Home to the Sea, The. *Mikhail Sholokhov.* MP12(III-1585), MPCE(I-577), MP8(II-1234), MP6(II-796), MPEur(249), MPv4(138), MP2(I-272), MWL2(272).
*Don Juan. *George Gordon, Lord Byron.* MP12(III-1590), MPCE(I-580), MP8(II-1237), MP6(II-798), MPPo(66), MP1(I-217), MWL1(217).
*Don Juan. *Molière (Jean Baptiste Poquelin).* MP12(III-1595), MPCE(I-583), MP8(II-1240), MP6(II-800), MPDr(221), MP3(I-296), MWL3(296).
Don Juan de Oñate and the Founding of New Mexico. *George P. Hammond.* HAmer(I-44).
Don Juan of Austria. *William Stirling-Maxwell.* HEur(I-183).
Don Juan Tenorio. *José Zorrilla y Moral.* MP12(III-1599), MPCE(I-585), MP8(II-1243), MP6(II-803), MPDr(224), MPv4(141), MP2(I-274), MWL2(274).
*Don Quixote de la Mancha. *Miguel de Cervantes Saavedra.* MP12(III-1603), MPCE(I-587), MP8(II-1246), MP6(II-805), MPEur(252), MP1(I-220), MWL1(220).
Don Segundo Sombra. *Ricardo Güiraldes.* MP12(III-1609), MPCE(I-590), MP8(II-1250), MP6(II-809), MPAm(148), MPv4(143), MP2(I-277), MWL2(277).
Doña Bárbara. *Rómulo Gallegos.* MP12(III-1614), MPCE(I-593), MP8(II-1253), MP6(II-811), MPAm(151), MPv4(146), MP2(I-279), MWL2(279).
*Doña Flor and Her Two Husbands. *Jorge Amado.* SCL12(III-2024), A71(63).
*Doña Perfecta. *Benito Pérez Galdós.* MP12(III-1618), MPCE(I-596), MP8(II-1256), MP6(II-813), MPEur(256), MP3(I-298), MWL3(298).
Donovan's Brain. *Curt Siodmak.* SF(II-579).
Don't Go Near the Water. *William Brinkley.* SCL12(III-2028), SCL7(II-1215), A57(58).

Doomsday Syndrome, The. *John Maddox.* SCL12(III-2032), A73(122).

Doors of His Face, The Lamps of His Mouth, and Other Stories, The. *Roger Zelazny.* SF(II-583).

Dorr Rebellion and the Growth of Political Democracy (Event). HAmer(II-766).

Dorr War: Or, the Constitutional Struggle in Rhode Island, The. *Arthur M. Mowry.* HAmer(II-768).

Dos de Mayo Insurrection in Spain (Event). HEur(II-581).

Dostoevsky. *Nicholas Berdyaev.* MP12(III-1621), MP8(II-1258), MP4(I-245), MWL4(245).

Dostoevsky. *Anna Dostoevsky.* LA77(I-230).

Dostoevsky. *Joseph Frank.* LA77(I-236).

Dostoevsky. *David Magarshack.* SCL12(III-2036), SCL7(II-1219), A64(67).

Double Helix, The. *James D. Watson.* SCL12(III-2039), SCL7(II-1222), A69(98). A different analysis on this title appears in: HEur(III-1575).

Double Honeymoon. *Evan S. Connell, Jr.* LA77(I-242).

Double Indemnity. Cine(I-478).

Double Star. *Robert A. Heinlein.* SF(II-587).

Double Witness, The. *Ben Belitt.* LA78(I-276).

Double-Cross in the War of 1939-1945, The. *J. C. Masterman.* SCL12(III-2043), A73(126).

*Double-Dealer, The. *William Congreve.* MP12(III-1624), MPCE(I-598), MP8(II-1261), MP6(II-815), MPDr(227), MPv3(135), MP2(I-281), MWL2(281).

*Down There. *Joris Karl Huysmans.* MP12(III-1627), MP8(II-1263), MP6(II-817), MPEur(258), MP3(I-300), MWL3(300).

*Downfall, The. *Émile Zola.* MP12(III-1629), MPCE(I-600), MP8(II-1265), MP6(II-819), MPEur(260), MP1(I-223), MWL1(223).

Downward to the Earth. *Robert Silverberg.* SF(II-591).

"Draco," *in* The Cambridge Ancient History. *F. E. Adcock.* HAnc(I-155).

Dracula. Cine(I-482).

*Dracula. *Bram Stoker.* MP12(III-1633), MPCE(I-601), MP8(II-1268), MP6(II-821), MPEng(170), MPv3(137), MP2(I-283), MWL2(283).

Drafting of the *Breviarium* of Alaric II (Event). HAnc(II-1005).

Dragon: Fifteen Stories, The. *Yevgeny Zamyatin.* SCL12(III-2048), SCL7(II-1226), A67(87).

Dragon by the Tail: American, British, Japanese, and Russian Encounters with China and One Another. *John Paton Davies, Jr.* HWor(II-660).

Dragon in the Sea, The. *Frank Herbert.* SF(II-595).

Dragon Masters, The. *Jack Vance.* SF(II-600).

*Dragon Seed. *Pearl S. Buck.* MP12(III-1638), MPCE(I-604),

Drums. *James Boyd.* MP12(III-1656), MP8(II-1288), MP6(II-831), MPAm(157), MP1(I-228), MWL1(228).

Drums Along the Mohawk. Cine(I-485).

Drums Along the Mohawk. *Walter D. Edmonds.* MP12(III-1659), MPCE(I-610), MP8(II-1291), MP6(II-834), MPAm(160), MP1(I-230), MWL1(230).

Drums of Father Ned, The. *Sean O'Casey.* SCL12(III-2081), SCL7(II-1255), A61(64).

Druso. *Friedrich Freksa.* SF(II-639).

Dual Autobiography, A. *Will Durant* and *Ariel Durant.* LA78(I-280).

"Dual Vision of the *Theogony*, The," *in* Arion. *William Sale.* HAnc(I-142).

Dubin's Lives. *Bernard Malamud.* LA80(I-231).

*Duchess of Malfi, The. *John Webster.* MP12(III-1664), MPCE(I-613), MP8(II-1294), MP6(II-836), MPDr(229), MP1(I-232), MWL1(232).

Ductor dubitantium. *Jeremy Taylor.* RCh(I-497).

Duino Elegies. *Rainer Maria Rilke.* MP12(III-1669), MP8(II-1296), MP6(II-838), MPPo(69), MP3(I-307), MWL3(307).

Duke of Deception: Memories of My Father, The. *Geoffrey Wolff.* LA80(I-236).

Dulles: A Biography of Eleanor, Allen, and John Foster Dulles and Their Family Network. *Leonard Mosley.* LA79(I-170).

Dåum o tisíci patrech. *Jan Weiss.* SF(II-644).

*Dunciad, The. *Alexander Pope.* MP12(III-1672), MP8(II-1299), MP6(II-840), MPPo(72), MP3(I-310), MWL3(310).

Dune. *Frank Herbert.* SF(II-647).

Dune Messiah. *Frank Herbert.* SF(II-659).

du Pont Family, The. *John D. Gates.* LA80(I-240).

Duration and Simultaneity, with Reference to Einstein's Theory. *Henri Bergson.* HEur(III-1162).

Dust Bowl, The (Event). HAmer(III-1627).

Dust Bowl: The Southern Plains in the 1930s. *Donald Worster.* LA80(I-244).

Dust Bowl: Men, Dirt, and Depression, The. *Paul Bonnifield.* LA80(I-251).

Duty, Honor, Country: A History of West Point. *Stephen E. Ambrose.* HAmer(I-434).

Dwight L. Moody: American Evangelist, 1837-1899. *James F. Findlay, Jr.* HAmer(II-1175).

Dyer's Hand and Other Essays, The. *W. H. Auden.* SCL12(III-2084), SCL7(II-1258), A63(47).

Dying Earth, The. *Jack Vance.* SF(II-665).

Dying Inside. *Robert Silverberg.* SF(II-671).

Dylan. *Sidney Michaels.* SCL12(III-2088), SCL7(II-1262), A65(74).

Dylan Thomas. *Andrew Sinclair.* SCL12(III-2091), A76(69).

*Dynasts, The. *Thomas Hardy*. MP12(III-1675), MPCE(I-616), MP8(II-1302), MP6(II-843), MPDr(231), MP1(I-234), MWL1(234).

E Pluribus Unicorn. *Theodore Sturgeon*. SF(II-676).
*Eagle and the Serpent, The. *Martin Luis Guzmán*. MP12(III-1679), MP8(II-1305), MP4(I-253), MWL4(253).
Eagle or Sun? *Octavio Paz*. SCL12(III-2095), A72(102).
Ear in Bartram's Tree, An. *Jonathan Williams*. SCL12(III-2099), A70(105).
Earl Warren: The Judge Who Changed America. *Jack Harrison Pollack*. LA80(I-255).
Earlier Diplomatic History, 1492-1713. *Charles Petrie*. HEur(I-343).
"Earliest Text of the Old Roman Symbol: A Debate with Hans Leitzmann and J. N. D. Kelly, The," *in* Church History. *D. Larrimore Holland*. HAnc(II-755).
Early Birds: The Wonders and Heroics of the First Decades of Flight, The. *Arch Whitehouse*. HAmer(II-1350).
Early Christian Creeds. *J. N. D. Kelly*. Different analyses on this title appear in: HAnc(II-753; II-870).
Early Christian Doctrines. *J. N. D. Kelly*. HAnc(II-750).
Early Electrical Communication. *E. A. Marland*. HAmer(II-746).
Early English Stages, 1300-1660. *Glynne W. Wickham*. HAnc(III-1222).
Early Greek Philosophy. *John Burnet*. HAnc(I-272).
Early Hainish Novels, The. *Ursula K. Le Guin*. SF(II-681).
Early History of the Monastery of Cluny, The. *Lucy Margaret Smith*. HAnc(II-1186).
Early History of the Republican Party, 1854-1856, The. *Andrew W. Crandall*. HAmer(II-881).
Early Persecutions of the Christians, The. *Leon H. Canfield*. HAnc(II-694).
Early Pythagorean Politics in Practice and Theory. *Edwin L. Minar*. HAnc(I-196).
Early Sparta. *G. L. Huxley*. HAnc(I-137).
Early Theological Writings. *Georg Wilhelm Friedrich Hegel*. RCh(II-633).
*Earth. *Émile Zola*. MP12(III-1682), MPCE(I-617), MP8(II-1308), MP6(II-845), MPEur(270), MP3(I-312), MWL3(312).
Earth Abides. *George R. Stewart*. SF(II-687).
Earth Walk. *William Meredith*. SCL12(III-2104), A71(66).
Earthly Delights, Unearthly Adornments: American Writers as Image-Makers. *Wright Morris*. LA79(I-175).
Earthly Paradise, The. *William Morris*. MP12(III-1687), MP8(II-1311), MP4(I-255), MWL4(255).
Earthsea Trilogy, The. *Ursula K. Le Guin*. SF(II-692).
East and West Germany: A Modus Vivendi. *Karl E. Birnbaum*.

HWor(III-1170).

East of Eden.   Cine(I-488).

*East of Eden.   *John Steinbeck.*   MP12(III-1689),   MPCE(I-620),
MP8(II-1313),   MP6(II-848),   MPAm(163),   MP3(I-315),
MWL3(315).

East to West.   *Arnold J. Toynbee.*   SCL12(III-2108),   SCL7(II-1265),
A59(68),   BMA(142).

Easter Parade.   Cine(II-491).

Easter Parade, The.   *Richard Yates.*   LA77(I-247).

Eastern Question: An Historical Study in Diplomacy, The.   *Sir J. A. R.
Marriott.*   HEur(I-477).

Eastern Question, 1774-1923: A Study in International Relations, The.   *M. S.
Anderson.*   Different analyses on this title appear in: HEur(III-1205;
III-1243).

Eastward Ho!   *George Chapman* with *Ben Jonson* and *John Marston.*
MP12(III-1693),   MPCE(I-622),   MP8(II-1316),   MP6(II-850),
MPDr(234),   MP3(I-317),   MWL3(317).

Easy Rider.   Cine(II-494).

Ebony and Ivory.   *Llewelyn Powys.*   MP12(III-1697),   MP8(II-1319),
MP6(II-853),   MPEng(173),   MP3(I-320),   MWL3(320).

Ebony Tower, The.   *John Fowles.*   SCL12(III-2111),   A75(75).

Ecce Homo.   *Sir John Robert Seeley.*   RCh(II-747).

Ecclesiastical History.   *Eusebius Pamphili, Bishop of Caesarea.*   Different
analyses on this title appear in: RCh(I-87),   RCa(I-88).

Ecclesiastical History of the English Nation.   *Saint Bede.*   RCh(I-181).

Ecclesiastical History of the English People, The.   *Saint Bede.*   RCa(I-258).

Ecclesiazusae, The.   *Aristophanes.*   MP12(III-1699),   MPCE(I-623),
MP8(II-1321),   MP6(II-855),   MPDr(237),   MP3(I-322),
MWL3(322).

*Eclogues.   *Vergil (Publius Vergilius Maro).*   MP12(III-1702),
MP8(II-1323),   MP4(I-257),   MWL4(257).

Economic and Social History of Medieval Europe.   *Henri Pirenne.*
HAnc(III-1362).

Economic and Social History of the Middle Ages (300-1300), An.   *James
Westfall Thompson.*   HAnc(III-1423).

Economic Crisis of Stagflation, The (Event).   HWor(II-1062).

Economic Development of France and Germany, 1815-1914, The.   *J. H.
Clapham.*   HEur(II-1046).

Economic Development of the Third World Since 1900, The.   *Paul Bairoch.*
HWor(II-559).

Economic History of the United States, Vol. III: The Farmer's Age:
Agriculture, 1815-1860, The.   *Paul W. Gates.*   HAmer(II-682).

Economic History of the United States, Vol. IV: The Transportation
Revolution, 1815-1860, The.   *George R. Taylor.*   HAmer(I-549).

Economic History of the United States, Vol. V: The Farmer's Last Frontier:

Agriculture, 1860-1897, The. *Fred Albert Shannon.* HAmer(II-964).
Economic History of the United States, Vol. VIII: Prosperity Decade:
From War to Depression, 1917-1929, The. *George Soule.*
Different analyses on this title appear in: HAmer(III-1540;
III-1546).
Economic Mobilization for War and Formation of the War Production Board
(Event). HAmer(III-1680).
Economic Origins of Jeffersonian Democracy. *Charles A. Beard.*
HAmer(I-358).
Economic Rationality and Soviet Politics. *Alec Nove.* HEur(III-1331).
Economics and the Public Purpose. *John Kenneth Galbraith.*
SCL12(III-2115), A74(109).
Economics in the Public Service: Administrative Aspects of the Employment
Act. *Edwin G. Nourse.* HAmer(III-1773).
Economists, The. *Leonard Silk.* LA77(I-251).
Ecumenical Movement: What It Is and What It Does, The. *Norman
Goodall.* HEur(III-1553).
Edge of Darkness, The. *Mary Ellen Chase.* SCL12(III-2119),
SCL7(II-1268), A58(80).
Edge of Day, The. *Laurie Lee.* SCL12(III-2122), SCL7(II-1271),
A61(67).
*Edge of Sadness, The. *Edwin O'Connor.* SCL12(III-2126),
SCL7(II-1275), A62(103).
Edge of the Sea, The. *Rachel Carson.* SCL12(III-2130),
SCL7(II-1279), A55(89), BMA(145).
Edge of the Storm, The. *Agustín Yáñez.* SCL12(III-2133),
SCL7(II-1282), A64(70).
Edge of the Sword: Israel's War of Independence, The. *Netanel Lorch.*
HWor(II-636).
Edge of the Woods, The. *Heather Ross Miller.* SCL12(III-2136),
SCL7(II-1285), A65(77).
Edict of Nantes (Event). HEur(I-214).
Edison: A Biography. *Matthew Josephson.* SCL12(IV-2139),
SCL7(II-1288), A60(63), BMA(148). A different analysis on this title
appears in: HAmer(II-1112).
Edison: The Man Who Made the Future. *Ronald W. Clark.* LA78(I-284).
Edison Demonstrates the First Practical Incandescent Lamp (Event).
HAmer(II-1110).
Edison's Conquest of Mars. *Garrett P. Serviss.* SF(II-698).
Edict of Restitution (Event). HEur(I-270).
Edith Wharton: A Biography. *R. W. B. Lewis.* SCL12(IV-2143),
A76(73).
Editing of the Chronicles of Julius Africanus (Event). HAnc(II-789).
Edmund Campion. *Evelyn Waugh.* MP12(III-1705), MPCE(I-624),
MP8(II-1326), MP6(II-857), MPNf(93), MP1(I-237),

Einstein: The Life and Times. *Ronald W. Clark.* SCL12(IV-2168), A72(110).

Einstein Intersection, The. *Samuel R. Delany.* SF(II-703).

Einstein Publishes *Special Theory of Relativity* (Event). HEur(III-1160).

Eirenicon, An. *Edward B. Pusey.* RCh(II-751).

Eisenhower and Berlin, 1945: The Decision to Halt at the Elbe. *Stephen E. Ambrose.* HAmer(III-1751).

Eisenhower and the American Crusades. *Herbert S. Parmet.* HAmer(III-1846).

Eisenhower Doctrine on the Middle East Enuniciated, The (Event). HWor(II-757).

Either/Or. *Søren Kierkegaard.* Ph(II-612).

El Alamein. *General Michael Carver.* See Alamein, El.

El Señor Presidente. *Miguel Ángel Asturias.* MP12(III-1726), MP8(II-1342), MP4(I-260), MWL4(260).

El Zarco. *Ignacio Manuel Altamirano.* See Zarco, El.

*Elder Statesman, The. *T. S. Eliot.* MP12(III-1728), MP8(II-1344), MP4(I-262), MWL4(262), SCL12(IV-2173), SCL7(II-1297), A60(67), BMA(152).

Eleanor: The Years Alone. *Joseph P. Lash.* SCL12(IV-2181), A73(143).

Eleanor and Franklin. *Joseph P. Lash.* SCL12(IV-2177), A72(115).

Eleanor of Aquitaine. *Desmond Seward.* LA80(I-277).

Election of Andrew Jackson, The. *Robert V. Remini.* HAmer(I-633).

Election of Carter to the Presidency in 1976 (Event). HWor(III-1302).

Election of Charles V as Emperor (Event). HEur(I-64).

Election of Coolidge to the Presidency, and the Ascendancy of Big Business (Event). HAmer(III-1542).

Election of 1884 (Event). HAmer(II-1140).

Election of 1840 (Event). HAmer(II-760).

Election of 1824 (Event). HAmer(I-607).

Election of Eisenhower to the Presidency in 1952 (Event). HAmer(III-1843).

Election of Franklin D. Roosevelt to the Presidency in 1932 (Event). HAmer(III-1609).

Election of Hugh Capet to the Throne of France (Event). HAnc(III-1200).

Election of Hayes to the Presidency, and the End of Reconstruction (Event). HAmer(II-1099).

Election of Jackson to the Presidency in 1828 (Event). HAmer(I-631).

Election of Jefferson to the Presidency in 1800 (Event). HAmer(I-426).

Election of Kennedy to the Presidency (Event). HAmer(III-1871).

Election of Lincoln to the Presidency in 1860 (Event). HAmer(II-935).

Election of Lyndon B. Johnson to the Presidency, and the Emergence of the Great Society (Event). HAmer(III-1918).

Election of McKinley to the Presidency in 1896 (Event). HAmer(II-1268).

Election of Michael Romanov as Tsar (Event). HEur(I-247).

Election of 1976: Reports and Interpretations, The. *Gerald M. Pomper,* et

Emancipation Proclamation, The. *John Hope Franklin.* HAmer(II-982).

Embedding, The. *Ian Watson.* SF(II-712).

*Embezzler, The. *Louis Auchincloss.* SCL12(IV-2206), SCL7(II-1317), A67(91).

Emergence of Austria (Event). HAnc(III-1364).

Emergence of Consumer Awareness (Event). HWor(II-856).

Emergence of Greek Medicine (Event). HAnc(I-302).

Emergence of Modern Turkey, The. *Bernard Lewis.* HWor(I-227).

Emergence of Modern Western Painting (Event). HAnc(III-1587).

Emergence of Papal Decretals (Event). HAnc(II-914).

Emergence of Perspective in Painting (Event). HAnc(III-1691).

Emergence of the American Indian Reform Movement (Event). HWor(II-865).

Emergence of the Common Law in England (Event). HAnc(III-1386).

Emergence of the Drug Culture (Event). HWor(II-814).

Emergence of the English Vernacular (Event). HAnc(III-1287).

Emergence of the First Political Parties (Event). HAmer(I-350).

Emergence of the New South, 1913-1945, The. *George Brown Tindall.* SCL12(IV-2209), SCL7(II-1320), A68(94).

Emergence of the Palestinian-Arab National Movement, 1918-1929, The. *Yehoshuah Porath.* HWor(I-237).

Emergence of "Theology" as a Concept (Event). HAnc(II-757).

Emerging South, The. *Thomas D. Clark.* SCL12(IV-2212), SCL7(II-1323), A62(106), BMA(163).

Emerson: A Collection of Critical Essays. *Milton R. Konvitz* and *Stephen E. Whicher,* eds. HAmer (II-851).

Emigrants, The. *Johan Bojer.* MP12(III-1749), MPCE(I-639), MP8(II-1362), MP6(II-874), MPEur(279), MP1(I-244), MWL1(244).

Emigrants, The. *José Maria Ferreira de Castro.* SCL12(IV-2216), SCL7(II-1327), A63(51).

Emigrants of Ahadarra, The. *William Carleton.* MP12(III-1752), MPCE(I-640), MP8(II-1364), MP6(II-876), MPEng(177), MP3(I-328), MWL3(328).

Emigration of European Intellectuals to America (Event). HWor(I-295).

*Émile. *Jean Jacques Rousseau.* MP12(III-1755), MP8(II-1366), MP6(II-878), MPEur(281), MP3(I-330), MWL3(330).

*Emilia Galotti. *Gotthold Ephraim Lessing.* MP12(III-1758), MPCE(I-641), MP8(II-1369), MP6(II-881), MPDr(247), MP3(I-333), MWL3(333).

Emily Dickinson. *Thomas H. Johnson.* SCL12(IV-2219), SCL7(II-1330), A55(92).

*Eminent Victorians. *Lytton Strachey.* MP12(III-1760), MP8(II-1371), MP6(II-882), MPNf(98), MP3(I-335), MWL3(335).

*Emma. *Jane Austen.* MP12(III-1763), MPCE(I-642), MP8(II-1374),

End of It, The. *Mitchell Goodman.* SCL12(IV-2236), SCL7(II-1343), A62(112).

End of Obscenity, The. *Charles Rembar.* SCL12(IV-2239), SCL7(II-1346), A69(110).

End of the American Era, The. *Andrew Hacker.* HWor(I-531).

End of the Ancient World and the Beginnings of the Middle Ages, The. *Ferdinand Lot.* Different analyses on this title appear in: HAnc(II-864; II-998).

End of the Battle, The. *Evelyn Waugh.* SCL12(IV-2244), SCL7(II-1351), A62(115), BMA(167).

End of the Old Order in Rural Europe, The. *Jerome Blum.* LA79(I-188).

*End of the Road, The. *John Barth.* MP12(III-1772), MP8(II-1379), MP4(I-273), MWL4(273).

End of the Roman World, The. *John James Stewart Perowne.* HAnc(II-938).

End of the War in Asia, The. *Louis Allen.* LA80(I-285).

End of Time, The. *Josef Pieper.* RCa(II-964).

End to Torment: A Memoir of Ezra Pound by H. D. *Hilda Doolittle.* LA80(I-290).

End Zone. *Don DeLillo.* SCL12(IV-2250), A73(148).

*Enderby. *Anthony Burgess.* SCL12(IV-2255), SCL7(II-1356), A69(115).

Endless Love. *Scott Spencer.* LA80(I-294).

*Endymion. *John Lyly.* MP12(III-1774), MPCE(I-647), MP8(II-1381), MP6(II-889), MPDr(251), MP3(I-337), MWL3(337).

Enemies, A Love Story. *Isaac Bashevis Singer.* SCL12(IV-2260), A73(154).

Enemy Camp, The. *Jerome Weidman.* SCL12(IV-2264), SCL7(II-1361), A59(71).

*Enemy of the People, An. *Henrik Ibsen.* MP12(III-1777), MPCE(I-649), MP8(II-1383), MP6(II-891), MPDr(253), MPv3(146), MP2(I-292), MWL2(292).

Energy and Conflict: The Life and Times of Edward Teller. *Stanley A. Blumberg* and *Gwinn Owens.* HWor(II-686).

Enforcement of Clerical Celibacy (Event). HAnc(III-1257).

Engine Summer. *John Crowley.* SF(II-721).

England and the Catholic Church Under Queen Elizabeth. *Arnold Oskar Meyer.* HEur(I-177).

England and the Near East: The Crimea. *Harold W. V. Temperley.* HEur(II-814).

England, 1870-1914. *R. C. K. Ensor.* HEur(II-1061).

England in the Age of the American Revolution. *Lewis B. Namier.* HAmer(I-227).

England in the Reigns of James II and William III. *David Ogg.*

HEur(I-388).

England Under the Stuarts. *George Macaulay Trevelyan.*
MP12(III-1781), MP8(II-1386), MP4(I-275), MWL4(275).

England's Road to Social Security. *Karl De Schweinitz.* HEur(III-1226).

English Auden: Poems, Essays and Dramatic Writings, 1927-1939,
The. *W. H. Auden.* LA79((I-193).

English Church in the Fourteenth and Fifteenth Centuries, The. *William W.
Capes.* HAnc(III-1632).

English Civil War: Conservatism and Revolution, 1603-1649, The. *Robert
Ashton.* LA80(I-297).

English Local Government. *Sidney Webb* and *Beatrice Webb.*
HEur(II-733).

English Monks and the Suppression of the Monasteries. *Geoffrey
Bakerville.* HEur(I-112).

English Navigation Laws, The. *Lawrence A. Harper.* HAmer(I-125).

*English Notebooks, The. *Nathaniel Hawthorne.* MP12(III-1784),
MP8(II-1389), MP4(I-277), MWL4(277).

English Reform Bill of 1867, The. *Joseph Park.* HEur(II-933).

English Reformation, The. *A. G. Dickens.* Different analyses on this title
appear in: HEur(I-107; I-127).

English Utilitarians, The. *Sir Leslie Stephen.* Different analyses on this title
appear in: HEur(I-535; II-631).

English Versions of the Bible. *Hugh Pope.* HEur(I-245).

Enid Bagnold's Autobiography. *Enid Bagnold.* SCL12(IV-2266),
A72(121).

Enid Starkie. *Joanna Richardson.* SCL12(IV-2270), A75(82).

Enlightenment: An Interpretation, Volume I, The. *Peter Gay.*
SCL12(IV-2273), SCL7(II-1363), A67(94).

Enlightenment: An Interpretation, Volume II, The. *Peter Gay.*
SCL12(IV-2278), A70(109).

Enneads. *Plotinus.* Ph(I-245).

*Enoch Arden. *Lord Alfred Tennyson.* MP12(III-1787), MPCE(I-651),
MP8(II-1392), MP6(II-894), MPPo(75), MP1(I-249),
MWL1(249).

Enormous Changes at the Last Minute. *Grace Paley.* SCL12(IV-2282),
A75(85).

*Enormous Room, The. *E. E. Cummings.* MP12(III-1789),
MPCE(I-652), MP8(II-1394), MP6(II-895), MPAm(166),
MP1(I-250), MWL1(250).

Enquiry Concerning Human Understanding, An. *David Hume.*
MP12(III-1793), MP8(II-1397), MP6(II-897), MPNf(101),
MP3(I-399), MWL3(339).

Enquiry Concerning the Principles of Morals, An. *David Hume.* Ph(I-488).

Entangling Alliances: Politics and Diplomacy Under George
Washington. *Alexander De Conde.* HAmer(I-393).

Entente Cordiale, The (Event).   HEur(III-1152).

Enthusiasm. *Ronald Knox.*   RCa(II-961).

Entrance of the United States into World War I (Event).   HAmer(III-1450).

Entrance to Porlock, The. *Frederick Buechner.*   SCL12(IV-2286), A72(124).

Enunciation of the *Dictatus Papae* (Event).   HAnc(III-1263).

Enunciation of the "Golden Bull" (Event).   HAnc(III-1635).

Environmental Legislation Passed Since 1960 (Event).   HWor(II-872).

Epic of Gilgamesh, The. *N. K. Sanders.*   HAnc(I-42).

*Epic of Gilgamesh, The. *Unknown.*   MP12(III-1796),   MPCE(II-653), MP8(II-1400),   MP6(II-900),   MPPo(77),   MP3(I-342), MWL3(342).

*Epigrams of Martial. *Martial (Marcus Valerius Martialis).* MP12(III-1800),   MP8(II-1403),   MP6(II-903),   MPPo(80), MP3(I-344),   MWL3(344).

Epigrams of Meleager, The. *Meleager.*   MP12(III-1802),   MP8(II-1405), MP4(I-280),   MWL4(280).

Epinicia, The. *Pindar.*   MP12(III-1805),   MP8(II-1408),   MP6(II-905), MPPo(82),   MP3(I-346),   MWL3(346).

Episode of Sparrows, An. *Rumer Godden.*   SCL12(IV-2290), SCL7(II-1367),   A55(95).

Epistle of Barnabas, The. *Unknown, but attributed to the Apostle Barnabas.*   RCh(I-3).

Epistle of Paul to the Romans, The. *Charles Harold Dodd.*   HAnc(II-635).

Epistle to a Godson. *W. H. Auden.*   SCL12(IV-2293),   A73(157).

Epistle to Diognetus, The. *Unknown.*   Different analyses on this title appear in: RCh(I-48),   RCa(I-62).

Epistle to the Philippians. *Saint Polycarp of Smyrna.*   RCh(I-17).

Epistle to the Romans, The. *Karl Barth.*   RCh(II-894).

Epistle XXI: To the Most Clement Emperor and Most Blessed Augustus. *Saint Ambrose.*   RCa(I-127).

Epistles *and* The Martyrdom of Saint Polycarp, The. *Saint Polycarp of Smyrna.*   RCa(I-16).

Epistles of Horace, The. *Horace (Quintus Horatius Flaccus).* MP12(III-1808),   MP8(II-1411),   MP4(I-282),   MWL4(282).

Epistles of Saint Ignatius of Antioch, The. *Saint Ignatius of Antioch.* RCa(I-7).

Epitaph for Dixie, An. *Harry S. Ashmore.*   SCL12(IV-2296), SCL7(II-1370),   A59(73).

*Epitaph of a Small Winner. *Joaquim Maria Machado de Assís.* MP12(III-1811),   MPCE(II-655),   MP8(II-1414), MP6(II-907),   MPAm(169),   MPv4(148),   MP2(I-294), MWL2(294).

Epp. *Axel Jensen.*   SF(II-725).

Equus. *Peter Shaffer.*   SCL12(IV-2299),   A75(89).

Era of Excess: A Social History of the Prohibition Movement. *Andrew Sinclair.* HAmer(III-1509).

Era of Good Feelings, The. *George Dangerfield.* Different analyses on this title appear in: HAmer(I-520; I-560; I-611).

Era of Reconstruction, 1865-1877, The. *Kenneth M. Stampp.* SCL12(IV-2302), SCL7(II-1373), A66(87).

Era of the Clipper Ships (Event). HAmer(II-807).

Era of Theodore Roosevelt and the Birth of Modern America, 1900-1912, The. New American Nation *series. George E. Mowry.* HAmer(II-1327).

Erasers, The. *Alain Robbe-Grillet.* SCL12(IV-2308), SCL7(II-1379), A65(83).

Erec and Enide. *Chrétien de Troyes.* MP12(III-1816), MPCE(II-658), MP8(II-1417), MP6(II-909), MPPo(85), MP3(I-348), MWL3(348).

Erection of Slater's Spinning Mill at Pawtucket (Event). HAmer(I-362).

*Erewhon. *Samuel Butler.* MP12(III-1822), MPCE(II-661), MP8(II-1421), MP6(II-913), MPEng(182), MP1(I-252), MWL1(252).

Erewhon *and* Erewhon Revisited. *Samuel Butler.* SF(II-729).

Erie Water West: A History of the Erie Canal, 1792-1854. *Ronald E. Shaw.* HAmer(I-548).

"Eritrean Battlefront: The Cubans Move In," *in* The Nation. *Dan Connell.* HWor(III-1319).

Ernest Hemingway. *Carlos Baker.* SCL12(IV-2311), A70(112).

Ernest Hemingway and His World. *Anthony Burgess.* LA79(I-196).

Ernest Hemingway Publishes *The Sun Also Rises* (Event). HAmer(III-1560). *See also* Sun Also Rises, The.

Ernest Renan: A Critical Biography. *H. W. Wardman.* HEur(II-895).

Esau and Jacob. *Joaquim Maria Machado de Assís.* SCL12(IV-2316), SCL7(II-1382), A66(93).

Escape of Socrates, The. *Robert Pick.* SCL12(IV-2320), SCL7(II-1386), A54(58).

Essais. *Michel Eyquem de Montaigne.* MP12(III-1825), MP8(II-1423), MP6(II-915), MPNf(104), MP3(I-352), MWL3(352).

Essay Concerning Human Understanding, An. *John Locke.* MP12(III-1828), MP8(II-1426), MP6(II-917), MPNf(107), MP3(I-354), MWL3(354). A different analysis on this title appears in: Ph(I-428).

*Essay of Dramatic Poesy, An. *John Dryden.* MP12(III-1831), MP8(II-1429), MP4(I-285), MWL4(285).

Essay on Catholicism, Liberalism, and Socialism. *Juan Francisco Maria de la Saludad Donoso Cortés.* RCa(II-650).

*Essay on Criticism. *Alexander Pope.* MP12(III-1834), MP8(II-1432), MP4(II-287), MWL4(287).

Essay on Human Love. *Jean Guitton.* RCa(II-923).

Essay on Indifference in Matters of Religion. *Félicité Robert de Lamennais.*
RCa(II-632).

Essay on Liberty. *John Stuart Mill.* Ph(II-644).

*Essay on Man. *Alexander Pope.* MP12(IV-1837), MP8(II-1435),
MP4(I-290), MWL4(290).

Essay on Metaphysics, An. *Robin George Collingwood.* Ph(II-1046).

Essay on the Development of Christian Doctrine, An. *John Henry Cardinal
Newman.* RCa(II-644).

Essay on the Metaphysics of Descartes, An. *Marthinus Versfeld.*
HEur(I-297).

Essay Towards a New Theory of Vision, An. *George Berkeley.*
MP12(IV-1840), MP8(II-1438), MP4(I-292), MWL4(292).

*Essays. *Sir Francis Bacon.* MP12(IV-1842), MP8(II-1440),
MP6(II-920), MPNf(110), MP3(I-357), MWL3(357).

Essays: First and Second Series. *Ralph Waldo Emerson.* MP12(IV-1845),
MP8(II-1443), MP6(II-922), MPNf(113), MP3(I-359),
MWL3(359).

Essays in Feminism. *Vivian Gornick.* LA80(I-302).

Essays of a Biologist. *Julian Huxley.* MP12(IV-1848), MP8(II-1446),
MP4(I-294), MWL4(294).

Essays of Aldous Huxley, The. *Aldous Huxley.* MP12(IV-1851),
MP8(II-1449), MP4(I-297), MWL4(297).

Essays of E. B. White. *E. B. White.* LA78(I-295).

Essays of Edgar Allan Poe, The. *Edgar Allan Poe.* MP12(IV-1854),
MP8(II-1452), MP4(I-299), MWL4(299).

*Essays of Elia and Last Essays of Elia. *Charles Lamb.* MP12(IV-1857),
MP8(II-1455), MP6(II-925), MPNf(116), MP3(I-362),
MWL3(362).

*Essays of G. K. Chesterton, The. *Gilbert Keith Chesterton.*
MP12(IV-1859), MP8(III-1457), MP4(I-302), MWL4(302).

Essays of Henry David Thoreau, The. *Henry David Thoreau.*
MP12(IV-1863), MP8(III-1461), MP4(I-305), MWL4(305).

*Essays of Max Beerbohm, The. *Max Beerbohm.* MP12(IV-1866),
MP8(III-1464), MP4(I-307), MWL4(307).

Essays on the Intellectual Powers of Man and Essays on the Active Powers of
the Human Mind. *Thomas Reid.* Ph(I-538).

Essence of Christianity, The. *Ludwig Feuerbach.* RCh(II-697).

Establishment of Alcuin's Palace School (Event). HAnc(II-1136).

Establishment of Castile's School of Translation (Event). HAnc(III-1524).

Establishment of Christianity and the Proscription of Paganism, The. *Maude
Aline Huttmann.* HAnc(II-907).

Establishment of Harvard College and Enactment of the Massachusetts School
Law (Event). HAmer(I-103).

Establishment of Oberlin College (Event). HAmer(II-708).

Establishment of Separate but Equal Doctrine for Black and White Public

Facilities (*Plessy* v. *Ferguson*) (Event).   HAmer(II-1261).

Establishment of the Commonwealth in England (Event).   HEur(I-329).

Establishment of the *Cursus Honorum* (Event).   HAnc(I-448).

Establishment of the Democratic Republic of Vietnam, The (Event).
     HWor(II-696).

Establishment of the Independent Treasury (Event).   HAmer(II-748).

Establishment of the Julian Calendar (Event).   HAnc(I-536).

Establishment of the Kingdom of Israel (Event).   HAnc(I-106).

Establishment of the League of Nations (Event).   HEur(III-1289).

Establishment of the Liturgical Year (Event).   HAnc(II-1091).

Establishment of the Organization of Petroleum Exporting Countries (OPEC)
     (Event).   HWor(II-912).

Establishment of the Rhine-Danube Frontier (Event).   HAnc(II-584).

Establishment of the Russian Patriarchate (Event).   HEur(I-198).

Establishment of the School of Prince Henry the Navigator (Event).
     HAnc(III-1686).

Establishment of the See of Canterbury (Event).   HAnc(II-1058).

Establishment of the Southeast Asia Treaty Organization (SEATO) (Event).
     HWor(II-703).

Establishment of the Third French Republic (Event).   HEur(II-974).

Establishment of the Union of South Africa (Event).   HWor(I-87).

Establishment of the United Kingdom (Event).   HAnc(I-90).

Establishment of the United States Military Academy (Event).
     HAmer(I-432).

Establishment of the United States Public Health Service (Event).
     HAmer(III-1394).

Establishment of Tudor Rule in England (Event).   HEur(I-6).

Establishment of Vivarium (Event).   HAnc(II-1046).

Establishment of Yahweh's Covenant with Israel (Event).   HAnc(I-84).

Estate of Memory, An. *Ilona Karmel.*   SCL12(IV-2323),   A70(117).

*Esther Waters. *George Moore.*   MP12(IV-1870),   MPCE(II-662),
     MP8(III-1468),   MP6(II-927),   MPEng(184),   MP1(I-254),
     MWL1(254).

Eternal Now, The. *Paul Tillich.*   SCL12(IV-2326),   SCL7(II-1389),
     A64(72).

*Ethan Frome. *Edith Wharton.*   MP12(IV-1873),   MPCE(II-664),
     MP8(III-1471),   MP6(II-929),   MPAm(172),   MP1(I-256),
     MWL1(256).

Ethica Nicomachea. *Aristotle.*   Ph(I-157).

Ethical Studies. *Francis Herbert Bradley.*   Ph(II-676).

Ethics. *Dietrich Bonhoeffer.*   RCh(II-1101).

Ethics. *Nicolai Hartmann.*   Ph(II-868).

Ethics. *Frank Chapman Sharp.*   Ph(II-901).

Ethics. *Benedictus de Spinoza.*   MP12(IV-1876),   MP8(III-1473),
     MP6(II-931),   MPNf(118),   MP3(I-364),   MWL3(364). A different

analysis on this title appears in: Ph(I-416).

Ethics and Language. *Charles Leslie Stevenson.*   Ph(II-1089).

Ethics in a World of Power: The Political Ideas of Friedrich
   Meinecke. *Richard W. Sterling.*   HWor(I-57).

Ethos of the Song of Roland, The. *G. F. Jones.*   HAnc(III-1310).

Etymologies, The. *Saint Isidore of Seville.*   RCa(I-248).

Eucharistic Words of Jesus, The. *Joachim Jerimias.*   HAnc(II-599).

Eugene Aram. *Edward George Earle Bulwer-Lytton.*   MP12(IV-1879),
   MPCE(II-665),   MP8(III-1476),   MP6(II-933),   MPEng(187),
   MPv3(148),   MP2(I-297),   MWL2(297).

*Eugene Onegin. *Alexander Pushkin.*   MP12(IV-1883),   MPCE(II-666),
   MP8(III-1479),   MP6(II-936),   MPPo(89),   MPv4(150),
   MP2(I-299),   MWL2(299).

*Eugénie Grandet. *Honoré de Balzac.*   MP12(IV-1886),
   MPCE(II-667),   MP8(III-1482),   MP6(II-938),   MPEur(284),
   MP1(I-258),   MWL1(258).

Eunuch, The. *Terence (Publius Terentius Afer).*   MP12(IV-1891),
   MPCE(II-670),   MP8(III-1485),   MP6(II-940),   MPDr(256),
   MPv4(152),   MP2(I-302),   MWL2(302).

*Euphues and His England. *John Lyly.*   MP12(IV-1894),
   MPCE(II-671),   MP8(III-1487),   MP6(II-942),   MPEng(190),
   MP3(I-366),   MWL3(366).

*Euphues, the Anatomy of Wit. *John Lyly.*   MP12(IV-1898),
   MPCE(II-674),   MP8(III-1489),   MP6(II-944),   MPEng(192),
   MP3(I-368),   MWL3(368).

Europe and Italy's Acquisition of Libya, 1911-1912. *William C. Askew.*
   HEur(III-1230).

Europe Emerges. *Robert L. Reynolds.*   Different analyses on this title
   appear in: HAnc(II-1102; III-1305; III-1424).

Europe in Decay: A Study of Disintegration, 1936-1940. *Lewis B. Namier.*
   HEur(III-1443).

Europe in the Nineteenth Century, 1815-1914. *E. Lipson.*   HEur(II-688).

Europe in the Seventeenth Century. *David Ogg.*   Different analyses on this
   title appear in: HEur(I-350; I-355).

European Alliances and Alignments, 1871-1890. *William L. Langer.*
   Different analyses on this title appear in: HEur(II-989; II-1010).

European Discovery of America: The Northern Voyages, A.D. 500-1600,
   The. *Samuel Eliot Morison.*   SCL12(IV-2329),   A72(129). A
   different analysis on this title appears in: HAmer(I-25).

European Discovery of America: The Southern Voyages, 1492-1616,
   The. *Samuel Eliot Morison.*   SCL12(IV-2334),   A75(92).

Eusebius of Caesarea. *D. S. Wallace-Hadrill.*   HAnc(II-843).

Eusebius Writes His *Ecclesiastical History* (Event).   HAnc(II-840). *See also*
   Ecclesiastical History.

Euthyphro. *Plato.*   Ph(I-49).

Evolution of the Christian Year, The. *A. Allan McArthur.* Different analyses on this title appear in: HAnc(II-880; II-1095).

"Evolution of the Doctrine of Territorial Incorporation, The" *in* The American Law Review. *Frederic R. Coudert, Jr.* HAmer(II-1322).

Evolution of the English Farm, The. *M. E. Seebohm.* HAnc(II-1171).

Evolution of the Monastic Ideal, The. *Herbert B. Workman.* HAnc(II-1187).

Evolution of the Zollverein, The. *Arnold H. Price.* HEur(II-713).

Exact Sciences in Antiquity, The. *Otto Neugebauer.* Different analyses on this title appear in: HAnc(I-23; II-715).

Excommunication of Theodosius (Event). HAnc(II-920).

Execution of Jesus: A Judicial and Historical Investigation, The. *W. R. Wilson.* HAnc(II-604).

Execution of Louis XVI (Event). HEur(I-520).

Executioner's Song, The. *Norman Mailer.* LA80(I-306).

Executive Privilege: A Constitutional Myth. *Raoul Berger.* SCL12(IV-2353), A75(98).

Exegesis of Maimonides (Event). HAnc(III-1391).

*Exemplary Novels. *Miguel de Cervantes Saavedra.* MP12(IV-1933), MP8(III-1512), MP6(II-963), MPEur(287), MP3(I-370), MWL3(370).

Exile and the Kingdom. *Albert Camus.* MP12(IV-1936), MP8(III-1515), MP4(I-311), MWL4(311), SCL12(IV-2356), SCL7(II-1404), A59(78), BMA(172).

Exile Waiting, The. *Vonda McIntyre.* SF(II-739).

*Exiles. *James Joyce.* MP12(IV-1939), MPCE(II-693), MP8(III-1518), MP6(II-966), MPDr(267), MP3(I-373), MWL3(373).

Existential Errands. *Norman Mailer.* SCL12(IV-2360), A73(160).

Existentialism in Literature (Event). HWor(I-252).

Exodus: A Commentary. *Martin Noth.* HAnc(I-78).

Exorcist, The. Cine(II-506).

Expansion and Coexistence: The History of Soviet Foreign Policy, 1917-1967. *Adam B. Ulam.* HEur(III-1437).

Expansion of the Vietnam War into Cambodia, The. *Peter A. Poole.* HWor(II-1086).

Expeditions of John C. Frémont (Event). HAmer(II-795).

*Expensive People. *Joyce Carol Oates.* SCL12(IV-2364), SCL7(II-1408), A69(122).

Experience and Substance. *De Witt Henry Parker.* Ph(II-1070).

Exploding Metropolis, The. *The Editors of* Fortune. SCL12(IV-2369), SCL7(II-1413), A59(81).

Exploitation of the Arch (Event). HAnc(I-501).

Exploration and Empire. *William H. Goetzmann.* SCL12(IV-2372), SCL7(II-1416), A67(101). A different analysis on this title appears in:

HAmer(II-797).

Explosion of the First Hydrogen Bomb (Event).   HWor(II-683).

Explosion of the First Nuclear Bomb (Event).   HEur(III-1561).

Expulsion of the Jews from Spain (Event).   HAnc(III-1752).

Expulsion of Yugoslavia from the Cominform (Event).   HWor(II-640).

Extant Fragments of the Works of Dionysius.   *Dionysius the Great.*
    RCh(I-77).

Extant Writings of Julius Africanus, The.   *Sextus Julius Africanus.*
    RCh(I-61).

Extant Writings of Saint Francis of Assisi, The.   *Saint Francis of Assisi.*
    RCa(I-349).

*Extreme Occident, The.   *Petru Dumitriu.*   SCL12(IV-2375),
    SCL7(II-1419),   A67(104).

Eye for an I, An.   *Harriet Zinnes.*   SCL12(IV-2379),   SCL7(II-1423),
    A66(100).

Eye in the Sky.   *Philip K. Dick.*   SF(II-744).

Eye of the Story: Selected Essays and Reviews, The.   *Eudora Welty.*
    LA79(I-200).

*Eye-Beaters, Blood, Victory, Madness, Buckhead and Mercy, The.   *James
    Dickey.*   (SCL12(IV-2383),   A71(69).

Ezra Pound.   *C. David Heymann.*   LA77(I-264).

Fabians, The.   *Norman MacKenzie* and *Jeanne MacKenzie.*   LA78(I-300).

*Fable, A.   *William Faulkner.*   MP12(IV-1942),   MPCE(II-694),
    MP8(III-1521),   MP6(II-968),   MPAm(174),   MP3(I-375),
    MWL3(375). A different analysis on this title appears in:
    SCL12(IV-2387),   SCL7(II-1427),   A54(61),   BMA(176).

*Fable for Critics, A.   *James Russell Lowell.*   MP12(IV-1948),
    MP8(III-1524),   MP4(I-313),   MWL4(313).

*Fables.   *Jean de La Fontaine.*   MP12(IV-1951),   MP8(III-1527),
    MP6(II-970),   MPPo(97),   MP3(I-378),   MWL3(378). A different
    analysis on this title appears in: SCL12(IV-2392),   SCL7(II-1431),
    A54(65).

Face of Battle, The.   *John Keegan.*   LA78(I-305).

Face of Defeat, The.   *David Pryce-Jones.*   SCL12(IV-2395),   A74(113).

"Face-off in Panama: U.S. Imperialists, Old and New," *in* At Issue: Politics in
    the World Arena.   *Penny Lernoux.*   HWor(III-1334).

Facing the Lions.   *Tom Wicker.*   SCL12(IV-2402),   A74(120).

"Fact and Fancy in the Vinland Sagas," *in* Old Norse Literature and
    Mythology, A Symposium.   *Erik Wahlgren.*   HAmer(I-16).

*Faerie Queen, The.   *Edmund Spenser.*   MP12(IV-1953),
    MPCE(II-698),   MP8(III-1529),   MP6(II-972),   MPPo(99),
    MP1(I-264),   MWL1(264).

Fahrenheit 451.   Cine(II-510).

Fahrenheit 451.   *Ray Bradbury.*   SF(II-749).

Failure of Akhenaten's Cultural Revival (Event). HAnc(I-64).

Failure of Julian's Pagan Revival (Event). HAnc(II-888).

Failure of the Prussian Reform Movement, 1807-1819, The. *Walter M. Simon.* HEur(II-577).

Failure of the Roman Republic, The. *R. E. Smith.* Different analyses on this title appear in: HAnc(I-484; I-499).

Failure of the Seventh Crusade (Event). HAnc(III-1496).

Fair Maid of Perth, The. *Sir Walter Scott.* MP12(IV-1958), MPCE(II-701), MP8(III-1532), MP6(II-975), MPEng(201), MP3(I-380), MWL3(380).

Fair Sister, The. *William Goyen.* SCL12(IV-2405), SCL7(II-1434), A64(75).

Fairly Good Time, A. *Mavis Gallant.* SCL12(IV-2408), SCLs(91).

Fairly Honourable Defeat, A. *Iris Murdoch.* SCL12(IV-2411), A72(134).

Faith and History. *Reinhold Niebuhr.* RCh(II-1104).

Faith and Knowledge. *John Hick.* RCh(II-1156).

Faith, Hope, and Charity. *Saint Augustine.* RCa(I-184).

Faith of a Moralist, The. *Alfred Edward Taylor.* RCh(II-954).

Faith of the Christian Church, The. *Gustaf Aulén.* RCh(II-912).

*Faithful Shepherdess, The. *John Fletcher.* MP12(IV-1962), MPCE(II-703), MP8(III-1535), MP6(II-978), MPDr(270), MP3(I-383), MWL3(383).

Falconer. *John Cheever.* LA78(I-309).

Falkners of Mississippi: A Memoir, The. *Murry C. Falkner.* SCL12(IV-2415), SCL7(II-1437), A68(97).

*Fall, The. *Albert Camus.* MP12(IV-1965), MP8(III-1537), MP4(I-316), MWL4(316). A different analysis on this title appears in: SCL12(IV-2418), SCL7(II-1440), A58(83), BMA(180).

Fall of a Sparrow, The. *Nigel Balchin.* SCL12(IV-2422), SCL7(II-1443), A57(64).

Fall of a Titan, The. *Igor Gouzenko.* SCL12(IV-2425), SCL7(II-1446), A54(68).

Fall of Acre (Event). HAnc(III-1574).

Fall of Babylon (Event). HAnc(I-179).

Fall of Cambodia to the Khmer Rouge, The (Event). HWor(III-1212).

Fall of Constantinople (Event). HAnc(III-1718).

Fall of Granada (Event). HAnc(III-1747).

Fall of Jerusalem and the Christian Church, The. *S. G. F. Brandon.* HAnc(II-651).

Fall of Khrushchev, The (Event). HWor(II-974).

Fall of Khrushchev, The. *William Hyland* and *Richard Wallace Shryock.* HWor(II-978).

Fall of La Rochelle (Event). HEur(I-259).

Fall of Paris, The. *Alistair Horne.* SCL12(IV-2428), SCL7(II-1449), A67(107).

Fall of Robespierre (Event).   HEur(I-529).

"Fall" of Rome (Event).   HAnc(II-980).

Fall of Rome: Can It Be Explained?, The.   *Mortimer Chambers*.
    HAnc(II-981).

Fall of South Vietnam, The (Event).   HWor(III-1227).

"Fall of the Athenian Empire, The," *in* Vol. V *of* The Cambridge Ancient
    History.   *W. S. Ferguson*.   HAnc(I-310).

Fall of the House of Habsburg, The.   *Edward Crankshaw*.
    SCL12(IV-2432),   SCL7(II-1453),   A64(77).

*Fall of the House of Usher, The.   *Edgar Allan Poe*.   MP12(IV-1968),
    MPCE(II-705),   MP8(III-1540),   MP6(II-980),   MPAm(177),
    MPv4(155),   MP2(I-316),   MWL2(316).

False Starts.   *Malcolm Braly*.   LA77(I-269).

Familiar Essays of William Hazlitt, The.   *William Hazlitt*.
    MP12(IV-1974),   MP8(III-1542),   MP4(I-319),   MWL4(319).

Familiar Territory: Observations on American Life.   *Joseph Epstein*.
    LA80(I-310).

Family Album, A.   *David Darryl Galloway*.   LA79(I-204).

Family Arsenal, The.   *Paul Theroux*.   LA77(I-274).

Family of Gilje, The.   *Jonas Lie*.   MP12(IV-1977),   MPCE(II-709),
    MP8(III-1545),   MP6(II-982),   MPEur(290),   MPv3(163),
    MP2(I-318),   MWL2(318).

Family Feeling.   *Helen Yglesias*.   LA77(I-277).

Family Letters of Robert and Elinor Frost, The.   *Robert Frost* and *Elinor
    Frost*.   SCL12(IV-2435),   A73(164).

*Family Moskat, The.   *Isaac Bashevis Singer*.   SCL12(IV-2438),
    SCL7(II-1456),   A66(103).

Family of Pascual Duarte, The.   *Camilo José Cela*.   MP12(IV-1980),
    MP8(III-1548),   MP4(I-321),   MWL4(321). A different analysis on this
    title appears in: SCL12(IV-2441),   SCL7(II-1459),   A65(86).

*Family Reunion, The.   *T. S. Eliot*.   MP12(IV-1983),   MPCE(II-710),
    MP8(III-1551),   MP6(II-984),   MPDr(272),   MPv4(157),
    MP2(I-321),   MWL2(321).

Fancy Strut.   *Lee Smith*.   SCL12(IV-2446),   A74(124).

Fantasia.   Cine(II-513).

Fantasticks, The.   *Tom Jones* and *Harvey Schmidt*.   SCL12(IV-2449),
    SCLs(94).

*Far Away and Long Ago.   *W. H. Hudson*.   MP12(IV-1986),
    MPCE(II-711),   MP8(III-1554),   MP6(II-986),   MPNf(121),
    MPv3(165),   MP2(I-323),   MWL2(323).

Far Cry, A.   *Earl Rovit*.   SCL12(IV-2454),   SCL7(II-1463),   A68(100).

*Far Field, The.   *Theodore Roethke*.   SCL12(IV-2459),   SCL7(III-1469),
    A65(89).

Far from the Madding Crowd.   Cine(II-517).

*Far from the Madding Crowd.   *Thomas Hardy*.   MP12(IV-1990),

Fathers and Children. *Michael Paul Rogin.* SCL12(IV-2499), A76(90).

*Fathers and Sons. *Ivan Turgenev.* MP12(IV-2015), MPCE(II-727),
    MP8(III-1571), MP6(II-997), MPEur(296), MP1(I-273),
    MWL1(273).

Fathers of the Greek Church, The. *Hans von Campenhausen.* Different
    analyses on this title appear in: HAnc(II-775; II-803; II-896).

"Fatti di Maggio" Riots (Event). HEur(II-1109).

Faulkner: A Biography. *Joseph Blotner.* SCL12(IV-2503), A75(101).

*Faust. *Johann Wolfgang von Goethe.* MP12(IV-2020), MPCE(II-730),
    MP8(III-1574), MP6(II-1000), MPDr(278), MP1(I-276),
    MWL1(276).

Fausto and Anna. *Carlo Cassola.* SCL12(IV-2509), SCL7(III-1495),
    A61(75).

FBI. *Sanford J. Ungar.* LA77(I-287).

FBI Story, The. *Don Whitehead.* SCL12(IV-2512), SCL7(III-1498),
    A57(67).

FDR's Last Year. *Jim Bishop.* SCL12(IV-2516), A75(107).

Fear *and* Typewriter in the Sky. *L. Ron Hubbard.* SF(II-761).

*Fear of Flying. *Erica Jong.* SCL12(IV-2520), A74(127).

Fearful Void, The. *Geoffrey Moorehouse.* SCL12(IV-2524), A75(111).

Feast of July, The. *H. E. Bates.* SCL12(IV-2528), SCL7(III-1502),
    A54(71).

*Feast of Lupercal, The. *Brian Moore.* SCL12(IV-2531),
    SCL7(III-1505), A58(86).

Feast of Saint Barnabas, The. *Jesse Hill Ford.* SCL12(IV-2534),
    A70(123).

Feast of Words: The Triumph of Edith Wharton, A. *Cynthia Griffin Wolff.*
    LA78(I-314).

Federal Antitrust Policy: Origination of an American Tradition, The. *Hans
    B. Thorelli.* HAmer(II-1208).

Federal Government Assumes Control of Interstate Commerce (*Gibbons* v.
    Ogden) (Event). HAmer(I-600).

Federal Government of Switzerland, The. *George A. Codding.*
    HEur(II-797).

Federal Republic in Spain, The. *C. A. M. Hennessy.* HEur(II-947).

Federal Reserve System: Purpose and Function, The. *Federal Reserve
    System Board of Governors.* HAmer(III-1434).

Federalist, The. *Alexander Hamilton, James Madison* and *John Jay.*
    (MP12(IV-2025), MP8(III-1577), MP6(II-1002), MPNf(124),
    MP3(I-384), MWL3(384).

Federalist: A Classic on Federalism and Free Government, The. *Gottfried
    Dietze.* HAmer(I-338).

Federalist Era, 1789-1801, The. New American Nation *series.* *John C.
    Miller.* HAmer(I-343).

*Felix Holt, Radical. *George Eliot.* MP12(IV-2029), MPCE(II-733),

Norris. HAmer(III-1624).

Figures in a Landscape. *Barry England.* SCL12(IV-2577),
SCL7(III-1528), A68(108).

Figures of Thought: Speculations on the Meaning of Poetry & Other
Essays. *Howard Nemerov.* LA79(I-209).

File No. 113. *Émile Gaboriau.* MP12(IV-2058), MPCE(II-740),
MP8(III-1604), MP6(II-1013), MPEur(299), MP1(I-278),
MWL1(278).

File on Stanley Patton Buchta, The. *Irvin Faust.* SCL12(IV-2580),
SCLs(102).

Film. Cine(II-531).

*Filostrato, Il. *Giovanni Boccaccio.* MP12(IV-2062), MPCE(II-742),
MP8(III-1607), MP4(I-340), MWL4(340).

Final Circle of Paradise, The. *Arkady Strugatsky* and *Boris Strugatsky.*
SF(II-776).

Final Days, The. *Carl Bernstein* and *Bob Woodward.* Different analyses on
this title appear in: HWor(III-1134; III-1204).

Final Entries, 1945: The Diaries of Joseph Goebbels. *Joseph Goebbels.*
LA79(I-212).

Final Payments. *Mary Gordon.* LA79(I-218).

Final Solutions. *Frederick Seidel.* SCL12(IV-2584), SCL7(III-1531),
A64(86).

Financial Expert, The. *R. K. Narayan.* SCL12(IV-2586), SCLs(105).

*Financier, The. *Theodore Dreiser.* MP12(IV-2067), MPCE(II-745),
MP8(III-1610), MP6(II-1015), MPAm(184), MP1(I-280),
MWL1(280).

"Finding Bar Kokhba's Despatches: The Exciting Story of an Archaeological
Expedition Among the Dead Sea Caves," *in* Illustrated London
News. *Yigael Yadin.* HAnc(II-705).

Findings. *Wendell Berry.* SCL12(IV-2589), A70(129).

Fine Madness, A. *Elliot Baker.* SCL12(IV-2592), SCL7(III-1533),
A65(95).

Finest Stories of Seán O'Faoláin, The. *Seán O'Faoláin.* SCL12(IV-2597),
SCL7(III-1538), A58(88).

Finn Cycle, The. *Unknown.* MP12(IV-2071), MPCE(II-747),
MP8(III-1612), MP6(II-1017), MPEng(210), MP3(I-392),
MWL3(392).

*Finnegans Wake. *James Joyce.* MP12(IV-2076), MP8(III-1615),
MP6(II-1020), MPEng(213), MP3(I-395), MWL3(395).

Fire from Heaven. *Mary Renault.* SCL12(IV-2601), A70(132).

Fire in the Lake. *Frances FitzGerald.* SCL12(IV-2605), A73(166).

Fire Next Time, The. *James Baldwin.* SCL12(IV-2611),
SCL7(III-1541), A64(88).

Fire over England. Cine(II-534).

Fire Screen, The. *James Merrill.* SCL12(IV-2614), A71(73).

First Principles. *Herbert Spencer*. Ph(II-649).

First Russian Revolution: The Decembrist Revolt, The. *Anatole G. Mazour*. HEur(II-667).

First Showing of *The Great Train Robbery* (Event). HAmer(II-1333).

First Successful Voyage of the *Clermont* (Event). HAmer(I-471).

First Superfortress Bombing Raid on Japan, The (Event). HWor(I-487).

First Test of a Submarine in Warfare (Event). HAmer(I-267).

First Thousand-Bomber Raid on Germany (Event). HEur(III-1461).

First Two Centuries of Florentine History, The. *Pasquale Villari*. HAnc(III-1305).

First World War, The. *Richard Thoumin*. HWor(I-103).

First, You Cry. *Betty Rollin*. LA77(I-291).

Fiscal Crisis of the State, The. *James O'Connor*. HWor(II-850).

Fisher Maiden, The. *Björnstjerne Björnson*. MP12(IV-2079), MPCE(II-750), MP8(III-1618), MP6(II-1022), MPEur(302), MPv3(170), MP2(I-330), MWL2(330).

Fishes, Birds and Sons of Men. *Jesse Hill Ford*. SCL12(IV-2648), SCL7(III-1565), A68(111).

Five Centuries of Religion, Vol. I: St. Barnard, His Predecessors and Successors, 1000-1200. *George G. Coulton*. HAnc(II-1031)

Five Easy Pieces. Cine(II-538).

Five for Sorrow, Ten for Joy. *Rumer Godden*. LA80(I-325).

Five Roman Emperors. *Bernard W. Henderson*. HAnc(II-677).

Five Smooth Stones. *Ann Fairbairn*. SCL12(IV-2651), SCL7(III-1568), A67(115).

Five Stages of Grief, The. *Linda Pastan*. LA79(I-222).

Five Stories of Ferrara. *Giorgio Bassani*. SCL12(IV-2654), A72(149).

Five Theological Orations. *Saint Gregory of Nazianzus*. RCh(I-113), RCa(I-116).

Five Women Who Loved Love. *Ibara Saikaku*. MP12(IV-2082), MPCE(II-751), MP8(III-1620), MP6(II-1024), MPEur(304), MP3(I-398), MWL3(398).

*Fixer, The. *Bernard Malamud*. SCL12(IV-2657), SCL7(III-1571), A67(118).

Flame Trees of Thika, The. *Elspeth Huxley*. SCL12(IV-2662), SCL7(III-1575), A60(77).

Flaming Star. Cine(II-541).

Flatland: A Romance of Many Dimensions. *Edwin A. Abbott*. SF(II-792).

Flaubert. *Benjamin F. Bart*. HEur(II-831).

Flaubert: The Making of the Master. *Enid Starkie*. SCL12(IV-2666), A72(151).

Flaubert: The Master. *Enid Starkie*. SCL12(IV-2671), SCL7(III-1579), A68(114).

Flaubert Publishes *Madame Bovary* (Event). HEur(II-827). *See also* Madame Bovary.

SF(II-807).

Fool Killer, The. *Helen Eustis.* SCL12(IV-2705), SCL7(III-1610), A54(80).

Fool of Quality, The. *Henry Brooke.* MP12(IV-2107), MPCE(II-755), MP8(III-1643), MP6(II-1030), MPEng(216), MPv4(164), MP2(I-333), MWL2(333).

Fool's Errand, A. *Albion W. Tourgée.* MP12(IV-2110), MPCE(II-756), MP8(III-1646), MP4(I-356), MWL4(356).

For a Bitter Season. *George Garrett.* SCL12(IV-2708), SCL7(III-1613), A68(118).

For the Union Dead. *Robert Lowell.* SCL12(IV-2712), SCL7(III-1617), A65(105).

For Whom the Bell Tolls. Cine(II-553).

*For Whom the Bell Tolls. *Ernest Hemingway.* MP12(IV-2114), MPCE(II-758), MP8(III-1649), MP6(II-1032), MPAm(186), MP1(I-282), MWL1(282).

Force and Matter. *Friedrich Karl Christian Ludwig Büchner.* Ph(II-633).

Ford: Decline and Rebirth, 1933-1962. *Allan Nevins* and *Frank Ernest Hill.* SCL12(IV-2715), SCL7(III-1619), A64(96).

Ford: Expansion and Challenge, 1915-1933. *Allan Nevins* and *Frank Ernest Hill.* SCL12(IV-2718), SCL7(III-1622), A58(96).

Ford: The Times, the Man, the Company. *Allan Nevins.* SCL12(IV-2721), SCL7(III-1625), A54(83). A different analysis on this title appears in: HAmer(III-1423).

Foreign *Clientelae* (264-70 B.C.). *E. Badian.* HAnc(I-336).

Foreign Correspondent. Cine(II-556).

Foreign Policies of France, 1944 to 1968, The. *Guy De Carmoy.* HEur(III-1650).

Foreign Policies of the Taft Administration, The. *Walter V. Scholes* and *Marie V. Scholes.* HAmer(III-1382).

Foreign Policy of Canning, 1822-1827: England, the Neo-Holy Alliance, and the New World, The. *Harold W. V. Temperley.* HEur(II-656).

Foreign Policy of Castlereagh, 1812-1815, The. *Sir Charles Webster.* HEur(II-626).

Foreign Policy of Castlereagh, 1815-1822, The. *Sir Charles Webster.* HEur(II-657).

Foreign Policy of Hitler's Germany: Diplomatic Revolution in Europe, 1933-1936, The. *Gerhard L. Weinberg.* Different analyses on this title appear in: HWor(I-346; I-352).

Foreign Policy of John Foster Dulles, The (Event). HWor(II-690).

Foreign Policy of the Attalids of Pergamum, The. *Roger B. McShane.* HAnc(I-489).

"Forerunners of the Gracchi," *in* Journal of Roman Studies. *L. R. Taylor.* HAnc(I-224).

Forest of the Night. *Madison Jones.* SCL12(IV-2724), SCL7(III-1628),

A61(87).

Forever Panting. *Peter De Vries.* SCL12(IV-2728), A74(131).

Forever War, The. *Joe Haldeman.* SF(II-813).

Forever Young. *Jonathan Cott.* LA79(I-231).

Forewords and Afterwords. *W. H. Auden.* SCL12(IV-2731), A74(134).

Forging of the "Donation of Constantine" (Event). HAnc(II-1121).

Fork River Space Project, The. *Wright Morris.* LA78(I-319).

Form of the Personal, The. *John Macmurray.* RCh(II-1162).

Formalization of Geometry (Event). HAnc(I-383).

Formalization of the Idea of Usury (Event). HAnc(III-1519).

Formalization of the Liturgy of the Mass (Event). HAnc(II-1069).

Formation of the American Anti-Slavery Society (Event). HAmer(II-719).

Formation of the Arab League (Event). HWor(I-494).

Formation of the Commonwealth of Australia and the Dominion of New Zealand, The (Event). HWor(I-14).

Formation of the Dominion of New England (Event). HAmer(I-163).

Formation of the First International (Event). HEur(II-897).

Formation of the German Empire (Event). HEur(II-963).

"Formation of the Israelite State in Palestine, The," *in* Essays on Old Testament History and Religion. *Albrecht Alt.* HAnc(I-92).

Formation of the League of Cambrai (Event). HEur(I-31).

Formation of the North German Confederation (Event). HEur(II-918).

Formation of the Peace Corps (Event). HAmer(III-1877).

Formation of the Republican Party (Event). HAmer(II-877).

Formation of the Roman Symbol (Event). HAnc(II-752).

Formation of the Russian Social Democratic Labor Party (Event). HEur(II-1105).

Formation of the Schmalkaldic League (Event). HEur(I-91).

Formation of the Scipionic Circle (Event). HAnc(I-453).

Formation of the Three Emperors' League (Event). HEur(II-988).

Formation of the United Nations (Event). HEur(III-1507).

Formation of the World Council of Churches (Event). HEur(III-1550).

Formative Years of Social Security, The. *Arthur J. Altmeyer.* HAmer(III-1646).

"Form-Critical Problem of the Hexateuch, The," (1938), *reprinted in* The Problem of the Hexateuch and Other Essays. *Gerhard Von Rad.* HAnc(I-99).

Formosa, China and the United Nations: Formosa in the World Community. *Harold D. Laswell* and *Lung-chu Chen.* HWor(III-1114).

Formulation of Logic (Event). HAnc(I-348).

Formulation of the Dawes Plan (Event). HAmer(III-1537).

Formulation of the Multiple-Element Hypothesis (Event). HAnc(I-270).

Formulation of the Nicene Creed (Event). HAnc(II-867).

Formulation of the "Twelve Tables" of Roman Law (Event). HAnc(I-253).

Formulation of Ulpian's Dictum (Event). HAnc(II-784).

Forrestal Diaries, The. *Walter Millis.* HAmer(III-1786).
*Forsyte Saga, The. *John Galsworthy.* MP12(IV-2119), MPCE(II-761),
    MP8(III-1652), MP6(II-1034), MPEng(219), MP1(I-284),
    MWL(284).
*Fortitude. *Hugh Walpole.* MP12(IV-2124), MPCE(II-764),
    MP8(III-1655), MP6(II-1037), MPEng(222), MP1(I-286),
    MWL1(286).
Fortress, The. *Hugh Walpole.* MP12(IV-2128), MPCE(II-766),
    MP8(III-1657), MP6(II-1039), MPEng(224), MP1(I-288),
    MWL1(288).
*Fortunata and Jacinta. *Benito Pérez Galdós.* MP12(IV-2132),
    MPCE(II-768), MP8(III-1660), MP6(II-1041), MPEur(309),
    MPv4(166), MP2(I-336), MWL2(336).
*Fortunes of Nigel, The. *Sir Walter Scott.* MP12(IV-2137),
    MPCE(II-771), MP8(III-1663), MP6(II-1043), MPEng(227),
    MPv3(171), MP2(I-338), MWL2(338).
Fortunes of Richard Mahony, The. *Henry Handel Richardson.*
    MP12(IV-2142), MPCE(II-774), MP8(III-1666), MP6(II-1046),
    MPEng(230), MPv4(168), MP2(I-341), MWL2(341).
Forty Days of Musa Dagh, The. *Franz Werfel.* MP12(IV-2145),
    MPCE(II-776), MP8(III-1669), MP6(II-1048), MPEur(312),
    MP1(I-291), MWL1(291).
42nd Street. Cine(II-561).
Found, Lost, Found. *J. B. Priestley.* LA78(I-325).
Foundation of Christian Doctrine. *Menno Simons.* RCh(I-367).
Foundation Trilogy, The. *Isaac Asimov.* SF(II-819).
Foundations of Freedom, The. *John Lilburne.* RCh(I-470).
Founders of Modern Medicine, The. *Elie (Ilya Mechnikov) Metchnikoff.*
    HEur(III-1175).
Founders of the Middle Ages. *E. K. Rand.* HAnc(II-1021).
Founding of Alexandria (Event). HAnc(I-353).
Founding of Cluny (Event). HAnc(II-1184).
Founding of Constantinople (Event). HAnc(II-862).
Founding of Harvard College, The. *Samuel Eliot Morison.* HAmer(I-105).
Founding of Luxeuil and Bobbio (Event). HAnc(II-1052).
Founding of Maryland, The. *Matthew P. Andrews.* HAmer(I-117).
Founding of Monte Cassino and the Rule of Saint Benedict (Event).
    HAnc(II-1029).
Founding of Moscow University (Event). HEur(I-432).
Founding of New England, The. *James Truslow Adams.* HAmer(I-167).
Founding of Pennsylvania (Event). HAmer(I-157).
Founding of Quebec and French Exploration of the Great Lakes (Event).
    HAmer(I-52).
Founding of Rhode Island (Event). HAmer(I-97).
Founding of San Francisco (Event). HAmer(I-272).

France in Ferment. *Alexander Werth.* HEur(III-1388).
France Under the Bourbon Restoration. *Frederick B. Artz.* HEur(II-684).
France Under the Republic: The Development of Modern France, 1870-1939,
    Book IV: The Republic in Danger. *Denis W. Brogan.* HEur(II-1055).
France Under the Republic: The Development of Modern France, 1870-1939,
    Book VI: The Republic Saved. *Denis W. Brogan.* Different analyses
    on this title appear in: HEur(II-975; II-1068; III-1144).
France Withdraws from NATO (Event). HEur(III-1648).
Franchise Act of 1884 (Event). HEur(II-1038).
Francis Bacon. *Fulton H. Anderson.* HEur(I-256).
Francis Bacon. *Catherine Drinker Bowen.* SCL12(IV-2760),
    SCL7(III-1648), A64(99).
Francis Bacon: Philosopher of Industrial Science. *Benjamin Farrington.*
    HEur(I-257).
Francis Bacon Publishes *Novum Organum* (Event). HEur(I-254). *See also*
    Novum Organum.
Francis the First. *Francis Hackett.* HEur(I-85).
Franciscan Missions of California, The. *John A. Berger.* HAmer(I-275).
Franco-Prussian War, The (Event). HEur(II-954).
Franco-Prussian War: The German Invasion of France, 1870-1871,
    The. *Michael Howard.* HEur(II-955).
Franco-Russian Alliance (Event). HEur(II-1070).
Franco-Russian Alliance, 1890-1914, The. *William L. Langer.*
    HEur(II-1072).
Frankenstein. Cine(II-570).
*Frankenstein. *Mary Godwin Shelley.* MP12(IV-2154), MPCE(II-778),
    MP8(III-1677), MP6(II-1056), MPEng(235), MP1(I-295),
    MWL1(295). A different analysis on this title appears in: SF(II-832).
Frankenstein Unbound. *Brian W. Aldiss.* SF(II-840).
Franklin D. Roosevelt and American Foreign Policy, 1932-1945. *Robert
    Dallek.* LA80(I-328).
Franklin D. Roosevelt, Vol. III: The Triumph. *Frank Freidel.*
    HAmer(III-1611).
Franklin D. Roosevelt: Launching the New Deal. *Frank Freidel.*
    SCL12(IV-2764), A74(137).
*Franny and Zooey. *J. D. Salinger.* MP12(IV-2157), MP8(III-1679),
    MP4(I-359), MWL4(359), SCL12(IV-2767), SCL7(III-1651),
    A62(127), BMA(195).
Fraternity. *John Galsworthy.* MP12(IV-2159), MPCE(II-780),
    MP8(III-1681), MP6(II-1058), MPEng(237), MPv4(171),
    MP2(I-343), MWL2(343).
Freaks: Myths and Images of the Secret Self. *Leslie Fiedler.* LA79(I-235).
Frederick the Great. *Pierre Gaxotte.* HEur(I-416).
Frederick the Great: The Ruler, the Writer, the Man. *G. P. Gooch.*
    HEur(I-417).

*Free Fall. *William Golding.* MP12(IV-2163), MP8(III-1684), MP4(I-361), MWL4(361), SCL12(IV-2770), SCL7(III-1654), A61(94), BMA(198).

Free Public School Movement, The (Event). HAmer(I-576).

Free Soil, Free Labor, Free Men: The Ideology of the Republican Party Before the Civil War. *Eric Foner.* HAmer(II-879).

Freedmen in the Early Roman Empire. *A. M. Duff.* HAnc(II-624).

Freedom and Fate: An Inner Life of Ralph Waldo Emerson. *Stephen E. Whicher.* HAmer(I-656).

Freedom and the Spirit. *Nikolai Berdyaev.* RCh(II-929).

Freedom of the Poet, The. *John Berryman.* LA77(I-299).

Freedom of the Will. *Jonathan Edwards.* Different analyses on this title appear in: Ph(I-501), RCh(II-598).

Freedom or Death. *Nikos Kazantzakis.* MP12(IV-2166), MP8(III-1687), MP4(I-364), MWL4(364), SCL12(IV-2775), SCL7(III-1658), A57(76).

Freedom Road. *Howard Fast.* SCL12(IV-2779), SCLs(111).

Freedom Spent. *Richard Harris.* LA77(I-304).

Freedom's Fetters: The Alien and Sedition Laws and American Civil Liberties. *James M. Smith.* HAmer(I-418).

Freezing Down. *Anders Bodelsen.* SF(II-845).

Frémont: Pathmarker of the West. *Allan Nevins.* HAmer(II-798).

French and Indian War, The (Event). HAmer(I-200).

French Connection, The. Cine(II-574).

French Exploration of the Mississippi Valley (Event). HAmer(I-144).

French Foreign Policy Under De Gaulle. *Alfred Grosser.* HEur(III-1651).

French Governmental Crisis of 1934 (Event). HEur(III-1386).

French Labor Movement, The. *Val R. Lorwin.* HEur(II-1045).

*French Lieutenant's Woman, The. *John Fowles.* SCL12(IV-2783), A70(139).

*French Revolution, The. *Thomas Carlyle.* MP12(IV-2169), MP8(III-1690), MP6(II-1060), MPNf(128), MP3(I-404), MWL3(404).

French Revolution, The. *Albert Mathiez.* HEur(I-530).

French Revolution: Conflicting Interpretations, The. *Frank A. Kofker* and *James M. Laux.* HEur(I-517).

French Revolution: From Its Origins to 1793, The. *Georges Lefebvre.* Different analyses on this title appear in: HEur(I-504; I-522).

French Revolution and Napoleon, The. *Leo Gershoy.* Different analyses on this title appear in: HEur(I-549; II-600).

French Wars of Religion, The. *J. H. M. Salmon.* Different analyses on this title appear in: HEur(I-165; I-206).

Freud. *Max Schur.* SCL12(IV-2788), A73(177).

Freud Publishes *The Interpretation of Dreams* (Event). HEur(III-1139). *See also* Interpretation of Dreams, The.

Friar Bacon and Friar Bungay. *Robert Greene*. MP12(IV-2172),
MPCE(II-782), MP8(III-1693), MP6(II-1062), MPDr(281),
MPv4(173), MP2(I-345), MWL2(345).

Friedrich Meinecke and German Politics in the Twentieth Century. *Robert A.
Pois*. HWor(I-59).

Friedrich Meinecke Publishes *Cosmopolitanism and the National State*
(Event). HWor(I-54).

Friedrich Nietzsche, Philosopher of Culture. *Frederick Copleston, S. J.*
HEur(II-1026).

Friedrich von Holstein: Politics and Diplomacy in the Era of Bismarck and
Wilhelm II. *Norman Rich*. HWor(I-49).

Friend in Power, A. *Carlos Baker*. SCL12(IV-2792), SCL7(III-1661),
A59(92).

Friend of Kafka, A. *Isaac Bashevis Singer*. SCL12(IV-2795), A71(80).

Friendly Fire. *C. D. B. Bryan*. LA77(I-309).

Frithiof's Saga. *Esaias Tegnér*. MP12(IV-2175), MPCE(II-783),
MP8(III-1696), MP6(II-1065), MPPo(109), MPv3(174),
MP2(I-348), MWL2(348).

Fritz Fischer Publishes *Germany's Aims in the First World War* (Event).
HWor(II-918).

*Frogs, The. *Aristophanes*. MP12(IV-2178), MPCE(II-784),
MP8(III-1698), MP6(II-1067), MPDr(284), MP1(I-297),
MWL1(297).

From a Logical Point of View. *Willard Van Orman Quine*. HAnc(II-837).

From Atomos to Atom. *Andrew G. Van Melsen*. HAnc(I-266).

From *Brown* to *Bakke*, The Supreme Court and School Integration:
1954-1978. *J. Harvie Wilkinson III*. LA80(I-334).

From Here to Eternity. Cine(II-577).

From Homer to Menander. *L. A. Post*. HAnc(I-369).

From Joseph to Joshua: Biblical Traditions in the Light of
Archaeology. *H. H. Rowley*. HAnc(I-77).

From Marco Polo Bridge to Pearl Harbor: Japan's Entry into World War
II. *David J. Lu*. HWor(I-441).

From Puritan to Yankee: Character and Social Order in Connecticut,
1690-1765. *Richard L. Bushman*. HAmer(I-179).

From Russia with Love. Cine(II-582).

From Schumacher to Brandt: The Story of German Socialism,
1945-1965. *David Childs*. HEur(III-1693).

From the Danube to the Yalu. *General Mark W. Clark*.
SCL12(IV-2798), SCL7(III-1664), A54(86), BMA(202).

From the Diary of a Snail. *Günter Grass*. SCL12(IV-2801), A74(140).

From the Dreadnought to Scapa Flow, Vol. I: The Road to War. *Arthur J.
Marder*. HEur(III-1189).

From the Dreadnought to Scapa Flow, Vol. III: Jutland and After. *Arthur J.
Marder*. HEur(III-1269).

*From the Earth to the Moon. *Jules Verne.*   SF(II-850).

From the Hand of the Hunter. *John Braine.*   SCL12(IV-2804),
     SCL7(III-1667),   A61(98).

*From the Terrace. *John O'Hara.*   SCL12(IV-2807),   SCL7(III-1670),
     A59(94).

"From the Union with Hungary to the Union with Lithuania: Jadwiga
     1374-99," *in* The Cambridge History of Poland. From the Origins to
     Sobieski (to 1696). *Oscar Halecki.*   HAnc(III-1653).

From the Wagner Act to Taft-Hartley: A Study of National Labor Policy and
     Labor Relations. *Harry A. Millis* and *Emily Clark Brown.*
     HWor(II-575).

From Vienna to Versailles. *L. C. B. Seaman.*   HEur(II-851).

Fronde, The. *Paul Rice Doolin.*   HEur(I-325).

Front Page, The.   Cine(II-586).

*Frontenacs, The. *François Mauriac.*   SCL12(IV-2810),   SCL7(III-1673),
     A62(130).

Frontier Camp Meeting: Religion's Harvest Time, The. *Charles A.
     Johnson.*   HAmer(I-422).

Frontier in American History, The. *Frederick Jackson Turner.*
     MP12(IV-2182),   MP8(III-1700),   MP4(I-366),   MWL4(366).

*Fruit of the Tree, The. *Edith Wharton.*   MP12(IV-2185),
     MPCE(II-787),   MP8(III-1703),   MP6(II-1068),   MPAm(189),
     MP3(I-406),   MWL3(406).

Fulfillment: The Epic Story of Zionism. *Rufus Learsi (Israel Goldberg).*
     HEur(II-1091).

Full Fathom Five. *John Stewart Carter.*   SCL12(IV-2813),
     SCL7(III-1676),   A66(109).

*Funeral, The. *Sir Richard Steele.*   MP12(IV-2188),   MPCE(II-788),
     MP8(III-1706),   MP6(II-1070),   MPDr(286),   MPv4(175),
     MP2(I-350),   MWL2(350).

Funny Girl.   Cine(II-589).

Funny Thing Happened on the Way to the Forum, A.   Cine(II-592).

Further Fables for Our Time. *James Thurber.*   SCL12(IV-2818),
     SCL7(III-1681),   A57(79).

Fury.   Cine(II-596).

Fury. *Lawrence O'Donnell.*   SF(II-855).

Future of China After Mao, The. *Ross Terrill.*   Different analyses on this
     title appear in: LA79(I-240),   HWor(III-1267).

Future of Mankind, The. *Karl Jaspers.*   SCL12(IV-2821),
     SCL7(III-1684),   A62(132).

Future Shock. *Alvin Toffler.*   SCL12(IV-2825),   A71(82).

Gabriela, Clove and Cinnamon. *Jorge Amado.*   MP12(IV-2192),
     MP8(III-1709),   MP4(I-369),   MWL4(369),   SCL12(IV-2834),
     SCL7(III-1687),   A63(62).

Gaius' Edition of the *Institutes* of Roman Law (Event).   HAnc(II-721).
Galen of Pergamum. *George Sarton.*   HAnc(II-739).
Galen's System of Physiology and Medicine. *Rudolph E. Siegel.*
     HAnc(II-740).
Galileo Galilei. *Ludovico Geymonat.*   HEur(I-288).
Galileo Publishes *Dialogue on the Two Great World Systems* (Event).
     HEur(I-285).
Gallipoli. *Alan Moorehead.*   SCL12(IV-2837),   SCL7(III-1690),
     A57(81),   BMA(205). A different analysis on this title appears in:
     HWor(I-133).
Gallipoli Campaign, The (Event).   HWor(I-129).
*Gambler, The. *Fyodor Mikhailovich Dostoevski.*   MP12(IV-2195),
     MPCE(II-790),   MP8(III-1712),   MP6(II-1073),   MPEur(315),
     MPv3(176),   MP2(I-352),   MWL2(352).
Game of Disarmament: How the United States and Russia Run the Arms
     Race, The. *Alva Myrdal.*   Different analyses on this title appear in:
     HWor(II-569; II-1058).
Game of Hearts, The. *Harriette Wilson.*   SCL12(IV-2840),
     SCL7(III-1693),   A55(101).
Gandhi and Civil Disobedience. *Judith M. Brown.*   HWor(I-178).
Gandhi's Truth. *Erik H. Erikson.*   SCL12(IV-2843),   A71(91).
Garden, The. *Yves Berger.*   SCL12(IV-2848),   SCL7(III-1696),
     A64(102).
Garden, The. *L. A. G. Strong.*   MP12(IV-2200),   MPCE(II-793),
     MP8(III-1715),   MP6(II-1075),   MPEng(240),   MPv4(177),
     MP2(I-354),   MWL2(354).
*Garden of Earthly Delights, A. *Joyce Carol Oates.*   SCL12(IV-2854),
     SCL7(III-1702),   A68(122).
Garden of the Finzi-Continis, The. *Giorgio Bassani.*   SCL12(IV-2859),
     SCL7(III-1706),   A66(114).
Gardener, and Other Poems, The. *John Hall Wheelock.*   SCL12(V-2863),
     SCL7(III-1710),   A62(135).
Gardener's Dog, The. *Lope de Vega.*   MP12(IV-2203),   MPCE(II-794),
     MP8(III-1718),   MP6(II-1077),   MPDr(289),   MPv3(178),
     MP2(I-356),   MWL2(356).
Garibaldi and His Enemies. *Christopher Hibbert.*   HEur(II-864).
Garibaldi and The Thousand. *George Macaulay Trevelyan.*   HEur(II-862).
Garibaldi's Thousand "Redshirts" Land in Italy (Event).   HEur(II-860).
*Gargantua and Pantagruel. *François Rabelais.*   MP12(IV-2208),
     MPCE(II-797),   MP8(III-1721),   MP6(II-1079),   MPEur(318),
     MP1(I-298),   MWL1(298).
Garvey and Garveyism. *Amy-Jacques Garvey.*   HAmer(III-1446).
Gas Turbines and Jet Propulsion for Aircraft. *G. Geoffrey Smith.*
     HWor(I-359).
Gaslight.   Cine(II-600).

Gate to the Sea. *Bryher.* SCL12(V-2866), SCL7(III-1713), A59(96).
Gates of Eden: American Culture in the Sixties. *Morris Dickstein.*
    LA78(I-328).
Gateway. *Frederik Pohl.* SF(II-858).
Gathering of Zion: The Story of the Mormon Trail, The. *Wallace Stegner.*
    HAmer(II-815).
Gathering the Tribes. *Carolyn Forché.* LA77(I-314).
Gaucho: Martin Fierro, The. *José Hernández.* MP12(IV-2213),
    MPCE(II-800), MP8(III-1724), MP6(II-1082), MPPo(111),
    MPv3(180), MP2(I-358), MWL2(358).
Gaudy Place, The. *Fred Chappell.* SCL12(V-2868), A74(144).
Gay Divorcee, The. Cine(II-605).
Gelasius' Statements on Church-State Relationships (Event). HAnc(II-989).
Gelehrtenrepublik, Die. *Arno Schmidt.* SF(II-865).
Gene: A Critical History, The. *Elof Axel Carlson.* HWor(I-10).
General Gage in America: Being Principally a History of His Role in the
    American Revolution. *John R. Alden.* HAmer(I-253).
General Introduction to Psychoanalysis, A. *Sigmund Freud.*
    MP12(IV-2218), MP8(III-1726), MP4(I-371), MWL4(371).
General MacArthur Administers the Reconstruction of Japan (Event).
    HWor(II-584).
General Strike, The. *Julian Symons.* HEur(III-1326).
General Strike of 1926 in Great Britain (Event). HEur(III-1324).
General Theory of Value. *Ralph Barton Perry.* Ph(II-874).
Generation of Materialism, 1871-1900, A. Vol. XVI *of* The Rise of Modern
    Europe *series.* *Carlton J. H. Hayes .* HEur(II-991).
Generation of 1914, The. *Robert Wohl.* LA80(I-337).
Generations. *Lucille Clifton.* LA77(I-318).
Generous Man, A. *Reynolds Price.* SCL12(V-2872), SCLs(115).
Genesis of the Trivium and Quadrivium (Event). HAnc(II-1000).
Genetic Research (Event). HWor(I-7).
Geneva Disarmament Conference, The (Event). HWor(I-276).
Geneva Summit Conference, The (Event). HWor(II-721).
"Genius," The. *Theodore Dreiser.* MP12(IV-2221), MPCE(II-803),
    MP8(III-1729), MP6(II-1084), MPAm(192), MP3(I-409),
    MWL3(409).
Genius and Lust. *Norman Mailer.* LA77(I-322).
Genius for War: The German Army and General Staff, 1807-1945, A. *T. N.
    Dupuy.* LA78(I-332).
Gentle Barbarian: The Life and Work of Turgenev, The. *V. S. Pritchett.*
    LA78(I-340).
*Gentleman Dancing Master, The. *William Wycherley.* MP12(IV-2226),
    MPCE(II-805), MP8(III-1732), MP6(II-1086), MPDr(292),
    MP3(I-411), MWL3(411).
*Gentleman Usher, The. *George Chapman.* MP12(IV-2230),

MPCE(II-807),   MP8(III-1735),   MP6(II-1089),   MPDr(295),
MP3(I-413),   MWL3(413).
Gentleman's Agreement.   Cine(II-610).
Gentlemen Prefer Blondes.   Cine(II-613).
Geoffrey Chaucer of England.   *Marchette Chute*.   HAnc(III-1657).
Geography III.   *Elizabeth Bishop*.   LA77(I-326).
"Geometrical Background to the 'Merton School': An Exploration into the
    Application of Mathematics to Natural Philosophy in the Fourteenth
    Century, The," *in* The British Journal for the History of Science.   *A. G.
    Molland*.   HAnc(III-1617).
George.   *Emlyn Williams*.   SCL12(V-2875),   SCL7(III-1715),   A63(65).
George Bancroft: Brahmin Rebel.   *Russel B. Nye*.   HAmer(II-732).
George Bernard Shaw.   *Archibald Henderson*.   SCL12(V-2878),
    SCL7(III-1718),   A57(84).
George C. Marshall.   *Robert H. Ferrell*, ed.   HAmer(III-1796).
George C. Marshall: Education of a General, 1880-1939.   *Forrest C. Pogue*.
    SCL12(V-2882),   SCL7(III-1722),   A64(107).
George C. Marshall: Ordeal and Hope, 1939-1942.   *Forrest C. Pogue*.
    SCL12(V-2885),   SCL7(III-1725),   A67(122). A different analysis on
    this title appears in: HAmer(III-1717).
George C. Marshall: Organizer of Victory, 1943-1954.   *Forrest C. Pogue*.
    SCL12(V-2890),   A74(148).
George Eliot: A Biography.   *Gordon S. Haight*.   SCL12(V-2895),
    SCL7(III-1729),   A69(130).
George Eliot: The Emergent Self.   *Ruby V. Redinger*.   SCL12(V-2901),
    A76(98).
George Meredith and English Comedy.   *V. S. Pritchett*.   SCL12(V-2906),
    A71(96).
George Stephenson, Father of Railways.   *Ada L. Barrett*.   HEur(II-610).
George Washington.   *James Thomas Flexner*.   SCL12(V-2910),   A73(181).
George Washington: A Biography, Vol. VI: Patriot and President.   *Douglas
    Southall Freeman*.   HAmer(I-343).
Georgia: A Short History.   *E. Merton Coulter*.   HAmer(I-184).
Georgia Scenes.   *Augustus Baldwin Longstreet*.   MP12(IV-2233),
    MP8(III-1738),   MP6(II-1091),   MPAm(195),   MP3(I-416),
    MWL3(416).
*Georgics.   *Vergil (Publius Vergilius Maro)*.   MP12(IV-2236),
    MP8(III-1741),   MP4(I-373),   MWL4(373).
German and Irish Immigration (Event).   HAmer(II-754).
German Army, 1933-1945: Its Political and Military Failure, The.   *Matthew
    Cooper*.   LA79(I-245).
"German Counteroffensive in the Ardennes, The" *in* Command
    Decisions.   *Charles V. P. von Luttichau*.   HEur(III-1499).
German Experience with Social Insurance.   *Walter Sulzbach*.
    HEur(II-1030).

German Generals Talk, The. *B. H. Liddell Hart.* HWor(I-482).
German Invasion of Norway (Event). HEur(III-1446).
German Invasion of Poland (Event). HEur(III-1440).
German Invasion of Russia (Event). HWor(I-450).
German Lesson, The. *Siegfried Lenz.* SCL12(V-2914), A73(184).
German Peasants' War (Event). HEur(I-76).
German Rearmament and the West, 1932-1933. *Edward W. Bennett.*
    LA80(I-344).
"Germany: Charles IV," *in* Vol. VII *of* The Cambridge Medieval
    History. *W. T. Waugh.* HAnc(III-1636).
"Germany: Lewis the Bavarian," *in* Vol. III *of* The Cambridge Medieval
    History. *W. T. Waugh.* HAnc(III-1622).
Germany and Italy Declare War on the United States (Event).
    HWor(I-465).
Germany and the Ottoman Empire, 1914-1918. *Ulrich Trumpener.*
    HWor(I-117).
Germany Between East and West: The Reunification Problem. *Frederick H.
    Hartmann.* Different analyses on this title appear in: HEur(III-1627),
    HWor(II-651).
Germany 1866-1945. *Gordon A. Craig.* LA79(I-249).
Germany Invades the Balkans (Event). HWor(I-444).
Germany Remilitarizes the Rhineland (Event). HWor(I-348).
Germany Renounces the Versailles Treaty (Event). HWor(I-342).
Germany Tried Democracy. *S. William Halperin.* HEur(III-1297).
*Germinal. *Émile Zola.* MP12(IV-2238), MPCE(II-808),
    MP8(III-1743), MP6(II-1093), MPEur(321), MPv3(182),
    MP2(I-360), MWL2(360).
*Germinie Lacerteux. *Edmond de Goncount* and *Jules de Goncount.*
    MP12(IV-2242), MPCE(II-809), MP8(III-1746), MP6(II-1096),
    MPEur(324), MPv4(180), MP2(I-363), MWL2(363).
Geronimo Rex. *Barry Hannah.* SCL12(V-2918), A73(188).
Gettysburg. *Elsie Singmaster.* MP12(IV-2246), MPCE(II-811),
    MP8(III-1749), MP6(II-1098), MPAm(198), MPv4(182),
    MP2(I-365), MWL2(365).
Ghost at Noon, A. *Alberto Moravia.* SCL12(V-2921), SCL7(III-1734),
    A55(104).
Ghost of Guy Thyrle, The. *Edgar Fawcett.* SF(II-869).
Ghost Story. *Peter Straub.* LA80(I-349).
Ghost Voyage, The. *Gontran de Poncins.* SCL12(V-2925),
    SCL7(III-1737), A54(89).
Ghost Writer, The. *Philip Roth.* LA80(I-354).
*Ghosts. *Henrik Ibsen.* MP12(IV-2250), MPCE(II-813),
    MP8(III-1752), MP6(II-1101), MPDr(298), MP1(I-301),
    MWL1(301).
Giai Phong!: The Fall and Liberation of Saigon. *Tiziano Terzani.*

HWor(III-1246).

Giant.   Cine(II-616).

Giant Dwarfs, The.   *Gisela Elsner.*   SCL12(V-2928),   SCL7(III-1740),
A66(118).

Giants: Russia and America, The.   *Richard J. Barnet.*   LA78(I-345).

Giants in the Earth.   *O. E. Rölvaag.*   MP12(IV-2255),   MPCE(II-817),
MP8(III-1754),   MP6(II-1103),   MPAm(201),   MP1(I-303),
MWL1(303).

Giants of Geology.   *Carroll Lane* and *Mildred Adams Fenton.*
HEur(II-681).

Gideon's Trumpet.   *Anthony Lewis.*   SCL12(V-2931),   SCL7(III-1743),
A65(107). A different analysis on this title appears in: HAmer(III-1895).

Gifford Pinchot: Forester–Politician.   *M. Nelson McGeary.*
HAmer(III-1376).

*Gift, The.   *Vladimir Nabokov.*   SCL12(V-2934),   SCL7(III-1746),
A64(110).

Gift from the Sea.   *Anne Morrow Lindbergh.*   SCL12(V-2937),
SCL7(III-1749),   A55(107).

Gigi.   Cine(II-621).

*Gil Blas of Santillane.   *Alain René Le Sage.*   MP12(IV-2260),
MPCE(II-820),   MP8(III-1757),   MP6(II-1105),   MPEur(327),
MP1(I-305),   MWL1(305).

Gilda.   Cine(II-627).

*Gilded Age, The.   *Mark Twain* and *Charles Dudley Warner.*
MP12(IV-2263),   MPCE(II-822),   MP8(III-1759),   MP6(II-1107),
MPAm(204),   MPv3(185),   MP2(I-368),   MWL2(368).

*Giles Goat-Boy.   *John Barth.*   SCL12(V-2940),   SCL7(III-1752),
A67(126). A different analysis on this title appears in: SF(II-873).

*Ginger Man, The.   *J. P. Donleavy.*   SCL12(V-2946),   SCL7(III-1757),
A59(98).

Ginger Tree, The.   *Oswald Wynd.*   LA78(I-349).

Girl Crazy.   Cine(II-630).

Girl in the Golden Atom, The.   *Ray Cummings.*   SF(II-878).

*Girl in Winter, A.   *Philip Larkin.*   SCL12(V-2949),   SCL7(III-1760),
A63(67).

Girl, the Gold Watch, & Everything, The.   *John D. MacDonald.*
SF(II-883).

Girl Who Sang with the Beatles and Other Stories, The.   *Robert
Hemenway.*   SCL12(V-2952),   A71(99).

*Girls of Slender Means, The.   *Muriel Spark.*   SCL12(V-2956),
SCL7(III-1763),   A64(112).

Give Us This Day.   *Sidney Stewart.*   SCL12(V-2960),   SCL7(III-1767),
A58(99).

Giving Good Weight.   *John J. McPhee.*   LA80(I-358).

Gladiator.   *Philip Wylie.*   SF(II-888).

Gladiator-at-Law. *Frederik Pohl* and *Cyril M. Kornbluth.* SF(II-894).
*Glass Bead Game, The. *Hermann Hesse.* SF(II-899).
Glass Key, The. *Dashiell Hammett.* MP12(IV-2267), MPCE(II-823),
 MP8(III-1762), MP6(II-1110), MPAm(207), MP1(I-307),
 MWL1(307).
*Glass Menagerie, The. *Tennessee Williams.* MP12(IV-2270),
 MP8(III-1764), MP6(II-1111), MPDr(300), MP3(I-418),
 MWL3(418).
Global Reach. *Richard J. Barnet* and *Ronald E. Miller.* SCL12(V-2963),
 A76(103).
Glories of Mary. *Saint Alphonsus Mary de' Liguori.* RCa(II-624).
"Glorious Revolution," The (Event). HEur(I-357).
Glory and the Dream, The. *William Manchester.* SCL12(V-2967),
 A75(115).
Glos pana. *Stanislaw Lem.* SF(II-905).
Glosses on Porphyry, The. *Peter Abelard.* Ph(I-290).
Gnomes & Occasions. *Howard Nemerov.* SCL12(V-2970), A74(153).
Gnostic Gospels, The. *Elaine Pagels.* LA80(I-363).
*Go Down, Moses. *William Faulkner.* MP12(IV-2272), MP8(III-1766),
 MP4(I-375), MWL4(375).
Go East, Young Man. *William O. Douglas.* SCL12(V-2974), A75(118).
*Go Tell It on the Mountain. *James Baldwin.* MP12(IV-2276),
 MP8(III-1770), MP4(I-379), MWL4(379).
Goat Song. *Franz Werfel.* MP12(IV-2279), MPCE(II-825),
 MP8(III-1773), MP6(II-1113), MPDr(302), MPv4(185),
 MP2(I-370), MWL2(370).
Go-Between, The. Cine(II-633).
Go-Between, The. *L. P. Hartley.* SCL12(V-2977), SCL7(III-1770),
 A54(92).
God Against the Gods, A. *Allen Drury.* LA77(I-332).
*God and His Gifts, A. *Ivy Compton-Burnett.* SCL12(V-2980),
 SCL7(III-1773), A65(110).
God and Intelligence in Modern Philosophy. *Fulton J. Sheen.* RCa(II-788).
God and Temple; the Presence of God in Israel's Worship. *R. E. Clements.*
 HAnc(I-102).
God in Christ. *Horace Bushnell.* RCh(II-716).
God in Modern Philosophy. *James D. Collins.* RCa(II-1071).
God Was in Christ. *Donald M. Baillie.* RCh(II-1093).
Goddess and Other Women, The. *Joyce Carol Oates.* SCL12(V-2983),
 A75(121).
Gödel, Escher, Bach: An Eternal Golden Braid. *Douglas R. Hofstadter.*
 LA80(I-367).
Godfather, The. Cine(II-638).
Godfather, Part II, The. Cine(II-644).
*Gods Are Athirst, The. *Anatole France.* MP12(IV-2282),

Golden Spur, The. *Dawn Powell.* SCL12(V-3024), SCL7(III-1803), A63(76).

Golden Weather, The. *Louis D. Rubin, Jr.* SCL12(V-3026), SCL7(III-1805), A62(138).

*Goncourt Journals, The. *Edmond de Goncourt* and *Jules de Goncourt.* MP12(IV-2307), MP8(III-1795), MP4(I-387), MWL4(387).

*Gondoliers, The. *W. S. Gilbert.* MP12(IV-2310), MPCE(II-836), MP8(III-1798), MP6(II-1126), MPDr(307), MPv4(188), MP2(I-377), MWL2(377).

Gone a Hundred Miles. *Heather Ross Miller.* SCL12(V-3030), SCL7(III-180), A69(135).

Gone with the Wind. Cine(II-654).

Gone with the Wind. *Margaret Mitchell.* MP12(IV-2313), MP8(III-1800), MP6(II-1128), MPAm(214), MP3(I-424), MWL3(424).

Good as Gold. *Joseph Heller.* LA80(I-372).

*Good Companions, The. *J. B. Priestley.* MP12(IV-2316), MPCE(II-838), MP8(III-1803), MP6(II-1131), MPEng(243), MP1(I-311), MWL1(311).

*Good Earth, The. *Pearl S. Buck.* MP12(IV-2319), MPCE (II-839), MP8(III-1806), MP6(II-1133), MPAm(217), MP1(I-313), MWL1(313).

Good Light, The. *Karl Bjarnhof.* SCL12(V-3033), SCL7(III-1812), A61(104).

*Good Man Is Hard to Find, A. *Flannery O'Connor.* SCL12(V-3036), SCL7(III-1815), A55(109).

Good Morning, Midnight. *Jean Rhys.* SCL12(V-3039), A71(102).

Good News Yesterday and Today, The. *Josef Andreas Jungmann, S. J.* RCa(II-843).

Good Shepherd, The. *C. S. Forester.* SCL12(V-3042), SCL7(III-1818), A55(112).

Good Soldier: Schweik, The. *Jaroslav Hašek.* MP12(IV-2324), MPCE(II-842), MP8(III-1809), MP4(I-390), MWL4(390).

Good Times/Bad Times. *James Kirkwood.* SCL12(V-3045), SCL7(III-1821), A69(138).

Good Word & Other Words, The. *Wilfrid Sheed.* LA80(I-375).

Goodbye. *William Sansom.* SCL12(V-3048), SCL7(III-1824), A67(131).

Goodbye Columbus. Cine(II-660).

*Goodbye, Columbus. *Philip Roth.* SCL12(V-3051), SCLs(117).

Goodbye, Mr. Chips. Cine(II-663).

*Goodbye, Mr. Chips. *James Hilton.* MP12(IV-2328), MPCE(II-844), MP8(III-1812), MP6(II-1135), MPEng(246), MP1(I-316), MWL1(316).

Goodbye to a River. *John Graves.* SCL12(V-3055),

SCL7(III-1827),   A61(107).
Goodbye to Uncle Tom.   *J. C. Furnas*.   SCL12(V-3058),
    SCL7(III-1830),   A57(87).
*Gorboduc.   *Thomas Norton* and *Thomas Sackville*.   MP12(IV-2332),
    MPCE(II-846),   MP8(III-1814),   MP6(II-1137),   MPDr(309),
    MPv3(189),   MP2(I-379),   MWL2(379).
Goshawk, Antelope.   *Dave Smith*.   LA80(I-380).
Gorgias.   *Plato*.   Ph(I-70).
"Gospel According to Luke, The," *in* The Jerome Biblical
    Commentary.   *Carroll Stuhlmueller, C. P.*   HAnc(I-569).
"Gospel According to Matthew, The," *in* The Jerome Biblical Commentary.
    John L. McKenzie.   HAnc(I-569).
Gospel and the Church, The.   *Alfred Loisy*.   RCh(II-832).
Gossip from the Forest.   *Thomas Keneally*.   LA77(I-336).
Gothic Cathedral: Origins of Gothic Architecture and the
    Medieval Concept of Order, The.   *Otto Von Simson*.
    HAnc(III-1419).
Governing of Men, The.   *Alexander H. Leighton*.   HAmer(III-1705).
Government Acts to Assure Loyalty at Home in Wartime (Event).
    HAmer(III-1703).
Government in Public Health.   *Harry S. Mustard*.   HAmer (III-1397).
Governor and the Rebel, The.   *Wilcomb E. Washburn*.   HAmer(I-154).
Grace Abounding to the Chief of Sinners.   *John Bunyan*.   RCh(I-506).
Graduate, The.   Cine(II-667).
Grain of Mustard Seed, A.   *May Sarton*.   SCL12(V-3061),   A72(155).
Grammar of Assent, A.   *John Henry Cardinal Newman*.   Different analyses
    on this title appear in: Ph(II-666),   RCa(II-678).
Grand Hotel.   Cine(II-672).
Grand Hotel.   *Vicki Baum*.   MP12(IV-2335),   MPCE(II-848),
    MP8(III-1816),   MP6(II-1139),   MPEur(335),   MP1(I-318),
    MWL1(318).
Grand Inquisitor, The.   *Fyodor Mikhailovich Dostoevski*.   RCh(II-786).
Grand Mademoiselle, The.   *Francis Steegmuller*.   SCL12(V-3064),
    SCL7(III-1833),   A57(90).
Grandfather Stories.   *Samuel Hopkins Adams*.   SCL12(V-3067),
    SCL7(III-1836),   A55(115).
Grandfathers, The.   *Conrad Richter*.   SCL12(V-3071),   SCL7(III-1840),
    A65(115).
Grandissimes, The.   *George W. Cable*.   MP12(IV-2338),   MPCE(II-849),
    MP8(III-1819),   MP6(II-1141),   MPAm(220),   MP1(I-320),
    MWL1(320).
Grandmothers, The.   *Glenway Wescott*.   MP12(IV-2341),
    MPCE(II-851),   MP8(III-1821),   MP6(II-1143),   MPAm(222),
    MP1(I-322),   MWL1(322).
Granger Movement: A Study of Agricultural Organization and Its Political,

Economic, and Social Manifestations, 1870-1880, The. *Solon J. Buck.*
HAmer(II-1045).
Granite and Rainbow. *Virginia Woolf.* SCL12(V-3077),
SCL7(III-1846), A59(101).
Granite Lady. *Susan Fromberg Schaeffer.* SCL12(V-3080), A75(125).
Grant Moves South. *Bruce Catton.* SCL12(V-3083), SCL7(III-1849),
A61(109), BMA(208).
Granting of the Charter of Lorris (Event). HAnc(III-1323).
Grapes of Wrath, The. Cine (II-675).
*Grapes of Wrath, The. *John Steinbeck.* MP12(IV-2344),
MPCE(II-835), MP8(III-1824), MP6(II-1146), MPAm(225),
MP1(I-324), MWL1(324).
Grasp of Consciousness, The. *Jean Piaget.* LA77(I-341).
Grasshoppers and Elephants: Why Vietnam Fell. *Wilfred Burchett.*
HWor(III-1164).
*Gravity's Rainbow. *Thomas Pynchon.* SCL12(V-3087), A74(166). A
different analysis on this title appears in: SF(II-915).
Gray Fox. *Burke Davis.* SCL12(V-3092), SCL7(III-1853), A57(93).
Gray Matters. *William Hjortsberg.* SF(II-921).
Great American Cattle Trails. *Harry Sinclair Drago.* HAmer(II-1023).
Great American Jackpot, The. *Herbert Gold.* SCL12(V-3095), A70(143).
*Great American Novel, The. *Philip Roth.* SCL12(V-3098), A74(170).
Great Armenian Massacre, The (Event). HWor(I-107).
Great Awakening, The (Event). HAmer(I-176).
Great Blood Purge, The (Event). HEur(III-1391).
Great Britain and Japan, 1911-1915: A Study of British Far Eastern
Policy. *Peter Lowe.* HWor(I-125).
Great Britain and the Bagdad Railway, 1888-1914. *Maybelle K. Chapman.*
HEur(II-1136).
"Great Britain and the Powers, 1904-1914," *in* The Cambridge History of the
British Empire. *F. H. Hinsley.* HEur(III-1200).
Great Britain Issues the 1939 White Paper Restricting Jewish Emigration to
Palestine (Event). HWor(I-411).
Great Britain Joins the Common Market (Event). HWor(III-1146).
Great Britain Purchases Suez Canal Shares (Event). HEur(II-998).
Great Britain Strengthens the Royal Navy (Event). HEur(II-1057).
Great Britain Withdraws from the Concert of Europe (Event).
HEur(II-654).
Great Captains, The. *Henry Treece.* SCL12(V-3102), SCL7(III-1856),
A57(96).
Great Catechism, The. *Saint Gregory of Nyssa.* Different analyses on this
title appear in: RCh(I-125), RCa(I-120).
Great Christian Doctrine of Original Sin Defended, The. *Jonathan
Edwards.* RCh(II-602).
Great Conspiracy Trial, The. *Jason Epstein.* SCL12(V-3105), A71(105).

Great Crash, 1929, The. *John Kenneth Galbraith.* HAmer(III-1579).

Great Days. *Donald Barthelme.* LA80(I-385).

Great Democracies, The. *Winston S. Churchill.* SCL12(V-3109), SCL7(III-1859), A59(103), BMA(212).

Great Depression, 1929-1939, The (Event). HAmer(III-1582).

Great Dictator, The. Cine(II-678).

Great Escape, The. Cine (II-682).

Great Expectations. Cine (II-685).

*Great Expectations. *Charles Dickens.* MP12(IV-2349), MPCE(II-856), MP8(III-1827), MP6(II-1148), MPEng(248), MP1(I-326), MWL1(326).

Great Fear: The Anti-Communist Purge Under Truman and Eisenhower, The. *David Caute.* LA79(I-255).

Great Galeoto, The. *José Echegaray.* MP12(IV-2355), MPCE(II-859), MP8(III-1830), MP6(II-1150), MPDr(311), MPv3(191), MP2(I-381), MWL2(381).

Great Gatsby, The. Cine(II-690).

*Great Gatsby, The. *F. Scott Fitzgerald.* MP12(IV-2358), MPCE(II-860), MP8(III-1832), MP6(II-1152), MPAm(228), MP1(I-329), MWL1(329).

Great Hunger, The. *Cecil Woodham-Smith.* SCL12(V-3113), SCL7(III-1862), A64(115). A different analysis on this title appears in: HEur(II-761).

Great Jurists of the World. Vol. II *of* Continental Legal History *series.* *Sir John McDonnell* and *Edward Manson,* eds. HAnc(II-723).

Great Lakes Frontier: An Epic of the Old Northwest, The. *John Anthony Caruso.* HAmer(I-529).

Great Learning, The. Attributed to *Tseng Tzu* or *Tzu Ssu.* Ph(I-212).

Great McGinty, The. Cine(II-693).

Great Meadow, The. *Elizabeth Madox Roberts.* MP12(IV-2363), MPCE(II-863), MP8(III-1835), MP6(II-1155), MPAm(231), MPv3(193), MP2(I-383), MWL2(383).

Great Migration, The (Event). HAmer(I-527).

Great Plains, The. *Walter Prescott Webb.* MP12(IV-2367), MP8(III-1838), MP4(I-393), MWL4(393).

Great Puritan Migration, The (Event). HAmer(I-85).

Great Railway Bazaar, The. *Paul Theroux.* SCL12(V-3117), A76(107).

Great Republic: A History of the American People, The. *Bernard Bailyn* et al. LA78(I-360).

Great Revolt in Castile, The. *Henry L. Seaver.* HEur(I-74).

Great River. *Paul Horgan.* SCL12(V-3121), SCL7(III-1866), A54(98), BMA(216).

Great Russian Civil War, The (Event). HWor(I-152).

Great Terror, The. *Robert Conquest.* SCL12(V-3125), SCL7(III-1870), A69(140). A different analysis on this title appears in: HWor(I-338).

Great Testament, The. *François Villon.* MP12(IV-2370),
  MP8(III-1841), MP6(II-1157), MPPo(113), MP3(I-426),
  MWL3(426).
Great Valley, The. *Mary Johnston.* MP12(IV-2372), MPCE(II-865),
  MP8(III-1843), MP6(II-1159), MPAm(234), MP3(I-428),
  MWL3(428).
Great Victorian Collection, The. *Brian Moore.* SCL12(V-3129),
  A76(111).
Great Wall of France, The. *Vivian Rowe.* HEur(III-1360).
Great War and Modern Memory, The. *Paul Fussell.* SCL12(V-3132),
  A76(114).
Great White Hope, The. *Howard Sackler.* SCL12(V-3136), A70(146).
Greatest Show on Earth, The. Cine(II-697).
Greatness of Oliver Cromwell, The. *Maurice Ashley.* Different analyses on
  this title appear in: HEur(I-315; I-333).
Greatness That Was Babylon, The. *H. W. F. Saggs.* HAnc(I-181).
Greek and Macedonian Art of War, The. *F. E. Adcock.* HAnc(I-311).
Greek Athletes and Athletics. *H. A. Harris.* HAnc(I-118).
Greek City from Alexander to Justinian, The. *A. H. M. Jones.*
  HAnc(I-355).
Greek Coins. *C. M. Kraay* and *Max Hirmer.* HAnc(I-147).
"Greek Medicine in Its Relation to Religion and Magic," *in* Bulletin of the
  Institute of the History of Medicine. *Ludwig Edelstein.* HAnc(I-304).
*Greek Passion, The. *Nikos Kazantzakis.* MP12(IV-2375),
  MP8(III-1846), MP4(I-395), MWL4(395), SCL12(V-3140),
  SCL7(III-1874), A54(102).
Greek Sculpture. *R. Lullies* and *M. Hirmer.* HAnc(I-278).
Greek Stones Speak: The Story of Archaeology in Greek Lands, The. *Paul
  MacKendrick.* HAnc(I-300).
Greek Thinkers: A History of Ancient Philosophy. *Theodor Gomperz.*
  HAnc(I-288).
Greek Tyrants, The. *A. Andrewes.* HAnc(I-136).
Greeks and Their Gods, The. *W. K. C. Guthrie.* HAnc(I-161).
Green Bay Tree, The. *Louis Bromfield.* MP12(IV-2378),
  MPCE(II-866), MP8(III-1849), MP6(II-1161), MPAm(237),
  MP1(I-331), MWL1(331).
Green Grow the Lilacs. *Lynn Riggs.* MP12(IV-2382), MPCE(II-868),
  MP8(III-1852), MP6(II-1163), MPDr(313), MP3(I-430),
  MWL3(430).
Green House, The. *Mario Vargas Llosa.* SCL12(V-3144), A70(150).
*Green Man, The. *Kingsley Amis.* SCL12(V-3148), SCLs(121).
*Green Mansions. *W. H. Hudson.* MP12(IV-2386), MPCE(II-870),
  MP8(III-1855), MP6(II-1165), MPEng(251), MP1(I-333),
  MWL1(333).
Green Mare, The. *Marcel Aymé.* SCL12(V-3152), SCL7(III-1877),

A57(99).

Green Mountain Boys, The. *Daniel Pierce Thompson.* MP12(IV-2389),
    MPCE(II-871), MP8(III-1858), MP6(II-1168), MPAm(240),
    MPv4(190), MP2(I-385), MWL2(385).

Greenback Era, The. *Irwin Unger.* SCL12(V-3155), SCLs(125). A
    different analysis on this title appears in: HAmer(II-1085).

Greene's Groatsworth of Wit Bought with a Million of Repentance. *Robert
    Greene.* MP12(IV-2394), MP8(III-1862), MP4(I-397),
    MWL4(397).

Greengage Summer, The. *Rumer Godden.* SCL12(V-3158),
    SCL7(III-1880), A59(106).

Greening of America, The. *Charles Reich.* SCL12(V-3161), A71(108).

Greenwillow. *B. J. Chute.* SCL12(V-3165), SCL7(III-1883), A57(102).

Gregory the Great: His Place in History and Thought. *Frederick Homes
    Dudden.* HAnc(II-1066).

Gregory's Recognition of "Vulgar Christianity" (Event). HAnc(II-1063).

Grettir the Strong. *Unknown.* MP12(IV-2396), MPCE(II-873),
    MP8(III-1864), MP6(II-1172), MPEur(338), MP1(I-335),
    MWL1(335).

Greybeard. *Brian W. Aldiss.* SF(II-926).

Gringa, La. *Florencio Sánchez.* MP12(IV-2401), MPCE(II-876),
    MP8(III-1867), MP6(II-1175), MPDr(316), MPv4(194),
    MP2(I-389), MWL2(389).

Groundwork. *Robert Morgan.* LA80(I-388).

*Group, The. *Mary McCarthy.* SCL12(V-3169), SCL7(III-1887),
    A64(119).

Group Portrait with Lady. *Heinrich Böll.* SCL12(V-3173), A74(174).

Grover Cleveland: A Study in Courage. *Allan Nevins.* HAmer(II-1142).

Grove's First Incandescent Electric Lamp (Event). HEur(II-753).

Growing into Love. *X. J. Kennedy.* SCL12(V-3178), A70(154).

Growing Up in America. *Fred M. Hechinger* and *Grace Hechinger.*
    HWor(I-515).

Growth of Manichaean Gnosticism (Event). HAnc(II-807).

Growth of Papal Government in the Middle Ages, The. *Walter Ullmann.*
    Different analyses on this title appear in: HAnc(II-991; II-1122; II-1132;
    III-1266; III-1273).

Growth of Philosophic Radicalism, The. *Elie Halévy.* Different analyses on
    this title appear in: HEur(I-536; II-631).

Growth of Southern Nationalism, 1848-1861, The. *Avery O. Craven.*
    HAmer(II-856).

Growth of the Athenian Economy, The. *A. French.* HAnc(I-171).

Growth of the Fairs of Champagne (Event). HAnc(III-1421).

Growth of the Idea of God, The. *Shailer Mathews.* RCh(II-965).

Growth of the Old Testament, The. *H. H. Rowley.* HAnc(II-667).

Growth of the Separatist Movement in Quebec (Event). HWor(II-820).

*Growth of the Soil. *Knut Hamsun.* MP12(IV-2404), MPCE(II-878), MP8(III-1870), MP6(II-1177), MPEur(341), MP1(I-338), MWL1(338).

Growth or Decline?: The Church Today. *Emmanuel Cardinal Suhard.* RCa(II-920).

Grüne Heinrich, Der. *Gottfried Keller.* MP12(IV-2408), MPCE(II-880), MP8(III-1873), MP6(II-1179), MPEur(344), MP3(I-432), MWL3(432).

Guadalcanal: The First Offensive, *in* The United States Army in World War II: The War in the Pacific *series. John Miller, Jr.* HAmer(III-1712).

*Guard of Honor. *James Gould Cozzens.* MP12(IV-2412), MPCE(II-881), MP8(III-1876), MP6(III-1183), MPAm(244), MP3(I-435), MWL3(435).

guerre au XXe siècle, La. *Albert Robida.* SF(II-932).

Guerrillas. *V. S. Naipaul.* SCL12(V-3182), A76(118).

*Guest and His Going, A. *P. H. Newby.* SCL12(V-3186), SCL7(III-1890), A61(113).

Guest the One-Eyed. *Gunnar Gunnarsson.* MP12(IV-2416), MP8(III-1878), MP6(III-1185), MPEur(347), MP3(I-437), MWL3(437).

Guggenheims: An American Epic, The. *John H. Davis.* LA79(I-260).

Guide, The. *R. K. Narayan.* MP12(IV-2418), MP8(III-1880), MP4(I-399), MWL4(399). A different analysis on this title appears in: SCL12(V-3189), SCL7(III-1893), A59(109).

Guide for the Perplexed, A. *E. F. Schumacher.* LA78(I-364).

Guide for the Perplexed. *Maimonides.* Different analyses on this title appear in: Ph(I-300), HAnc(III-1392).

Guillaume de Machaut. *Siegmund Levarie.* HAnc(III-1413).

Gulliver's Travels. *Jonathan Swift.* MP12(IV-2421), MPCE(II-884), MP8(III-1883), MP6(III-1187), MPEng(254), MP1(I-341), MWL1(341).

Gull's Hornbook, The. *Thomas Dekker.* MP12(IV-2426), MP8(III-1886), MP4(I-401), MWL4(401).

Guilty Pleasures. *Donald Barthelme.* SCL12(V-3192), A75(128).

Gulag Archipelago: One, Parts I-II, The. *Alexander Solzhenitsyn.* SCL12(V-3195), A75(131).

*Gulag Archipelago: Two, Parts III-IV, The. *Alexander Solzhenitsyn.* SCL12(V-3199), A76(122).

Gulag Archipelago: Three, Parts V-VII, 1918-1956, The. *Alexander Solzhenitsyn.* LA78(I-370).

Guns of August, The. *Barbara W. Tuchman.* SCL12(V-3202), SCL7(III-1896), A63(78).

Guns of Navarone, The. Cine(II-700).

Guns, Sails, and Empires. *Carlo M. Cipolla.* HAnc(III-1511).

Gustavus Adolphus: A History of Sweden, 1611-1632. Vol. II:

1626-1632.   *Michael Roberts.*   HEur(I-275).

Gustavus Adolphus and The Thirty Years War.   *C. R. L. Fletcher.*
    HEur(I-276).

*Guy Mannering.   *Sir Walter Scott.*   MP12(IV-2429),   MPCE(II-887),
    MP8(III-1889),   MP6(III-1189),   MPEng(257),   MPv3(196),
    MP2(I-391),   MWL2(391).

*Guy of Warwick.   *Unknown.*   MP12(IV-2433),   MPCE(II-888),
    MP8(III-1892),   MP6(III-1191),   MPPo(115),   MP3(I-439),
    MWL3(439).

*Guzmán de Alfarache.   *Mateo Alemán.*   MP12(IV-2437),
    MPCE(II-890),   MP8(III-1895),   MP6(III-1194),   MPEur(349),
    MPv4(197),   MP2(I-393),   MWL2(393).

Guzman, Go Home.   *Alan Sillitoe.*   SCL12(V-3206),   A70(157).

Habit of Being, The.   *Flannery O'Connor.*   LA80(I-391).

Hadrian.   *John James Stewart Perowne.*   HAnc(II-704).

Hadrian's Memoirs.   *Marguerite Yourcenar.*   MP12(V-2443),
    MP8(III-1900),   MP4(I-404),   MWL4(404). A different analysis on this
    title appears in: SCL12(V-3213),   SCL7(III-1900),   A54(105).

Hadrian VII.   *Peter Luke.*   SCL12(V-3209),   A70(161).

Hagia Sophia.   *Heinz Kähler.*   HAnc(II-1043).

Hagia Sophia.   *Emerson Howland Swift.*   HAnc(II-1042).

Hair of Harold Roux, The.   *Thomas Williams.*   SCL12(V-3216),   A75(135).

Hajji Baba of Ispahan.   *James Morier.*   MP12(V-2446),   MPCE(II-892),
    MP8(III-1903),   MP6(III-1199),   MPEng(260),   MP1(I-343),
    MWL1(343).

Hakluyt's Voyages.   *Richard Hakluyt.*   MP12(V-2450),   MPCE(II-894),
    MP8(III-1906),   MP6(III-1201),   MPNf(131),   MP1(I-346),
    MWL1(346).

Halcyon Drift.   *Brian Stableford.*   SF(II-936).

Half Past Human.   *T. J. Bass.*   SF(II-940).

Half Sun Half Sleep.   *May Swenson.*   SCL12(V-3220),   SCL7(III-1903),
    A68(130).

Half-Way Covenant, The (Event).   HAmer(I-127).

Hall of Mirrors, A.   *Robert Stone.*   SCL12(V-3224),   SCL7(III-1907),
    A68(134).

Hallelujah!   Cine(II-704).

Hamlet.   Cine(II-708).

*Hamlet.   *William Shakespeare.*   MP12(V-2457),   MPCE(II-897),
    MP8(III-1912),   MP6(III-1206),   MPDr(319),   MP1(I-348),
    MWL1(348).

*Hamlet, The.   *William Faulkner.*   MP12(V-2454),   MPCE(II-896),
    MP8(III-1909),   MP6(III-1204),   MPAm(246),   MPv3(198),
    MP2(I-398),   MWL2(398).

Hammarskjöld.   *Brian Urquhart.*   SCL12(V-3228),   A74(179).

Hampdenshire Wonder, The. *John Davys Beresford.* SF(II-945).
*Hampshire Days. *W. H. Hudson.* MP12(V-2462), MP8(III-1914), MP4(I-406), MWL4(406).
Han Fei Tzu. *Han Fei.* Ph(I-201).
Handbook of Greek and Roman Architecture, A. *D. S. Robertson.* HAnc(I-279).
Handbook of the New Library of Congress in Washington. *Herbert Small.* HAmer(II-1281).
Handbook to the Septuagint, A. *R. R. Ottley.* HAnc(I-420).
Handcarts to Zion: The Story of a Unique Western Migration, 1856-1860 *LeRoy R. Hafen* and *Ann W. Hafen.* HAmer(II-816).
*Handful of Dust, A. *Evelyn Waugh.* MP12(V-2464), MPCE(II-900), MP8(III-1916), MP6(III-1208), MPEng(263), MP1(I-350), MWL1(350).
*Handley Cross. *Robert Smith Surtees.* MP12(V-2467), MPCE(II-901), MP8(III-1919), MP6(III-1210), MPEng(266), MP1(I-352), MWL1(352).
Handy Andy. *Samuel Lover.* MP12(V-2470), MPCE(II-902), MP8(III-1922), MP6(III-1213), MPEng(269), MPv3(200), MP2(I-400), MWL2(400).
Hanger Stout, Awake! *Jack Matthews.* SCL12(V-3232), SCL7(III-1911), A68(137).
Hangman's House. *Donn Byrne.* MP12(V-2473), MPCE(II-903), MP8(III-1925), MP6(III-1215), MPEng(272), MPv4(201), MP2(I-403), MWL2(403).
Hannah Arendt: The Recovery of the Public World. *Melvyn A. Hill,* ed. LA80(I-395).
Hannibal. *T. A. Dodge.* HAnc(I-440).
Hanseatic Control of Norwegian Commerce During the Late Middle Ages, The. *John A. Gade.* HAnc(III-1433).
*Happy Birthday, Wanda June. *Kurt Vonnegut, Jr.* SCL12(V-3235), A72(158).
Happy Exiles, The. *Felicity Shaw.* SCL12(V-3240), SCL7(III-1915), A57(105).
*Happy Families Are All Alike. *Peter Taylor.* SCL12(V-3242), SCL7(III-1918), A60(80).
Happy Marriage, The. *R. V. Cassill.* SCL12(V-3245), SCL7(III-1921), A67(133).
Happy Rural Seat. *Richard Gill.* SCL12(V-3249), A73(191).
Hapsburg Monarchy, 1867-1914, The. *Arthur J. May.* HEur(II-942).
*Hard Blue Sky, The. *Shirley Ann Grau.* SCL12(V-3253), SCL7(III-1925), A59(111).
Hard Day's Night, A. Cine(II-712).
Hard Hours, The. *Anthony Hecht.* SCL12(V-3257), SCL7(III-1928), A68(140).

Hard Scrabble: Observations on a Patch of Land. *John Graves*.
 SCL12(V-3262),   A75(139).
*Hard Times. *Charles Dickens*. MP12(V-2477),   MPCE(II-904),
 MP8(III-1928),   MP6(III-1217),   MPEng(275),   MPv3(203),
 MP2(I-405),   MWL2(405).
Hard Times. *Studs Terkel*. SCL12(V-3267),   A71(112).
Hard to Be a God. *Arkady Strugatsky* and *Boris Strugatsky*. SF(II-950).
Harmless People, The. *Elizabeth Marshall Thomas*. SCL12(V-3271),
 SCL7(III-1933),   A60(82).
Harmonium. *Wallace Stevens*. MP12(V-2480),   MP8(III-1931),
 MP6(III-1220),   MPPo(118),   MP3(I-442),   MWL3(442).
Harold and Maude. Cine(II-716).
Harold Nicolson: Diaries and Letters, 1930-1939. *Sir Harold Nicolson*.
 SCL12(V-3274),   SCL7(III-1936),   A67(138).
Harold Nicolson: Diaries and Letters, 1939-1945. *Sir Harold Nicolson*.
 SCL12(V-3279),   SCL7(III-1941),   A68(145).
Harold Nicolson: Diaries and Letters, 1945-1962. *Sir Harold Nicolson*.
 SCL12(V-3283),   SCL7(III-1945),   A69(144).
Harp of a Thousand Strings. *H. L. Davis*. MP12(V-2484),
 MPCE(II-905),   MP8(III-1935),   MP6(III-1223),   MPAm(249),
 MPv4(204),   MP2(I-407),   MWL2(407).
*Harp-Weaver and Other Poems, The. *Edna St. Vincent Millay*.
 MP12(V-2489),   MP8(III-1938),   MP6(III-1225),   MPPo(122),
 MP3(I-445),   MWL3(445).
Harriet Beecher Stowe Publishes *Uncle Tom's Cabin* (Event).
 HAmer(II-859). *See also* Uncle Tom's Cabin.
Harrison Gray Otis, 1765-1848: The Urbane Federalist. *Samuel Eliot
 Morison*.   HAmer(I-519).
Harry Hopkins: A Biography. *Henry H. Adams*.   LA78(I-375).
Harry S Truman. *Margaret Truman*. SCL12(V-3288),   A74(183).
Hartford Convention, The (Event). HAmer(I-517).
Harun al-Rashid. *H. St. John Philby*.   HAnc(II-1144).
Harvest on the Don. *Mikhail Sholokhov*. SCL12(V-3292),
 SCL7(III-1950),   A62(142).
Harvey. Cine(II-720).
Hat on the Bed, The. *John O'Hara*.   SCL12(V-3295),   SCL7(III-1953),
 A64(121).
*Havelok the Dane. *Unknown*. MP12(V-2492),   MPCE(II-908),
 MP8(III-1941),   MP6(III-1228),   MPPo(125),   MPv3(205),
 MP2(I-410),   MWL2(410).
Hawaii. *James A. Michener*.   SCL12(V-3298),   SCL7(III-1956),
 A60(85).
Hawkline Monster, The. *Richard Brautigan*. SCL12(V-3302),   A75(144).
Hawthorne: A Collection of Critical Essays. *A. N. Kaul*.   HAmer(II-851).
Hayes-Tilden Election, The. *Paul L. Haworth*.   HAmer(II-1101).

*Hazard of New Fortunes, A. *William Dean Howells.* MP12(V-2495), MPCE(II-910), MP8(III-1944), MP6(III-1230), MPAm(252), MPv4(206), MP2(I-412), MWL2(412).

He Slew the Dreamer: My Search for the Truth About James Earl Ray and the Murder of Martin Luther King. *William Bradford Huie.* HAmer(III-1929).

He Who Flees the Lion. *J. Klein-Haparash.* SCL12(V-3305), SCL7(III-1960), A64(124).

He Who Rides a Tiger. *Bhabani Bhattacharya.* SCL12(V-3308), SCL7(III-1963), A54(108).

Headlong Hall. *Thomas Love Peacock.* MP12(V-2498), MPCE(II-911), MP8(III-1947), MP6(III-1232), MPEng(278), MPv4(209), MP2(I-414), MWL2(414).

*Hear Us O Lord from Heaven Thy Dwelling Place. *Malcolm Lowry.* SCL12(V-3311), SCL7(III-1966), A62(145), BMA(220).

Hearing Secret Harmonies. *Anthony Powell.* LA77(I-347).

Hearst-Pulitzer Circulation War (Event). HAmer(II-1243).

Heart Attack: You Don't Have to Die. *Christian N. Barnard.* HWor(II-1020).

*Heart Is a Lonely Hunter, The. *Carson McCullers.* MP12(V-2501), MPCE(II-912), MP8(III-1949), MP6(III-1234), MPAm(255), MPv4(210), MP2(I-416), MWL2(416).

Heart of a Dog, The. *Michail Bulgakov.* SF(II-956).

*Heart of Darkness. *Joseph Conrad.* MP12(V-2505), MPCE(II-914), MP8(III-1952), MP6(III-1236), MPEng(280), MP3(I-447), MWL3(447).

Heart of Man, The. *Gerald Vann, O. P.* RCa(II-889).

*Heart of Midlothian, The. *Sir Walter Scott.* MP12(V-2510), MPCE(II-917), MP8(III-1955), MP6(III-1239), MPEng(283), MP1(I-355), MWL1(355).

*Heart of the Matter, The. *Graham Greene.* MP12(V-2515), MPCE(II-920), MP8(III-1958), MP6(III-1241), MPEng(286), MPv3(207), MP2(I-418), MWL2(418).

Heartbeat Away, A. *Richard M. Cohen* and *Jules Witcover.* HWor(III-1190).

*Heartbreak House. *George Bernard Shaw.* MP12(V-2520), MP8(III-1961), MP6(III-1243), MPDr(321), MP3(I-449), MWL3(449).

Heartbreak Tango. *Manuel Puig.* SCL12(V-3315), A74(187).

Hearts and Minds. *Axel Madsen.* LA78(I-379).

Heart's Needle. *W. D. Snodgrass.* SCL12(V-3317), SCL7(III-1970), A60(88), BMA(224).

Heat and Dust. *Ruth Prawer Jhabvala.* LA77(I-352).

*Heat of the Day, The. *Elizabeth Bowen.* MP12(V-2523), MPCE(II-923), MP8(III-1964), MP6(III-1246), MPEng(289),

MPv4(213),   MP2(I-420),   MWL2(420).
Heaven Can Wait.   Cine(II-724).
Heaven Can Wait.   Cine(II-727).
*Heaven's My Destination.   *Thornton Wilder.*   MP12(V-2528),
    MPCE(II-926),   MP8(III-1967),   MP6(III-1249),   MPAm(258),
    MP1(I-357),   MWL1(357).
Heaven's Tableland: The Dust Bowl Story.   *Vance Johnson.*
    HAmer(III-1630).
Hebrew Exodus from Egypt (Event).   HAnc(I-75).
*Hedda Gabler.   *Henrik Ibsen.*   MP12(V-2532),   MPCE(II-928),
    MP8(III-1970),   MP6(III-1251),   MPDr(324),   MP1(I-359),
    MWL1(359).
Heights of Macchu Picchu, The.   *Pablo Neruda.*   SCL12(V-3321),
    SCL7(III-1974),   A68(149).
Heiké Story, The.   *Eiji Yoshikawa.*   SCL12(V-3325),   SCL7(III-1978),
    A57(107).
*Heimskringla, The.   *Snorri Sturluson.*   MP12(V-2537),   MPCE(II-931),
    MP8(III-1972),   MP6(III-1253),   MPEur(354),   MPv4(215),
    MP2(I-423),   MWL2(423).
Heiress, The.   Cine(II-730).
Heirs of Stalin: Dissidence and the Soviet Regime, 1953-1970, The.   *Abraham
    Rothberg.*   HWor(II-994).
Heirs of the Kingdom, The.   *Zoé Oldenbourg.*   SCL12(V-3328),   A72(163).
*Helen.   *Euripides.*   MP12(V-2544),   MPCE(II-934),   MP8(III-1977),
    MP6(III-1258),   MPDr(326),   MP3(I-452),   MWL3(452).
Heliopolis.   *Ernst Jünger.*   SF(II-960).
Hell in a Very Small Place: The Siege of Dien Bien Phu, *in* Great Battles of
    History *series.*   *Bernard B. Fall.*   HEur(III-1581).
Hellenism.   *Arnold Toynbee.*   SCL12(V-3333),   SCL7(III-1981),
    A60(91).
Hellenistic Civilization.   *Sir William W. Tarn* and *G. T. Griffith.*
    HAnc(I-341).
Hellenistic Civilization and the Jews.   *Victor Tcherikover.*   HAnc(I-461).
Hellenistic Military and Naval Developments.   *Sir William W. Tarn.*
    HAnc(I-359).
Hello, Darkness: The Collected Poems of L. E. Sissman.   *L. E. Sissman.*
    LA79(I-264).
Hell's Angels.   Cine(II-734).
*Helmets.   *James Dickey.*   SCL12(V-3336),   SCL7(III-1984),   A65(121).
Helsinki Agreement, The (Event).   HWor(III-1257).
"Helsinki Declaration: Brobdingnag or Lilliput?, The," *in* American Journal of
    International Law.   *Harold S. Russell.*   HWor(III-1260).
*Henderson the Rain King.   *Saul Bellow.*   MP12(V-2547),
    MP8(III-1979),   MP4(I-408),   MWL4(408),   SCL12(V-3339),
    SCL7(III-1987),   A60(94).

Henry Adams: The Major Phase. *Ernest Samuels.* SCL12(V-3346), SCL7(III-1993), A65(124).

Henry Adams: The Middle Years. *Ernest Samuels.* SCL12(V-3343), SCL7(III-1990), A59(114), BMA(228). A different analysis on this title appears in: HAmer(II-1186).

Henry Adams Publishes *History of the United States of America During the First Administrations of Jefferson and Madison* (Event). HAmer(II-1184). *See also* History of the United States of America During the First Administrations of Jefferson and Madison.

Henry Barnard, School Administrator. *Anna Lou Blair.* HAmer(II-1034).

*Henry Esmond. *William Makepeace Thackeray.* MP12(V-2550), MPCE(II-935), MP8(III-1982), MP6(III-1259), MPEng(292), MP1(I-361), MWL1(361).

Henry James: Autobiography. *Henry James.* SCL12(V-3363), A57(110).

Henry James, Vol. II: The Conquest of London, 1870-1881 *and* Vol. III: The Middle Years, 1882-1895. *Leon Edel.* SCL12(V-3355), SCL7(III-2002), A63(81).

Henry James, Vol. V: The Master, 1901-1916. *Leon Edel.* SCL12(V-3359), A73(195).

Henry James Letters, Vol. I. *Henry James.* SCL12(V-3367), A75(147).

Henry Knox. *North Callahan.* SCL12(V-3371), SCLs(128).

Henry's Fate & Other Poems, 1967-1972. *John Berryman.* LA78(I-384).

Henry VIII. *J. J. Scarisbrick.* SCL12(V-3350), SCL7(III-1997), A69(148).

*Henry the Eighth. *William Shakespeare.* MP12(V-2555), MPCE(II-938), MP8(III-1985), MP6(III-1262), MPDr(328), MPv3(209), MP2(I-427), MWL2(427).

*Henry the Fifth. *William Shakespeare.* MP12(V-2558), MPCE(II-939), MP8(III-1988), MP6(III-1265), MPDr(331), MP1(I-364), MWL1(364).

Henry IV Ascends the Throne of France (Event). HEur(I-202).

*Henry the Fourth, Part One. *William Shakespeare.* MP12(V-2562), MPCE(II-942), MP8(III-1990), MP6(III-1266), MPDr(333), MPv3(212), MP2(I-430), MWL2(430).

*Henry the Fourth, Part Two. *William Shakespeare.* MP12(V-2567), MPCE(II-945), MP8(III-1993), MP6(III-1269), MPDr(336), MPv3(214), MP2(I-432), MWL2(432).

*Henry the Sixth, Part One. *William Shakespeare.* MP12(V-2572), MPCE(II-948), MP8(III-1996), MP6(III-1271), MPDr(339), MPv3(216), MP2(I-434), MWL2(434).

*Henry the Sixth, Part Two. *William Shakespeare.* MP12(V-2576), MPCE(II-949), MP8(III-1999), MP6(III-1274), MPDr(342), MPv3(219), MP2(I-437), MWL2(437).

*Henry the Sixth, Part Three. *William Shakespeare.* MP12(V-2580), MPCE(II-950), MP8(III-2002), MP6(III-1276), MPDr(345),

MPv3(221),   MP2(I-439),   MWL2(439).

Heraclitus. *Philip Wheelwright.* HAnc(I-213).

Heraclitus: Fragments. *Heraclitus of Ephesus.* Ph(I-11).

Heraclitus, the Cosmic Fragments. *G. S. Kirk.* HAnc(I-212).

Herakles. *Archibald MacLeish.* SCL12(V-3374),   SCL7(III-2005),
    A68(152).

*Herakles Mad. *Euripides.* MP12(V-2584),   MPCE(II-952),
    MP8(III-2005),   MP6(III-1279),   MPDr(348),   MP3(I-454),
    MWL3(454).

Herbe Rouge, L'. *Boris Vian.* SF(II-965).

Herbert Hoover: A Public Life. *David Burner.* LA80(I-400).

Herbert Hoover and the Great Depression. *Harris G. Warren.*
    HAmer(III-1596).

"Herbert Hoover and the Origins of the Reconstruction Finance Corporation,"
    in Mississippi Valley Historical Review. *Gerald Nash.*
    HAmer(III-1596).

Hercules and His Twelve Labors. *Unknown.* MP12(V-2587),
    MPCE(II-953),   MP8(III-2007),   MP6(III-1280),   MPEur(359),
    MP1(I-366),   MWL1(366).

Herdsmen, The. *Elizabeth Marshall Thomas.* SCL12(V-3379),
    SCL7(III-2010),   A66(123).

Here Abide Monsters. *Andre Norton.* SF(II-969).

Here at the New Yorker. *Brendan Gill.* SCL12(V-3383),   A76(125).

Here Comes Mr. Jordan. Cine(II-737).

Here I Stand: A Life of Martin Luther. *Roland H. Bainton.* HEur(I-56).

Heresy in the Later Middle Ages. *Gordon Leff.* HAnc(III-1384).

*Hereward the Wake. *Charles Kingsley.* MP12(V-2591),
    MPCE(II-956),   MP8(III-2009),   MP6(III-1282),   MPEng(295),
    MP1(I-367),   MWL1(367).

Heritage. *Anthony West.* SCL12(V-3386),   SCL7(III-2014),   A55(118).

*Heritage and Its History, A. *Ivy Compton-Burnett.* MP12(V-2594),
    MP8(III-2012),   MP4(I-411),   MWL4(411). A different
    analysis on this title appears in: SCL12(V-3389),   SCL7(III-2017),
    A61(116).

Heritage of Persia, The. *Richard N. Frye.* HAnc(I-430).

Hermaphrodeity. *Alan Friedman.* SCL12(V-3393),   A73(199).

*Hero of Our Time, A. *Mikhail Yurievich Lermontov.* MP12(V-2597),
    MPCE(II-957),   MP8(III-2015),   MP6(III-1285),   MPEur(361),
    MP3(I-456),   MWL3(456).

Herodotus, Father of History. *John L. Myers.* HAnc(I-261).

Herod's Children. *Ilse Aichinger.* SCL12(V-3396),   SCL7(III-2021),
    A64(126).

*Heroides. *Ovid (Publius Ovidius Naso).* MP12(V-2601),
    MP8(III-2019),   MP4(I-413),   MWL4(413).

Heron, The. *Giorgio Bassani.* SCL12(V-3400),   A71(115).

Herovit's World. *Barry N. Malzberg.* SF(II-972).
*Herself Surprised. *Joyce Cary.* MP12(V-2603), MPCE(II-959),
MP8(III-2021), MP6(III-1288), MPEng(298), MP3(I-459),
MWL3(459).
*Herzog. *Saul Bellow.* SCL12(V-3404), SCL7(III-2025), A65(127).
Hesiod's Composition of the *Theogony* (Event). HAnc(I-139).
Hesiod's Theogony. *Edited with* Prolegomena and Commentary. *M. L.
West.* HAnc(I-140).
*Hesperides. *Robert Herrick.* MP12(V-2606), MP8(III-2024),
MP6(III-1290), MPPo(128), MP3(I-461), MWL3(461).
Hester Street. Cine(II-741).
H. G. Wells. *Lovat Dickson.* SCL12(V-3408), A70(164).
H. G. Wells. *Norman MacKenzie* and *Jean MacKenzie.* SCL12(V-3413),
A74(190).
Hidden Persuaders, The. *Vance Packard.* SCL12(V-3416),
SCL7(III-2028), A58(104), BMA(231).
High and Low. *John Betjeman.* SCL12(V-3419), SCL7(III-2031),
A68(157).
High Crusade, The. *Poul Anderson.* SF(II-977).
High New House, A. *Thomas Williams.* SCL12(V-3423),
SCL7(III-2035), A64(130).
High Noon. Cine(II-745).
High Sierra. Cine(II-748).
High Tide at Gettysburg. *Glenn Tucker.* SCL12(V-3428),
SCL7(III-2040), A59(117).
High Valley, The. *Kenneth E. Read.* SCL12(V-3431), SCL7(III-2043),
A66(127).
High Water. *Richard Bissell.* SCL12(V-3434), SCL7(III-2046),
A54(111).
High, Wide and Lonesome. *Hal Borland.* SCL12(V-3437),
SCL7(III-2049), A57(113).
High Wind Rising, A. *Elsie Singmaster.* MP12(V-2609),
MPCE(II-960), MP8(III-2027), MP6(III-1293), MPAm(261),
MPv3(224), MP2(I-442), MWL2(442).
*High Windows. *Philip Larkin.* SCL12(V-3440), A75(151).
Higher Education in Transition: A History of American Colleges and
Universities, 1936-1968. *John S. Brubacher* and *Willis Rudy.*
HAmer(I-315).
Highway, The. *Edgar B. Schieldrop.* HEur(II-1036).
Hill of Dreams, The. *Arthur Machen.* MP12(V-2613), MPCE(II-961),
MP8(III-2030), MP6(III-1295), MPEng(301), MPv3(226),
MP2(I-445), MWL2(445).
Hillingdon Hall. *Robert Smith Surtees.* MP12(V-2616), MPCE(II-962),
MP8(III-2033), MP6(III-1297), MPEng(304), MPv4(220),
MP2(I-447), MWL2(447).

Himself! The Life and Times of Mayor Richard J. Daley. *Eugene Kennedy.*
    LA79(I-273).
Hind and the Panther, The. *John Dryden.* RCa(II-611).
*Hippolytus. *Euripides.* MP12(V-2620), MPCE(II-964),
    MP8(III-2036), MP6(III-1300), MPDr(350), MPv3(229),
    MP2(I-449), MWL2(449).
Hiroshima Diary. *Michihiko Hachiya.* SCL12(V-3443),
    SCL7(III-2052), A55(121), BMA(234).
His Girl Friday. Cine(II-751).
*His Toy, His Dream, His Rest. *John Berryman.* SCL12(V-3447),
    SCL7(III-2056), A69(152).
Historia Calamitatum. *Pierre Abélard.* MP12(V-2624), MP8(III-2039),
    MP6(III-1302), MPNf(134), MP3(I-464), MWL3(464). A different
    analysis on this title appears in: RCa(I-307).
Historia Numorum. *Barclay V. Head.* HAnc(I-145).
Historia Pontificalis of John of Salisbury, The. *M. Chibnall.*
    HAnc(III-1373).
Historians Against History: The Frontier Thesis and the National Covenant in
    American Historical Writing Since 1830. *David W. Noble.*
    HAmer(II-733).
Historian's Approach to Religion, An. *Arnold Toynbee.* SCL12(V-3452),
    SCL7(III-2060), A57(116), BMA(238).
Historic Highways of America, Vol. X: The Cumberland Road. *Archer B.
    Hulbert.* HAmer(I-494).
Historical and Critical Dictionary, The. *Pierre Bayle.* Ph(I-441).
Historical Commentary on Thucydides, A. *A. W. Gomme.* HAnc(I-293).
Historical Introduction to the Study of Roman Law. *H. F. Jolowicz.*
    Different analyses on this title appear in: HAnc(I-256; I-493).
Histories, The. *Herodotus.* HAnc(I-239).
Histories, The. *Ammianus Marcellinus.* HAnc(II-900).
History and Description of Roman Political Institutions, A. *Frank Frost
    Abbott.* HAnc(I-396).
History and Social Influence of the Potato, The. *Redcliffe N. Salaman.*
    HEur(I-426).
History in a Changing World. *Geoffrey Barraclough.* HAnc(III-1198).
History of Agricultural Education in the United States, A. *Alfred Charles
    True.* HAmer(II-976).
History of American Poetry, 1900-1940, A. *Horace Gregory* and *Marya A.
    Zaturenska.* HAmer(III-1403).
History of Architecture on the Comparative Method, A. *Sir Banister
    Fletcher.* HAnc(III-1418).
History of Astronomy from Thales to Kepler, A (*formerly entitled* History of
    the Planetary Systems from Thales to Kepler). *J. L. E. Dreyer.*
    HAnc(II-714).
History of Broadcasting in the United States, Vol. I: A Tower in Babel: To

1933, A. *Erik Barnouw*. HAmer(III-1521).

History of Broadcasting in the United States, Vol. II: The Golden Web: 1933 to 1953, A. *Erik Barnouw*. HAmer(III-1676).

History of Christian Philosophy in the Middle Ages. *Étienne Gilson*. HAnc(II-836).

History of Classical Scholarship, Vol. I: From Sixth Century B.C. to the End of the Middle Ages, A. *John Edwin Sandys*. Different analyses on this title appear in: HAnc(I-356; II-1025; III-1233).

*History of Colonel Jacque, The. *Daniel Defoe*. MP12(V-2627), MPCE(II-966), MP8(III-2042), MP6(III-1304), MPEng(307), MPv4(222), MP2(I-451), MWL2(451).

History of Dogma, The. *Adolph Harnack*. HAnc(II-869).

History of Domesticated Animals, A. *Friedrich E. Zeuner*. HAnc(I-3).

History of Early Christian Literature, A. *Edgar Johnson Goodspeed*. HAnc(II-699).

History of Early Medieval Europe, 476 to 911, A. *Margaret Deanesly*. HAnc(II-1162).

History of Egypt Under the Ptolemaic Dynasty, A. *Edwyn Robert Bevan*. HAnc(I-406).

History of Engineering and Science in the Bell System: The Early Years, 1875-1925, A. *M. D. Fagen, ed.* HWor(I-4).

History of England, The. *John Lingard*. RCa(II-638).

*History of England, The. *Thomas Babington Macaulay*. MP12(V-2631), MP8(III-2045), MP6(III-1307), MPNf(137), MP3(I-466), MWL3(466).

History of England, Vol. IV: England Under the Tudors, A. *Geoffrey Rudolph Elton*. HEur(I-7).

History of English Law Before the Time of Edward I, The. *Sir Frederick Pollock* and *Frederick William Maitland*. HAnc(III-1389).

History of Events Resulting in Indian Consolidation West of the Mississippi, The. *Annie H. Abel*. HAmer(I-669).

History of France from the Death of Louis XI, A. *John S. C. Bridge*. Different analyses on this title appear in: HEur(I-22; I-32).

*History of Frederick II of Prussia. *Thomas Carlyle*. MP12(V-2634), MP8(III-2048), MP4(I-415), MWL4(415).

History of Freedom and Other Essays, The. *John Emerich Edward Dalberg Acton*. RCa(II-739).

History of French Literature, A. *L. Cazamian*. HAnc(III-1224).

History of Genetics, A. *A. H. Sturtevant*. HWor(I-12).

History of Greece to 322 B.C., A. *B. G. L. Hammond*. HAnc(I-340).

History of Greek Literature, A. *Moses Hadas*. Different analyses on this title appear in: HAnc(I-113; I-262).

History of Greek Mathematics, A. *Sir Thomas L. Heath*. HAnc(I-385).

History of Greek Religion, A. *Martin P. Nilsson*. HAnc(I-121).

History of Hungary. *Denis Sinor*. HAnc(III-1211).

History of Ireland in the Eighteenth Century, A. *William Edward Hartpole Lecky.* HEur(II-553).

History of Islamic Spain, A. *W. Montgomery Watt.* HAnc(II-1191).

History of Israel, The. *Martin Noth.* Different analyses on this title appear in: HAnc(I-94; I-191).

History of Jesus Christ, The. *R. L. Bruckberger.* HAnc(I-570).

History of Jewish Literature, A. *Meyer Waxman.* HAnc(III-1335).

History of King Richard III. *Sir Thomas More.* MP12(V-2637), MP8(III-2051), MP4(I-417), MWL4(417).

History of Latin Literature, A. *Moses Hadas.* HAnc(I-534).

History of Latvia, A. *Alfred Bilmanis.* HAnc(III-1474).

History of Magic and Experimental Science: Vol. II, A. *Lynn Thorndike.* HAnc(III-1542).

History of Marine Navigation, A. *Per Collinder.* HAnc(III-1507).

History of Mathematical Notations, A. *Florian Cajori.* HAnc(III-1284).

History of Mathematics, A. *Florian Cajori.* HAnc(III-1285).

History of Mathematics, A. *J. F. Scott.* HAnc(II-719).

History of Medicine, A. *Henry E. Sigerist.* HAnc(I-305).

History of Medieval Islam, A. *J. J. Saunders.* HAnc(II-1079).

History of Medieval Political Theory in the West, A. *R. W. Carlyle.* HAnc(II-1089).

History of Mr. Polly, The. *H. G. Wells.* MP12(V-2640), MPCE(II-967), MP8(III-2054), MP6(III-1310), MPEng(310), MPv4(225), MP2(I-454), MWL2(454).

History of Modern Germany, Vol. I: The Reformation, A. *Hajo Holborn.* Different analyses on this title appear in: HEur(I-79; I-89; I-93; I-150; I-292).

History of Modern Germany, Vol. II: 1648-1840, A. *Hajo Holborn.* Different analyses on this title appear in: HEur(I-379; I-483).

*History of New York, by Diedrich Knickerbocker, A. *Washington Irving.* MP12(V-2643), MP8(III-2056), MP6(III-1312), MPNf(140), MP3(I-469), MWL3(469).

History of Norway, A. *Karen Larsen.* HEur(III-1167).

History of Oberlin College: From Its Foundation Through the Civil War, A. *Robert S. Fletcher.* HAmer(II-710).

History of Partition, 1912-1925, The. *Denis Gwynn.* HEur(III-1237).

History of Penance, A. *Oscar D. Watkins.* HAnc(II-764).

History of Philosophy: The Hellenistic and Roman Age, The. *Emile Brehier.* HAnc(I-474).

History of Portugal, A. *Charles E. Nowell.* Different analyses on this title appear in: HEur(I-306; II-647; II-677; II-724; III-1221).

History of Printing, A. *John Clyde Oswald.* HAnc(III-1716).

History of Rome, The. *Theodore Mommsen.* HAnc(I-283).

History of Russia, A. *Vasily O. Kluchevsky.* Different analyses on this title appear in: HEur(I-248; I-466).

History of Russia, A. *Sir Bernard Pares*. HEur(I-200).

History of Sacerdotal Celibacy in the Christian Church. *Henry Charles Lea*. HAnc(III-1259).

History of Science, Vol. II: Hellenistic Science and Culture in the Last Three Centuries B.C., A. *George Sarton*. HAnc(I-401).

History of South Africa, Social and Economic, A. *C. W. De Kiewiet*. HWor(I-90).

History of Soviet Russia, Vol. I-III: The Bolshevik Revolution, 1917-1923, A. *Edward Hallett Carr*. HWor(I-322).

History of Surgical Anesthesia, The. *Thomas E. Keys*. HAmer(II-793).

"History, Red Power and the New Indian," *in* The American Indian. *Raymond Friday Locke*, ed. HWor(II-868).

History of Technology, Vol. I: From Early Times to the Fall of the Ancient Empires, A. *C. N. Bromhead, R. J. Forbes, H. H. Coghlan, Herbert Maryon* and *H. J. Plenderleith*. HAnc(I-17).

History of Technology, Vol. II: The Mediterranean Civilization and the Middle Ages, A. *Charles Singer*. HAnc(I-229).

"History of the Allotment Policy," *in* Readjustment of Indian Affairs. *D. S. Otis*. HAmer(II-1164).

History of the Ancient World, Vol. II: Rome, A. *Mikhail I. Rostovtzeff*. HAnc(II-832).

History of the Arabs. *Philip K. Hitti*. Different analyses on this title appear in: HAnc(II-1077; II-1107).

History of the Athenian Constitution to the End of the Fifth Century, B.C., A. *C. H. Hignett*. Different analyses on this title appear in: HAnc(I-156; I-206).

History of the Balkan Peninsula: From the Earliest Times to the Present Day, The. *Ferdinand Schevill*. HAnc(III-1663).

History of the Byzantine Empire, 324-1453. *A. A. Vasiliev*. Different analyses on this title appear in: HAnc(II-863; II-890; II-1154; III-1438).

History of the Byzantine State. *George Ostrogorsky*. HAnc(II-1155).

History of the Catholic Church in the United States, A. *John Dawson Gilmary Shea*. RCa(II-702).

History of the Cold War: From the Korean War to the Present. *André Fontaine*. HWor(II-727).

History of the Commonwealth and Protectorate, 1649-1656. *Samuel Rawson Gardiner*. HEur(I-332).

History of the Conquest of Mexico. *C. Harvey Gardiner*, ed. HEur(I-61).

History of the Conquest of Mexico. *William Hickling Prescott*. MP12(V-2646), MP8(III-2059), MP6(III-1314), MPNf(143), MP3(I-471), MWL3(471). A different analysis on this title appears in: HEur(I-61).

History of the Council of Trent, A. *Hubert Jedin*. HEur(I-145).

History of the Councils. *Karl Joseph von Hefele*. RCa(II-686).

History of the Crusades, Vol. I: The First Crusade and the Foundation of the

Kingdom of Jerusalem, A. *Steven Runciman*. HAnc(III-1280).

History of the Crusades, Vol. I: The First Hundred Years, A. *Kenneth M. Setton*. HAnc(III-1278).

History of the Crusades, Vol. III: The Kingdom of Acre and the Later Crusades, A. *Steven Runciman*. Different analyses on this title appear in: HAnc(III-1439; III-1498).

History of the Decline and Fall of the Medieval Papacy, The. *L. E. Elliott-Binns*. HAnc(III-1647).

*History of the Decline and Fall of the Roman Empire, The. *Edward Gibbon*. MP12(V-2649),   MP8(III-2062),   MP6(III-1317), MPNf(146),   MP3(I-474),   MWL3(474). A different analysis on this title appears in: HAnc(II-983).

History of the Development of the Doctrine of the Person of Christ. *Isaac August Dorner*. RCh(II-692).

History of the Ecumenical Movement, 1517-1948, A. *Ruth Rouse* and *Stephen Charles Neill,* eds. HEur(III-1552).

History of the English Corn Laws, 1660-1846, A. *Donald G. Barnes*. HEur(II-768).

History of the English Language, A. *Albert C. Baugh*. HAnc(III-1288).

History of the First Bulgarian Empire, A. *Steven Runciman*. HAnc(III-1218).

History of the Franks. *Saint Gregory, Bishop of Tours*. Different analyses on this title appear in: RCa(I-244),   HAnc(II-997).

History of the French Revolution. *Jules Michelet*. Different analyses on this title appear in: HEur(I-503; I-508).

History of the German Resistance, 1933-1945, The. *Peter Hoffmann*. LA78(I-388).

History of the Inquisition of the Middle Ages, The. *Henry Charles Lea*. HAnc(III-1486).

History of the Jewish People in the Time of Jesus Christ, The. *Emil Schürer*. HAnc(II-650).

History of the Jews in Christian Spain, A. *Yitzhak Baer*. HAnc(III-1754).

History of the League of Nations, A. *John I. Knudsen*. HEur(III-1293).

History of the League of Nations, A. *F. P. Walters*. HEur(III-1292).

History of the League of Sainte Union, 1576-1595, A. *Maurice Wilkinson*. HEur(I-205).

History of the Microscope, The. *Reginald S. Clay* and *Thomas H. Court*. HAnc(III-1557).

History of the Monroe Doctrine, A. *Dexter Perkins*. HAmer(I-596).

History of the Ottoman Empire and Modern Turkey, Vol. II: Reform, Revolution, and Republic: The Rise of Modern Turkey, 1808-1975. *Stanford J. Shaw* and *Ezel Kural Shaw*. Different analyses on this title appear in: LA78(I-393),   HWor(I-228).

History of the Papacy from the Great Schism to the Sack of Rome, A. *Mandell Creighton*. Different analyses on this title appear in:

HAnc(III-1595),   HEur(I-29; I-47).

History of the Papacy in the Nineteenth Century. *J. B. Bury.*
HEur(II-906).

*History of the Peloponnesian War. *Thucydides.* MP12(V-2652),
MP8(III-2065),   MP6(III-1319),   MPNf(149),   MP3(I-476),
MWL3(476).

*History of the Persian Wars, The. *Herodotus.* MP12(V-2655),
MP8(III-2068),   MP6(III-1322),   MPNf(152),   MP3(I-479),
MWL3(479).

History of the Popes from the Close of the Middle Ages, The. *Ludwig von
Pastor.* Different analyses on this title appear in: RCa(II-796),
HEur(I-46).

History of the Public Land Policies, A. *Benjamin H. Hibbard.*
HAmer(I-584).

History of the Rebellion and Civil Wars in England. *Edward Hyde, Earl of
Clarendon.* MP12(V-2658),   MP8(III-2071),   MP4(I-420),
MWL4(420).

History of the Reformation in Scotland. *John Knox.* RCh(I-409).

*History of the Reign of King Henry VII. *Sir Francis Bacon.*
MP12(V-2660),   MP8(III-2073),   MP4(I-421),   MWL4(421).

History of the Second World War. *B. H. Liddell Hart.* SCL12(V-3456),
A72(167).

History of the Southern Confederacy, A. *Clement Eaton.* HAmer(II-944).

History of the United Nations Charter: The Role of the United States,
1940-1945, A. *Ruth B. Russell* and *Jeannette E. Muther.* Different
analyses on this title appear in: HEur(III-1509),   HAmer(III-1744).

History of the United States Atomic Energy Commission, Vol. I: The New
World, 1939-1946, A. *Richard G. Hewlett* and *Oscar E. Anderson, Jr.*
HWor(I-391).

History of the United States of America During the Administrations of
Jefferson and Madison, Vol. II. *Henry Adams.* HAmer(I-445).

History of the United States of America, from the Discovery of the
Continent. *George Bancroft.* HAmer(I-142).

History of the Waldensians of Italy, from Their Origin to the
Reformation. *Emilio Comba.* HAnc(III-1383).

History of the Weimar Republic, A. *Erich Eyck.* HEur(III-1297).

History of the Westward Movement. *Frederick Merk.* LA79(I-277).

History of the Work of the Cistercians in Yorkshire 1131-1300, A. *Francis A.
Mullin.* HAnc(III-1428).

History of United States Naval Operations in World War II, Vol. I: The Battle
of the Atlantic, September 1939-May 1943. *Samuel Eliot Morison.*
HWor(I-407).

History of United States Naval Operations in World War II, Vol. V: The
Struggle for Guadalcanal, August, 1942-February, 1943. *Samuel Eliot
Morison.* HAmer(III-1713).

History of United States Naval Operations in World War II, Vol. XII: Leyte:
     June, 1944-January, 1945. *Samuel Eliot Morison.* HAmer(III-1733).
History of Zionism, A. *Walter Ze'ev Laqueur.* HWor(I-239).
History, Time and Deity. *S. G. F. Brandon.* HAnc(II-792).
Hitler: A Study in Tyranny. *Alan L. C. Bullock.* SCL12(V-3462),
     SCL7(III-2064), A65(130). Different analyses on this title appear in:
     HEur(III-1392; III-1442).
Hitler Among the Germans. *Rudolph Binion.* LA77(I-357).
Hitler and His Generals: The Hidden Crisis, January-June 1938. *Harold C.
     Deutsch.* HWor(I-378).
Hitler and I. *Otto Strasser.* HEur(III-1393).
Hitler Comes to Power in Germany (Event). HWor(I-311).
Hitler Establishes Control of the Diplomatic and Military Hierarchy
     (Event). HWor(I-375).
Hitler Moves East, 1941-1943. *Paul Carell.* HEur(III-1474).
Hitler vs. Roosevelt: The Undeclared Naval War. *Thomas A. Bailey* and
     Paul B. Ryan. LA80(I-404).
Hitler's *Mein Kampf*: An Analysis. *Werner Maser.* HWor(I-191).
Hitler's Spies: German Military Intelligence in World War II. *David Kahn.*
     LA79(I-281).
Hitler's Strategy 1940-1941: The Balkan Clue. *Martin Van Creveld.*
     HWor(I-446).
Hitler's War. *David Irving.* LA78(I-398).
Hive, The. *Camilo José Cela.* MP12(V-2663), MP8(III-2076),
     MP4(I-424), MWL4(424).
Hiza-Kurige. *Jippensha Ikku.* MP12(V-2667), MP8(III-2080),
     MP6(III-1324), MPEur(365), MP3(I-481), MWL3(481).
H. L. Mencken. *Douglas C. Stenerson.* SCL12(V-3466), A72(173).
*H.M.S. Pinafore. *W. S. Gilbert.* MP12(V-2669), MPCE(II-968),
     MP8(III-2082), MP6(III-1325), MPDr(353), MP1(I-370),
     MWL1(370).
Ho Chi Minh: A Political Biography. *Jean Lacouture.* HWor(II-698).
Hobson's Choice. Cine(II-754).
Hogan's Goat. *William Alfred.* SCL12(V-3470), SCL7(III-2068),
     A67(143).
Hogarth's Progress. *Peter Quennell.* SCL12(V-3474), SCL7(III-2072),
     A55(124).
Hold April. *Jesse Stuart.* SCL12(V-3478), SCL7(III-2076), A63(84).
Holiday. Cine(II-758).
Hollow Universe, The. *George De Koninck.* RCa(II-1084).
Holocaust and the Literary Imagination, The. *Lawrence L. Langer.*
     SCL12(V-3481), A76(128).
Holy Roman Empire, The. *James Bryce.* Different analyses on this title
     appear in: HAnc(III-1196; III-1319).
Holy State and the Profane State, The. *Thomas Fuller.* MP12(V-2672),

MP8(III-2084), MP4(I-428), MWL4(428).

*Holy Terrors, The. *Jean Cocteau.* MP12(V-2675), MPCE(II-970), MP8(III-2087), MP6(III-1327), MPEur(367), MP3(I-483), MWL3(483).

Holy the Firm. *Annie Dillard.* LA78(I-404).

Holy Week. *Louis Aragon.* SCL12(V-3485), SCL7(III-2079), A62(149).

Homage to Clio. *W. H. Auden.* SCL12(V-3488), SCL7(III-2082), A61(119).

*Homage to Mistress Bradstreet. *John Berryman.* MP12(V-2678), MP8(III-2090), MP4(I-430), MWL4(430). A different analysis on this title appears in: SCL12(V-3490), SCL7(III-2084), A57(119).

Home from the Hill. *William Humphrey.* SCL12(V-3494), SCL7(III-2087), A59(119).

*Home Is the Sailor. *Jorge Amado.* SCL12(V-3497), SCL7(III-2090), A65(133).

*Homecoming. *C. P. Snow.* SCL12(V-3500), SCL7(III-2093), A57(123).

Homemade World, A. *Hugh Kenner.* SCL12(V-3504), A76(132).

Homer's Composition of the *Iliad* (Event). HAnc(I-110). *See also* Iliad, The.

Homilies. *Aelfric.* RCa(I-272).

Homilies of Saint John Chrysostom. *Saint John Chrysostom.* RCa(I-154).

Homilies on the Statues. *Saint John Chrysostom.* RCh(I-117).

Homo Viator. *Gabriel Marcel.* RCa(II-893).

*Honest Whore, Part One, The. *Thomas Dekker.* MP12(V-2680), MPCE(II-971), MP8(III-2092), MP6(III-1329), MPDr(355), MP3(I-485), MWL3(485).

Honest Whore, Part Two, The. *Thomas* with *Thomas Middleton Dekker.* MP12(V-2684), MPCE(II-973), MP8(III-2095), MP6(III-1332), MPDr(358), MP3(I-487), MWL3(487).

Honey in the Horn. *H. L. Davis.* MP12(V-2688), MPCE(II-975), MP8(III-2098), MP6(III-1334), MPAm(264), MP1(I-371), MWL1(371).

Honorary Consul, The. *Graham Greene.* SCL12(V-3508), A74(193).

Hoosier Schoolmaster, The. *Edward Eggleston.* MP12(V-2691), MPCE(II-976), MP8(III-2101), MP6(III-1336), MPAm(267), MP1(I-373), MWL1(373).

Hoover-Stimson Doctrine (Event). HAmer(III-1599).

Hopscotch. *Julio Cortázar.* SCL12(V-3515), SCL7(III-2097), A67(146).

*Horace. *Pierre Corneille.* MP12(V-2695), MPCE(II-978), MP8(III-2104), MP6(III-1339), MPDr(361), MP3(I-490), MWL3(490).

Horatio. *Hyam Plutzik.* SCL12(V-3520), SCL7(III-2102), A62(152).

Horror of Dracula. Cine(II-762).

Horse Knows the Way, The. *John O'Hara.* SCL12(V-3523),

Huguenot Warrior: The Life and Times of Henri de Rohan, 1579-1638. *Jack Alden Clarke.* HEur(I-260).
Huguenots and Henry of Navarre, The. *Henry M. Baird.* HEur(I-216).
Hugo Black and the Judicial Revolution. *Gerald T. Dunne.* LA78(I-418).
*Human Comedy, The. *William Saroyan.* MP12(V-2766), MPCE(II-1017), MP8(III-2154), MP6(III-1378), MPAm(288), MP1(I-392), MWL1(392).
Human Destiny. *Pierre Lecomte du Noüy.* RCa(II-913).
Human Factor, The. *Graham Greene.* LA79(I-286).
Human Nature and Conduct. *John Dewey.* Ph(II-835).
"Human Rights and East-West Relations," *in* Foreign Affairs. *Karl E. Birnbaum.* HWor(III-1261).
Human Situation: Lectures at Santa Barbara, 1959, The. *Aldous Huxley.* LA78(I-422).
Humanism of Cicero, The. *H. A. K. Hunt.* HAnc(I-543).
Humanitarian Reform Movement, The (Event). HAmer(I-642).
Humanity of Christ, The. *Romano Guardini.* RCa(II-1064).
Humanoids, The *and* "With Folded Hands". *Jack Williamson.* SF(II-981).
Humboldt. *Helmut de Terra.* SCL12(V-3565), SCL7(III-2137), A55(128).
*Humboldt's Gift. *Saul Bellow.* SCL12(V-3569), A76(136).
Humoresque. Cine(II-782).
Humphry Clinker. *Tobias Smollett.* MP12(V-2769), MPCE(II-1018), MP8(III-2156), MP6(III-1380), MPEng(330), MP1(I-394), MWL1(394).
Hunchback of Notre Dame, The. Cine(II-786).
*Hunchback of Notre Dame, The. *Victor Hugo.* MP12(V-2774), MPCE(II-1021), MP8(III-2159), MP6(III-1383), MPEur(376), MP1(I-397), MWL1(397).
Hundred Days, The (Event). HAmer(III-1615).
Hundred Years War: The English in France, 1337-1453, The. *Desmond Seward.* LA79(I-291).
Hungarian Revolution (Event). HEur(III-1595).
Hungarian Revolution, The. *David Pryce-Jones.* HEur(III-1597).
"Hungary and Byzantium in the Middle Ages," *in* Vol. IV *of* The Cambridge Medieval History. *Gy Moravcsik.* HAnc(III-1213).
Hungary and Her Successors: The Treaty of Trianon and Its Consequences, 1919-1937. *Carlile Aylmer Macartney.* HWor(I-185).
Hungary at the Paris Peace Conference: The Diplomatic History of the Treaty of Trianon. *Francis Deák.* HWor(I-183).
*Hunger. *Knut Hamsun.* MP12(V-2780), MPCE(II-1024), MP8(III-2163), MP6(III-1386), MPEur(380), MP1(I-400), MWL1(400). A different analysis on this title appears in: SCL12(V-3573), SCL7(III-2141), A68(160).
Hungerfield and Other Poems. *Robinson Jeffers.* SCL12(V-3577),

SCLs(130).

Hunting Hypothesis, The. *Robert Ardrey.* LA77(I-367).

Huon de Bordeaux. *Unknown.* MP12(V-2784), MPCE(II-1026), MP8(III-2165), MP6(III-1388), MPEur(382), MP3(I-494), MWL3(494).

Hurricane, The. Cine(II-793).

Hustler, The. Cine(II-796).

Hyde Park. *James Shirley.* MP12(V-2787), MPCE(II-1027), MP8(III-2168), MP6(III-1391), MPDr(366), MP3(I-497), MWL3(497).

Hydriotaphia: Urn-Burial. *Sir Thomas Browne.* MP12(V-2791), MP8(III-2171), MP4(I-432), MWL4(432).

Hymns of Ephraem the Syrian, The. *Ephraem the Syrian.* RCh(I-103).

Hymns of Saint Ambrose, The. *Saint Ambrose.* RCa(I-152).

Hymns of Saint Thomas Aquinas, The. *Saint Thomas Aquinas.* RCa(I-421).

*Hypatia. *Charles Kingsley.* MP12(V-2794), MPCE(II-1029), MP8(III-2174), MP6(III-1393), MPEng(333), MP1(I-402), MWL1(402).

*Hypochondriac, The. *Molière (Jean Baptiste Poquelin).* MP12(V-2798), MPCE(II-1031), MP8(III-2178), MP6(III-1396), MPDr(369), MPv3(235), MP2(I-474), MWL2(474).

I Am a Camera. Cine(II-800).

I Am a Fugitive from a Chain Gang. Cine(II-803).

I Am Legend. *Richard Matheson.* SF(II-986).

*I Am Mary Dunne. *Brian Moore.* SCL12(V-3580), SCL7(III-2145), A69(160).

I Am Thinking of My Darling. *Vincent McHugh.* SF(II-991).

I and Thou. *Martin Buber.* Different analyses on this title appear in: Ph(II-856), RCh(II-917).

*I, Claudius. *Robert Graves.* MP12(V-2803), MPCE(II-1034), MP8(III-2181), MP6(III-1398), MPEng(337), MP1(I-406), MWL1(406).

I Don't Need You Any More. *Arthur Miller.* SCL12(V-3584), SCL7(III-2149), A68(164).

I Hear America Swinging. *Peter De Vries.* LA77(I-372).

I Heard My Sister Speak My Name. *Thomas Savage.* LA78(I-427).

*I Know Why the Caged Bird Sings. *Maya Angelou.* SCL12(VI-3587), SCLs(133).

I Married a Witch. Cine(II-806).

*I Remember! I Remember! *Seán O'Faoláin.* SCL12(VI-3590), SCL7(III-2152), A63(86).

I, Robot. *Isaac Asimov.* SF(II-995).

I See a Dark Stranger. Cine(II-809).

Ignatius His Conclave. *John Donne.* MP12(V-2834), MP8(IV-2206), MP4(I-437), MWL4(437).

I.G.Y., the Year of the New Moons. *John Tuzo Wilson.* HWor(II-768).

Il Filostrato. *Giovanni Boccaccio.* *See* Filostrato, Il.

*Iliad, The. *Homer.* MP12(V-2837), MPCE(II-1046), MP8(IV-2209), MP6(III-1415), MPPo(138), MP1(I-423), MWL1(423).

Illness as Metaphor. *Susan Sontag.* LA79(I-295).

Illusion of Peace: Foreign Policy in the Nixon Years, The. *Tad Szulc.* LA79(I-300).

Illusion of Technique: A Search for Meaning in a Technological Civilization, The. *William Barrett.* LA80(I-409).

Illustrated Man, The. *Ray Bradbury.* SF(II-1008).

I'm Expecting to Live Quite Soon. *Paul West.* SCL12(VI-3615), A71(122).

I'm Radcliffe! Fly Me! *Liva Baker.* LA77(I-376).

Image of America. *R. L. Bruckberger.* SCL12(VI-3618), SCL7(III-2162), A60(99).

Images of Truth. *Glenway Wescott.* SCL12(VI-3621), SCL7(III-2165), A63(89).

*Imaginary Conversations. *Walter Savage Landor.* MP12(V-2842), MP8(IV-2212), MP6(III-1418), MPNf(158), MP3(I-499), MWL3(499).

Imaginations. *William Carlos Williams.* SCL12(VI-3625), A71(124).

Imitation of Christ, The. *Thomas à Kempis.* MP12(V-2845), MP8(IV-2215), MP6(III-1421), MPNf(161), MP3(I-501), MWL3(501). Different analyses on this title appear in: RCh(I-308), RCa(I-491).

*Imitations. *Robert Lowell.* SCL12(VI-3629), SCLs(137).

Immediate Experience: Movies, Comics, Theatre, and Other Aspects of Popular Culture, The. *Robert Warshow.* HAmer(III-1505).

Immediate Origins of the War, The. *Pierre Renouvin.* HEur(III-1343).

Immortale Dei. *Pope Leo XIII.* RCa(II-695).

Immortals, The. *James E. Gunn.* SF(II-1014).

Impact of Television on Society, The (Event). HWor(II-669).

Impact of the War upon American Education, The. *Isaac L. Kandel.* HAmer(III-1727).

Impatient Crusader: Florence Kelley's Life Story. *Josephine Goldmark.* HAmer(III-1372).

Impeachment of Andrew Johnson (Event). HAmer(II-1026).

Imperial Civil Service of Rome, The. *Harold B. Mattingly.* HAnc(II-623).

Imperial Earth. *Arthur C. Clarke.* SF(III-1019).

Imperial Experience in Sub-Saharan Africa Since 1870, The. *Henry S. Wilson.* LA78(I-436).

Imperial Federation: A Study of New Zealand Policy and Opinion,

1880-1914. *Keith Sinclair.* HWor(I-21).

Imperial Presidency, The. *Arthur M. Schlesinger, Jr.* SCL12(VI-3632), A74(204).

"Imperial Recovery, The," *in* Vol. XI *of* The Cambridge Ancient History. *Harold B. Mattingly.* HAnc(II-831).

Imperial Spain, 1469-1716. *John H. Elliott.* Different analyses on this title appear in: HEur(I-4; I-42; I-74; I-156; I-190; I-374).

Imperial Visit to Canossa (Event). HAnc(III-1269).

Imperial Woman. *Pearl S. Buck.* SCL12(VI-3635), SCL7(III-2169), A57(130).

"Imperialism: An Historiographical Revision," *in* The Economic History Review. *D. K. Fieldhouse.* HWor(I-35).

"Imperialism and Expansionism in Ethiopia from 1865-1900," *in* Colonialism in Africa, 1870-1960, Vol. I: The History and Politics of Colonialism, 1870-1914. *Harold G. Marcus.* HEur(II-1097).

Imperialism at Bay: The United States and the Decolonization of the British Empire, 1941-1945. *Wm. Roger Louis.* LA79(I-305).

Imperialism, the Highest Stage of Capitalism: A Popular Outline. *V. I. Lenin.* HWor(I-34).

Importance of Being Earnest, The. Cine(II-817).

*Importance of Being Earnest, The. *Oscar Wilde.* MP12(V-2847), MPCE(II-1049), MP8(IV-2217), MP6(III-1423), MPDr(372), MPv3(237), MP2(I-476), MWL2(476).

Improper Bostonian: Dr. Oliver Wendell Holmes, The. *Edwin P. Hoyt.* LA80(I-414).

Improvement of Communication with the Pacific Coast as an Issue in American Politics, 1783-1864. *Robert R. Russel.* HAmer(II-868).

Improvements in Horse Transportation (Event). HAnc(II-1169).

Improvements in Shipbuilding and Navigation (Event). HAnc(III-1503).

In a Shallow Grave. *James Purdy.* LA77(I-380).

In a Summer Season. *Elizabeth Taylor.* SCL12(VI-3638), SCL7(III-2172), A62(155).

In a Wild Sanctuary. *William Harrison.* SCL12(VI-3641), A70(174).

In Between the Sheets and Other Stories. *Ian McEwan.* LA80(I-417).

*In Cold Blood. *Truman Capote.* SCL12(VI-3645), SCL7(III-2175), A67(158).

*In Dubious Battle. *John Steinbeck.* MP12(V-2850), MPCE(II-1050), MP8(IV-2219), MP6(III-1425), MPAm(293), MPv3(239), MP2(I-478), MWL2(478).

In Evil Hour. *Gabriel García Márquez.* LA80(I-421).

In Hiding. *Ronald Fraser.* SCL12(VI-3650), A73(201).

In His Steps. *Charles M. Sheldon.* RCh(II-808).

In Mediterranean Air. *Ann Stanford.* LA78(I-439).

*In Memoriam. *Lord Alfred Tennyson.* MP12(V-2853), MP8(IV-2221), MP4(I-439), MWL4(439).

*In My Father's Court. *Isaac Bashevis Singer.* SCL12(VI-3654), SCL7(III-2179), A67(162).

In My Father's House. *Ernest J. Gaines.* LA79(I-311).

In Name Only. Cine(II-822).

In Old Chicago. Cine(II-825).

In Parenthesis. *David Jones.* SCL12(VI-3657), SCL7(III-2182), A63(93).

In Praise of Darkness. *Jorge Luis Borges.* SCL12(VI-3660), A75(154).

In Praise of Love: An Introduction to the Love-Poetry of the Renaissance. *Maurice Valency.* HAnc(III-1299).

In Quest and Crisis: Emperor Joseph I and the Habsburg Monarchy. *Charles W. Ingrao.* LA80(I-426).

In Quest of Quasars: An Introduction to Stars and Starlike Objects. *Ben Bova.* HWor(II-901).

In Search of Enemies: A CIA Story. *John Stockwell.* HWor(III-1221).

In Search of History: A Personal Adventure. *Theodore H. White.* LA79(I-314).

*In the American Grain. *William Carlos Williams.* MP12(V-2856), MP8(IV-2224), MP4(I-442), MWL4(442).

In the Boom Boom Room. *David Râbe.* SCL12(VI-3664), A76(144).

In the Clearing. *Robert Frost.* SCL12(VI-3667), SCL7(III-2185), A63(95), BMA(245).

In the Days of McKinley. *Margaret Leech.* SCL12(VI-3674), SCL7(III-2192), A60(102).

In the Days of Simon Stern. *Arthur A. Cohen.* SCL12(VI-3678), A74(208).

*In the Heart of the Heart of the Country. *William H. Gass.* SCL12(VI-3682), SCL7(III-2196), A69(164).

In the Heat of the Night. Cine(II-829).

In the Name of the People. *Adam B. Ulam.* LA78(I-442).

In the Ocean of Night. *Gregory Benford.* SF(III-1026).

In the Rose of Time. *Robert Fitzgerald.* SCL12(VI-3686), SCL7(III-2200), A58(109).

In the Time of Greenbloom. *Gabriel Fielding.* SCL12(VI-3688), SCL7(III-2202), A58(111).

*In the Wilderness. *Sigrid Undset.* MP12(V-2861), MPCE(II-1051), MP8(IV-2229), MP6(III-1427), MPEur(391), MPv3(241), MP2(I-480), MWL2(480).

In Which We Serve. Cine(II-833).

*Inadmissible Evidence. *John Osborne.* SCL12(VI-3691), SCL7(III-2205), A66(129).

Inauguration of Barnum's Circus (Event). HAmer(II-1066).

Inauguration of George Washington as First President (Event). HAmer(I-341).

Inauguration of the Dominate (Event). HAnc(II-829).

Inauguration of the Feast of Christmas (Event).   HAnc(II-884).
Inauguration of the Olympic Games (Event).   HAnc(I-115).
Inazuma-byôshi.   *Santô Kyôden*.   MP12(V-2864),   MPCE(II-1052),
    MP8(IV-2232),   MP6(III-1429),   MPEur(394),   MP3(I-503),
    MWL3(503).
Incandescent Light, The.   *Floyd A. Lewis*.   HEur(II-754).
Incarnation of the Word of God, The.   *Saint Athanasius*.   Different analyses
    on this title appear in: RCh(I-83),   RCa(I-84).
Incarnations.   *Robert Penn Warren*.   SCL12(VI-3694),   SCL7(III-2208),
    A69(167).
Incense to Idols.   *Sylvia Ashton-Warner*.   SCL12(VI-3697),
    SCL7(III-2211),   A61(124).
Inception of Christian Apologetics (Event).   HAnc(II-707).
Inception of Church-State Problems (Event).   HAnc(II-852).
*Incognito.   *Petru Dumitriu*.   MP12(V-2868),   MP8(IV-2235),
    MP4(I-446),   MWL4(446). A different analysis on this title appears in:
    SCL12(VI-3700),   SCL7(IV-2215),   A65(139).
Incoherence of the Incoherence, The.   *Averroës*.   Ph(I-294).
Incomplete Enchanter, The.   *L. Sprague De Camp* and *Fletcher Pratt*.
    SF(III-1031).
Incredible Shrinking Man, The.   Cine(II-836).
Incredible Victory.   *Walter Lord*.   HWor(I-474).
*Independent People.   *Halldór Laxness*.   MP12(V-2872),
    MPCE(II-1053),   MP8(IV-2239),   MP6(III-1432),   MPEur(397),
    MP1(I-425),   MWL1(425).
Index of Arabic Manuscripts on Medicine and Pharmacy at the National
    Library of Cairo.   *Sami K. Hamarneh*.   HAnc(III-1228).
India Today.   *Frank Moraes*.   SCL12(VI-3705),   SCL7(IV-2219),
    A61(127).
Indian Affairs in Colonial New York: The Seventeenth Century.   *Allen W.
    Trelease*.   HAmer(I-82).
Indian Heritage of America, The.   *Alvin M. Josephy, Jr*.   HAmer(I-2).
Indian Removal: The Emigration of the Five Civilized Tribes of
    Indians.   *Grant Foreman*.   HAmer(I-670).
*Indian Summer.   *William Dean Howells*.   MP12(V-2877),
    MPCE(II-1056),   MP8(IV-2242),   MP6(III-1434),   MPAm(295),
    MPv4(240),   MP2(I-482),   MWL2(482).
*Indiana.   *George Sand*.   MP12(V-2880),   MPCE(II-1057),
    MP8(IV-2245),   MP6(III-1436),   MPEur(400),   MPv3(243),
    MP2(I-485),   MWL2(485).
Indiana Historical Collections, Vol. XIV: William Henry Harrison: A Political
    Biography, The.   *Dorothy B. Goebel*.   HAmer(I-501).
Indians.   *Arthur Kopit*.   SCL12(VI-3708),   A70(177).
India-Pakistan War and the Creation of Bangladesh, The (Event).
    HWor(II-1091).

"Induction of Follicular Growth, Ovulation and Luteinization in the Human Ovary," *in* Journal of Reproduction and Fertility. *Robert G. Edwards* and *P. C. Steptoe.* HWor(III-1328).

Industrial America in the World War. *Grosvenor B. Clarkson.* HAmer(III-1462).

Industrial Biography: Iron Workers and Tool Makers. *Samuel Smiles.* HEur(I-526).

Industrial Revolution in the Eighteenth Century, The. *Paul Mantoux.* HEur(I-407).

Industry Comes of Age: Business, Labor, and Public Policy, 1860-1897. *Edward Chase Kirkland.* HAmer(II-1159).

Inês de Castro. *António Ferreira.* MP12(V-2883), MPCE(II-1059), MP8(IV-2247), MP6(III-1438), MPDr(374), MP3(I-506), MWL3(506).

Infants of the Spring. *Anthony Powell.* LA78(I-447).

*Infernal Machine and Other Plays, The. *Jean Cocteau.* SCL12(VI-3712), SCL7(IV-2222), A65(143).

"Infinity in Plotinus," *in* Gregorianum. *Leo Sweeney.* HAnc(II-825).

Infinity of Mirrors, An. *Richard Condon.* SCL12(VI-3716), SCL7(IV-2226), A65(146).

Inflation and Labor Unrest (Event). HWor(II-572).

Informer, The. Cine(II-839).

*Informer, The. *Liam O'Flaherty.* MP12(V-2886), MPCE(II-1061), MP8(IV-2249), MP6(III-1440), MPEng(343), MPv4(243), MP2(I-486), MWL2(486).

Ingoldsby Legends, The. *Thomas Ingoldsby.* MP12(V-2891), MP8(IV-2252), MP4(I-449), MWL4(449).

*Inheritors, The. *William Golding.* MP12(V-2894), MP8(IV-2255), MP4(I-452), MWL4(452), SCL12(VI-3719), SCL7(IV-2229), A63(101). A different analysis on this title appears in: SF(III-1063).

Inkling, The. *Fred Chappell.* SCL12(VI-3723), SCL7(IV-2233), A66(132).

Innocent, The. *Madison Jones.* SCL12(VI-3727), SCL7(IV-2237), A58(114).

Innocent Eréndira and Other Stories. *Gabriel García Márquez.* LA79(I-318).

Innocent Party, The. *John Hawkes.* SCL12(VI-3730), SCL7(IV-2240), A67(165).

"Innocent III," *in* Vol. VI *of* The Cambridge Medieval History. *E. F. Jacobs.* HAnc(III-1459).

*Innocent Voyage, The. *Richard Hughes.* MP12(V-2897), MPCE(II-1064), MP8(IV-2258), MP6(III-1442), MPEng(346), MPv4(245), MP2(I-488), MWL2(488).

Innovations in Medieval Prosody (Event). HAnc(III-1349).

Inquiry Concerning Political Justice, An. *William Godwin.*

MP12(V-2901), MP8(IV-2261), MP4(I-454), MWL4(454).

Inquiry into Meaning and Truth, An. *Bertrand Russell.* Ph(II-1052).

Inquisition: A Critical and Historical Study of the Coercive Power of the Church, The. *E. Vacandard.* HAnc(III-1488).

Inquisitor's House, The. *Robert Somerlott.* SCL12(VI-3733), A70(181).

Inside Africa. *John Gunther.* SCL12(VI-3737), SCL7(IV-2243), A55(131).

Inside Russia Today. *John Gunther.* SCL12(VI-3740), SCL7(IV-2246), A59(125).

Inside the Blood Factory. *Diane Wakoski.* SCL12(VI-3744), SCL7(IV-2250), A69(169).

Inside the Third Reich. *Albert Speer.* SCL12(VI-3747), A71(128).

Insight. *Bernard J. F. Lonergan, S. J.* RCa(II-1043).

Insolent Chariots, The. *John Keats.* SCL12(VI-3755), SCL7(IV-2253), A59(128), BMA(252).

Inspector, The. *Jan de Hartog.* SCL12(VI-3758), SCL7(IV-2256), A61(130).

*Inspector General, The. *Nikolai V. Gogol.* MP12(V-2904), MPCE(II-1065), MP8(IV-2264), MP6(III-1444), MPDr(376), MPv3(245), MP2(I-491), MWL2(491).

Instigations: Ezra Pound and Remy de Gourmont. *Richard Sieburth.* LA80(II-431).

Institutes, A Textbook of the History and System of Roman Private Law, The. *Rudolph Sohm.* HAnc(II-1006).

Institutes of Gaius, The. *Francis de Zulueta.* HAnc(II-722).

Institutes of the Christian Religion, The. *John Calvin.* RCh(I-358).

Institutes of the Monastic Life, The. *John Cassian.* RCa(I-193).

Institution of the Alimentary System (Event). HAnc(II-675).

Institution of the Formulary System (Event). HAnc(I-491).

Institution of the Inquisition (Event). HAnc(III-1484).

Institution of the Plebeian Tribunate (Event). HAnc(I-221).

Instructions in Favor of Christian Discipline. *Commodianus.* RCh(I-71).

Instrument, The. *John O'Hara.* SCL12(VI-3760), SCL7(IV-2258), A68(166).

Insular Cases, The (Event). HAmer(II-1318).

Insurgency: Personalities and Politics of the Taft Era. *Kenneth W. Heckler.* HAmer(III-1392).

Insuring the Essentials. *Barbara Armstrong.* HEur(II-1031).

Intellectual Life, The. *Antonin Gilbert Sertillanges.* RCa(II-771).

Intellectual Life of Colonial New England, The. *Samuel Eliot Morison.* HAmer(I-106).

Intellectual Migration: Europe and America, 1930-1960, The. *Donald Fleming* and *Bernard Bailyn,* eds. HWor(I-297).

Inter Ice Age 4. *Kobo Abé.* SF(III-1040).

Interior Castle, The. *Saint Teresa of Ávila.* RCa(I-561).

Interiors. Cine(II-844).

International Cell Biology, 1976-1977. *B. R. Brinkley* and *Keith Porter,*
eds. HWor(I-506).

International Geophysical Year, The (Event). HWor(II-764).

International Monetary System, 1945-1976: An Insider's View, The. *Robert
Solomon.* Different analyses on this title appear in: HWor(III-1100;
III-1106).

International Politics of the Nigerian Civil War, 1967-1970, The. *John J.
Stremlau.* HWor(II-1007).

Interpretation of Dreams, The. *Sigmund Freud.* MP12(V-2908),
MP8(IV-2267), MP6(III-1447), MPNf(163), MP3(I-508),
MWL3(508).

Intervention and Dollar Diplomacy in the Caribbean, 1900-1921. *Dana G.
Munro.* HAmer(III-1381).

Interview with the Vampire. *Anne Rice.* LA77(I-384).

Introduction of Arabic Numerals (Event). HAnc(III-1282).

Introduction of Christianity into Germany (Event). HAnc(II-1126).

Introduction of the Wheel (Event). HAnc(I-5).

Introduction to Descriptive Linguistics, An. *H. A. Gleason.* HAnc(I-13).

Introduction to Divine and Human Readings by Cassiodorus Senator,
An. *Leslie Webber Jones.* HAnc(II-1048).

Introduction to Lasers and Their Applications, An. *Donald C. O'Shea,* et
al. HWor(II-884).

Introduction to Mathematical Philosophy. *Bertrand Russell.* Ph(II-816).

Introduction to Metaphysics, An. *Henri Bergson.* Ph(II-749).

Introduction to Philo Judaeus, An. *Erwin R. Goodenough.* HAnc(II-614).

Introduction to Roman Law, An. *Barry Nicholas.* HAnc(II-1036).

Introduction to Semantics. *Rudolf Carnap.* Ph(II-1075).

Introduction to the Apocrypha, An. *B. M. Metzger.* HAnc(I-446).

Introduction to the Devout Life. *Saint Francis of Sales.* Different analyses
on this title appear in: RCh(I-428), RCa(I-568).

Introduction to the New Testament. *W. Marxsen.* HAnc(II-634).

Introduction to the Old Testament. *Robert H. Pfeiffer.* HAnc(II-666).

Introduction to the Old Testament in Greek, An. *H. B. Swete.*
HAnc(I-419).

Introduction to the Philosophy of Religion. *Peter Anthony Bertocci.*
RCh(II-1130).

Introduction to the Principles of Morals and Legislation, An. *Jeremy
Bentham.* Ph(I-551).

Introduction to the Study of Roman Law. *J. W. Cecil Turner.*
HAnc(I-494).

Introduction to the Talmud and Midrash. *Hermann L. Strack.*
HAnc(II-986).

*Intruder in the Dust. *William Faulkner.* MP12(V-2911),
MPCE(II-1067), MP8(IV-2270), MP6(III-1449), MPAm(298),

MP3(I-511),   MWL3(511).

Invasion of Europe by the Barbarians, The. *J. B. Bury.* HAnc(II-961).

Invasion of Italy (Event).   HEur(III-1486).

Invasion of Normandy: Operation "Overlord," The (Event). HAmer(III-1721).

Invasion of North Africa (Event).   HAmer(III-1715).

Invasion of the Black Death (Event).   HAnc(III-1625).

Invasion of the Body Snatchers.   Cine(II-848).

Inventing America: Jefferson's Declaration of Independence. *Garry Wills.* LA79(I-322).

Invention and Innovation in the Radio Industry: Massachusetts Institute of Technology Studies of Innovation. *W. Rupert Maclaurin.* HAmer(III-1523).

Invention of America: An Inquiry into the Historical Nature of the New World and the Meaning of Its History, The. *Edmundo O'Gorman.* HEur(I-19).

Invention of Bronze (Event).   HAnc(I-16).

Invention of Coinage (Event).   HAnc(I-44).

Invention of Gunpowder (Event).   HAnc(III-1509).

Invention of Lithography, The. *Alois Senefelder.* HEur(I-544).

Invention of Printing (Event).   HAnc(III-1713).

Invention of the Diesel Engine (Event).   HEur(II-1100).

Invention of the Electric Telegraph (Event).   HAmer(II-742).

Invention of the Jet Engine (Event).   HWor(I-355).

Invention of the Laser (Event).   HWor(II-881).

Invention of the Transistor (Event).   HWor(II-612).

Invention of Xerography (Event).   HWor(I-382).

Inverted World. *Christopher Priest.*   SF(III-1045).

Invincible, The. *Stanislaw Lem.*   SF(III-1050).

*Invisible Man. *Ralph Ellison.*   MP12(V-2915),   MP8(IV-2272), MP4(I-457),   MWL4(457).

*Invisible Man, The. *H. G. Wells.*   MP12(V-2918),   MPCE(II-1070), MP8(IV-2275),   MP6(III-1451),   MPEng(349),   MP1(I-428), MWL1(428). A different analysis on this title appears in: SF(III-1057).

Invisible Scar, The. *Caroline Bird.*   HAmer(III-1585).

Invisible Writing, The. *Arthur Koestler.*   SCL12(VI-3763), SCL7(IV-2261),   A54(117).

*Iolanthe. *W. S. Gilbert.*   MP12(V-2922),   MPCE(II-1072), MP8(IV-2278),   MP6(III-1454),   MPDr(379),   MPv4(247), MP2(I-493),   MWL2(493).

*Ion. *Euripides.*   MP12(V-2925),   MPCE(II-1074),   MP8(IV-2280), MP6(III-1456),   MPDr(381),   MP3(I-513),   MWL3(513).

*Iphigenia in Aulis. *Euripides.*   MP12(V-2928),   MPCE(II-1075), MP8(IV-2283),   MP6(III-1458),   MPDr(384),   MPv3(247), MP2(I-495),   MWL2(495).

*Iphigenia in Taurus. *Euripides.* MP12(V-2931), MPCE(II-1076), MP8(IV-2285), MP6(III-1460), MPDr(386), MPv3(249), MP2(I-497), MWL2(497).

Ippolita. *Alberto Denti di Pirajno.* SCL12(VI-3767), SCL7(IV-2264), A62(157).

Iranian Revolution, The (Event). HWor(III-1338).

Ireland and the American Emigration, 1850-1900. *Arnold Schrier.* HEur(II-762).

"Irenaeus of Lugdunum and the Apostolic Succession," *in* Journal of Ecclesiastical History. *Einar Molland.* HAnc(II-745).

Irish Famine and the Great Emigration (Event). HEur(II-757).

Irish Home Rule Bill (Event). HEur(III-1233).

Irish Melodies. *Thomas Moore.* MP12(V-2935), MP8(IV-2288), MP4(I-460), MWL4(460).

Irish Question, 1840-1921, The. *Nicholas Mansergh.* HEur(III-1236).

Iron Afloat: The Story of the Confederate Armorclads. *William N. Still, Jr.* HAmer(II-958).

Iron Cage: An Historical Interpretation of Max Weber, The. *Arthur Mitzman.* HWor(I-43).

Iron Dream, The. *Norman Spinrad.* SF(III-1062).

Iron Heel, The. *Jack London.* SF(III-1068).

Isidore of Seville Writes the *Etymologies* (Event). HAnc(II-1086).

Islam Inflamed. *James Morris.* SCL12(VI-3769), SCL7(IV-2266), A58(117).

*Island. *Aldous Huxley.* SCL12(VI-3772), SCL7(IV-2269), A63(105). A different analysis on this title appears in: SF(III-1073).

Island, The. *Robert Creeley.* SCL12(VI-3775), SCL7(IV-2272), A64(138).

Island of Doctor Moreau, The. *H. G. Wells.* SF(III-1079).

Islanders, The. *Philip Booth.* SCL12(VI-3778), SCL7(IV-2275), A62(159).

Islandia. *Austin Tappan Wright.* SF(III-1084).

*Islands in the Stream. *Ernest Hemingway.* SCL12(VI-3781), A71(135).

Isolationism in America, 1935-1941. *Manfred Jonas.* HAmer(III-1652).

Israel from Its Beginnings to the Middle of the Eighth Century. *Adolphe Lods.* HAnc(I-107).

*Israel Potter. *Herman Melville.* MP12(V-2938), MPCE(II-1079), MP8(IV-2291), MP6(III-1462), MPAm(300), MP3(I-515), MWL3(515).

Israel-Arab Reader, The. *Walter Ze'ev Laqueur.* HWor(I-413).

Israel's Golden Age: The Story of the United Kingdom. *John Dick Fleming.* HAnc(I-108).

Issuance of Alexander Hamilton's *Report on Public Credit* (Event). HAmer(I-356).

Issuance of Draco's Code (Event). HAnc(I-153).

Issuance of the Decree *Licet Juris* (Event).   HAnc(III-1620).
Issuance of the *Lex Hortensia* (Event).   HAnc(I-393).
It Can't Happen Here.   *Sinclair Lewis.*   SF(III-1089).
It Happened One Night.   Cine(II-852).
It Has Happened Here.   *Virgil T. Blossom.*   HWor(II-773).
It Is Better than It Was.   *Pedro Calderón de la Barca.*   MP12(V-2942),
     MPCE(II-1081),   MP8(IV-2294),   MP6(III-1464),   MPDr(389),
     MP3(I-517),   MWL3(517).
It Is Worse than It Was.   *Pedro Calderón de la Barca.*   MP12(V-2945),
     MPCE(II-1082),   MP8(IV-2296),   MP6(III-1466),   MPDr(391),
     MP3(I-519),   MWL3(519).
Italian, The.   *Mrs. Ann Radcliffe.*   MP12(V-2948),   MPCE(II-1083),
     MP8(IV-2298),   MP6(III-1468),   MPEng(352),   MP3(I-521),
     MWL3(521).
Italian Defeat at Adowa and the Downfall of Crispi (Event).   HEur(II-1094)
Italian Democracy in the Making: The Political Scene in the Giolittian Era,
     1900-1914.   *Arcangelo William Salomone.*   HWor(I-141).
Italian Ethiopian Campaign (Event).   HEur(III-1401).
Italian Parliament Passes the Law of Papal Guarantees (Event).
     HEur(II-978).
Italian Renaissance Sculpture.   *John Pope-Hennessy.*   HAnc(III-1668).
Italy: A Modern History.   *Denis Mack Smith.*   Different analyses on this
     title appear in: HEur(II-960; II-1097; II-1111).
Italy After Fascism: A Political History, 1943-1965.   *Giuseppe Mammarella.*
     HEur(III-1539).
Italy and the Vatican at War.   *S. William Halperin.*   Different analyses on
     this title appear in: HEur(II-960; II-980).
Italy Annexes Tripoli (Event).   HEur(III-1228).
Italy Enters World War I (Event).   HWor(I-138).
Italy from Liberalism to Fascism, 1870-1925.   *Christopher Seton-Watson.*
     HEur(II-1097).
"Italy in 1848" *in François Fejto's* The Opening Of an Era, 1848.   *Delio
     Cantimori.*   HEur(II-779).
Italy in the Making, 1815-1846.   *G. F. H. Berkeley.*   HEur(II-701).
Italy Is Proclaimed a Kingdom (Event).   HEur(II-870).
Italy Today.   *Bolton King* and *Thomas Okey.*   HEur(II-1112).
Italy's Foreign and Colonial Policy, 1914-1937.   *M. H. H. Macartney* and *P.
     Cremona.*   HEur(III-1404).
Itching Parrot, The.   *José Joaquín Fernández de Lizardi.*   MP12(V-2955),
     MPCE(II-1085),   MP8(IV-2304),   MP6(III-1473),   MPAm(303),
     MPv3(251),   MP2(I-499),   MWL2(499).
It's a Wonderful Life.   Cine(II-856).
Ivan the Great of Moscow.   *J. L. I. Fennell.*   Different analyses on this title
     appear in: HAnc(III-1739; III-1743).
Ivan III's Organization of the "Third Rome" (Event).   HAnc(III-1738).

*Ivanhoe. *Sir Walter Scott.* MP12(V-2959), MPCE(II-1087), MP8(IV-2307), MP6(III-1475), MPEng(358), MP1(I-430), MWL1(430).

Jack: A Biography of Jack London. *Andrew Sinclair.* LA78(I-454).

Jack of Newberry. *Thomas Deloney.* MP12(V-2964), MPCE(II-1090), MP8(IV-2310), MP6(III-1478), MPEng(361), MPv4(249), MP2(I-501), MWL2(501).

Jack Sheppard. *William Harrison Ainsworth.* MP12(V-2969), MPCE(II-1093), MP8(IV-2313), MP6(III-1480), MPEng(364), MPv3(254), MP2(I-504), MWL2(504).

Jacksonian Persuasion: Politics and Belief, The. *Marvin Meyers.* Different analyses on this title appear in: HAmer(I-634; II-677).

Jacob's Ladder, The. *Denise Levertov.* SCL12(VI-3786), SCL7(IV-2278), A64(140).

Jagged Orbit, The. *John Brunner.* SF(III-1094).

Jailbird. *Kurt Vonnegut, Jr.* LA80(II-436).

Jalna. *Mazo de la Roche.* MP12(V-2973), MPCE(II-1094), MP8(IV-2316), MP6(III-1483), MPAm(306), MPv4(252), MP2(I-506), MWL2(506).

James Boswell: The Earlier Years, 1740-1769. *Frederick A. Pottle.* SCL12(VI-3789), SCL7(IV-2281), A67(168).

"James Chadwick," *in* Biographical Memoirs of Fellows of the Royal Society. *Harrie Massey* and *Norman Feather.* HWor(I-287).

James Edward Oglethorpe, Imperial Idealist. *Amos A. Ettinger.* HAmer(I-185).

James Forrestal. *Arnold A. Rogow.* SCL12(VI-3793), SCL7(IV-2285), A65(148).

James G. Blaine: A Political Idol of Other Days. *David S. Muzzey.* Different analyses on this title appear in: HAmer(II-1144; II-1192).

James Joyce. *Richard Ellmann.* SCL12(VI-3797), SCL7(IV-2289), A60(105).

James Madison: 1809-1812. *Irving Brant.* SCL12(VI-3800), SCL7(IV-2292), A57(132).

James Madison: 1812-1836. *Irving Brant.* SCL12(VI-3804), SCL7(IV-2296), A62(162).

James Monroe. *Harry Ammon.* SCL12(VI-3808), A72(181).

James Russell Lowell. *Martin B. Duberman.* SCL12(VI-3813), SCL7(IV-2300), A67(171).

James I Becomes King of England and Scotland (Event). HEur(I-224).

James Watt. *L. T. C. Rolt.* HEur(I-461).

James Watt and the History of Steam Power. *Ivor B. Hart.* HEur(I-462).

James Watt Develops His Steam Engine (Event). HEur(I-460).

Jane Eyre. Cine(II-860).

*Jane Eyre. *Charlotte Brontë.* MP12(V-2976), MPCE(II-1095),

MP8(IV-2319),   MP6(III-1485),   MPEng(367),   MP1(I-432),
MWL1(432).

Janus: A Summing Up. *Arthur Koestler*.   LA79(I-326).

Japan Occupies Indochina (Event).   HWor(I-438).

Japan Occupies the Dutch East Indies, Singapore, and Burma (Event).
MWor(I-457).

Japan Presents China with the Twenty-One Demands (Event).   HWor(I-121).

Japanese, The. *Edwin O. Reischauer*.   LA78(II-459).

Japanese Inn. *Oliver Statler*.   SCL12(VI-3817),   SCL7(IV-2304),
A62(165).

Japanese Military Campaigns in China (Event).   HWor(I-361).

Japanese-Trained Armies in Southeast Asia: Independence and Volunteer
Forces in World War II. *Joyce C. Lebra*.   HWor(I-461).

Japan's American Interlude. *Kazuo Kawai*.   HWor(II-586).

Jason and the Golden Fleece. *Unknown*.   MP12(V-2981),
MPCE(II-1098),   MP8(IV-2322),   MP6(III-1488),   MPEur(402),
MP1(I-435),   MWL1(435).

Java Head. *Joseph Hergesheimer*.   MP12(V-2985),   MPCE(II-1101),
MP8(IV-2324),   MP6(III-1489),   MPAm(309),   MP1(I-437),
MWL1(437).

Jaws.   Cine(II-863).

Jay Cooke, Private Banker. *Henrietta M. Larson*.   HAmer(II-988).

Jay's Treaty: A Study in Commerce and Diplomacy. *Samuel Flagg Bemis*.
HAmer(I-391).

Jazz Singer, The.   Cine(II-866).

*J. B. *Archibald MacLeish*.   SCL12(VI-3820),   SCL7(IV-2307),
A59(131),   BMA(255).

*Jean Santeuil. *Marcel Proust*.   SCL12(VI-3823),   SCL7(IV-2310),
A57(135).

*Jean-Christophe. *Romain Rolland*.   MP12(V-2988),   MPCE(II-1102),
MP8(IV-2327),   MP6(III-1491),   MPEur(404),   MP1(I-439),
MWL1(439).

Jean-Jacques Rousseau: Conscience of an Era. *Frances Winwar*.
HEur(I-449).

Jean-Paul Sartre Publishes *Being and Nothingness* (Event).   HEur(III-1482).

Jeb Stuart: The Last Cavalier. *Burke Davis*.   SCL12(VI-3827),
SCL7(IV-2313),   A58(120).

Jedediah Smith and the Opening of the West. *Dale L. Morgan*.
HAmer(I-621).

Jedediah Smith, Trader and Trail Breaker. *Maurice S. Sullivan*.
HAmer(I-622).

Jedediah Smith's Exploration of the Far West (Event).   HAmer(I-619).

Jefferson and Hamilton: The Struggle for Democracy in America. *Claude G.
Bowers*.   MP12(V-2993),   MP8(IV-2330),   MP4(I-462),
MWL4(462).

Jefferson and His Time, Vol. III: Jefferson and the Ordeal of
  Liberty. *Dumas Malone.* HAmer(I-429).
Jefferson and the Ordeal of Liberty. *Dumas Malone.* SCL12(VI-3830),
  SCL7(IV-2316), A63(108).
Jefferson and the Presidency: Leadership in the Young Republic. *Robert M.
  Johnstone, Jr.* LA79(I-331).
Jefferson Davis: American Patriot. *Hudson Strode.* SCL12(VI-3835),
  SCL7(IV-2320), A55(134), BMA(258).
Jefferson Davis: Confederate President. *Hudson Strode.*
  SCL12(VI-3838), SCL7(IV-2323), A60(108), BMA(261).
Jefferson Davis: Private Letters, 1823-1889. *Hudson Strode.*
  SCL12(VI-3841), SCL7(IV-2326), A67(175).
Jefferson Davis: The Sphinx of the Confederacy. *Clement Eaton.*
  LA78(II-464).
Jefferson Davis: Tragic Hero. *Hudson Strode.* SCL12(VI-3845),
  SCL7(IV-2330), A65(152).
Jefferson the President: First Term, 1801-1805. *Dumas Malone.*
  SCL12(VI-3849), A71(140).
Jefferson the President: Second Term, 1805-1809. *Dumas Malone.*
  SCL12(VI-3854), A75(158).
Jeffersonian Republicans: The Formation of Party Organization, 1789-1801,
  The. *Noble E. Cunningham, Jr.* HAmer(I-352).
Jeffersonian System, 1801-1811, Vol. XII: The American Nation: A History,
  The. *Edward Channing.* HAmer(I-428).
Jennie: The Life of Lady Randolph Churchill, Volume II. *Ralph G.
  Martin.* SCL12(VI-3857), A72(186).
*Jennie Gerhardt. *Theodore Dreiser.* MP12(V-2996), MPCE(II-1105),
  MP8(IV-2333), MP6(III-1494), MPAm(312), MP3(I-526),
  MWL3(526).
Jeremiah: Prophet of Courage and Hope. *J. Philip Hyatt.* HAnc(I-151).
Jeremiah, Man and Prophet. *Sheldon H. Blank.* HAnc(I-151).
Jeremy's Version. *James Purdy.* SCL12(VI-3862), A71(144).
Jerome Writes the *Contra Vigilantium* (Event). HAnc(II-929).
Jerusalem. *Michel Join-Lambert.* HAnc(I-103).
*Jerusalem Delivered. *Torquato Tasso.* MP12(V-3000),
  MPCE(II-1107), MP8(IV-2336), MP6(III-1496), MPPo(141),
  MP1(I-441), MWL1(441). A different analysis on this title appears in:
  RCa(I-548).
Jesse Stuart. *Ruel E. Foster.* SCL12(VI-3866), SCL7(IV-2334),
  A69(172).
Jesuits: A History of the Society of Jesus, The. *René Fülöp-Miller.*
  HEur(I-101).
Jesus and His Times. *Henri Daniel-Rops.* RCa(II-1006).
Jesus and the Word. *Rudolf Bultmann.* HAnc(II-591).
Jesus the Lord. *Karl Heim.* RCh(II-1008).

Jet Propulsion Progress: The Development of Aircraft Gas Turbines. *Leslie E. Neville* and *Nathaniel F. Silsbee*. HWor(I-358).

*Jew of Malta, The. *Christopher Marlowe*. MP12(V-3004), MPCE(II-1109),   MP8(IV-2339),   MP6(III-1499),   MPDr(393), MP1(I-444),   MWL1(444).

Jewess of Toledo, The. *Franz Grillparzer*. MP12(V-3008), MPCE(II-1112),   MP8(IV-2341),   MP6(III-1500),   MPDr(395), MP3(I-528),   MWL3(528).

Jewish Background of the Christian Liturgy, The. *W. O. E. Oesterley*. HAnc(II-596).

Jewish Gnosticism, Markabah Mysticism, and Talmudic Tradition. *Gershom G. Scholem*. HAnc(III-1562).

Jews and Arabs: Their Contacts Through the Ages. *S. D. Goitein*. HWor(I-414).

Jews in Spain, The. *Abraham Neuman*. HAnc(III-1754).

Jews in the Eyes of the Germans: From the Enlightenment to Imperial Germany. *Alfred D. Low*. LA80(II-439).

Jezebel. Cine(II-870).

Joan of Arc. *Lucien Fabre*. HAnc(III-1699).

Joan of Arc. *Francis C. Lowell*. HAnc(III-1700).

Joan of Arc. *Edward Lucie-Smith*. LA78(II-472).

Joan of Arc's Relief of Orléans (Event). HAnc(III-1697).

Joanna Godden. *Sheila Kaye-Smith*. MP12(V-3012),   MPCE(II-1113), MP8(IV-2344),   MP6(III-1503),   MPEng(370),   MPv4(254), MP2(I-509),   MWL2(509).

Joel Chandler Harris. *Paul M. Cousins*. SCL12(VI-3872), SCL7(IV-2340),   A69(177).

Johann Sebastian Bach. *Philipp Spitta*. HEur(I-382).

Johann Sebastian Bach: The Culmination of an Era. *Karl Geiringer* and *Irene Geiringer*. HEur(I-383).

John A. Hobson Publishes *Imperialism: A Study* (Event). HWor(I-31).

John Adams. *Page Smith*. SCL12(VI-3876),   SCL7(IV-2344),   A63(112).

John Brown and the Legend of Fifty-Six. *James C. Malin*. HAmer(II-893).

John Brown's Body. *Stephen Vincent Benét*. MP12(V-3016), MPCE(II-1115),   MP8(IV-2347),   MP6(III-1505),   MPPo(144), MP1(I-445),   MWL1(445).

John Brown's Raid on Harpers Ferry (Event). HAmer(II-918).

John C. Calhoun, Vol. I: Nationalist, 1782-1828. *Charles M. Wiltse*. HAmer(I-544).

John C. Calhoun, Vol. II: Nullifer, 1829-1839. *Charles M. Wiltse*. HAmer(II-706).

John Calvin: The Man and His Ethics. *Georgia Harkness*. HEur(I-120).

John Donne: A Life. *R. C. Bald*. SCL12(VI-3880),   A71(148).

John Dryden: The Poet, The Dramatist, The Critic. *T. S. Eliot*. MP12(V-3020),   MP8(IV-2350),   MP4(I-465),   MWL4(465).

LA80(II-444).

*Jorrocks' Jaunts and Jollites. *Robert Smith Surtees*. MP12(V-3033), MPCE(II-1123), MP8(IV-2362), MP6(III-1514), MPEng(382), MPv3(261), MP2(I-518), MWL2(518).

Joseph: The Man Closest to Jesus. *Francis L. Filas, S. J.* RCa(II-1115).

*Joseph Andrews. *Henry Fielding*. MP12(V-3036), MPCE(II-1124), MP8(IV-2365), MP6(III-1517), MPEng(385), MP1(I-448), MWL1(448).

Joseph Conrad. *Jocelyn Baines*. SCL12(VI-3903), SCL7(IV-2362), A61(132), BMA(272).

Joseph Conrad: The Three Lives. *Frederick R. Karl*. LA80(II-449).

Joseph Stalin. *Robert Warth*. HEur(III-1569).

Joseph II's Reforms (Event). HEur(I-480).

Joseph Vance. *William De Morgan*. MP12(V-3041), MPCE(II-1127), MP8(IV-2368), MP6(III-1519), MPEng(388), MP1(I-450), MWL1(450).

Journal of a Tour to the Hebrides. *James Boswell*. MP12(V-3044), MP8(IV-2371), MP4(I-467), MWL4(467).

Journal of Christopher Columbus, The. *Christopher Columbus*. HAnc(III-1759).

Journal of Edwin Carp, The. *Richard Haydn*. SCL12(VI-3909), SCL7(IV-2368), A54(123).

Journal of Francis Asbury, The. *Francis Asbury*. RCh(II-654).

Journal of George Fox, The. *George Fox*. RCh(I-546).

Journal of John Wesley, The. *John Wesley*. RCh(II-581).

Journal of John Woolman, The. *John Woolman*. RCh(II-612).

*Journal of the Plague Year, A. *Daniel Defoe*. MP12(V-3047), MP8(IV-2374), MP4(I-469), MWL4(469).

*Journal of Thoreau, The. *Henry David Thoreau*. MP12(V-3050), MP8(IV-2377), MP4(I-471), MWL4(471).

Journal to Eliza. *Laurence Sterne*. MP12(V-3053), MP8(IV-2380), MP4(I-474), MWL4(474).

*Journal to Stella. *Jonathan Swift*. MP12(V-3056), MP8(IV-2383), MP4(I-476), MWL4(476).

Journals: Early Fifties Early Sixties. *Allen Ginsberg*. LA78(II-483).

Journals of André Gide, The. *André Gide*. MP12(VI-3059), MP8(IV-2386), MP4(I-478), MWL4(478).

Journals of Dorothy Wordsworth. *William Wordsworth*. MP12(VI-3062), MP8(IV-2389), MP4(I-481), MWL4(481).

Journals of George Whitefield. *George Whitefield*. RCh(II-577).

Journals of Henry Melchoir Mühlenberg, The. *Henry Melchior Mühlenberg*. RCh(II-620).

Journals of Lewis and Clark, The. *Meriwether Lewis* and *William Clark*. MP12(VI-3065), MP8(IV-2392), MP4(I-484), MWL4(484).

Journals, with Letters and Related Documents. *Zebulon Montgomery Pike*.

Peck) (Event).   HAmer(I-485).
Judith Paris. *Hugh Walpole.*   MP12(VI-3084),   MPCE(II-1136),
  MP8(IV-2405),   MP6(III-1530),   MPEng(394),   MP1(I-457),
  MWL1(457).
Julia and the Bazooka. *Anna Kavan.*   SCL12(VI-3956),   A76(154).
Julian. *Gore Vidal.*   SCL12(VI-3959),   SCL7(IV-2387),   A65(155).
Julian the Apostate. *Guiseppe Ricciotti.*   HAnc(II-891).
Julius Caesar.   Cine(II-881).
*Julius Caesar. *William Shakespeare.*   MP12(VI-3089),   MPCE(II-1139),
  MP8(IV-2408),   MP6(III-1532),   MPDr(402),   MPv3(263),
  MP2(I-522),   MWL2(522).
Julius Caesar, Man, Soldier, and Tyrant. *John F. C. Fuller.*   HAnc(I-518).
July Revolution in France (Event).   HEur(II-682).
Jung Publishes *Psychological Types* (Event).   HEur(III-1310).
*Jungle, The. *Upton Sinclair.*   MP12(VI-3094),   MPCE(II-1142),
  MP8(IV-2411),   MP6(III-1535),   MPAm(315),   MP1(I-459),
  MWL1(459).
*Jungle Books, The. *Rudyard Kipling.*   MP12(VI-3097),
  MPCE(II-1143),   MP8(IV-2413),   MP6(III-1537),   MPEng(397),
  MP1(I-461),   MWL1(461).
*Juno and the Paycock. *Sean O'Casey.*   MP12(VI-3100),
  MPCE(II-1144),   MP8(IV-2416),   MP6(III-1539),   MPDr(405),
  MP3(I-533),   MWL3(533).
*Jurgen. *James Branch Cabell.*   MP12(VI-3105),   MPCE(II-1147),
  MP8(IV-2418),   MP6(III-1541),   MPAm(317),   MP1(I-464),
  MWL1(464).
Just Above My Head. *James Baldwin.*   LA80(II-456).
Just Representations: A James Gould Cozzens Reader. *James Gould
  Cozzens.*   LA79(I-343).
Justice. *John Galsworthy.*   MP12(VI-3108),   MPCE(II-1148),
  MP8(IV-2421),   MP6(III-1543),   MPDr(407),   MP1(I-466),
  MWL1(466).
Justice Crucified: The Story of Sacco and Vanzetti. *Roberta Strauss
  Feuerlicht.*   LA78(II-487).
Justice Oliver Wendell Holmes. *Mark DeWolfe Howe.*   SCL12(VI-3963),
  SCL7(IV-2391),   A58(122),   BMA(278).
Justin Martyr: His Life and Thought. *L. W. Barnard.*   HAnc(II-710).
*Justine. *Lawrence Durrell.*   SCL12(VI-3967),   SCL7(IV-2395),
  A58(125),   BMA(282).

Kadesh Inscriptions of Ramesses II, The. *Sir Alan H. Gardiner.*
  HAnc(I-73).
Kaiser, The. *Virginia Cowles.*   HEur(III-1210).
Kaitei Gunkan. *Shunro Oshikawa.*   SF(III-1106).
Kalevala, The. *Elias Lönnrot.*   MP12(VI-3111),   MPCE(II-1150),

King Kong. Cine(II-900).

*King Lear. *William Shakespeare.* MP12(VI-3148), MPCE(II-1163), MP8(IV-2453), MP6(III-1565), MPDr(418), MPv3(268), MP2(I-526), MWL2(526).

King Must Die, The. *Mary Renault.* SCL12(VI-4015), SCL7(IV-2427), A59(133), BMA(284).

King of Hearts. Cine(II-905).

King of Kings. Cine(II-908).

King of Pontus. *Alfred Duggan.* SCL12(VI-4019), SCL7(IV-2431), A60(121).

King of Rome, The. *André Castelot.* SCL12(VI-4022), SCL7(IV-2434), A61(143), BMA(287).

King of the Golden River, The. *John Ruskin.* MP12(VI-3153), MPCE(II-1166), MP8(IV-2456), MP6(III-1567), MPEng(407), MPv4(260), MP2(I-529), MWL2(529).

King of the Jews. *Leslie Epstein.* LA80(II-458).

King of the Mountains, The. *Edmond François About.* MP12(VI-3156), MPCE(II-1167), MP8(IV-2459), MP6(III-1570), MPEur(410), MPv4(263), MP2(I-531), MWL2(531).

King Paradox. *Pío Baroja.* MP12(VI-3159), MPCE(II-1168), MP8(IV-2462), MP6(III-1572), MPEur(413), MPv4(265), MP2(I-533), MWL2(533).

King, Queen, Knave. *Vladimir Nabokov.* SCL12(VI-4026), SCL7(IV-2438), A69(181).

King Ranch, The. *Tom Lea.* SCL12(VI-4030), SCL7(IV-2442), A58(127).

King Rat. Cine(II-911).

King Solomon's Mines. *H. Rider Haggard.* MP12(VI-3163), MPCE(II-1169), MP8(IV-2465), MP6(III-1574), MPEng(410), MP1(I-475), MWL1(475).

*King, the Greatest Alcalde, The. *Lope de Vega.* MP12(VI-3168), MPCE(II-1171), MP8(IV-2469), MP6(III-1577), MPDr(421), MPv3(270), MP2(I-536), MWL2(536).

Kingdom of Christ, The. *Frederick Denison Maurice.* RCh(II-688).

Kingdom of God, The. *Gregorio Martínez Sierra.* MP12(VI-3173), MPCE(II-1175), MP8(IV-2471), MP6(III-1579), MPDr(423), MP3(I-545), MWL3(545).

Kingdom of This World, The. *Alejo Carpentier.* SCL12(VI-4033), SCL7(IV-2445), A58(130).

Kings Depart: The Tragedy of Germany: Versailles and the German Revolution, The. *Richard M. Watt.* HEur(III-1288).

*Kings in Exile. *Alphonse Daudet.* MP12(VI-3176), MPCE(II-1176), MP8(IV-2474), MP6(III-1582), MPEur(416), MPv3(272), MP2(I-538), MWL2(538).

King's Indian: Stories and Tales, The. *John Gardner.* SCL12(VI-4036),

A75(164).

King's Row. *Henry Bellamann.* MP12(VI-3179), MPCE(II-1177), MP8(IV-2476), MP6(III-1583), MPAm(322), MP1(I-478), MWL1(478).

King's Story, A. *Duke of Windsor.* HEur(III-1422).

King's Two Bodies, The. *Ernst Kantorowicz.* HAnc(III-1345).

King's War: 1641-1647, The. *C. V. Wedgwood.* SCL12(VI-4039), SCL7(IV-2448), A60(124), BMA(291).

Kingship of God. *Martin Buber.* HAnc(I-87).

Kipps. *H. G. Wells.* MP12(VI-3182), MPCE(II-1178), MP8(IV-2478), MP6(III-1585), MPEng(414), MPv4(267), MP2(I-540), MWL2(540).

Kiss Kiss. *Roald Dahl.* SCL12(VI-4042), SCL7(IV-2451), A61(147).

Kissinger. *Bruce Mazlish.* HWor(II-1052).

Kith. *P. H. Newby.* LA78(II-491).

Klute. Cine(II-915).

*Knight of the Burning Pestle, The. *Francis Beaumont.* MP12(VI-3185), MPCE(II-1179), MP8(IV-2480), MP6(III-1587), MPDr(426), MPv3(274), MP2(I-542), MWL2(542).

Knightly Quest, The. *Tennessee Williams.* SCL12(VI-4045), SCL7(IV-2454), A67(179).

Knights, The. *Aristophanes.* MP12(VI-3189), MPCE(II-1180), MP8(IV-2483), MP6(III-1590), MPDr(429), MP1(I-480), MWL1(480).

Knights of the Limits, The. *Barrington J. Bayley.* SF(III-1126).

*Knock on Any Door. *Willard Motley.* SCL12(VI-4048), SCLs(151).

Knocking on the Door. *Alan Paton.* LA77(I-396).

Know Thyself. *Peter Abelard.* RCh(I-212).

Knowledge of God and the Service of God, The. *Karl Barth.* Ph(II-1027).

Koch Receives the Nobel Prize for Service to Medicine (Event). HEur(III-1174).

Kolyma: The Arctic Death Camps. *Robert Conquest.* LA79(I-354).

Korea: The Limited War. *David Rees.* HAmer(III-1826).

Korean Decision, June 24-30, 1950, The. *Glenn D. Paige.* HAmer(III-1827).

Korean War, The (Event). HAmer(III-1823).

Kramer vs. Kramer. Cine(II-919).

*Kreutzer Sonata, The. *Count Leo Tolstoy.* MP12(VI-3192), MPCE(II-1183), MP8(IV-2485), MP6(III-1591), MPEur(418), MP1(I-481), MWL1(481).

Krishna Fluting. *John Berry.* SCL12(VI-4052), SCL7(IV-2457), A60(126).

*Kristin Lavransdatter. *Sigrid Undset.* MP12(VI-3195), MPCE(II-1185), MP8(IV-2488), MP6(III-1594), MPEur(421), MP1(I-483), MWL1(483).

Kulturkampf (Event).   HEur(II-969).
Kung-sun Lung Tzu.   *Kung-sun Lung*.   Ph(I-195).

La Colonia Felice.   *Carlo Dossi*.   *See* Colonia Felice, La.
La Gringa.   *Florencio Sánchez*.   *See* Gringa, La.
La guerre au XXe siècle.   *Albert Robida*.   *See* guerre au XXe siècle, La.
La Naissance des dieux.   *Charles Henneberg*.   *See* Naissance des dieux, La.
La Nave.   *Tomas Salvador*.   *See* Nave, La.
La Sepoltura.   *Gianni Montanari*.   *See* Sepoltura, La
La Teseide.   *Giovanni Boccaccio*.   *See* Teseide, La.
La Vida.   *Oscar Lewis*.   *See* Vida, La
Labor and the New Deal.   *Milton Derber* and *Edwin Young, eds.*
   HAmer(III-1640).
Labyrinth of Solitude, The.   *Octavio Paz*.   MP12(VI-3200),
   MP8(IV-2491),   MP4(I-489),   MWL4(489),   SCL12(VI-4057),
   SCL7(IV-2462),   A63(117).
L'Action.   *Maurice Blondel*.   *See* Action, L'.
Ladder of Divine Ascent, The.   *Saint John Climacus*.   Different analyses on
   this title appear in: RCh(I-179),   RCa(I-254).
Ladder of Perfection, The.   *Walter Hilton*.   Different analyses on this title
   appear in: RCh(I-316),   RCa(I-494).
*Lady, The.   *Conrad Richter*.   SCL12(VI-4061),   SCL7(IV-2465),
   A58(133).
*Lady Chatterley's Lover.   *D. H. Lawrence*.   SCL12(VI-4064),
   SCL7(IV-2468),   A60(129).
Lady Eve, The.   Cine(II-929).
Lady for Ransom, The.   *Alfred Duggan*.   MP12(VI-3203),
   MP8(IV-2494),   MP4(I-492),   MWL4(492),   SCL12(VI-4070),
   SCL7(IV-2473),   A54(135).
*Lady from the Sea.   *Henrik Ibsen*.   MP12(VI-3206),   MPCE(II-1188),
   MP8(IV-2497),   MP6(III-1596),   MPDr(431),   MPv3(277),
   MP2(I-544),   MWL2(544).
Lady into Fox.   *David Garnett*.   MP12(VI-3210),   MPCE(II-1190),
   MP8(IV-2500),   MP6(III-1598),   MPEng(416),   MP1(I-486),
   MWL1(486).
Lady of the Lake, The.   *Sir Walter Scott*.   MP12(VI-3213),
   MPCE(II-1191),   MP8(IV-2502),   MP6(III-1600),   MPPo(151),
   MPv3(279),   MP2(I-547),   MWL2(547).
Lady Oracle.   *Margaret Atwood*.   LA77(I-400).
Lady Vanishes, The.   Cine(II-933).
*Lady Windermere's Fan.   *Oscar Wilde*.   MP12(VI-3216),
   MPCE(II-1192),   MP8(IV-2505),   MP6(III-1602),   MPDr(434),
   MP1(I-488),   MWL1(488).
Ladykillers, The.   Cine(II-939).
Lady's Not for Burning, The.   *Christopher Fry*.   MP12(VI-3219),

MPCE(II-1193),   MP8(IV-2507),   MP6(III-1604),   MPDr(436),
    MPv4(269),   MP2(I-549),   MWL2(549).
Lafayette: A Biography. *Peter Buckman*.   LA78(II-495).
Lafcadio Hearn. *Elizabeth Stevenson*.   SCL12(VI-4073),
    SCL7(IV-2476),   A62(175).
L'Aiglon. *Edmond Rostand.   See* Aiglon, L'.
Lais, Le. *François Villon*.   MP12(VI-3226),   MP8(IV-2512),
    MP4(I-494),   MWL4(494).
Lais of Marie de France, The. *Marie de France*.   MP12(VI-3230),
    MPCE(II-1196),   MP8(IV-2516),   MP4(I-497),   MWL4(497).
Lalla Rookh. *Thomas Moore*.   MP12(VI-3237),   MPCE(II-1197),
    MP8(IV-2522),   MP6(III-1609),   MPPo(154),   MP3(I-548),
    MWL3(548).
*Lamb, The. *François Mauriac*.   SCL12(VI-4076),   SCL7(IV-2479),
    A57(141).
Lament for the Molly Maguires. *Arthur H. Lewis*.   SCL12(VI-4079),
    SCL7(IV-2482),   A65(164).
L'Amorosa Fiammetta. *Giovanni Boccaccio.   See* Amorosa Fiammetta, L'.
Lamp Post, The. *Martin Gregor-Dellin*.   SCL12(VI-4082),
    SCL7(IV-2485),   A65(167).
Lamy of Santa Fe. *Paul Horgan*.   SCL12(VI-4085),   A76(157).
Lancelot. *Walker Percy*.   LA78(II-501).
Land Divided: A History of the Panama Canal and Other Isthmian Canal
    Projects, The. *Gerstle Mack*.   HAmer(II-1343).
Land Law of 1820 (Event).   HAmer(I-582).
Land Office Business: The Settlement and Administration of American Public
    Lands, 1789-1837, The. *Malcolm J. Rohrbough*.   HAmer(I-585).
Land That Time Forgot, The. *Edgar Rice Burroughs*.   SF(III-1130).
Land They Fought For, The. *Clifford Dowdey*.   SCL12(VI-4089),
    SCL7(IV-2488),   A55(137).
Land Use Policy and Problems in the United States. *Howard W. Ottoson*.
    HAmer(II-966).
Land Without Justice. *Milovan Djilas*.   SCL12(VI-4093),
    SCL7(IV-2492),   A59(137).
Landa's *Relación de las Coasas de Yucatan*: A Translation. *D. De Landa*.
    HAmer(I-9).
Landing of the Pilgrims at Plymouth (Event).   HAmer(I-74).
Landing of United Nations Forces at Inchon, The (Event).   HWor(II-676).
Language, Counter-Memory, Practice: Selected Essays and
    Interviews. *Michel Foucault*.   LA78(II-504).
Language, Truth and Logic. *Alfred Jules Ayer*.   Ph(II-1010).
Languages of Pao, The. *Jack Vance*.   SF(III-1135).
Lanterns and Lances. *James Thurber*.   SCL12(VI-4097),
    SCL7(IV-2496),   A62(178).
Lardners, The. *Ring Lardner, Jr*.   LA77(I-404).

Laser Technology and Applications. *Samuel L. Marshall,* ed.
    HWor(II-883).
Last Athenian, The. *Viktor Rydberg.* MP12(VI-3243), MPCE(II-1200),
    MP8(IV-2528), MP6(III-1613), MPEur(427), MPv4(274),
    MP2(I-553), MWL2(553).
Last Analysis, The. *Saul Bellow.* SCL12(VI-4099), SCL7(IV-2498),
    A66(138).
Last and First Men. *Olaf Stapledon.* SF(III-1140).
Last Angry Man, The. *Gerald Green.* SCL12(VI-4102),
    SCL7(IV-2501), A58(136).
Last Battle, The. *Cornelius Ryan.* HAmer(III-1750).
Last Castle, The. *Jack Vance.* SF(III-1144).
Last Chance: Nuclear Proliferation and Arms Control, The. *William
    Epstein.* HWor(II-567).
Last Chopper: The Denounement of the American Role in Vietnam,
    1963-1975, The. *Weldon A. Brown.* HWor(III-1163).
*Last Chronicle of Barset, The. *Anthony Trollope.* MP12(VI-3246),
    MPCE(II-1201), MP8(IV-2531), MP6(III-1615), MPEng(418),
    MPv3(281), MP2(I-556), MWL2(556).
Last Convertible, The. *Anton Myrer.* LA79(I-359).
Last Day the Dogbushes Bloomed, The. *Lee Smith.* SCL12(VI-4105),
    SCL7(IV-2504), A69(185).
Last Days of Pompeii, The. *Edward George Earle Bulwer-Lytton.*
    MP12(VI-3249), MPCE(II-1203), MP8(IV-2533), MP6(III-1617),
    MPEng(420), MP1(I-490), MWL1(490).
Last Days of United Pakistan, The. *G. W. Choudhury.* HWor(II-1094).
Last Detail, The. Cine(II-942).
*Last Gentleman, The. *Walker Percy.* SCL12(VI-4109),
    SCL7(IV-2508), A67(184).
Last Hundred Days, The. *John Toland.* HWor(II-580).
Last Hunt, The. *Milton Lott.* SCL12(VI-4112), SCL7(IV-2511),
    A54(138).
Last Hurrah, The. Cine(II-945).
*Last Hurrah, The. *Edwin O'Connor.* SCL12(VI-4115),
    SCL7(IV-2514), A57(144), BMA(294).
Last Innocence, The. *Célia Bertin.* SCL12(VI-4119), SCL7(IV-2518),
    A55(141).
Last Kaiser, The. *Michael Tyler-Whittle.* LA78(II-509).
Last Man, The. *Mary Wollstonecraft Shelley.* SF(III-1151).
Last of Summer, The. *Kate O'Brien.* MP12(VI-3253), MPCE(II-1205),
    MP8(IV-2535), MP6(III-1619), MPEng(422), MPv4(276),
    MP2(I-558), MWL2(558).
Last of the Barons, The. *Edward George Earle Bulwer-Lytton.*
    MP12(VI-3257), MPCE(II-1207), MP8(IV-2538), MP6(III-1622),
    MPEng(425), MP1(I-492), MWL1(492).

Last of the Crazy People, The. *Timothy Findley.* SCL12(VI-4122),
    SCL7(IV-2521), A68(173).
Last of the Just, The. *André Schwarz-Bart.* SCL12(VI-4125),
    SCL7(IV-2524), A61(149).
*Last of the Mohicans, The. *James Fenimore Cooper.* MP12(VI-3261),
    MPCE(II-1208), MP8(IV-2541), MP6(III-1624), MPAm(324),
    MP1(I-494), MWL1(494).
Last of the Vikings, The. *Johan Bojer.* MP12(VI-3266),
    MPCE(II-1211), MP8(IV-2544), MP6(III-1627), MPEur(430),
    MPv4(278), MP2(I-560), MWL2(560).
Last of the Wine, The. *Mary Renault.* MP12(VI-3271), MP8(IV-2547),
    MP4(I-503), MWL4(503), SCL12(VI-4128), SCL7(IV-2527),
    A57(147), BMA(298).
*Last Picture Show, The. *Larry McMurtry.* SCL12(VI-4132), SCLs(154).
Last Puritan, The. *George Santayana.* MP12(VI-3274),
    MPCE(II-1214), MP8(IV-2550), MP6(III-1629), MPAm(327),
    MP1(I-497), MWL1(497).
Last Starship from Earth, The. *John Boyd.* SF(III-1156).
*Last Tales. *Isak Dinesen.* SCL12(VI-4135), SCL7(IV-2530),
    A58(138).
*Last Temptation of Christ, The. *Nikos Kazantzakis.* SCL12(VI-4138),
    SCL7(IV-2533), A61(153).
Last Things. *C. P. Snow.* SCL12(VI-4142), A71(161).
*Last Tycoon, The. *F. Scott Fitzgerald.* MP12(VI-3277),
    MPCE(II-1216), MP8(IV-2553), MP6(III-1631), MPAm(330),
    MP3(I-552), MWL3(552).
Last Unicorn, The. *Peter S. Beagle.* SCL12(VI-4146), SCL7(IV-2537),
    A69(188).
Last Valley, The. *A. B.Guthrie, Jr.* SCL12(VI-4151), A76(161).
Late George Apley, The. *John P. Marquand.* MP12(VI-3280),
    MPCE(II-1218), MP8(IV-2555), MP6(III-1633), MPAm(332),
    MP1(I-499), MWL1(499).
Late Lord Byron, The. *Doris Langley Moore.* SCL12(VI-4154),
    SCL7(IV-2542), A62(180), BMA(301).
Late Mattia Pascal, The. *Luigi Pirandello.* MP12(VI-3285),
    MPCE(II-1221), MP8(IV-2558), MP6(III-1636), MPEur(433),
    MPv4(281), MP2(I-562), MWL2(562).
Latent Image: The Discovery of Photography. *Beaumont Newhall.*
    HEur(II-751).
Later Crusades, 1189-1311, Vol. II: A History of the Crusades, The. *Kenneth
    M. Setton.* HAnc(III-1500).
Later Roman Empire 284-602—A Social, Economic, and Administrative
    Survey, The. *A. H. M. Jones.* HAnc(II-936).
Lathe of Heaven, The. *Ursula K. Le Guin.* SF(III-1161).
"Latin Bible, The," *in* The Bible in Its Ancient and English

Versions. *H. F. D. Sparks.* HAnc(II-911).
Laughable Loves. *Milan Kundera.* SCL12(VI-4158), A75(167).
Laughter. *Henri Bergson.* MP12(VI-3289), MP8(IV-2561),
 MP4(I-505), MWL4(505).
Laura. Cine(II-948).
Laurette. *Marguerite Courtney.* SCL12(VI-4161), SCL7(IV-2546),
 A55(144), BMA(305).
Laval. *Hubert Cole.* SCL12(VI-4165), SCL7(IV-2550), A64(146).
Lavender Hill Mob, The. Cine(II-952).
Lavengro. *George Henry Borrow.* MP12(VI-3292), MPCE(II-1223),
 MP8(IV-2564), MP6(III-1638), MPEng(428), MP1(I-501),
 MWL1(501).
Lavka snovidenyi. *Ilya Varshavsky.* SF(III-1165).
Law, The. *Roger Vailland.* SCL12(VI-4168), SCL7(IV-2553),
 A59(141).
Law and Covenant in Israel and in the Ancient Near East. *George E.
 Mendenhall.* HAnc(I-86).
Law and Economic Policy in America: The Evolution of the Sherman
 Act. *William L. Letwin.* HAmer(II-1210).
Law of Obscenity, The. *Frederick F. Schauer.* HWor(III-1176).
Law of the Commonwealth and Chief Justice Shaw: The Evolution of
 American Law, 1830-1860, The. *Leonard W. Levy.* HAmer(II-788).
Lawless Breed, The. Cine(II-956).
Lawrence and Oppenheimer. *Nuel Pharr Davis.* HWor(II-687).
Lawrence of Arabia. Cine(II-959).
Laws. *Plato.* Ph(I-131).
"Lay Investiture and Its Relation to the Conflict of Empire and Papacy," *in*
 Proceedings of the British Academy. *Zachery N. Brooke.*
 HAnc(III-1320).
Lay of Igor's Campaign, The. *Unknown.* MP12(VI-3296),
 MP8(IV-2567), MP4(I-507), MWL4(507).
Lay of the Last Minstrel, The. *Sir Walter Scott.* MP12(VI-3299),
 MPCE(II-1225), MP8(IV-2570), MP6(III-1641), MPPo(157),
 MPv3(283), MP2(I-564), MWL2(564).
Laying of the First Transatlantic Cable (Event). HEur(II-834).
Laying of the First Transatlantic Cable (Event). HAmer(II-895).
Lazarillo de Tormes. *Unknown.* MP12(VI-3302), MPCE(II-1226),
 MP8(IV-2573), MP6(III-1643), MPEur(436), MPv3(285),
 MP2(II-567), MWL2(567).
Lazarus. *André Malraux.* LA78(II-515).
Le Docteur Lerne. *Maurice Renard.* *See* Docteur Lerne, Le.
Le Lais. *François Villon.* *See* Lais, Le.
Le Menteur. *Pierre Corneille.* *See* Menteur, Le.
Le Meraviglie del duemila. *Emilio Salgari.* *See* Meraviglie del duemila, Le.
Le Morte d'Arthur. *Sir Thomas Malory.* *See* Morte d'Arthur, Le.

Le Prisonnier de la planète Mars. *Gustave LeRouge. See* Prisonnier de la
    planète Mars, Le.
Le Roman de la Rose. *L. Thuasne. See* Roman de la Rose, Le.
Le voyageur imprudent. *René Barjavel. See* voyageur imprudent, Le.
"Leading Ideas of the New Period, The," *in* Vol. V *of* The Cambridge Ancient
    History. *W. S. Ferguson.* HAnc(I-405).
Leaf Storm. *Gabriel García Márquez.* SCL12(VI-4171), A73(215).
League of Arab States: A Study in the Dynamics of Regional Organization,
    The. *Robert W. Macdonald.* HWor(I-498).
Leaping Clear. *Irving Feldman.* LA77(I-408).
Leatherstocking Saga, The. *Allan Nevins,* ed. SCL12(VI-4176),
    SCL7(IV-2556), A54(141).
Leave Her to Heaven. Cine(II-963).
*Leaves of Grass. *Walt Whitman.* MP12(VI-3307), MP8(IV-2576),
    MP6(III-1646), MPPo(160), MP3(I-554), MWL3(554).
Lebanese Civil War, The (Event). HWor(III-1235).
Lebanon: The Collapse of a State. *Abbas Kelidar* and *Michael Burrell.*
    HWor(III-1241).
Lectures on Calvinism. *Abraham Kuyper.* RCh(II-969).
Lectures on Godmanhood. *Vladimir Solovyev.* RCh(II-782).
Lectures on Preaching. *Phillips Brooks.* RCh(II-778).
Lectures on Revivals of Religion. *Charles Grandison Finney.* RCh(II-675).
Lectures on the Philosophy of Life. *Friedrich von Schlegel.* RCa(II-635).
Lee's Lieutenants: A Multiple Biography of the Military Leaders in Lee's
    Command During the Civil War, Vol. I: Manassas to Malvern
    Hill. *Douglas Southall Freeman.* HAmer(II-955).
Lee's Lieutenants: A Multiple Biography of the Military Leaders in Lee's
    Command During the Civil War, Vol. II: Cedar Mountain to
    Chancellorville. *Douglas Southall Freeman.* HAmer(II-955).
Lee's Lieutenants: A Multiple Biography of the Military Leaders in Lee's
    Command During the Civil War, Vol. III: Gettysburg to
    Appomattox. *Douglas Southall Freeman.* HAmer(II-955).
Left Hand of Darkness, The. *Ursula K. Le Guin.* SF(III-1171).
Left-Handed Woman, The. *Peter Handke.* LA79(I-363).
Legacy of the German Refugee Intellectuals, The. *Robert Boyers,* ed.
    HWor(I-299).
"Legal Significance of the Statute of Praemunire of 1353, The," *in* Anniversary
    Essays in Medieval History. *Edgar B. Graves.* HAnc(III-1632).
Legalization of French Trade Unions (Event). HEur(II-1044).
Legend of Good Women, The. *Geoffrey Chaucer.* MP12(VI-3311),
    MP8(IV-2580), MP6(III-1649), MPPo(164), MP3(I-557),
    MWL3(557).
Legend of Henry Ford, The. *Keith Sward.* HAmer(III-1424).
*Legend of Sleepy Hollow, The. *Washington Irving.* MP12(VI-3314),
    MPCE(II-1229), MP8(IV-2583), MP6(III-1651), MPAm(335),

MPv4(283), MP2(II-569), MWL2(569).

Legend of the Moor's Legacy. *Washington Irving.* MP12(VI-3317), MPCE(II-1231), MP8(IV-2585), MP6(III-1653), MPAm(337), MPv4(285), MP2(II-571), MWL2(571).

Legend of Tyl Ulenspiegel, The. *Charles de Coster.* MP12(VI-3321), MPCE(II-1233), MP8(IV-2588), MP6(III-1656), MPEur(439), MPv3(287), MP2(II-573), MWL2(573).

Legends of Genesis: The Biblical Saga and History, The. *Hermann Gunkel.* HAnc(I-98).

Legends of the Fall. *Jim Harrison.* LA80(II-462).

Legion of Time, The. *Jack Williamson.* SF(III-1178).

Legislation of Solon (Event). HAnc(I-168).

Leisure the Basis of Culture. *Josef Pieper.* RCa(II-940).

Lenin's New Economic Policy (Event). HEur(III-1304).

Lensman Series, The. *Edward E. Smith.* SF(III-1183).

Léon Blum, Humanist in Politics. *Joel Colton.* HEur(III-1414).

Leon Trotsky. *Irving Howe.* LA79(I-368).

Leonardo da Vinci: An Account of His Development As an Artist. *Kenneth Clark.* HAnc(III-1762).

Leonardo da Vinci Paints the *Last Supper* (Event). HAnc(III-1761).

*Leopard, The. *Giuseppe di Lampedusa.* MP12(VI-3324), MP8(IV-2591), MP4(I-510), MWL4(510). A different analysis on this title appears in: SCL12(VI-4179), SCL7(IV-2559), A61(156), BMA(309).

Leopard's vershini Kilimandzharo. *Olga Larionova.* SF(III-1188).

Leopards and Lilies. *Alfred Duggan.* MP12(VI-3327), MP8(IV-2594), MP4(I-512), MWL4(512), SCL12(VI-4184), SCL7(IV-2563), A54(144).

Leopold I of Austria. *John P. Spielman.* LA78(II-518).

Lermontov: Tragedy in the Caucasus. *Laurence Kelly.* LA79(I-373).

Les Blancs. *Lorraine Hansberry. See* Blancs, Les.

Les Misérables. *Victor Hugo. See* Misérables, Les.

Les Navigateurs de l'infini. *J. H. Rosny, the Elder. See* Navigateurs de l'infini, Les.

Les Troubadours dans leur vie et dans leurs oeuvres. *Ernest Hoepffner. See* Troubadours dans leur vie et dans leurs oeuvres, Les.

Les Xipéhuz. *J. H. Rosny, the Elder. See* Xipéhuz, Les.

Lesabéndio. *Paul Scheerbart.* SF(III-1193).

Lest Darkness Fall. *L. Sprague De Camp.* SF(III-1198).

*Let Me Count the Ways. *Peter De Vries.* SCL12(VI-4191), SCL7(IV-2566), A66(141).

*Let No Man Write My Epitaph. *Willard Motley.* SCL12(VI-4195), SCLs(157).

Let Not Your Hart. *James Seay.* SCL12(VI-4199), A71(164).

Let the Seller Beware. *James Bishop, Jr.* and *Henry Hubbard.*

HWor(II-862).

*Let Us Now Praise Famous Men. *James Agee.*   MP12(VI-3330),
     MP8(IV-2597),   MP4(I-515),   MWL4(515). A different analysis on this
     title appears in: SCL12(VI-4202),   SCL7(IV-2570),   A61(160),
     BMA(313).

Letter from an Unknown Woman.   Cine(II-966).

"Letter from Washington," *in* The New Yorker.   *Richard H. Rovere.*
     HWor(II-713).

Letter of the Church of Rome to the Church of Corinth, The.   *Saint Clement
     I.*   RCa(I-4).

Letter to the Grand Duchess Christina.   *Galileo Galilei.*   RCa(II-579).

Letters.   *John Barth.*   LA80(II-466).

Letters and Sermons of Saint Leo the Great, The.   *Saint Leo the Great.*
     RCa(I-211).

Letters from an American Farmer.   *Michel-Guillaume Jean de Crèvecœur.*
     MP12(VI-3333),   MP8(IV-2600),   MP6(III-1658),   MPNf(169),
     MP3(I-560),   MWL3(560).

Letters from the Earth.   *Mark Twain.*   SCL12(VI-4209),
     SCL7(IV-2576),   A63(120).

*Letters from the Underworld.   *Fyodor Mikhailovich Dostoevski.*
     MP12(VI-3336),   MPCE(II-1235),   MP8(IV-2603),   MP6(III-1661),
     MPEur(442),   MPv3(290),   MP2(II-576),   MWL2(576).

Letters Home.   *Sylvia Plath.*   SCL12(VI-4211),   A76(164).

Letters of Anton Chekhov.   *Anton Chekhov.*   SCL12(VI-4215),   A74(221).

Letters of Bernard DeVoto.   *Bernard DeVoto.*   SCL12(VI-4220),
     A76(168).

Letters of Carl Sandburg, The.   *Carl Sandburg.*   SCL12(VI-4225),
     SCL7(IV-2578),   A69(193).

Letters of Charles Lamb, The.   *Charles Lamb.*   MP12(VI-3341),
     MP8(IV-2606),   MP4(I-517),   MWL4(517).

Letters of C. S. Lewis.   *C. S. Lewis.*   SCL12(VI-4229),   SCL7(IV-2582),
     A67(187).

Letters of D. H. Lawrence, Vol. I: September 1901-May 1913, The.   *D. H.
     Lawrence.*   LA80(II-469).

Letters of E. B. White.   *E. B. White.*   LA77(I-413).

Letters of Emily Dickinson, The.   *Emily Dickinson.*   MP12(VI-3344),
     MP8(IV-2609),   MP4(I-520),   MWL4(520). A different analysis on
     this title appears in: SCL12(VI-4233),   SCL7(IV-2586),   A59(144),
     BMA(316).

Letters of F. Scott Fitzgerald, The.   *F. Scott Fitzgerald.*   MP12(VI-3347),
     MP8(IV-2612),   MP4(I-523),   MWL4(523),   SCL12(VI-4237),
     SCL7(IV-2589),   A64(149).

Letters of James Agee to Father Flye.   *James Agee.*   SCL12(VI-4241),
     SCL7(IV-2593),   A63(122).

Letters of James Joyce.   *James Joyce.*   SCL12(VI-4245),

Letters of Wallace Stevens. *Wallace Stevens.* SCL12(VI-4276),
    SCL7(IV-2616),   A67(190).
Letters of Walpole, The. *Horace Walpole.* MP12(VI-3368),
    MP8(IV-2633),   MP6(III-1663),   MPNf(172),   MP3(I-563),
    MWL3(563).
Letters of William Cowper, The. *William Cowper.* MP12(VI-3371),
    MP8(IV-2636),   MP4(I-541),   MWL4(541).
Letters on Literature and Politics, 1912-1972. *Edmund Wilson.*
    LA78(II-522).
Letters to Felice. *Franz Kafka.* SCL12(VI-4280),   A74(226).
Letters to Friends, Family, and Editors. *Franz Kafka.* LA78(II-526).
*Letters to His Son. *Philip Dormer Stanhope, Lord Chesterfield.*
    MP12(VI-3374),   MP8(IV-2639),   MP6(III-1666),   MPNf(175),
    MP3(I-565),   MWL3(565).
*Letting Go. *Philip Roth.* SCL12(VII-4283),   SCL7(IV-2620),
    A63(129).
L'Eve future. *Adam Villiers de l'Isle Adam.* *See* Eve future, L'.
Level Seven. *Mordecai Roshwald.* SF(III-1204).
Leviathan. *Thomas Hobbes.* MP12(VI-3376),   MP8(IV-2641),
    MP6(III-1667),   MPNf(177),   MP3(I-567),   MWL3(567). A different
    analysis on this title appears in: Ph(I-392).
Levittowners, The. *Herbert J. Gans.* HWor(II-552).
Lewis and Clark: Partners in Discovery. *John Bakeless.* HAmer(I-452).
Lewis and Clark Expedition (Event). HAmer(I-450).
Lex rex. *Samuel Rutherford.* RCh(I-462).
Leyte: June 1944-January 1945. *Samuel Eliot Morison.* SCL12(VII-4287),
    SCL7(IV-2624),   A59(147).
L'Herbe Rouge. *Boris Vian.* *See* Herbe Rouge, L'.
*Liber Amoris. *William Hazlitt.* MP12(VI-3379),   MP8(IV-2644),
    MP6(III-1670),   MPNf(180),   MP3(I-570),   MWL3(570).
Liber de Corpore et Sanguine Domini. *Lanfranc.* RCa(I-283).
Liberal Tradition in America: An Interpretation of American Political Thought
    Since the Revolution, The. *Louis Hartz.* HAmer(I-651).
Liberation of Lord Byron Jones, The. *Jesse Hill Ford.* SCL12(VII-4290),
    SCL7(IV-2627),   A66(144).
Liberator, The. *John I. Thomas.* SCL12(VII-4294),   SCL7(IV-2631),
    A64(157).
Library of Congress Occupies Its Own Building (Event). HAmer(II-1279).
Lie, The. *Alberto Moravia.* SCL12(VII-4297),   SCL7(IV-2634),
    A67(194).
*Lie Down in Darkness. *William Styron.* MP12(VI-3382),
    MP8(IV-2647),   MP4(I-544),   MWL4(544).
Lieh Kuo Chih. *Feng Meng-lung.* MP12(VI-3385),   MPCE(II-1238),
    MP8(IV-2650),   MP6(III-1673),   MPEur(445),   MP3(I-572),
    MWL3(572).

Life of Samuel Johnson, LL.D., The. *Sir John Hawkins, Knt.*
   SCL12(VII-4356),   SCL7(IV-2659),   A62(184).
Life of Sir Alexander Fleming, The. *André Maurois.* HEur(III-1336).
Life of Sir John Eliot, The. *Harold Hulme.* HEur(I-266).
Life of Stephen F. Austin, Founder of Texas, 1793-1836, The. *Eugene C. Barker.* HAmer(II-739).
Life of the Mind: One/Thinking, Two/Willing, The. *Hannah Arendt.*
   LA79(I-393).
Life of the Mind in America, The. *Perry Miller.* SCL12(VII-4359),
   SCLs(160).
Life of Washington Irving, The. *Stanley T. Williams.* HAmer(I-483).
*Life on the Mississippi. *Mark Twain.*   MP12(VI-3412),
   MPCE(II-1244),   MP8(IV-2673),   MP6(III-1687),   MPNf(189),
   MP1(I-504),   MWL1(504).
Life/Situations: Essays Written and Spoken. *Jean-Paul Sartre.*
   LA78(II-529).
*Life Studies. *Robert Lowell.*   SCL12(VII-4362),   SCL7(IV-2662),
   A60(133),   BMA(329).
Life with Father. *Clarence Day, Jr.*   MP12(VI-3415),   MPCE(II-1246),
   MP8(IV-2676),   MP6(III-1689),   MPAm(340),   MP1(I-506),
   MWL1(506).
Lifeboat.   Cine(II-974).
Lifted Veil, The. *George Eliot.*   SF(III-1213).
*Ligeia. *Edgar Allan Poe.*   MP12(VI-3418),   MPCE(II-1247),
   MP8(IV-2679),   MP6(III-1691),   MPAm(343),   MPv4(290),
   MP2(II-583),   MWL2(583).
*Light Around the Body, The. *Robert Bly.*   SCL12(VII-4365),
   SCL7(IV-2665),   A68(176).
Light for the World: Edison and the Power Industry. *Robert Silverberg.*
   HAmer(II-1114).
*Light in August. *William Faulkner.*   MP12(VI-3423),   MPCE(II-1250),
   MP8(IV-2681),   MP6(III-1693),   MPAm(345),   MP1(I-509),
   MWL1(509).
Light in the Piazza, The. *Elizabeth Spencer.*   SCL12(VII-4369),
   SCL7(IV-2668),   A61(163).
Light Infantry Ball, The. *Hamilton Basso.*   SCL12(VII-4372),
   SCL7(IV-2671),   A60(136).
Lighthouse of the Skies. *Bessie Zaban Jones.*   HAmer(II-833).
Lights in the Sky Are Stars, The. *Fredric Brown.*   SF(III-1217).
Like a Bulwark. *Marianne Moore.*   SCL12(VII-4376),   SCL7(IV-2675),
   A57(156),   BMA(332).
Liliom. *Ferenc Molnar.*   MP12(VI-3428),   MPCE(II-1253),
   MP8(IV-2684),   MP6(III-1695),   MPDr(444),   MP1(I-511),
   MWL1(511).
Limbo. *Bernard Wolfe.*   SF(III-1221).

Lime Twig, The. *John Hawkes.* MP12(VI-3431), MP8(IV-2686), MP4(I-551), MWL4(551), SCL12(VII-4380), SCL7(IV-2678), A62(186).

Limelight. Cine(II-978).

Limits of Liberty: Studies of Mill's *On Liberty.* *Peter Radcliff.* HEur(II-845).

Lincoln and His Generals. *T. Harry Williams.* HAmer(II-954).

Lincoln and His Party in the Secession Crisis. *David M. Potter.* HAmer(II-948).

Lincoln and the First Shot. *Richard N. Current.* HAmer(II-949).

Lincoln and the War Governors. *William B. Hesseltine.* HAmer(II-994).

Lincoln Finds a General. *Kenneth P. Williams.* SCL12(VII-4384), SCL7(IV-2681), A60(140), BMA(335). A different analysis on this title appears in: HAmer(II-1001).

Lincoln the President, Vol. I: Springfield to Bull Run. *James G. Randall.* HAmer(II-938).

Lincoln the President, Vol II: Bull Run to Gettysburg. *James G. Randall.* HAmer(II-983).

Lincoln the President, Vol. IV: Last Full Measure. *James G. Randall* and *Richard N. Current.* SCL12(VII-4389), SCL7(IV-2686), A55(147), BMA(340).

Lincoln-Douglas Debates (Event). HAmer(II-906).

Lindbergh. *Leonard Mosley.* LA77(I-433).

Lindmann. *Frederic Raphael.* SCL12(VII-4393), SCL7(IV-2690), A65(174).

Linguistic Introduction to the History of English, A. *Leonard Newmark* and *Morton W. Bloomfield.* HAnc(III-1289).

Link, The. *August Strindberg.* MP12(VI-3434), MPCE(II-1255), MP8(IV-2689), MP6(III-1697), MPDr(446), MP3(II-581), MWL3(581).

Lion and the Throne, The. *Catherine Drinker Bowen.* SCL12(VII-4395), SCL7(IV-2692), A58(150), BMA(344).

Lion for Love: A Critical Biography of Stendhal, A. *Robert Alter.* LA80(II-497).

Lion in the Garden. *James B. Meriwether* and *Michael Millgate,* eds. SCL12(VII-4398), SCL7(IV-2695), A68(179).

Lion of Flanders, The. *Hendrik Conscience.* MP12(VI-3438), MPCE(II-1257), MP8(IV-2691), MP6(III-1699), MPEur(448), MP3(II-583), MWL3(583).

Listeners, The. *James E. Gunn.* SF(III-1226).

Lister and Antiseptic Surgery (Event). HEur(II-935).

Lister and His Achievement. *William Watson Cheyne.* HEur(II-938).

Literary Essays of Virginia Woolf, The. *Virginia Woolf.* MP12(VI-3442), MP8(IV-2694), MP4(I-553), MWL4(553).

Literary History of Rome from the Origins to the Close of the Golden Age,

A. *J. Wight Duff.* Different analyses on this title appear in: HAnc(I-468; I-524; I-533).

Literary History of Rome in the Silver Age from Tiberius to Hadrian, A. *J. Wight Duff.* Different analyses on this title appear in: HAnc(I-533; I-654).

Literary Women. *Ellen Moers.* LA77(I-439).

Literature and Dogma. *Matthew Arnold.* RCh(II-770).

Lithography and Lithographers. Some Chapters in the History of the Art. *Elizabeth Robins Pennell* and *Joseph Pennell.* HEur(I-545).

Little Big Man. Cine(II-981).

*Little Big Man. *Thomas Berger.* SCL12(VII-4401), SCL7(IV-2698), A65(176).

Little Book of Eternal Wisdom, The. *Blessed Henry Suso, O. P.* RCa(I-458).

Little Brown Brother: How the United States Purchased and Pacified the Philippine Islands at the Century's Turn. *Leon Wolff.* HAmer(II-1293).

Little Clay Cart, The. *Shudraka.* MP12(VI-3444), MPCE(II-1258), MP8(IV-2696), MP6(III-1702), MPDr(448), MP3(II-586), MWL3(586).

*Little Dorrit. *Charles Dickens.* MP12(VI-3448), MPCE(II-1260), MP8(IV-2699), MP6(III-1704), MPEng(436), MPv3(295), MP2(II-585), MWL2(585).

Little Flowers of St. Francis, The. *Unknown.* Different analyses on this title appear in: RCh(I-264), RCa(I-448).

Little Foxes, The. Cine(II-984).

*Little Foxes, The. *Lillian Hellman.* MP12(VI-3451), MPCE(II-1261), MP8(IV-2702), MP6(III-1706), MPDr(451), MP3(II-588), MWL3(588).

Little Fuzzy. *H. Beam Piper.* SF(III-1230).

Little Girls, The. *Elizabeth Bowen.* SCL12(VII-4408), SCL7(IV-2705), A64(160).

Little Hotel, The. *Christina Stead.* SCL12(VII-4411), A76(181).

Little Hut, The. *André Roussin.* SCL12(VII-4415), SCL7(IV-2708), A54(153).

Little Karoo, The. *Pauline Smith.* SCL12(VII-4418), SCL7(IV-2711), A60(144).

Little Learning, A. *Evelyn Waugh.* SCL12(VII-4421), SCL7(IV-2714), A65(183).

*Little Minister, The. *James M. Barrie.* MP12(VI-3454), MPCE(II-1263), MP8(IV-2704), MP6(III-1708), MPEng(439), MP1(I-513), MWL1(513).

Little Rock School Desegregation Crisis, The (Event). HWor(II-770).

Little Women. Cine(II-988).

*Little Women. *Louisa May Alcott.* MP12(VI-3458), MPCE(II-1264),

Logic of Modern Physics, The. *Percy Williams Bridgman.* Ph(II-880).
Logic, the Theory of Inquiry. *John Dewey.* Ph(II-1033).
*Lolita. *Vladimir Nabokov.* SCL12(VII-4455), SCL7(IV-2733),
    A59(150).
London Yankees: Portraits of American Writers and Artists in England,
    1894-1914, The. *Stanley Weintraub.* LA80(II-508).
Loneliest Campaign: The Truman Victory of 1948, The. *Irwin Ross.*
    HAmer(III-1803).
Loneliness of the Long Distance Runner, The. Cine(II-996).
*Loneliness of the Long-Distance Runner, The. *Alan Sillitoe.*
    SCL12(VII-4458), SCL7(IV-2736), A61(165).
Lonely Hunter, The. *Virginia Spencer Carr.* SCL12(VII-4461), A76(185).
Lonely in America. *Suzanne Gordon.* LA77(I-445).
*Lonely Passion of Judith Hearne, The. *Brian Moore.* SCL12(VII-4465),
    SCL7(IV-2739), A57(159).
Lonely Vigil: Coastwatchers of the Solomons. *Walter Lord.* LA78(II-534).
Lonesome Traveler and Other Stories, The. *John William Corrington.*
    SCL12(VII-4469), SCL7(IV-2742), A69(200).
Long Afternoon of Earth, The. *Brian W. Aldiss.* SF(III-1235).
Long and Happy Life, A. *Reynolds Price.* MP12(VI-3474),
    MP8(IV-2721), MP4(I-561), MWL4(561). A different analysis on
    this title appears in: SCL12(VII-4475), SCL7(IV-2748), A63(135).
Long Day's Journey into Night. Cine(III-999).
*Long Day's Journey into Night. *Eugene O'Neill.* SCL12(VII-4480),
    SCL7(IV-2753), A57(162), BMA(347).
*Long Journey, The. *Johannes V. Jensen.* MP12(VI-3477),
    MPCE(II-1268), MP8(IV-2724), MP6(III-1718), MPEur(451),
    MPv4(294), MP2(II-589), MWL2(589).
Long Loud Silence, The. *Wilson Tucker.* SF(III-1238).
*Long March, The. *William Styron.* SCL12(VII-4484), SCLs(168).
Long Night, The. *Andrew Lytle.* MP12(VI-3483), MPCE(II-1271),
    MP8(IV-2728), MP6(III-1722), MPAm(350), MPv4(298),
    MP2(II-593), MWL2(593).
Long Shadow of Little Rock: A Memoir, The. *Daisy Bates.* HWor(II-772).
Long Ships, The. *Frans G. Bengtsson.* SCL12(VII-4487),
    SCL7(IV-2756), A54(159).
Long Street, The. *Donald Davidson.* SCL12(VII-4490),
    SCL7(IV-2759), A62(192), BMA(350).
Long Tomorrow, The. *Leigh Brackett.* SF(III-1242).
Long Voyage, The. *Jorge Semprun.* SCL12(VII-4494), SCL7(IV-2763),
    A65(188).
Long Voyage Home, The. Cine(III-1003).
Longer Rules *and* The Shorter Rules, The. *Saint Basil of Caesarea.*
    RCh(I-99).
Longest Day: June 6, 1944, The. *Cornelius Ryan.* SCL12(VII-4499),

MWL1(524).

Losing Battles. *Eudora Welty*. SCL12(VII-4538), A71(175).

Losing Ground. *Erik P. Eckholm*. LA77(I-450).

Loss of El Dorado, The. *V. S. Naipaul*. SCL12(VII-4542), A71(178).

Loss of Spanish Colonies to the United States (Event). HEur(II-1119).

Loss of the Self. *Wylie Sypher*. HWor(I-257).

Lost Centuries, The. *General Sir John Glubb*. HAnc(III-1578).

Lost Honor of Katharina Blum, The. *Heinrich Böll*. SCL12(VII-4545), A76(192).

Lost Horizon. Cine(III-1006).

*Lost Horizon. *James Hilton*. MP12(VI-3512), MPCE(II-1280), MP8(IV-2753), MP6(III-1735), MPEng(453), MP1(I-527), MWL1(527). A different analysis on this title appears in: SF(III-1265).

*Lost Illusions. *Honoré de Balzac*. MP12(VI-3518), MPCE(II-1284), MP8(IV-2756), MP6(III-1738), MPEur(455), MPv3(297), MP2(II-595), MWL2(595).

Lost in the Funhouse. *John Barth*. SCL12(VII-4548), SCL7(IV-2784), A69(205).

*Lost Lady, A. *Willa Cather*. MP12(VI-3521), MPCE(II-1285), MP8(IV-2759), MP6(III-1740), MPAm(359), MP1(I-529), MWL1(529).

*Lost Ones, The. *Samuel Beckett*. SCL12(VII-4551), A73(228).

Lost Pathfinder, Zebulon Montgomery Pike, The. *W. Eugene Hollon*. HAmer(I-469).

Lost Revolution, The. *Robert Shaplen*. SCL12(VII-4555), SCL7(IV-2787), A66(151).

Lost Tribes and Promised Lands: The Origins of American Racism. *Ronald Sanders*. LA79(I-398).

Lost Weekend, The. Cine(III-1009).

Lost Weekend, The. *Charles Jackson*. MP12(VI-3524), MPCE(II-1286), MP8(IV-2762), MP6(III-1742), MPAm(362), MP1(I-531), MWL1(531).

Lost World, The. *Arthur Conan Doyle*. SF(III-1270).

*Lost World, The. *Randall Jarrell*. SCL12(VII-4558), SCL7(IV-2790), A66(154).

Lost World of Thomas Jefferson, The. *Daniel J. Boorstin*. HAmer(I-196).

Louis XIV. *Vincent Buranelli*. HEur(I-348).

Louis XIV. *John B. Wolf*. Different analysis on this title appear in: HEur(I-351; I-355).

Louis XIV Invades the Netherlands (Event). HEur(I-345).

Louis XIV Moves the French Court to Versailles (Event). HEur(I-349).

Louis Napoleon Bonaparte Becomes Emperor of France (Event). HEur(II-808).

Louisiana in French Diplomacy, 1759-1804. *E. Wilson Lyon*. HAmer(I-447).

Louisiana Purchase, The (Event).   HAmer(I-445).

Louisiana Story.   Cine(III- 1012).

*Love & Fame. *John Berryman.*   SCL12(VII-4561),   A72(201).

Love and Its Derangements. *Joyce Carol Oates.*   SCL12(VII-4565),
    A71(181).

Love and Napalm: Export U. S. A.   *J. G. Ballard.*   SF(III-1274).

Love and Will. *Rollo May.*   SCL12(VII-4570),   A70(187).

Love and Work. *Reynolds Price.*   SCL12(VII-4573),   SCL7(IV-2793),
    A69(208).

Love Finds Andy Hardy.   Cine(III-1015).

*Love for Love. *William Congreve.*   MP12(VI-3527),   MPCE(II-1287),
    MP8(IV-2764),   MP6(III-1744),   MPDr(453),   MPv3(299),
    MP2(II-597),   MWL2(597).

*Love in a Wood. *William Wycherley.*   MP12(VI-3530),
    MPCE(II-1289),   MP8(IV-2767),   MP6(III-1746),   MPDr(456),
    MP3(II-595),   MWL3(595).

Love in the Afternoon.   Cine(III-1018).

Love in the Ruins. *Walker Percy.*   SCL12(VII-4577),   A72(205). A
    different analysis on this title appears in: SF(III-1278).

Love Me Tonight.   Cine(III-1022).

Love of God, The. *Saint Francis of Sales.*   RCa(II-584).

Love of Learning and the Desire for God, The.   *Jean Leclerq.*
    HAnc(II-1049).

Love Parade, The.   Cine(III-1026).

Love Poems. *Anne Sexton.*   SCL12(VII-4580),   SCL7(IV-2797),
    A69(212).

Love Story. *Erich Segal.*   SCL12(VII-4583),   A71(189).

Love, the Law of Life. *Toyohiko Kagawa.*   RCh(II-921).

Love with the Proper Stranger.   Cine(III-1029).

Lovecraft Mythos, The. *H. P. Lovecraft.*   SF(III-1284).

*Love-Girl and the Innocent, The. *Aleksandr I. Solzhenitsyn.*
    SCL12(VII-4587),   A71(186).

Lovely Ambition, The. *Mary Ellen Chase.*   SCL12(VII-4591),
    SCL7(IV-2800),   A61(168).

Lovers, The. *Philip José Farmer.*   SF(III-1289).

Lovers & Agnostics. *Kelly Cherry.*   SCL12(VII-4594),   A76(195).

Lovers and Tyrants. *Francine du Plessix Gray.*   LA77(I-455).

Lover's Discourse: Fragments, A. *Roland Barthes.*   LA79(I-404).

Love's Body. *Norman O. Brown.*   SCL12(VII-4597),   SCL7(IV-2803),
    A67(205).

Love's Labour's Lost. *William Shakespeare.*   MP12(VI-3534),
    MPCE(II-1291),   MP8(IV-2770),   MP6(III-1748),   MPDr(459),
    MPv3(301),   MP2(II-599),   MWL2(599).

Loving. *Henry Green.*   MP12(VI-3537),   MPCE(II-1292),
    MP8(IV-2773),   MP6(III-1750),   MPEng(456),   MPv4(300),

MP2(II-602), MWL2(602).

*Lower Depths, The. *Maxim Gorky.* MP12(VI-3540), MPCE(II-1293), MP8(IV-2776), MP6(III-1752), MPDr(462), MPv3(303), MP2(II-604), MWL2(604).

Low's Autobiography. *David Low.* SCL12(VII-4601), SCL7(IV-2807), A58(155).

Loyalists and Redcoats. *Paul H. Smith.* HAmer(I-297).

Loyalties. *John Galsworthy.* MP12(VI-3544), MPCE(II-1295), MP8(IV-2779), MP6(III-1754), MPDr(465), MP1(I-533), MWL1(533).

L-Shaped Room, The. Cine(II-925).

Luce and His Empire. *W. A. Swanberg.* SCL12(VII-4604), A73(231).

*Lucien Leuwen. *Stendhal (Marie-Henri Beyle).* MP12(VI-3547), MPCE(II-1297), MP8(IV-2781), MP6(III-1756), MPEur(458), MPv4(302), MP2(II-606), MWL2(606).

Lucifer in Harness. *Edwin Fussell.* SCL12(VII-4607), A74(242).

Lucinella. *Lore Segal.* LA77(I-460).

*Luck of Ginger Coffey, The. *Brian Moore.* SCL12(VII-4610), SCL7(IV-2810), A61(171).

*Luck of Roaring Camp and Other Sketches, The. *Bret Harte.* MP12(VI-3551), MP8(IV-2784), MP6(III-1758), MPAm(364), MP3(II-597), MWL3(597).

Lucky Eyes and a High Heart: The Biography of Maud Gonne. *Nancy Cardozo.* LA79(I-409).

*Lucky Jim. *Kingsley Amis.* MP12(VI-3554), MP8(IV-2787), MP4(I-569), MWL4(569).

Lucky Life. *Gerald Stern.* LA78(II-540).

Lucretius and His Influence. *George Depue Hadzsits.* HAnc(I-514).

Lucretius Writes the *De Rerun Natura* (Event). HAnc(I-511). *See also* De Rerum Natura.

Lumen. *Camille Flammarion.* SF(III-1294).

Lunar Landscapes. *John Hawkes.* SCL12(VII-4613), A70(190).

L'Univers Vagabond. *Leon Groc* and *Jacqueline Zorn.* *See* Univers Vagabond, L'.

*Lusiads, The. *Luis Vaz de Camoëns.* MP12(VI-3557), MPCE(II-1299), MP8(IV-2790), MP6(III-1761), MPPo(167), MPv3(306), MP2(II-608), MWL2(608).

Luther Posts His Ninety-Five Theses (Event). HEur(I-54).

Lyell Publishes *The Principles of Geology* (Event). HEur(II-678).

Lyfe of Sir Thomas More, Knighte. *William Roper.* RCa(I-543).

Lyndon B. Johnson: The Exercise of Power. *Rowland Evans* and *Robert Novak.* HAmer(III-1921).

Lyndon Johnson and the American Dream. *Doris Kearns.* LA77(II-465).

Lyric Poetry of Byron, The. *George Gordon, Lord Byron.* MP12(VI-3562), MP8(IV-2793), MP4(I-571), MWL4(571).

Lyric Poetry of Lowell, The. *James Russell Lowell.* MP12(VI-3565),
     MP8(IV-2796), MP4(I-574), MWL4(574).
*Lyric Poetry of Milton, The. *John Milton.* MP12(VI-3569),
     MP8(IV-2800), MP4(I-577), MWL4(577).
*Lyric Poetry of Spenser, The. *Edmund Spenser.* MP12(VI-3573),
     MP8(IV-2804), MP4(I-581), MWL4(581).
Lyrical and Critical Essays. *Albert Camus.* SCL12(VII-4616),
     SCL7(IV-2813), A69(215).
*Lysistrata. *Aristophanes.* MP12(VI-3578), MPCE(II-1301),
     MP8(IV-2809), MP6(III-1763), MPDr(467), MPv3(308),
     MP2(II-610), MWL2(610).
Lytton Strachey. *Michael Holroyd.* SCL12(VII-4620), SCL7(IV-2817),
     A69(218).

*Mabinogion, The. *Unknown.* MP12(VI-3582), MPCE(II-1303),
     MP8(IV-2811), MP6(III-1765), MPEng(459), MP3(II-600),
     MWL3(600).
*Macbeth. *William Shakespeare.* MP12(VI-3589), MPCE(II-1306),
     MP8(IV-2815), MP6(III-1769), MPDr(469), MP1(I-534),
     MWL1(534)
McCarthy and His Enemies: The Record and Its Meaning. *William F.
     Buckley* and *L. Brent Bozell.* HAmer(III-1820).
McCarthy Hearings, The (Event). HAmer(III-1817).
Macaulay: The Shaping of the Historian. *John Clive.* SCL12(VII-4624),
     A74(246).
McCormick's Invention of the Reaper (Event). HAmer(II-679).
Machiavelli and the Renaissance. *Federico Chabod.* HEur(I-37).
Machiavelli Writes *The Prince* (Event). HEur(I-35). *See also* Prince, The.
Machine Stops, The. *E. M. Forster.* SF(III-1299).
Macht der drei, Die. *Hans Dominik.* SF(III-1304).
*Mackerel Plaza, The. *Peter De Vries.* SCL12(VII-4628),
     SCL7(IV-2821), A59(152).
McKinley, Bryan, and the People. *Paul W. Glad.* HAmer(II-1270).
Macroscope. *Piers Anthony.* SF(III-1308).
*McTeague. *Frank Norris.* MP12(VI-3594), MPCE(III-1309),
     MP8(IV-2818), MP6(III-1771), MPAm(367), MP1(I-537),
     MWL1(537).
*Madame Bovary. *Gustave Flaubert.* MP12(VI-3599),
     MPCE(III-1312), MP8(IV-2821), MP6(III-1774), MPEur(461),
     MP1(I-539), MWL1(539).
Madame Curie. Cine(III-1033).
Madder Music. *Peter De Vries.* LA78(II-546).
Mademoiselle de Maupin. *Théophile Gautier.* MP12(VI-3604),
     MPCE(III-1315), MP8(IV-2824), MP6(III-1776), MPEur(464),
     MP1(I-542), MWL1(542).

MP12(VI-3638),   MPCE(III-1331),   MP8(IV-2848),
MP6(IV-1795),   MPDr(480),   MPv4(304),   MP2(II-612),
MWL2(612).

Mail Boat, The. *Alexander Randolph*.   SCL12(VII-4650),
SCL7(IV-2828),   A54(165).

Maimonidean Criticism and the Maimonidean Controversy, 1180-1240. *Daniel
J. Silver*.   HAnc(III-1393).

Main Currents in American Thought. *Vernon Louis Parrington*.
MP12(VI-3642),   MP8(IV-2851),   MP4(I-586),   MWL4(586).

Main Currents in Sociological Thought. *Raymond Aron*.   HEur(II-806).

*Main Street. *Sinclair Lewis*.   MP12(VI-3645),   MPCE(III-1333),
MP8(IV-2854),   MP6(IV-1798),   MPAm(375),   MP1(I-549),
MWL1(549).

*Main-Travelled Roads. *Hamlin Garland*.   MP12(VI-3650),
MP8(IV-2857),   MP6(IV-1800),   MPAm(378),   MP3(II-615),
MWL3(615).

Major and the Minor, The.   Cine(III-1043).

*Major Barbara. *George Bernard Shaw*.   MP12(VI-3652),
MP8(IV-2859),   MP6(IV-1802),   MPDr(483),   MP3(II-617),
MWL3(617).

Major Trends in Jewish Mysticism. *Gershom G. Scholem*.   HAnc(III-1561).

Make Room! Make Room! *Harry Harrison*.   SF(III-1312).

Makepeace Experiment, The. *Abram Tertz*.   SCL12(VII-4653),
SCL7(IV-2831),   A66(161).

Making of Adolf Hitler: The Birth and Rise of Nazism, The. *Eugene
Davidson*.   LA78(II-552).

Making of an Assassin, The. *George McMillan*.   LA77(II-470).

Making of an un-American: A Dialogue with Experience, The. *Paul
Cowan*.   HAmer(III-1881).

Making of Charles Dickens, The. *Christopher Hibbert*.
SCL12(VII-4656),   SCL7(IV-2834),   A68(182).

Making of Europe, The. *Christopher Dawson*.   RCa(II-824).

Making of Modern Italy, The. *Arrigo Solmi*.   HEur(II-926).

Making of the Australian Constitution, The. *John Andrew La Nauze*.
HWor(I-20).

Making of the Electrical Age, The. *Harold I. Sharlin*.   HEur(II-651).

Making of the Good Neighbor Policy, The. *Bryce Wood*.   HWor(I-264).

Making of the President, 1960, The. *Theodore H. White*.
SCL12(VII-4660),   SCL7(IV-2838),   A62(195),   BMA(356). A
different analysis on this title appears in: HAmer(III-1873).

Making of the President, 1964, The. *Theodore H. White*.
SCL12(VII-4664),   SCL7(IV-2842),   A66(164). A different analysis on
this title appears in: HAmer (III-1920).

Making of the President, 1968, The. *Theodore H. White*.
SCL12(VII-4669),   A70(193). A different analysis on this title appears

in: HAmer(III-1935).

Making of the President 1972, The. *Theodore H. White.*
SCL12(VII-4675), A74(255).

Malcolm. *James Purdy.* MP12(VI-3655), MP8(IV-2862),
MP4(I-588), MWL4(588). A different analysis on this title appears in:
SCL12(VII-4680), SCL7 (IV-2847), A60(149).

Malcolm Lowry. *Douglas Day.* SCL12(VII-4684), A74(260).

Malcontent, The. *John Marston.* MP12(VI-3658), MPCE(III-1336),
MP8(IV-2865), MP6(IV-1804), MPDr(486), MP3(II-619),
MWL3(619).

Male Animal, The. Cine(III-1046).

*Malefactors, The. *Caroline Gordon.* SCL12(VII-4688), SCLs(176).

Malevil. *Robert Merle.* SF(III-1317).

Maltaverne. *Françoise Mauriac.* SCL12(VII-4691), A71(192).

Maltese Falcon, The. Cine(III-1049).

*Maltese Falcon, The. *Dashiell Hammett.* MP12(VI-3661),
MPCE(III-1337), MP8(IV-2868), MP6(IV-1806), MPAm(380),
MP1(I-551), MWL1(551).

Malthus Publishes *An Essay on the Principle of Population* (Event).
HEur(I-533).

Man a Machine. *Julien Offray de La Mettrie.* Ph(I-482).

*Man Against the Sky, The. *Edwin Arlington Robinson.* MP12(VI-3664),
MP8(IV-2871), MP6(IV-1809), MPPo(173), MP3(II-622),
MWL3(622).

*Man and Superman. *George Bernard Shaw.* MP12(VI-3667),
MP8(IV-2874), MP6(IV-1811), MPDr(489), MP3(II-624),
MWL3(624).

Man and the State. *Jacques Maritain.* RCa(II-973).

*Man and Two Women, A. *Doris Lessing.* SCL12(VII-4695),
SCL7(IV-2851), A64(169).

Man Called Intrepid, A. *William S. Stevenson.* LA77(II-475).

Man for All Seasons, A. Cine(III-1053).

Man in Motion. *Michael Mewshaw.* SCL12(VII-4698), A71(195).

Man in the Gray Flannel Suit, The. *Sloan Wilson.* SCL12(VII-4703),
SCL7(IV-2854), A55(150).

Man in the High Castle, The. *Philip K. Dick.* SF(III-1323).

Man in the White Suit, The. Cine(III-1056).

Man Just Ahead of You, The. *Robert M. Coates.* SCL12(VII-4706),
SCL7(IV-2857), A65(193).

Man of Feeling, The. *Henry Mackenzie.* MP12(VII-3669),
MPCE(III-1338), MP8(IV-2876), MP6(IV-1813), MPEng(463),
MPv4(307), MP2(II-615), MWL2(615).

Man of La Mancha. *Dale Wasserman.* SCL12(VII-4709),
SCL7(IV-2860), A67(209).

Man of Mode, The. *Sir George Etherege.* MP12(VII-3672),

MPCE(III-1339),   MP8(IV-2879),   MP6(IV-1815),   MPDr(491),
MPv4(309),   MP2(II-617),   MWL2(617).
Man Plus. *Frederik Pohl.*   SF(III-1328).
*Man Who Cried I Am, The. *John A. Williams.*   SCL12(VII-4714),
SCLs(179).
Man Who Folded Himself, The. *David Gerrold.*   SF(III-1333).
Man Who Loved Children, The. *Christina Stead.*   SCL12(VII-4718),
SCL7(IV-2865),   A66(168).
Man Who Made News, James Gordon Bennett, The. *Oliver Carlson.*
HAmer(II-715).
Man Who Never Was, The. *Ewen Montagu.*   SCL12(VII-4721),
SCL7(IV-2868),   A54(168).
Man Who Shook Hands, The. *Diane Wakoski.*   LA79(I-414).
Man Who Shot Liberty Valance, The.   Cine(III-1059).
Man Who Sold Louisiana: The Career of Françoise Barbé-Marbois, The.   *E.
Wilson Lyon.*   HAmer(I-447).
*Man Who Was Thursday, The. *Gilbert Keith Chesterton.*
MP12(VII-3676),   MPCE(III-1341),   MP8(IV-2882),
MP6(IV-1818),   MPEng(466),   MPv3(310),   MP2(II-619),
MWL2(619).
Man Who Would Be King, The.   Cine(III-1063).
Man with a Bull-Tongue Plow. *Jesse Stuart.*   MP12(VII-3680),
MP8(IV-2885),   MP6(IV-1820),   MPPo(176),   MP3(II-626),
MWL3(626).
Man with the Broken Ear, The. *Edmond About.*   SF(III-1340).
*Man Without a Country, The. *Edward Everett Hale.*   MP12(VII-3683),
MPCE(III-1343),   MP8(IV-2888),   MP6(IV-1822),   MPAm(383),
MP1(I-553),   MWL1(553).
Man Without Qualities: Volume II, The. *Robert Musil.*
SCL12(VII-4724),   SCL7(IV-2871),   A54(171).
Manchild in the Promised Land. *Claude Brown.*   SCL12(VII-4727),
SCL7(IV-2874),   A66(171).
Manchurian Crisis and the Rise of Japanese Militarism, The (Event).
HWor(I-269).
*Mandarins, The. *Simone de Beauvoir.*   SCL12(VII-4732),
SCL7(IV-2878),   A57(165).
Mandate for Change, 1953-1956. *Dwight D. Eisenhower.*
SCL12(VII-4736),   SCL7(IV-2881),   A64(172).
Mandelbaum Gate, The. *Muriel Spark.*   SCL12(VII-4740),
SCL7(IV-2885),   A66(175).
Man-Eater of Malgudi, The. *R. K. Narayan.*   SCL12(VII-4743),
SCL7(IV-2888),   A62(199).
*Manette Salomon. *Edmond de Goncourt* and *Jules de Goncourt.*
MP12(VII-3686),   MPCE(III-1345),   MP8(IV-2890),
MP6(IV-1824),   MPEur(469),   MP3(II-628),   MWL3(628).

March of Conquest, The. *Telford Taylor*. HEur(III-1459).
March of the Iron Men: A Social History of Union Through
    Invention. *Roger Burlingame*. HAmer(II-841).
March of the Ten Thousand (Event). HAnc(I-313).
Marching On. *James Boyd*. MP12(VII-3714), MPCE(III-1356),
    MP8(IV-2912), MP6(IV-1840), MPAm(390), MP1(I-566),
    MWL1(566).
Marconi: The Man and His Wireless. *Orrin E. Dunlap, Jr.* HEur(II-1082).
Marconi Develops Wireless Telegraphy (Event). HEur(II-1080).
Marcus Aurelius. *A. R. Birley*. HAnc(II-728).
Marcus Aurelius: His Life and His World. *A. S. L. Farquharson*.
    HAnc(II-727).
Marcus Aurelius Writes the *Meditations* (Event). HAnc(II-725). *See also*
    Meditations.
Marcus Porcius Cato, On Agriculture; Marcus Terentius Varro, On
    Agriculture. *William Davis Hooper*. HAnc(I-467).
*Mardi. *Herman Melville*. MP12(VII-3717), MPCE(III-1357),
    MP8(IV-2915), MP6(IV-1842), MPAm(393), MPv3(314),
    MP2(II-623), MWL2(623).
Margaret Fuller: From Transcendentalism to Revolution. *Paula Blanchard*.
    LA79(I-422).
Maria Chapdelaine. *Louis Hémon*. MP12(VII-3721), MPCE(III-1359),
    MP8(V-2919), MP6(IV-1844), MPAm(396), MPv3(316),
    MP2(II-626), MWL2(626).
Maria Magdalena. *Friedrich Hebbel*. MP12(VII-3725),
    MPCE(III-1360), MP8(V-2922), MP6(IV-1846), MPDr(494),
    MPv4(311), MP2(II-628), MWL2(628).
Maria Theresa Succeeds to the Austrian Throne (Event). HEur(I-419).
Marianne. *Pierre de Marivaux*. MP12(VII-3728), MPCE(III-1361),
    MP8(V-2925), MP6(IV-1849), MPEur(478), MP3(II-631),
    MWL3(631).
Marianne Thornton. *E. M. Forster*. SCL12(VII-4766), SCL7(IV-2904),
    A57(170).
Marius' Creation of the Private Army (Event). HAnc(I-496).
Marius the Epicurean. *Walter Pater*. MP12(VII-3732),
    MPCE(III-1363), MP8(V-2928), MP6(IV-1851), MPEng(472),
    MPv3(318), MP2(II-630), MWL2(630).
Marjorie Morningstar. *Herman Wouk*. SCL12(VII-4769),
    SCL7(IV-2907), A55(153).
Mark of Zorro, The. Cine(III-1070).
Mark Twain: A Collection of Critical Essays. Twentieth-Century Views
    series. *Henry Nash Smith*. HAmer(II-1149).
Mark Twain: An American Prophet. *Maxwell Geismar*.
    SCL12(VII-4772), A71(200).
Mark Twain and Huck Finn. *Walter Blair*. HAmer(II-1148).

Mark Twain Publishes *The Adventures of Huckleberry Finn* (Event).
　　HAmer(II-1146). *See also* Huckleberry Finn.
Market Harborough. *George J. Whyte-Melville.* MP12(VII-3736),
　　MPCE(III-1365),　MP8(V-2931),　MP6(IV-1853),　MPEng(475),
　　MPv4(314),　MP2(II-632),　MWL2(632).
Markings. *Dag Hammarskjöld.* SCL12(VII-4775),　SCL7(IV-2910),
　　A65(195).
Marlborough and the Rise of the British Army. *Christopher T. Atkinson.*
　　HEur(I-394).
Marlborough, His Life, and Times. *Winston S. Churchill.* HEur(I-392).
Marlborough's Duchess. *Louis Kronenberger.* SCL12(VII-4779),
　　SCL7(IV-2914),　A59(155).
Marmion. *Sir Walter Scott.* MP12(VII-3739),　MPCE(III-1366),
　　MP8(V-2934),　MP6(IV-1856),　MPPo(181),　MPv3(320),
　　MP2(II-635),　MWL2(635).
Marnie. Cine(III-1076).
Marquand: An American Life. *Millicent Bell.* LA80(II-517).
*Marquise Went Out at Five, The. *Claude Mauriac.* SCL12(VII-4783),
　　SCL7(IV-2918),　A63(139).
*Marriage à la Mode. *John Dryden.* MP12(VII-3742),
　　MPCE(III-1367),　MP8(V-2937),　MP6(IV-1858),　MPDr(497),
　　MP3(II-634),　MWL3(634).
Marriage and Celibacy. *Max Thurian.* HAnc(III-1260).
Marriage of Ferdinand and Isabella (Event).　HEur(I-1).
Marriage of Figaro, The. *Pierre A. Caron de Beaumarchais.*
　　MP12(VII-3745),　MPCE(III-1369),　MP8(V-2939),
　　MP6(IV-1860),　MPDr(499),　MPv3(323),　MP2(II-637),
　　MWL2(637).
*Marriages and Infidelities. *Joyce Carol Oates.* SCL12(VII-4786),
　　A73(234).
Married Man, A. *Piers Paul Read.* LA80(II-522).
Marry Me. *John Updike.* LA77(II-485).
Mars at Last. *Mark Washburn.* HWor(III-1299).
Marse Chan. *Thomas Nelson Page.* MP12(VII-3748),　MPCE(III-1370),
　　MP8(V-2941),　MP6(IV-1861),　MPAm(399),　MPv4(316),
　　MP2(II-638),　MWL2(638).
Marshall Mission to China, The (Event). HAmer(III-1765).
Marshall Plan and Its Meaning, The. *Harry Bayard Price.* HEur(III-1535).
Marshall Plan Is Announced, The (Event). HEur(III-1532).
Marsilius of Padua: The Defender of Peace, Vol. I: Marsilius of Padua and
　　Medieval Political Philosophy. *Alan Gewirth.* HAnc(III-1611).
Martereau. *Nathalie Sarraute.* SCL12(VII-4790),　SCL7(IV-2921),
　　A60(156).
*Martial Spirit: A Study of Our War with Spain, The. *Walter Millis.*
　　HAmer(II-1288).

Martian Chronicles, The.   *Ray Bradbury*.   SF(III-1348).

Martian Odyssey and Other Science Fiction Tales, A.   *Stanley G. Weinbaum*.   SF(III-1353).

Martian Time Slip.   *Philip K. Dick*.   SF(III-1357).

Martians, Go Home.   *Fredric Brown*.   SF(III-1362).

*Martin Chuzzlewit.   *Charles Dickens*.   MP12(VII-3751), MPCE(III-1372),   MP8(V-2943),   MP6(IV-1863),   MPEng(478), MPv3(324),   MP2(II-640),   MWL2(640).

Martin Luther: A Selection from His Writings.   *John Dillenberger*.   HEur(I-56).

Marty.   Cine(III-1079).

Martyred, The.   *Richard E. Kim*.   SCL12(VII-4793),   SCL7(IV-2924), A65(199).

Martyrdom and Persecution in the Early Church.   *W. H. C. Frend*.   Different analyses on this title appear in: HAnc(II-639; II-814).

Martyrdom of Ignatius of Antioch (Event).   HAnc(II-696).

Martyrdom of Saint Peter in Rome (Event).   HAnc(II-643).

Marxism: An Historical and Critical Study.   *George Lichtheim*.   Different analyses on this title appear in: HEur(II-784; II-900).

Mary.   *Vladimir Nabokov*.   SCL12(VII-4796),   A71(202).

Mary Barton.   *Mrs. Elizabeth Gaskell*.   MP12(VII-3756),   MP8(V-2947), MP4(I-594),   MWL4(594).

Mary Queen of Scots.   *Lady Antonia Fraser*.   SCL12(VII-4800), A70(198).

Mary Wollstonecraft.   *Eleanor Flexner*.   SCL12(VII-4806),   A73(238).

Masaryk Case, The.   *Claire Sterling*.   HWor(II-631).

M*A*S*H.   Cine(III-1083).

Mass Culture: The Popular Arts in America.   *Bernard Rosenberg* and *David Manning White*.   HAmer(III-1503).

Mass for the Dead, A.   *William Gibson*.   SCL12(VII-4810), SCL7(IV-2927),   A69(222).

Mass of the Roman Rite, The.   *Josef A. Jungmann, S. J.*   Different analyses on this title appear in: RCa(II-949),   HAnc(II-1071).

Massacre at Montségur.   *Zoé Oldenbourg*.   SCL12(VII-4817), SCL7(IV-2934),   A63(142).

Massacre of St. Bartholomew, The.   *Henri Noguères*.   HEur(I-188).

Massacre of St. Bartholomew's Day (Event).   HEur(I-184).

*Master Builder, The.   *Henrik Ibsen*.   MP12(VII-3759), MPCE(III-1373),   MP8(V-2950),   MP6(IV-1866),   MPDr(501), MPv3(328),   MP2(II-643),   MWL2(643).

*Master of Ballantrae, The.   *Robert Louis Stevenson*.   MP12(VII-3764), MPCE(III-1377),   MP8(V-2952),   MP6(IV-1868),   MPEng(482), MP1(I-568),   MWL1(568).

Master of Go, The.   *Yasunari Kawabata*.   SCL12(VII-4820),   A73(242).

Master Roger Williams.   *Ola E. Winslow*.   HAmer(I-100).

Meaning of God in Human Experience, The. *William Ernest Hocking.* RCh(II-869).

Meaning of Hitler, The. *Sebastian Haffner.* LA80(II-528).

Meaning of Man, The. *Jean Mouroux.* RCa(II-933).

Meaning of Revelation, The. *H. Richard Niebuhr.* RCh(II-1054).

Meaning of Stoicism, The. *Ludwig Edelstein.* HAnc(I-391).

Meaning of Truth, The. *William James.* Ph(II-784).

Meaning of Yalta, The. *John L. Snell.* HEur(III-1504).

Means and Ends in American Abolitionism: Garrison and His Critics on Strategy and Tactics, 1834-1850. *Aileen S. Kraditor.* HAmer(II-722).

Meany: A Biography of the Unchallenged Strong Man of American Labor. *Joseph C. Goulden.* HWor(II-733).

*Measure for Measure. *William Shakespeare.* MP12(VII-3793), MPCE(III-1387), MP8(V-2975), MP6(IV-1884), MPDr(506), MPv3(330), MP2(II-648), MWL2(648).

Measure My Love. *Helga Sandburg.* SCL12(VII-4854), SCL7(IV-2954), A60(158).

Measure of Man, The. *Joseph Wood Krutch.* SCL12(VII-4858), SCLs(182).

Mechanicals, The. *L. T. C. Rolt.* HEur(II-1103).

*Medea. *Euripides.* MP12(VII-3798), MPCE(III-1390), MP8(V-2978), MP6(IV-1887), MPDr(509), MP1(II-573), MWL1(573).

Mediaeval Mind: A History of the Development of Thought and Emotion in the Middle Ages, The. *Henry Osborn Taylor.* HAnc(II-1003).

Medieval Foundation of England, The. *Sir Arthur Bryant.* SCL12(VII-4861), SCL7(IV-2958), A68(196).

Mediator Dei. *Pope Pius XII.* RCa(II-915).

"Medical Education and Practice in Medieval Islam," *in O'Malley's* The History of Medical Education. *Sami K. Hamarneh.* Different analyses on this title appear in: HAnc(II-1181; III-1228).

Medical Nemesis. *Ivan D. Illich.* LA77(II-489).

Medical Writings of Rhazes (Event). HAnc(II-1179).

Medieval Cities. *Henri Pirenne.* HAnc(II-1133).

Medieval Manichee: A Study of the Christian Dualist Heresy, The. *Steven Runciman.* HAnc(III-1444).

Medieval Philosophy. *Frederick C. Copleston, S. J.* HAnc(II-836).

Medieval Technology and Social Change. *Lynn White, Jr.* Different analyses on this title appear in: HAnc(II-1101; II-1170; III-1512).

Medieval Town, The. *John H. Mundy* and *Peter Riesenberg.* HAnc(III-1326).

Medieval Town, The. *Fritz Rörig.* HAnc(III-1432).

Medieval University, The. *Lowrie J. Daly, S. J.* HAnc(III-1481).

Medieval University, The. *H. Wieruszowski.* HAnc(III-1403).

Meditations. *Marcus Aurelius (Marcus Aurelius Antoninus).*

MP12(VII-3802), MP8(V-2980), MP6(IV-1888), MPNf(201), MP3(II-644), MWL3(644). A different analysis on this title appears in: Ph(I-229).

Meditations on First Philosophy. *René Descartes.* Ph(I-386).

Meditations on the Life of Christ. *Saint Bonaventure.* RCa(I-455).

Mediterranean and the Mediterranean World in the Age of Philip II, The. *Fernand Braudel.* SCL12(VII-4863), A76(202).

Medusa and the Snail: More Notes of a Biology Watcher, The. *Lewis Thomas.* LA80(II-533).

Meek Heritage. *Frans Eemil Sillanpää.* MP12(VII-3804), MPCE(III-1393), MP8(V-2982), MP6(IV-1890), MPEur(488), MPv4(320), MP2(II-650), MWL2(650).

Meet John Doe. Cine(III-1087).

Meet Me in St. Louis. Cine(III-1091).

Meet Me in the Green Glen. *Robert Penn Warren.* SCL12(VII-4867), A72(219).

Meet Your Ancestors. *Roy Chapman Andrews.* HEur(II-825).

Meeting at Potsdam. *Charles L. Mee, Jr.* SCL12(VII-4870), A76(206).

Meeting House and Counting House: The Quaker Merchants of Colonial Philadelphia, 1682-1763. *Frederick B. Tolles.* HAmer(I-159).

Meeting of Love and Knowledge, The. *Martin Cyril D'Arcy, S. J.* RCa(II-1040).

Meeting of the Fourth Lateran Council (Event). HAnc(III-1457).

Meeting of the Washington Disarmament Conference (Event). HAmer(III-1531).

Megalopolis: The Urbanized Northeastern Seaboard of the United States. *Jean Gottmann.* HAmer(III-1815).

Melbourne. *Lord David Cecil.* SCL12(VII-4874), SCL7(V-2961), A54(174), BMA(364).

Mellons: The Chronicle of America's Richest Family, The. *David E. Koskoff.* LA79(I-434).

Melmoth the Wanderer. *Charles Robert Maturin.* MP12(VII-3809), MPCE(III-1396), MP8(V-2985), MP6(IV-1893), MPEng(488), MPv3(332), MP2(II-653), MWL2(653).

Melville: A Collection of Critical Essays. *Richard Chase*, ed. HAmer(II-851).

*Member of the Wedding, The. *Carson McCullers.* MP12(VII-3815), MPCE(III-1400), MP8(V-2988), MP6(IV-1895), MPAm(401); MPv4(322), MP2(II-655), MWL2(655).

Memed, My Hawk. *Yashar Kemal.* SCL12(VII-4877), SCL7(V-2964), A62(202).

*Memento Mori. *Muriel Spark.* MP12(VII-3820), MP8(V-2991), MP4(I-601), MWL4(601).

Memoir of Jacques Cartier, A. *James P. Baxter.* HAmer(I-30).

Memoir of Samuel Slater: The Father of American Manufacturers. *George S. White.* HAmer(I-364).
Memoirs. *Giovanni Jacopo Casanova de Seingalt.* MP12(VII-3823), MP8(V-2994), MP6(IV-1897), MPNf(203), MP3(II-646), MWL3(646).
Memoirs. *Tennessee Williams.* LA77(II-494).
Memoirs: 1925-1950. *George F. Kennan.* SCL12(VII-4892), SCL7(V-2975), A68(198). A different analysis on this title appears in: HEur(III-1557).
Memoirs: 1950-1963. *George F. Kennan.* SCL12(VII-4900), A73(246).
Memoirs by Harry S Truman, Vol. I: Years of Decision. *Harry S Truman.* SCL12(VII-4880), SCL7(V-2967), A55(156). A different analysis on this title appears in: HAmer(III-1762).
Memoirs by Harry S Truman, Vol. II: Years of Trial and Hope. *Harry S Truman.* SCL12(VII-4884), SCL7(V-2971), A57(173). A different analysis on this title appears in: HAmer(III-1785).
Memoirs and Opinions. *Allen Tate.* SCL12(VII-4888), A76(210).
Memoirs Found in a Bathtub. *Stanislaw Lem.* SF(III-1370).
Memoirs of a Cavalier, The. *Daniel Defoe.* MP12(VII-3826), MPCE(III-1403), MP8(V-2997), MP6(IV-1900), MPEng(491), MP3(II-649), MWL3(649).
Memoirs of a Fox-Hunting Man. *Siegfried Sassoon.* MP12(VII-3830), MPCE(III-1404), MP8(V-3000), MP6(IV-1903), MPEng(494), MP1(II-575), MWL1(575).
Memoirs of a Midget. *Walter de la Mare.* MP12(VII-3833), MPCE(III-1405), MP8(V-3003), MP6(IV-1905), MPEng(497), MP1(II-577), MWL1(577).
*Memoirs of a Physician. *Alexandre Dumas (père).* MP12(VII-3836), MPCE(III-1406), MP8(V-3005), MP6(IV-1907), MPEur(491), MP3(II-651), MWL3(651).
Memoirs of a Survivor, The. *Doris Lessing.* SCL12(VII-4906), A76(214).
Memoirs of an Ex-Prom Queen. *Alix Kates Shulman.* SCL12(VII-4910), A73(251).
Memoirs of an Infantry Officer. *Siegfried Sassoon.* MP12(VII-3842), MPCE(III-1409), MP8(V-3009), MP6(IV-1910), MPEng(499), MP1(II-579), MWL1(579).
Memoirs of Count Witte, The. *Sergei Witte.* HEur(III-1172).
Memoirs of Earl Warren, The. *Earl Warren.* LA78(II-567).
Memoirs of Field-Marshal Montgomery, The. *Viscount Montgomery.* SCL12(VII-4913), SCL7(V-2983), A59(162).
*Memoirs of Hecate County. *Edmund Wilson.* SCL12(VII-4917), SCL7(V-2987), A60(162).
Memoirs of King Abdullah of Transjordan. *Abdullah ibn-Husein, Amir of Transjordan.* HWor(I-496).
Memoirs of the Second World War. *Winston S. Churchill.* HEur(III-1529).

Memoirs of W. B. Yeats. *W. B. Yeats.* SCL12(VII-4921), A74(264).
*Memories of a Catholic Girlhood. *Mary McCarthy.* SCL12(VII-4926), SCL7(V-2991), A58(158).
"Memory of Socrates, The," *in* Paideia: The Ideals of Greek Culture. *Werner W. Jaeger.* HAnc(I-321).
Men and Women. *Robert Browning.* MP12(VII-3846), MP8(V-3012), MP4(I-603), MWL4(603).
Men Die. *H. L. Humes.* SCL12(VII-4929), SCL7(V-2994), A60(165).
Men Like Gods. *H. G. Wells.* SF(III-1375).
Men of Waterloo. *John Sutherland.* HEur(II-620).
Men of West Point: The First 150 Years of the United States Military Academy. *Ernest R. DuPuy.* HAmer(I-435).
Men to Match My Mountains. *Irving Stone.* SCL12(VII-4932), SCL7(V-2997), A57(177).
*Menaechmi, The. *Plautus (Titus Maccius Plautus).* MP12(VII-3849), MPCE(III-1411), MP8(V-3015), MP6(IV-1912), MPDr(511), MP3(II-654), MWL3(654).
Mendel Announces His Laws on Genetics (Event). HEur(II-908).
Meng Tzu. *Mencius.* Ph(I-180).
Meno. *Plato.* Ph(I-64).
*Menteur, Le. *Pierre Corneille.* MP12(VII-3852), MPCE(III-1412), MP8(V-3017), MP6(IV-1914), MPDr(513), MP3(II-656), MWL3(656).
Meraviglie del duemila, Le. *Emilio Salgari.* SF(III-1380).
*Merchant of Venice, The. *William Shakespeare.* MP12(VII-3855), MPCE(III-1413), MP8(V-3020), MP6(IV-1917), MPDr(516), MP1(II-581), MWL1(581).
*Mercier and Camier. *Samuel Beckett.* SCL12(VII-4935), A76(218).
Merciful Disguises. *Mona Van Duyn.* SCL12(VII-4938), A74(269).
Mercy of God, The. *Jean Cau.* SCL12(VII-4942), SCL7(V-3000), A64(175).
Merger of the AFL and the CIO (Event). HWor(II-730).
Meridian. *Alice Walker.* LA77(II-501).
Meriwether Lewis: A Biography. *Richard Dillon.* SCL12(VII-4944), SCL7(V-3003), A66(182). A different analysis on this title appears in: HAmer(I-453).
Mermaid Madonna, The. *Stratis Myrivilis.* SCL12(VII-4949), SCL7(V-3008), A60(168).
Mermaids, The. *Eva Boros.* SCL12(VII-4952), SCL7(V-3011), A57(180).
Merry Monarch. *Hasketh Pearson.* SCL12(VII-4955), SCL7(V-3014), A61(177), BMA(367).
*Merry Wives of Windsor, The. *William Shakespeare.* MP12(VII-3860), MPCE(III-1416), MP8(V-3023), MP6(IV-1919), MPDr(519), MPv3(334), MP2(II-657), MWL2(657).

Message in the Bottle, The. *Walker Percy.* SCL12(VII-4959), A76(221).

Messer Marco Polo. *Donn Byrne.* MP12(VII-3863), MPCE(III-1417), MP8(V-3026), MP6(IV-1921), MPEng(502), MP1(II-584), MWL1(584).

*Metamorphoses, The. *Ovid (Publius Ovidius Naso).* MP12(VII-3866), MP8(V-3028), MP6(IV-1923), MPPo(184), MP3(II-658), MWL3(658). A different analysis on this title appears in: HAnc(II-574).

Metamorphosis of Greece Since World War II, The. *William H. McNeill.* LA79(I-438).

Metaphysics. *Aristotle.* Ph(I-152).

"Metaphysics of the Law of Obscenity, The," *in* The Supreme Court and the Constitution. *Harry Kalven, Jr.* HWor(III-1178).

Methods of Ethics, The. *Henry Sidwick.* Ph(II-671).

Metropolis. *Thea von Harbou.* SF(III-1383).

Metropolitan Opera, The. *Irving Kolodin.* HAmer(II-1137).

Methodism. *Rupert E. Davies.* HEur(I-412).

Meuse-Argonne Offensive (Event). HAmer(III-1466).

Mexican Adventure, The. *Daniel Dawson.* HEur(II-878).

Mexican Adventure of Maximilian (Event). HEur(II-876).

Mexican Revolution, The (Event). HWor(I-69).

Mexican Revolution: The Constitutionalist Years. *Charles Curtis Cumberland.* HWor(I-74).

Mexican War, The. *Otis A. Singletary.* HAmer(II-829).

*MF. *Anthony Burgess.* SCL12(VII-4963), A72(223).

Micah Clarke. *Arthur Conan Doyle.* MP12(VII-3869), MPCE(III-1418), MP8(V-3031), MP6(IV-1925), MPEng(504), MP1(II-585), MWL1(585).

Michael and His Lost Angel. *Henry Arthur Jones.* MP12(VII-3873), MPCE(III-1420), MP8(V-3034), MP6(IV-1928), MPDr(522), MPv4(325), MP2(II-660), MWL2(660).

Michael Faraday: A Biography. *L. Pearce Williams.* HEur(II-650).

Michaelmas. *Algis Budrys.* SF(III-1387).

Microbe Hunters. *Paul De Kruif.* HEur(III-1177).

Microcosmus. *Rudolf Hermann Lotze.* Ph(II-638).

*Midcentury. *John Dos Passos.* SCL12(VII-4966), SCL7(V-3018), A62(205).

Mid-Channel. *Arthur Wing Pinero.* MP12(VII-3877), MP8(V-3037), MP6(IV-1930), MPDr(525), MP3(II-661), MWL3(661).

*Middle Age of Mrs. Eliot, The. *Angus Wilson.* SCL12(VIII-4971), SCL7(V-3023), A60(171).

Middle East Reader, The. *Irene L. Gendzier,* ed. HWor(I-147).

Middle-Class Democracy and the Revolution in Massachusetts, 1691-1780. *Robert E. Brown.* HAmer(I-292).

*Middlemarch. *George Eliot.* MP12(VII-3879), MPCE(III-1422), MP8(V-3039), MP6(IV-1932), MPEng(507), MP1(II-588),

MWL1(588).

Midnight Cowboy. Cine(III-1095).

Midnight Cowboy. *James Leo Herlihy.* SCL12(VIII-4975),
SCL7(V-3026), A66(186).

Midnight Oil. *V. S. Pritchett.* SCL12(VIII-4978), A73(254).

*Midpoint and Other Poems. *John Updike.* SCL12(VIII-4983),
A70(203).

*Midsummer Night's Dream, A. *William Shakespeare.* MP12(VII-3885),
MPCE(III-1425), MP8(V-3042), MP6(IV-1935), MPDr(527),
MPv3(337), MP2(II-662), MWL2(662).

Midway: The Battle That Doomed Japan. *Mitsuo Fuchida* and *Masatake
Okumiya.* SCL12(VIII-4987), SCL7(V-3029), A55(160). A
different analysis on this title appears in: HWor(I-476).

Midwestern Progressive Politics, 1870-1958. *Russel B. Nye.*
HAmer(II-1309).

Midwich Cuckoos, The. *John Wyndham.* SF(III-1391).

Mightiest Machine, The. *John W. Campbell, Jr.* SF(III-1396).

*Mighty and Their Fall, The. *Ivy Compton-Burnett.* MP12(VII-3890),
MP8(V-3045), MP4(I-606), MWL4(606), SCL12(VIII-4991),
SCL7(V-3033), A63(145), BMA(371).

Mighty Stonewall. *Frank E. Vandiver.* SCL12(VIII-4995),
SCL7(V-3036), A58(161).

Miguel Seizes the Portuguese Throne (Event). HEur(II-675).

*Mikado, The. *W. S. Gilbert.* MP12(VII-3893), MPCE(III-1428),
MP8(V-3048), MP6(IV-1937), MPDr(530), MP1(II-591),
MWL1(591).

Mildred Pierce. Cine(III-1098).

*Military Philosophers, The. *Anthony Powell.* SCL12(VIII-4998),
A70(207).

Mill and Liberalism. *Maurice Cowling.* HEur(II-846).

*Mill on the Floss, The. *George Eliot.* MP12(VII-3896),
MPCE(III-1429), MP8(V-3050), MP6(IV-1939), MPEng(510),
MP1(II-593), MWL1(593).

Mill on the Po, The. *Riccardo Bacchelli.* MP12(VII-3901),
MPCE(III-1432), MP8(V-3053), MP6(IV-1941), MPEur(495),
MPv3(339), MP2(II-664), MWL2(664).

Millennium of Europe, The. *Oscar Halecki.* RCa(II-1128).

Million and One Nights: A History of the Modern Motion Picture Through
1925, A. *Terry Ramsaye.* HAmer(II-1337).

Million Dollar Legs. Cine(III-1101).

Million Dollar Mermaid. Cine(III-1104).

Millions of Strange Shadows. *Anthony Hecht.* LA78(II-572).

Military History and Atlas of the Napoleonic Wars, A. *Vincent J. Esposito*
and *John Robert Elting.* HEur(II-571).

Military History of the Western World, Vol. I: From the Earliest Times to the

Battle of Lepanto, A. *John F. C. Fuller.* Different analyses on this title appear in: HAnc(II-580; II-978; II-1119).

Military History of the Western World, Vol. II: From the Defeat of the Spanish Armada, 1588, to the Battle of Waterloo, A. *John F. C. Fuller.* HEur(I-315).

Milton and the English Revolution. *Christopher Hill.* LA79(I-444).

Milton and the Puritan Dilemma. *Arthur E. Barker.* HEur(I-322).

Milton in the Puritan Revolution. *Don M. Wolfe.* HEur(I-321).

Milton Publishes *Areopagitica* (Event). HEur(I-317). *See also* Areopagitica.

Min and Bill. Cine(III-1107).

Minamata. *W. Eugene Smith* and *Aileen M. Smith.* SCL12(VIII-5003), A76(225).

Mind and Art of Henry Adams, The. *Jacob C. Levenson.* HAmer(II-1187).

Mind and Heart of Love, The. *Martin Cyril D'Arcy, S. J.* RCa(II-909).

Mind and Its Place in Nature, The. *Charlie Dunbar Broad.* Ph(II-862).

Mind and Nature: A Necessary Unity. *Gregory Bateson.* LA80(II-536).

Mind and the World Order. *Clarence Irving Lewis.* Ph(II-914).

Mind of Primitive Man, The. *Franz Boas.* MP12(VII-3906), MP8(V-3056), MP4(I-608), MWL4(608).

Mind Parasites, The. *Colin Wilson.* SCL12(VIII-5008), SCL7(V-3039), A68(205). A different analysis on this title appears in: SF(III-1401).

Mind, Self, and Society. *George Herbert Mead.* Ph(II-992).

Mindbridge. *Joe Haldeman.* SF(III-1407).

Mind-Reader, The. *Richard Wilbur.* LA77(II-505).

Mind's Road to God, The. *Saint Bonaventure.*
    See Journey of the Mind to God.

Mindswap. *Robert Sheckley.* SF(III-1413).

*Ministry of Fear, The. *Graham Greene.* MP12(VII-3909), MPCE(III-1434), MP8(V-3059), MP6(IV-1944), MPEng(513), MPv3(341), MP2(II-666), MWL2(666).

*Minna von Barnhelm. *Gotthold Ephraim Lessing.* MP12(VII-3912), MPCE(III-1435), MP8(V-3062), MP6(IV-1946), MPDr(532), MPv4(327), MP2(II-668), MWL2(668).

Mirabell: Books of Number. *James Merrill.* LA79(I-448).

Miracle of Morgan's Creek, The. Cine(III-1111).

Miracle of the Met: An Informal History of the Metropolitan Opera, 1883-1967, The. *Quaintaince Eaton.* HAmer(II-1138).

Mirror for Observers, A. *Edgar Pangborn.* SF(III-1417).

Mirror for Witches, A. *Esther Forbes.* MP12(VII-3917), MPCE(III-1438), MP8(V-3065), MP6(IV-1948), MPAm(404), MPv4(329), MP2(II-671), MWL2(671).

Mirrors & Windows: Poems. *Howard Nemerov.* SCL12(VIII-5012), SCL7(V-3043), A59(164).

*Misanthrope, The. *Molière (Jean Baptiste Poquelin).* MP12(VII-3921), MPCE(III-1440), MP8(V-3068), MP6(IV-1950), MPDr(535),

MP1(II-595),   MWL1(595).
Miscellanies. *Abraham Cowley.*   MP12(VII-3926),   MP8(V-3070),
    MP6(IV-1952),   MPPo(187),   MP3(II-663),   MWL3(663).
*Miser, The. *Molière (Jean Baptiste Poquelin).*   MP12(VII-3928),
    MPCE(III-1443),   MP8(V-3072),   MP6(IV-1954),   MPDr(537),
    MPv3(343),   MP2(II-673),   MWL2(673).
Miserables, Les.   Cine(III-1114).
*Misérables, Les. *Victor Hugo.*   MP12(VII-3931),   MPCE(III-1445),
    MP8(V-3074),   MP6(IV-1956),   MPEur(498),   MP1(II-597),
    MWL1(597).
Misfits, The.   Cine(III-1117).
Mishima: A Biography. *John Nathan.*   SCL12(VIII-5014),   A75(194).
Misidentification of Dionysius the Areopagite (Event).   HAnc(II-1011).
Miss Herbert. *Christina Stead.*   LA77(II-509).
*Miss Julie. *August Strindberg.*   MP12(VII-3936),   MPCE(III-1448),
    MP8(V-3077),   MP6(IV-1959),   MPDr(539),   MPv4(332),
    MP2(II-675),   MWL2(675).
*Miss Leonora When Last Seen. *Peter Taylor.*   SCL12(VIII-5018),
    SCL7(V-3045),   A65(202).
*Miss Lonelyhearts. *Nathanael West.*   MP12(VII-3941),
    MPCE(III-1451),   MP8(V-3080),   MP6(IV-1961),   MPAm(407),
    MP3(II-664),   MWL3(664).
Miss Ravenel's Conversion. *John William De Forest.*   MP12(VII-3945),
    MPCE(III-1453),   MP8(V-3083),   MP6(IV-1964),   MPAm(410),
    MPv3(345),   MP2(II-677),   MWL2(677).
Missile Crisis, The. *Elie Abel.*   HAmer(III-1890).
Missing Persons and Other Essays. *Heinrich Böll.*   LA78(II-577).
Mission and Achievement of Jesus, The. *Reginald H. Fuller.*
    HAnc(II-592).
Mission of Gravity. *Hal Clement.*   SF(III-1424).
Mission to the Moon: A Critical Examination of NASA and the Space
    Program. *Erlend A. Kennan* and *Edmund H. Harvey, Jr.*
    HAmer(III-1943).
Mississippi Question, 1795-1803: A Study in Trade, Politics, and Diplomacy,
    The. *Arthur P. Whitaker.*   HAmer(I-398).
Mississippi Valley in British Politics, The. *Clarence W. Alvord.*
    HAmer(I-209).
Missolonghi Manuscript, The. *Frederic Prokosch.*   SCL12(VIII-5021),
    SCL7(V-3048),   A69(228).
Missouri Controversy, 1819-1821, The. *Glover Moore.*   HAmer(I-555).
Mr. Balfour's Poodle. *Roy Jenkins.*   HEur(III-1216).
Mr. Baruch. *Margaret L. Coit.*   SCL12(VIII-5024),   SCL7(V-3051),
    A58(163).
*Mr. Bridge. *Evan S. Connell, Jr.*   SCL12(VIII-5027),   A70(212).
Mr. Britling Sees It Through. *H. G. Wells.*   MP12(VII-3949),

MPCE(III-1455),   MP8(V-3086),   MP6(IV-1966),   MPEng(516),
  MP1(II-600),   MWL1(600).
*Mr. Bullivant and His Lambs.   *Ivy Compton-Burnett.*   MP12(VII-3952),
  MP8(V-3089),   MP4(I-611),   MWL4(611).
Mr.Clemens and Mark Twain.   *Justin Kaplan.*   SCL12(VIII-5030),
  SCL7(V-3054),   A67(221).
Mr. Facey Romford's Hounds.   *Robert Smith Surtees.*   MP12(VII-3954),
  MPCE(III-1456),   MP8(V-3091),   MP6(IV-1968),   MPEng(519),
  MPv4(334),   MP2(II-679),   MWL2(679).
Mr. Gallion's School.   *Jesse Stuart.*   SCL12(VIII-5034),   SCL7(V-3058),
  A68(209).
Mr. Midshipman Easy.   *Frederick Marryat.*   MP12(VII-3960),
  MPCE(III-1458),   MP8(V-3096),   MP6(IV-1973),   MPEng(524),
  MP1(II-602),   MWL1(602).
Mister Roberts.   Cine(III-1121).
Mister Roberts.   *Thomas Heggen.*   MP12(VII-3964),   MPCE(III-1460),
  MP8(V-3099),   MP6(IV-1975),   MPAm(413),   MP1(II-605),
  MWL1(605).
Mr. Roosevelt's Navy: The Private War of the U.S. Atlantic Fleet,
  1939-1942.   *Patrick Abbazia.*   HWor(I-408).
*Mr. Sammler's Planet.   *Saul Bellow.*   SCL12(VIII-5037),   A71(208).
Mr. Skeffington.   Cine(III-1125).
Mr. Smith Goes to Washington.   Cine(III-1128).
Mr. Sponge's Sporting Tour.   *Robert Smith Surtees.*   MP12(VII-3967),
  MPCE(III-1461),   MP8(V-3102),   MP6(IV-1977),   MPEng(527),
  MPv3(347),   MP2(II-684),   MWL2(684).
Mr. Weston's Good Wine.   *T. F. Powys.*   MP12(VII-3970),
  MPCE(III-1462),   MP8(V-3105),   MP6(IV-1980),   MPEng(530),
  MPv4(338),   MP2(II-686),   MWL2(686).
*Mrs. Dalloway.   *Virginia Woolf.*   MP12(VII-3973),   MPCE(III-1463),
  MP8(V-3108),   MP6(IV-1982),   MPEng(533),   MP1(II-607),
  MWL1(607).
Mrs. Dane's Defence.   *Henry Arthur Jones.*   MP12(VII-3978),
  MPCE(III-1466),   MP8(V-3111),   MP6(IV-1984),   MPDr(542),
  MPv4(341),   MP2(II-688),   MWL2(688).
Mrs. Miniver.   Cine(III-1131).
*Mistress of the Inn, The.   *Carlo Goldoni.*   MP12(VII-3982),
  MPCE(III-1468),   MP8(V-3114),   MP6(IV-1986),   MPDr(545),
  MPv4(343),   MP2(II-691),   MWL2(691).
Mistress to an Age.   *J. Christopher Herold.*   SCL12(VIII-5042),
  SCL7(V-3061),   A59(167),   BMA(374).
Mrs. Wallop.   *Peter De Vries.*   SCL12(VIII-5046),   A71(213).
Mit brennender Sorge.   *Pope Pius XI.*   RCa(II-860).
*Mithridate.   *Jean Baptiste Racine.*   MP12(VII-3987),   MPCE(III-1471),
  MP8(V-3117),   MP6(IV-1989),   MPDr(548),   MP3(II-667),

Mortgage on the Brain, The. *Vincent Harper.* SF(III-1459).
*Mortgaged Heart, The. *Carson McCullers.* SCL12(VIII-5083),
     A72(225).
Mosby's Memoirs and Other Stories. *Saul Bellow.* SCL12(VIII-5086),
     SCL7(V-3091), A69(234).
Moscow. *Theodor Plevier.* SCL12(VIII-5091), SCL7(V-3096),
     A54(177).
Moshe Dayan. *Moshe Dayan.* LA77(II-513).
Mosquitoes, Malaria and Man: A History of the Hostilities Since
     1880. *Gordon Harrison.* LA79(II-466).
Moss on the North Side. *Sylvia Wilkinson.* SCL12(VIII-5094),
     SCL7(V-3099), A67(225).
Most Likely to Succeed. *John Dos Passos.* SCL12(VIII-5098),
     SCL7(V-3103), A54(180).
Mote in God's Eye, The. *Larry Niven* and *Jerry Pournelle.* SF(III-1463).
*Mother. *Maxim Gorky.* MP12(VII-4072), MP8(V-3176),
     MP6(IV-2034), MPEur(517), MP3(II-676), MWL3(676).
*Mother, The. *Grazia Deledda.* MP12(VII-4068), MPCE(III-1510),
     MP8(V-3173), MP6(IV-2032), MPEur(514), MPv4(356),
     MP2(II-708), MWL2(708).
*Mother and Son. *Ivy Compton-Burnett.* MP12(VII-4076),
     MP8(V-3179), MP4(I-617), MWL4(617), SCL12(VIII-5101),
     SCL7(V-3106), A55(163), BMA(378).
Mother Hubberd's Tale. *Edmund Spenser.* MP12(VII-4078),
     MP8(V-3181), MP4(I-619), MWL4(619).
*Mother Night. *Kurt Vonnegut, Jr.* SCL12(VIII-5104), SCLs(185).
Mother's Breast and the Father's House, The. *Reed Whittemore.*
     SCL12(VIII-5108), A75(198).
Mother's Kisses, A. *Bruce Jay Friedman.* SCL12(VIII-5111),
     SCL7(V-3109), A65(205).
Motor Car, 1765-1914, The. *Anthony Bird.* HEur(II-1034).
Moulin Rouge. Cine(III-1154).
*Mountolive. *Lawrence Durrell.* SCL12(VIII-5114), SCL7(V-3112),
     A60(174), BMA(381).
*Mourning Becomes Electra. *Eugene O'Neill.* MP12(VII-4081),
     MPCE(III-1514), MP8(V-3184), MP6(IV-2037), MPDr(559),
     MPv3(354), MP2(II-710), MWL2(710).
Mouse That Roared, The. Cine(III-1159).
Mousetrap and Other Plays, The. *Agatha Christie.* LA79(II-470).
*Moveable Feast, A. *Ernest Hemingway.* MP12(VII-4087),
     MP8(V-3187), MP4(I-621), MWL4(621). A different analysis on this
     title appears in: SCL12(VIII-5119), SCL7(V-3116), A65(208). A
     different analysis on this title appears in: HAmer(III-1563).
*Moviegoer, The. *Walker Percy.* SCL12(VIII-5122), SCL7(V-3119),
     A62(212).

*Moving On. *Larry McMurtry.* SCL12(VIII-5126), SCLs(188).

Moving Target, The. *W. S. Merwin.* SCL12(VIII-5129), SCL7(V-3123), A64(177).

Moynihan Report and the Politics of Controversy, The. *Lee Rainwater* and *William L. Yancey.* HAmer(III-1868).

Much Abused Letter, A. *George Tyrrell.* RCh(II-844).

*Much Ado About Nothing. *William Shakespeare.* MP12(VII-4090), MPCE(III-1518), MP8(V-3190), MP6(IV-2039), MPDr(562), MPv3(356), MP2(II-712), MWL2(712).

Mulata, The. *Miguel Angel Asturias.* SCL12(VIII-5134), SCL7(V-3128), A68(212).

Mulligan Stew. *Gilbert Sorrentino.* LA80(II-544).

Multinational Empire: Nationalism and National Reform in the Habsburg Monarchy, 1848-1918, Vol. I: Empire and Nationalities, The. *Robert Kann.* Different analyses on this title appear in: HEur(I-482; II-941).

Mumbo Jumbo. *Ishmael Reed.* SCL12(VIII-5139), A73(259).

Mungo Park the African Traveler. *Kenneth Lupton.* LA80(II-550).

Munich. *Keith Eubank.* HEur(III-1432).

Munich: Prologue to Tragedy. *John W. Wheeler-Bennett.* HEur(III-1431).

Munich: The Price of Peace. *Telford Taylor.* LA80(II-555).

Munich Crisis, The (Event). HEur(III-1429).

Municipal Corporations Act (Event). HEur(II-737).

*Murder in the Cathedral. *T. S. Eliot.* MP12(VII-4094), MPCE(III-1521), MP8(V-3192), MP6(IV-2041), MPDr(564), MPv4(358), MP2(II-714), MWL2(714).

Murder, My Sweet. Cine(III-1164).

Murder of Dollfuss (Event). HEur(III-1395).

Murder of Thomas à Becket (Event). HAnc(III-1375).

Murmurs of Earth: The Voyager Interstellar Record. *Carl Sagan,* et al. HWor(III-1314).

Museum Pieces. *William Plomer.* SCL12(VIII-5142), SCL7(V-3133), A54(183).

*Museums and Women and Other Stories. *John Updike.* SCL12(VIII-5145), A73(262).

Music in the Medieval World. *Albert Seay.* HAnc(III-1412).

*Music School, The. *John Updike.* SCL12(VIII-5148), SCL7(V-3136), A67(228).

Muslims of British India, The. *Peter Hardy.* HWor(II-609).

Mussolini Formulates The Doctrine of Fascism (Event). HEur(III-1299).

Mussolini's Italy. *Herman Finer.* HEur(III-1300).

Mussolini's "March on Rome" (Event). HEur(III-1319).

Mussolini's Roman Empire. *Denis Mack Smith.* LA77(II-520).

Mutiny on the Bounty. Cine(III-1167).

Mutiny on the Bounty. *Charles Nordhoff* and *James Norman Hall.* MP12(VII-4099), MPCE(III-1524), MP8(V-3195),

MP6(IV-2044),   MPAm(427),   MP1(II-628),   MWL1(628).

"M. V. Lomonosov and the Founding of Moscow University," *in* Readings in Russian History and Culture.   *I. Spector* and *M. Spector*. HEur(I-433).

*My Ántonia.   *Willa Cather*.   MP12(VII-4103),   MPCE(III-1526), MP8(V-3198),   MP6(IV-2046),   MPAm(430),   MP1(II-630), MWL1(630).

My Autobiography.   *Charles Chaplin*.   SCL12(VIII-5152), SCL7(V-3140),   A65(211).

My Bones Being Wiser.   *Vassar Miller*.   SCL12(VIII-5156),   SCLs(191).

My Brother's Keeper.   *Stanislaus Joyce*.   SCL12(VIII-5159), SCL7(V-3144),   A59(171).

My Experience in the World War.   *John J. Pershing*.   HAmer(III-1470).

My Fair Lady.   Cine(III-1170).

My Fair Lady.   *Alan Jay Lerner*.   SCL12(VIII-5163),   SCL7(V-3148), A57(182),   BMA(385).

My Father, Marconi.   *Degna M. Marconi*.   HEur(II-1081).

My Father's House.   *Philip B.Kunhardt, Jr.*   SCL12(VIII-5166), SCLs(194).

My Father's Son.   *Frank O'Connor*.   SCL12(VIII-5169),   A70(215).

My Favorite Wife.   Cine(III-1175).

My God and My All: The Life of St. Francis of Assisi.   *Elizabeth Goudge*. HAnc(III-1449).

My Lady Suffolk.   *Evelyn Read*.   SCL12(VIII-5172),   SCL7(V-3151), A64(183).

My Lai 4.   *Seymour M. Hersh*.   SCL12(VIII-5175),   A71(216).

My Land Has a Voice.   *Jesse Stuart*.   SCL12(VIII-5180),   SCL7(V-3154), A67(231).

*My Life and Hard Times.   *James Thurber*.   MP12(VII-4108), MP8(V-3201),   MP6(IV-2048),   MPNf(206),   MP3(II-678), MWL3(678).

My Life as a Man.   *Philip Roth*.   SCL12(VIII-5183),   A75(201).

My Life for My Sheep.   *Alfred Duggan*.   SCL12(VIII-5187), SCL7(V-3157),   A55(166).

My Man Godfrey.   Cine(III-1178).

My Petition for More Space.   *John Hersey*.   SCL12(VIII-5190),   A75(205).

My Several Worlds.   *Pearl S. Buck*.   SCL12(VIII-5194),   SCL7(V-3160), A54(186).

My Years with Xerox: The Billions Nobody Wanted.   *John H. Dessauer*. HWor(I-384).

Mysteries of Christianity, The.   *Matthias Joseph Scheeben*.   RCa(II-672).

Mysteries of Paris, The.   *Eugène Sue*.   MP12(VII-4111), MPCE(III-1529),   MP8(V-3204),   MP6(IV-2051),   MPEur(520), MP1(II-632),   MWL1(632).

*Mysteries of Udolpho, The.   *Mrs. Ann Radcliffe*.   MP12(VII-4115),

MPCE(III-1531), MP8(V-3207), MP6(IV-2054), MPEng(552), MP1(II-635), MWL1(635).

Mysterious Island, The. *Jules Verne.* MP12(VII-4121), MPCE(III-1535), MP8(V-3210), MP6(IV-2056), MPEur(523), MP3(II-681), MWL3(681).

*Mystery and Manners. *Flannery O'Connor.* SCL12(VIII-5197), SCLs(196).

Mystery of Being, The. *Gabriel Marcel.* Different analyses on this title appear in: Ph(II-1120), RCa(II-966).

*Mystery of Edwin Drood, The. *Charles Dickens.* MP12(VII-4125), MPCE(III-1537), MP8(V-3213), MP6(IV-2059), MPEng(555), MPv3(358), MP2(II-717), MWL2(717).

Mystical Body of Christ, The. *Pope Pius XII.* RCa(II-886).

Mystical Element of Religion, The. *Baron Friedrich John von Hügel.* RCa(II-749).

Mystical Theology, The. *Dionysius the Pseudo-Areopagite.* RCa(I-218).

Mystical Theology of Saint Bernard, The. *Étienne Gilson.* HAnc(III-1332).

Mysticism and Logic. *Bertrand Russell.* HWor(I-84).

"Myth and Reality in Greek Tragedy," *in* The Discovery of the Mind: The Greek Origins of European Thought. *Bruno Snell.* HAnc(I-250).

Myth Makers: Literary Essays, The. *V. S. Pritchett.* LA80(II-560).

Myth of Liberation, The. *Bennett Kovrig.* HWor(II-595).

*Myth of Sisyphus, The. *Albert Camus.* MP12(VII-4128), MP8(V-3216), MP4(I-624), MWL4(624).

Myth, Oil, and Politics: Introduction to the Political Economy of Petroleum. *Charles F. Doran.* HWor(III-1142).

Myths and Realities: Societies of the Colonial South. *Carl Bridenbaugh.* HAmer(I-215).

NAACP: A History of the National Association for the Advancement of Colored People, Vol. 1: 1909-1920. *Charles Flint Kellogg.* HAmer(III-1386).

Nabokov: His Life in Part. *Andrew Field.* LA78(II-590).

Nabokov-Wilson Letters: Correspondence Between Vladimir Nabokov and Edmund Wilson, 1940-1971, The. *Vladimir Nabokov* and *Edmund Wilson.* LA80(II-564).

Nabou. *Günther Krupkat.* SF(III-1468).

Naissance des dieux, La. *Charles Henneberg.* SF(III-1472).

*Naked and the Dead, The. *Norman Mailer.* SCL12(VIII-5200), SCLs(199).

Naked Ape, The. *Desmond Morris.* SCL12(VIII-5204), SCL7(V-3163), A69(239).

Naked Sun, The. *Isaac Asimov.* SF(III-1476).

Naked to Mine Enemies. *Charles W. Ferguson.* SCL12(VIII-5209), SCL7(V-3168), A59(174).

Naked Year, The. *Boris Pilnyak.* MP12(VII-4131), MPCE(III-1538),
     MP8(V-3219), MP6(IV-2061), MPEur(526), MPv4(360),
     MP2(II-719), MWL2(719).
Names: A Memoir, The. *N. Scott Momaday.* LA78(II-594).
Names and Faces of Heroes, The. *Reynolds Price.* SCL12(VIII-5213),
     SCL7(V-3172), A64(185).
*Nana. *Émile Zola.* MP12(VII-4135), MPCE(III-1540),
     MP8(V-3222), MP6(IV-2064), MPEur(529), MP1(II-638),
     MWL1(638).
Nanga Parbat. *Karl M. Herrligkoffer.* SCL12(VIII-5216),
     SCL7(V-3175), A54(189).
Napoleon: From 18 Brumaire to Tilsit, 1799-1807. *Georges Lefebvre.*
     Different analyses on this title appear in: HEur(I-548; II-558; II-565).
Napoleon and the Birth of Modern Spain. *Gabriel H. Lovett.* Different
     analyses on this title appear in: HEur(II-583; II-596).
Napoleon as Military Commander. *James Marshall-Cornwall.* Different
     analyses on this title appear in: HEur(II-557; II-591).
Napoleon Bonaparte. *Vincent Cronin.* SCL12(VIII-5219), A73(265).
Napoleon Bonaparte. *James M. Thompson.* HEur(II-592).
*Napoleon of Notting Hill, The. *Gilbert Keith Chesterton.*
     MP12(VII-4140), MPCE(III-1543), MP8(V-3225),
     MP6(IV-2066), MPEng(558), MPv3(361), MP2(II-721),
     MWL2(721).
Napoleon Rises to Power in France (Event). HEur(I-547).
Napoleon Symphony. *Anthony Burgess.* LA77(II-525).
Napoleon's Invasion of Russia (Event). HEur(II-585).
Napoleon's Invasion of Russia. *E. V. Tarle.* HEur(II-587).
Napoleon III and Cavour Meet at Plombières (Event). HEur(II-838).
Napoleon III and the Emperor Francis Joseph Meet at Villafranca (Event).
     HEur(II-849).
*Narrative of Arthur Gordon Pym, The. *Edgar Allan Poe.*
     MP12(VII-4143), MPCE(III-1544), MP8(V-2068), MPAm(433),
     MP1(II-640), MWL1(640). A different analysis on this title appears in:
     SF(III-1480).
Narrative of the Life of David Crockett, A. *David Crockett.*
     MP12(VII-4146), MPCE(III-1545), MP8(V-3231),
     MP6(IV-2071), MPNf(209), MPv3(363), MP2(II-724),
     MWL2(724).
Narratives of Exploration and Adventure. *John Charles Frémont.*
     SCL12(VIII-5223), SCL7(V-3178), A57(185).
Nashville. Cine(III-1181).
Nasty Swans, The. *Arkady Strugatsky* and *Boris Strugatsky.* SF(III-1488).
Nat Turner's Slavery Insurrection (Event). HAmer(II-685).
Nathan the Wise. *Gotthold Ephraim Lessing.* MP12(VII-4149),
     MPCE(III-1546), MP8(V-3234), MP6(IV-2073), MPDr(567),

MP3(II-683), MWL3(683).

Nation of Strangers, A. *Vance Packard.* SCL12(VIII-5227), A73(269).

Nation on Trial: America and the War of 1812, A. *Patrick White.* HAmer(I-509).

National Association for the Advancement of Colored People Formed (Event). HAmer(III-1384).

National Consciousness in Divided Germany. *Gebhard Ludwig Schweigler.* HWor(III-1171).

National Insurance Act (Event). HEur(III-1223).

National Land System, 1785-1820, The. *Payson Jackson Treat.* HAmer(I-308).

National Policy for the Environment: NEPA and Its Aftermath, A. *Richard A. Liroff.* HWor(II-876).

National Road, The. *Philip D. Jordan.* HAmer(I-493).

National Workshops: A Study in the French Revolution of 1848, The. *Donald Cope McKay.* HEur(II-787).

Nationalism: A Religion. *Carlton J. H. Hayes.* RCa(II-1091).

Nationalism and Liberty: The Swiss Example. *Hans Kohn.* HAnc(III-1606).

Native Son. *Richard Wright.* MP12(VII-4152), MPCE(III-1547), MP8(V-3236), MP6(IV-2075), MPAm(436), MP1(II-643), MWL1(643).

NATO: The Entangling Alliance. *Robert E. Osgood.* HAmer(III-1809).

Natural and the Supernatural, The. *John Wood Oman.* RCh(II-973).

Natural Histories. *Leslie Ullman.* LA80(II-569).

Natural Religion and Christian Theology. *Charles E. Raven.* RCh(II-1143).

Natural Theology. *William Paley.* RCh(II-641).

Nature and Destiny of Man, The. *Reinhold Niebuhr.* Different analyses on this title appear in: Ph(II-1064), RCh(II-1059).

Nature and Mind. *Frederick James E. Woodbridge.* Ph(II-1021).

Nature, Man and God. *William Temple.* RCh(II-999).

Nature, Mind, and Death. *Curt John Ducasse.* Ph(II-1132).

Nature of Faith, The. *Gerhard Ebeling.* RCh(II-1184).

Nature of Passion, The. *R. Prawer Jhabvala.* SCL12(VIII-5230), SCL7(V-3181), A58(166).

Nature of Physical Reality: Philosophy of Modern Physics, The. *Henry Margenau.* HWor(I-172).

Nature of the Atonement, The. *John McLeod Campbell.* RCh(II-731).

Nature of Thought, The. *Brand Blanshard.* Ph(II-1040).

Nature of Truth, The. *Harold Henry Joachim.* Ph(II-773).

Naughty Marietta. Cine(III-1186).

Nausea. *Jean-Paul Sartre.* MP12(VII-4157), MPCE(III-1550), MP8(V-3239), MP6(IV-2077), MPEur(532), MPv3(365), MP2(II-726), MWL2(726).

Naval Law of Themistocles, The (Event). HAnc(I-226).

T. Washington. *August Meier.* HAmer(II-1251).

Nephew, The. *James Purdy.* SCL12(VIII-5244), SCL7(V-3194),
A61(185).

Nero's Persecution of the Christians (Event). HAnc(II-638).

Nerves. *Lester Del Rey.* SF(III-1510).

Nest of Simple Folk, A. *Seán O'Faoláin.* MP12(VII-4165),
MPCE(III-1554), MP8(V-3245), MP6(IV-2082), MPEng(561),
MPv4(363), MP2(II-728), MWL2(728).

Network. Cine(III-1190).

Never Call Retreat. *Bruce Catton.* SCL12(VIII-5247), SCL7(V-3197),
A66(189). A different analysis on this title appears in: HAmer(II-1013).

Never Give a Sucker an Even Break. Cine(III-1193).

New Age Now Begins, A. *Page Smith.* LA77(II-529).

New & Collected Poems, 1917-1976. *Archibald MacLeish.* LA77(II-534).

New and Selected Poems. *Irving Feldman.* LA80(II-580).

New & Selected Poems. *William Jay Smith.* SCL12(VIII-5252),
A72(228).

New and Selected Poems. *David Wagoner.* SCL12(VIII-5255), A70(217).

New & Selected Things Taking Place. *May Swenson.* LA79(II-472).

*New Atlantis. *Sir Francis Bacon.* MP12(VII-4168), MPCE(III-1555),
MP8(V-3248), MP6(IV-2084), MPNf(212), MP3(II-685),
MWL3(685).

New Bonapartist Generals in the Crimean War: Distrust and Decision-Making
in the Anglo-French Alliance, The. *Brison D. Gooch.* HEur(II-815).

New Class, The. *Milovan Djilas.* SCL12(VIII-5259), SCL7(V-3202),
A58(169).

*New Criticism, The. *John Crowe Ransom.* MP12(VII-4171),
MP8(V-3250), MP4(I-626), MWL4(626).

New Critique of Theoretical Thought, A. *Herman Dooyeweerd.*
RCh(II-1016).

New Deal Collective Bargaining Policy, The. *Irving Bernstein.*
HAmer(III-1639).

New England Mind, Vol. I: The Seventeenth Century, The. *Perry Miller.*
HAmer(I-129).

New England Mind, Vol. II: From Colony to Province, The. *Perry Miller.*
HAmer(I-129).

New English Bible, The. *Oxford/Cambridge University Presses.*
SCL12(VIII-5262), SCL7(V-3205), A62(215).

New Essays on the Human Understanding. *Gottfried Wilhelm von Leibniz.*
Ph(I-518).

New Golden Land, The. *Hugh Honour.* LA77(II-538).

*New Grub Street, The. *George Gissing.* MP12(VII-4174),
MPCE(III-1556), MP8(V-3253), MP6(IV-2086), MPEng(564),
MP1(II-647), MWL1(647).

New Harmony, Indiana, and the Communitarian Movement (Event).

HAmer(I-511).

*New Héloïse, The. *Jean Jacques Rousseau.* MP12(VII-4177),
MPCE(III-1557), MP8(V-3256), MP6(IV-2088), MPEur(535),
MPv3(367), MP2(II-730), MWL2(730).

New History of India, A. *Stanley Wolpert.* LA78(II-598).

New History of Portugal, A. *Harold V. Livermore.* Different analyses on
this title appear in: HEur(I-306; II-646; II-676; II-723; III-1220).

New Immigration and the Establishment of Ellis Island Immigration Station,
The (Event). HAmer(II-1219).

"New Laws" of Spain, The (Event). HEur(I-129).

*New Life, A. *Bernard Malamud.* SCL12(VIII-5264), SCL7(V-3207),
A62(217).

New Life of Anton Chekhov, A. *Ronald Hingley.* LA77(II-543).

"New Light on the History of the Federal Judiciary Act of 1789," *in* Harvard
Law Review. *Charles Warren.* HAmer(I-348).

New Lives. *Dorothy Rabinowitz.* LA77(II-549).

*New Men, The. *C. P. Snow.* SCL12(VIII-5267), SCL7(V-3210),
A55(172), BMA(388).

New Mencken Letters, The. *Carl Bode,* ed. LA78(II-603).

New Nation: A History of the United States During the Confederation,
1781-1789, The. *Merrill Jensen.* Different analyses on this title appear
in: HAmer(I-290; I-327).

New Philosophy of Henri Bergson, The. *Eduard Le Roy.* HEur(III-1184).

New Poems. *Eugenio Montale.* LA77(II-553).

New Poems. *Pablo Neruda.* SCL12(VIII-5270), A73(272).

New Poems. *Kenneth Rexroth.* SCL12(VIII-5273), A75(209).

New Poems: 1965-1969. *A. D. Hope.* SCL12(VIII-5276), A71(220).

New Poetry Movement, The (Event). HAmer(III-1399).

New Poor Law, The (Event). HEur(II-730).

New Reformation. *Paul Goodman.* SCL12(VIII-5280), A71(223).

New Science, The. *Giovanni Battista Vico.* Different analyses on this title
appear in: Ph(I-477), RCa(II-618).

New Solutions of New Testament Problems. *Edgar Johnson Goodspeed.*
HAnc(II-782).

New South Creed, The. *Paul M. Gaston.* SCL12(VIII-5283), A71(225).

New Testament Apologetic. *Barnabas Lindars.* HAnc(II-707).

*New Way to Pay Old Debts, A. *Philip Massinger.* MP12(VII-4180),
MPCE(III-1558), MP8(V-3259), MP6(IV-2090), MPDr(569),
MPv3(369), MP2(II-732), MWL2(732).

New World, The. *Winston S. Churchill.* SCL12(VIII-5286),
SCL7(V-3213), A57(188), BMA(391).

New York Jew. *Alfred Kazin.* LA79(II-475).

*Newcomes, The. *William Makepeace Thackeray.* MP12(VII-4185),
MPCE(III-1561), MP8(V-3261), MP6(IV-2092), MPEng(567),
MP1(II-650), MWL1(650).

News from Nowhere. *William Morris.* SF(III-1516).

News of the Nile. *R. H. W. Dillard.* SCL12(VIII-5290), A72(231).

Next Chapter, The. *André Maurois.* SF(III-1521).

Next 200 Years: A Scenario for America and the World, The. *Herman Kahn,*
William Brown and *Leon Martel.* Different analyses on this title appear
in: LA77(II-559), HWor(II-547).

Nez Perce Indians and the Opening of the Northwest, The. *Alvin M.*
Josephy, Jr. SCL12(VIII-5293), SCL7(V-3217), A66(193).

*Nibelungenlied, The. *Unknown.* MP12(VII-4190), MPCE(III-1564),
MP8(V-3264), MP6(IV-2095), MPEur(538), MP1(II-652),
MWL1(652).

"Nibelungenlied: eine stauffische Elegie oder ein Deutsches Nationalepos?,
Das," *in* Dichtung und Volkstum. *Hans Naumann.* HAnc(III-1406).

Nibelungenlied: Entstehung und Gestalt, Das. *Friedrich Panzer.*
HAnc(III-1407).

Nicholas and Alexandra. *Robert K. Massie.* SCL12(VIII-5296),
SCL7(V-3220), A68(217).

Nicholas Biddle: Nationalist and Public Banker, 1786-1844. *Thomas P.*
Govan. HAmer(I-542).

*Nicholas Nickleby. *Charles Dickens.* MP12(VII-4195),
MPCE(III-1567), MP8(V-3267), MP6(IV-2098), MPEng(570),
MPv3(371), MP2(II-734), MWL2(734).

"Nicholas of Cusa," *in* Vol. III *of* A History of Philosophy. *Frederick C.*
Copleston, S.J. HAnc(III-1711).

Nicholas of Cusa Writes *De Docta Ignorantia* (Event). HAnc(III-1708). *See*
also Of Learned Ignorance.

Nicholas I: Emperor and Autocrat of All the Russias. *W. Bruce Lincoln.*
LA79(II-479).

*Nick of the Woods. *Robert Montgomery Bird.* MP12(VII-4199),
MPCE(III-1569), MP8(V-3270), MP6(IV-2101), MPAm(442),
MPv4(365), MP2(II-737), MWL2(737).

Nickel Miseries. *Ivan Gold.* SCL12(VIII-5301), SCLs(202).

Nickel Mountain. *John Gardner.* SCL12(VIII-5304), A74(273).

Niels Lyhne. *Jens Peter Jacobsen.* MP12(VII-4205), MPCE(III-1571),
MP8(V-3275), MP6(IV-2105), MPEur(541), MPv3(374),
MP2(II-741), MWL2(741).

Nietzsche Publishes *Thus Spake Zarathustra* (Event). HEur(II-1024). *See*
also Thus Spake Zarathustra.

Nigerian Civil War, The (Event). HWor(II-1003).

*Nigger of the Narcissus, The. *Joseph Conrad.* MP12(VII-4209),
MPCE(III-1573), MP8(V-3278), MP6(IV-2107), MPEng(573),
MPv3(376), MP2(II-743), MWL2(743).

Night and Day. *Tom Stoppard.* LA80(II-586).

Night at Sea, A. *Margaret Lane.* SCL12(VIII-5309), SCL7(V-3225),
A66(196).

Night at the Opera, A.   Cine(III-1196).
Night Comes to the Cumberlands. *Harry M. Caudill.*   SCL12(VIII-5313),
    SCL7(V-3229),   A64(188).
Night Flight. *Antoine de Saint-Exupéry.*   MP12(VII-4212),
    MPCE(III-1574),   MP8(V-3281),   MP6(IV-2110),   MPEur(544),
    MP3(II-687),   MWL3(687).
Night in the Luxembourg, A. *Remy de Gourmont.*   MP12(VII-4215),
    MPCE(III-1575),   MP8(V-3284),   MP6(IV-2112),   MPEur(547),
    MP1(II-655),   MWL1(655).
Night Light. *Donald Justice.*   SCL12(VIII-5317),   SCL7(V-3233),
    A68(221).
Night of the Hunter, The.   Cine(III-1200).
Night of the Hunter, The. *Davis Grubb.*   SCL12(VIII-5320),
    SCL7(V-3236),   A54(192).
*Night of the Iguana, The. *Tennessee Williams.*   SCL12(VIII-5323),
    SCL7(3239),   A63(154).
Night of Time, The. *René Fülöp-Miller.*   SCL12(VIII-5327),
    SCL7(V-3242),   A55(175).
*Night Rider. *Robert Penn Warren.*   MP12(VII-4218),   MP8(V-3286),
    MP4(I-628),   MWL4(628).
Night to Remember, A.   Cine(III-1203).
Night to Remember, A. *Walter Lord.*   SCL12(VIII-5330),
    SCL7(V-3245),   A55(178).
Night Visitor and Other Stories, The. *B. Traven.*   SCL12(VIII-5334),
    SCL7(V-3249),   A67(239).
Nightmare. *J. Anthony Lukas.*   LA77(II-565).
Nightmare Abbey. *Thomas Love Peacock.*   MP12(VII-4221),
    MPCE(III-1577),   MP8(V-3289),   MP6(IV-2113),   MPEng(576),
    MP1(II-657),   MWL1(657).
Nightmare Alley.   Cine(III-1207).
Nightmares of Eminent Persons. *Bertrand Russell.*   SCL12(VIII-5337),
    SCL7(V-3253),   A55(181).
Nights and Days. *James Merrill.*   SCL12(VIII-5341),   SCL7(V-3257),
    A67(243).
Night-Side. *Joyce Carol Oates.*   LA78(II-608).
Nightwalker and Other Poems. *Thomas Kinsella.*   SCL12(VIII-5345),
    SCL7(V-3261),   A69(243).
Nightwings. *Robert Silverberg.*   SF(III-1526).
Nijinsky. *Richard Buckle.*   SCL12(VIII-5351),   A73(275).
Nine Hours to Rama. *Stanley Wolpert.*   SCL12(VIII-5355),
    SCL7(V-3267),   A63(157).
900 Days, The. *Harrison E. Salisbury.*   SCL12(VIII-5358),   A70(221).
Nine Rivers from Jordan. *Denis Johnston.*   SCL12(VIII-5363),
    SCL7(V-3270),   A55(184).
1918: The Last Act. *Barrie Pitt.*   SCL12(VIII-5366),   SCL7(V-3273),

SF(IV-1548).

Norma Rae.   Cine(III-1220).

Norman Conquest, The.   *D. J. A. Matthews.*   HAnc(III-1251).

Norman Thomas.   *W. A. Swanberg.*   LA77(II-570).

Norsemen Discover the New World (Event).   HAmer(I-11).

Norstrilia.   *Cordwainer Smith.*   SF(IV-1555).

North Atlantic Treaty Organization Pact Signed (Event).   HEur(III-1555).

North Carolina: The History of a Southern State.   *Hugh T. Lefler and Albert R. Newsome.*   HAmer(I-136).

North Eastern Railway.   *William W. Tomlinson.*   HEur(II-661).

North Pole, Its Discovery in 1909 Under the Auspices of the Peary Arctic Club, The.   *Robert Edwin Peary.*   HWor(I-65).

North Toward Home.   *Willie Morris.*   SCL12(VIII-5394), SCL7(V-3293),   A68(227).

*Northanger Abbey.   *Jane Austen.*   MP12(VII-4238),   MPCE(III-1583), MP8(V-3302),   MP6(IV-2124),   MPEng(586),   MPv3(378), MP2(II-750),   MWL2(750).

"Northern Frontier Under Augustus, The," *in* Vol. X *of* The Cambridge Ancient History.   *Ronald Syme.*   HAnc(II-586).

Northern Lass, The.   *Richard Brome.*   MP12(VII-4243), MPCE(III-1586),   MP8(V-3305),   MP6(IV-2126),   MPDr(574), MP3(II-689),   MWL3(689).

Northrop Frye on Culture and Literature.   *H. Northrop Frye.* LA79(II-496).

Northwest Passage.   *Kenneth Roberts.*   MP12(VII-4247),   MP8(V-3308), MP4(I-631),   MWL4(631).

Norway Becomes Independent (Event).   HEur(III-1164).

Norwegian Campaign of 1940, The.   *J. L. Moulton.*   HEur(III-1449).

*Nostromo.   *Joseph Conrad.*   MP12(VII-4250),   MPCE(III-1588), MP8(V-3311),   MP6(IV-2129),   MPEng(589),   MPv3(380), MP2(II-752),   MWL2(752).

Not by Bread Alone.   *Vladimir Dudintsev.*   SCL12(VIII-5398), SCL7(V-3297),   A58(172).

Not for Publication.   *Nadine Gordimer.*   SCL12(VIII-5402), SCL7(V-3301),   A66(200).

*Not Honour More.   *Joyce Cary.*   SCL12(VIII-5406),   SCL7(V-3305), A55(187).

Not This Pig.   *Philip Levine.*   SCL12(VIII-5410),   SCL7(V-3308), A69(248).

"Note on the Fall of Babylon, A," *in* Journal of the Ancient Near Eastern Society of Columbia University.   *Howard Wohil.*   HAnc(I-182).

*Notebook 1967-68.   *Robert Lowell.*   SCL12(VIII-5414),   A70(225).

Notebooks: 1935-1942.   *Albert Camus.*   SCL12(VIII-5418), SCL7(V-3312),   A64(194).

Notebooks: 1942-1951.   *Albert Camus.*   SCL12(VIII-5421),

O Lovely England. *Walter de la Mare*. SCL12(VIII-5452),
    SCL7(V-3337), A57(197).
O Lucky Man! Cine(III-1231).
*O Pioneers! *Willa Cather*. MP12(VII-4265), MPCE(III-1591),
    MP8(V-3324), MP6(IV-2134), MPAm(447), MP1(II-663),
    MWL1(663).
O Taste and See. *Denise Levertov*. SCL12(VIII-5455), SCL7(V-3340),
    A65(217).
O the Chimneys. *Nelly Sachs*. SCL12(VIII-5457), SCL7(V-3342),
    A68(231).
O to Be a Dragon. *Marianne Moore*. SCL12(VIII-5460),
    SCL7(V-3345), A60(177), BMA(401).
OAS Suspends the Embargo Against Cuba, The (Event). HWor(III-1251).
Oath of the Tennis Court (Event). HEur(I-506).
Obedience to Authority. *Stanley Milgram*. SCL12(VIII-5464), A75(212).
Oblomov. *Ivan Alexandrovich Goncharov*. MP12(VII-4270),
    MPCE(III-1594), MP8(V-3326), MP6(IV-2136), MPEur(549),
    MPv3(383), MP2(II-755), MWL2(755).
Obscenities. *Michael Casey*. SCL12(VIII-5470), A73(283).
"Obseruations in the Art of English Poesie," *in* Elizabethan
    and Jacobean Quartos. *Thomas Campion*.
    HAnc(III-1350).
Obstacle Race: The Fortunes of Women Painters and Their Work,
    The. *Germaine Greer*. LA80(II-600).
Occupation of California and the Southwest (Event). HAmer(II-818).
Octavius. *Minucius Felix*. Different analyses on this title appear in:
    RCh(I-51), RCa(I-50).
October Country, The. *Ray Bradbury*. SF(IV-1571).
October Light. *John Gardner*. LA77(II-580).
October Manifesto, The (Event). HEur(III-1169).
October Revolution, The (Event). HEur(III-1271).
October Revolution, The. *Roy A. Medvedev*. LA80(II-605).
October the First Is Too Late. *Fred Hoyle*. SF(IV-1574).
Odd Couple, The. Cine(III-1234).
Odd John: A Story Between Jest and Earnest. *Olaf Stapledon*.
    SF(IV-1583).
Odd Woman, The. *Gail Godwin*. SCL12(VIII-5473), A75(218).
Ode to Aphrodite. *Sappho*. MP12(VII-4273), MP8(V-3329),
    MP6(IV-2139), MPPo(189), MP3(II-694), MWL3(694).
*Odyssey: A Modern Sequel, The. *Nikos Kazantzakis*.
    SCL12(VIII-5476), SCLs(205).
*Odyssey, The. *Homer*. MP12(VII-4275), MPCE(III-1595),
    MP8(V-3331), MP6(IV-2140), MPPo(191), MP1(II-665),
    MWL1(665).
Odyssey of a Friend. *Whittaker Chambers*. SCL12(VIII-5481), A71(235).

Old and the Young, The. *Luigi Pirandello.* MP12(VIII-4305),
  MPCE(III-1610), MP8(V-3349), MP6(IV-2153), MPEur(552),
  MP1(II-676), MWL1(676).
*Old Bachelor, The. *William Congreve.* MP12(VIII-4309),
  MPCE(III-1612), MP8(V-3352), MP6(IV-2156), MPDr(581),
  MPv3(387), MP2(II-759), MWL2(759).
Old Bruin: Commodore Matthew C. Perry, 1794-1858. *Samuel Eliot
  Morison.* SCL12(VIII-5510), SCL7(V-3366), A68(234). A different
  analysis on this title appears in: HAmer(II-887).
Old Calabria. *Norman Douglas.* MP12(VIII-4313), MP8(V-3355),
  MP4(I-641), MWL4(641).
*Old Curiosity Shop, The. *Charles Dickens.* MP12(VIII-4316),
  MPCE(III-1614), MP8(V-3358), MP6(IV-2158), MPEng(595),
  MPv3(389), MP2(II-761), MWL2(761).
*Old Fortunatus. *Thomas Dekker.* MP12(VIII-4319), MPCE(III-1615),
  MP8(V-3361), MP6(IV-2160), MPDr(584), MP3(II-696),
  MWL3(696).
*Old Glory, The. *Robert Lowell.* SCL12(VIII-5513), SCL7(V-3369),
  A66(209).
Old Love. *Isaac Bashevis Singer.* LA80(II-614).
Old Maid, The. *Edith Wharton.* MP12(VIII-4322), MPCE(III-1616),
  MP8(V-3364), MP6(IV-2162), MPAm(454), MP1(II-679),
  MWL1(679).
*Old Man and the Sea, The. *Ernest Hemingway.* MP12(VIII-4325),
  MPCE(III-1617), MP8(V-3367), MP6(IV-2165), MPAm(457),
  MPv4(374), MP2(II-764), MWL2(764).
*Old Men at the Zoo, The. *Angus Wilson.* SCL12(VIII-5517),
  SCL7(V-3373), A62(222).
*Old Mortality. *Katherine Anne Porter.* MP12(VIII-4330),
  MPCE(III-1620), MP8(V-3370), MP6(IV-2167), MPAm(460),
  MPv4(376), MP2(II-766), MWL2(766).
Old Mortality. *Sir Walter Scott.* MP12(VIII-4334), MPCE(III-1621),
  MP8(V-3373), MP6(IV-2170), MPEng(598), MP1(II-681),
  MWL1(681).
Old Northwest: Pioneer Period, 1815-1840, The. *R. Carlyle Buley.*
  HAmer(I-530).
Old One and the Wind: Poems, The. *Clarice Short.* SCL12(VIII-5520),
  A74(282).
Old Patagonian Express: By Train Through the Americas, The. *Paul
  Theroux.* LA80(II-619).
Old Red and Other Stories. *Caroline Gordon.* SCL12(VIII-5523),
  SCL7(V-3376), A64(198).
Old Regime and the Revolution, The. *Alexis de Tocqueville.* Different
  analyses on this title appear in: HAnc(III-1736), HWor(III-1342).
Old Regime in Canada, The. *Francis Parkman.* MP12(VIII-4338),

MP8(V-3376),   MP4(I-643),   MWL4(643).
Old St. Paul's. *William Harrison Ainsworth.* MP12(VIII-4341),
   MPCE(III-1622),   MP8(V-3379),   MP6(IV-2172),   MPEng(601),
   MPv3(391),   MP2(II-768),   MWL2(768).
Old Soldiers Never Die. *Wolf Mankowitz.* SCL12(VIII-5525),
   SCL7(V-3378),   A57(200).
Old Tippecanoe: William Henry Harrison and His Time. *Freeman Cleaves.*
   HAmer(II-763).
*Old Wives' Tale, The. *Arnold Bennett.* MP12(VIII-4344),
   MPCE(III-1623),   MP8(V-3382),   MP6(IV-2175),   MPEng(604),
   MP1(II-684),   MWL1(684).
Old Wives' Tale, The. *George Peele.* MP12(VIII-4349),
   MPCE(III-1626),   MP8(V-3385),   MP6(IV-2177),   MPDr(587),
   MPv4(379),   MP2(II-771),   MWL2(771).
Old Woman, the Wife, and the Archer, The. *Donald Keene,* ed.
   SCL12(VIII-5528),   SCL7(V-3381),   A62(224).
*Oldtown Folks. *Harriet Beecher Stowe.* MP12(VIII-4353),
   MPCE(III-1627),   MP8(V-3388),   MP6(IV-2179),   MPAm(463),
   MPv4(381),   MP2(II-773),   MWL2(773).
"Oligarchic Movement in Athens, The," *in* Vol. V of The Cambridge Ancient
   History. *W. S. Ferguson.*   HAnc(I-310).
Oliver! Cine (III-1252).
Oliver Cromwell's Letters and Speeches. *Oliver Cromwell.* RCh(I-493).
Oliver Twist.   Cine(III-1256).
*Oliver Twist. *Charles Dickens.* MP12(VIII-4358),   MPCE(III-1628),
   MP8(V-3392),   MP6(IV-2183),   MPEng(607),   MP1(II-686),
   MWL1(686).
Olympio. *André Maurois.* SCL12(VIII-5531),   SCL7(V-3384),
   A57(203).
Omega: The Last Days of the World. *Camille Flammarion.* SF(IV-1592).
*Omensetter's Luck. *William H. Gass.* SCL12(VIII-5535),   SCLs(209).
Omnivore. *Piers Anthony.* SF(IV-1596).
*Omoo. *Herman Melville.* MP12(VIII-4364),   MPCE(III-1631),
   MP8(V-3396),   MP6(IV-2186),   MPAm(467),   MP1(II-689),
   MWL1(689).
On a Lonesome Porch. *Ovid Williams Pierce.* SCL12(VIII-5540),
   SCL7(V-3387),   A61(188).
On Being and Essence. *Saint Thomas Aquinas.* RCa(I-364).
On Being Blue. *William Gass.* LA77(II-594).
On Borrowed Time. *Leonard Mosley.* SCL12(VIII-5544),   A70(228).
On Crimes and Punishments. *Cesare Bonesana Beccaria.* HWor(III-1282).
On Ecclesiastical Unity. *John Gerson.* RCh(I-299).
On Education. *Juan Luis Vives.* RCa(I-519).
On First Principles. *Origen.*   Different analyses on this title appear in:
   RCh(I-57),   RCa(I-65).

On the Resurrection of the Dead. *Athenagoras.* RCa(I-30).
*On the Road. *Jack Kerouac.* SCL12(VIII-5556), SCL7(V-3398), A58(179).
On the Soul. *Saint Thomas Aquinas.* RCa(I-409).
On the Soul. *Aristotle.* Ph(I-147).
On the Steps of Humility and Pride. *Saint Bernard.* RCa(I-296).
*On the Sublime. *Unknown.* MP12(VIII-4378), MP8(V-3409), MP4(I-650), MWL4(650).
On the Theology of Death. *Karl Rahner.* RCa(II-1047).
On the Town. Cine(III-1259).
On the Trinity. *Saint Augustine.* RCh(I-134).
On the Trinity. *Saint Hilary of Poitiers.* RCh(I-106).
On the Unity of the Catholic Church. *Saint Cyprian of Carthage.* Different analyses on this title appear in: RCh(I-73), RCa(I-75).
On the Virtues in General. *Saint Thomas Aquinas.* RCa(I-413).
On the Waterfront. Cine(III-1262).
*Once and Future King, The. *T. H. White.* MP12(VIII-4381), MP8(V-3412), MP4(II-653), MWL4(653). A different analysis on this title appears in: SCL12(VIII-5560), SCL7(V-3401), A59(183), BMA(410).
Once for the Last Bandit. *Samuel Hazo.* SCL12(VIII-5565), A73(289).
Once to Sinai. *H. F. M. Prescott.* SCL12(VIII-5569), SCL7(V-3406), A59(187).
*Ondine. *Jean Giraudoux.* SCL12(VIII-5572), SCL7(V-3409), A54(201).
One Day. *Wright Morris.* SCL12(VIII-5575), SCL7(V-3412), A66(213).
*One Day in the Life of Ivan Denisovich. *Aleksandr I. Solzhenitsyn.* SCL12(VIII-5581), SCL7(V-3418), A64(203).
*One Fat Englishman. *Kingsley Amis.* SCL12(VIII-5585), SCL7(V-3421), A65(219).
One Flew Over the Cuckoo's Nest. Cine(III-1265).
*One Flew Over the Cuckoo's Nest. *Ken Kesey.* SCL12(VIII-5587), SCL7(V-3423), A63(160).
One Hour with You. Cine(III-1268).
100 Men and a Girl. Cine(III-1272).
One Hundred Years of Solitude. *Gabriel García Márquez.* SCL12(VIII-5590), A71(240).
One in Twenty. *Bryan Magee.* SCL12(VIII-5596), SCL7(V-3426), A67(252).
One Kind of Freedom: The Economic Consequences of Emancipation. *Roger L. Ransom* and *Richard Sutch.* LA78(II-622).
One Night of Love. Cine(III-1275).
One Story of Radar. *Albert Percival Rowe.* HWor(I-327).

One to Count Cadence. *James Crumley.* SCL12(VIII-5600), A70(231).

O'Neill. *Arthur Gelb* and *Barbara Gelb.* SCL12(VIII-5603),
SCL7(V-3429), A63(162), BMA(415).

O'Neill: Son and Artist. *Louis Sheaffer.* SCL12(VIII-5606), A74(285).

Onion Field, The. *Joseph Wambaugh.* SCL12(VIII-5610), A74(289).

Only Angels Have Wings. Cine(III-1279).

Only Child, An. *Frank O'Connor.* SCL12(VIII-5614), SCL7(V-3432),
A62(227).

Only in America. *Harry Golden.* SCL12(VIII-5617), SCL7(V-3435),
A59(190).

Only One Earth: The Care and Maintenance of a Small Planet. *Barbara
Ward* and *René Dubos.* HWor(II-1074).

Only Yesterday: An Informal History of the 1920's. *Frederick Lewis Allen.*
HAmer(III-1579).

Open Letter to the Christian Nobility of the German Nation, An. *Martin
Luther.* RCh(I-330).

Opening of the Chisholm Trail and Rise of the Cattle Kingdom (Event).
HAmer(II-1020).

Opening of the Metropolitan Opera (Event). HAmer(II-1135).

Opening of the St. Lawrence Seaway (Event). HWor(II-783).

Opening of the Santa Fe Trade (Event). HAmer(I-588).

Opening of the Stockton and Darlington Railway (Event). HEur(II-660).

Openings. *Wendell Berry.* SCL12(VIII-5620), SCL7(V-3438),
A69(255).

Opera de Temporibus. *The Venerable Bede.* HAnc(II-860).

Operation of the Pony Express (Event). HAmer(II-925).

Operation Sunrise: The Secret Surrender. *Bradley F. Smith* and *Elena
Agarossi.* LA80(II-631).

Operators, The. *Frank Gibney.* SCL12(VIII-5624), SCL7(V-3441),
A61(191).

Ophiuchi Hotline, The. *John Varley.* SF(IV-1608).

Oppermanns, The. *Lion Feuchtwanger.* HWor(I-244).

Optimist's Daughter, The. *Eudora Welty.* SCL12(VIII-5627), A73(293).

Opus majus. *Roger Bacon.* RCa(I-398).

Opus Oxoniense. *John Duns Scotus.* RCa(I-427).

Opus Posthumous. *Wallace Stevens.* SCL12(VIII-5630), SCL7(V-3444),
A58(182).

Oraşele Înecate. *Felix Aderca.* SF(IV-1613).

Oration and Panegyric Addressed to Origen, The. *Saint Gregory
Thaumaturgus.* RCa(I-69).

Oration on the Dignity of Man. *Giovanni Pico della Mirandola.*
MP12(VIII-4385), MP8(V-3416), MP4(II-655), MWL4(655). A
different analysis on this title appears in: RCa(I-487).

Orbitsville. *Bob Shaw.* SF(IV-1617).

Orchard Keeper, The. *Cormac McCarthy.* SCL12(VIII-5634),

SCL7(V-3448), A66(218).

Orde Wingate. *Christopher Sykes.* SCL12(VIII-5638), SCL7(V-3452), A60(181).

*Ordeal of Gilbert Pinfold, The. *Evelyn Waugh.* MP12(VIII-4387), MP8(V-3418), MP4(II-657), MWL4(657).

Ordeal of Power: A Political Memoir of the Eisenhower Years, The. *Emmet J. Hughes.* HAmer(III-1845).

*Ordeal of Richard Feverel, The. *George Meredith.* MP12(VIII-4390), MPCE(III-1632), MP8(V-3421), MP6(IV-2193), MPEng(611), MP1(II-692), MWL1(692).

Ordeal of the Constitution: The Antifederalists and the Ratification Struggle of 1787-1788, The. *Robert A. Rutland.* HAmer(I-333).

Ordeal of the Union, Vol. II: A House Dividing, 1852-1857. *Allan Nevins.* HAmer(II-874).

Ordeal of the Union, Vol. V: The War for the Union, Part I: The Impoverished War, 1861-1862. *Allan Nevins.* HAmer(II-960).

Ordeal of the Union, Vol. VI: The War for the Union, Part II: War Becomes Revolution, 1862-1863. *Allan Nevins.* HAmer(II-960).

Ordeal of the Union, Vol. VII: The War for the Union, Part III: The Organized War, 1863-1864. *Allan Nevins.* HAmer(II-960).

Ordeal of the Union, Vol. VIII: The War for the Union. Part IV: The Organized War to Victory, 1864-1865. *Allan Nevins.* HAmer(II-960).

Order and History, Vol. III: Plato and Aristotle. *Eric Voegelin.* HAnc(I-345).

Ordinary People. *Judith Guest.* LA77(II-597).

Ordinary Woman, An. *Lucille Clifton.* SCL12(VIII-5642), A75(221).

Ordinatio: Oxford Commentary on the Sentences of Peter Lombard. *John Duns Scotus.* RCh(I-251).

Ordways, The. *William Humphrey.* SCL12(VIII-5645), SCL7(V-3456), A66(221).

Oregon Question: Essays in Anglo-American Diplomacy and Politics, The. *Frederick Merk.* HAmer(II-781).

Oregon Trail, The. *Francis Parkman.* MP12(VIII-4394), MPCE(III-1633), MP8(V-3425), MP6(IV-2196), MPNf(222), MP1(II-695), MWL1(695).

Orfeo. *Politian.* MP12(VIII-4398), MPCE(III-1635), MP8(V-3428), MP6(IV-2199), MPDr(590), MP3(II-702), MWL3(702).

Organization and Administration of the Union Army, 1861-1865, The. *Fred Albert Shannon.* HAmer(II-993).

Organization Man, The. *William H. Whyte, Jr.* SCL12(VIII-5649), SCL7(V-3459), A58(185). A different analysis on this title appears in: HWor (I-530).

Organization of American States (Event). HAmer(III-1789).

Organization of the American Federation of Labor (Event). HAmer(II-1152).

Organization of the German Confederation (Event). HEur(II-602).
Organization of the National Grange of the Patrons of Husbandry (Event).
    HAmer(II-1043).
Organization of the People's Party (Event). HAmer(II-1225).
Organization of the Standard Oil Trust (Event). HAmer(II-1116).
Organon. *Aristotle.* Ph(I-137).
Oriental Religions in Roman Paganism, The. *Franz Cumont.* HAnc(I-435).
Origen. *Jean Daniélou, S. J.* Different analyses on this title appear in:
    HAnc(II-777; II-798).
Origen: *Contra Celsum. Origen. See* Contra Celsum.
Origen and His Work. *Eugene De Faye.* Different analyses on this title
    appear in: HAnc(II-759; II-797).
"Origen and the Tradition of Natural Law Concepts," *in* Dumbarton Oaks
    Papers. *W. A. Banner.* HAnc(II-804).
Origen's Teaching on the Natural Law (Event). HAnc(II-801).
Origin and Form of Early Greek Tragedy, The. *G. F. Else.* HAnc(I-251).
"Origin of Christmas, The," *in* The Early Church, Studies in Early Christian
    History and Theology. *Oscar Cullmann.* HAnc(II-885).
Origin of *Municipia* (Event). HAnc(I-333).
Origin of Printing in Europe, The. *Pierce Butler.* HAnc(III-1715).
Origin of the Brunists, The. *Robert Coover.* SCL12(VIII-5652),
    SCL7(V-3462), A67(255).
"Origin of the Cambridge Modern History, The," *in* The Cambridge Historical
    Journal. *G. N. Clark.* HWor(I-27).
Origin of the Jesuits, The. *James Brodrick, S. J.* Different analyses on this
    title appear in: RCa(II-868), HEur(I-100).
Origin of the New Testament, The. *Adolph Harnack.* HAnc(II-781).
Origin of Writing (Event). HAnc(I-10).
Origins. *Richard E. Leakey* and *Roger Lewin.* HWor(I-222).
Origins of Modern Germany, The. *Geoffrey Barraclough.* Different
    analyses on this title appear in: HAnc(III-1366; III-1475; III-1623;
    III-1638), HEur(I-66).
Origins of Modern Spain, The. *John B. Trend.* HEur(II-1121).
Origins of Prohibition, The. *John Allen Krout.* HAmer(III-1511).
Origins of Russia, The. *George Vernadsky.* HAnc(II-1175).
Origins of the American Revolution, 1759-1766. *Bernhard Knollenberg.*
    HAmer(I-223).
Origins of the Great Schism, The. *Walter Ullmann.* HAnc(III-1683).
Origins of the Second World War, The. *Maurice Baumont.* LA79(II-516).
Origins of the Second World War, The. *A. J. P. Taylor.* Different analyses
    on this title appear in: HWor(I-202; I-344).
Origins of the Triple Alliance. *Archibald C. Coolidge.* HEur(II-1022).
Origins of the War of 1870, The. *Robert Howard Lord.* HEur(II-951).
Origins of the War of 1914, The. *Luigi Albertini.* Different analyses on this
    title appear in: HEur(II-1021; III-1231; III-1247).

Origins of the Whig Party. *E. Malcolm Carroll.* HAmer(II-692).
Origins of the World War, Vol. I: Before Sarajevo, The. *Sidney B. Fay.*
   Different analyses on this title appear in: HEur(II-1073; III-1154;
   III-1195).
Origins of the World War, Vol. II: After Sarajevo, The. *Sidney B. Fay.*
   HEur(III-1245).
Orion Book of Balloons, The. *Charles Dollfus.* HEur(I-500).
*Orlando. *Virginia Woolf.* MP12(VIII-4400), MPCE(III-1636),
   MP8(V-3430), MP6(IV-2201), MPEng(615), MP1(II-698),
   MWL1(698).
*Orlando Furioso. *Ludovico Ariosto.* MP12(VIII-4404),
   MPCE(III-1637), MP8(V-3433), MP6(IV-2203), MPPo(194),
   MPv3(394), MP2(II-776), MWL2(776).
*Orlando Innamorato. *Matteo Maria Boiardo.* MP12(VIII-4410),
   MPCE(III-1640), MP8(V-3437), MP6(IV-2207), MPPo(198),
   MP3(II-703), MWL3(703).
*Orley Farm. *Anthony Trollope.* MP12(VIII-4415), MPCE(III-1641),
   MP8(V-3441), MP6(IV-2210), MPEng(618), MPv3(397),
   MP2(II-780), MWL2(780).
*Oroonoko. *Mrs. Aphra Behn.* MP12(VIII-4421), MPCE(III-1644),
   MP8(V-3445), MP6(IV-2214), MPEng(622), MPv4(385),
   MP2(II-783), MWL2(783).
Orphan, The. *Thomas Otway.* MP12(VIII-4425), MPCE(III-1646),
   MP8(V-3448), MP6(IV-2216), MPDr(592), MP3(II-707),
   MWL3(707).
Orpheus and Eurydice. *Unknown.* MP12(VIII-4428),
   MPCE(III-1648), MP8(V-3450), MP6(IV-2218), MPEur(555),
   MP1(II-700), MWL1(700).
*Orpheus Descending with Battle of Angels. *Tennessee Williams.*
   SCL12(VIII-5656), SCL7(V-3466), A59(193).
Orsinian Tales. *Ursula K. Le Guin.* LA77(II-601).
*Orthodoxy. *Gilbert Keith Chesterton.* RCa(II-744).
Ossius of Cordova: A Contribution to the History of the Constantinian
   Period. *Victor De Clercq.* HAnc(II-875).
Oswald Spengler: A Critical Estimate. *H. Stuart Hughes.* HEur(III-1280).
*Othello. *William Shakespeare.* MP12(VIII-4431), MPCE(III-1651),
   MP8(V-3452), MP6(IV-2219), MPDr(594), MP1(II-701),
   MWL1(701).
Other, The. *Thomas Tryon.* SCL12(VIII-5659), A72(236).
Other America: Poverty in the United States, The. *Michael Harrington.*
   HAmer(III-1867).
Other Days, Other Eyes. *Bob Shaw.* SF(IV-1622).
Other Men's Daughters. *Richard Stern.* SCL12(VIII-5662), A74(294).
Other One, The. *Sidonie Gabrielle Claudine Colette.* MP12(VIII-4436),
   MPCE(III-1654), MP8(V-3455), MP6(IV-2221), MPEur(557),

Outer Space: Prospects for Man and Society. *Lincoln P. Bloomfield.*
HEur(III-1620).
Outlawed Party: Social Democracy in Germany, 1878-1890, The. *Vernon L.
Lidtke.* Different analyses on this title appear in: HEur(II-994;
II-1015).
Outlawing the Spoils: A History of the Civil Service Reform Movement,
1865-1883. *Ari Hoogenboom.* HAmer(II-1131).
Outline of the Theology of the New Testament, An. *Hans Conzelmann.*
HAnc(II-610).
Outlines of Pyrrhonism. *Sextus Empiricus.* Ph(I-234).
Outlyer and Ghazals. *Jim Harrison.* SCL12(VIII-5688), A72(243).
Outpost of Empire: The Story of the Founding of San Francisco. *Herbert E.
Bolton.* HAmer(I-274).
Outsider, The. *Colin Wilson.* SCL12(IX-5693), SCL7(V-3487),
A57(206).
*Overcoat, The. *Nikolai V. Gogol.* MP12(VIII-4452),
MPCE(III-1660), MP8(V-3470), MP6(IV-2230), MPEur(560),
MPv4(387), MP2(II-790), MWL2(790).
Overthrow of Allende and the Politics of Chile, 1964-1976, The. *Paul E.
Sigmund.* LA78(II-630).
Ovid Writes the *Metamorphoses* (Event). HAnc(II-573). *See also*
Metamorphoses, The.
Ox-Box Incident, The. Cine(III-1290).
Ox-Bow Incident, The. *Walter Van Tilburg Clark.* MP12(VIII-4457),
MPCE(III-1663), MP8(V-3473), MP6(IV-2233), MPAm(470),
MP1(II-706), MWL1(706).
Oxford History of England, Vol. VII: The Earlier Tudors, 1485-1558,
The. *John Duncan Mackie.* HEur(I-9).
Oxford History of England, Vol. IX: The Early Stuarts, 1603-1660,
The. *Godfrey Davies.* HEur(II-229).
Oxford History of England, Vol. X: The Later Stuarts, 1660-1714,
The. *George Clark.* HEur(I-403).
Oxford History of South Africa, The. *Monica Wilson* and *Leonard
Thompson,* eds. HWor(I-89).
Oxygen och Aromasia. *Claës Lundin.* SF(IV-1637).
Oysters of Locmariaquer, The. *Eleanor Clark.* SCL12(IX-5696),
SCLs(213).

Pacem in terris. *Pope John XXIII.* RCa(II-1131).
Pacific Railroad Surveys (Event). HAmer(II-865).
Pacific War: World War II and the Japanese, 1931-1945, The. *Saburō
Ienaga.* LA79(II-520).
Pagan Mysteries in the Renaissance. *Edgar Wind.* HAnc(III-1768).
Paideia: The Ideals of Greek Culture. *Werner W. Jaeger.* HAnc(I-289).
*Painted Bird, The. *Jerzy Kosinski.* SCL12(IX-5699), SCL7(V-3491),

A66(224).

Painter of Signs, The. *R. K. Narayan.* LA77(II-605).

Palace, The. *Claude Simon.* SCL12(IX-5702), SCL7(V-3494),
A64(206).

Palace of Industry, 1851: A Study of the Great Exhibition and Its
Fruits. *C. R. Fay.* HEur(II-801).

*Pale Fire. *Vladimir Nabokov.* MP12(VIII-4462), MP8(V-3476),
MP4(II-662), MWL4(662). A different analysis on this title appears in:
SCL12(IX-5705), SCL7(V-3497), A63(165), BMA(418).

*Pale Horse, Pale Rider. *Katherine Anne Porter.* MP12(VIII-4465),
MP8(V-3479), MP4(II-665), MWL4(665).

Palestine Triangle: The Struggle for the Holy Land, 1935-48, The. *Nicholas
Bethell.* LA80(II-634).

Palm-Wine Drinkard, The. *Amos Tutuola.* MP12(VIII-4469),
MP8(V-3483), MP4(II-668), MWL4(668).

*Pamela. *Samuel Richardson.* MP12(VIII-4472), MPCE(III-1666),
MP8(V-3486), MP6(IV-2235), MPEng(631), MP1(II-708),
MWL1(708).

Panama Canal Scandal in France (Event). HEur(II-1066).

Pan-Americanism: From Monroe to the Present. *Alonso Aguilar.*
HAmer(II-1193).

Panarion. *Saint Epiphanius of Salamis.* RCh(I-111).

Panzer Leader. *Heinz Guderian.* HWor(I-484).

Papa Hemingway. *A. E. Hotchner.* SCL12(IX-5710), SCL7(V-3501),
A67(259).

Papacy and European Diplomacy, 1869-1878, The. *Lillian Parker Wallace.*
HEur(II-972).

Paper Chase, The. Cine(III-1293).

Paper Horse, A. *Robert Watson.* SCL12(IX-5714), SCL7(V-3504),
A63(168).

Papers of Benjamin Franklin, The. *Leonard W. Labaree* and *Whitfield J.
Bell, Jr.,* eds. SCL12(IX-5717), SCL7(V-3507), A60(184).

Papillon. *Henri Charrière.* SCL12(IX-5720), A71(245).

Parables of the Kingdom, The. *Charles Harold Dodd.* RCh(II-1012).

Paraclesis, The. *Desiderius Erasmus.* RCa(I-505).

*Parade's End. *Ford Madox Ford.* MP12(VIII-4477), MPCE(II-1669),
MP8(V-3489), MP6(IV-2238), MPEng(634), MPv4(389),
MP2(II-792), MWL2(792).

*Paradise Lost. *John Milton.* MP12(VIII-4482), MPCE(III-1671),
MP8(V-3493), MP6(IV-2241), MPPo(202), MP1(II-711),
MWL1(711). A different analysis on this title appears in: RCh(I-511).

Paradise Lost: The Decline of the Auto-Industrial Age. *Emma Rothschild.*
SCL12(IX-5725), A74(298).

Paradise Reclaimed. *Halldór Laxness.* SCL12(IX-5730),
SCL7(V-3509), A63(171).

Passage of the Chinese Exclusion Act and the First Immigration Law
    (Event).   HAmer(II-1123).
Passage of the Dawes Act (Event).   HAmer(II-1161).
Passage of the Employment Act of 1946 (Event).   HAmer(III-1770).
Passage of the Federal Reserve Act (Event).   HAmer(III-1432).
Passage of the First National Draft Law (Event).   HAmer(II-991).
Passage of the Homestead Act (Event).   HAmer(II-962).
Passage of the Indian Removal Act (Event).   HAmer(I-666).
Passage of the Interstate Commerce Act (Event).   HAmer(II-1157).
Passage of the Judiciary Act (Event).   HAmer(I-345).
Passage of the Kansas-Nebraska Act (Event).   HAmer(II-871).
Passage of the Maryland Act of Toleration (Event).   HAmer(I-115).
Passage of the Morrill Land Grant Act (Event).   HAmer(II-974).
Passage of the National Bank Acts of 1863 and 1864 (Event).
    HAmer(II-985).
Passage of the National Labor Relations Act (Event).   HAmer(III-1637).
Passage of the National Security Act (Event).   HAmer(III-1783).
Passage of the Neutrality Acts (Event).   HAmer(III-1649).
Passage of the Northwest Ordinance (Event).   HAmer(I-324).
Passage of the Pendleton Act Reforming the Civil Service (Event).
    HAmer(II-1128).
Passage of the Pre-emption Act of 1841 (Event).   HAmer(II-772).
Passage of the Reconstruction Finance Corporation Legislation (Event).
    HAmer(III-1594).
Passage of the Sherman Antitrust Act (Event).   HAmer(II-1206).
Passage of the Social Security Act (Event).   HAmer(III-1643).
Passage to Ararat.   *Michael J. Arlen.*   SCL12(IX-5756),   A76(238).
*Passage to India, A.   *E. M. Forster.*   MP12(VIII-4500),
    MPCE(III-1676),   MP8(V-3506),   MP6(IV-2253),   MPEng(638),
    MP1(II-713),   MWL1(713).
Passing of French Algeria, The.   *David C. Gordon.*   HEur(III-1631).
Passing of the Great Reform Bill, The.   *J. R. M. Butler.*   HEur(II-708).
Passing of the Habsburg Monarchy, 1914-1918, The.   *Arthur J. May.*
    HWor(I-161).
Passion Artist, The.   *John Hawkes.*   LA80(II-644).
*Passion Flower, The.   *Jacinto Benavente.*   MP12(VIII-4505),
    MPCE(III-1679),   MP8(V-3509),   MP6(IV-2255),   MPDr(600),
    MP3(II-718),   MWL3(718).
Passion Play.   *Jerzy Kosinski.*   LA80(II-649).
Passions and Ancient Days.   *Constantine P. Cavafy.*   SCL12(IX-5760),
    A72(250).
Passions and Other Stories.   *Isaac Bashevis Singer.*   SCL12(IX-5763),
    A76(242).
Passions of the Soul, The.   *René Descartes.*   MP12(VIII-4510),
    MP8(V-3512),   MP4(II-670),   MWL4(670).

Paul Bunyan. *James Stevens*. MP12(VIII-4537), MPCE(III-1687), MP8(V-3535), MP6(IV-2270), MPAm(475), MP1(II-717), MWL1(717).

Paul Writes His Letter to the Romans (Event). HAnc(II-632).

Pavane. *Keith Roberts*. SF(IV-1660).

Pax Britannica. *James Morris*. SCL12(IX-5781), SCL7(V-3526), A69(260).

Peace, The. *Aristophanes*. MP12(VIII-4541), MPCE(III-1689), MP8(V-3538), MP6(IV-2272), MPDr(605), MP3(II-726), MWL3(726).

Peace Conspiracy: Wang Ching-wei and the China War, 1937-1941, The. *Gerald E. Bunker*. HWor(I-365).

Peace of Augsburg (Event). HEur(I-148).

Peace of Christmas Eve, The. *Fred L. Engleman*. HAmer(I-525).

Peace of Karlowitz (Event). HEur(I-368).

Peace of Paris, The (Event). HEur(I-451).

"Peace of Paris, The" *in* The Cambridge History of the British Empire. *Harold W. V. Temperley*. HEur(I-453).

Peace of Soul. *Fulton J. Sheen*. RCa(II-958).

Peace of the Pyrenees (Event). HEur(I-341).

"Peace of Utrecht and the Supplementary Pacifications, The," *in* The Cambridge Modern History. *A. W. Ward*. HEur(I-402).

Peace of Westphalia (Event). HEur(I-308).

"Peace of Westphalia, The," *in* The Cambridge Modern History. *A. W. Ward*. HEur(I-311).

Peacemakers, The. *Richard B. Morris*. SCL12(IX-5785), SCL7(V-3530), A66(230). A different analysis on this title appears in HAmer(I-302).

Peacock Spring, The. *Rumer Godden*. LA77(II-614).

Pearl Harbor: Warning and Decision. *Roberta Wohlstetter*. HAmer(III-1700).

Peasant Nationalism and Communist Power: The Emergence of Revolutionary China, 1937-1945. *Chalmers A. Johnson*. Different analyses on this title appear in: HWor(I-214; I-363).

*Peasants, The. *Ladislas Reymont*. MP12(VIII-4544), MPCE(III-1690), MP8(V-3540), MP6(IV-2274), MPEur(566), MP1(II-720), MWL1(720).

Peasants' War in Germany, The. *E. Belfort Bax*. HEur(I-79).

Peder Victorious. *O. E. Rölvaag*. MP12(VIII-4549), MPCE(III-1693), MP8(V-3543), MP6(IV-2276), MPAm(478), MPv4(397), MP2(II-802), MWL2(802).

Pedro Martinez. *Oscar Lewis*. SCL12(IX-5789), SCL7(V-3534), A65(221).

Pedro Páramo. *Juan Rulfo*. MP12(VIII-4552), MP8(V-3546), MP4(II-678), MWL4(678). A different analysis on this title appears in:

A66(233).

People of the Lake: Mankind and Its Beginnings. *Richard E. Leakey* and *Roger Lewin*. LA79(II-535).

People Shapers, The. *Vance Packard*. LA78(II-649).

*People, Yes, The. *Carl Sandburg*. MP12(VIII-4593), MP8(V-3577), MP6(IV-2303), MPPo(214), MP3(II-734), MWL3(734).

Pepita Jimenez. *Juan Valera*. MP12(VIII-4595), MPCE(III-1711), MP8(V-3579), MP6(IV-2305), MPEur(584), MPv4(406), MP2(II-813), MWL2(813).

Perception. *Henry Habberley Price*. Ph(II-968).

*Peregrine Pickle. *Tobias Smollett*. MP12(VIII-4599), MPCE(III-1713), MP8(V-3582), MP6(IV-2308), MPEng(648), MP1(II-731), MWL1(731).

*Perelandra. *C. S. Lewis*. SF(IV-1669).

Perfection of the Greek Choral Lyric (Event). HAnc(I-215).

Performance. Cine(III-1310).

Pericles on 31st Street. *Harry Mark Petrakis*. SCL12(IX-5812), SCLs(219).

*Pericles, Prince of Tyre. *William Shakespeare*. MP12(VIII-4603), MPCE(III-1714), MP8(V-3586), MP6(IV-2311), MPDr(612), MPv4(408), MP2(II-816), MWL2(816).

Perjury: The Hiss-Chambers Case. *Allen Weinstein*. LA79(II-540).

Permanent Errors. *Reynolds Price*. SCL12(IX-5815), A71(250).

*Persecution and Assassination of Jean-Paul Marat, The. *Peter Weiss*. SCL12(IX-5818), SCLs(222).

Pershing Military Expedition into Mexico (Event). HAmer(III-1438).

Pershing's Mission in Mexico. *Haldeen Braddy*. HAmer(III-1442).

Persian Invasion of Greece (Event). HAnc(I-237).

Persian Letters. *Charles de Montesquieu*. MP12(VIII-4607), MP8(V-3589), MP6(IV-2313), MPNf(234), MP3(II-736), MWL3(736).

*Persians, The. *Aeschylus*. MP12(VIII-4609), MPCE(III-1716), MP8(V-3591), MP6(IV-2316), MPDr(615), MPv3(409), MP2(II-818), MWL2(818).

Person and Place of Jesus Christ, The. *Peter Taylor Forsyth*. RCh(II-861).

Personae. *Ezra Pound*. MP12(VIII-4612), MP8(V-3593), MP4(II-681), MWL4(681).

Personal Anthology, A. *Jorge Luis Borges*. SCL12(IX-5822), SCL7(V-3547), A67(262).

Personal Politics: The Roots of Women's Liberation in the Civil Rights Movement and the New Left. *Sara Evans*. LA80(II-655).

Personal Realism. *James Bissett Pratt*. Ph(II-1016).

Personalism. *Borden Parker Bowne*. RCh(II-851).

Perspectives on the Computer Revolution. *Zenon W. Pylyshyn*, ed. HWor(II-540).

SCL12(IX-5831), SCL7(V-3557), A60(189). A different analysis on this title appears in: RCa(II-1017).

Phidias Creates the Statue of Zeus at Olympia (Event). HAnc(I-297).

Philadelphia Story, The. Cine(III-1330).

*Philaster. *Francis Beaumont* and *John Fletcher*. MP12(VIII-4639), MPCE(III-1727), MP8(V-3616), MP6(IV-2331), MPDr(622), MPv3(411), MP2(II-825), MWL2(825).

Philebus. *Plato*. Ph(I-120).

Philip II of Spain Becomes King of Portugal (Event). HEur(I-189).

Philippics, The. *Demosthenes*. MP12(VIII-4644), MP8(V-3619), MP6(IV-2333), MPNf(236), MP3(II-738), MWL3(738).

Philippine Insurrection, The (Event). HAmer(II-1290).

Philo. *Harry A. Wolfson*. HAnc(II-613).

Philoctetes. *Sophocles*. MP12(VIII-4647), MPCE(III-1730), MP8(V-3622), MP6(IV-2335), MPDr(625), MP3(II-741), MWL3(741).

Philo's Hellenization of Judaism (Event). HAnc(II-612).

Philosopher and Theology, The. *Étienne Gilson*. RCa(II-1088).

Philosopher at Large: An Intellectual Autobiography. *Mortimer J. Adler*. LA78(II-654).

Philosopher or Dog? *Joaquim Maria Machado de Assís*. MP12(VIII-4650), MP8(V-3625), MP4(II-686), MWL4(686), SCL12(IX-5836), SCL7(V-3561), A54(204).

Philosopher's Stone, The. *Colin Wilson*. SF(IV-1674).

Philosophiae Naturalis Principia Mathematica. *Sir Isaac Newton*. MP12(VIII-4653), MP8(V-3628), MP6(IV-2337), MPNf(239), MP3(II-743), MWL3(743).

Philosophical Bases of Theism, The. *George Dawes Hicks*. RCh(II-1031).

Philosophical Efforts Toward an Objective View of Planet Earth (Event). HWor(II-1069).

Philosophical Fragments. *Søren Kierkegaard*. Ph(II-619).

Philosophical Investigations. *Ludwig Wittgenstein*. Ph(II-1160).

Philosophical Studies. *George Edward Moore*. Ph(II-842).

Philosophical Theology. *Frederick Robert Tennant*. RCh(II-933).

Philosophical Treatises and Moral Reflections of Seneca. *Seneca (Lucius Annaeus Seneca)*. MP12(VIII-4656), MP8(V-3631), MP4(II-688), MWL4(688).

Philosophy and Logical Syntax. *Rudolf Carnap*. Ph(II-997).

Philosophy and Psycho-Analysis. *John Wisdom*. Ph(II-1153).

Philosophy in the Middle Ages: An Introduction. *Paul Vignaux*. HAnc(III-1567).

Philosophy of Art. *Hippolyte Taine*. MP12(VIII-4659), MP8(V-3634), MP6(IV-2340), MPNf(242), MP3(II-745), MWL3(745).

Philosophy of Democratic Government. *Yves René Marie Simon*. RCa(II-982).

*Pictures of Fidelman. *Bernard Malamud.* SCL12(IX-5852), A70(238).
Pieces of Life. *Mark Schorer.* LA78(II-657).
*Pierre. *Herman Melville.* MP12(VIII-4690), MPCE(III-1744),
    MP8(VI-3659), MP6(IV-2359), MPAm(484), MPv4(415),
    MP2(II-829), MWL2(829).
*Pigeon Feathers. *John Updike.* SCL12(IX-5857), SCL7(V-3577),
    A63(182).
Pike's Exploration of the Southwest (Event). HAmer(I-467).
Pilgrim, The. *Michael Serafian.* HEur(III-1639).
Pilgrim at Tinker Creek. *Annie Dillard.* SCL12(IX-5861), A75(236).
Pilgrim Hawk, The. *Glenway Wescott.* MP12(VIII-4693),
    MP8(VI-3662), MP4(II-691), MWL4(691). A different analysis on
    this title appears in: SCL12(IX-5865), SCL7(V-3581), A68(240).
Pilgrimage. *Dorothy M. Richardson.* MP12(VIII-4696), MP8(VI-3665),
    MP6(IV-2362), MPEng(674), MP3(II-757), MWL3(757).
Pilgrimage: The Book of the People *and* The People: No Different
    Flesh. *Zenna Henderson.* SF(IV-1682).
Pilgrimage of Charlemagne, The. *Unknown.* MP12(VIII-4700),
    MPCE(III-1745), MP8(VI-3669), MP6(V-2367), MPPo(216),
    MP3(II-760), MWL3(760).
*Pilgrim's Progress, The. *John Bunyan.* MP12(VIII-4705),
    MPCE(III-1747), MP8(VI-3672), MP6(V-2369), MPEng(678),
    MP1(II-748), MWL1(748). A different analysis on this title appears in:
    RCh(I-530).
*Pillars of Society, The. *Henrik Ibsen.* MP12(VIII-4710),
    MPCE(III-1750), MP8(VI-3675), MP6(V-2371), MPDr(633),
    MPv3(416), MP2(II-831), MWL2(831).
Pillow Talk. Cine(III-1339).
*Pilot, The. *James Fenimore Cooper.* MP12(VIII-4714),
    MPCE(III-1752), MP8(VI-3678), MP6(V-2374), MPAm(487),
    MP1(II-750), MWL1(750).
Pinckney's Treaty: A Study of America's Advantages from Europe's
    Distresses. *Samuel Flagg Bemis.* HAmer(I-400).
Pindar. *Gilbert Norwood.* HAnc(I-217).
"Pindar: The Last Greek Aristocrat," *in* The Great Way to Western
    Civilization. *Edith Hamilton.* HAnc(I-218).
Ping-Pong. *Arthur Adamov.* MP12(VIII-4719), MP8(VI-3681),
    MP4(II-694), MWL4(694).
Pink Panther, The. Cine(III-1343).
Pinky. Cine(III-1346).
Pio Nono: A Study in European Politics and Religion in the Nineteenth
    Century. *Edward E. Hales.* Different analyses on this title appear in:
    HEur(II-773; II-905; II-981).
Pioneer: A History of The Johns Hopkins University, 1874-1889. *Hugh
    Hawkins.* HAmer(II-1079).

Pioneering in Big Business, 1882-1911: History of Standard Oil Company, New Jersey. *Ralph W. Hidy* and *Muriel E. Hidy.* HAmer(II-1120).
*Pioneers, The. *James Fenimore Cooper.* MP12(VIII-4722), MPCE(III-1755), MP8(VI-3684), MP6(V-2377), MPAm(490), MP1(II-753), MWL1(753).
Pioneers of France in the New World. *Francis Parkman.* HAmer(I-31).
*Pirates of Penzance, The. *W. S. Gilbert.* MP12(VIII-4726), MPCE(III-1756), MP8(VI-3687), MP6(V-2379), MPDr(636), MPv4(418), MP2(II-834), MWL2(834).
*Pit, The. *Frank Norris.* MP12(VIII-4729), MPCE(III-1757), MP8(VI-3689), MP6(V-2381), MPAm(493), MP1(II-756), MWL1(756).
Pius IX Publishes the *Syllabus of Errors* (Event). HEur(II-902).
Place in the Sun, A. Cine(III-1349).
Place on Earth, A. *Wendell Berry.* SCL12(IX-5870), SCL7(V-3586), A68(244).
*Plague, The. *Albert Camus.* MP12(VIII-4734), MPCE(III-1764), MP8(VI-3692), MP6(V-2383), MPEur(587), MPv4(419), MP2(II-836), MWL2(836).
Plague Dogs, The. *Richard Adams.* LA79(II-546).
Plague of Demons, A. *Keith Laumer.* SF(IV-1687).
Plagues and Peoples. *William H. McNeill.* LA77(II-618).
Plaideurs, Les. *Jean Baptiste Racine.* MP12(VIII-4740), MP8(VI-3695), MP6(V-2386), MPDr(638), MP3(II-763), MWL3(763).
Plain Account of Christian Perfection, A. *John Wesley.* RCh(II-608).
*Plain Dealer, The. *William Wycherley.* MP12(VIII-4743), MPCE(III-1766), MP8(VI-3697), MP6(V-2387), MPDr(640), MPv3(418), MP2(II-838), MWL2(838).
Plain Speaking. *Merle Miller.* SCL12(IX-5874), A75(240).
Plainsman, The. Cine(III-1352).
Plan of Salvation, The. *Benjamin Warfield.* RCh(II-890).
Planet of the Apes. Cine(III-1355).
Planet of the Apes. *Pierre Boulle.* SF(IV-1692).
Plantation Boy. *José Lins do Rêgo.* MP12(VIII-4748), MP8(VI-3700), MP4(II-696), MWL4(696). A different analysis on this title appears in: SCL12(IX-5877), SCL7(V-3590), A67(264).
*Platero and I. *Juan Ramón Jiménez.* MP12(VIII-4752), MP8(VI-3704), MP6(V-2390), MPEur(590), MP3(II-764), MWL3(764). A different analysis on this title appears in: SCL12(IX-5882), SCL7(V-3595), A58(188), BMA(436).
Plato, an Introduction. *Paul Friedlander.* HAnc(I-325).
Plato Develops the Theory of Ideas (Event). HAnc(I-323).
*Play It as It Lays. *Joan Didion.* SCL12(IX-5886), A71(253).
*Playboy of the Western World, The. *John Millington Synge.*

*Poetry of Waller, The. *Edmund Waller.* MP12(IX-5194),
　　MP8(VI-4140), MP4(II-989), MWL4(989).
Poetry of Warren, The. *Robert Penn Warren.* MP12(IX-5197),
　　MP8(VI-4143), MP4(II-992), MWL4(992).
Poetry of Whittier, The. *John Greenleaf Whittier.* MP12(IX-5200),
　　MP8(VI-4146), MP4(II-995), MWL4(995).
*Poetry of Wilbur, The. *Richard Wilbur.* MP12(IX-5203),
　　MP8(VI-4149), MP4(II-997), MWL4(997).
Poetry of Wilde, The. *Oscar Wilde.* MP12(IX-5206), MP8(VI-4152),
　　MP4(II-1000), MWL4(1000).
Poetry of Williams, The. *William Carlos Williams.* MP12(IX-5209),
　　MP8(VI-4155), MP4(II-1002), MWL4(1002).
Poetry of Wither, The. *George Wither.* MP12(IX-5212),
　　MP8(VI-4158), MP4(II-1004), MWL4(1004).
Poetry of Wordsworth, The. *William Wordsworth.* MP12(IX-5215),
　　MP8(VI-4161), MP4(II-1007), MWL4(1007).
Poetry of Wyatt and Surrey, The. *Sir Thomas Wyatt* and *Henry Howard, Earl
　　of Surrey.* MP12(IX-5219), MP8(VI-4165), MP4(II-1010),
　　MWL4(1010).
*Poetry of Yeats, The. *William Butler Yeats.* MP12(IX-5224),
　　MP8(VI-4170), MP6(V-2471), MPPo(300), MP3(II-836),
　　MWL3(836).
Poets in a Landscape. *Gilbert Highet.* SCL12(IX-5947), SCL7(V-3644),
　　A58(193).
Poet's Work: 29 Masters of 20th Century Poetry on the Origins and Practice of
　　Their Art, The. *Reginald Gibbons, ed.* LA80(II-668).
*Point Counter Point. *Aldous Huxley.* MP12(IX-5227),
　　MPCE(III-1778), MP8(VI-4173), MP6(V-2474), MPEng(684),
　　MP1(II-760), MWL1(760).
Points of My Compass, The. *E. B. White.* SCL12(IX-5950),
　　SCL7(V-3647), A63(194).
Poison Belt, The. *Arthur Conan Doyle.* SF(IV-1702).
"Poland and Lithuania in the Fourteenth and Fifteenth Centuries," *in* Vol.
　　VIII *of* The Cambridge Medieval History. *Alexander Bruce-Boswell.*
　　HAnc(III-1652).
Polar Exploration (Event). HWor(I-63).
Polarization of American Society in the 1960's (Event). HAmer(III-1861).
Policraticus. *John of Salisbury.* RCh(I-216).
Policraticus *and* Metalogicon. *John of Salisbury.* RCa(I-335).
Polish Politics and the Revolution of November, 1830. *R. F. Leslie.*
　　HEur(II-694).
Political Aspects of St. Augustine's "City of God," The. *John Neville
　　Figgis.* HAnc(II-942).
Political Doctrine of the Mongols, The. *Grzegorz Leopold Seidler.*
　　HAnc(III-1465).

MWL3(839).

*Ponder Heart, The. *Eudora Welty.* MP12(IX-5234), MP8(VI-4179), MP4(II-1014), MWL4(1014), SCL12(IX-5964), SCL7(V-3650), A54(213).

Ponedel'nik nachinaetsia v subbotu. *Arkady Strugatsky* and *Boris Strugatsky.* SF(IV-1710).

Pontificate of Pope IX (Event). HEur(II-770).

Pony Express: The Great Gamble. *Roy S. Bloss.* HAmer(II-928).

*Poor People. *Fyodor Mikhailovich Dostoevski.* MP12(IX-5237), MPCE(III-1781), MP8(VI-4182), MP6(V-2479), MPEur(593), MPv3(422), MP2(II-847), MWL2(847).

*Poor White. *Sherwood Anderson.* MP12(IX-5241), MPCE(III-1783), MP8(VI-4185), MP6(V-2481), MPAm(496), MP1(II-762), MWL1(762).

*Poorhouse Fair, The. *John Updike.* MP12(IX-5244), MP8(VI-4187), MP4(II-1016), MWL4(1016), SCL12(IX-5967), SCL7(V-3653), A60(202), BMA(448). A different analysis on this title appears in: SF(IV-1714).

"Pope Gelasius and His Teaching on the Relation of Church and State," *in* Catholic Historical Review. *A. K. Ziegler.* HAnc(II-992).

Pope Paul VI Publishes *Humanae Vitae* (Event). HEur(III-1659).

Popes Through History, Vol. II: The Ancient Popes, The. *E. G. Weltin.* Different analyses on this title appear in: HAnc(II-821; II-955).

Popular Education and Democratic Thought in America. *Rush Welter.* HAmer(I-579).

Popularization of Experimental Science (Event). HAnc(III-1539).

Population Explosion and the Move to Suburbia, The (Event). HAmer(III-1811).

Population Shift to the Sunbelt, The (Event). HWor(II-1077).

Populist Revolt: A History of the Farmers' Alliance and the People's Party, The. *John D. Hicks.* HAmer(II-1227).

Porgy. *DuBose Heyward.* MP12(IX-5247), MPCE(III-1785), MP8(VI-4190), MP6(V-2483), MPAm(498), MP1(II-764), MWL1(764).

Porphyry's Commentaries on the *Categories* of Aristotle (Event). HAnc(II-834).

*Portnoy's Complaint. *Philip Roth.* SCL12(IX-5971), A70(242).

*Portrait in Brownstone. *Louis Auchincloss.* SCL12(IX-5976), SCL7(V-3657), A63(196).

Portrait of a Decade: The Second American Revolution. *Anthony Lewis* and *The New York Times.* Different analyses on this title appear in: HAmer(III-1850; III-1858).

Portrait of a Diplomatist: Sir Arthur Nicolson, Bart, First Lord Carnock: A Study in Old Diplomacy. *Harold Nicolson.* HEur(III-1199).

Portrait of a General: Sir Henry Clinton in the War of

Powdered Eggs. *Charles Simmons*. SCL12(IX-5993), SCL7(V-3669), A65(223).

Powell of the Colorado. *William Culp Darrah*. HAmer(II-1106).

Powell Publishes *Report on the Lands of the Arid Region of the United States* (Event). HAmer(II-1104).

*Power. *Lion Feuchtwanger*. MP12(IX-5277), MPCE(III-1797), MP8(VI-4208), MP6(V-2494), MPEur(599), MP1(II-773), MWL1(773).

"Power," *in* A History of Technology. *Robert J. Forbes*. HAnc(I-7).

Power and the Glory, The. Cine(III-1368).

*Power and the Glory, The. *Graham Greene*. MP12(IX-5280), MPCE(III-1798), MP8(VI-4211), MP6(V-2497), MPEng(689), MPv4(427), MP2(II-851), MWL2(851).

Power Broker: Robert Moses and the Fall of New York, The. *Robert A. Caro*. SCL12(IX-5996), A75(243).

Power in the Kremlin: From Khrushchev to Kosygin. *Michel Tatu*. Different analyses on this title appear in: HWor(II-909; II-977).

Power, Morals and the Founding Fathers: Essays in the Interpretation of the American Enlightenment. *Adrienne Koch*. HAmer(I-198).

*Power of Darkness, The. *Count Leo Tolstoy*. MP12(IX-5283), MPCE(III-1799), MP8(VI-4214), MP6(V-2499), MPDr(655), MP3(II-841), MWL3(841).

Power on the Left: American Radical Movements Since 1946. *Lawrence Lader*. LA80(II-680).

Power Politics. *Margaret Atwood*. SCL12(IX-6000), A74(316).

Power Shift. *Kirkpatrick Sale*. SCL12(IX-6004), A76(249).

Powers That Be, The. *David Halberstam*. LA80(II-684).

Practical Christianity. *Rufus Matthew Jones*. RCh(II-819).

Practice of the Presence of God, The. *Brother Lawrence (Nicholas Herman)*. RCh(I-543).

Pragmatism. *William James*. MP12(IX-5287), MP8(VI-4217), MP6(V-2501), MPNf(251), MP3(II-843), MWL3(843). A different analysis on this title appears in: Ph(II-779).

Prague Spring: A Report on Czechoslovakia, 1968. *Zbynek A. Zeman*. HEur(III-1669).

*Prairie, The. *James Fenimore Cooper*. MP12(IX-5290), MPCE(III-1801), MP8(VI-4220), MP6(V-2504), MPAm(503), MP1(II-776), MWL1(776).

*Praise of Folly, The. *Desiderius Erasmus*. MP12(IX-5294), MP8(VI-4223), MP6(V-2506), MPNf(254), MP3(II-846), MWL3(846). Different analyses on this title appear in: RCh(I-326), RCa(I-501).

Prayer. *George Arthur Buttrick*. RCh(II-1064).

Prayer for Katerina Horovitzova, A. *Arnost Lustig*. SCL12(IX-6008), A74(320).

Preaching of John Huss, The (Event). HAnc(III-1675).
Preaching of the First Crusade (Event). HAnc(III-1276).
Preaching of the Pentecostal Gospel (Event). HAnc(II-607).
Preces privatae. *Lancelot Andrewes.* RCh(I-473).
Precious Bane. *Mary Webb.* MP12(IX-5296), MPCE(III-1803),
    MP8(VI-4225), MP6(V-2508), MPEng(692), MP1(II-778),
    MWL1(778).
Pre-Conquest Church in England, The. *Margaret Deanesly.* HAnc(II-1061).
Preface to Plato. *Eric A. Havelock.* HAnc(I-326).
Preface to Shakespeare. *Samuel Johnson.* MP12(IX-5299),
    MP8(VI-4228), MP4(II-1024), MWL4(1024).
Preferences. *Richard Howard.* SCL12(IX-6012), A75(247).
Prehistoric Avebury. *Aubrey Burl.* LA80(II-688).
Prehistory of North America. *Jesse D. Jennings.* HAmer(I-3).
Prejudice: Japanese-Americans, Symbol of Racial Intolerance. *Carey
    McWilliams.* HAmer(III-1706).
Prejudices: Six Series. *H. L. Mencken.* MP12(IX-5302),
    MP8(VI-4231), MP6(V-2510), MPNf(256), MP3(II-847),
    MWL3(847).
Prelude, A. *Edmund Wilson.* SCL12(IX-6015), SCL7(V-3672),
    A68(251).
*Prelude, The. *William Wordsworth.* MP12(IX-5304), MP8(VI-4233),
    MP6(V-2512), MPPo(303), MP3(II-849), MWL3(849).
Prelude to Calamity: The Nazi Revolution 1933-35, with a Background Survey
    of the Weimar Era. *Eliot B. Wheaton.* HWor(I-314).
Prelude to Civil War: The Nullification Controversy in South Carolina,
    1816-1836. *William W. Freehling.* HAmer(II-705).
Prelude to Greatness: Lincoln in th 1850's. *Don E. Fehrenbacher.*
    HAmer(II-908).
Prelude to Infamy: The Story of Chancellor Dollfuss of Austria. *Gordon
    Brook-Shepherd.* HEur(III-1397).
Prelude to Riot: A View of Urban America from the Bottom. *Paul Jacobs.*
    HAmer(III-1926).
Prelude to the Partition of West Africa. *John D. Hargreaves.*
    HEur(II-1050).
Presence of Grace, The. *J. F. Powers.* SCL12(IX-6017),
    SCL7(V-3674), A57(209).
Presences: Seven Dramatic Pieces. *Peter Taylor.* SCL12(IX-6020),
    A74(324).
Present at the Creation. *Dean Acheson.* SCL12(IX-6024), A71(256).
Presentation of Leo's *Tome* (Event). HAnc(II-963).
Presentation of the Recapitulation Theory (Event). HAnc(II-747).
Presentation Piece. *Marilyn Hacker.* SCL12(IX-6030), A75(250).
Presidency of John Adams: The Collapse of Federalism, 1795-1800,
    The. *Stephen G. Kurtz.* HAmer(I-410).

President, The. *R. V. Cassill.* SCL12(IX-6034), SCL7(V-3677),
    A65(226).
Presidential Lottery. *James A. Michener.* SCL12(IX-6039), A70(246).
Presocratic Philosopher: A Critical History with a Selection of Texts,
    The. *G. S. Kirk* and *J. E. Raven.* HAnc(I-267).
Pressure for Prison Reform (Event). HWor(II-886).
Pressure of Minorities for Personal Equality (Event). HWor(II-893).
Price, The. *Arthur Miller.* SCL12(IX-6043), SCL7(V-3682), A69(264).
Price of Glory: Verdun, 1916, The. *Alistair Horne.* SCL12(IX-6047),
    SCL7(V-3686), A64(215). A different analysis on this title appears in:
    HEur(III-1264).
Price of My Soul, The. *Bernadette Devlin.* HWor(III-1121).
Price Was High: The Last Uncollected Stories of F. Scott Fitzgerald, The. *F.
    Scott Fitzgerald.* LA80(II-693).
Pricksongs & Descants. *Robert Coover.* SCL12(IX-6050), A70(250).
*Pride and Prejudice. *Jane Austen.* MP12(IX-5307), MPCE(III-1804),
    MP8(VI-4236), MP6(V-2515), MPEng(695), MP1(II-780),
    MWL1(780).
Priest to the Temple, A. *George Herbert.* RCh(I-485).
Primacy or World Order: American Foreign Policy Since the Cold
    War. *Stanley Hoffmann.* LA79(II-551).
Prime of Miss Jean Brodie, The. Cine(III-1371).
*Prime of Miss Jean Brodie, The. *Muriel Spark.* SCL12(IX-6055),
    SCL7(V-3689), A63(199).
Primer of Dutch Seventeenth Century Overseas Trade, A. *D. W. Davies.*
    HAmer(I-83).
Primitive Church, The. *B. H. Streeter.* HAnc(II-683).
Primitive Time-Reckoning. *Martin P. Nilsson.* HAnc(I-537).
*Prince, The. *Niccolò Machiavelli.* MP12(IX-5314), MP8(VI-4240),
    MP6(V-2518), MPNf(258), MP3(II-852), MWL3(852). Different
    analyses on this title appear in: Ph(I-354), RCa(I-523).
*Prince and the Pauper, The. *Mark Twain.* MP12(IX-5317),
    MPCE(III-1808), MP8(VI-4243), MP6(V-2521), MPAm(506),
    MPv3(427), MP2(II-854), MWL2(854).
Prince Eugen of Savoy. *Nicholas Henderson.* SCL12(IX-6059),
    SCL7(V-3692), A66(242).
Prince Henry, the Navigator. *C. Raymond Beazley.* HAnc(III-1688).
Prince of Homburg, The. *Heinrich von Kleist.* MP12(IX-5321),
    MPCE(III-1810), MP8(VI-4246), MP6(V-2523), MPDr(658),
    MP3(II-854), MWL3(854).
Prince of Our Disorder, A. *John E. Mack.* LA77(II-637).
*Princess, The. *Alfred, Lord Tennyson.* MP12(IX-5324),
    MP8(VI-4248), MP4(II-1026), MWL4(1026).
*Princess Casamassima, The. *Henry James.* MP12(IX-5327),
    MPCE(III-1811), MP8(VI-4251), MP4(II-1029), MWL4(1029).

Process and Reality. *Alfred North Whitehead.* Ph(II-921).
Proclamation of an Independent Jewish State (Event). HWor(II-634).
Proclamation of 1763 (Event). HAmer(I-207).
Proclamation of the People's Republic of China (Event). HWor(II-654).
Proclamation of the Republic of Portugal (Event). HEur(III-1219).
Proclamation of the Second Spanish Republic (Event). HEur(III-1368).
Producers, The. Cine(III-1388).
Professing Poetry. *John Wain.* LA79(II-561).
Professionalization of History (Event). HAnc(I-259).
*Professor, The. *Charlotte Brontë.* MP12(IX-5353), MPCE(III-1819),
    MP8(VI-4274), MP6(V-2536), MPEng(705), MPv3(429),
    MP2(II-864), MWL2(864).
Professor of Desire, The. *Philip Roth.* LA78(II-669).
*Professor's House, The. *Willa Cather.* MP12(IX-5357),
    MPCE(III-1821), MP8(VI-4277), MP6(V-2539), MPAm(509),
    MPv3(431), MP2(II-867), MWL2(867).
Profiles in Courage. *John F. Kennedy.* SCL12(IX-6079),
    SCL7(V-3705), A57(212).
Progress and Religion. *Christopher Dawson.* RCa(II-798).
Progress of Hellenism in Alexander's Empire, The. *J. P. Mahaffy.*
    HAnc(I-315).
Progressive Historians: Turner, Beard, Parrington, The. *Richard
    Hofstadter.* HWor(I-207).
"Project for a New Edition of Vincent of Beauvais, A," *in* Speculum. *B. L.
    Ullman.* HAnc(III-1536).
Prolegomena to Ethics. *Thomas Hill Green.* Ph(II-681).
Prologue to Conflict: The Crisis and Compromise of 1850. *Holman
    Hamilton.* HAmer(II-857).
Prologue to Parmenides. *Giorgio De Santillana.* HAnc(I-233).
Prologue to War: England and the United States, 1805-1812. *Bradford
    Perkins.* HAmer(I-507).
Prometheus: The Life of Balzac. *André Maurois.* SCL12(IX-6083),
    SCL7(VI-3709), A67(276).
*Prometheus Bound. *Aeschylus.* MP12(IX-5361), MPCE(III-1823),
    MP8(VI-4280), MP6(V-2541), MPDr(665), MP1(II-786),
    MWL1(786).
*Prometheus Unbound. *Percy Bysshe Shelley.* MP12(IX-5365),
    MPCE(III-1826), MP8(VI-4282), MP6(V-2543), MPPo(306),
    MP1(II-788), MWL1(788).
Promise of Space, The. *Arthur C. Clarke.* HWor(II-754).
Promised Land, The. *Henrik Pontoppidan.* MP12(IX-5368),
    MPCE(III-1827), MP8(VI-4284), MP6(V-2545), MPEur(605),
    MPv3(434), MP2(II-869), MWL2(869).
Promises. *Robert Penn Warren.* SCL12(IX-6087), SCL7(VI-3713),
    A58(198), BMA(455).

Promulgation of Hammurabi's Code (Event). HAnc(I-45).

Promulgation of Justinian's *Code* (Event). HAnc(II-1035).

Promulgation of the Statute of Praemunire (Event). HAnc(III-1630).

Promulgation of Theodosius' Edicts (Event). HAnc(II-904).

Pronouncement of the Bull *Unam Sanctam* (Event). HAnc(III-1592).

Propaganda and Civil Liberties in World War I (Event). HAmer(III-1454).

Propaganda Technique in World War I. *Harold D. Lasswell.* HAmer(III-1458).

Prophet, The. *Sholem Asch.* SCL12(IX-6091), SCL7(VI-3717), A55(211).

Prophet, The. *Kahlil Gibran.* MP12(IX-5372), MP8(VI-4287), MP4(II-1036), MWL4(1036).

Prophetic Faith in Israel. *Sheldon H. Blank.* HAnc(I-185).

Prophetic Minority, A. *Jack Newfield.* HAmer(III-1863).

Proscriptions of the Second Triumvirate (Event). HAnc(I-546).

Proserpine and Ceres. *Unknown.* MP12(IX-5374), MPCE(III-1829), MP8(VI-4289), MP6(V-2547), MPEur(608), MP1(II-789), MWL1(789).

"Pro-Slavery Argument," The (Event). HAmer(I-648).

Pro-Slavery Thought in the Old South. *William S. Jenkins.* HAmer(I-650).

Proslogion. *Saint Anselm of Canterbury.* Different analyses on this title appear in: RCh(I-197), RCa(I-280).

*Prospects Are Pleasing, The. *Honor Tracy.* SCL12(IX-6095), SCL7(VI-3721), A59(207).

Protagoras. *Plato.* Ph(I-59).

"Protestant Collapse, 1620-1630, The," *in* The Cambridge Modern History. *A. W. Ward.* HEur(I-272).

Protestant Diplomacy and the Near East: Missionary Influence on American Policy, 1810-1927. *Joseph L. Grabill.* HWor(I-114).

Protestant Search for Political Realism, 1919-1941, The. *Donald B. Meyer.* HAmer(III-1607).

Proud Tower, The. *Barbara W. Tuchman.* SCL12(IX-6098), SCL7(VI-3724), A66(246). A different analysis on this title appears in: HEur(III-1194).

Proust: The Early Years. *George D. Painter.* SCL12(IX-6105), SCL7(VI-3731), A60(206), BMA(459).

Proust: The Later Years. *George D. Painter.* SCL12(IX-6109), SCL7(VI-3735), A66(252).

Proust Screenplay, The. *Harold Pinter.* LA78(II-673).

Prussian Reform After Defeat at Jena (Event). HEur(II-572).

Prussian Revolution of 1848 (Event). HEur(II-790).

P. S. Wilkinson. *C. D. B. Bryan.* SCL12(IX-6113), SCLs(231).

Psycho. Cine(III-1391).

Psychology of Jung: A Critical Interpretation, The. *Avis M. Dry.* HEur(III-1311).

Psychopathic God: Adolf Hitler, The. *Robert G. L. Waite.* Different
    analyses on this title appear in: LA78(II-677),   HWor(I-193).
Public Awareness of Environmental Dangers (Event).   HWor(III-542).
Public Enemy, The.   Cine(III-1395).
Public Finance. *Harley Leist Lutz.*   HAmer(III-1418).
Public Image, The. *Muriel Spark.*   SCL12(IX-6117),   SCL7(VI-3739),
    A69(268).
Publication of Celsus' *True Word* (Event).   HAnc(II-731).
Publication of Galen's Medical Writings (Event).   HAnc(II-737).
Publication of the Cambridge Histories (Event).   HWor(I-24).
Publication of the Kinsey Reports (Event).   HWor(II-619).
Publication of Kant's Three *Critiques* (Event).   HEur(I-491). *See also*
    Critique of Judgment, Critique of Practical Reason, *and* Critique of Pure
    Reason.
Publication of Reinhold Niebuhr's *Moral Man and Immoral Society,* and the
    Rise of Neoörthodoxy (Event).   HAmer(III-1604).
Publication of the *Communist Manifesto* (Event).   HEur(II-781).
Publication of the *Encyclopédie* (Event).   HEur(I-428).
Publication of *The Federalist* (Event).   HAmer(I-335). *See also* Federalist,
    The.
Publication of the King James Bible (Event).   HEur(I-241).
Publication of *The Southern Literary Messenger* (Event).   HAmer(II-725).
Publication of Washington's Farewell Address (Event).   HAmer(I-403).
Publicity and Diplomacy: With Special Reference to England and Germany,
    1890-1914. *Oron J. Hale.*   HEur(III-1212).
Pulitzer. *W. A. Swanberg.*   SCL12(IX-6121),   SCL7(VI-3743),
    A68(254).
Pullman: An Experiment in Industrial Order and Community Planning,
    1880-1930. *Stanley Buder.*   HAmer(II-1239).
Pullman Strike, The (Event).   HAmer(II-1237).
Pullman Strike: The Story of a Unique Experiment and of a Great Labor
    Upheaval, The. *Almont Lindsey.*   HAmer(II-1239).
Pump House Gang, The. *Tom Wolfe.*   SCL12(IX-6125),
    SCL7(VI-3747),   A69(271).
Puppet Masters, The. *Robert A. Heinlein.*   SF(IV-1730).
Purchase of Alaska (Event).   HAmer(II-1037).
*Pure and the Impure, The. *Colette.*   SCL12(IX-6128),
    SCL7(VI-3750),   A68(257).
Puritan Carpenter, The. *Julia Randall.*   SCL12(IX-6131),
    SCL7(VI-3753),   A66(256).
Puritan Dilemma: The Story of John Winthrop, The. *Edmund S. Morgan.*
    HAmer(I-87).
Puritan Village. *Sumner Chilton Powell.*   SCL12(IX-6134),   SCLs(234).
Puritan Way of Death, The. *David E. Stannard.*   LA78(II-682).
Purple Cloud, The. *M. P. Shiel.*   SF(IV-1735).

*Purple Dust. *Sean O'Casey*. MP12(IX-5378), MPCE(III-1832), MP8(VI-4291), MP6(V-2549), MPDr(667), MP3(II-857), MWL3(857).

*Purple Land, The. *W. H. Hudson*. MP12(IX-5382), MPCE(III-1834), MP8(VI-4294), MP6(V-2551), MPEng(708), MP1(II-791), MWL1(791).

Pushcart Prize, III: Best of the Small Presses, The. *Bill Henderson*, ed. LA79(II-565).

Pushkin. *Henri Troyat*. SCL12(IX-6138), A72(262).

Puzzleheaded Girl, The. *Christina Stead*. SCL12(IX-6142), SCL7(VI-3756), A68(260).

Pygmalion. Cine(III-1399).

*Pygmalion. *George Bernard Shaw*. MP12(IX-5385), MP8(VI-4296), MP6(V-2553), MPDr(670), MP3(II-859), MWL3(859).

Pyramid, The. *William Golding*. SCL12(IX-6146), SCL7(VI-3760), A68(264).

Pyramids of Egypt, The. *I. E. S. Edwards*. HAnc(I-27).

Pythagoras and Early Pythagoreans. *J. A. Philip*. HAnc(I-197).

Quadragesimo anno. *Pope Pius XI*. RCa(II-812).

*Quality Street. *James M. Barrie*. MP12(IX-5387), MPCE(III-1835), MP8(VI-4298), MP6(V-2555), MPDr(672), MP1(II-793), MWL1(793).

Quando le Radici. *Lino Aldani*. SF(IV-1739).

Quantum Physics Research (Event). HWor(I-166).

*Quare Fellow, The. *Brendan Behan*. SCL12(IX-6150), SCL7(VI-3764), A58(201).

Quarry, The. *Richard Eberhart*. SCL12(IX-6153), SCL7(VI-3767), A65(230).

Quarup. *Antonio Callado*. SCL12(IX-6156), SCLs(238).

Quasars, Their Importance in Astronomy and Physics. *Frenz D. Kahn* and *Henry P. Palmer*. HWor(II-902).

Quasi-War: The Politics and Diplomacy of the Undeclared War with France, 1797-1801, The. *Alexander De Conde*. HAmer(I-412).

Queen Alexandra. *Georgina Battiscombe*. SCL12(IX-6162), A70(259).

Queen Anne. *David Green*. SCL12(IX-6166), A72(266).

Queen Christina. Cine(III-1404).

Queen Mary. *James Pope-Hennessy*. SCL12(IX-6170), SCL7(VI-3770), A61(200), BMA(463).

Queen of France. *André Castelot*. SCL12(IX-6174), SCL7(VI-3773), A58(204).

Queen Victoria. *Cecil Woodham-Smith*. SCL12(IX-6177), A73(300).

Queen Victoria. *Lytton Strachey*. MP12(IX-5390), MP8(VI-4300), MP4(II-1038), MWL4(1038).

Queen Victoria: Born to Succeed. *Elizabeth, Countess of Longford*.

HAmer(III-1519).

Raditzer. *Peter Matthiessen.* SCL12(IX-6222), SCL7(VI-3810), A62(239).

Rage of Edmund Burke: Portrait of an Ambivalent Conservative, The. *Isaac Kramnick.* LA78(II-686).

Ragtime. *E. L. Doctorow.* SCL12(IX-6227), A76(256).

Raider, The. *Jesse Hill Ford.* LA77(II-642).

Railroads and Regulation, 1877-1916. *Gabriel Kolko.* HAmer(II-1160).

Railway Revolution, The. *L. T. C. Rolt.* HEur(II-609).

Rain. Cine(III-1415).

Rainbird, The. *Sara Lidman.* SCL12(IX-6232), SCL7(VI-3815), A63(205).

*Rainbow, The. *D. H. Lawrence.* MP12(IX-5410), MPCE(III-1842), MP8(VI-4316), MP6(V-2564), MPEng(713), MP1(II-800), MWL1(800).

Rainbow Grocery, The. *William Dickey.* LA79(II-570).

Rainbow on the Road. *Esther Forbes.* SCL12(IX-6235), SCL7(VI-3818), A54(219).

Rainmaker, The. Cine(III-1419).

Raintree County. *Ross Lockridge, Jr.* MP12(IX-5415), MPCE(III-1845)), MP8(VI-4319), MP6(V-2566), MPAm(512), MPv4(437), MP2(II-874), MWL2(874).

*Raise High the Roof Beam, Carpenters. *J. D. Salinger.* SCL12(IX-6238), SCL7(VI-3821), A64(220).

Raisin in the Sun, A. Cine(III-1422).

*Raisin in the Sun, A. *Lorraine Hansberry.* SCL12(IX-6242), SCL7(VI-3824), A60(215).

Rakehells of Heaven, The. *John Boyd.* SF(IV-1746).

Rakóssy. *Cecelia Holland.* SCL12(IX-6245), SCL7(VI-3827), A67(280).

Raleigh and the British Empire. *David B. Quinn.* HAmer(I-48).

Raleigh's Attempts at Colonization in the New World (Event). HAmer(I-46).

Ralph 124C 41 +. *Hugo Gernsback.* SF(IV-1751).

Ralph Roister Doister. *Nicholas Udall.* MP12(IX-5418), MPCE(III-1846), MP8(VI-4322), MP6(V-2569), MPDr(674), MPv3(438), MP2(II-876), MWL2(876).

Ramayana, The. *Aubrey Menen.* SCL12(IX-6249), SCL7(VI-3831), A54(222).

*Ramayana, The. *Valmiki.* MP12(IX-5421), MPCE(III-1847), MP8(VI-4324), MP6(V-2571), MPPo(308), MP3(II-861), MWL3(861).

*Rambler, The. *Samuel Johnson.* MP12(IX-5426), MP8(VI-4327), MP4(II-1044), MWL4(1044).

Rameau's Nephew. *Denis Diderot.* MP12(IX-5429), MP8(VI-4330),

MP6(V-2573),   MPEur(616),   MP3(II-863),   MWL3(863).

Ranke: The Meaning of History.   *Leonard Krieger.*   LA78(II-690).

*Rape of Lucrece, The.   *William Shakespeare.*   MP12(IX-5432),
    MPCE(III-1850),   MP8(VI-4333),   MP6(V-2575),   MPPo(311),
    MPv3(440),   MP2(II-878),   MWL2(878).

Rape of the Fair Country, The.   *Alexander Cordell.*   SCL12(IX-6252),
    SCL7(VI-3834),   A60(218).

*Rape of the Lock, The.   *Alexander Pope.*   MP12(IX-5436),
    MPCE(III-1853),   MP8(VI-4335),   MP6(V-2577),   MPPo(313),
    MP1(II-802),   MWL1(802).

Rapprochement with the People's Republic of China (Event).
    HWor(III-1124).

Rasputin and the Empress.   Cine(III-1425).

*Rasselas.   *Samuel Johnson.*   MP12(IX-5441),   MPCE(III-1857),
    MP8(VI-4337),   MP6(V-2579),   MPEng(716),   MP1(II-804),
    MWL1(804).

Ratification of the Bill of Rights (Event).   HAmer(I-367).

Ratification of the Panama Canal Treaties (Event).   HWor(III-1331).

Rationalization of Ethics (Event).   HAnc(I-328).

Ratner's Star.   *Don DeLillo.*   LA77(II-647).

Ravenshoe.   *Henry Kingsley.*   MP12(IX-5446),   MPCE(III-1860),
    MP8(VI-4340),   MP6(V-2581),   MPEng(719),   MPv4(440),
    MP2(II-880),   MWL2(880).

Raw and the Cooked, The.   *Claude Lévi-Strauss.*   SCL12(IX-6255),
    A70(263).

Razor's Edge, The.   Cine(III-1429).

R. E. Lee.   *Douglas Southall Freeman.*   MP12(IX-5497),
    MP8(VII-4381),   MP6(V-2608),   MPNf(261),   MP3(II-874),
    MWL3(874). A different analysis on this title appears in: HAmer(II-999).

Reaching Judgment at Nuremberg.   *Bradley F. Smith.*   LA78(II-695).

Reaction and Revolution, 1814-1832. Vol. XIII *of* The Rise of Modern Europe
    series.   *Frederick B. Artz.*   HEur(II-689).

Reading the Song of Roland.   *E. Vance.*   HAnc(III-1311).

*Real Life of Sebastian Knight, The.   *Vladimir Nabokov.*
    MP12(IX-5450),   MP8(VI-4343),   MP4(II-1046),   MWL4(1046),
    SCL12(IX-6258),   SCL7(VI-3837),   A60(220).

Real Losses, Imaginary Gains.   *Wright Morris.*   LA77(II-652).

Real Majority, The.   *Richard M. Scammon.*   SCL12(IX-6261),   A71(262).

Reality of Faith, The.   *Friedrich Gogarten.*   RCh(II-1167).

Reality of God and Religion and Agnosticism, The.   *Friedrich Von Hügel.*
    HAnc(I-380).

Realms of Being.   *George Santayana.*   Ph(II-895).

Realms of Gold, The.   *Margaret Drabble.*   SCL12(IX-6265),   A76(261).

Reason and Existenz.   *Karl Jaspers.*   Ph(II-1004).

Reason and Revelation in the Middle Ages.   *Étienne Gilson.*   Different analyses on this title appear in: HAnc(III-1397; III-1566).

Reason Why, The. *Cecil Woodham-Smith*. SCL12(IX-6269), SCL7(VI-3840), A54(225).

Reasonableness of Christianity, The. *John Locke*. RCh(II-551).

Rebecca. Cine(III-1434).

Rebecca. *Daphne du Maurier*. MP12(IX-5452), MPCE(III-1862), MP8(VI-4345), MP6(V-2584), MPEng(722), MP1(II-806), MWL1(806).

Rebel, The. *Albert Camus*. SCL12(IX-6272), SCL7(VI-3843), A54(228). A different analysis on this title appears in: Ph(II-1127).

Rebel Generation, The. *Johanna van Ammers-Küller*. MP12(IX-5456), MPCE(III-1864), MP8(VI-4348), MP6(V-2586), MPEur(619), MP3(II-865), MWL3(865).

Re-Birth. *John Wyndham*. SF(IV-1755).

Rebuilding of Italy, The. *Muriel Grindrod*. HEur(III-1541).

Recapitulation. *Wallace Stegner*. LA80(II-702).

Recognition of the University of Salerno (Event). HAnc(III-1478).

Recognitions, The. *William Gaddis*. SCL12(IX-6275), SCLs(243).

Reconstruction in Philosophy. *John Dewey*. HAnc(I-366).

Reconstruction of Southern Education, The. *Gary Orfield*. HWor(II-968).

Reconstruction of the South (Event). HAmer(II-1003).

Recovery of Confidence, The. *John W. Gardner*. SCL12(IX-6280), A71(265).

Re-Creation of Western Empire (Event). HAnc(II-1146).

*Recruiting Officer, The. *George Farquhar*. MP12(IX-5459), MPCE(III-1865), MP8(VI-4351), MP6(V-2588), MPDr(676), MPv4(442), MP2(II-882), MWL2(882).

*Rector of Justin, The. *Louis Auchincloss*. SCL12(IX-6284), SCL7(VI-3846), A65(234).

*Red and the Black, The. *Stendhal (Marie-Henri Beyle)*. MP12(IX-5463), MPCE(III-1866), MP8(VI-4354), MP6(V-2591), MPEur(622), MP1(II-808), MWL1(808).

*Red Badge of Courage, The. *Stephen Crane*. MP12(IX-5468), MPCE(III-1869), MP8(VI-4357), MP6(V-2593), MPAm(515), MP1(II-811), MWL1(811).

Red Cock Flies to Heaven, The. *Miodrag Bulatovic*. SCL12(IX-6291), SCL7(VI-3852), A63(208).

Red Dust. Cine(III-1438).

Red Fort, The. *James Leasor*. SCL12(IX-6294), SCL7(VI-3855), A58(206).

*Red Room, The. *August Strindberg*. MP12(IX-5473), MPCE(III-1872), MP8(VI-4360), MP6(V-2596), MPEur(625), MP3(II-868), MWL3(868).

*Red Rover, The. *James Fenimore Cooper*. MP12(IX-5477), MPCE(III-1874), MP8(VI-4363), MP6(V-2598), MPAm(518),

MP1(II-813),   MWL1(813).

Red Scare, The (Event).   HAmer(III-1491).

Red Scare: A Study in National Hysteria, 1919-1920, The.   *Robert K. Murray*.   HAmer(III-1494).

Red Shoes, The.   Cine(III-1441).

Red Sky at Morning.   *Richard Bradford*.   SCL12(IX-6297), SCL7(VI-3858),   A69(274).

Red Star in Space.   *Martin Caidin*.   HWor(II-780).

Red Wolves and Black Bears.   *Edward Hoagland*.   LA77(II-658).

*Redburn.   *Herman Melville*.   MP12(IX-5481),   MPCE(III-1876), MP8(VI-4366),   MP6(V-2600),   MPAm(521),   MPv3(442), MP2(II-885),   MWL2(885).

*Redskins, The.   *James Fenimore Cooper*.   MP12(IX-5484), MPCE(III-1877),   MP8(VI-4369),   MP6(V-2602),   MPAm(524), MP3(II-870),   MWL3(870).

Reeling.   *Pauline Kael*.   LA77(II-662).

Refinement of Latin Prose (Event).   HAnc(I-531).

Refinements in Banking (Event).   HAnc(III-1359).

Reflections: Essays, Aphorisms, Autobiographical Writings.   *Walter Benjamin*.   LA79(II-575).

Reflections on Language.   *Noam Chomsky*.   LA77(II-668).

Reflections on the Psalms.   *C. S. Lewis*.   SCL12(IX-6300), SCL7(VI-3861),   A59(209).

Reflexions on Poetry & Poetics.   *Howard Nemerov*.   SCL12(IX-6303), A73(304).

Reform Act of 1867: Disraeli's "Leap in the Dark," The (Event). HEur(II-929).

Reform Act of 1832 (Event).   HEur(II-704).

Reform and Insurrection in Russian Poland, 1856-1865.   *R. F. Leslie*. HEur(II-888).

Reform and Revolution in China: The 1911 Revolution in Hunan and Hubei.   *Joseph W. Esherick*.   HWor(I-97).

Reform of the International Monetary System (Event).   HWor(III-1104).

Reform of the Spanish Church (Event).   HAnc(III-1728).

Reform Program of Mustafa Kemal, The (Event).   HWor(I-225).

Reformation, The.   *Will Durant*.   SCL12(IV-6307),   SCL7(VI-3864), A58(209),   BMA(473).

Reformation Era, 1500-1650, The.   *Harold J. Grimm*.   Different analyses on this title appear in: HEur(I-94; I-151).

Reformation Europe, 1517-1559.   *Geoffrey Rudolph Elton*.   HEur(I-155).

"Reformation in Difficulties: France, 1519-1559, The," *in* Vol. II *of* The New Cambridge Modern History.   *F. C. Spooner*.   HAnc(III-1704).

Reformation in England, The.   *Philip Hughes*.   Different analyses on this title appear in: HEur(I-105; I-125; I-171).

Reforms of Cleisthenes, The (Event).   HAnc(I-205).

"Reforms of Diocletian, The," *in* Vol. XII *of* The Cambridge Ancient
    History. *W. Ensslin.* HAnc(II-831).
Reforms of Peter the Great (Event). HEur(I-364).
Refutation of All Heresies. *Saint Hippolytus.* RCa(I-58).
Regarding Wave. *Gary Snyder.* SCL12(IX-6311), A72(273).
Regiment of Women. *Thomas Berger.* SCL12(IX-6314), A74(328).
Regiomontanus on Triangles. *Barnabas Hughes, O. F. M.* HAnc(II-718).
Regional History of the Railways of Great Britain, Vol. IV: North East
    England, A. *K. Hoole.* HEur(II-663).
Regularization of Papal Elections (Event). HAnc(III-1243).
Regulating Competition in Oil. *Anthony R. Copp.* HWor(II-915).
Rehearsal for Reconstruction. *Willie Lee Rose.* SCL12(IX-6318),
    SCL7(VI-3868), A65(240).
Reichstag Fire, The (Event). HEur(III-1377).
Reichstag Fire: Legend and Truth, The. *Fritz Tobias.* HEur(III-1380).
Reign of George III, 1760-1815, The. *J. Steven Watson.* HEur(II-554).
Reign of King John, The. *Sidney Painter.* HAnc(III-1455).
Reinhart in Love. *Thomas Berger.* SCL12(IX-6321), SCLs(247).
*Reivers, The. *William Faulkner.* MP12(IX-5489), MP8(VI-4373),
    MP4(II-1048), MWL4(1048), SCL12(IX-6325), SCL7(VI-3871),
    A63(211).
Relapse, The. *Sir John Vanbrugh.* MP12(IX-5493), MPCE(III-1879),
    MP8(VI-4377), MP6(V-2606), MPDr(679), MPv4(444),
    MP2(II-887), MWL2(887).
Relativity: A Point of View. *Kelly Cherry.* LA78(II-700).
Relativity and Cosmology. *William J. Kaufmann.* HWor(II-839).
Relativity for the Million. *Martin Gardner.* HEur(III-1162).
Relearning the Alphabet. *Denise Levertov.* SCL12(IX-6331), A71(269).
Religio medici. *Sir Thomas Browne.* RCh(I-450).
Religion and Economic Action. *Kurt Samuelsson.* HWor(I-41).
"Religion and Public Education: The Post-Schempp Years," *in* Religion and
    Public Education. *William E. Ball.* HWor(II-952).
Religion and the American Mind. *Alan E. Heimert.* SCL12(IX-6334),
    SCL7(VI-3876), A67(283). A different analysis on this title appears in:
    HAmer(I-178).
Religion and the State: The Making and Testing of an American
    Tradition. *Evarts B. Greene.* HAmer(I-320).
Religion in America. *William G. McLoughlin* and *Robert N. Bellah,* eds.
    HWor(I-511).
Religion in the Making. *Alfred North Whitehead.* RCh(II-925).
Religion of Numa and Other Essays on the Religion of Ancient Rome,
    The. *Jesse Benedict Carter.* HAnc(I-202).
Religion of the Manichees, The. *F. C. Burkitt.* HAnc(II-809).
Religion Within the Limits of Reason Alone. *Immanuel Kant.*
    RCh(II-626).

Religious A Priori, The. *Ernst Troeltsch*. RCh(II-865).
Religious History of America, A. *Edwin Scott Gaustad*. HWor(I-509).
Religious History of Modern France, Vol. I: From the Revolution to the Third
    Republic. *Adrien Dansette*. HEur(I-518).
Religious History of Modern France, Vol. II: Under the Third
    Republic. *Adrien Dansette*. HEur(III-1145).
Religious Orders in England, The. *David Knowles, O. S. B.* HEur(I-113).
Reluctant Belligerent: American Entry into World War II, The. *Robert A.*
    Divine. Different analyses on this title appear in: HAmer(III-1651),
    HWor(I-467).
Rembrandt's Hat. *Bernard Malamud*. SCL12(IX-6339), A74(332).
Rembrandt's House. *Anthony Bailey*. LA79(II-580).
Remember the House. *Santha Rama Rau*. SCL12(IX-6343),
    SCL7(VI-3881), A57(218).
Remembered Darkness, A. *John Ratti*. SCL12(IX-6346), A70(265).
Remembering Poets: Reminiscences and Opinions. *Donald Hall*.
    LA79(II-584).
*Remembrance of Things Past. *Marcel Proust*. MP12(IX-5500),
    MPCE(III-1880), MP8(VII-4384), MP6(V-2610), MPEur(628),
    MP1(II-815), MWL1(815).
*Remembrance Rock. *Carl Sandburg*. MP12(IX-5505),
    MPCE(III-1883), MP8(VII-4387), MP6(V-2613), MPAm(528),
    MPv3(444), MP2(II-889), MWL2(889).
Reminiscenses. *Douglas MacArthur*. SCL12(IX-6350), SCL7(VI-3884),
    A65(243). A different analysis on this title appears in: HAmer(III-1833).
Renaissance, The. *Walter Pater*. MP12(IX-5511), MP8(VII-4392),
    MP4(II-1052), MWL4(1052).
Renaissance and Renascences in Western Art. *Erwin Panofsky*.
    HAnc(III-1693).
Renaissance Diplomacy. *Garrett Mattingly*. HEur(I-24).
Renan Publishes *Life of Jesus* (Event). HEur(II-892). *See also* Life of Jesus,
    The.
Rendezvous with Rama. *Arthur C. Clarke*. SF(IV-1759).
René Lévesque: Portrait of a Québécois. *Jean Provencher*. HWor(II-824).
Renée Mauperin. *Edmond de Goncourt* and *Jules de Goncourt*.
    MP12(IX-5514), MPCE(III-1885), MP8(VII-4395),
    MP6(V-2618), MPEur(631), MPv4(447), MP2(II-894),
    MWL2(894).
"Reorganization of the Roman Government in 366 B.C. and the So-called
    Licinio-Sextian Laws, The," *in* Historia. *Kurt Von Fritz*.
    HAnc(I-394).
Repeal of the Corn Laws (Event). HEur(II-764).
Report of the President's Commission on the Assassination of President John
    F. Kennedy. *J. Lee Rankin, Earl Warren* and others.
    SCL12(IX-6354), SCL7(VI-3888), A65(246).

Report on Probability A. *Brian W. Aldiss.* SF(IV-1764).
*Report to Greco. *Nikos Kazantzakis.* SCL12(IX-6360),
     SCL7(VI-3894), A66(265).
Representations. *Steven Marcus.* LA77(II-673).
Representative Men. *Ralph Waldo Emerson.* MP12(IX-5518),
     MP8(VII-4398), MP4(II-1054), MWL4(1054).
*Republic. *Plato.* MP12(IX-5522), MP8(VII-4402), MP6(V-2620),
     MPNf(263), MP3(II-876), MWL3(876). A different analysis on this
     title appears in: Ph(I-88).
Republic in Suspense: Politics, Parties, and Personalities in Postwar
     Germany. *Klaus Bolling.* HEur(III-1692).
Republic of Letters: A History of Postwar American Literary Opinion,
     The. *Grant Webster.* LA80(II-705).
Republic of the Southern Cross, The. *Valery Bryusov.* SF(IV-1768).
Republican Ascendancy, 1921-1933. New American Nation *series. John D.*
     Hicks. HAmer(III-1545).
Republican Congressional Insurgency (Event). HAmer(III-1390).
Republican Era, 1869-1901, The. *Leonard D. White.* HAmer(II-1133).
Republican Resurgence in the Elections of 1918 and 1920 (Event).
     HAmer(III-1472).
Republican Roosevelt, The. *John Morton Blum.* HAmer(II-1327).
Requiem for a Dream. *Hubert Selby, Jr.* LA79(II-589).
Requiem for a Heavyweight. Cine(III-1444).
*Requiem for a Nun. *William Faulkner.* MP12(X-5525),
     MP8(VII-4405), MP4(II-1058), MWL4(1058).
Rerum novarum. *Pope Leo XIII.* RCa(II-699).
Reruns. *Jonathan Baumbach.* SCL12(IX-6364), A75(254).
Rescue the Dead. *David Ignatow.* SCL12(IX-6368), SCL7(VI-3898),
     A69(277).
Research into the Origins of Man (Event). HWor(I-218).
Resignation in Protest. *Edward Weisband* and *Thomas M. Franck.*
     SCL12(IX-6371), A76(265).
Resignation of Vice-President Spiro T. Agnew (Event). HWor(III-1188).
Resistance: European Resistance to Nazism, 1940-1945. *M. R. D. Foot.*
     LA78(II-704).
Resistance, Rebellion, and Death. *Albert Camus.* SCL12(IX-6375),
     SCL7(VI-3901), A62(243).
Responses. *Richard Wilbur.* LA77(II-679).
Responsibilities of the Novelist, The. *Frank Norris.* MP12(X-5528),
     MP8(VII-4408), MP4(II-1061), MWL4(1061).
Rest Is Done with Mirrors, The. *Carolyn See.* SCL12(IX-6379),
     A71(271).
*Restlessness of Shanti Andia, The. *Pío Baroja.* SCL12(X-6385),
     SCL7(VI-3905), A60(223).
Restoration of Charles II (Event). HEur(I-337).

Restoration of Charles II, 1658-1660, The. *Godfrey Davies.* HEur(I-338).
Restoration of Ferdinand VII to the Throne of Spain (Event). HEur(II-594).
Restoration of Maria II to the Throne of Portugal (Event). HEur(II-722).
Restoration of the French Bourbon Kings (Event). HEur(II-598).
Restoration, Revolution, Reaction: Economics and Politics in Germany, 1815-1871. *Theodore S. Hamerow.* Different analyses on this title appear in: HEur(II-791; II-884).
*Resurrection. *Count Leo Tolstoy.* MP12(X-5531), MPCE(III-1887), MP8(VII-4411), MP6(V-2623), MPEur(634), MP3(II-879), MWL3(879).
Retief: Ambassador to Space. *Keith Laumer.* SF(IV-1775).
Retracing the Arts to Theology. *Saint Bonaventura. See* On the Reduction of the Arts to Theology.
Retrieval System, The. *Maxine Kumin.* LA79(II-593).
Return, The. *Walter de la Mare.* MP12(X-5536), MPCE(III-1890), MP8(VII-4414), MP6(V-2625), MPEng(725), MPv4(449), MP2(II-896), MWL2(896).
Return from the Captivity (Event). HAnc(I-189).
Return of H*Y*M*A*N*K*A*P*L*A*N, The. *Leo Rosten.* SCL12(X-6389), SCL7(VI-3908), A60(226).
Return of Lady Brace, The. *Nancy Wilson Ross.* SCL12(X-6392), SCL7(VI-3911), A58(212).
*Return of the King, The. *J. R. R. Tolkien.* MP12(X-5540), MPCE(III-1891), MP8(VII-4417), MP4(II-1063), MWL4(1063).
*Return of the Native, The. *Thomas Hardy.* MP12(X-5545), MPCE(III-1894), MP8(VII-4420), MP6(V-2628), MPEng(728), MP1(II-818), MWL1(818).
Return to Thebes. *Allen Drury.* LA78(II-708).
Reunification of Vietnam, The (Event). HWor(III-1243).
Reunion. *Merle Miller.* SCL12(X-6394), SCL7(VI-3913), A54(231).
Reunion and Reaction: The Compromise of 1877 and the End of Reconstruction. *C. Vann Woodward.* HAmer(II-1102).
Revelation and Reason. *Heinrich Emil Brunner.* Ph(II-1058).
Revelation of Jeremiah, The (Event). HAnc(I-149).
Revelations of Divine Love, The. *Lady Julian (Juliana) of Norwich.* Different analyses on this title appear in: RCh(I-284), RCa(I-476).
*Revenge of Bussy d'Ambois, The. *George Chapman.* MP12(X-5550), MPCE(III-1897), MP8(VII-4423), MP6(V-2630), MPDr(682), MP3(II-881), MWL3(881).
Revenger's Tragedy, The. *Cyril Tourneur.* MP12(X-5554), MPCE(III-1898), MP8(VII-4426), MP6(V-2633), MPDr(685), MP3(II-883), MWL3(883).
Revenue Act of 1767 and the Townshend Crisis (Event). HAmer(I-225).
Revenue Laws of Ptolemy Philadelphus (Event). HAnc(I-413).

Revival of Classical Themes in Painting (Event). HAnc(III-1766).
Revival of Roman Law (Event). HAnc(III-1344).
Revocation of the Edict of Nantes (Event). HEur(I-353).
Revolt in Aspromonte. *Corrado Alvardo.* SCL12(X-6397),
SCL7(VI-3916), A63(216).
Revolt of Gunner Asch, The. *Hans Hellmut Kirst.* SCL12(X-6400),
SCL7(VI-3919), A57(221).
*Revolt of the Angels, The. *Anatole France.* MP12(X-5558),
MPCE(III-1900), MP8(VII-4429), MP6(V-2636), MPEur(637),
MP1(II-821), MWL1(821).
Revolt of the Catalans (Event). HEur(I-299).
Revolt of the Catalans, The. *John H. Elliott.* Different analyses on this title
appear in: HEur(I-301; I-306).
Revolt of the Maccabees (Event). HAnc(I-459).
*Revolt of the Masses, The. *José Ortega y Gasset.* MP12(X-5562),
MP8(VII-4432), MP6(V-2638), MPNf(266), MP3(II-886),
MWL3(886).
Revolution at Berkeley. *Michael V. Miller* and *Susan Gilmore,* eds.
HAmer(III-1915).
Revolution Betrayed: What Is the Soviet Union and Where Is It Going?,
The. *Leon Trotsky.* HEur(III-1349).
Revolution in Taste, A. *Louis Simpson.* LA80(II-709).
"Revolution of 1688, The" *in* English Constitutional Conflicts of the
Seventeenth Century, 1603-1689. *J. R. Tanner.* HEur(I-362).
Revolutions of 1848: A Social History. *Priscilla Robertson.* HEur(II-788).
Revolutions of 1848 in Italy (Event). HEur(II-775).
Reynard the Fox. *Unknown.* MP12(X-5565), MPCE(III-1902),
MP8(VII-4435), MP6(V-2640), MPEur(640), MPv4(451),
MP2(II-899), MWL2(899).
RFK Must Die: The History of the Robert Kennedy Assassination and Its
Aftermath. *Robert Blair Kaiser.* HAmer(III-1930).
Rhadamistus and Zenobia. *Prosper Jolyot de Crébillon.* MP12(X-5570),
MPCE(III-1905), MP8(VII-4438), MP6(V-2643), MPDr(688),
MP3(II-888), MWL3(888).
Rhetoric. *Aristotle.* Ph(I-169).
Rhineland Crisis: A Study in Multilateral Diplomacy, The. *James Thomas
Emmerson.* Different analyses on this title appear in: LA78(II-712),
HWor(I-350).
*Rhinoceros. *Eugène Ionesco.* MP12(X-5574), MP8(VII-4441),
MP4(II-1066), MWL4(1066).
Rhodesia: A Study of the Deterioration of a White Society. *Frank
Clements.* HEur(III-1644).
Rhodesia: Racial Conflict or Coexistence? *Patrick O'Meara.* HWor(II-984).
Rhodesia and Independence. *Kenneth Young.* HEur(III-1646).
Rhodesian Declaration of Independence (Event). HEur(III-1642).

Ricardo Publishes *Principles of Political Economy* (Event).   HEur(II-629).
*Riceyman Steps.   *Arnold Bennett*.   MP12(X-5577),   MPCE(III-1907),
    MP8(VII-4444),   MP6(V-2645),   MPEng(731),   MP1(II-823),
    MWL1(823).
Rich Nations and the Poor Nations, The.   *Barbara Ward*.
    SCL12(X-6403),   SCL7(VI-3922),   A63(218).
*Richard the Second.   *William Shakespeare*.   MP12(X-5580),
    MPCE(III-1908),   MP8(VII-4446),   MP6(V-2647),   MPDr(691),
    MPv3(449),   MP2(II-901),   MWL2(901).
*Richard the Third.   *William Shakespeare*.   MP12(X-5585),
    MPCE(III-1911),   MP8(VII-4449),   MP6(V-2649),   MPDr(694),
    MPv3(451),   MP2(II-903),   MWL2(903).
Richard Wagner.   *Robert W. Gutman*.   SCL12(X-6406),   SCL7(VI-3925),
    A69(280).
Richard Wright Reader.   *Richard Wright*.   LA79(II-597).
Richelieu: His Rise to Power.   *Carl J. Burckhardt*.   HEur(I-282).
Riddle of History, The.   *Bruce Mazlish*.   HEur(III-1280).
Riddle of the Tower, The.   *John D. Beresford* and *Esme Wynne-Tyson*.
    SF(IV-1780).
Riddle of the Universe, The.   *Ernst Heinrich Haeckel*.   Ph(II-734).
Ride the High Country.   Cine(III-1447).
Riders in the Chariot.   *Patrick White*.   MP12(X-5590),   MP8(VII-4452),
    MP4(II-1069),   MWL4(1069). A different analysis on this title appears
    in: SCL12(X-6411),   SCL7(VI-3930),   A62(246).
Riders on the Earth.   *Archibald MacLeish*.   LA79(II-601).
Right and the Good, The.   *W. David Ross*.   Ph(II-929).
Right Stuff, The.   *Tom Wolfe*.   LA80(II-713).
Right to Be Indian, The.   *Ernest Shusky*.   HWor(II-869).
*Right You Are—If You Think So.   *Luigi Pirandello*.   MP12(X-5593),
    MPCE(III-1914),   MP8(VII-4455),   MP6(V-2651),   MPDr(697),
    MP3(II-891),   MWL3(891).
Rim of Morning, The.   *William Sloane*.   SF(IV-1784).
Rim Worlds Series, The.   *Arthur Bertram Chandler*.   SF(IV-1789).
*Rime of Petrarch, Le.   *Francesco Petrarch*.   MP12(X-5597),
    MP8(VII-4458),   MP6(V-2654),   MPPo(315),   MP3(II-893),
    MWL3(893).
*Rime of the Ancient Mariner, The.   *Samuel Taylor Coleridge*.
    MP12(X-5600),   MPCE(III-1916),   MP8(VII-4461),   MP6(V-2656),
    MPPo(318),   MP1(II-825),   MWL1(825).
*Ring and the Book, The.   *Robert Browning*.   MP12(X-5603),
    MPCE(III-1919),   MP8(VII-4463),   MP6(V-2658),   MPPo(320),
    MP1(II-826),   MWL1(826).
Ring Around the Sun.   *Clifford D. Simak*.   SF(IV-1794).
Ring of Bright Water.   *Gavin Maxwell*.   SCL12(V-6416),
    SCL7(VI-3934),   A62(250).

*Ring Round the Moon. *Jean Anouilh.* MP12(X-5608), MP8(VII-4466), MP6(V-2660), MPDr(700), MP3(II-896), MWL3(896).

Ringworld. *Larry Niven.* SF(IV-1799).

Riot in Cell Block 11. Cine(III-1451).

*Rip Van Winkle. *Washington Irving.* MP12(X-5611), MPCE(III-1922), MP8(VII-4469), MP6(V-2662), MPAm(533), MPv4(454), MP2(II-905), MWL2(905).

Rise and Fall of New France, The. *George M. Wrong.* HAmer(I-56).

Rise and Fall of the Cyprus Republic, The. *Kyriacos C. Markides.* HWor(III-1196).

Rise and Fall of the Third Reich, The. *William L. Shirer.* SCL12(X-6420), SCL7(VI-3938), A61(206), BMA(477). A different analysis on this title appears in: HEur(III-1379).

Rise of American Civilization, The. *Charles A. Beard* and *Mary R. Beard.* MP12(X-5614), MP8(VII-4471), MP4(II-1071), MWL4(1071).

Rise of Brandenburg-Prussia to 1786, The. *Sidney B. Fay.* HEur(I-399).

Rise of Courtly Love (Event). HAnc(III-1296).

Rise of Italian Fascism, The. *Angelo Tasca.* HEur(III-1322).

Rise of Mass Culture, The (Event). HAmer(III-1501).

Rise of Modern Europe, Vol. VII: The Emergence of the Great Powers, 1685-1715, The. *John B. Wolf.* HEur(I-361).

Rise of Modern Europe, Vol. IX: Competition for Empire, 1740-1763, The. *Walter L. Dorn.* Different analyses on this title appear in: HEur(I-421; I-438; I-454).

Rise of Modern Europe, Vol. XI: A Decade of Revolution, 1789-1799, The. *Crane Brinton.* HEur(I-512).

Rise of Modern Europe, Vol. XII: Europe and the French Imperium, 1799-1814, The. *Geoffrey Bruun.* HEur(II-566).

Rise of Modern Europe, Vol. XVI: A Generation of Materialism, 1871-1900, The. *Carleton J. H. Hayes.* HEur(II-991).

Rise of Parthia (Event). HAnc(I-427).

Rise of Philosophy (Event). HAnc(I-173).

*Rise of Silas Lapham, The. *William Dean Howells.* MP12(X-5618), MPCE(III-1924), MP8(VII-4475), MP6(V-2664), MPAm(535), MP1(II-828), MWL1(828).

Rise of the Christian Platonists (Event). HAnc(II-773).

Rise of the Hansa (Event). HAnc(III-1430).

Rise of the Megalopolis, The (Event). HWor(II-550).

Rise of the Parti Québécois 1967-1976, The. *John Saywell.* HWor(II-822).

Rise of the Pharisees (Event). HAnc(I-477).

Rise of the Social Gospel in American Protestantism, 1865-1915, The. *C. Howard Hopkins.* HAmer(II-1198).

Rise of the Spanish Empire in the Old World and in the New, Vol. II: The Catholic Kings, The. *Roger B. Merriman.* HEur(I-3).

Rise of the Spanish Empire in the Old World and in the New, Vol. IV: The Prudent King, The. *Roger B. Merriman*. HEur(I-191).

Rise of the West, The. *William H. McNeill*. SCL12(X-6428), SCL7(VI-3945), A64(223).

Rise of the West, 1754-1830, The. New American Nation *series*. *Francis S. Philbrick*. HAmer(I-326).

Rise of the Whig Party (Event). HAmer(II-690).

Rise of Theodore Roosevelt, The. *Edmund Morris*. LA80(II-717).

Rise of Transcendentalism (Event). HAmer(I-654).

Rite of Passage. *Alexei Panshin*. SF(IV-1805).

*Rivals, The. *Richard Brinsley Sheridan*. MP12(X-5624), MPCE(III-1927), MP8(VII-4478), MP6(V-2666), MPDr(703), MP1(II-831), MWL1(831).

Rivals: America and Russia Since World War II, The. *Adam B. Ulam*. HWor(II-910).

River Congo, The. *Peter Forbath*. LA78(II-717).

River Niger, The. *Joseph Walker*. SCL12(X-6431), A74(336).

River of Earth. *James Still*. MP12(X-5629), MPCE(III-1930), MP8(VII-4481), MP6(V-2669), MPAm(538), MP1(II-833), MWL1(833).

Rivers and Mountains. *John Ashberry*. SCL12(X-6436), SCL7(VI-3948), A67(287).

Riverworld Series. *Philip José Farmer*. SF(IV-1809).

Rivet in Grandfather's Neck, The. *James Branch Cabell*. MP12(X-5632), MPCE(III-1931), MP8(VII-4484), MP6(V-2671), MPAm(541), MP3(II-898), MWL3(898).

RN: The Memoirs of Richard Nixon. *Richard M. Nixon*. Different analyses on this title appear in: LA79(II-605), HWor(III-1191).

Road to Harpers Ferry, The. *Joseph Chamberlain Furnas*. HAmer(II-922).

Road to Morocco. Cine(III-1454).

Road to Normalcy: The Presidential Campaign and Election of 1920, The. The Johns Hopkins University Studies in History and Political Science *series*. *Wesley M. Bagby*. HAmer(III-1475).

Road to Pearl Harbor, The. *Herbert Feis*. HWor(I-440).

Roads That Led to Rome, The. *Victor W. Von Hagen*. HAnc(I-376).

Roadside Picnic. *Arkady Strugatsky* and *Boris Strugatsky*. SF(IV-1817).

*Roan Stallion. *Robinson Jeffers*. MP12(X-5636), MPCE(III-1932), MP8(VII-4487), MP6(V-2673), MPPo(323), MP1(II-835), MWL1(835).

Roar Lion Roar. *Irvin Faust*. SCL12(X-6439), SCL7(VI-3951), A66(269).

Roaring Twenties, The. Cine(III-1458).

*Rob Roy. *Sir Walter Scott*. MP12(X-5638), MPCE(III-1933), MP8(VII-4489), MP6(V-2675), MPEng(733), MP1(II-837), MWL1(837).

The.   *Charles G. Haines.*   HAmer(I-347).

Role of the Warsaw Pact in Soviet Policy.   *Thomas W. Wolfe.*
HWor(II-719).

Roll, Jordan, Roll.   *Eugene D. Genovese.*   SCL12(X-6462),   A75(258).

*Roman Actor, The.   *Philip Massinger.*   MP12(X-5665),
MPCE(III-1947),   MP8(VII-4508),   MP6(V-2687),   MPDr(706),
MP3(II-901),   MWL3(901).

"Roman Alimentary Program and Italian Agriculture, The," *in* Transactions
and Proceedings of the American Philological Association.   *Frank C.
Bourne.*   HAnc(II-678).

"Roman and Canon Law in the Middle Ages," *in* Vol. V. *of* The Cambridge
Medieval History.   *Harold Dexter Hazeltine.*   HAnc(III-1494).

"Roman Aqueducts as Monuments of Architecture, The," *in* American
Journal of Archaeology.   *H. C. Butler.*   HAnc(II-628).

Roman Britain and the English Settlements.   *R. G. Collingwood* and *J. N. L
Myers.*   HAnc(II-619).

Roman Campagna in Classical Times, The.   *Thomas Ashby.*   HAnc(I-374).

Roman Citizenship, The.   *Adrian N. Sherwin-White.*   Different analyses on
this title appear in: HAnc(I-335; I-508).

Roman Conquest of Britain (Event).   HAnc(II-616).

Roman de la Rose, Le.   *L. Thuasne.*   HAnc(III-1468).

Roman Destruction of the Temple at Jerusalem (Event).   HAnc(II-648).

Roman Law: An Historical Introduction.   *Hans Julius Wolff.*
HAnc(II-1037).

Roman Law in Medieval Europe.   *Paul Vinogradoff.*   HAnc(II-1008).

"Roman Monumental Arches," *in* Supplementary Papers of the American
School of Classical Studies in Rome.   *D. Curtis.*   HAnc(I-504).

Roman Poets of the Augustan Age: Horace and the Elegiac Poets,
The.   *W. Y. Sellar.*   HAnc(II-576).

Roman Political Life.   *Abel H. J. Greenidge.*   HAnc(I-451).

Roman Politics 220-150 B.C.   *H. H. Scullard.*   HAnc(I-449).

Roman Public Life.   *Abel H. J. Greenidge.*   HAnc(I-222).

Roman Revolution, The.   *Ronald Syme.*   Different analyses on this title
appear in: HAnc(I-547; I-565).

Roman Roads.   *Victor W. Von Hagen.*   HAnc(I-376).

Roman Science: Origins, Development, and Influence to the Later Middle
Ages.   *William H. Stahl.*   HAnc(II-656).

Roman Wall.   *Bryher.*   SCL12(X-6466),   SCL7(VI-3974),   A54(234).

Romance of a Schoolmaster, The.   *Edmondo de Amicis.*   MP12(X-5669),
MPCE(III-1949),   MP8(VII-4511),   MP6(V-2689),   MPEur(643),
MPv4(455),   MP2(II-909),   MWL2(909).

Romance of Leonardo da Vinci, The.   *Dmitri Merejkowski.*
MP12(X-5672),   MPCE(III-1950),   MP8(VII-4514),   MP6(V-2691),
MPEur(646),   MPv3(456),   MP2(II-911),   MWL2(911).

*Romance of the Forest, The.   *Mrs. Ann Radcliffe.*   MP12(X-5675),

MPCE(III-1951),   MP8(VII-4517),   MP6(V-2694),   MPEng(748),
MPv4(458),   MP2(II-914),   MWL2(914).
Romance of the Three Kingdoms. *Lo Kuan-chung.* MP12(X-5681),
MPCE(III-1952),   MP8(VII-4522),   MP6(V-2698),   MPEur(649),
MP3(II-903),   MWL3(903).
*Romantic Comedians, The. *Ellen Glasgow.* MP12(X-5684),
MPCE(III-1954),   MP8(VII-4524),   MP6(V-2700),   MPAm(544),
MP1(II-846),   MWL1(846).
*Romantic Egoists, The. *Louis Auchincloss.* SCL12(X-6469),
SCL7(VI-3977),   A54(237).
Romantic Ladies, The. *Molière (Jean Baptiste Poquelin).*
MP12(X-5689),   MPCE(III-1957),   MP8(VII-4527),   MP6(V-2702),
MPDr(709),   MPv3(458),   MP2(II-918),   MWL2(918).
Romantic Manifesto, The. *Ayn Rand.* SCL12(X-6472),   A72(276).
Romany Rye, The. *George Henry Borrow.* MP12(X-5693),
MPCE(III-1960),   MP8(VII-4529),   MP6(V-2704),   MPEng(753),
MP1(II-849),   MWL1(849).
"Rome and Carthage: The First Punic War," *in* Vol. VII *of* The Cambridge
Ancient History. *Frank Tenney.* HAnc(I-410).
Rome and the City of God. *Karl Frederick Morrison.* HAnc(II-854).
Rome and the Counter-Reformation in England. *Philip Hughes.*
HEur(I-178).
Rome Becomes the Capital of Italy (Event).   HEur(II-958).
Rome Haul. *Walter D. Edmonds.* MP12(X-5697),   MPCE(IV-1962),
MP8(VII-4532),   MP6(V-2707),   MPAm(547),   MP1(II-851),
MWL1(851).
*Romeo and Juliet. *William Shakespeare.* MP12(X-5700),
MPCE(IV-1963),   MP8(VII-4535),   MP6(V-2709),   MPDr(711),
MP1(II-853),   MWL1(853).
*Romola. *George Eliot.* MP12(X-5705),   MPCE(IV-1966),
MP8(VII-4538),   MP6(V-2712),   MPEng(756),   MP1(II-856),
MWL1(856).
Roof of Tiger Lilies, A. *Donald Hall.* SCL12(X-6475),
SCL7(VI-3980),   A65(252).
Room at the Top.   Cine(III-1469).
*Room at the Top. *John Braine.* MP12(X-5709),   MP8(VII-4541),
MP4(II-1078),   MWL4(1078),   SCL12(X-6479),   SCL7(VI-3984),
A58(214),   BMA(484).
*Room with a View, A. *E. M. Forster.* MP12(X-5712),
MPCE(IV-1968),   MP8(VII-4544),   MP6(V-2714),   MPEng(759),
MP3(II-905),   MWL3(905).
Roosevelt: The Lion and the Fox. *James MacGregor Burns.*
SCL12(X-6489),   SCL7(VI-3993),   A57(224). A different analysis on
this title appears in: HAmer(III-1671).
Roosevelt: The Soldier of Freedom. *James MacGregor Burns.*

MP8(VII-4555), MP6(V-2722), MPEng(765), MPv3(462), MP2(II-924), MWL2(924).

Royal Charles: Charles II and the Restoration. *Lady Antonia Fraser.* LA80(II-732).

Royal Charles, Ruler, and Rake. *David Loth.* HEur(I-339).

Royal Flash. *George McDonald Fraser.* SCL12(X-6517), A71(280).

Royal Hunt of the Sun, The. *Peter Shaffer.* SCL12(X-6521), SCL7(VI-4014), A66(275).

Royo County. *Robert Roper.* SCL12(X-6525), A74(342).

Ruan. *Bryher.* SCL12(X-6528), SCL7(VI-4018), A61(216).

*Rubáiyát of Omar Khayyám, The. *Edward FitzGerald.* MP12(X-5730), MP8(VII-4558), MP6(V-2725), MPPo(325), MP3(II-907), MWL3(907).

Rudolf Diesel: Pioneer of the Age of Power. *W. Robert Nitske* and *Charles Marrow Wilson.* HEur(II-1101).

*Rule a Wife and Have a Wife. *John Fletcher.* MP12(X-5732), MPCE(IV-1977), MP8(VII-4560), MP6(V-2727), MPDr(717), MP3(II-909), MWL3(909).

Rule and Exercise of Holy Living and Holy Dying, The. *Jeremy Taylor.* RCh(I-477).

"Rule of Democracy 1905-1914, The," *in* A History of the English People in the Nineteenth Century. *Elie Halévy.* HEur(III-1217).

Rule of St. Benedict, The. *Saint Benedict of Nursia.* Different analyses on this title appear in: RCh(I-172), RCa(I-234).

Rum, Religion, and Votes: 1928 Re-Examined. *Ruth C. Silva.* HAmer(III-1569).

Run to the Waterfall. *Arturo Vivante.* LA80(II-736).

*Runaway Horses. *Yukio Mishima.* SCL12(X-6531), A74(345).

Rungless Ladder: Harriet Beecher Stowe and New England Puritanism, The. *Charles H. Foster.* HAmer(II-861).

Runner, The. *Gary Gildner.* LA79(II-613).

Running Dog. *Don DeLillo.* LA79(II-617).

Run-Through. *John Houseman.* SCL12(X-6535), A73(308).

Rupert Brooke. *Christopher Hassall.* SCL12(X-6538), SCL7(VI-4021), A65(256).

*R.U.R. *Karel Čapek.* MP12(X-5736), MPCE(IV-1979), MP8(VII-4563), MP6(V-2729), MPDr(720), MPv4(464), MP2(II-927), MWL2(927). A different analysis on this title appears in: SF(IV-1837).

Rural Russia Under the Old Regime. *G. T. Robinson.* HEur(II-868).

*Ruslan and Lyudmila. *Alexander Pushkin.* MP12(X-5740), MP8(VII-4566), MP4(II-1080), MWL4(1080).

Russia: A History and Interpretation. *Michael T. Florinsky.* Different analyses on this title appear in: HAnc(III-1464; III-1740; III-1745), HEur(I-199; I-249; I-366; II-1065; III-1171; III-1182; III-1681).

Russia and the Balkans, 1870-1880. *B. H. Sumner.* HEur(II-1011).
Russia and the West Under Lenin and Stalin. *George F. Kennan.*
 SCL12(X-6543), SCL7(VI-4025), A62(254), BMA(487). A
 different analysis on this title appears in: HWor(I-322).
Russia at War, 1941-1945. *Alexander Werth.* SCL12(X-6548),
 SCL7(VI-4030), A65(260).
Russia in Revolution, 1900-1930. *Harrison E. Salisbury.* LA79(II-622).
Russia Invades East Prussia (Event). HWor(I-101).
Russia Leaves the War, Volume I. *George F. Kennan.* SCL12(X-6552),
 SCL7(VI-4034), A57(227), BMA(492).
Russia Puts a Man in Space (Event). HEur(III-1618).
Russia, the Atom and the West. *George F. Kennan.* SCL12(X-6556),
 SCL7(VI-4038), A59(214). A different analysis on this title appears in:
 HEur(III-1564).
Russia Under the Old Regime. *Richard Pipes.* SCL12(X-6559),
 A75(265).
Russian Beauty and Other Stories, A. *Vladimir Nabokov.*
 SCL12(X-6564), A74(349).
Russian Empire 1801-1917, The. *Hugh Seton-Watson.* SCL12(X-6567),
 SCL7(VI-4041), A68(283).
Russian Far Eastern Policy, 1881-1904: With Special Emphasis on the Causes
 of the Russo-Japanese War. *Andrew Malozemoff.* HEur(III-1151).
Russian Religion Mind: Kievan Christianity: The Tenth to the Thirteenth
 Centuries, The. *George P. Fedotov.* HAnc(III-1207).
Russian Revolution, 1917, The. *N. N. Sukhanov.* SCL12(X-6571),
 SCL7(VI-4045), A55(217).
Russian Revolution, 1917-1921, The. *William Henry Chamberlain.*
 Different analyses on this title appear in: HEur(III-1274),
 HWor(I-155).
Russian Thinkers. *Isaiah Berlin.* LA79(II-627).
Russians, The. *Hedrick Smith.* LA77(II-694).
Russia's Education Heritage. *William H. E. Johnson.* HEur(I-434).
Russo-American Relations, 1815-1867. *Benjamin Platt Thomas.*
 HAmer(II-1040).
Russo-German Alliance, August, 1939-June, 1941, The. *A. Rossi.*
 HEur(III-1438).
Russo-German War, 1941-1945, The. *Albert Seaton.* HWor(I-452).
Russo-Japanese War (Event). HEur(III-1148).
Ryan's Daughter. Cine(III-1480).

Sabrina. Cine(III-1484).
Sack of Rome, The (Event). HAnc(II-935).
Sacraments, The. *G. C. Berkouwer.* HAnc(III-1341).
Sacred and Profane Love Machine, The. *Iris Murdoch.* SCL12(X-6574),
 A75(270).

Sands of Dunkirk, The. *Richard Collier.* SCL12(X-6626), SCL7(VI-4070), A62(258).

Sanine. *Mikhail Artsybashev.* MP12(X-5787), MPCE(IV-1996), MP8(VII-4606), MP6(V-2753), MPEur(660), MP3(II-921), MWL3(921).

Sanreizan Hiroku. *Ryo Hanmura.* SF(IV-1854).

Santa Fe Trail, The. *Robert L. Duffus.* HAmer(I-590).

Santa Maria: My Crusade for Portugal. *Henrique Galvao.* HEur(III-1676).

Santaroga Barrier, The. *Frank Herbert.* SF(IV-1859).

*Sappho. *Alphonse Daudet.* MP12(X-5790), MPCE(III-1998), MP8(VII-4609), MP6(V-2755), MPEur(663), MP1(II-865), MWL1(865).

Sappho. *Franz Grillparzer.* MP12(X-5793), MPCE(IV-1999), MP8(VII-4611), MP6(V-2757), MPDr(730), MP3(II-923), MWL3(923).

Sara Teasdale: Woman & Poet. *William Drake.* LA80(II-741).

Saragossa. *Benito Pérez Galdós.* MP12(X-5796), MPCE(IV-2000), MP8(VII-4614), MP6(V-2759), MPEur(665), MPv4(471), MP2(II-935), MWL2(935).

Sarah Bernhardt and Her World. *Joanna Richardson.* LA78(II-740).

*Sartor Resartus. *Thomas Carlyle.* MP12(X-5799), MP8(VII-4617), MP6(V-2761), MPNf(271), MP3(II-925), MWL3(925).

*Sartoris. *William Faulkner.* MP12(X-5801), MP8(VII-4619), MP4(II-1091), MWL4(1091).

Satana dei Miracoli. *Ugo Malaguti.* SF(IV-1863).

*Satanstoe. *James Fenimore Cooper.* MP12(X-5804), MPCE(IV-2002), MP8(VII-4623), MP6(V-2763), MPAm(553), MP3(II-927), MWL3(927).

Satellite Spin-Off: The Achievements of Space Flight, The. *Günter Paul.* HWor(II-755).

Satires. *Nicolas Boileau-Despréaux.* MP12(X-5809), MP8(VII-4627), MP4(II-1094), MWL4(1094).

*Satires. *Juvenal (Decimus Junius Juvenalis).* MP12(X-5812), MP8(VII-4630), MP6(V-2767), MPPo(327), MP3(II-931), MWL3(931).

*Satires. *Lucian.* MP12(X-5814), MP8(VII-4632), MP4(II-1097), MWL4(1097).

*Satiromastix. *Thomas Dekker.* MP12(X-5817), MPCE(IV-2004), MP8(VII-4635), MP6(V-2769), MPDr(733), MP3(II-933), MWL3(933).

*Saturday Night and Sunday Morning. *Alan Sillitoe.* SCL12(X-6629), SCL7(VI-4073), A60(229).

*Satyricon, The. *Petronius (Gaius Petronius Arbiter).* MP12(X-5820), MPCE(IV-2005), MP8(VII-4638), MP6(V-2771), MPEur(668), MPv3(466), MP2(II-938), MWL2(938).

Saurus. *Eden Phillpotts.* SF(IV-1866).

Savage God, The. *A. Alvarez.* SCL12(X-6634), A73(314).

Savage Mind, The. *Claude Lévi-Strauss.* SCL12(X-6637), SCLs(251).

Savage State, The. *George Conchon.* SCL12(X-6641), SCL7(VI-4077),
A66(278).

Save Every Lamb. *Jesse Stuart.* SCL12(X-6644), SCL7(VI-4080),
A65(263).

Scale of Perfection, The. *Walter Hilton.* RCh(I-316). *See* Laer of
Perfection, The.

Scandals of the Grant Administration (Event). HAmer(II-1054).

Scandals of the Harding Administration (Event). HAmer(III-1525).

"Scandinavia," *in* The Cambridge Modern History. *Ludvig Stavenow.*
HEur(III-1168).

Scarface: The Shame of the Nation. Cine(III-1490).

*Scarlet Letter, The. *Nathaniel Hawthorne.* MP12(X-5826),
MPCE(IV-2008), MP8(VII-4641), MP6(V-2773), MPAm(557),
MP1(II-867), MWL1(867).

Scarlet Pimpernel, The. Cine(IV-1493).

Scarlet Thread, The. *Doris Betts.* SCL12(X-6647), SCL7(VI-4083),
A66(281).

Scepticism and Animal Faith. *George Santayana.* MP12(X-5831),
MP8(VII-4644), MP6(V-2776), MPNf(273), MP3(II-935),
MWL3(935).

Schatten Affair, The. *Frederic Morton.* SCL12(X-6650),
SCL7(VI-4086), A66(283).

School for Dictators, The. *Ignazio Silone.* SCL12(X-6653),
SCL7(VI-4089), A64(228).

School for Husbands, The. *Molière (Jean Baptiste Poquelin).*
MP12(X-5834), MPCE(IV-2011), MP8(VII-4647), MP6(V-2779),
MPDr(736), MP3(II-938), MWL3(938).

*School for Scandal, The. *Robert Brinsley Sheridan.* MP12(X-5838),
MPCE(IV-2013), MP8(VII-4650), MP6(V-2781), MPDr(739),
MP1(II-869), MWL1(869).

School for Wives, The. *Molière (Jean Baptiste Poquelin).*
MP12(X-5843), MPCE(IV-2016), MP8(VII-4653), MP6(V-2783),
MPDr(742), MPv3(469), MP2(II-940), MWL2(940).

Science and Health With Key to the Scriptures. *Mary Baker Eddy.*
RCh(II-775).

Science and Politics in the Ancient World. *Benjamin Farrington.*
HAnc(I-513).

Science and the Modern World. *Alfred North Whitehead.* HWor(I-83).

Science Awakening. *B. L. Van Der Waerden.* HAnc(I-23).

Science Fiction of Edgar Allan Poe, The. *Edgar Allan Poe.* SF(IV-1871).

Science of Culture: A Study of Man and Civilization, The. *Leslie A. White.*
HAnc(I-68).

Science of Mechanics in the Middle Ages, The. *Marshall Clagett.*
    HAnc(III-1616).
Science, Religion and Christianity. *Hans Urs von Balthasar.* RCa(II-1021).
Scientific Revolution, 1500-1800, The. *A. R. Hall.* HEur(I-136).
Scientists Against Time. *James P. Baxter.* HAmer(III-1694).
Scientists Under Hitler: Politics and the Physics Community in the Third
    Reich. *Alan D. Beyerchen.* LA78(II-743).
Scipio Aemilianus. *A. E. Astin.* HAnc(I-456).
Scipio Africanus: Soldier and Politician. *H. H. Scullard.* HAnc(I-439).
Scopes Trial, The (Event). HAmer(III-1549).
*Scornful Lady, The. *Francis Beaumont* and *John Fletcher.*
    MP12(X-5848), MPCE(IV-2019), MP8(VII-4655), MP6(V-2785),
    MPDr(744), MP3(II-940), MWL3(940).
Scorpion, The. *Albert Memmi.* SCL12(X-6656), A72(285).
Scott Fitzgerald. *Andrew Turnbull.* SCL12(X-6659), SCL7(VI-4092),
    A63(234).
Scottish Chiefs, The. *Jane Porter.* MP12(X-5851), MPCE(IV-2021),
    MP8(VII-4658), MP6(V-2788), MPEng(775), MPv3(471),
    MP2(II-942), MWL2(942).
Scott's Last Expedition. *Captain Robert Falcon Scott.* MP12(X-5855),
    MP8(VII-4661), MP4(II-1100), MWL4(1100).
Scottsboro. *Dan T. Carter.* SCL12(X-6663), A70(269). A different
    analysis on this title appears in: HAmer(III-1590).
Scottsboro Trials, The (Event). HAmer(III-1588).
Scoundrel Time. *Lillian Hellman.* LA77(II-702).
Screwtape Letters, The. *C. S. Lewis.* RCh(II-1068).
Scripture-Doctrine of the Trinity, The. *Samuel Clarke.* RCh(II-562).
Scrolls from the Dead Sea, The. *Edmund Wilson.* SCL12(X-6667),
    SCL7(VI-4096), A55(220).
Sculpture and Sculptors of the Greeks, The. *Gisela M. A. Richter.*
    HAnc(I-299).
Sculpture in Italy: 1400-1500. *Charles Seymour, Jr.* HAnc(III-1667).
Sea and the Jungle, The. *H. M. Tomlinson.* MP12(X-5858),
    MP8(VII-4664), MP6(V-2790), MPNf(276), MP3(II-942),
    MWL3(942).
Sea Dreamer, The. *Gérard Jean-Aubry.* SCL12(X-6670),
    SCL7(VI-4099), A58(222).
Sea Fights and Shipwrecks. *Hanson W. Baldwin.* SCL12(X-6674),
    SCL7(VI-4103), A55(223).
Sea Hawk, The. Cine(IV-1497).
*Sea of Grass, The. *Conrad Richter.* MP12(X-5861), MPCE(IV-2022),
    MP8(VII-4667), MP6(V-2793), MPAm(560), MP1(II-872),
    MWL1(872).
Sea Road to the Indies. *Henry H. Hart.* HEur(I-12).
*Sea Wolf, The. *Jack London.* MP12(X-5865), MPCE(IV-2024),

Second Polish Rebellion (Event). HEur(II-886).

Second Shepherd's Play, The. *Unknown.* MP12(X-5886), MPCE(IV-2031), MP8(VII-4687), MP6(V-2804), MPDr(753), MPv4(473), MP2(II-949), MWL2(949).

Second Skin. *John Hawkes.* SCL12(X-6715), SCL7(VI-4123), A65(266).

Second Tree from the Corner, The. *E. B. White.* SCL12(X-6718), SCL7(VI-4126), A54(246).

Second Vatican Council (Event). HEur(III-1633).

Second War of the Worlds, The. *Arkady Strugatsky* and *Boris Strugatsky.* SF(IV-1879).

Second World War, Vols. I-VI, The. *Winston S. Churchill.* MP12(X-5890), MP8(VII-4689), MP6(V-2806), MPNf(279), MP3(II-947), MWL3(947).

Second World War, Vol. II: Their Finest Hour, The. *Winston S. Churchill.* HEur(III-1452).

Second World War, Vol. VI: Triumph and Tragedy, The. *Winston S. Churchill.* HEur(III-1520).

Secret, The. *Alba de Céspedes.* SCL12(X-6721), SCL7(VI-4129), A59(219).

*Secret Agent, The. *Joseph Conrad.* MP12(X-5893), MPCE(IV-2034), MP8(VII-4692), MP6(V-2808), MPEng(778), MP3(II-949), MWL3(949).

Secret Conversations of Henry Kissinger, The. *Matti Golan.* LA77(II-709).

Secret Diary of Harold L. Ickes: Volume II, The. *Harold L. Ickes.* SCL12(X-6724), SCL7(VI-4132), A54(249).

Secret Diplomacy of the Habsburgs, 1598-1625, The. *Charles Howard Carter.* HEur(I-222).

Secret of Luca, The. *Ignazio Silone.* SCL12(X-6727), SCL7(VI-4135), A59(222).

"Secret Societies and the First International," *in Drachkovitch's* The Revolutionary Internationals, 1864-1943. *Boris I. Nicolaevsky.* HEur(II-899).

Secretary, Martin Bormann: The Man Who Manipulated Hitler, The. *Jochen von Lang.* LA80(II-746).

Secretary Stimson: A Study in Statecraft. *Richard N. Current.* HAmer(III-1602).

Seduction and Betrayal: Women and Literature. *Elizabeth Hardwick.* SCL12(X-6730), A75(279).

Seed, The. *Pierre Gascar.* SCL12(X-6735), SCL7(VI-4138), A60(235).

Seed and the Sower, The. *Laurens Van Der Post.* SCL12(X-6738), SCL7(VI-4141), A64(231).

*Seed Beneath the Snow, The. *Ignazio Silone.* SCL12(X-6741), SCL7(VI-4144), A66(286).

Seed of Light. *Edmund Cooper.* SF(IV-1884).

Seedling Stars, The. *James Blish.* SF(IV-1888).

Seeds of Contemplation. *Thomas Merton.* RCa(II-955).

Seedtime on the Cumberland. *Harriette Simpson Arnow.*
SCL12(X-6747), SCL7(VI-4150), A61(222).

"Seeking an End to Cosmic Loneliness," in New York Times. *Timothy Ferris.* HWor(II-831).

Segaki. *David Stacton.* SCL12(X-6750), SCL7(VI-4153), A60(237).

Segregation. *Robert Penn Warren.* SCL12(X-6753), SCL7(VI-4156),
A57(236).

*Seize the Day. *Saul Bellow.* SCL12(X-6756), SCLs(254).

*Sejanus. *Ben Jonson.* MP12(X-5896), MPCE(IV-2035),
MP8(VII-4695), MP6(V-2811), MPDr(755), MP3(II-951),
MWL3(951).

Selected and Collected Poems. *Bill Knott.* LA78(II-748).

Selected Essays of Delmore Schwartz. *Delmore Schwartz.*
SCL12(X-6765), A72(291).

Selected Letters. *Baron Friedrich von Hügel.* RCh(II-938).

Selected Letters of Conrad Aiken. *Conrad Aiken.* LA79(II-652).

Selected Letters of Dylan Thomas. *Dylan Thomas.* SCL12(X-6768),
SCL7(VI-4159), A67(295).

Selected Letters of James Joyce. *James Joyce.* SCL12(X-6772),
A76(279).

Selected Letters of John O'Hara. *John O'Hara.* LA79(II-656).

Selected Letters of Malcolm Lowry. *Malcolm Lowry.* SCL12(X-6776),
SCL7(VI-4163), A66(291).

Selected Letters of Robert Frost. *Robert Frost.* SCL12(X-6780),
SCL7(VI-4167), A65(269).

Selected Poems. *A. R. Ammons.* SCL12(X-6787), SCL7(VI-4173),
A68(287).

Selected Poems. *Margaret Atwood.* LA79(II-661).

Selected Poems. *Joseph Brodsky.* SCL12(X-6790), A75(284).

Selected Poems. *Austin Clarke.* LA77(II-715).

Selected Poems. *Rubén Dario.* SCL12(X-6793), SCL7(VI-4176),
A66(295).

Selected Poems. *Randall Jarrell.* SCL12(X-6799), SCL7(VI-4182),
A55(225).

Selected Poems. *Robert Lowell.* LA77(II-720).

Selected Poems. *John Masefield.* LA79(II-666).

Selected Poems. *Thomas Merton.* SCL12(X-6802), SCL7(VI-4185),
A68(290).

Selected Poems. *John Crowe Ransom.* MP12(X-5899),
MP8(VII-4698), MP6(V-2813), MPPo(332), MP3(II-954),
MWL3(954). A different analysis on this title appears in:
SCL12(X-6806), SCLs(262).

Selected Poems. *Louis Simpson.* SCL12(X-6811), SCL7(VI-4189),

A66(300).

Selected Poems. *Robert Watson.* SCL12(X-6814), A75(287).

Selected Poems: New and Old 1923-1966. *Robert Penn Warren.* SCL12(X-6817), SCL7(VI-4192), A67(298).

Selected Poems: 1944-1970. *Gwendolyn Brooks.* SCL12(X-6822), SCLs(266).

Selected Poems: 1928-58. *Stanley Kunitz.* SCL12(X-6825), SCLs(268).

Selected Poems, 1950-1975. *Thom Gunn.* LA80(II-750).

Selected Poems, 1923-1975. *Robert Penn Warren.* LA78(II-753).

Selected Poems 1923-1967. *Jorge Luis Borges.* SCL12(X-6828), A73(321).

Selected Stories. *Nadine Gordimer.* LA77(II-725).

Selected Stories. *V. S. Pritchett.* LA79(II-669).

Selected Tales. *Nikolai Leskov.* SCL12(X-6832), SCL7(VI-4197), A62(261).

Selected Writings on the Spiritual Life. *Saint Peter Damian.* RCh(I-190).

Self Condemned. *Wyndham Lewis.* SCL12(X-6835), SCL7(VI-4200), A55(228).

Self-Portrait in a Convex Mirror. *John Ashbery.* SCL12(X-6838), A76(283).

Self-Tormentor, The. *Terence (Publius Terentius Afer).* MP12(X-5902), MPCE(IV-2037), MP8(VII-4701), MP6(V-2815), MPDr(758), MP3(II-956), MWL3(956).

Seljuks in Asia Minor, The. *Tamara Talbot Rice.* HAnc(III-1254).

Sempiternin. *Lajos Mesterházi.* SF(IV-1892).

Senator Joe McCarthy. *Richard H. Rovere.* HAmer(III-1819).

Senefelder Invents Lithography (Event). HEur(I-542).

*Sense and Sensibility. *Jane Austen.* MP12(X-5905), MPCE(IV-2038), MP8(VII-4704), MP6(V-2818), MPEng(781), MPv3(478), MP2(II-951), MWL2(951).

Sense of Beauty, The. *George Santayana.* Ph(II-718).

Sense of Dark, A. *William Malliol.* SCL12(X-6842), SCL7(VI-4203), A68(293).

Sense of Reality, A. *Graham Greene.* SCL12(X-6845), SCL7(VI-4206), A64(234).

*Sentimental Education, A. *Gustave Flaubert.* MP12(X-5909), MPCE(IV-2039), MP8(VII-4707), MP6(V-2820), MPEur(671), MP1(II-876), MWL1(876).

*Sentimental Journey, A. *Laurence Sterne.* MP12(X-5914), MPCE(IV-2042), MP8(VII-4710), MP6(V-2823), MPEng(784), MP1(II-879), MWL1(879).

*Separate Peace, A. *John Knowles.* SCL12(X-6847), SCL7(VI-4208), A61(225).

Separate Reality, A. *Carlos Castaneda.* SCL12(X-6851), A72(294).

Separate Tables. Cine(IV-1506).

Separation of the Church and the State in France (Event).   HEur(III-1143).
Sepoltura, La.   *Gianni Montanari*.   SF(IV-1896).
Sergeant Getúlio.   *João Ubaldo Ribeiro*.   LA79(II-672).
Sergeant York.   Cine(IV-1509).
Sergei Witte and the Industrialization of Russia.   *Theodore H. Von Laue*.
    HEur(II-1064).
Sergei Witte Begins the Industrialization of Russia (Event).   HEur(II-1062).
Serious Call to a Devout and Holy Life, A.   *William Law*.   RCh(II-566).
Sermo contra Auxentium.   *Saint Ambrose*.   RCa(I-132).
Sermons and Treatises.   *Johannes Eckhart*.   RCh(I-245).
Serpico.   Cine(IV-1512).
Servile State, The.   *Hilaire Belloc*.   RCa(II-754).
*Set This House on Fire.   *William Styron*.   MP12(X-5919),
    MP8(VII-4713),   MP4(II-1106),   MWL4(1106),   SCL12(X-6854),
    SCL7(VI-4211),   A61(228),   BMA(502).
Settlement of Connecticut (Event).   HAmer(I-91).
Settlement of Georgia (Event).   HAmer(I-182).
Settlement of Jamestown (Event).   HAmer(I-59).
Settlement of the Carolinas (Event).   HAmer(I-132).
Settlement of the Iconoclastic Struggle (Event).   HAnc(II-1152).
*Seven Against Thebes.   *Aeschylus*.   MP12(X-5922),   MPCE(IV-2045),
    MP8(VII-4716),   MP6(V-2825),   MPDr(761),   MPv3(480),
    MP2(II-953),   MWL2(953).
Seven Books of History Against the Pagans.   *Paulus Orosius*.   Different
    analyses on this title appear in: RCh(I-145),   RCa(I-178).
Seven Brides for Seven Brothers.   Cine(IV-1515).
Seven Epistles of Ignatius, The.   *Saint Ignatius, Bishop of Antioch*.
    RCh(I-7).
*Seven Gothic Tales.   *Isak Dinesen*.   MP12(X-5926),   MP8(VII-4719),
    MP6(V-2827),   MPEur(674),   MP3(II-958),   MWL3(958).
Seven into Space.   *Joseph Bell*.   HWor(II-937).
Seven Islands, The.   *Jon Godden*.   SCL12(X-6859),   SCL7(VI-4215),
    A57(238).
Seven Liberal Arts: A Study in Mediaeval Culture, The.   *Paul Abelson*.
    HAnc(II-1001).
Seven Men Among the Penguins.   *Mario Marret*.   SCL12(X-6862),
    SCL7(VI-4218),   A55(231).
*Seven Pillars of Wisdom.   *T. E. Lawrence*.   MP12(X-5929),
    MP8(VII-4722),   MP6(V-2830),   MPNf(282),   MP3(II-961),
    MWL3(961).
Seven Plays.   *Bertolt Brecht*.   SCL12(X-6865),   SCL7(VI-4221),
    A62(264),   BMA(506).
Seven Short Plays.   *Lady Gregory*.   MP12(X-5932),   MP8(VII-4725),
    MP6(V-2832),   MPDr(764),   MP3(II-963),   MWL3(963).
Seven Storey Mountain, The.   *Thomas Merton*.   RCa(II-930).

Shakespeare. *John Drinkwater*. HEur(I-211).

Shakespeare and Company. *Sylvia Beach*. SCL12(X-6903),
　　SCL7(VI-4242), A60(240).

Shakespeare Writes His Dramas (Event). HEur(I-208).

Shall We Dance. Cine(IV-1529).

Shane. Cine(IV-1534).

Shape of the Liturgy, The. *Dom Gregory Dix, O. S. B.* Different analyses
　　on this title appear in: HAnc(II-881; II-1096).

Shape of Things to Come, The. *H. G. Wells*. SF(IV-1902).

Shattered Peace. *Daniel H. Yergin*. LA78(II-766).

She. *H. Rider Haggard*. MP12(X-5952), MPCE(IV-2055),
　　MP8(VII-4741), MP6(V-2843), MPEng(787), MP1(II-886),
　　MWL1(886). A different analysis on this title appears in: SF(IV-1908).

She Done Him Wrong. Cine(IV-1539).

*She Stoops to Conquer. *Oliver Goldsmith*. MP12(X-5957),
　　MPCE(IV-2058), MP8(VII-4744), MP6(V-2846), MPDr(766),
　　MP1(II-889), MWL1(889).

Sheep Look Up, The. *John Brunner*. SF(IV-1913).

*Sheep Well, The. *Lope de Vega*. MP12(X-5962), MPCE(IV-2061),
　　MP8(VII-4747), MP6(V-2848), MPDr(769), MPv4(477),
　　MP2(II-960), MWL2(960).

SheLa. *Aubrey Menen*. SCL12(X-6906), SCL7(VI-4245), A63(237).

Shelburne Essays. *Paul Elmer More*. MP12(X-5966), MP8(VII-4750),
　　MP4(II-1112), MWL4(1112).

*Sheltered Life, The. *Ellen Glasgow*. MP12(X-5969),
　　MPCE(IV-2063), MP8(VII-4753), MP6(V-2850), MPAm(575),
　　MP1(II-891), MWL1(891).

*Shepheardes Calendar, The. *Edmund Spenser*. MP12(X-5972),
　　MP8(VII-4756), MP4(II-1114), MWL4(1114).

Shepherd, The. *Hermas*. Different analyses on this title appear in:
　　RCh(I-13), RCa(I-12).

*Shepherds of the Night. *Jorge Amado*. SCL12(X-6909),
　　SCL7(VI-4248), A67(303).

Sherman, Soldier, Realist, American. *B. H. Liddell Hart*. HAmer(II-1011).

Sherman's March to the Sea (Event). HAmer(II-1010).

Shield of Achilles, The. *W. H. Auden*. SCL12(X-6912),
　　SCL7(VI-4251), A55(234), BMA(509).

Shih Ching, The. *Confucius*. MP12(X-5976), MP8(VII-4760),
　　MP6(V-2853), MPPo(335), MP3(II-965), MWL3(965).

Shikasta. *Doris Lessing*. LA80(II-753).

*Ship of Fools. *Katherine Anne Porter*. MP12(X-5979),
　　MP8(VII-4763), MP4(II-1118), MWL4(1118), SCL12(X-6915),
　　SCL7(VI-4254), A63(240).

Ship Who Sang, The. *Anne McCaffrey*. SF(IV-1917).

Ships and Seamen of the American Revolution. *Jack Coggins*.

HAmer(I-270).

*Shirley. *Charlotte Brontë*.   MP12(X-5985),   MPCE(IV-2064),
    MP8(VII-4769),   MP6(V-2855),   MPEng(790),   MP3(II-968),
    MWL3(968).

Shoal of Time: A History of the Hawaiian Islands. *Gavan Davis*.
    HWor(II-794).

Shockwave Rider, The. *John Brunner*.   SF(IV-1922).

*Shoemaker's Holiday, The. *Thomas Dekker*.   MP12(X-5988),
    MPCE(IV-2065),   MP8(VII-4772),   MP6(V-2857),   MPDr(772),
    MPv3(485),   MP2(II-962),   MWL2(962).

Shoes of the Fisherman, The. *Morris L. West*.   SCL12(X-6923),
    SCL7(VI-4261),   A64(238).

Shogun. *James Clavell*.   SCL12(X-6926),   A76(287).

*Shooting Star, The. *Wallace Stegner*.   SCL12(X-6930),
    SCL7(VI-4264),   A62(272).

Shootist, The.   Cine(IV-1542).

Short and Clear Exposition of the Christian Faith, A. *Ulrich Zwingli*.
    RCh(I-363).

Short Fiction of Arthur C. Clarke, The. *Arthur C. Clarke*.   SF(IV-1926).

Short Fiction of Avram Davidson, The. *Avram Davidson*.   SF(IV-1930).

Short Fiction of Dmitri Bilenkin, The. *Dmitri Bilenkin*.   SF(IV-1934).

Short Fiction of Edmond Hamilton, The. *Edmond Hamilton*.   SF(IV-1939).

Short Fiction of Fitz-James O'Brien, The. *Fitz-James O'Brien*.
    SF(IV-1944).

Short Fiction of Frederik Pohl, The. *Frederik Pohl*.   SF(IV-1948).

Short Fiction of Fredric Brown, The. *Fredric Brown*.   SF(IV-1954).

Short Fiction of Fritz Leiber, Jr., The. *Fritz Leiber, Jr*.   SF(IV-1958).

Short Fiction of Gennadiy Samoilovich Gor, The. *Gennadiy Samoilovich
    Gor*.   SF(IV-1963).

Short Fiction of Harlan Ellison, The. *Harlan Ellison*.   SF(IV-1978).

Short Fiction of Herman Melville, The. *Herman Melville*.   SF(IV-1989).

Short Fiction of H. G. Wells, The. *H. G. Wells*.   SF(IV-1967).

Short Fiction of H. P. Lovecraft, The. *H. P. Lovecraft*.   SF(IV-1973).

Short Fiction of J. G. Ballard, The. *J. G. Ballard*.   SF(IV-1994).

Short Fiction of James Tiptree, Jr., The. *James Tiptree, Jr*.   SF(IV-1999).

Short Fiction of John W. Campbell, Jr., The. *John W. Campbell, Jr*.
    SF(IV-2003).

Short Fiction of Jorge Luis Borges, The. *Jorge Luis Borges*.   SF(IV-2008).

Short Fiction of Judith Merril, The. *Judith Merril*.   SF(IV-2014).

Short Fiction of Kirill Bulychev, The. *Kirill Bulychev*.   SF(IV-2019).

Short Fiction of Larry Niven, The. *Larry Niven*.   SF(IV-2023).

Short Fiction of Murray Leinster, The. *Murray Leinster*.   SF(IV-2030).

Short Fiction of Nathaniel Hawthorne, The. *Nathaniel Hawthorne*.
    SF(IV-2035).

Short Fiction of Ray Bradbury, The. *Ray Bradbury*.   SF(IV-2042).

Short Fiction of Robert Sheckley, The. *Robert Sheckley.* SF(IV-2046).

Short Fiction of Rudyard Kipling, The. *Rudyard Kipling.* SF(V-2051).

Short Fiction of Theodore Sturgeon, The. *Theodore Sturgeon.* SF(V-2056).

Short Fiction of Thomas M. Disch, The. *Thomas M. Disch.* SF(V-2059).

Short Fiction of William Tenn, The. *William Tenn.* SF(V-2065).

Short Friday and Other Stories. *Isaac Bashevis Singer.* SCL12(X-6933), SCL7(VI-4267), A65(280).

Short History of British Expansion: The Modern Empire and Commonwealth, A. *James A. Williamson.* HEur(III-1374).

Short History of Genetics, A. *L. C. Dunn.* HEur(II-910).

Short History of Machine Tools, A. *L. T. C. Rolt.* HEur(I-527).

Short History of Switzerland, A. *E. Bonjour, H. S. Offler and G. R. Potter.* HEur(II-796).

Short Letter, Long Farewell. *Peter Handke.* SCL12(X-6936), A75(296).

Short Novels of Thomas Wolfe, The. *Thomas Wolfe.* SCL12(X-6940), SCLs(271).

Short Stories of A. E. Coppard, The. *A. E. Coppard.* MP12(X-5993), MP8(VII-4775), MP4(II-1123), MWL4(1123).

Short Stories of D. H. Lawrence. *D. H. Lawrence.* MP12(X-5995), MP8(VII-4777), MP4(II-1125), MWL4(1125).

Short Stories of E. M. Forster, The. *E. M. Forster.* MP12(X-5998), MP8(VII-4780), MP4(II-1127), MWL4(1127).

Short Stories of Ernest Hemingway, The. *Ernest Hemingway.* MP12(X-6002), MP8(VII-4784), MP4(II-1130), MWL4(1130).

Short Stories of Eudora Welty, The. *Eudora Welty.* MP12(X-6005), MP8(VII-4787), MP4(II-1133), MWL4(1133).

Short Stories of Flannery O'Connor, The. *Flannery O'Connor.* MP12(X-6008), MP8(VII-4790), MP4(II-1136), MWL4(1136).

Short Stories of John Cheever, The. *John Cheever.* MP12(X-6011), MP8(VII-4793), MP4(II-1139), MWL4(1139).

Short Stories of John Updike, The. *John Updike.* MP12(X-6014), MP8(VII-4796), MP4(II-1142), MWL4(1142).

Short Stories of Katherine Mansfield. *Katherine Mansfield.* MP12(X-6018), MP8(VII-4800), MP6(V-2860), MPEng(793), MP3(II-970), MWL3(970).

*Short Stories of O. Henry. *O. Henry.* MP12(X-6021), MP8(VII-4803), MP6(V-2862), MPAm(578), MP3(II-972), MWL3(972).

Short Stories of Peter Taylor, The. *Peter Taylor.* MP12(X-6024), MP8(VII-4806), MP4(II-1145), MWL4(1145).

*Short Stories of Saki, The. *Saki.* MP12(X-6027), MP8(VII-4809), MP4(II-1148), MWL4(1148).

Shorter Cambridge Medieval History, Vol. I: The Late Roman Empire to the Twelfth Century, The. *Charles W. Previte-Orton.* Different analyses on this title appear in: HAnc(II-976; II-1160).

Silence of Desire, A. *Kamala Markandaya.* SCL12(X-6965),
  SCL7(VI-4285), A61(232).
Silent Spring. *Rachel Carson.* SCL12(X-6968), SCL7(VI-4288),
  A63(249). A different analysis on this title appears in: HWor(I-428).
Silent Woman, The. *Ben Jonson.* MP12(X-6046), MPCE(IV-2075),
  MP8(VII-4823), MP6(V-2874), MPDr(777), MP3(II-980),
  MWL3(980).
Silk Stockings. Cine(IV-1553).
Silken Eyes. *Françoise Sagan.* LA78(II-776).
*Silmarillion, The. *J. R. R. Tolkien.* LA78(II-780).
Simon de Montfort. *Margaret Wade Labarge.* HAnc(III-1530).
*Simple Honorable Man, A. *Conrad Richter.* MP12(X-6050),
  MP8(VII-4826), MP4(II-1151), MWL4(1151), SCL12(X-6971),
  SCL7(VI-4291), A63(251).
Simple Justice. *Richard Kluger.* LA77(II-735).
Simplicissimus the Vagabond. *H. J. C. von Grimmelshausen.*
  MP12(X-6053), MPCE(IV-2077), MP8(VII-4829),
  MP6(V-2877), MPEur(679), MPv4(481), MP2(II-966),
  MWL2(966).
Since Yesterday: The Nineteen-Thirties in America, September 3,
  1929-September 3, 1939. *Frederick Lewis Allen.* HAmer(III-1584).
Sincerely, Willis Wayde. *John P. Marquand.* SCL12(X-6974),
  SCL7(VI-4294), A55(237).
Sincerity and Authenticity. *Lionel Trilling.* SCL12(X-6977), A73(325).
Sinclair Lewis. *Mark Schorer.* SCL12(X-6980), SCL7(VI-4297),
  A62(275), BMA(512).
Sing as We Go. Cine(IV-1557).
Singapore: The Chain of Disaster. *S. Woodburn Kirby.* HWor(I-460).
Singapore: The Japanese Version. *Colonel Masanobe Tsuji.*
  SCL12(X-6985), SCL7(VI-4301), A62(279).
Singin' and Swingin' and Gettin' Merry Like Christmas. *Maya Angelou.*
  LA77(II-738).
Singin' in the Rain. Cine(IV-1560).
*Single Pebble, A. *John Hersey.* SCL12(X-6989), SCL7(VI-4305),
  A57(244).
Singularities. *John Simon.* LA77(II-742).
Sinister Barrier. *Eric Frank Russell.* SF(V-2075).
Sinister Twilight, A. *Noel Barber.* SCL12(X-6993), SCL7(VI-4308),
  A69(288).
Sino-Soviet Conflict, 1956-1961, The. *Donald S. Zagoria.* HEur(III-1585).
*Sir Charles Grandison. *Samuel Richardson.* MP12(X-6056),
  MPCE(IV-2078), MP8(VII-4832), MP6(V-2879), MPEng(800),
  MP3(II-983), MWL3(983).
*Sir Gawain and the Green Knight. *Unknown.* MP12(X-6060),
  MPCE(IV-2080), MP8(VII-4835), MP6(V-2882), MPPo(340),

MPv3(487),   MP2(II-969),   MWL2(969).
*Sir John van Olden Barnavelt. *John Fletcher* and *Philip Massinger*.
    MP12(X-6063),   MPCE(IV-2082),   MP8(VII-4837),
    MP6(V-2884),   MPDr(780),   MP3(II-985),   MWL3(985).
*Sir Roger de Coverley Papers, The. *Joseph Addison, Sir Richard Steele* and
    Eustace Budgell.   MP12(X-6067),   MP8(VII-4840),   MP6(V-2887),
    MPNf(288),   MP3(II-988),   MWL3(988).
Sir Thomas More Publishes *Utopia* (Event).   HEur(I-49). *See also* Utopia.
Sir Walter Raleigh. *Willard M. Wallace*.   HAmer(I-50).
Sir Walter Ralegh. *A. L. Rowse*.   SCL12(X-6997),   SCL7(VI-4312),
    A63(254).
Sir William. *David Stacton*.   SCL12(X-7000),   SCL7(VI-4315),
    A64(244).
*Sirens of Titan, The. *Kurt Vonnegut, Jr*.   SF(V-2079).
Sirius: A Fantasy of Love and Discord. *Olaf Stapledon*.   SF(V-2085).
Sissie. *John A. Williams*.   SCL12(X-7004),   SCLs(279).
*Sister Carrie. *Theodore Dreiser*.   MP12(X-6070),   MPCE(IV-2084),
    MP8(VII-4843),   MP6(V-2889),   MPAm(581),   MP1(II-895),
    MWL1(895).
Sister Philomène. *Edmond de Goncourt* and *Jules de Goncourt*.
    MP12(X-6075),   MPCE(IV-2087),   MP8(VII-4845),
    MP6(V-2891),   MPEur(682),   MP3(II-990),   MWL3(990).
Sitting Pretty.   Cine(IV-1564).
Sitwells: A Family Biography, The. *John Pearson*.   LA80(II-763).
Six Articles of Henry VIII, The (Event).   HEur(I-123).
Six Books of the Republic, The. *Jean Bodin*.   RCa(I-552).
*Six Characters in Search of an Author. *Luigi Pirandello*.
    MP12(X-6079),   MPCE(IV-2089),   MP8(VII-4848),
    MP6(V-2893),   MPDr(783),   MP3(II-993),   MWL3(993).
Six Days or Forever: Tennessee Versus John Thomas Scopes. *Ray Ginger*.
    HAmer(III-1553).
Sixteenth Amendment, The (Event).   HAmer(III-1415).
Sixty Days That Shook the West: The Fall of France, 1940. *Jacques
    Benoist-Méchin*.   HEur(III-1452).
Skepticism of the Middle Academy (Event).   HAnc(I-471).
Sketch of the History of the Mayo Clinic and the Mayo Foundation. *Mayo
    Clinic Division of Publications*.   HAmer(II-1182).
*Skin of Our Teeth, The. *Thornton Wilder*.   MP12(X-6084),
    MPCE(IV-2092),   MP8(VII-4851),   MP6(V-2896),   MPDr(786),
    MP3(II-995),   MWL3(995).
Sky Suspended: The Battle of Britain, The. *Drew Middleton*.
    HWor(I-436).
Skylark, The. *Ralph Hodgson*.   SCL12(X-7008),   SCL7(VI-4319),
    A61(235).
Skylark Series, The. *Edward E. Smith*.   SF(V-2091).

Slammer. *Ben Greer.* SCL12(X-7011), A76(294).
Slan. *A. E. van Vogt.* SF(V-2096).
*Slapstick. *Kurt Vonnegut, Jr.* LA77(II-749).
*Slaughterhouse-Five. *Kurt Vonnegut, Jr.* SCL12(X-7015), A70(273). A different analysis on this title appears in: SF(V-2101).
*Slave, The. *Isaac Bashevis Singer.* SCL12(X-7020), SCL7(VI-4322), A63(256).
Slavs, Their Early History and Civilization, The. *Francis Dvornik.* HAnc(III-1208).
Sleep of Baby Filbertson, The. *James Leo Herlihy.* SCL12(X-7023), SCLs(282).
Sleepers Joining Hands. *Robert Bly.* SCL12(X-7027), A74(361).
Sleeping in the Woods. *David Wagoner.* SCL12(X-7031), A75(300).
Sleepless Nights. *Elizabeth Hardwick.* LA80(II-768).
Sleepwalkers, The. *Hermann Broch.* MP12(X-6089), MPCE(IV-2095), MP8(VII-4854), MP6(V-2898), MPEur(685), MPv4(483), MP2(II-970), MWL2(970).
*Sleepwalkers, The. *Arthur Koestler.* SCL12(X-7034), SCL7(VI-4325), A60(245).
Sleuth. Cine(IV-1567).
Slipknot, The. *Plautus (Titus Maccius Plautus).* MP12(X-6094), MPCE(IV-2098), MP8(VII-4857), MP6(V-2900), MPDr(789), MP3(II-997), MWL3(997).
*Small House at Allington, The. *Anthony Trollope.* MP12(X-6097), MPCE(IV-2099), MP8(VII-4860), MP6(V-2903), MPEng(803), MPv3(489), MP2(II-973), MWL2(973).
Small Souls. *Louis Couperus.* MP12(X-6101), MPCE(IV-2100), MP8(VII-4864), MP6(V-2906), MPEur(688), MP3(II-1000), MWL3(1000).
Smile. Cine(IV-1572).
Smithsonian: America's Treasure House, The. *Webster Prentiss True.* HAmer(II-835).
*Smoke. *Ivan Turgenev.* MP12(X-6105), MPCE(IV-2101), MP8(VII-4867), MP6(V-2908), MPEur(691), MP1(II-897), MWL1(897).
*Snake Pit, The. *Sigrid Undset.* MP12(X-6109), MPCE(IV-2103), MP8(VII-4870), MP6(V-2911), MPEur(694), MPv3(492), MP2(II-976), MWL2(976).
Sneaky People. *Thomas Berger.* SCL12(X-7038), A76(298).
*Snow Country *and* Thousand Cranes. *Yasunari Kawabata.* SCL12(X-7042), A70(277).
Snow Leopard, The. *Peter Matthiessen.* LA79(II-685).
*Snow White. *Donald Barthelme.* SCL12(X-7047), SCL7(VI-4329), A68(296).
Snow White and the Seven Dwarfs. Cine(IV-1575).

Soul of Wood and Other Stories. *Jokov Lind.* SCL12(XI-7132),
    SCL7(VI-4377), A66(303).
Soul on Ice. *Eldridge Cleaver.* SCL12(XI-7135), SCL7(VI-4380),
    A68(301).
Souls on Fire. *Elie Wiesel.* SCL12(XI-7140), A73(337).
*Sound and the Fury, The. *William Faulkner.* MP12(XI-6194),
    MPCE(IV-2134), MP8(VII-4937), MP6(V-2947), MPAm(589),
    MP1(II-917), MWL1(917).
Sound of Music, The. Cine(IV-1586).
Sound of the Mountain, The. *Yasunari Kawabata.* SCL12(XI-7144),
    A71(304).
*Sound of Waves, The. *Yukio Mishima.* MP12(XI-6199),
    MP8(VII-4940), MP4(II-1171), MWL4(1171), SCL12(XI-7147),
    SCL7(VI-4385), A57(255).
Source of Human Good, The. *Henry Nelson Wieman.* RCh(II-1084).
"Sources and Development of Arabic Medical Therapy and Pharmacology," *in*
    Sudhoffs Archiv. *Sami K. Hamarneh.* Different analyses on this title
    appear in: HAnc(II-1181; III-1228).
South Africa: A Modern History. *T. R. H. Davenport.* HWor(III-1276).
South Asian Crisis: India, Pakistan and Bangladesh: A Political and Historical
    Analysis of the 1971 War. *Robert Victor Jackson.* HWor(II-1095).
South Carolina Regulators, The. *Richard M. Brown.* HAmer(I-216).
South Pacific. Cine(IV-1589).
South Pole: An Account of the Norwegian Antarctic Expedition in the
    "Fram," 1910-1912, The. *Roald Amundsen.* HWor(I-66).
"South Today, The," *in* Time. HWor(II-1079).
South Wind. *Norman Douglas.* MP12(XI-6202), MPCE(IV-2137),
    MP8(VII-4943), MP6(V-2950), MPEng(810), MPv4(491),
    MP2(II-988), WL2(988).
South-East Asia in Turmoil. *Brian Crozier.* HWor(II-705).
Southern Colonies in the Seventeenth Century, 1607-1689, The. *Wesley F.
    Craven.* HAmer(I-61).
Southern Heritage, The. *James McBride Dabbs.* SCL12(XI-7150),
    SCLs(288).
Southern Literary Messenger, 1834-1864, The. *Benjamin B. Minor.*
    HAmer(II-728).
Southerner, The. Cine(IV-1594).
Soviet Bloc: Unity and Conflict, The. *Zbigniew K. Brzezinski.*
    HEur(III-1598).
Soviet Economic Development Since 1917. *Maurice Dobb.* HEur(III-1305).
Soviet Invasion of Eastern Europe (Event). HWor(I-479).
Soviet Political Mind: Studies in Stalinism and Post-Stalin Change,
    The. *Robert C. Tucker.* HEur(III-1332).
Soviet Politics: The Dilemma of Power. *Barrington Moore, Jr.* HEur(III-1307).
Soviet Russia in China. *Chiang Kai-shek.* SCL12(XI-7154),

Spanish Republic and the Civil War, 1931-1939, The. *Gabriel Jackson.*
    Different analyses on this title appear in: HEur(III-1370; III-1418).
Spanish Revolution of 1868 (Event). HEur(II-945).
Spanish Revolution of 1820 (Event). HEur(II-634).
Spanish Struggle for Justice in the Conquest of America, The. *Lewis*
    Hanke. HEur(I-131).
*Spanish Tragedy, The. *Thomas Kyd.* MP12(XI-6211),
    MPCE(IV-2141), MP8(VII-4951), MP6(VI-2956), MPDr(802),
    MPv3(499), MP2(II-990), MWL2(990).
Spanish-American Frontier, 1783-1795, The. *Arthur P. Whitaker.*
    HAmer(I-398).
Spanish-American War, The (Event). HAmer(II-1284).
Spartan Conquest of Messenia (Event). HAnc(I-134).
S. P. D. in the Bonn Republic: A Socialist Party Modernizes, The. *Harold*
    Kent Schellenger, Jr. HEur(III-1693).
Speak, Memory. *Vladimir Nabokov.* SCL12(XI-7161), SCL7(VI-4395),
    A68(305).
Special Envoy to Churchill and Stalin, 1941-1946. *W. Averell Harriman* and
    Elie Abel. SCL12(XI-7165), A76(306).
Specimen Days. *Walt Whitman.* MP12(XI-6216), MP8(VII-4953),
    MP4(II-1173), MWL4(1173).
Spectator Bird, The. *Wallace Stegner.* LA77(II-769).
Spectral Boy, The. *Donald Peterson.* SCL12(XI-7168), SCL7(VI-4399),
    A66(306).
Spectral Emanations: New and Selected Poems. *John Hollander.*
    LA79(II-699).
Speculations About Jakob. *Uwe Johnson.* MP12(XI-6219),
    MP8(VII-4956), MP4(II-1176), MWL4(1176), SCL12(XI-7171),
    SCL7(VI-4402), A64(247).
Speedboat. *Renata Adler.* LA77(II-776).
Spellbound. Cine(IV-1597).
Spencer Holst Stories. *Spencer Holst.* LA77(II-780).
Spengler Publishes *Decline of the West* (Event). HEur(III-1279). *See also*
    Decline of the West, The.
Spider King, The. *Lawrence Schoonover.* SCL12(XI-7174),
    SCL7(VI-4405), A54(258).
Spider's House, The. *Paul Bowles.* SCL12(XI-7177), SCL7(VI-4408),
    A55(243).
*Spinoza of Market Street, The. *Isaac Bashevis Singer.* SCL12(XI-7180),
    SCL7(VI-4411), A62(285).
Spinster. *Sylvia Ashton-Warner.* SCL12(XI-7183), SCL7(VI-4414),
    A60(249).
Spiral Staircase, The. Cine(IV-1601).
*Spire, The. *William Golding.* SCL12(XI-7186), SCL7(VI-4417),
    A65(287).

Stopping Place, A. *A. G. Mojtabai.* LA80(II-785).

Stop-time. *Frank Conroy.* SCL12(XI-7248), SCL7(VI-4451), A68(308).

Stories. *Doris Lessing.* LA79(II-708).

*Stories and Texts for Nothing. *Samuel Beckett.* SCL12(XI-7252), SCL7(VII-4455), A68(312).

Stories of John Cheever, The. *John Cheever.* LA79(II-713).

Stories of Liam O'Flaherty, The. *Liam O'Flaherty.* SCL12(XI-7255), SCL7(VII-4458), A57(258).

Stories of William Sansom, The. *William Sansom.* SCL12(XI-7259), SCL7(VII-4461), A64(254).

Stories That Could Be True: New and Collected Poems. *William Stafford.* LA78(II-799).

Storm and Other Poems, The. *William Pitt Root.* SCL12(XI-7262), A70(284).

Storming of the Bastille (Event). HEur(I-510).

Story of a Bad Boy, The. *Thomas Bailey Aldrich.* MP12(XI-6265), MPCE(IV-2163), MP8(VII-4991), MP6(VI-2980), MPAm(610), MP1(II-927), MWL1(927).

Story of a Country Town, The. *Edgar Watson Howe.* MP12(XI-6268), MPCE(IV-2164), MP8(VII-4994), MP6(VI-2982), MPAm(613), MP1(II-929), MWL1(929).

Story of a Life, The. *Konstantin Paustovsky.* SCL12(XI-7265), SCLs(295).

Story of a Soul, The. *Saint Thérèse of Lisieux.* RCa(II-729).

Story of an African Farm, The. *Olive Schreiner.* MP12(XI-6272), MPCE(IV-2165), MP8(VII-4997), MP6(VI-2985), MPEur(720), MP1(II-932), MWL1(932).

Story of Burnt Njal, The. *Unknown.* MP12(XI-6276), MPCE(IV-2166), MP8(VII-5000), MP6(VI-2987), MPEur(723), MPv3(501), MP2(II-997), MWL2(997).

Story of G.I. Joe, The. Cine(IV-1638).

Story of Gösta Berling, The. *Selma Lagerlöf.* MP12(XI-6281), MPCE(IV-2168), MP8(VII-5003), MP6(VI-2990), MPEur(726), MP1(II-934), MWL1(934).

Story of Medicine in the Middle Ages, The. *David Riesman.* HAnc(III-1480).

Story of My Boyhood and Youth, The. *John Muir.* MP12(XI-6286), MP8(VII-5006), MP4(II-1183), MWL4(1183).

Story of the Apocrypha, The. *Edgar Johnson Goodspeed.* HAnc(I-445).

Story of the Armory Show, The. *Milton W. Brown.* HAmer(III-1413).

Story of the Baltimore and Ohio Railroad, The. *Edward Hungerford.* HAmer(I-627).

Story of the Guitar. *Kao Tse-ch'eng.* MP12(XI-6288), MPCE(IV-2171), MP8(VII-5008), MP6(VI-2992), MPDr(806),

A73(349).

Street of Crocodiles, The. *Bruno Schulz.* LA78(II-804).

Street Scene. *Elmer Rice.* MP12(XI-6304), MPCE(IV-2176), MP8(VII-5021), MP6(VI-2999), MPDr(811), MP3(II-1026), MWL3(1026).

Streetcar Named Desire, A. Cine(IV-1641).

*Streetcar Named Desire, A. *Tennessee Williams.* MP12(XI-6308), MP8(VII-5023), MP4(II-1189), MWL4(1189).

Strength of Fields, The. *James Dickey.* LA80(II-794).

Strictly Speaking. *Edwin Newman.* SCL12(XI-7295), A75(311).

Strife. *John Galsworthy.* MP12(XI-6311), MPCE(IV-2178), MP8(VII-5026), MP6(VI-3001), MPDr(813), MP1(II-936), MWL1(936).

*Strike the Father Dead. *John Wain.* SCL12(XI-7299), SCL7(VII-4476), A63(259).

Striking the Earth. *John Woods.* LA77(II-784).

String Too Short to Be Saved. *Donald Hall.* SCL12(XI-7302), SCL7(VII-4479), A62(2906).

Stringer. *Ward Just.* SCL12(XI-7305), A75(315).

Stromata, *or* Miscellanies, The. *Saint Clement of Alexandria.* Different analyses on this title appear in: RCh(I-43), RCa(I-44).

Strong Opinions. *Vladimir Nabokov.* LA77(II-789).

Structure of Politics at the Accession of George III, The. *Lewis B. Namier.* HAmer(I-227).

Struggle, The. Cine(IV-1645).

Struggle for Catholic Emancipation, The. *Denis Gwynn.* HEur(II-672).

Struggle for Europe, The. *Chester Wilmot.* Different analyses on this title appear in: HEur(III-1479; III-1493; III-1503), HAmer(III-1722).

Struggle for Indochina, The. *Ellen Joy Hammer.* HWor(II-700).

Struggle for Judicial Supremacy, The. *Robert H. Jackson.* HAmer(III-1669).

Struggle for Mastery in Europe, 1848-1918, The. *A. J. P. Taylor.* HEur(II-925).

Struggle for Oregon, The (Event). HAmer(II-778).

Struggle for Supremacy in Germany, 1859-1866, The. *Heinrich Friedjung.* HEur(II-915).

Struggle for the Horn of Africa, The (Event). HWor(III-1317).

Students Without Teachers. *Harold Taylor.* SCL12(XI-7308), A70(291).

Studies in Ancient Technology, Vol. VIII *and* IX. *Robert J. Forbes.* HAnc(I-61).

Studies in Ancient Technology, Vol. IX. *Robert J. Forbes.* HAnc(I-19).

Studies in Classic American Literature. *D. H. Lawrence.* MP12(XI-6314), MP8(VII-5028), MP4(II-1192), MWL4(1192).

Studies in Medieval Legal Thought. *Gaines Post.* HAnc(III-1346).

Studies on Hysteria. *Josef Breuer* and *Sigmund Freud.* MP12(XI-6317),

Summer of '42.   Cine(IV-1652).
*Summing Up, The.   *W. Somerset Maugham*.   MP12(XI-6332),
    MP8(VII-5045),   MP4(II-1198),   MWL4(1198).
Summit Conferences, 1919-1960, The.   *Keith Eubank*.   HWor(II-725).
Summoned by Bells.   *John Betjeman*.   SCL12(XI-7334),
    SCL7(VII-4490),   A61(245).
Summoning of the Council of Sardica (Event).   HAnc(II-872).
Summoning of the Model Parliament (Event).   HAnc(III-1581).
Summons of the Trumpet: U.S.-Vietnam in Perspective.   *Dave Richard*
    Palmer.   LA79(II-732).
*Sun Also Rises, The.   *Ernest Hemingway*.   MP12(XI-6335),
    MPCE(IV-2181),   MP8(VII-5048),   MP6(VI-3012),   MPAm(618),
    MP1(II-941),   MWL1(941).
Sunday Between Wars: The Course of American Life from 1865 to 1917,
    A.   *Ben Maddow*.   LA80(II-798).
Sunflower Splendor.   *Wu-chi Liu* and *Irving Yucheng Lo,* eds.
    LA77(II-792).
*Sunken Bell, The.   *Gerhart Hauptmann*.   MP12(XI-6341),
    MPCE(IV-2185),   MP8(VII-5051),   MP6(VI-3015),   MPDr(815),
    MP3(II-1035),   MWL3(1035).
*Sunlight Dialogues, The.   *John Gardner*.   SCL12(XI-7338),   A73(353).
Sunset Boulevard.   Cine(IV-1655).
Super Fly.   Cine(IV-1660).
Supership.   *Noël Mostert*.   SCL12(XI-7342),   A75(322).
*Suppliants, The.   *Aeschylus*.   MP12(XI-6345),   MPCE(IV-2186),
    MP8(VII-5054),   MP6(VI-3017),   MPDr(818),   MPv4(498),
    MP2(II-1002),   MWL2(1002).
Suppliants, The.   *Euripides*.   MP12(XI-6349),   MPCE(IV-2188),
    MP8(VII-5057),   MP6(VI-3020),   MPDr(821),   MP3(II-1038),
    MWL3(1038).
Suppositi, I.   *Ludovico Ariosto*.   MP12(XI-6352),   MPCE(IV-2190),
    MP8(VII-5059),   MP6(VI-3021),   MPDr(823),   MP3(II-1039),
    MWL3(1039).
Suppression of the Monasteries in England (Event).   HEur(I-110).
Supreme Court and the Electoral Process, The.   *Richard Claude*.
    HAmer(III-1885).
Supreme Court Decisions in Reapportionment Cases (Event).
    HAmer(III-1883).
Supreme Court Defines Rights of Accused Criminals (*Gideon* v. *Wainright*)
    (Event).   HAmer(III-1893).
Supreme Court in United States History, Vol. I: 1789-1821, The.   *Charles*
    Warren.   HAmer(I-441).
Supreme Court Orders Desegregation of the Public Schools (*Brown* v. *Board*
    of Education of Topeka) (Event).   HAmer(III-1849).
Supreme Court Packing Fight (Event).   HAmer(III-1667).

Supreme Court's First Exercise of the Right of Judicial Review (*Marbury* v. *Madison*) (Event). HAmer(I-437).

Surface of Earth, The. *Reynolds Price.* SCL12(XI-7345), A76(309).

"Surface of Mars, The," *in* Scientific American. *Raymond E. Arvidson,* et al. HWor(III-1297).

Surfacing. *Margaret Atwood.* SCL12(XI-7350), A74(377).

"Surgical Developments in Medieval Arabic Medicine," *in* Viewpoints: American Friends of the Middle East. *Sami K. Hamarneh.* HAnc(III-1228).

Surrender in Panama: The Case Against the Treaty. *Philip M. Crane.* HWor(III-1335).

Surrender of Cornwallis at Yorktown (Event). HAmer(I-294).

Surry of Eagle's Nest. *John Esten Cooke.* MP12(XI-6355), MPCE(IV-2191), MP8(VII-5061), MP6(VI-3023), MPAm(621), MP3(II-1042), MWL3(1042).

Survey of British Commonwealth Affairs, Vol. I: Problems of Nationality, 1918-1936. *W. K. Hancock.* HEur(III-1316).

Survival of the Bark Canoe, The. *John J. McPhee.* SCL12(XI-7354), A76(314).

Survival of the Pagan Gods: The Mythological Tradition and Its Place in Renaissance Humanism and Art, The. *Jean Seznec.* HAnc(III-1769).

Survivor: An Anatomy of Life in the Death Camps, The. *Terrence Des Pres.* Different analyses on this title appear in: LA77(II-797), HWor(I-400).

Suspicion. Cine(IV-1663).

Swallow Barn. *John P. Kennedy.* MP12(XI-6359), MPCE(IV-2192), MP8(VII-5064), MP6(VI-3026), MPAm(624), MPv4(500), MP2(II-1004), MWL2(1004).

Swamp Fox. *Robert Duncan Bass.* SCL12(XI-7357), SCLs(303).

Swastika and the Eagle: Hitler, the United States, and the Origins of World War II, The. *James V. Compton.* HWor(I-469).

Sweden Enters the Thirty Years' War (Event). HEur(I-274).

*Sweet Bird of Youth. *Tennessee Williams.* SCL12(XI-7361), SCL7(VII-4494), A60(263), BMA(526).

*Sweet Thursday. *John Steinbeck.* SCL12(XI-7365), SCL7(VII-4498), A54(264).

Swift Sword: The Historical Record of Israel's Victory, June, 1967. *Samuel L. Marshall.* HEur(III-1657).

Swimmers, The. *Allen Tate.* SCL12(XI-7369), A72(307).

Swiss Confederation Formed (Event). HEur(II-794).

"Swiss Confederation in the Middle Ages, The," *in* Vol. VII *of* The Cambridge Medieval History. *Paul E. Martin.* HAnc(III-1605).

*Swiss Family Robinson, The. *Johann Rudolf Wyss.* MP12(XI-6363), MPCE(IV-2194), MP8(VII-5066), MP6(VI-3028), MPEur(731), MP1(II-943), MWL1(943).

Swiss Victory at Morgarten (Event).   HAnc(III-1603).
Sword of God, The.   *René Hardy*.   SCL12(XI-7372),   SCL7(VII-4501),
     A54(267).
Sword of Rhiannon, The.   *Leigh Brackett*.   SF(V-2201).
Swords into Plowshares: The Problems and Progress of International
     Organization.   *Inis L. Claude, Jr*.   Different analyses on this title
     appear in: HEur(III-1510),   HAmer(III-1745).
Sylvia Plath: The Woman and the Work.   *Edward Butscher, ed*.
     LA78(II-809).
Symbolism.   *Johann Adam Möhler*.   RCa(II-640).
Symbols and Values in Zoroastrianism.   *Jacques Duchesne-Guillemin*.
     HAnc(I-166).
*Symposium.   *Plato*.   Ph(I-74).
Symzonia.   *"Captain Adam Seaborn."*   SF(V-2207).
Syndic, The.   *Cyril M. Kornbluth*.   SF(V-2211).
Synod of Jamnia (Event).   HAnc(II-664).
Syntagma Philosophicum.   *Pierre Gassendi*.   Ph(I-404).
Synthesis of DDT for Use as an Insecticide, The (Event).   HWor(I-425).
Synthetic Man, The.   *Theodore Sturgeon*.   SF(V-2215).
System of Doctrines.   *Samuel Hopkins*.   RCh(II-629).
System of Logic, A.   *John Stuart Mill*.   Ph(II-606).
Systematic Theology.   *Charles Hodge*.   RCh(II-766).
Systematic Theology.   *Augustus Hopkins Strong*.   RCh(II-797).
Systematic Theology.   *Paul Tillich*.   Different analyses on this title appear
     in: Ph(II-1138),   RCh(II-1135).
Syzygy.   *Michael G. Coney*.   SF(V-2218).

t zero.   *Italo Calvino*.   SF(V-2223).
Taft Story, The.   *William Smith White*.   SCL12(XI-7375),   SCLs(307).
*Take a Girl Like You.   *Kingsley Amis*.   SCL12(XI-7379),
     SCL7(VII-4504),   A62(293).
Take the A Train.   *Michael Blankfort*.   LA79(II-737).
Takeover, The.   *Muriel Spark*.   LA77(II-802).
Tale for Midnight, A.   *Frederic Prokosch*.   SCL12(XI-7383),
     SCL7(VII-4508),   A55(246).
Tale for the Mirror.   *Hortense Calisher*.   SCL12(XI-7386),
     SCL7(VII-4511),   A63(262).
*Tale of a Tub, A.   *Jonathan Swift*.   MP12(XI-6366),   MP8(VII-5069),
     MP4(II-1201),   MWL4(1201).
Tale of Asa Bean, The.   *Jack Matthews*.   SCL12(XI-7389),   A72(310).
Tale of Genji, The.   *Lady Murasaki Shikibu*.   MP12(XI-6369),
     MPCE(IV-2195),   MP8(VII-5072),   MP6(VI-3031),   MPEur(734),
     MPv4(502),   MP2(II-1006),   MWL2(1006).
Tale of Two Cities, A.   Cine(IV-1667).
*Tale of Two Cities, A.   *Charles Dickens*.   MP12(XI-6373),

MP1(II-959),   MWL1(959).

Tarzan of the Apes. *Edgar Rice Burroughs.*   SF(V-2229).

Tarzan, the Ape Man.   Cine(IV-1675).

Task, The. *William Cowper.*   MP12(XI-6425),   MP8(VIII-5116),
MP6(VI-3063),   MPPo(355),   MP3(II-1054),   MWL3(1054).

Taswell-Langmead's English Constitutional History.   *Theodore F. T.
Plucknett.*   HAnc(III-1584).

Tau Zero. *Poul Anderson.*   SF(V-2236).

Taxation and Democracy in America. *Sidney Ratner.*   HAmer(III-1417).

Taxi Driver.   Cine(IV-1678).

T. E. Lawrence. *Desmond Stewart.*   LA78(II-813).

*Tea and Sympathy. *Robert Anderson.*   SCL12(XI-7402),
SCL7(VII-4514),   A54(270),   BMA(530).

Teacher's Pet.   Cine(IV-1682).

Teaching as a Subversive Activity. *Neil Postman* and *Charles Weingartner.*
SCL12(XI-7405),   A70(303).

Teaching of Amos, The (Event).   HAnc(I-125).

Teaching of Euhemerus, The (Event).   HAnc(I-378).

Teaching of Second Isaiah, The (Event).   HAnc(I-184).

Teachings of the Magi, The. *R. C. Zaehner.*   HAnc(I-165).

Teachings of the Sophists, The (Event).   HAnc(I-286).

Teahouse of the August Moon, The. *John Patrick.*   SCL12(XI-7410),
SCL7(VII-4517),   A54(273),   BMA(533).

Teapot Dome: Oil and Politics in the 1920's. *Burl Noggle.*
HAmer(III-1528).

Technical Report on Salk Poliomyelitis Vaccine.   *United States Department of
Health, Education and Welfare.*   HAmer(III-1840).

"Technique of Nationalist Socialist Seizure of Power, The," *in Eschenburg's*
The Path to Dictatorship, 1918-1933. *Karl Dietrich Bracher.*
HEur(III-1384).

Tecumseh, Vision of Glory. *Glenn Tucker.*   HAmer(I-500).

Teitelbaum's Window. *Wallace Markfield.*   SCL12(XI-7413),   A71(311).

Telegraph in America: Its Founders, Promoters, and Noted Men, The. *James
D. Reid.*   HAmer(II-933).

Telephone: The First Hundred Years. *John Brooks.*   HWor(II-616).

*Telephone Poles. *John Updike.*   SCL12(XI-7416),   SCL7(VII-4520),
A64(257).

Television as a Cultural Force. *Richard Adler* and *Douglass Cater,* eds.
HWor(II-673).

Tell Freedom. *Peter Abrahams.*   SCL12(XI-7420),   SCL7(VII-4524),
A54(276).

Tell Me a Riddle. *Tillie Olsen.*   SCL12(XI-7424),   SCL7(VII-4527),
A62(296).

Tell Me, Tell Me. *Marianne Moore.*   SCL12(XI-7426),
SCL7(VII-4529),   A67(313).

Tell Me That You Love Me, Junie Moon. *Marjorie Kellogg.*
SCL12(XI-7430), SCL7(VII-4533), A69(305).
Temper of Our Time, The. *Eric Hoffer.* SCL12(XI-7434),
SCL7(VII-4537), A67(316).
*Tempest, The. *William Shakespeare.* MP12(XI-6427),
MPCE(IV-2217), MP8(VIII-5118), MP6(VI-3065), MPDr(833),
MP1(II-961), MWL1(961).
Temple, The. *George Herbert.* MP12(XI-6432), MP8(VIII-5121),
MP6(VI-3068), MPPo(357), MP3(II-1056), MWL3(1056).
Temple Beau, The. *Henry Fielding.* MP12(XI-6435), MPCE(IV-2220),
MP8(VIII-5124), MP6(VI-3071), MPDr(836), MPv4(504),
MP2(II-1013), MWL2(1013).
*Temple of Dawn, The. *Yukio Mishima.* SCL12(XI-7438), A74(381).
*Temple of the Golden Pavilion, The. *Yukio Mishima.* SCL12(XI-7443),
SCL7(VII-4541), A60(266).
Temple of the Past, The. *Stefan Wul.* SF(V-2241).
*Temporary Kings. *Anthony Powell.* SCL12(XI-7448), A74(386).
Temptation of Jack Orkney, The. *Doris Lessing.* SCL12(XI-7452),
A73(356).
*Temptation of Saint Anthony, The. *Gustave Flaubert.* MP12(XI-6438),
MPCE(IV-2221), MP8(VIII-5127), MP6(VI-3073), MPEur(746),
MP3(II-1059), MWL3(1059).
*Ten North Frederick. *John O'Hara.* SCL12(XI-7456),
SCL7(VII-4545), A55(249).
Ten Thousand: A Study in Social Organization and Action in Xenophon's
Anabasis, The. *G. B. Nussbaum.* HAnc(I-316).
Ten Thousand Things, The. *Maria Dermoût.* SCL12(XI-7460),
SCL7(VII-4548), A59(229).
*Tenant of Wildfell Hall, The. *Anne Brontë.* MP12(XI-6442),
MPCE(IV-2222), MP8(VIII-5130), MP6(VI-3076), MPEng(825),
MP1(II-963), MWL1(963).
*Tenants, The. *Bernard Malamud.* SCL12(XI-7463), A72(313).
Tenants of Moonbloom, The. *Edward Lewis Wallant.* MP12(XI-6445),
MP8(VIII-5132), MP4(II-1205), MWL4(1205), SCL12(XI-7467),
SCL7(VII-4551), A64(261).
*Tender Is the Night. *F. Scott Fitzgerald.* MP12(XI-6448),
MPCE(IV-2223), MP8(VIII-5135), MP6(VI-3078), MPAm(635),
MPv3(511), MP2(II-1016), MWL2(1016).
Tent of Miracles. *Jorge Amado.* SCL12(XI-7470), A72(317).
Terezín Requiem, The. *Josef Bor.* SCL12(XI-7473), SCL7(VII-4554),
A64(264).
Terms of Endearment. *Larry McMurtry.* SCL12(XI-7478), A76(317).
Termush, Atlanterhavskysten. *Sven Holm.* SF(V-2245).
Terra Nostra. *Carlos Fuentes.* LA77(II-807).
Terrible Beauty, A. *Arthur J. Roth.* SCL12(XI-7482),

SCL7(VII-4559),   A59(231).

Territorial Rights.   *Muriel Spark.*   LA80(II-804).

Terrorism.   *Walter Ze'ev Laqueur.*   HWor(II-1034).

*Teseide, La.   *Giovanni Boccaccio.*   MP12(XI-6453),   MPCE(IV-2226),
MP8(VIII-5138),   MP4(II-1208),   MWL4(1208).

*Tess of the D'Urbervilles.   *Thomas Hardy.*   MP12(XI-6457),
MPCE(IV-2228),   MP8(VIII-5141),   MP6(VI-3080),   MPEng(827),
MP1(II-965),   MWL1(965).

Test Ban and Disarmament: The Path of Negotiation.   *Arthur H. Dean.*
HWor(II-960).

Testimony: The Memoirs of Dmitri Shostakovich.   *Dmitri Shostakovich.*
LA80(II-808).

Testimony and Demeanor.   *John Casey.*   LA80(II-811).

Testing Tree, The.   *Stanley Kunitz.*   SCL12(XI-7485),   A72(319).

Texas Revolution (Event).   HAmer(II-736).

Texas Revolution, The.   *William C. Binkley.*   HAmer(II-738).

Texas Trilogy, A.   *Preston Jones.*   LA77(II-812).

Thackeray: The Age of Wisdom.   *Gordon N. Ray.*   SCL12(XI-7488),
SCL7(VII-4562),   A59(234),   BMA(536).

Thackeray: The Uses of Adversity.   *Gordon N. Ray.*   SCL12(XI-7492),
SCL7(VII-4566),   A55(252),   BMA(540).

Thaddeus of Warsaw.   *Jane Porter.*   MP12(XI-6462),   MPCE(IV-2231),
MP8(VIII-5144),   MP6(VI-3083),   MPEng(830),   MP1(II-967),
MWL1(967).

Thaddeus Stevens: Scourge of the South.   *Fawn M. Brodie.*
SCL12(XI-7496),   SCLs(315). A different analysis on this title appears
in: HAmer(II-1029).

Thank You, Fog.   *W. H. Auden.*   SCL12(XI-7500),   A75(325).

That Championship Season.   *Jason Miller.*   SCL12(XI-7504),   A73(360).

That Hamilton Woman.   Cine(IV-1685).

*That Hideous Strength.   *C. S. Lewis.*   SF(V-2250).

*That Uncertain Feeling.   *Kingsley Amis.*   MP12(XI-6466),
MP8(VIII-5147),   MP4(II-1210),   MWL4(1210).

That Wilder Image: The Painting of America's Native School from Thomas
Cole to Winslow Homer.   *James Thomas Flexner.*   HAmer(I-615).

Theaetetus.   *Plato.*   Ph(I-98).

Theater Essays of Arthur Miller, The.   *Arthur Miller.*   LA79(II-742).

Theatre of Blood.   Cine(IV-1689).

*Thebais, The.   *Statius (Publius Papinius Statius).*   MP12(XI-6469),
MP8(VIII-5150),   MP6(VI-3085),   MPPo(360),   MP3(II-1062),
MWL3(1062).

Their Brothers' Keepers: Moral Stewardship in the United States,
1800-1865.   *Clifford S. Griffin.*   HAmer(I-645).

*them.   *Joyce Carol Oates.*   SCL12(XI-7509),   A70(307).

Theodicy.   *Gottfried Wilhelm von Leibniz.*   Ph(I-454).

Theodor Herzl Publishes *Der Judenstaat* (Event). HEur(II-1089).
Theodore Roosevelt: The Formative Years. *Carlton Putnam.*
  SCL12(XI-7516), SCL7(VII-4570), A59(237).
Theodore Roosevelt and the Progressive Movement. *George E. Mowry.*
  HAmer(III-1393).
Theodore Roosevelt Assumes the Presidency (Event). HAmer(II-1325).
Theologica Germanica. *Unknown.* RCh(I-276).
Theology and Sanity. *Francis Joseph Sheed.* RCa(II-906).
Theology as an Empirical Science. *Douglas Clyde Macintosh.* RCh(II-899).
Theology for the Social Gospel, A. *Walter Rauschenbusch.* RCh(II-886).
Theology of the New Testament. *Rudolf Bultmann.* RCh(II-1097).
Theophilus North. *Thornton Wilder.* SCL12(XI-7520), A74(391).
Theophilus to Autolycus. *Saint Theophilus of Antioch.* Different analyses
  on this title appear in: RCh(I-32), RCa(I-33).
Theory of Moral Sentiments. *Adam Smith.* Ph(I-506).
Theory of the Leisure Class, The. *Thorsten Veblen.* MP12(XI-6471),
  MP8(VIII-5152), MP4(II-1213), MWL4(1213).
There Are Crimes and Crimes. *August Strindberg.* MP12(XI-6473),
  MPCE(IV-2233), MP8(VIII-5154), MP6(VI-3087), MPDr(839),
  MP3(II-1064), MWL3(1064).
*Therefore Be Bold. *Herbert Gold.* SCL12(XI-7523), SCL7(VII-4574),
  A61(248).
*Thérèse. *François Mauriac.* MP12(XI-6477), MPCE(IV-2235),
  MP8(VIII-5157), MP6(VI-3090), MPEur(749), MP3(II-1066),
  MWL3(1066).
These Lovers Fled Away. *Howard Spring.* SCL12(XI-7526),
  SCL7(VII-4577), A55(256).
These Thousand Hills. *A. B. Guthrie, Jr.* SCL12(XI-7529),
  SCL7(VII-4580), A57(263).
These Three. Cine(IV-1693).
*Thesmophoriazusae, The. *Aristophanes.* MP12(XI-6483),
  MPCE(IV-2239), MP8(VIII-5159), MP6(VI-3092), MPDr(842),
  MP3(II-1068), MWL3(1068).
They Burn the Thistles. *Yashar Kemal.* LA78(II-817).
They Called Him Stonewall. *Burke Davis.* SCL12(XI-7533),
  SCL7(VII-4583), A54(279).
They Came to Cordura. *Glendon Swarthout.* SCL12(XI-7536),
  SCL7(VII-4586), A59(241).
They Gathered at the River: The Story of the Great Revivalists and Their
  Impact upon Religion in America. *Bernard A. Weisberger.*
  HAmer(II-1176).
They Hanged My Saintly Billy. *Robert Graves.* SCL12(XI-7540),
  SCL7(VII-4589), A58(231).
They Shall Be Free. *Allan Knight Chalmers.* HAmer(III-1591).
They Shoot Horses, Don't They? *Horace McCoy.* MP12(XI-6486),

MP8(VIII-5161),   MP4(II-1214),   MWL4(1214).

They Were Expendable.   Cine(IV-1698).

They'd Rather Be Right.   *Mark Clifton*.   SF(V-2255).

Thief of Bagdad, The.   Cine(IV-1703).

Thin Disguise: Turning Point in Negro History—Plessy vs. Ferguson: A
  Documentary Presentation, 1864-1869, The.   *Otto H. Olsen*.
  HAmer(II-1265).

Thin Man, The.   Cine(IV-1709).

Thin Man, The.   *Dashiell Hammett*.   MP12(XI-6489),   MPCE(IV-2240),
  MP8(VIII-5164),   MP6(VI-3093),   MPAm(638),   MP1(II-970),
  MWL1(970).

Thin Mountain Air, The.   *Paul Horgan*.   LA78(II-821).

*Thin Red Line, The.   *James Jones*.   SCL12(XI-7543), SCL7(VII-4592),
  A63(265).

Thing, The.   Cine(IV-1712).

*Things of This World.   *Richard Wilbur*.   SCL12(XI-7546),
  SCL7(VII-4595),   A57(266).

Things That I Do in the Dark: Selected Poetry.   *June Jordan*.
  LA78(II-826).

Things to Come.   Cine(IV-1716).

Third Book About Achim, The.   *Uwe Johnson*.   SCL12(XI-7549),
  SCL7(VII-4598),   A68(318).

Third Man, The.   Cine(IV-1719).

Third Policeman, The.   *Flann O'Brien*.   SCL12(XI-7552),
  SCL7(VII-4601),   A68(321).

Third Republic of France: The First Phase, 1871-1894, The.   *Guy
  Chapman*.   Different analyses on this title appear in: HEur(II-1054;
  II-1067).

Third Revolution: A Study of Psychiatry and Religion, The.   *Karl Stern*.
  HEur(III-1141).

"Third World's" Struggle for Equality, The (Event).   HWor(II-557).

Thirteen Books of Euclid's Elements, The.   *Sir Thomas L. Heath*.
  HAnc(I-386).

Thirteenth Apostle, The.   *Eugene Vale*.   SCL12(XI-7555),
  SCL7(VII-4604),   A60(270).

Thirteenth Century, 1216-1307, The.   *Frederick M. Powicke*.
  HAnc(III-1583).

Thirteenth Tribe, The.   *Arthur Koestler*.   LA77(II-817).

Thirties and After: Poetry, Politics, People 1933-1970, The.   *Stephen
  Spender*.   LA79(II-745).

Thirty Years That Shook Physics.   *George Gamow*.   HWor(I-169).

Thirty Years War, The.   *C. V. Wedgwood*.   Different analyses on this title
  appear in: HEur(I-252; I-271; I-291; I-310).

Thirty-Nine Articles of the Church of England, The (Event).   HEur(I-168).

39 Steps, The.   Cine(IV-1723).

Thirty-Nine Steps, The. *John Buchan.* MP12(XI-6493), MPCE(IV-2242), MP8(VIII-5167), MP6(VI-3096), MPEng(833), MP1(II-972), MWL1(972).

This Above All. *Eric Knight.* MP12(XI-6497), MPCE(IV-2244), MP8(VIII-5170), MP6(VI-3098), MPEng(836), MP1(II-974), MWL1(974).

This Blessèd Earth, New and Selected Poems, 1927-1977. *John Hall Wheelock.* LA79(II-749).

This Endangered Planet: Prospects and Proposals for Human Survival. *Richard A. Falk.* HWor(II-1072).

This Hallowed Ground. *Bruce Catton.* SCL12(XI-7558), SCL7(VII-4607), A57(269), BMA(544).

This High Man: The Life of Robert H. Goddard. *Milton Lehman.* HAmer(III-1557).

This Immortal. *Roger Zelazny.* SF(V-2260).

This Sporting Life. Cine(IV-1726).

This Way for the Gas, Ladies and Gentlemen. *Tadeusz Borowski.* SCL12(XI-7561), SCL7(VII-4610), A68(324).

Thomas. *Shelley Mydans.* SCL12(XI-7565), SCL7(VII-4614), A66(309).

Thomas à Kempis, His Age and His Book. *J. E. G. De Montmorency.* HAnc(III-1672).

Thomas à Kempis Writes the *Imitation of Christ* (Event). HAnc(III-1670). *See also* Imitation of Christ, The.

Thomas Becket. *Richard Winston.* SCL12(XI-7570), SCL7(VII-4619), A68(328). A different analysis on this title appears in: HAnc(III-1378).

Thomas Wolfe. *Elizabeth Nowell.* SCL12(XI-7574), SCL7(VII-4622), A61(251), BMA(547).

Thoreau: A Collection of Critical Essays. *Sherman Paul,* ed. HAmer(II-851).

Thorn Birds, The. *Colleen McCullough.* LA78(II-831).

Thornton Wilder: His World. *Linda Simon.* LA80(II-815).

Thought and Character of William James: Briefer Version, The. *Ralph Barton Perry.* HAmer(III-1366).

Thought and Letters in Western Europe, A.D. 500 to 900. *Max L. W. Laistner.* HAnc(II-1139).

Thoughts on the Interpretation of Nature. *Denis Diderot.* Ph(I-495).

Thousand Clowns, A. Cine(IV-1728).

Thousand Days, A. *Arthur M. Schlesinger, Jr.* SCL12(XI-7578), SCL7(VII-4626), A66(313). A different analysis on this title appears in: HAmer(III-1891).

Thread That Runs So True, The. *Jesse Stuart.* SCL12(XI-7584), SCLs(318).

Three. *Sylvia Ashton-Warner.* SCL12(XI-7592), A71(314).

Three Black Pennys, The. *Joseph Hergesheimer.* MP12(XI-6500),

To Purge This Land with Blood: A Biography of John Brown. *Stephen B. Oates.* HAmer(II-921).

To Set the Record Straight: The Break-in, the Tapes, the Conspirators, the Pardon. *John J. Sirica.* LA80(II-822).

To Teach, To Love. *Jesse Stuart.* SCL12(XI-7690), A71(327).

To the Farewell Address: Ideas of Early American Foreign Policy. *Felix Gilbert.* Different analyses on this title appear in: HAmer(I-286; I-406).

*To the Lighthouse. *Virginia Woolf.* MP12(XI-6573), MPCE(IV-2275), MP8(VIII-5228), MP6(VI-3142), MPEng(850), MP1(II-993), MWL1(993).

*Tobacco Road. *Erskine Caldwell.* MP12(XI-6578), MPCE(IV-2278), MP8(VIII-5231), MP6(VI-3144), MPAm(653), MP1(II-996), MWL1(996).

Tocqueville and American Civilization. *Max Lerner.* HAmer(II-675).

*Toilers of the Sea, The. *Victor Hugo.* MP12(XI-6581), MPCE(IV-2279), MP8(VIII-5233), MP6(VI-3146), MPEur(758), MPv3(515), MP2(II-1037), MWL2(1037).

Toleration and the Reformation. *Joseph Lecler, S. J.* HEur(I-217).

Tolkien: A Biography. *Humphrey Carpenter.* LA78(II-851).

Tolstoy. *Henri Troyat.* SCL12(XI-7695), SCL7(VII-4706), A69(312).

Tolstoy, My Father. *Ilya Tolstoy.* SCL12(XI-7699), A72(325).

Tolstoy's Letters. *Lev Tolstoy.* LA79(II-754).

Tom Barber. *Forrest Reid.* SCL12(XI-7703), SCL7(VII-4710), A55(269).

Tom Brown's School Days. *Thomas Hughes.* MP12(XI-6585), MPCE(IV-2281), MP8(VIII-5236), MP6(VI-3148), MPEng(853), MPv4(524), MP2(II-1039), MWL2(1039).

Tom Burke of Ours. *Charles Lever.* MP12(XI-6588), MPCE(IV-2282), MP8(VIII-5238), MP6(VI-3150), MPEng(855), MPv4(526), MP2(II-1041), MWL2(1041).

Tom Cringle's Log. *Michael Scott.* MP12(XI-6594), MPCE(IV-2284), MP8(VIII-5243), MP6(VI-3155), MPEng(860), MP1(II-997), MWL1(997).

Tom Jones. Cine(IV-1760).

*Tom Jones. *Henry Fielding.* MP12(XI-6598), MPCE(IV-2285), MP8(VIII-5246), MP6(VI-3158), MPEng(863), MP1(II-1000), MWL1(1000).

*Tom Sawyer. *Mark Twain.* MP12(XI-6604), MPCE(IV-2288), MP8(VIII-5250), MP6(VI-3161), MPAm(655), MP1(II-1003), MWL1(100).

Tom Swift Novels, The. *"Victor Appleton."* SF(V-2298).

Tom Thumb the Great. *Henry Fielding.* MP12(XI-6609), MPCE(IV-2291), MP8(VIII-5253), MP6(VI-3164), MPDr(860), MPv4(531), MP2(II-1046), MWL2(1046).

Tomb of St. Peter—New Discoveries in the Sacred Grottoes of the Vatican,
   The. *Margherita Guarducci.* HAnc(II-645).
Tome. *Saint Leo I.* Different analyses on this title appear in: RCh(I-159),
   RCa(I-201).
Tomorrow and Yesterday. *Heinrich Böll.* SCL12(XI-7707),
   SCL7(VII-4714), A58(236).
Tono-Bungay. *H. G. Wells.* MP12(XI-6613), MPCE(IV-2293),
   MP8(VIII-5256), MP6(VI-3166), MPEng(867), MP1(II-1006),
   MWL1(1006).
Top Hat. Cine(IV-1764).
Topper. Cine(IV-1770).
Torchbearer of the Revolution: The Story of Bacon's Rebellion and Its
   Leader. *Thomas J. Wertenbaker.* HAmer(I-153).
Tormented Warrior: Ludendorff and the Supreme Command. *Roger
   Parkinson.* LA80(II-827).
Toro! Toro! Toro! *William Hjortsberg.* SCL12(XI-7711), A75(329).
Touch. *Thom Gunn.* SCL12(XI-7713), SCL7(VII-4717), A69(315).
Touch of the Poet, A. *Eugene O'Neill.* SCL12(XI-7716),
   SCL7(VII-4720), A58(239), BMA(558).
Toward Lexington: The Role of the British Army in the Coming of the
   American Revolution. *John Shy.* HAmer(I-233).
Toward the Final Solution: A History of European Racism. *George L.
   Mosse.* LA79(II-761).
Toward Understanding Saint Thomas. *M. D. Chenu, O. P.* HAnc(III-1546).
"Towards a Revised History of the New Testament Canon," *in* Studia
   Evangelica IV: Texte und Untersuchengen. *A. C. Sundberg.*
   HAnc(II-770).
Tower of Glass. *Robert Silverberg.* SF(V-2303).
Tower of London, The. *William Harrison Ainsworth.* MP12(XI-6618),
   MPCE(IV-2296), MP8(VIII-5259), MP6(VI-3168), MPEng(870),
   MP1(II-1008), MWL1(1008).
Towers of Trebizond, The. *Rose Macaulay.* SCL12(XI-7719),
   SCL7(VII-4723), A58(242).
*Town, The. *William Faulkner.* MP12(XI-6623), MPCE(IV-2299),
   MP8(VIII-5262), MP6(VI-3171), MPAm(658), MP3(II-1074),
   MWL3(1074). A different analysis on this title appears in:
   SCL12(XI-7722), SCL7(VII-4726), A58(245), BMA(561).
*Town, The. *Conrad Richter.* MP12(XI-6628), MPCE(IV-2302),
   MP8(VIII-5265), MP6(VI-3174), MPAm(661), MPv4(533),
   MP2(II-1048), MWL2(1048).
Toynbee and History. *Ashley Montagu, ed.* HWor(I-333).
*Toys in the Attic. *Lillian Hellman.* SCL12(XI-7275), SCL7(VII-4729),
   A61(263).
*Track of the Cat, The. *Walter Van Tilburg Clark.* MP12(XI-6633),
   MPCE(IV-2305), MP8(VIII-5268), MP6(VI-3176), MPAm(664),

MPv4(535), MP2(II-1051), MWL2(1051).
Track to Bralgu, The. *B. Wongar.* LA79(II-768).
Tract Concerning the First Principle, A. *John Duns Scotus.* Ph(I-329).
Tractatus Logico-Philosophicus. *Ludwig Wittgenstein.* Ph(II-829).
Tradition and Design in the Iliad. *C. M. Bowra.* HAnc(I-112).
Tragic Finale, The. *Wilfred Desan.* HEur(III-1483).
*Tragic Muse, The. *Henry James.* MP12(XI-6636), MPCE(IV-2306),
MP8(VIII-5271), MP4(II-1222), MWL4(1222).
Tragic Sense of Life in Men and in Peoples, The. *Miguel de Unamuno y
Jugo.* MP12(XI-6640), MP8(VIII-5274), MP4(II-1225),
MWL4(1225).
Trail of the Fox, The. *David Irving.* LA78(II-856).
*Train of Powder, A. *Rebecca West.* SCL12(XI-7729),
SCL7(VII-4732), A55(272).
Train Whistle Guitar. *Albert Murray.* SCL12(XI-7733), A75(331).
Training in Christianity. *Søren Kierkegaard.* RCh(II-720).
Traité du Libre Arbitre. *Yves René Marie Simon.* RCa(II-986).
Traitor, The. *James Shirley.* MP12(XI-6643), MPCE(IV-2307),
MP8(VIII-5277), MP6(VI-3178), MPDr(863), MP3(II-1077),
MWL3(1077).
Transatlantic Blues. *Wilfrid Sheed.* LA79(II-772).
Transatlantic Patterns: Cultural Comparisons of England with
America. *Martin Green.* LA78(II-860).
Transcendentalist Ministers: Church Reform in the New England Renaissance,
The. *William R. Hutchinson.* HAmer(I-657).
Transference of Pergamum to Rome (Event). HAnc(I-486).
Transformation in Christ. *Dietrich von Hildebrand.* RCa(II-946).
Transformation of Rhode Island, 1790-1860, The. *Peter J. Coleman.*
HAmer(II-769).
Transformation of Southern Politics, The. *Jack Bass* and *Walter DeVries.*
LA77(II-832).
Transformation of the School: Progressivism in American Education,
1876-1957, The. *Lawrence A. Cremin.* HAmer(II-1303).
Transformations of the American Party System: Political Coalitions from the
New Deal to the 1970s. *Everett Carll Ladd, Jr.* and *Charles D.
Hadley.* HWor(III-1307).
Transgressor, The. *Julian Green.* SCL12(XI-7737), SCL7(VII-4736),
A58(247).
Transient and Permanent in Christianity, The. *Theodore Parker.*
RCh(II-700).
"Translator's Introduction," *in* Being and Nothingness. *Hazel Barnes.*
HEur(III-1484).
"Transmission of Learning and Literary Influences to Western Europe," *in*
Vol. II *of* The Cambridge History of Islam. *Francesco Gabrieli.*
HAnc(II-1192).

Transmission of the Alphabet (Event).   HAnc(I-80).

Transparent Things.   *Vladimir Nabokov.*   SCL12(XI-7741),   A73(364).

"Transplants: Will Future Vindicate the Failures?," *in* Chicago Sun
    Times.   *Christian N. Barnard.*   HWor(II-1019).

Trap, The.   *Dan Jacobson.*   SCL12(XI-7745),   SCL7(VII-4739),
    A55(275).

Travel and Discovery in the Renaissance, 1420-1620.   *Boies Penrose.*
    HEur(I-13).

Travelers.   *Ruth Prawer Jhabvala.*   SCL12(XI-7748),   A74(394).

Traveling Through the Dark.   *William Stafford.*   SCL12(XI-7751),
    SCLs(325).

Travellers, The.   *Jean Stubbs.*   SCL12(XI-7754),   SCL7(VII-4742),
    A64(274).

Travels in Arabia Deserta.   *Charles M. Doughty.*   MP12(XI-6647),
    MP8(VIII-5280),   MP6(VI-3180),   MPNf(300),   MP3(II-1079),
    MWL3(1079).

Travels of Jaimie McPheeters, The.   *Robert Lewis Taylor.*
    SCL12(XI-7759),   SCL7(VII-4747),   A59(251).

Travels of Marco Polo (Event).   HAnc(III-1550).

Travels of Marco Polo, The.   *Marco Polo.*   MP12(XI-6650),
    MPCE(IV-2309),   MP8(VIII-5283),   MP6(VI-3183),   MPNf(303),
    MP1(II-1011),   MWL1(1011). A different analysis on this title appears
    in: HAnc(III-1553).

Travels to the Interior Districts of Africa.   *Mungo Park.*   MP12(XI-6656),
    MP8(VIII-5287),   MP4(II-1227),   MWL4(1227).

*Travels with a Donkey.   *Robert Louis Stevenson.*   MP12(XI-6659),
    MPCE(IV-2312),   MP8(VIII-5290),   MP6(VI-3186),   MPNf(307),
    MP1(II-1014),   MWL1(1014).

Travels with Charley.   *John Steinbeck.*   SCL12(XI-7763),
    SCL7(VII-4751),   A63(270).

Travels with My Aunt.   *Graham Greene.*   SCL12(XI-7765),   A71(332).

*Travesties.   *Tom Stoppard.*   SCL12(XI-7769),   A76(325).

Travesty.   *John Hawkes.*   LA77(II-837).

Tread the Dark: New Poems.   *David Ignatow.*   LA79(II-777).

*Treasure Island.   *Robert Louis Stevenson.*   MP12(XI-6662),
    MPCE(IV-2313),   MP8(VIII-5292),   MP6(VI-3187),   MPEng(873),
    MP1(II-1015),   MWL1(1015).

Treasure of the Sierra Madre, The.   Cine(IV-1773).

Treatise Concerning Religious Affections, A.   *Jonathan Edwards.*
    RCh(II-590).

Treatise Concerning the Principles of Human Knowledge, A.   *George
    Berkeley.*   PH(I-447).

Treatise Concerning the Pursuit of Learning.   *Hugh of St. Victor.*
    RCa(I-300).

Treatise Concerning the Search After Truth.   *Nicholas de Malebranche.*

RCh(I-522).

Treatise of Excommunication, A. *Thomas Erastus.* RCh(I-414).

*Treatise of Human Nature (Book I), A. *David Hume.* Ph(I-471).

Treatise of Reformation Without Tarrying for Any. *Robert Browne.* RCh(I-400).

Treatise on Christian Liberty, A. *Martin Luther.* RCh(I-339).

Treatise on Laws. *Francisco Suarez, S. J.* RCa(II-575).

Treatise on the Church. *John Huss.* RCh(I-304).

Treatise on the Four Gospels. *Joachim of Fiore.* RCh(I-224).

Treatise on the Holy Spirit. *Saint Basil.* RCa(I-107).

Treatise on the Laws and Customs of England. *Henry of Bracton.* RCa(I-367).

Treatise on the Laws of Ecclesiastical Polity. *Richard Hooker.* RCh(I-418).

Treatise on the Mysteries. *Saint Hilary of Poitiers.* RCa(I-103).

Treatise on the Passion. *Saint Thomas More.* RCa(I-538).

Treatise on the Promises. *Saint Dionysius of Alexandria.* RCa(I-78).

Treatises and Sermons of Meister Eckhart, The. *Johannes Eckhart.* RCa(I-451).

Treatises of Cicero, The. *Cicero (Marcus Tullius Cicero).* MP12(XI-6669), MP8(VIII-5295), MP4(II-1229), MWL4(1229).

Treatises on Marriage. *Tertullian.* RCa(I-54).

Treaty for Antarctica, A. *Howard J. Taubenfeld.* HWor(II-802).

Treaty of Câteau-Cambrésis (Event). HEur(I-158).

Treaty of Kuchkuk Kainarji (Event). HEur(I-475).

Treaty of 1921 Between Britain and Ireland (Event). HEur(III-1314).

Treaty of Prague (Event). HEur(I-290).

Treaty of Trianon (Event). HWor(I-181)).

Treaty of Utrecht (Event). HEur(I-400).

Treaty of Verdum (Event). HAnc(II-1158).

Treaty of Versailles (Event). HEur(III-1283).

Treaty of Vervins (Event). HEur(I-220).

Treaty of Washington, 1871: A Study in Imperial History, The. *Goldwin A. Smith.* HAmer(II-1074).

Treblinka. *Jean-François Steiner.* SCL12(XI-7773), SCL7(VII-4753), A68(337).

Tree Grows in Brooklyn, A. *Betty Smith.* MP12(XI-6672), MPCE(IV-2317), MP8(VIII-5298), MP6(VI-3190), MPAm(667), MP1(II-1018), MWL1(1018).

Tree of Man, The. *Patrick White.* MP12(XI-6676), MP8(VIII-5301), MP4(II-1232), MWL4(1232), SCL12(XI-7776), SCL7(VII-4756), A55(278).

Tree of the Folkungs, The. *Verner von Heidenstam.* MP12(XI-6679), MPCE(IV-2319), MP8(VIII-5304), MP6(VI-3192), MPEur(761), MPv4(537), MP2(II-1053), MWL2(1053).

*Tree on Fire, A. *Alan Sillitoe.* SCL12(XI-7779), SCL7(VII-4759), A69(318).
*Trees, The. *Conrad Richter.* MP12(XI-6683), MPCE(IV-2321), MP8(VIII-5307), MP6(VI-3195), MPAm(670), MPv4(540), MP2(II-1055), MWL2(1055).
*Trial, The. *Franz Kafka.* MP12(XI-6687), MPCE(IV-2322), MP8(VIII-5310), MP6(VI-3197), MPEur(764), MP1(II-1020), MWL1(1020).
*Trial by Jury. *W. S. Gilbert.* MP12(XI-6692), MPCE(IV-2325), MP8(VIII-5313), MP6(VI-3200), MPDr(866), MPv4(542), MP2(II-1058), MWL2(1058).
Trial of Jesus, The. *Josef Blinzler.* HAnc(II-603).
Trial of John Peter Zenger and Freedom of the Press (Event). HAmer(I-188).
Trial of Peter Zenger, The. *Vincent Buranelli.* HAmer(I-190).
Trial of the Germans: An Account of the Twenty-Two Defendants Before the International Military Tribunal at Nuremburg, The. *Eugene Davidson.* HEur(III-1524).
Trialogus. *John Wycliffe.* RCh(I-294).
Tribe That Lost Its Head, The. *Nicholas Monsarrat.* SCL12(XI-7783), SCL7(VII-4763), A57(275).
Tribunate of Tiberius Sempronius Gracchus (Event). HAnc(I-481).
Trick to Catch the Old One, A. *Thomas Middleton.* MP12(XI-6695), MPCE(IV-2326), MP8(VIII-5315), MP6(VI-3201), MPDr(868), MPv4(544), MP2(II-1059), MWL2(1059).
Trickster, The. *Plautus (Titus Maccius Plautus).* MP12(XI-6698), MPCE(IV-2328), MP8(VIII-5318), MP6(VI-3203), MPDr(871), MP3(II-1081), MWL3(1081).
Trilby. *George du Maurier.* MP12(XI-6701), MPCE(IV-2329), MP8(VIII-5321), MP6(VI-3205), MPEng(876), MP1(II-1023), MWL1(1023).
Trinity. *Leon Uris.* LA77(II-842).
Triple Alliance, The (Event). HEur(II-1019).
Triple Entente, The (Event). HEur(III-1197).
Tristan and Isolde. *Gottfried von Strassburg.* MP12(XI-6705), MPCE(IV-2331), MP8(VIII-5324), MP6(VI-3208), MPPo(362), MP3(II-1083), MWL3(1083).
*Tristram. *Edwin Arlington Robinson.* MP12(XI-6709), MPCE(IV-2334), MP8(VIII-5326), MP6(VI-3210), MPPo(364), MP1(II-1025), MWL1(1025).
*Tristram Shandy. *Laurence Sterne.* MP12(XI-6712), MPCE(IV-2335), MP8(VIII-5329), MP6(VI-3212), MPEng(879), MP1(1027), MWL1(1027).
Triton. *Samuel R. Delany.* SF(V-2307).

Triumph in the West. *Sir Arthur Bryant.* SCL12(XI-7787), SCL7(VII-4767), A60(278), BMA(564).

Triumph of Conservatism: A Reinterpretation of American History, 1900-1916, The. *Gabriel Kolko.* HAmer(III-1435).

*Triumph of Death, The. *Gabriele D'Annunzio.* MP12(XI-6717), MPCE(IV-2338), MP8(VIII-5332), MP6(VI-3215), MPEur(767), MPv4(546), MP2(II-1061), MWL2(1061).

Triumph of the Alphabet, The. *Alfred C. Moorhouse.* HAnc(I-82).

Triumph of the Novel, The. *Albert J. Guerard.* LA77(II-847).

Triumph, or Tragedy: Reflections on Vietnam. *Richard N. Goodwin.* SCL12(XI-7790), SCL7(VII-4770), A67(328).

*Troilus and Cressida. *William Shakespeare.* MP12(XI-6720), MPCE(IV-2339), MP8(VIII-5334), MP6(VI-3217), MPDr(874), MPv4(548), MP2(II-1063), MWL2(1063).

*Troilus and Criseyde. *Geoffrey Chaucer.* MP12(XI-6725), MPCE(IV-2342), MP8(VIII-5337), MP6(VI-3220), MPPo(367), MP1(II-1030), MWL1(1030).

*Trojan Women, The. *Euripides.* MP12(XI-6729), MPCE(IV-2345), MP8(VIII-5339), MP6(VI-3221), MPDr(877), MP3(II-1085), MWL3(1085).

Tropic of Capricorn. *Henry Miller.* MP12(XI-6733), MP8(VIII-5341), MP4(II-1234), MWL4(1234).

Trotsky Sent into Exile (Event). HEur(III-1347).

Troubadours dans leur vie et dans leurs oeuvres, Les. *Ernest Hoepffner.* HAnc(III-1300).

Trouble with Harry, The. Cine(IV-1777).

True Adventures of Huckleberry Finn, The. *John Seelye.* SCL12(XII-7793), A70(313).

True Christianity. *Johann Arndt.* RCh(I-422).

True Grit. Cine(IV-1780).

True Grit. *Charles Portis.* SCL12(XII-7796), SCL7(VII-4773), A69(321).

True History, The. *Lucian.* MP12(XI-6737), MPCE(IV-2348), MP8(VIII-5345), MP6(VI-3223), MPEur(769), MP3(II-1087), MWL3(1087).

True Humanism. *Jacques Maritain.* RCh(II-1020).

True Intellectual System of the Universe, The. *Ralph Cudworth.* RCh(I-534).

"Truman and Eisenhower Doctrines in the Light of the Doctrine of Non-Intervention, The," *in* Political Science Quarterly. *Doris A. Graber.* HWor(II-761).

Truman and the 80th Congress. *Susan M. Hartmann.* HAmer(III-1802).

Truman Doctrine with Its Policy of Containment, The (Event). HAmer(III-1776).

"Truman Foreign Policy: A Traditional View," *in* The Truman Period as a
    Research Field: A Reappraisal. *Robert H. Ferrell.* HWor(II-665).
Truman Presidency: The History of a Triumphant Succession, The. *Cabell
    Phillips.* HAmer(III-1761).
Truman-MacArthur Confrontation, The (Event). HAmer(III-1829).
Truman-MacArthur Controversy and the Korean War, The. *John W.
    Spanier.* HAmer(III-1831).
Trustee from the Toolroom. *Nevil Shute.* SCL12(XII-7800),
    SCL7(VII-4777),   A61(266).
Trusting and the Maimed, The. *James Plunkett.* SCL12(XII-7803),
    SCL7(VII-4780),   A55(281).
Truth of the Christian Religion, The. *Hugo Grotius.* RCh(I-432).
Truth Suspected. *Juan Ruiz de Alarcón.* MP12(XI-6740),
    MPCE(IV-2349),   MP8(VIII-5347),   MP6(VI-3225),   MPDr(879),
    MP3(II-1089),   MWL3(1089).
Tsar and Empire: Studies in Russian Myths. *Michael Cherniavsky.*
    HEur(I-234).
Tube of Plenty. *Erik Barnouw.* SCL12(XII-7806),   A76(329).
    A different analysis on this title appears in:
    HWor(II-671).
Tunc. *Lawrence Durrell.* SCL12(XII-7810),   SCL7(VII-4783),
    A69(324).
Tunc *and* Nunquam. *Lawrence Durrell.* SF(V-2311).
Tunnel, The. *Bernhard Kellermann.* SF(V-2316).
*Tunnel of Love, The. *Peter De Vries.* SCL12(XII-7814),
    SCL7(VII-4787),   A54(282).
Tunnel Sottomarino, Il. *Luigi Motta.* SF(V-2321).
Tunnel Through the Deeps, The. *Harry Harrison.* SF(V-2324).
Turcaret. *Alain René Le Sage.* MP12(XI-6744),   MPCE(IV-2352),
    MP8(VIII-5349),   MP6(VI-3227),   MPDr(881),   MP3(II-1091),
    MWL3(1091).
Turgenev: His Life and Times. *Leonard Schapiro.* LA80(II-832).
Turkestan Down to the Mongol Invasion. *W. Barthold.* HAnc(III-1255).
Turkey, the Great Powers, and the Bagdad Railway. *Edward M. Earle.*
    HEur(II-1135).
Turkish Conquest of Serbia (Event). HAnc(III-1660).
Turn of the Screw, The. *Henry James.* MP12(XI-6748),
    MPCE(IV-2353),   MP8(VIII-5352),   MP6(VI-3229),   MPAm(673),
    MPv3(517),   MP2(II-1066),   MWL2(1066).
Turn of the Tide, The. *Sir Arthur Bryant.* SCL12(XII-7818),
    SCL7(VII-4790),   A58(250),   BMA(567).
Turning Point of the Revolution: Or Burgoyne in America, The. *Hoffman
    Nickerson.* HAmer(I-280).
Turtle Diary. *Russell Hoban.* LA77(II-852).
Turtle Island. *Gary Snyder.* SCL12(XII-7821),   A75(335).

RCa(II-628).

Two Essays on Analytical Psychology. *Carl G. Jung.* MP12(XII-6769), MP8(VIII-5366), MP4(II-1240), MWL4(1240).

*Two Gentlemen of Verona. *William Shakespeare.* MP12(XII-6772), MPCE(IV-2362), MP8(VIII-5369), MP6(VI-3239), MPDr(887), MPv3(524), MP2(II-1074), MWL2(1074).

Two Hague Conferences, The. *Joseph H. Choate.* HEur(II-1126).

*Two Noble Kinsmen, The. *John Fletcher* and *William Shakespeare.* MP12(XII-6775), MPCE(IV-2363), MP8(VIII-5371), MP6(VI-3241), MPDr(889), MPv4(551), MP2(II-1076), MWL2(1076).

Two Planets. *Kurd Lasswitz.* SF(V-2334).

Two Queens of Baghdad: Mother and Wife of Harun al-Rashid. *Nabia Abbott.* HAnc(II-1144).

Two Sides of an Island. *Martin Halpern.* SCL12(XII-7841), SCL7(VII-4803), A64(278).

Two Sources of Morality and Religion, The. *Henri Bergson.* Different analyses on this title appear in: Ph(II-959), RCh(II-990).

Two Tales. *Shmuel Yosef Agnon.* SCL12(XII-7844), SCL7(VII-4806), A67(331).

2018 A.D. or The King Kong Blues. *Sam J. Lundwall.* SF(V-2339).

2001: A Space Odyssey. Cine(IV-1798).

2001: A Space Odyssey. *Arthur C. Clarke.* SF(V-2343).

*Two Towers, The. *J. R. R. Tolkien.* MP12(XII-6778), MPCE(IV-2365), MP8(VIII-5373), MP4(II-1242), MWL4(1242).

Two Under the Indian Sun. *Jon Godden* and *Rumer Godden.* SCL12(XII-7847), SCL7(VII-4809), A67(333).

*Two Weeks in Another Town. *Irwin Shaw.* SCL12(XII-7851), SCL7(VII-4813), A61(268).

*Two Women. *Alberto Moravia.* MP12(XII-6782), MP8(VIII-5376), MP4(II-1245), MWL4(1245), SCL12(XII-7855), SCL7(VII-4817), A59(254).

*Two Years Before the Mast. *Richard Henry Dana, Jr.* MP12(XII-6785), MPCE(IV-2366), MP8(VIII-5379), MP6(VI-3243), MPNf(309), MP1(II-1033), MWL1(1033).

Two-Edged Sword, The. *John L.McKenzie, S. J.* RCa(II-1028).

Two-Part Inventions. *Richard Howard.* SCL12(XII-7858), A75(337).

*Typee. *Herman Melville.* MP12(XII-6791), MPCE(IV-2370), MP8(VIII-5382), MP6(VI-3245), MPAm(676), MP1(II-1035), MWL1(1035).

Tyrants Destroyed. *Vladimir Nabokov.* SCL12(XII-7861), A76(337).

Ubik. *Philip K. Dick.* SF(V-2350).

Ugly Duchess, The. *Lion Feuchtwanger.* MP12(XII-6796), MPCE(IV-2373), MP8(VIII-5385), MP6(VI-3247), MPEur(776),

MP1(II-1037),   MWL1(1037).

*Ulysses. *James Joyce.* MP12(XII-6799),   MPCE(IV-2374),
MP8(VIII-5388),   MP6(VI-3249),   MPEng(882),   MP1(II-1040),
MWL1(1040).

Ulysses S. Grant, Politician. *William B. Hesseltine.* HAmer(II-1056).

Un autre monde. *J. J. Grandville* and *Taxile Delord.* See autre monde, Un.

Unbearable Bassington, The. *Saki.* MP12(XII-6804),
MPCE(IV-2377),   MP8(VIII-5391),   MP6(VI-3252),   MPEng(885),
MP1(II-1042),   MWL1(1042).

Uncertain Greatness: Henry Kissinger and American Foreign Policy. *Roger
Morris.* LA78(II-869).

Uncle. *Julia Markus.* LA79(II-783).

Uncle of Europe. *Gordon Brook-Shepherd.* LA77(II-861).

Uncle Sam's Stepchildren: The Reformation of United States Indian Policy,
1865-1887. *Loring B. Priest.* HAmer(II-1163).

Uncle Silas. *Joseph Sheridan Le Fanu.* MP12(XII-6808),
MPCE(IV-2379),   MP8(VIII-5394),   MP6(VI-3254),   MPEng(888),
MPv4(553),   MP2(II-1078),   MWL2(1078).

*Uncle Tom's Cabin. *Harriet Beecher Stowe.*   MP12(XII-6814),
MPCE(IV-2381),   MP8(VIII-5398),   MP6(VI-3258),
MPAm(679),   MP1(II-1044),   MWL1(1044).
A different analysis on this title appears
in: HAmer(II-862).

*Uncle Vanya. *Anton Chekhov.* MP12(XII-6818),   MPCE(IV-2383),
MP8(VIII-5401),   MP6(VI-3260),   MPDr(891),   MPv4(557),
MP2(II-1082),   MWL2(1082).

Uncollected Stories of William Faulkner. *William Faulkner.* LA80(II-838).

Uncompleted Past, The. *Martin Duberman.* SCL12(XII-7865),   A70(315).

Undeclared War, 1940-1941, The. *William L. Langer* and *S. Everett
Gleason.* HAmer(III-1689).

Under Fire. *Henri Barbusse.* MP12(XII-6822),   MPCE(IV-2385),
MP8(VIII-5404),   MP6(VI-3263),   MPEur(779),   MP1(II-1047),
MWL1(1047).

*Under Milk Wood. *Dylan Thomas.* MP12(XII-6825),
MP8(VIII-5407),   MP4(II-1247),   MWL4(1247). A different analysis
on this title appears in: SCL12(XII-7870),   SCL7(VII-4820),
A54(285),   BMA(570).

*Under the Greenwood Tree. *Thomas Hardy.* MP12(XII-6829),
MPCE(IV-2386),   MP8(VIII-5411),   MP6(VI-3265),
MPEng(892),   MPv4(559),   MP2(II-1084),
MWL2(1084).

Under the Mountain Wall. *Peter Matthiessen.* SCL12(XII-7874),
SCL7(VII-4824),   A63(272).

*Under the Volcano. *Malcolm Lowry.* MP12(XII-6833),
MP8(VIII-5414),   MP4(II-1250),   MWL4(1250).

Under the Yoke. *Ivan Vazov.* MP12(XII-6836), MPCE(IV-2388), MP8(VIII-5417), MP6(VI-3267), MPEur(782), MPv4(561), MP2(II-1086), MWL2(1086).

Under Two Flags. *Ouida.* MP12(XII-6840), MPCE(IV-2390), MP8(VIII-5420), MP6(VI-3269), MPEng(895), MP1(II-1049), MWL1(1049).

*Under Western Eyes. *Joseph Conrad.* MP12(XII-6844), MPCE(IV-2391), MP8(VIII-5423), MP6(VI-3272), MPEng(898), MP3(II-1093), MWL3(1093).

*Underdogs, The. *Mariano Azuela.* MP12(XII-6847), MPCE(IV-2392), MP8(VIII-5425), MP6(VI-3274), MPAm(682), MPv4(564), MP2(II-1088), MWL2(1088).

Underground Man, The. *Ross Macdonald.* SCL12(XII-7878), A72(329).

Undine. *Friedrich de La Motte-Fouqué.* MP12(XII-6852), MPCE(IV-2395), MP8(VIII-5428), MP6(VI-3276), MPEur(785), MPv3(526), MP2(II-1091), MWL2(1091).

Undying Grass, The. *Yashar Kemal.* LA79(II-787).

Uneasy Chair: A Biography of Bernard DeVoto, The. *Wallace Stegner.* SCL12(XII-7884), A75(340).

Unequal Justice. *Jerold S. Auerbach.* LA77(II-866).

Unexpected Universe, The. *Loren Eiseley.* SCL12(XII-7891), A70(320).

Unfinished Quest of Richard Wright, The. *Michael Fabre.* SCL12(XII-7894), A74(401).

*Unfinished Woman, An. *Lillian Hellman.* SCL12(XII-7898), A70(322).

*Unfortunate Traveller, The. *Thomas Nash.* MP12(XII-6855), MPCE(IV-2396), MP8(VIII-5430), MP6(VI-3278), MPEng(900), MPv3(528), MP2(II-1092), MWL2(1092).

Unheimliche Erscheinungsformen auf Omega XI. *Johanna Braun* and *Gunter Braun.* SF(V-2357).

*Unicorn, The. *Iris Murdoch.* SCL12(XII-7902), SCL7(VII-4828), A64(281).

Uninvited, The. Cine(IV-1801).

Union Pacific Railroad: A Case in Premature Enterprise, The. *Robert William Fogel.* HAmer(II-972).

Unitarian Christianity. *William Ellery Channing.* RCh(II-650).

United Colonies of New England, 1643-1690, The. *Harry M. Ward.* HAmer(I-111).

United Nations Charter Convention (Event). HAmer(III-1741).

United States and Inter-American Security, 1889-1960, The. *J. Lloyd Mecham.* HAmer(III-1792).

United States and Latin America, The. *Herbert L. Matthews,* ed. HAmer(III-1791).

United States and Pancho Villa: A Study in Unconventional Diplomacy, The. *Clarence C. Clendennen.* HAmer(III-1441).

United States and the First Hague Conference, The. *Calvin de Armond*

The. *Hastings Rashdall.* HAnc(III-1493).
Unknown Orwell, The. *Peter Stansky* and *William Abrahams.*
  SCL12(XII-7912),   A73(367).
Unmade Bed, The. *Françoise Sagan.* LA79(II-791).
Unmaking of a President: Lyndon Johnson and Vietnam, The. *Herbert*
  Schandler. HWor(II-1038).
Unmarried Woman, An. Cine(IV-1805).
*Unnamable, The. *Samuel Beckett.* SCL12(XII-7917),
  SCL7(VII-4838),   A59(257).
*Unofficial Rose, An. *Iris Murdoch.* SCL12(XII-7920),
  SCL7(VII-4841),   A63(276).
Unperfect Society, The. *Milovan Djilas.* SCL12(XII-7924),   A70(326).
Unseen Revolution, The. *Peter F. Drucker.* LA77(II-872).
Unsettling of America: Culture and Agriculture, The. *Wendell Berry.*
  LA79(II-795).
Unsinkable Molly Brown, The. Cine(IV-1808).
Unsleeping Eye, The. *David Guy Compton.* SF(V-2366).
*Unspeakable Practices, Unnatural Acts. *Donald Barthelme.*
  SCL12(XII-7927),   SCL7(VII-4845),   A69(331).
Unspeakable Skipton, The. *Pamela Hansford Johnson.*
  SCL12(XII-7930),   SCL7(VII-4848),   A60(284).
Unsuspected Revolution: The Birth and Rise of Castroism, The. *Mario*
  Llerena. LA79(II-799).
Untoward Hills, The. *Albert Stewart.* SCL12(XII-7933),
  SCL7(VII-4851),   A63(279).
*Unvanquished, The. *William Faulkner.* MP12(XII-6860),
  MP8(VIII-5433),   MP4(II-1253),   MWL4(1253).
Unwelcome Immigrant: The American Image of the Chinese, 1785-1882,
  The. *Stuart Creighton Miller.* HAmer(II-1126).
Up Country. *Maxine Kumin.* SCL12(XII-7936),   A74(405).
Upon the Sweeping Flood. *Joyce Carol Oates.* SCL12(XII-7940),
  SCL7(VII-4854),   A67(336).
Uprising of the Comuneros (Event). HEur(I-72).
Upstate: Records and Recollections of Northern New York. *Edmund*
  Wilson. SCL12(XII-7944),   A72(335).
Upsurge of Venetian Trade with the East (Event). HAnc(III-1354).
Upton Sinclair Publishes *The Jungle* (Event). HAmer(III-1353). *See also*
  Jungle, The.
Urban Prospect, The. *Lewis Mumford.* HWor(II-554).
Urban Scene: Human Ecology and Demography, The. *Leo F. Schnore.*
  HAmer(III-1813).
Us He Devours. *James B. Hall.* SCL12(XII-7949),   SCL7(VII-4858),
  A65(299).
*U.S.A. *John Dos Passos.* MP12(XII-6863),   MPCE(IV-2399),
  MP8(VIII-5436),   MP6(VI-3280),   MPAm(685),   MP1(II-1051),

MWL1(1051).

Uses of Disorder, The. *Richard Sennett.* SCL12(XII-7952), A71(335).

Uses of Enchantment, The. *Bruno Bettelheim.* LA77(II-876).

Utilitarianism. *John Stuart Mill.* Ph(II-654).

*Utopia. *Sir Thomas More.* MP12(XII-6868), MP8(VIII-5439), MP6(VI-3283), MPNf(312), MP3(II-1095), MWL3(1095). Different analyses on this title appear in: Ph(I-348), RCa(I-509).

U-2 Incident and the Collapse of the Paris Summit Conference, The (Event). HWor(II-906).

*V. *Thomas Pynchon.* SCL12(XII-4955), SCL7(VII-4861), A64(284).

V Was for Victory. *John Morton Blum.* LA77(II-880).

*Valley of Bones, The. *Anthony Powell.* SCL12(XII-7958), SCL7(VII-4864), A65(302).

Valley of Darkness: The Japanese People and World War Two. *Thomas R. H. Havens.* LA79(II-804).

Vandal Seizure of Carthage (Event). HAnc(II-958).

Vanessa. *Hugh Walpole.* MP12(XII-6871), MPCE(IV-2402), MP8(VIII-5442), MP6(VI-3285), MPEng(903), MP1(II-1054), MWL1(1054).

Vanished Cities. *Herman Schreiber* and *George Schreiber.* SCL12(XII-7961), SCL7(VII-4867), A58(252).

*Vanity Fair. *William Makepeace Thackeray.* MP12(XII-6875), MPCE(IV-2404), MP8(VIII-5445), MP6(VI-3287), MPEng(906), MP1(II-1056), MWL1(1056).

Vantage Point, The. *Lyndon B. Johnson.* SCL12(XII-7964), A72(339).

Varieties of Religious Experience, The. *William James.* RCh(II-836).

Variety Photoplays. *Edward Field.* SCL12(XII-7968), SCL7(VII-4870), A68(343).

Vasari's Lives of the Artists. *Betty Burroughs.* HAnc(III-1589).

Vathek. *William Beckford.* MP12(XII-6881), MPCE(IV-2407), MP8(VIII-5449), MP6(VI-3291), MPEng(910), MPv3(530), MP2(II-1094), MWL2(1094).

Vatican Council Two. *Xavier Rynne.* HEur(III-1638).

Vatican Treaty, The (Event). HEur(III-1354).

V-E Day (Event). HAmer(III-1748).

Velvet Horn, The. *Andrew Lytle.* MP12(XII-6884), MP8(VIII-5451), MP4(II-1256), MWL4(1256). A different analysis on this title appears in: SCL12(XII-7971), SCL7(VII-4873), A58(255), BMA(573).

Venetia Is Ceded to Italy (Event). HEur(II-923).

Venetian Adventurer. *Henry H. Hart.* HAnc(III-1552).

Venetian Glass Nephew, The. *Elinor Wylie.* MP12(XII-6887), MPCE(IV-2408), MP8(VIII-5454), MP6(VI-3292), MPAm(688), MPv4(566), MP2(II-1096), MWL2(1096).

Venetian Red. *P. M. Pasinetti.* SCL12(XII-7975), SCL7(VII-4877),

A61(272).

Venetian Vespers, The. *Anthony Hecht.* LA80(II-841).

Venice and Its Story. *Thomas Okey.* HEur(I-34).

Venice, Its Individual Growth from the Earliest Beginnings to the Fall of the Republic. *Pompeo Molmenti.* HAnc(III-1357).

Venice Preserved. *Thomas Otway.* MP12(XII-6890), MPCE(IV-2409), MP8(VIII-5457), MP6(VI-3295), MPDr(894), MPv4(568), MP2(II-1098), MWL2(1098).

Ventriloquist, The. *Robert Huff.* LA78(II-873).

*Venus and Adonis. *William Shakespeare.* MP12(XII-6893), MPCE(IV-2411), MP8(VIII-5460), MP6(VI-3297), MPPo(369), MP1(II-1060), MWL1(1060).

Venus Plus X. *Theodore Sturgeon.* SF(V-2370).

Verdi. *George Martin.* SCL12(XII-7978), SCL7(VII-4880), A64(286).

Verdun. *Georges Blond.* HEur(III-1265).

Vergil Writes the *Aeneid* (Event). HAnc(I-556). *See also* Aeneid.

Verlaine. *Joanna Richardson.* SCL12(XII-7982), A72(343).

Vernon Louis Parrington Publishes *Main Currents in American Thought* (Event). HWor(I-205). *See also* Main Currents in American Thought.

Very Private Life, A. *Michael Frayn.* SCL12(XII-7986), SCL7(VII-4884), A69(334).

Vesalius Publishes *On the Fabric of the Human Body* (Event). HEur(I-133).

*Vicar of Bullhampton, The. *Anthony Trollope.* MP12(XII-6897), MPCE(IV-2414), MP8(VIII-5462), MP6(VI-3298), MPEng(912), MPv3(532), MP2(II-1101), MWL2(1101).

*Vicar of Wakefield, The. *Oliver Goldsmith.* MP12(XII-6901), MPCE(IV-2416), MP8(VIII-5465), MP6(VI-3301), MPEng(915), MP1(II-1061), MWL1(1061).

*Vicomte de Bragelonne, The. *Alexandre Dumas (père).* MP12(XII-6904), MPCE(IV-2417), MP8(VIII-5468), MP6(VI-3303), MPEur(787), MP1(II-1063), MWL1(1063).

*Victim, The. *Saul Bellow.* MP12(XII-6911), MP8(VIII-5472), MP4(II-1259), MWL4(1259).

Victorian Cities. *Asa Briggs.* HEur(II-738).

*Victory. *Joseph Conrad.* MP12(XII-6914), MPCE(IV-2420), MP8(VIII-5475), MP6(VI-3307), MPEng(918), MP1(II-1067), MWL1(1067).

Victory. *Oliver Warner.* SCL12(XII-7989), SCL7(VII-4887), A59(260), BMA(577).

Victory in the Pacific, 1945. *Samuel Eliot Morison.* SCL12(XII-7992), SCL7(VII-4890), A61(275).

Vida, La. *Oscar Lewis.* SCL12(VI-4055), SCL7(IV-2460), A67(182).

Vienna Settlement, The (Event). HEur(II-612).

Viet Cong Tet Offensive (Event). HWor(II-1036).

"Vietnam Since Reunification," *in* Problems of Communism. *William S.*

Turley.   HWor(III-1248).

Vietnam-Cambodia Conflict.   *Douglas Pike*.   HWor(III-1353).

Vietnam's Conquest of Cambodia (Event).   HWor(III-1346).

View from Highway 1, The.   *Michael J. Arlen*.   LA77(II-884).

View from Pompey's Head, The.   *Hamilton Basso*.   SCL12(XII-7995),
     SCL7(VII-4893),   A54(288).

*View from the Bridge, A.   *Arthur Miller*.   SCL12(XII-7999),
     SCL7(VII-4896),   A55(287),   BMA(580).

View from the UN.   *U Thant*.   LA79(II-809).

View of the Evidences of Christianity, A.   *William Paley*.   Ph(I-563).

View of Victorian Literature, A.   *Geoffrey Tillotson*.   LA79(II-814).

Views & Spectacles: New and Selected Shorter Poems.   *Theodore Weiss*.
     LA80(II-846).

Viking Landings on Mars, The (Event).   HWor(III-1294).

*Vile Bodies.   *Evelyn Waugh*.   MP12(XII-6918),   MPCE(IV-2421),
     MP8(VIII-5478),   MP6(VI-3309),   MPEng(921),   MPv4(570),
     MP2(II-1103),   MWL2(1103).

*Village, The.   *Ivan Alexeyevich Bunin*.   MP12(XII-6922),
     MPCE(IV-2422),   MP8(VIII-5481),   MP6(VI-3312),   MPEur(791),
     MPv3(534),   MP2(II-1105),   MWL2(1105).

Village, The.   *George Crabbe*.   MP12(XII-6927),   MP8(VIII-5484),
     MP6(VI-3314),   MPPo(371),   MP3(II-1097),   MWL3(1097).

*Villette.   *Charlotte Brontë*.   MP12(XII-6929),   MPCE(IV-2425),
     MP8(VIII-5486),   MP6(VI-3316),   MPEng(924),   MPv3(537),
     MP2(II-1108),   MWL2(1108).

"Vincent of Beauvais," *in* Vol. II *of* A History of Magic and Experimental
     Science During the First Thirteen Centuries of Our Era.   *Lynn
     Thorndike*.   HAnc(III-1535).

Vincent of Beauvais Compiles the *Speculum Maius* (Event).
     HAnc(III-1533).

Vindication of Natural Society, A.   *Edmund Burke*.   MP12(XII-6934),
     MP8(VIII-5489),   MP6(VI-3319),   MPNf(315),   MP3(II-1099),
     MWL3(1099).

*Violated, The.   *Vance Bourjaily*.   SCL12(XII-8003),   SCL7(VII-4899),
     A59(263).

*Violent Bear It Away, The.   *Flannery O'Connor*.   MP12(XII-6937),
     MP8(VIII-5492),   MP4(II-1261),   MWL4(1261),
     SCL12(XII-8007),   SCL7(VII-4903),   A61(278).

Violent Land, The.   *Jorge Amado*.   MP12(XII-6939),   MPCE(IV-2428),
     MP8(VIII-5494),   MP6(VI-3321),   MPAm(691),   MPv4(573),
     MP2(II-1110),   MWL2(1110).

Viper Jazz.   *James Tate*.   LA77(II-888).

Virgil, A Study in Civilized Poetry.   *Brooks Otis*.   HAnc(I-559).

Virgin of San Gil, The.   *Paul Olsen*.   SCL12(XII-8011),
     SCL7(VII-4906),   A66(322).

Voices of Silence, The. *André Malraux.* MP12(XII-6975), MP8(VIII-5522), MP4(II-1263), MWL4(1263).

*Volpone. *Ben Jonson.* MP12(XII-6978), MPCE(IV-2442), MP8(VIII-5525), MP6(VI-3343), MPDr(897), MP1(II-1076), MWL1(1076).

Voltaire. *Jean Orieux.* LA80(II-850).

Voltaire and Beccaria as Reformers of Criminal Law. *Marcello T. Maestro.* HEur(I-457).

Voltaire in Love. *Nancy Mitford.* SCL12(XII-8043), SCL7(VII-4923), A59(266).

Volunteer Army and the Allied Intervention in South Russia, 1917-1921, The. *George A. Brinkley.* HWor(I-154).

Volupté. *Charles Augustin Sainte-Beuve.* MP12(XII-6983), MPCE(IV-2445), MP8(VIII-5528), MP6(VI-3345), MPEur(797), MP3(II-1110), MWL3(1110).

Vortex: Pound, Eliot, and Lewis. *Timothy Materer.* LA80(II-855).

Voss. *Patrick White.* SCL12(XII-8046), SCL7(VII-4926), A58(258).

Vosstanie veshchei. *Lev Lunts.* SF(V-2373).

Voyage of Magellan. *Antonio Pigafetta.* SCL12(XII-8050), SCLs(328).

*Voyage of the Beagle, The. *Charles Darwin.* MP12(XII-6987), MPCE(IV-2446), MP8(VIII-5531), MP6(VI-3348), MPNf(322), MP1(II-1079), MWL1(1079).

Voyage of the Lucky Dragon, The. *Ralph E. Lapp.* SCL12(XII-8056), SCL7(VII-4930), A59(268).

Voyage of the Space Beagle, The. *A. E. van Vogt.* SF(V-2378).

Voyage to Arcturus, A. *David Lindsay.* SF(V-2383).

Voyager: A Life of Hart Crane. *John Unterecker.* SCL12(XII-8059), A70(328).

"*Voyager*'s Encore Performance," *in* Sky and Telescope. *J. Kelly Beatty.* HWor(III-1313).

Voyages and Explorations of Samuel De Champlain, 1604-1616, Narrated by Himself, The. *Edward G. Bourne* and *A. N. Bourne,* eds. HAmer(I-55).

Voyages of John Cabot, The (Event). HAmer(I-23).

voyageur imprudent, Le. *René Barjavel.* SF(V-2389).

"Vulgate," *in* A Dictionary of the Bible. *H. J. White.* HAnc(II-912).

*Waiting for Godot. *Samuel Beckett.* MP12(XII-6991), MPCE(IV-2449), MP8(VIII-5533), MP6(VI-3350), MPDr(900), MP3(II-1113), MWL3(1113). A different analysis on this title appears in: SCL12(XII-8062), SCL7(VII-4933), A57(281), BMA(583).

*Walden. *Henry David Thoreau.* MP12(XII-6996), MPCE(IV-2452), MP8(VIII-5536), MP6(VI-3352), MPNf(324), MPv4(580), MP2(II-1117), MWL2(1117).

Walden Two. *B. F. Skinner.* SF(V-2392).

Walk Egypt. *Vinnie Williams*.   SCL12(XII-8066),   SCL7(VII-4936),
    A61(281).
Walk in the Sun, A.   Cine(IV-1816).
*Walking to Sleep. *Richard Wilbur*.   SCL12(XII-8069),   A70(331).
*Wallenstein. *Johann Christoph Friedrich von Schiller*.   MP12(XII-7001),
    MPCE(IV-2455),   MP8(VIII-5539),   MP6(VI-3355),   MPDr(903),
    MPv4(582),   MP2(II-1119),   MWL2(1119).
Walnut Door, The. *John Hersey*.   LA78(II-883).
Walter Hines Page: The Southerner as American, 1855-1918. *John Milton
    Cooper, Jr.*   LA78(II-888).
Walter Rauschenbusch. *Dores R. Sharpe*.   HAmer(II-1197).
Walter Rauschenbusch and the Social Gospel (Event).   HAmer(II-1195).
*Waltz of the Toreadors, The. *Jean Anouilh*.   SCL12(XII-8073),
    SCL7(VII-4939),   A58(261).
Wanderer, The. *Alain-Fournier*.   MP12(XII-7006),   MPCE(IV-2458),
    MP8(VIII-5542),   MP6(VI-3357),   MPEur(800)   MP1(II-1081),
    MWL1(1081).
Wanderer, The. *Fritz Leiber, Jr.*   SF(V-2396).
Wandering Jew, The. *Eugène Sue*.   MP12(XII-7010),   MPCE(IV-2460),
    MP8(VIII-5545),   MP6(VI-3359),   MPEur(803),   MP1(II-1083),
    MWL1(1083).
Wandering Scholar from Paradise, The. *Hans Sachs*.   MP12(XII-7014),
    MPCE(IV-2462),   MP8(VIII-5548),   MP6(VI-3362),   MPDr(906),
    MP3(II-1115),   MWL3(1115).
Waning of the Middle Ages, The. *Johan Huizinga*.   MP12(XII-7017),
    MP8(VIII-5550),   MP4(II-1266),   MWL4(1266).
Wanting Seed, The. *Anthony Burgess*.   SF(V-2402).
*Wapshot Chronicle, The. *John Cheever*.   MP12(XII-7020),
    MP8(VIII-5553),   MP4(II-1268),   MWL4(1268),
    SCL12(XII-8076),   SCL7(VII-4942),   A58(264),   BMA(586).
*Wapshot Scandal, The. *John Cheever*.   MP12(XII-7024),
    MP8(VIII-5557),   MP4(II-1271),   MWL4(1271). A different analysis
    on this title appears in: SCL12(XII-8080),   SCL7(VII-4946),
    A64(290).
War Against the Jews, 1933-1945, The. *Lucy S. Dawidowicz*.
    SCL12(XII-8087),   A76(344).
*War and Peace. *Count Leo Tolstoy*.   MP12(XII-7028),
    MPCE(IV-2463),   MP8(VIII-5561),   MP6(VI-3364),   MPEur(806),
    MP1(II-1085),   MWL1(1085).
War Between Russia and China. *Harrison E. Salisbury*.   HEur(III-1680).
War Between the Tates, The. *Alison Lurie*.   SCL12(XII-8091),   A75(347).
War Debts and World Prosperity. *Harold G. Moulton* and *Leo Pasvolsky*.
    HAmer(III-1539).
War for the Union: Vol. I, The. *Allan Nevins*.   SCL12(XII-8095),
    SCL7(VII-4953),   A60(286),   BMA(590).

War for the Union: Vol. II, The. *Allan Nevins.* SCL12(XII-8099), SCL7(VII-4957), A61(284), BMA(594).

War in Algeria, The. *Jules Roy.* SCL12(XII-8103), SCL7(VII-4961), A62(298).

War in France and Flanders, The. *Major L. F. Ellis.* HEur(III-1458).

War in the Air, The. *H. G. Wells.* SF(V-2407).

War in Vietnam, The (Event). HAmer(III-1906).

War Industries Board and Economic Mobilization for War, The (Event). HAmer(III-1460).

War Lords of Washington, The. *Bruce Catton.* HAmer(III-1684).

*War Lover, The. *John Hersey.* SCL12(XII-8106), SCL7(VII-4964), A60(290).

War of Atonement, October, 1973, The. *Chaim Herzog.* HWor(III-1186).

War of 1812, The (Event). HAmer(I-505).

War of Illusions: German Policies from 1911 to 1914. *Fritz Fischer.* Different analyses on this title appear in: HWor(I-51; II-923).

"War of the Austrian Succession, The" *in* The New Cambridge Modern History. *M. A. Thomson.* HEur(I-422).

War of the Three Henrys (Event). HEur(I-162).

War of the Wing-Men. *Poul Anderson.* SF(V-2411).

*War of the Worlds, The. *H. G. Wells.* MP12(XII-7035), MPCE(IV-2466), MP8(VIII-5566), MP6(VI-3368), MPEng(933), MP1(II-1090), MWL1(1090). A different analysis on this title apears in: SF(V-2416).

War Path: Hitler's Germany in the Years 1933-1939, The. *David Irving.* LA79(II-819).

War That Hitler Won: The Most Infamous Propaganda Campaign in History, The. *Robert Edwin Herzstein.* LA79(II-823).

War to End All Wars: The American Military Experience in World War I, The. *Edward M. Coffman.* HAmer(III-1469).

War with Mexico (Event). HAmer(II-825).

War with Mexico. *Justin H. Smith.* HAmer(II-821).

War with the Newts. *Karel Čapek.* SF(V-2424).

*Warden, The. *Anthony Trollope.* MP12(XII-7038), MPCE(IV-2467), MP8(VIII-5568), MP6(VI-3370), MPEng(935), MP1(II-1092), MWL1(1092).

Warrior of God. *Paul Roubiczek* and *Joseph Kalmer.* HAnc(III-1677).

Wars of Religion in France, 1559-1576, The. *James Westfall Thompson.* HEur(I-164).

Warsaw Pact: Case Studies in Communist Conflict Resolution, The. *Robin Alison Remington.* HWor(II-717).

Wartime. *Milovan Djilas.* LA78(II-894).

Warwick the Kingmaker. *Paul Murray Kendall.* SCL12(XII-8110), SCL7(VII-4967), A58(268).

Washing of the Spears, The. *Donald R. Morris.* SCL12(XII-8113),

*Way of All Flesh, The. *Samuel Butler*. MP12(XII-7061),
    MPCE(IV-2475),   MP8(VIII-5586),   MP6(VI-3383),   MPEng(943),
    MP1(II-1097),   MWL1(1097).
Way of Perfection, The. *Saint Teresa of Ávila*.   RCa(I-555).
Way of Truth *and* The Way of Opinion, The.   *Parmenides of Elea*.
    Ph(I-16).
*Way of the World, The. *William Congreve*.   MP12(XII-7066),
    MPCE(IV-2478),   MP8(VIII-5589),   MP6(VI-3385),   MPDr(910),
    MP1(II-1099),   MWL1(1099).
Way Out West.   Cine(IV-1823).
Way Station. *Clifford D. Simak*.   SF(V-2429).
Way to Christ, The. *Jakob Boehme*.   RCh(I-436).
Way to Go: The Coming Revival of U.S. Rail Passenger Service,
    The. *Thomas C. Southerland, Jr.* and *William McCleery*.
    HWor(I-524).
Way to Rainy Mountain, The. *N. Scott Momaday*.   SCL12(XII-8153),
    A70(335).
We. *Evgeny Zamyatin*.   SF(V-2433).
*We Bombed in New Haven. *Joseph Heller*.   SCL12(XII-8156),
    SCL7(VII-4989),   A69(340).
We Have Always Lived in the Castle. *Shirley Jackson*.   SCL12(XII-8159),
    SCL7(VII-4992),   A63(288).
We Hold These Truths. *John Courtney Murray, S. J.*   RCa(II-1098).
We the People: The Economic Origins of the Constitution. *Forrest
    McDonald*.   HAmer(III-1428).
We Who Built America: The Saga of the Emigrant. *Carl F. Wittke*.
    Different analyses on this title appear in: HAmer(II-757; II-1221).
Wealth of Nations, The. *Adam Smith*.   MP12(XII-7070),
    MP8(VIII-5591),   MP6(VI-3387),   MPNf(327),   MP3(II-1122),
    MWL3(1122).
Weapon Shops of Isher, The. *A. E. van Vogt*.   SF(V-2442).
Weathers and Edges. *Philip Booth*.   SCL12(XII-8161),
    SCL7(VII-4994),   A67(339).
*Weavers, The. *Gerhart Hauptmann*.   MP12(XII-7073),
    MPCE(IV-2481),   MP8(VIII-5594),   MP6(VI-3390),   MPDr(912),
    MPv4(584),   MP2(II-1124),   MWL2(1124).
*Web and the Rock, The. *Thomas Wolfe*.   MP12(XII-7077),
    MPCE(IV-2482),   MP8(VIII-5597),   MP6(VI-3392),   MPAm(703),
    MP1(II-1101),   MWL1(1101).
W. E. B. DuBois: Propagandist of the Negro Protest. *Elliott M. Rudwick*.
    HAmer(III-1388).
Web of Victory, The. *Earl Schenck Miers*.   SCL12(XII-8166),
    SCL7(VII-4999),   A55(293),   BMA(601).
Webster-Hayne Debate over States' Rights (Event).   HAmer(I-660).
Wedemeyer Reports! *General Albert C. Wedemeyer*.   SCL12(XII-8169),

SCL7(VII-5002),   A59(271).

Weedkiller's Daughter, The. *Harriette Simpson Arnow.*
    SCL12(XII-8172),   A70(337).

*Week on the Concord and Merrimack Rivers, A. *Henry David Thoreau.*
    MP12(XII-7081),   MP8(VIII-5600),   MP4(II-1277),   MWL4(1277).

Weekend in Dinlock. *Clancy Sigal.*   SCL12(XII-8175),
    SCL7(VII-5005),   A61(293).

Welcome to the Monkey House. *Kurt Vonnegut, Jr.*   SF(V-2447).

Wellington: Pillar of State. *Elizabeth, Countess of Longford.*
    SCL12(XII-8178),   A73(377).

Wellington: The Years of the Sword. *Elizabeth, Countess of Longford.*
    SCL12(XII-8182),   A71(342).

West Side Story. Cine(IV-1826).

Western Approaches, The. *Howard Nemerov.*   SCL12(XII-8186),
    A76(352).

Western Asceticism: The Teaching of SS Augustine, Gregory and Bernard on
    Contemplation and the Contemplative Life. *Dom Edward Cuthbert
    Butler.*   HAnc(III-1331).

"Western Europe and the Power of Spain," *in* The New Cambridge Modern
    History. *H. G. Koenigsberger.*   HEur(I-159).

Western Europe in the Middle Ages: A Short History. *Joseph R. Strayer.*
    HAnc(II-1148).

Western Greeks, The. *T. J. Dunbabin.*   HAnc(I-130).

Westerner, The. Cine(IV-1830).

*Westward Ho! *Charles Kingsley.*   MP12(XII-7084),   MPCE(IV-2484),
    MP8(VIII-5603),   MP6(VI-3395),   MPEng(946),   MP1(II-1103),
    MWL1(1103).

Westward to Vinland: The Discovery of Pre-Columbian Norse
    House-Sites in North America. *Helge Ingstad.*
    HAmer(I-15).

W. H. Auden: The Life of a Poet. *Charles Osborne.*   LA80(II-860).

What a Way to Go! *Wright Morris.*   SCL12(XII-8189),
    SCL7(VII-5008),   A63(290).

What Comes Next. *Jonathan Baumbach.*   SCL12(XII-8194),
    SCL7(VII-5013),   A69(343).

*What Every Woman Knows. *James M. Barrie.*   MP12(XII-7089),
    MPCE(IV-2487),   MP8(VIII-5606),   MP6(VI-3397),   MPDr(915),
    MP1(II-1106),   MWL1(1106).

What Happened in History. *V. Gordon Childe.*   HAnc(I-60).

What I Believe. *Count Leo Tolstoy.*   RCh(II-790).

What I'm Going to Do, I Think. *L. Woiwode.*   SCL12(XII-8197),
    A70(340).

What Is an Editor? Saxe Commins at Work. *Dorothy Berliner Commins.*
    LA79(II-839).

What Is Art? *Count Leo Tolstoy.*   Ph(II-723).

Where the Light Falls. *Chard Powers Smith.* SCL12(XII-8240),
    SCL7(VII-5039), A66(329).
Whig Party in the South, The. *Arthur C. Cole.* HAmer(II-692).
While Six Million Died: A Chronicle of American Apathy. *Arthur D.*
    Morse. HWor(I-306).
Whiskey Rebellion, The (Event). HAmer(I-377).
Whiskey Rebels: The Story of a Frontier Uprising. *Leland D. Baldwin.*
    HAmer(I-380).
Whispering Land, The. *Gerald M. Durrell.* SCL12(XII-8244),
    SCL7(VII-5043), A63(295).
Whistle. *James Jones.* LA79(II-843).
White Album, The. *Joan Didion.* LA80(II-862).
White Company, The. *Arthur Conan Doyle.* MP12(XII-7111),
    MPCE(IV-2495), MP8(VIII-5623), MP6(VI-3408), MPEng(952),
    MP1(II-1108), MWL1(1108).
*White Devil, The. *John Webster.* MP12(XII-7115), MPCE(IV-2496),
    MP8(VIII-5626), MP6(VI-3410), MPDr(920), MP3(II-1131),
    MWL3(1131).
White Heat. Cine(IV-1839).
White House Conference on Conservation, The (Event). HAmer(III-1374).
White House Years. *Henry A. Kissinger.* LA80(II-866).
White Man's Indian: Images of the American Indian from Columbus to the
    Present, The. *Robert F. Berkhofer, Jr.* LA79(II-847).
White Monks: A History of the Cistercian Order, The. *Louis J. Lekai.*
    HAnc(III-1427).
White Nile, The. *Alan Moorehead.* SCL12(XII-8246),
    SCL7(VII-5045), A62(304), BMA(604).
White Over Black: American Attitudes Toward the Negro,
    1550-1812. *Winthrop D. Jordan.* HAmer(I-71).
Whitehall and the Wilderness: The Middle West in British Colonial Policy,
    1760-1775. *Jack M. Sosin.* HAmer(I-210).
*White-Jacket. *Herman Melville.* MP12(XII-7118), MPCE(IV-2497),
    MP8(VIII-5629), MP6(VI-3412), MPAm(709), MPv3(542),
    MP2(II-1128), MWL2(1128).
Whitman: A Collection of Critical Essays. *Roy H. Pearce.* HAmer(II-851).
Whitney Invents the Cotton Gin (Event). HAmer(I-371).
*Whitsun Weddings, The. *Philip Larkin.* SCL12(XII-8249),
    SCL7(VII-5048), A66(333).
Who? *Algis Budrys.* SF(V-2474).
Who Is Teddy Villanova? *Thomas Berger.* LA78(II-899).
Who Shall Be the Sun? Poems Based on the Lore, Legends and Myths of
    Northwest Coast and Plateau Indians. *David Wagoner.* LA79(II-852).
Who Shall Live? *Victor R. Fuchs.* SCL12(XII-8254), A76(359).
Who Should Play God? The Artificial Creation of Life and What It Means for
    the Future of the Human Race. *Ted Howard* and *Jeremy Rifkin.*

William the Conqueror. *David C. Douglas.* SCL12(XII-8308), SCL7(VII-5088), A65(311).

Wilson: Campaigns for Progressivism and Peace, 1916-1917. *Arthur S. Link.* HAmer(III-1451).

Wilson: Confusions and Crises, 1915-1916. *Arthur S. Link.* SCL12(XII-8311), SCL7(VII-5091), A66(337).

Wilson: The New Freedom. *Arthur S. Link.* HAmer(III-1407).

Wilson: The Road to the White House. *Arthur S. Link.* HAmer(III-1407).

Winchester '73. Cine(IV-1848).

Wind from Nowhere, The. *J. G. Ballard.* SF(V-2478).

Wind in the Willows, The. *Kenneth Grahame.* MP12(XII-7159), MPCE(IV-2507), MP8(VIII-5662), MP6(VI-3431), MPEng(955), MPv4(591), MP2(II-1141), MWL2(1141).

Wind Mountain. *Fred Chappell.* LA80(II-877).

*Wind, Sand and Stars. *Antoine de Saint-Exupéry.* MP12(XII-7163), MP8(VIII-5665), MP4(II-1291), MWL4(1291).

Wind That Swept Mexico: The History of the Mexican Revolution, 1910-1942, The. *Anita Brenner.* HWor(I-76).

Wind Will Not Subside, The. *David Milton* and *Nancy Dall Milton.* LA77(II-918).

Window on Russia, A. *Edmund Wilson.* SCL12(XII-8315), A73(381).

Windsor Castle. *William Harrison Ainsworth.* MP12(XII-7166), MPCE(IV-2509), MP8(VIII-5668), MP6(VI-3434), MPEng(958), MP1(II-1117), MWL1(1117).

Wine of Astonishment, The. *Rachel MacKenzie.* SCL12(XII-8317), A75(360).

*Winesburg, Ohio. *Sherwood Anderson.* MP12(XII-7171), MPCE(IV-2510), MP8(VIII-5672), MP6(VI-3438), MPAm(717), MP1(II-1121), MWL1(1121).

Wings of Eagles, The. Cine(IV-1853).

*Wings of the Dove, The. *Henry James.* MP12(XII-7176), MPCE(IV-2513), MP8(VIII-5675), MP6(VI-3440), MPAm(720), MPv3(552), MP2(II-1143), MWL2(1143).

Winner Names the Age, The. *Lillian Smith.* LA79(II-879).

Winners, The. *Julio Cortázar.* SCL12(XII-8321), SCL7(VII-5095), A66(341).

Winston S. Churchill: The Prophet of Truth, Vol. V: 1922-1939. *Martin Gilbert,* ed. LA78(II-917).

Winter in the Air. *Sylvia Townsend Warner.* SCL12(XII-8324), SCL7(VII-5098), A57(284).

Winter in the Blood. *James Welch.* SCL12(XII-8327), A75(364).

Winter in the Hills, A. *John Wain.* SCL12(XII-8331), A71(352).

Winter News. *John Haines.* SCL12(XII-8336), SCL7(VII-5101), A67(344).

*Winter of Our Discontent, The. *John Steinbeck.* SCL12(XII-8340),

LA78(II-928).

Wolf Solent. *John Cowper Powys.* MP12(XII-7203), MPCE(IV-2523), MP8(VIII-5696), MP6(VI-3452), MPEng(962), MP3(II-1136), MWL3(1136).

Wolf-Man, The. *Freud's "Wolf-Man".* SCL12(XII-8362), A72(349).

*Woman at the Washington Zoo, The. *Randall Jarrell.* SCL12(XII-8365), SCL7(VII-5124), A61(309), BMA(613).

*Woman Hater, The. *Francis Beaumont* and *John Fletcher.* MP12(XII-7207), MPCE(IV-2524), MP8(VIII-5699), MP6(VI-3454), MPDr(937), MP3(II-1138), MWL3(1138).

*Woman in the Dunes, The. *Kobo Abé.* SCL12(XII-8369), SCL7(VII-5128), A65(318).

*Woman in White, The. *Wilkie Collins.* MP12(XII-7211), MPCE(IV-2525), MP8(VIII-5702), MP6(VI-3457), MPEng(965), MP1(II-1125), MWL1(1125).

Woman Killed with Kindness, A. *Thomas Heywood.* MP12(XII-7217), MPCE(IV-2529), MP8(VIII-5705), MP6(VI-3460), MPDr(940), MPv4(593), MP2(II-1151), MWL2(1151).

*Woman of Rome, The. *Alberto Moravia.* MP12(XII-7221), MPCE(IV-2531), MP8(VIII-5708), MP6(VI-3462), MPEur(825), MPv4(596), MP2(II-1153), MWL2(1153).

Woman on the Edge of Time. *Marge Piercy.* SF(V-2488).

Woman Said Yes, The. *Jessamyn West.* LA77(II-928).

Woman Warrior, The. *Maxine Hong Kingston.* LA77(II-932).

Woman Who Was Poor, The. *Léon Bloy.* RCa(II-726).

*Woman Within, The. *Ellen Glasgow.* SCL12(XII-8373), SCL7(VII-5132), A54(297).

*Woman's Life, A. *Guy de Maupassant.* MP12(XII-7224), MPCE(IV-2532), MP8(VIII-5711), MP6(VI-3464), MPEur(828), MP1(II-1127), MWL1(1127).

*Woman's Prize, The. *John Fletcher.* MP12(XII-7229), MPCE(IV-2535), MP8(VIII-5714), MP6(VI-3467), MPDr(943), MP3(II-1141), MWL3(1141).

Women, The. Cine(IV-1872).

Women: Their Changing Roles. HWor(II-1000).

*Women and Thomas Harrow. *John P. Marquand.* SCL12(XII-8377), SCL7(VII-5136), A59(277).

*Women Beware Women. *Thomas Middleton.* MP12(XII-7235), MPCE(IV-2538), MP8(VIII-5717), MP6(VI-3470), MPDr(946), MP3(II-1144), MWL3(1144).

*Women in Love. *D. H. Lawrence.* MP12(XII-7239), MP8(VIII-5720), MP4(II-1298), MWL4(1298).

Women of the Shadows. *Ann Cornelisen.* LA77(II-937).

*Women of Trachis, The. *Sophocles.* MP12(XII-7242), MPCE(IV-2540), MP8(VIII-5723), MP6(VI-3472), MPDr(949),

MP3(II-1146),   MWL3(1146).

Women's Rights: The Suffrage Movement in America, 1848-1920. *Olivia Coolidge.* HAmer(III-1516).

*Wonderland. *Joyce Carol Oates.* SCL12(XII-8381),   A72(352).

*Wooden Shepherdess, The. *Richard Hughes.* SCL12(XII-8384), A74(412).

*Woodlanders, The. *Thomas Hardy.* MP12(XII-7247), MPCE(IV-2543),   MP8(VIII-5726),   MP6(VI-3474),   MPEng(968), MPv4(598),   MP2(II-1156),   MWL2(1156).

Woodrow Wilson. *Arthur Walworth.* SCL12(XII-8388), SCL7(VII-5139),   A59(280).

Woodrow Wilson: The Years of Preparation. *John M. Mulder.* LA79(II-892).

Woodrow Wilson and the Peacemakers. *Thomas A. Bailey.* HAmer(III-1486).

Woodrow Wilson and the Progressive Era. *Arthur S. Link.* HAmer(III-1408).

Woodrow Wilson and World Politics: America's Response to War and Revolution. *N. Gordon Levin, Jr.* HAmer(III-1488).

Woodstock. *Sir Walter Scott.* MP12(XII-7251),   MPCE(IV-2545), MP8(VIII-5729),   MP6(VI-3477),   MPEng(971),   MPv3(559), MP2(II-1158),   MWL2(1158).

Word Child, A. *Iris Murdoch.* SCL12(XII-8391),   A76(366).

Word for World Is Forest, The. *Ursula K. Le Guin.* SF(V-2492).

Words, The. *Jean-Paul Sartre.* SCL12(XII-8395),   SCL7(VII-5142), A65(322).

Words for Dr. Y: Uncollected Poems with Three Stories. *Anne Sexton.* LA79(II-897).

Words That Won the War. *James R. Mock* and *Cedric Larson.* HAmer(III-1456).

Work Ethic in Industrial America, 1850-1920, The. *Daniel T. Rodgers.* LA79(II-904).

Working. *Studs Terkel.* SCL12(XII-8398),   A76(370).

Working It Out. *Sara Ruddick* and *Pamela Daniels,* eds.   LA78(II-937).

*Works and Days. *Hesiod.* MP12(XII-7254),   MP8(VIII-5732), MP6(VI-3479),   MPPo(381),   MP3(II-1149),   MWL3(1149).

Works of Jonathan Edwards. *Jonathan Edwards.* MP12(XII-7256), MP8(VIII-5734),   MP6(VI-3481),   MPNf(330),   MP3(II-1150), MWL3(1150).

Works of Lyman Beecher, The. *Lyman Beecher.* RCh(II-724).

Works Progress Administration Formed (Event).   HAmer(III-1632).

World According to Garp, The. *John Irving.* LA79(II-908).

World and the Individual, The. *Josiah Royce.* Ph(II-739).

World as Will and Idea, The. *Arthur Schopenhauer.* MP12(XII-7259), MP8(VIII-5737),   MP6(VI-3484),   MPNf(333),   MP3(II-1153),

MWL1(1137).

Xerxes' Invasion of Greece. *C. H. Hignett.* HAnc(I-240).
Xipéhuz, Les. *J. H. Rosny (the Elder).* SF(V-2516).
XYZ Affair, The (Event). HAmer(I-408).

Yalta. *Diane Shaver Clemens.* HAmer(III-1738).
Yalta Conference, The (Event). HEur(III-1501).
Yalta Conference, The (Event). HAmer(III-1736).
Yalta Myths: An Issue in U.S. Politics, 1945-1955, The. *Athan G. Theoharis.* HAmer(III-1739).
Yankee Doodle Dandy. Cine(IV-1888).
Yard of Sun, A. *Christopher Fry.* SCL12(XII-8451), A71(363).
Yazoo. *Willie Morris.* SCL12(XII-8456), A72(354).
Yazoo: Law and Politics in the New Republic, the Case of Fletcher vs. Peck. *C. Peter McGrath.* HAmer(I-489).
Year of My Rebirth, The. *Jesse Stuart.* SCL12(XII-8461), SCL7(VII-5174), A57(297), BMA(620).
Year of the French, The. *Thomas Flanagan.* LA80(II-880).
Year of the Quiet Sun, The. *Wilson Tucker.* SF(V-2520).
Year of the Whale, The. *Victor B. Scheffer.* SCL12(XII-8464), A70(354).
Yearling, The. *Marjorie Kinnan Rawlings.* MP12(XII-7286), MPCE(IV-2558), MP8(VIII-5757), MP6(VI-3500), MPAm(726), MP1(II-1140), MWL1(1140).
*Years, The. *Virginia Woolf.* MP12(XII-7290), MPCE(IV-2560), MP8(VIII-5760), MP6(VI-3503), MPEng(979), MP3(II-1156), MWL3(1156).
Years with Ross, The. *James Thurber.* SCL12(XII-8467), SCL7(VII-5177), A60(295).
Yellow Danger, The. *M. P. Shiel.* SF(V-2525).
*Yemassee, The. *William Gilmore Simms.* MP12(XII-7295), MPCE(IV-2563), MP8(VIII-5763), MP6(VI-3506), MPAm(729), MPv3(561), MP2(II-1165), MWL2(1165).
Yesterday. *Maria Dermoût.* SCL12(XII-8470), SCL7(VII-5180), A60(298).
Yevtushenko Poems. *Yevgeny Yevtushenko.* SCL12(XII-8472), SCL7(VII-5182), A67(347).
Yoke and the Arrows, The. *Herbert Lionel Matthews.* SCL12(XII-8476), SCL7(VII-5186), A58(279).
Yom Kippur War, The (Event). HWor(III-1182).
Yom Kippur War, The. *The Insight Team of the London Sunday* Times. HWor(III-1184).
Yonnondio: From the Thirties. *Tillie Olsen.* SCL12(XII-8479), A75(368).
Yoshida Memoirs: The Study of Japan in Crisis, The. *Shigeru Yoshida.*

Author Index

An asterisk appearing by a title indicates that extensive bibliographical sources for the work may be found in *Magill's Bibliography of Literary Criticism*. 4 vols. Salem Press, Englewood Cliffs. 1979.

Abbazia, Patrick
    Mr. Roosevelt's Navy: The Private War of the U.S. Atlantic Fleet, 1939-1942. HWor(I-408).
Abbey, Edward
    Desert Solitaire. SCL12(III-1894), SCL7(II-1134), A69(93).
Abbo, John A. *and* Jerome D. Hannan
    Sacred Cannons, The. HAnc(II-917).
Abbot, Henry L.
    Beginning of Modern Submarine Warfare. HAmer(I-269).
Abbott, Edwin A.
    Flatland: A Romance of Many Dimensions. SF(II-792).
Abbott, Frank Frost
    History and Description of Roman Political Institutions, A. HAnc(I-396).
Abbott, Nabia
    Two Queens of Baghdad: Mother and Wife of Harun al-Rashid. HAnc(II-1144).
Abdullah ibn-Husein, Amir of Transjordan
    Memoirs of King Abdullah of Transjordan. HWor(I-496).
Abé, Kobo
    Inter Ice Age 4. SF(III-1040).
    *Woman in the Dunes, The. SCL12(XII-8369), SCL7(VII-5128), A65(318).
Abel, Annie H.
    History of Events Resulting in Indian Consolidation West of the Mississippi, The. HAmer(I-669).
Abel, Elie

Missile Crisis, The.   HAmer(III-1890).

Abel, Elie *and* W. Averell Harriman
Special Envoy to Churchill and Stalin, 1941-1946.   SCL12(XI-7165),
A76(306).

Abelard, Peter
Glosses on Porphyry, The.   Ph(I-290).
Historia Calamitatum.   MP12(V-2624),   MP8(III-2039),
MP6(III-1302),   MPNf(134),   MP3(I-464),   MWL3(464). A different
analysis on this title appears in: RCa(I-307).
Know Thyself.   RCh(I-212).
Sic et non.   RCa(I-291).

Abelson, Paul
Seven Liberal Arts: A Study in Mediaeval Culture, The.   HAnc(II-1001).

Abernethy, Thomas P.
Burr Conspiracy, The.   HAmer(I-465).

About, Edmond François
King of the Mountains, The.   MP12(VI-3156),   MPCE(II-1167),
MP8(IV-2459),   MP6(III-1570),   MPEur(410),   MPv4(263),
MP2(I-531),   MWL2(531).
Man with the Broken Ear, The.   SF(III-1340).

Abrahams, Peter
Tell Freedom.   SCL12(XI-7420),   SCL7(VII-4524),   A54(276).
Wreath for Udomo, A.   SCL12(XII-8440),   SCL7(VII-5163),
A57(294).

Abrahams, William *and* Peter Stansky
Unknown Orwell, The.   SCL12(XII-7912),   A73(367).

Abrahams, William, *ed.*
Prize Stories 1978: The O. Henry Awards.   LA79(II-556).

Abse, Dannie
Collected Poems, 1948-1976.   LA78(I-192).

Acheson, Dean
Present at the Creation.   SCL12(IX-6024),   A71(256).

Acton, Harold
Bourbons of Naples, 1734-1825, The.   HEur(II-643).

Acton, John Emerich Edward Dalberg
History of Freedom and Other Essays, The.   RCa(II-739).

Adam, Karl
Christ of Faith, The.   RCa(II-1000).
Spirit of Catholicism, The.   RCa(II-778).

Adamov, Arthur
Ping-Pong.   MP12(VIII-4719),   MP8(VI-3681),   MP4(II-694),
MWL4(694).

Adams, Henry
Education of Henry Adams, The.   MP12(III-1708),   MPCE(I-626),
MP8(II-1328),   MP6(II-858),   MPNf(95),   MP1(I-238),

MWL1(238).

History of the United States of America During the Administrations of Jefferson and Madison, Vol. II. HAmer(I-445).

Mont-Saint-Michel and Chartres. MP12(VII-4049), MP8(V-3158), MP4(I-614), MWL4(614).

Adams, Henry H.
Harry Hopkins: A Biography. LA78(I-375).

Adams, James Truslow
Founding of New England, The. HAmer(I-167).

Adams, John
Defense of the Constitutions of Government of the United States of America, A. MP12(III-1426), MP8(II-1103), MP6(II-719), MPNf(77), MP3(I-263), MWL3(263).

Adams, Richard
Plague Dogs, The. LA79(II-546).
Watership Down. SCL12(XII-8149), A75(356).

Adams, Robert M.
Bad Mouth: Fugitive Papers on the Dark Side. LA78(I-81).

Adams, Samuel Hopkins
Grandfather Stories. SCL12(V-3067), SCL7(III-1836), A55(115).

Adamson, Joy
Born Free. SCL12(II-845), SCL7(I-480), A61(26).

Adcock, F. E
"Draco," in The Cambridge Ancient History. HAnc(I-155).
Greek and Macedonian Art of War, The. HAnc(I-311).
Thucydides and His History. HAnc(I-295).

Adcock, F. E., Marcus N. Todd, *and* E. M. Walker
Cambridge Ancient History, Vol. V: Athens, 478-401 B.C., The. HAnc(I-244).

Addison, Joseph, Sir Richard Steele *and* Eustace Budgell
*Sir Roger de Coverley Papers, The. MP12(X-6067), MP8(VII-4840), MP6(V-2887), MPNf(288), MP3(II-988), MWL3(988).

Aderca, Felix
Oraşele Înecate. SF(IV-1613).

Adler, Morris
World of the Talmud, The. HAnc(II-987).

Adler, Mortimer J.
Philosopher at Large: An Intellectual Autobiography. LA78(II-654).

Adler, Renata
Speedboat. LA77(II-776).

Adler, Richard *and* Douglass Cater, *eds.*
Television as a Cultural Force. HWor(II-673).

Aelfric
Homilies. RCa(I-272).

Aelred, Saint
    Spiritual Friendship.   RCa(I-319).
Aeschylus
    House of Atreus, The.   MP12(V-2719),   MPCE(II-991),
    MP8(III-2121),   MP6(III-1352),   MPDr(363),   MP1(I-378),
    MWL1(378).
    Persians, The.   MP12(VIII-4609),   MPCE(III-1716),
    MP8(V-3591),   MP6(IV-2316),   MPDr(615),   MPv3(409),
    MP2(II-818),   MWL2(818).
    Prometheus Bound.   MP12(IX-5361),   MPCE(III-1823),
    MP8(VI-4280),   MP6(V-2541),   MPDr(665),   MP1(II-786),
    MWL1(786).
    Seven Against Thebes.   MP12(X-5922),   MPCE(IV-2045),
    MP8(VII-4716),   MP6(V-2825),   MPDr(761),   MPv3(480),
    MP2(II-953),   MWL2(953).
    Suppliants, The.   MP12(XI-6345),   MPCE(IV-2186),
    MP8(VII-5054),   MP6(VI-3017),   MPDr(818),   MPv4(498),
    MP2(II-1002),   MWL2(1002).
Aesop
    Aesop's Fables.   MP12(I-51),   MP8(I-39),   MP6(I-31),
    MPEur(7),   MP3(I-15),   MWL3(15).
Afnan, Soheil M.
    Avicenna: His Life and Works.   HAnc(III-1227).
Agarossi, Elena *and* Bradley F. Smith
    Operation Sunrise: The Secret Surrender.   LA80(II-631).
Agee, James
    Collected Poems of James Agee, The.   SCL12(II-1398),
    SCL7(II-817),   A69(72).
    Collected Short Prose of James Agee, The.   SCL12(II-1405),
    SCL7(II-827),   A69(74).
    Death in the Family, A.   MP12(III-1354),   MP8(II-1046),
    MP4(I-192),   MWL4(192),   SCL12(III-1808),   SCL7(II-1088),
    A58(69),   BMA(117).
    Let Us Now Praise Famous Men.   MP12(VI-3330),   MP8(IV-2597),
    MP4(I-515),   MWL4(515). A different analysis on this title appears in:
    SCL12(VI-4202),   SCL7(IV-2570),   A61(160),   BMA(313).
    Letters of James Agee to Father Flye.   SCL12(VI-4241),
    SCL7(IV-2593),   A63(122).
Agnon, Shmuel Yosef
    Two Tales.   SCL12(XII-7844),   SCL7(VII-4806),   A67(331).
Aguilar, Alonso
    Pan-Americanism: From Monroe to the Present.   HAmer(II-1193).
Aichinger, Ilse
    Herod's Children.   SCL12(V-3396),   SCL7(III-2021),   A64(126).
Aiken, Conrad

Poetry of Aiken, The.   MP12(VIII-4798),   MP8(VI-3744),
MP4(II-711),   MWL4(711).
Selected Letters of Conrad Aiken.   LA79(II-652).

Ainsworth, William Harrison
Jack Sheppard.   MP12(V-2969),   MPCE(II-1093),   MP8(IV-2313),
MP6(III-1480),   MPEng(364),   MPv3(254),   MP2(I-504),
MWL2(504).
Old St. Paul's.   MP12(VIII-4341),   MPCE(III-1622),
MP8(V-3379),   MP6(IV-2172),   MPEng(601),   MPv3(391),
MP2(II-768),   MWL2(768).
Tower of London, The.   MP12(XI-6618),   MPCE(IV-2296),
MP8(VIII-5259),   MP6(VI-3168),   MPEng(870),   MP1(II-1008),
MWL1(1008).
Windsor Castle.   MP12(XII-7166),   MPCE(IV-2509),
MP8(VIII-5668),   MP6(VI-3434),   MPEng(958),   MP1(II-1117),
MWL1(1117).

Ajar, Émile
Momo.   LA79(I-454).

Alarcón, Pedro Antonio de
Three-Cornered Hat, The.   MP12(XI-6505),   MPCE(IV-2248),
MP8(VIII-5175),   MP6(VI-3102),   MPEur(751),   MP1(II-978),
MWL1(978).

Albee, Edward
All Over.   SCL12(I-221),   A72(1).
Ballad of the Sad Café, The.   SCL12(I-534),   SCL7(I-309),
A64(12).
Delicate Balance, A.   SCL12(III-1862),   SCL7(II-1117),   A67(75).
Seascape.   SCL12(X-6698),   A76(273).
Who's Afraid of Virginia Woolf?   MP12(XII-7121),
MP8(VIII-5632),   MP4(II-1282),   MWL4(1282),
SCL12(XII-8262),   SCL7(VII-5052),   A63(297),
BMA(607).

Albert the Great, Saint
Commentary on Aristotle's De anima.   RCa(I-360).
Summa de creaturis.   RCa(I-352).

Albertini, Luigi
Origins of the War of 1914, The.   Different analyses on this title appear
in: HEur(II-1021; III-1231; III-1247).

Albright, George L.
Official Explorations for Pacific Railroads, 1853-1855.   HAmer(II-868).

Alcott, Louisa May
Little Women.   MP12(VI-3458),   MPCE(II-1264),
MP8(IV-2707),   MP6(III-1711),   MPAm(348),   MP1(I-515),
MWL1(515).

Alcuin

Concerning Rhetoric and Virtue. RCa (I-261).
Aldani, Lino
    Quando le Radici. SF(IV-1739).
Alden, John R.
    American Revolution, 1775-1783, The. HAmer(I-259).
    General Gage in America: Being Principally a History of
    His Role in the American Revolution.
    HAmer(I-253).
Aldington, Richard
    Death of a Hero. MP12(III-1362), MPCE(I-501), MP8(II-1052),
    MP6(II-690), MPEng(140), MPv4(105), MP2(I-223),
    MWL2(223).
Aldiss, Brian W.
    Barefoot in the Head. SF(I-125).
    Cryptozoic! SF(I-443).
    Frankenstein Unbound. SF(II-840).
    Greybeard. SF(II-926).
    Long Afternoon of Earth, The. SF(III-1235).
    Report on Probability, A. SF(IV-1764).
Aldrich, Thomas Bailey
    Story of a Bad Boy, The. MP12(XI-6265), MPCE(IV-2163),
    MP8(VII-4991), MP6(VI-2980), MPAm(610), MP1(II-927),
    MWL1(927).
Alegría, Ciro
    *Broad and Alien Is the World. MP12(II-666), MPCE(I-244),
    MP8(I-515), MP6(I-342), MPAm(72), MPv4(50), MP2(I-116),
    MWL2(116).
Aleichem, Sholom
    Best of Sholom Aleichem, The. LA80(I-77).
Alemán, Mateo
    *Guzmán de Alfarache. MP12(IV-2437), MPCE(II-890),
    MP8(III-1895), MP6(III-1194), MPEur(349), MPv4(197),
    MP2(I-393), MWL2(393).
Alexander, James
    Brief Narrative of the Case and Trial of John Peter Zenger,
    Printer of the New York Weekly Journal, *A.*
    HAmer(I-191).
Alexander, Samuel
    Space, Time and Deity. Ph(II-823).
Alexander of Hales
    Summa universae theologiae. RCa(I-382).
Alfred, William
    Hogan's Goat. SCL12(V-3470), SCL7(III-2068),
    A67(143).
Allen, Frederick Lewis

Only Yesterday: An Informal History of the 1920's.   HAmer(III-1579).
Since Yesterday: The Nineteen-Thirties in America, September 3,
1929-September 3, 1939.   HAmer(III-1584).
Allen, Gay Wilson
Solitary Singer, The.   SCL12(XI-7082),   SCL7(VI-4352),
A55(240),   BMA(516).
William James: A Biography.   SCL12(XII-8296),   SCL7(VII-5076),
A68(349).
Allen, Hervey
Anthony Adverse.   MP12(I-246),   MPCE(I-84),   MP8(I-194),
MP6(I-125),   MPAm(25),   MP1(I-34),   MWL1(34).
Allen, Lee
American League Story, The.   HAmer(III-1500).
Allen, Louis
End of the War in Asia, The.   LA80(I-285).
Allen, Walter
Threescore and Ten.   SCL12(XI-7620),   SCL7(VII-4644),
A60(272).
Allen, William Sheridan
Nazi Seizure of Power: The Experience of a Single German Town
1930-1935, The.   HWor(I-316).
Alliluyeva, Svetlana
Twenty Letters to a Friend.   SCL12(XII-7830),   SCL7(VII-4796),
A68(340).
Alperovitz, Gar
Atomic Diplomacy: Hiroshima and Potsdam.   Different analyses on this
title appear in: HEur(III-1515),   HAmer(III-1756).
Alphonsus Mary de' Liguori, Saint
Glories of Mary.   RCa(II-624).
Alt, Albrecht
"Formation of the Israelite State in Palestine, The," in
Essays on Old Testament History and Religion.
HAnc(I-92).
Altamirano, Ignacio Manuel
Zarco, El.   MP12(XII-7323),   MPCE(IV-2576),   MP8(VIII-5784),
MP6(VI-3524),   MPAm(740),   MP3(II-1170),   MWL3(1170).
Alter, Robert
Lion for Love: A Critical Biography of Stendhal, A.   LA80(II-497).
Alther, Lisa
Kinflicks.   LA77(I-391).
Altmeyer, Arthur J.
Formative Years of Social Security, The.   HAmer(III-1646).
Altov, Henrich
Sozdan dla buzi.   SF(V-2117).
Alvardo, Corrado

Different analyses on this title appear in: HEur(III-1205; III-1243).

Anderson, Oscar E., Jr. *and* Richard G. Hewlett
History of the United States Atomic Energy Commission, Vol. I: The New World, 1939-1946, A.   HWor(I-391).

Anderson, Poul
Brain Wave.   SF(I-242).
High Crusade, The.   SF(II-977).
Tau Zero.   SF(V-2236).
Three Hearts and Three Lions.   SF(V-2264).
War of the Wing-Men.   SF(V-2411).

Anderson, Robert
*Tea and Sympathy.   SCL12(XI-7402),   SCL7(VII-4514),
A54(270),   BMA(530).

Anderson, R. C.
Naval Wars in the Levant.   HEur(I-182).

Anderson, Sherwood
*Dark Laughter.   MP12(III-1317),   MPCE(I-482),   MP8(II-1019),
MP6(II-667),   MPAm(125),   MP1(I-185),   MWL1(185).
*Poor White.   MP12(IX-5241),   MPCE(III-1783),   MP8(VI-4185),
MP6(V-2481),   MPAm(496),   MP1(II-762),   MWL1(762).
Story Teller's Story, A.   MP12(XI-6291),   MP8(VII-5010),
MP4(II-1184),   MWL4(1184).
*Winesburg, Ohio.   MP12(XII-7171),   MPCE(IV-2510),
MP8(VIII-5672),   MP6(VI-3438),   MPAm(717),   MP1(II-1121),
MWL1(1121).

Anderson, Troyer S.
Command of the Howe Brothers During the American Revolution, The.
HAmer(I-279).

Andrewes, A.
Greek Tyrants, The.   HAnc(I-136).

Andrewes, Lancelot
Preces privatae.   RCh(I-473).

Andrews, Charles M.
Colonial Period of American History, Vol. II: The Settlements, The.
Different analyses on this title appear in: HAmer(I-94; I-99; I-118).
Colonial Period of American History, Vol. IV: England's Commercial and Colonial Policy, The.   HAmer(I-123).

Andrews, Matthew P.
Founding of Maryland, The.   HAmer(I-117).

Andrews, Roy Chapman
Meet Your Ancestors.   HEur(II-825).

Andreyev, Leonid
Seven Who Were Hanged, The.   MP12(X-5939),   MPCE(IV-2050),
MP8(VII-4730),   MP6(V-2836),   MPEur(677),   MPv4(475),
MP2(II-957),   MWL2(957).

Andrić, Ivo
 Bosnian Chronicle.   SCL12(II-852),   SCL7(I-486),   A64(27).
 Bridge on the Drina, The.   MP12(II-656),   MP8(I-506),
 MP4(I-87),   MWL4(87). A different analysis on this title appears in:
 SCL12(II-917),   SCL7(I-522),   A60(30).
 Devil's Yard.   SCL12(III-1923),   SCL7(II-1156),   A63(42).
Andrikopoulos, Bonnie *and* Warren M. Hearn, *eds.*
 *Abortion in the Seventies: Proceedings of the Western Regional Conference
 on Abortion*.   HWor(III-1156).
Angelou, Maya
 I Know Why the Caged Bird Sings.   SCL12(VI-3587),   SCLs(133).
 Singin' and Swingin' and Gettin' Merry Like Christmas.   LA77(II-738).
Anouilh, Jean
 Ring Round the Moon.   MP12(X-5608),   MP8(VII-4466),
 MP6(V-2660),   MPDr(700),   MP3(II-896),   MWL3(896).
 Waltz of the Toreadors, The.   SCL12(XII-8073),   SCL7(VII-4939),
 A58(261).
Anselm of Canterbury, Saint
 Cur Deus homo.   Different analyses on this title appear in:
 RCh(I-202),   RCa(I-286).
 Monologion.   RCh(I-194).
 Monologion and *Proslogion*.   Ph(I-284).
 Proslogion.   Different analyses on this title appear in RCh(I-197),
 RCa(I-280).
Anthony, Piers
 Chthon.   SF(I-354).
 Macroscope.   SF(III-1308).
 Omnivore.   SF(IV-1596).
Apollinaire, Guillaume
 Poetry of Apollinaire, The.   MP12(VIII-4805),
 MP8(VI-3751),   MP4(II-718),   MWL4(718).
"Appleton, Victor"
 Tom Swift Novels, The.   SF(V-2298).
Aptheker, Herbert
 American Negro Slave Revolts.   HAmer(II-688).
Apuleius, Lucius
 Golden Ass of Lucius Apuleius, The.   MP12(IV-2292),
 MPCE(II-829),   MP8(III-1784),   MP6(II-1120),   MPEur(332),
 MP1(I-309),   MWL1(309).
Aquinas, Saint Thomas
 De veritate.   RCa(I-379).
 Hymns of Saint Thomas Aquinas, The.   RCa(I-421).
 On Being and Essence.   RCa(I-364).
 On Free Choice.   RCa(I-406).
 On Kingship.   RCa(I-391).

On Spiritual Creatures.   RCa(I-402).
On the Power of God.   RCa(I-394).
On the Soul.   RCa(I-409).
On the Virtues in General.   RCa(I-413).
Summa contra gentiles.   Different analyses on this title appear in:
Ph(I-314),   RCh(I-232),   RCa(I-385).
*Summa Theologica.   MP12(XI-6329),   MP8(VII-5042),
MP6(VI-3010),   MPNf(294),   MP3(II-1033),   MWL3(1033). Different
analyses on this title appear in: Ph(I-321),   RCh(I-241),   RCa(I-416).
Aragon, Louis
Holy Week.   SCL12(V-3485),   SCL7(III-2079),   A62(149).
Archer, Jules
Chinese and the Americans, The.   HWor(III-1128).
Ardrey, Robert
Hunting Hypothesis, The.   LA77(I-367).
Social Contract, The.   SCL12(X-7056),   A71(300).
Arendt, Hannah
Life of the Mind: One/Thinking, Two/Willing, The.   LA79(I-393).
On Revolution.   SCL12(VIII-5550),   SCL7(V-3393),   A64(200).
Aretino, Pietro
*Courtesan, The.   MP12(II-1168),   MPCE(I-424),   MP8(II-909),
MP6(I-595),   MPDr(179),   MP3(I-234),   MWL3(234).
Discourses.   MP12(III-1524),   MP8(II-1187),   MP4(I-239),
MWL4(239).
Arihara no Narihira
Tales of Ise.   MP12(XI-6378),   MP8(VII-5078),   MP6(VI-3036),
MPEur(737),   MP3(II-1044),   MWL3(1044).
Ariosto, Ludovico
*Orlando Furioso.   MP12(VIII-4404),   MPCE(III-1637),
MP8(V-3433),   MP6(IV-2203),   MPPo(194),   MPv3(394),
MP2(II-776),   MWL2(776).
Suppositi, I.   MP12(XI-6352),   MPCE(IV-2190),   MP8(VII-5059),
MP6(VI-3021),   MPDr(823),   MP3(II-1039),   MWL3(1039).
Aristides
Apology of Aristides, The.   Different analyses on this title appear in:
RCh(I-9),   RCa(I-10).
Aristophanes
*Acharnians, The.   MP12(I-26),   MPCE(I-10),   MP8(I-21),
MP6(I-18),   MPDr(6),   MP3(I-7),   MWL3(7).
*Birds, The.   MP12(I-547),   MPCE(I-199),   MP8(I-422),
MP6(I-282),   MPDr(80),   MPv3(57),   MP2(I-94),   MWL2(94).
*Clouds, The.   MP12(II-1006),   MPCE(I-369),   MP8(II-779),
MP6(I-514),   MPDr(158),   MP1(I-152),   MWL1(152).
Ecclesiazusae, The.   MP12(III-1699),   MPCE(I-623),
MP8(II-1321),   MP6(II-855),   MPDr(237),   MP3(I-322),

MWL3(322).

Frogs, The. MP12(IV-2178), MPCE(II-784), MP8(III-1698), MP6(II-1067), MPDr(284), MP1(I-297), MWL1(297).

Knights, The. MP12(VI-3189), MPCE(II-1180), MP8(IV-2483), MP6(III-1590), MPDr(429), MP1(I-480), MWL1(480).

Lysistrata. MP12(VI-3578), MPCE(II-1301), MP8(IV-2809), MP6(III-1763), MPDr(467), MPv3(308), MP2(II-610), MWL2(610).

Peace, The. MP12(VIII-4541), MPCE(III-1689), MP8(V-3538), MP6(IV-2272), MPDr(605), MP3(II-726), MWL3(726).

Plutus. MP12(VIII-4770), MPCE(III-1776), MP8(VI-3718), MP6(V-2399), MPDr(648), MPv3(420), MP2(II-845), MWL2(845).

Thesmophoriazusae, The. MP12(XI-6483), MPCE(IV-2239), MP8(VIII-5159), MP6(VI-3092), MPDr(842), MP3(II-1068), MWL3(1068).

Wasps, The. MP12(XII-7044), MPCE(IV-2469), MP8(VIII-5573), MP6(VI-3374), MPDr(908), MP3(II-1119), MWL3(1119).

Aristotle

Ethica Nicomachea. Ph(I-157).

Metaphysics. Ph(I-152).

On the Soul. Ph(I-147).

Organon. Ph(I-137).

Physics. Ph(I-143).

Poetics. MP12(VIII-4789), MP8(VI-3735), MP6(V-2409), MPNf(248), MP3(II-774), MWL3(774). A different analysis on this title appears in: Ph(I-174).

Politics. Ph(I-163).

Rhetoric. Ph(I-169).

Arlen, Michael J.

American Verdict, An. SCL12(I-265), A74(1).

Living Room War, The. HAmer(III-1677).

Passage to Ararat. SCL12(IX-5756), A76(238).

View from Highway 1, The. LA77(II-884).

Armah, Avi Kwei

Beautyful Ones Are Not Yet Born, The. SCL12(I-588), SCL7(I-346), A69(33).

Fragments. SCL12(IV-2757), A71(77).

Arminius, Jacobus

Declaration of Sentiments, The. RCh(I-424).

Armitage, Angus

World of Copernicus, The. HEur(I-140).

Armstrong, Barbara

Insuring the Essentials. HEur(II-1031).

Armstrong, Scott *and* Bob Woodward
      Brethren: Inside the Supreme Court, The.   LA80(I-104).
Arndt, Johann
      True Christianity.   RCh(I-422).
Arnold, Edwin L.
      Lieut. Gullivar Jones: His Vacation.   SF(III-1209).
Arnold, Matthew
      *Culture and Anarchy.   MP12(III-1242),   MP8(II-962),
      MP4(I-169),   MWL4(169).
      Literature and Dogma.   RCh(II-770).
      *Poetry of Arnold, The.   MP12(VIII-4808),   MP8(VI-3754),
      MP4(II-720),   MWL4(720).
      Sohrab and Rustum.   MP12(X-6125),   MPCE(IV-2108),
      MP8(VII-4884),   MP6(V-2917),   MPPo(344),   MP3(II-1002),
      MWL3(1002).
Arnow, Harriette Simpson
      Dollmaker, The.   SCL12(III-2009),   SCL7(II-1206),   A54(55).
      Flowering of the Cumberland.   SCL12(IV-2696),   SCL7(III-1600),
      A64(93).
      Seedtime on the Cumberland.   SCL12(X-6747),   SCL7(VI-4150),
      A61(222).
      Weedkiller's Daughter, The.   SCL12(XII-8172),   A70(337).
Aron, Raymond
      Main Currents in Sociological Thought.   HEur(II-806).
Artaud, Antonin
      Antonin Artaud.   LA77(I-52).
Artsybashev, Mikhail
      Sanine.   MP12(X-5787),   MPCE(IV-1996),   MP8(VII-4606),
      MP6(V-2753),   MPEur(660),   MP3(II-921),   MWL3(921).
Artz, Frederick B.
      France Under the Bourbon Restoration.   HEur(II-684).
      Reaction and Revolution, 1814-1832. Vol. XIII of *The Rise of Modern
      Europe* series.   HEur(II-689).
Arvidson, Raymond E., *et al*.
      "Surface of Mars, The," in *Scientific American.*   HWor(III-1297).
Asbury, Francis
      Journal of Francis Asbury, The.   RCh(II-654).
Asch, Sholem
      Apostle, The.   MP12(I-269),   MPCE(I-94),   MP8(I-211),
      MP6(I-138),   MPAm(28),   MP1(I-38),   MWL1(38).
      Nazarene, The.   MP12(VII-4161),   MPCE(III-1552),
      MP8(V-3242),   MP6(IV-2079),   MPAm(439),   MP1(II-645),
      MWL1(645).
      Prophet, The.   SCL12(IX-6091),   SCL7(VI-3717),   A55(211).
Ashabranner, Brent

Moment in History: The First Ten Years of the Peace Corps, A.
HAmer(III-1879).
Ashberry, John
Rivers and Mountains.   SCL12(X-6436),   SCL7(VI-3948),   A67(287).
Ashbery, John
As We Know.   LA80(I-31).
Houseboat Days.   LA78(I-408).
Self-Portrait in a Convex Mirror.   SCL12(X-6838),   A76(283).
Ashby, Thomas
Roman Campagna in Classical Times, The.   HAnc(I-374).
Ashley, Maurice
Greatness of Oliver Cromwell, The.   Different analyses on this title
appear in: HEur(I-315; I-333).
Ashmore, Harry S.
Epitaph for Dixie, An.   SCL12(IV-2296),   SCL7(II-1370),   A59(73).
Ashton, Robert
English Civil War: Conservatism and Revolution, 1603-1649, The.
LA80(I-297).
Ashton-Warner, Sylvia
Incense to Idols.   SCL12(VI-3697),   SCL7(III-2211),   A61(124).
Spinster.   SCL12(XI-7183),   SCL7(VI-4414),   A60(249).
Three.   SCL12(XI-7592),   A71(314).
Asimov, Isaac
Caves of Steel, The.   SF(I-318).
Collapsing Universe: The Story of Black Holes, The.   HWor(II-838).
Foundation Trilogy, The.   SF(II-819).
Gods Themselves, The.   SF(II-909).
I, Robot.   SF(II-995).
Naked Sun, The.   SF(III-1476).
Asinof, Eliot
Eight Men Out: The Black Sox and the 1919 World Series.
HAmer(III-1499).
Askew, William C.
Europe and Italy's Acquisition of Libya, 1911-1912.   HEur(III-1230).
Asprey, Robert B.
First Battle of the Marne, The.   HEur(III-1251).
Asser, John
Life of Alfred.   RCa(I-268).
Astin, A. E.
Scipio Aemilianus.   HAnc(I-456).
Astor, John Jacob
Journey in Other Worlds, A.   SF(III-1098).
Asturias, Miguel Ángel
El Señor Presidente.   MP12(III-1726),   MP8(II-1342),   MP4(I-260),
MWL4(260).

English Auden: Poems, Essays and Dramatic Writings, 1927-1939, The.
LA79(I-193).
Epistle to a Godson. SCL12(IV-2293), A73(157).
Forewords and Afterwords. SCL12(IV-2731), A74(134).
Homage to Clio. SCL12(V-3488), SCL7(III-2082), A61(119).
Poetry of Auden, The. MP12(VIII-4811), MP8(VI-3757),
MP6(V-2411), MPPo(228), MP3(II-777), MWL3(777).
Shield of Achilles, The. SCL12(X-6912), SCL7(VI-4251),
A55(234), BMA(509).
Thank You, Fog. SCL12(XI-7500), A75(325).
Aue, Hartmann von
Arme Heinrich, Der. MP12(I-307), MPCE(I-111), MP8(I-237),
MP6(I-158), MPPo(10), MP3(I-63), MWL3(63).
Auerbach, Jerold S.
Unequal Justice. LA77(II-866).
Augustine, Saint
City of God, The. Different analyses on this title appear in:
Ph(I-258), RCh(I-140), RCa(I-188).
Confessions. MP12(II-1057), MP8(II-823), MP6(I-539),
MPNf(58), MP3(I-213), MWL3(213). Different analyses on this title
appear in: Ph(I-252), RCh(I-128), RCa(I-165).
De magistro. RCa(I-140).
De trinitate. RCa(I-173).
Enarrations on the Psalms. RCa(I-196).
Enchiridion on Faith, Hope, and Love, The. RCh(I-149).
Faith, Hope, and Charity. RCa(I-184).
First Catechetical Instruction, The. RCa(I-161).
On the Trinity. RCh(I-134).
Aulén, Gustaf
*Christus Victor: An Historical Study of the Three Main Types of the
Atonement.* Different analyses on this title appear in: RCh(II-950),
HAnc(III-1293).
Faith of the Christian Church, The. RCh(II-912).
Austen, Jane
Emma. MP12(III-1763), MPCE(I-642), MP8(II-1374),
MP6(II-885), MPEng(179), MP1(I-246), MWL1(246).
Mansfield Park. MP12(VII-3704), MPCE(III-1352),
MP8(IV-2904), MP6(IV-1835), MPEng(469), MP1(I-562),
MWL1(562).
Northanger Abbey. MP12(VII-4238), MPCE(III-1583),
MP8(V-3302), MP6(IV-2124), MPEng(586), MPv3(378),
MP2(II-750), MWL2(750).
Persuasion. MP12(VIII-4615), MPCE(III-1717), MP8(V-3596),
MP6(IV-2318), MPEng(652), MP1(II-734), MWL1(734).
Pride and Prejudice. MP12(IX-5307), MPCE(III-1804),

HAnc(II-793).

Bair, Deirdre
    Samuel Beckett.   LA79(II-636).

Baird, Henry M.
    Huguenots and Henry of Navarre, The.   HEur(I-216).

Bairoch, Paul
    Economic Development of the Third World Since 1900, The.
    HWor(II-559).

Bakeless, John
    Background to Glory.   SCL12(I-517),   SCL7(I-295),   A58(26).
    Lewis and Clark: Partners in Discovery.   HAmer(I-452).

Baker, Carlos
    Ernest Hemingway.   SCL12(IV-2311),   A70(112).
    Friend in Power, A.   SCL12(IV-2792),   SCL7(III-1661),   A59(92).

Baker, Elliot
    Fine Madness, A.   SCL12(IV-2592),   SCL7(III-1533),   A65(95).

Baker, Liva
    I'm Radcliffe! Fly Me!   LA77(I-376).

Bakerville, Geoffrey
    English Monks and the Suppression of the Monasteries.   HEur(I-112).

Balaban, John
    After Our War.   SCL12(I-101),   A75(4).

Balchin, Nigel
    Fall of a Sparrow, The.   SCL12(IV-2422),   SCL7(II-1443),   A57(64).

Bald, R. C.
    John Donne: A Life.   SCL12(VI-3880),   A71(148).

Baldry, H. C.
    Unity of Mankind in Greek Thought, The.   Different analyses on this
    title appear in: HAnc(I-390; I-455).

Baldwin, Hanson W.
    Sea Fights and Shipwrecks.   SCL12(X-6674),   SCL7(VI-4103),
    A55(223).

Baldwin, James
    Fire Next Time, The.   SCL12(IV-2611),   SCL7(III-1541),   A64(88).
    *Go Tell It on the Mountain.   MP12(IV-2276),   MP8(III-1770),
    MP4(I-379),   MWL4(379).
    Just Above My Head.   LA80(II-456).
    No Name in the Street.   SCL12(VIII-5384),   A73(279).
    Nobody Knows My Name.   SCL12(VIII-5391),   SCL7(V-3290),
    A62(219),   BMA(398).

Baldwin, Leland D.
    Keelboat Age on Western Waters, The.   HAmer(I-473).
    Whiskey Rebels: The Story of a Frontier Uprising.   HAmer(I-380).

Bale, John
    *King John.   MP12(VI-3140),   MPCE(II-1160),   MP8(IV-2447),

Barber, Noel
    Sinister Twilight, A.   SCL12(X-6993),   SCL7(VI-4308),   A69(288).
Barbour, Philip L.
    Dimitry, Called the Pretender, Tsar and Great Prince of All Russia,
    1605-1606.   HEur(I-233).
Barbusse, Henri
    Under Fire.   MP12(XII-6822),   MPCE(IV-2385),   MP8(VIII-5404),
    MP6(VI-3263),   MPEur(779),   MP1(II-1047),   MWL1(1047).
Barclay, John
    Argenis.   MP12(I-302),   MPCE(I-110),   MP8(I-233),   MP6(I-154),
    MPEng(31),   MP3(I-59),   MWL3(59).
Barclay, Robert
    Apology for the True Christian Divinity, An.   RCh(I-526).
Barghoorn, Frederick C.
    Détente and the Democratic Movement in the U.S.S.R.
    HWor(II-995).
Barjavel, René
    voyageur imprudent, Le.   SF(V-2389).
Barker, Arthur E.
    Milton and the Puritan Dilemma.   HEur(I-322).
Barker, Ernest
    Politics of Aristotle, The.   HAnc(I-346).
Barker, Eugene C.
    Life of Stephen F. Austin, Founder of Texas, 1793-1836, The.
    HAmer(II-739).
Barker, George
    Poetry of Barker, The.   MP12(VIII-4814),   MP8(VI-3760),
    MP4(II-723),   MWL4(723).
Barker, Nancy Nichols
    Distaff Diplomacy: The Empress Eugénie and the Foreign Policy of the
    Second Empire.   HEur(II-852).
Barker, Ralph
    Blockade Busters.   LA78(I-108).
Barnard, Christian N.
    Heart Attack: You Don't Have to Die.   HWor(II-1020).
    "Transplants: Will Future Vindicate the Failures?," in Chicago Sun
    Times.   HWor(II-1019).
Barnard, L. W.
    Justin Martyr: His Life and Thought.   HAnc(II-710).
Barnes, Donald G.
    History of the English Corn Laws, 1660-1846, A.   HEur(II-768).
Barnes, Hazel
    "Translator's Introduction," in Being and Nothingness.   HEur(III-1484).
Barnes, Viola F.
    Dominion of New England: A Study in British Colonial Policy, The.

HAmer(I-165).

Barnet, Richard J.
Giants: Russia and America, The. LA78(I-345).

Barnet, Richard J. *and* Ronald E. Miller
Global Reach. SCL12(V-2963), A76(103).

Barnett, A. Doak
"Changing Strategic Balance in Asia, The," in *Sino-American Détente and Its Policy Implications.* HWor(III-1126).

Barnett, Lincoln
World We Live In, The. SCL12(XII-8430), SCL7(VII-5157), A55(299).

Barnouw, Erik
History of Broadcasting in the United States, Vol. I: A Tower in Babel: To 1933, A. HAmer(III-1521).
History of Broadcasting in the United States, Vol. II: The Golden Web: 1933 to 1953, A. HAmer(III-1676).
Tube of Plenty. SCL12(XII-7806), A76(329). A different analysis on this title appears in: HWor(II-671).

Baroja, Pío
*Caesar or Nothing. MP12(II-731), MPCE(I-268), MP8(I-567), MP6(I-375), MPEur(100), MP1(I-97), MWL1(97).
King Paradox. MP12(VI-3159), MPCE(II-1168), MP8(IV-2462), MP6(III-1572), MPEur(413), MPv4(265), MP2(I-533), MWL2533).
*Restlessness of Shanti Andia, The. SCL12(X-6385), SCL7(VI-3905), A60(223).

Barraclough, Geoffrey
History in a Changing World. HAnc(III-1198).
Origins of Modern Germany, The. Different analyses on this title appear in: HAnc(III-1366; III-1475; III-1623; III-1638), HEur(I-66).

Barrett, Ada L.
George Stephenson, Father of Railways. HEur(II-610).

Barrett, Helen M.
Boethius: Some Aspects of His Times and Work. HAnc(II-1020).

Barrett, William
Illusion of Technique: A Search for Meaning in a Technological Civilization, The. LA80(I-409).

Barrie, James M.
*Admirable Crichton, The. MP12(I-35), MPCE(I-13), MP8(I-28), MP6(I-24), MPDr(8), MP1(I-10), MWL1(10).
*Dear Brutus. MP12(III-1345), MPCE(I-493), MP8(II-1041), MP6(II-683), MPDr(199), MP1(I-196), MWL1(196).
*Little Minister, The. MP12(VI-3454), MPCE(II-1263), MP8(IV-2704), MP6(III-1708), MPEng(439), MP1(I-513), MWL1(513).

Barthes, Roland
    Critical Essays. SCL12(III-1619),   A73(104).
    Eiffel Tower and Other Mythologies, The. LA80(I-269).
    Lover's Discourse: Fragments, A. LA79(I-404).
    Roland Barthes. LA78(II-730).
Barthold, W.
    Turkestan Down to the Mongol Invasion. HAnc(III-1255).
Bartlett, Irving H.
    Daniel Webster. LA79(I-143).
Baruch, Bernard M.
    Baruch: The Public Years. SCL12(I-550),   SCL7(I-320),   A61(13).
Baruk, Henri
    *Patients Are People Like Us: The Experiences of Half a Century in
    Neuropsychiatry.* LA79(II-532).
Barzun, Jacques
    House of Intellect, The. SCL12(V-3551),   SCL7(III-2128),
    A60(96),   BMA(242).
Bashô, Matsuo
    Poetry of Bashô, The. MP12(VIII-4816),   MP8(VI-3762),
    MP6(V-2414),   MPPo(231),   MP3(II-779),   MWL3(779).
Basil, Saint
    Against Eunomius. RCa(I-98).
    Letters of Saint Basil, The. RCa(I-110).
    Longer Rules and *The Shorter Rules, The.* RCh(I-99).
    Treatise on the Holy Spirit. RCa(I-107).
Baskir, Lawrence M. *and* William A. Strauss
    *Chance and Circumstance: The Draft, the War and the Vietnam
    Generation.* LA79(I-88).
Bass, Jack *and* Walter DeVries
    Transformation of Southern Politics, The. LA77(II-832).
Bass, Robert Duncan
    Swamp Fox. SCL12(XI-7357),   SCLs(303).
Bass, T. J.
    Half Past Human. SF(II-940).
Bassani, Giorgio
    Five Stories of Ferrara. SCL12(IV-2654),   A72(149).
    Garden of the Finzi-Continis, The. SCL12(IV-2859),
    SCL7(III-1706),   A66(114).
    Heron, The. SCL12(V-3400),   A71(115).
Bassett, John S.
    Life of Andrew Jackson, The. HAmer(I-535).
Basso, Hamilton
    Light Infantry Ball, The. SCL12(VII-4372),   SCL7(IV-2671),
    A60(136).
    View from Pompey's Head, The. SCL12(XII-7995),

Beach, Sylvia
  Shakespeare and Company.   SCL12(X-6903),   SCL7(VI-4242),
  A60(240).
Beagle, Peter S.
  Last Unicorn, The.   SCL12(VI-4146),   SCL7(IV-2537),   A69(188).
Beaglehole, John C.
  Life of Captain James Cook, The.   SCL12(VII-4323),   A75(170).
Beale, Howard K.
  Charles A. Beard: An Appraisal.   HAmer(III-1430).
Beard, Charles A.
  Economic Origins of Jeffersonian Democracy.   HAmer(I-358).
Beard, Charles A. *and* Mary R. Beard
  Rise of American Civilization, The.   MP12(X-5614),
  MP8(VII-4471),   MP4(II-1071),   MWL4(1071).
Beattie, Ann
  Chilly Scenes of Winter.   LA77(I-154).
Beatty, J. Kelly
  "Far-Out Worlds of Voyager I—*Part 1, The,"* in *Sky and Telescope.*
  HWor(III-1313).
  "Far-Out Worlds of Voyager I—*Part 2, The,"* in *Sky and Telescope.*
  HWor(III-1313).
  *"*Voyager*'s Encore Performance,"* in *Sky and Telescope.*
  HWor(III-1313).
Beaumarchais, Pierre A. Caron de
  Barber of Seville, The.   MP12(I-423),   MPCE(I-147),   MP8(I-330),
  MP6(I-213),   MPDr(58),   MPv3(40)   MP2(I-70),   MWL2(70).
  Marriage of Figaro, The.   MP12(VII-3745),   MPCE(III-1369),
  MP8(V-2939),   MP6(IV-1860),   MPDr(499),   MPv3(323),
  MP2(II-637),   MWL2(637).
Beaumont, Francis
  *Knight of the Burning Pestle, The.   MP12(VI-3185),
  MPCE(II-1179),   MP8(IV-2480),   MP6(III-1587),   MPDr(426),
  MPv3(274),   MP2(I-542),   MWL2(542).
Beaumont, Francis *and* John Fletcher
  *Coxcomb, The.   MP12(II-1185),   MPCE(I-435),   MP8(II-919),
  MP6(I-603),   MPDr(181),   MP3(I-236),   MWL3(236).
  *King and No King, A.   MP12(VI-3133),   MPCE(II-1158),
  MP8(IV-2441),   MP6(III-1558),   MPDr(409),   MP3(I-541),
  MWL3(541).
  *Maid's Tragedy, The.   MP12(VI-3638),   MPCE(III-1331),
  MP8(IV-2848),   MP6(IV-1795),   MPDr(480),   MPv4(304),
  MP2(II-612),   MWL2(612).
  *Philaster.   MP12(VIII-4639),   MPCE(III-1727),   MP8(V-3616),
  MP6(IV-2331),   MPDr(622),   MPv3(411),   MP2(II-825),
  MWL2(825).

Scornful Lady, The.   MP12(X-5848),   MPCE(IV-2019),
MP8(VII-4655),   MP6(V-2785),   MPDr(744),   MP3(II-940),
MWL3(940).
Woman Hater, The.   MP12(XII-7207),   MPCE(IV-2524),
MP8(VIII-5699),   MP6(VI-3454),   MPDr(937),   MP3(II-1138),
MWL3(1138).
Beauvoir, Simon de
Coming of Age, The.   SCL12(III-1475),   A73(96).
All Said and Done.   SCL12(I-225),   A75(11).
Mandarins, The.   SCL12(VII-4732),   SCL7(IV-2878),   A57(165).
Beazley, C. Raymond
Prince Henry, the Navigator.   HAnc(III-1688).
Beccaria, Cesare Bonesana
On Crimes and Punishments.   HWor(III-1282).
Becker, Carl L.
*Declaration of Independence: A Study in the History of Political Ideas,
The*.   HAmer(I-263).
Becker, Stephen
Outcasts, The.   SCL12(VIII-5682),   SCL7(V-3481),   A68(237).
When the War Is Over.   SCL12(XII-8231),   A70(345).
Beckett, Samuel
Lost Ones, The.   SCL12(VII-4551),   A73(228).
Mercier and Camier.   SCL12(VII-4935),   A76(218).
Stories and Texts for Nothing.   SCL12(XI-7252),   SCL7(VII-4455),
A68(312).
Unnamable, The.   SCL12(XII-7917),   SCL7(VII-4838),   A59(257).
Waiting for Godot.   MP12(XII-6991),   MPCE(IV-2449),
MP8(VIII-5533),   MP6(VI-3350),   MPDr(900),   MP3(II-1113),
MWL3(1113). A different analysis on this title appears in:
SCL12(XII-8062),   SCL7(VII-4933),   A57(281),   BMA(583).
Beckford, William
Vathek.   MP12(XII-6881),   MPCE(IV-2407),   MP8(VIII-5449),
MP6(VI-3291),   MPEng(910),   MPv3(530),   MP2(II-1094),
MWL2(1094).
Beddoes, Thomas Lovell
Poetry of Beddoes, The.   MP12(VIII-4819),   MP8(VI-3765),
MP4(II-725),   MWL4(725).
Bede, Saint
Ecclesiastical History of the English Nation.   RCh(I-181).
Ecclesiastical History of the English People, The.   RCa(I-258).
Opera de Temporibus.   HAnc(II-860).
Bedient, Calvin
Eight Contemporary Poets.   SCL12(IV-2159),   A75(79).
Beecher, Henry Ward
Evolution and Religion.   RCh(II-793).

Beecher, Lyman
　　Works of Lyman Beecher, The.　RCh(II-724).
Beeman, Richard R.
　　Patrick Henry.　SCL12(IX-5774),　A75(232).
Beerbohm, Max
　　Essays of Max Beerbohm, The.　MP12(IV-1866),　MP8(III-1464),
　　MP4(I-307),　MWL4(307).
　　Zuleika Dobson.　MP12(XII-7334),　MPCE(IV-2578),
　　MP8(VIII-5793),　MP6(VI-3527),　MPEng(982),　MPv4(605),
　　MP2(II-1169),　MWL2(1169).
Behan, Brendan
　　Borstal Boy.　SCL12(II-849),　SCL7(I-483),　A60(25).
　　Quare Fellow, The.　SCL12(IX-6150),　SCL7(VI-3764),　A58(201).
Behn, Mrs. Aphra
　　Oroonoko.　MP12(VIII-4421),　MPCE(III-1644),　MP8(V-3445),
　　MP6(IV-2214),　MPEng(622),　MPv4(385),　MP2(II-783),
　　MWL2(783).
Behrman, S. N.
　　Burning Glass, The.　SCL12(II-977),　SCL7(I-558),　A69(54).
　　Portrait of Max.　SCL12(IX-5983),　SCL7(V-3660),　A61(198),
　　BMA(452).
Belitt, Ben
　　Double Witness, The.　LA78(I-276).
　　Nowhere but Light: Poems 1964-1969.　SCL12(VIII-5442),　A71(228).
Bell, Daniel
　　Cultural Contradictions of Capitalism, The.　LA77(I-184).
Bell, J. Bowyer
　　Time of Terror: How Democratic Societies Cope with Terrorism, A.
　　HWor(II-1032).
Bell, Joseph.
　　Seven into Space.　HWor(II-937).
Bell, Marvin
　　Probable Volume of Dreams, A.　SCL12(IX-6066),　A70(255).
Bell, Millicent
　　Marquand: An American Life.　LA80(II-517).
Bell, Oliver, *ed.*
　　America's Changing Population. HWor(II-1081).
Bell, Quentin
　　Virginia Woolf.　SCL12(XII-8015),　A73(372).
Bell, Sir H. Idris
　　Egypt from Alexander the Great to the Arab Conquest.　HAnc(I-416).
Bell, Whitfield J., Jr. *and* Leonard W. Labaree, *eds.*
　　Papers of Benjamin Franklin, The.　SCL12(IX-5717),
　　SCL7(V-3507),　A60(184).
Bellah, Robert N. *and* William G. McLoughlin, *eds.*

Religion in America.   HWor(I-511).
Bellamann, Henry
   King's Row.   MP12(VI-3179),   MPCE(II-1177),   MP8(IV-2476),
   MP6(III-1583),   MPAm(322),   MP1(I-478),   MWL1(478).
Bellamy, Edward
   Looking Backward: 2000-1887.   MP12(VI-3497),   MPCE(II-1274),
   MP8(IV-2741),   MP6(III-1729),   MPAm(356),   MP1(I-520),
   MWL1(520). A different analysis on this title appears in: SF(III-1246).
Bellarmine, Saint Robert Cardinal
   Political Writings.   RCa(II-564).
Bellay, Joachim du
   Poetry of du Bellay, The.   MP12(IX-4914),   MP8(VI-3860),
   MP4(II-788),   MWL4(788).
Belloc, Hilaire
   Path to Rome, The.   MP12(VIII-4521),   MP8(V-3523),
   MP6(IV-2259),   MPNf(228),   MP3(II-722),   MWL3(722). A different
   analysis on this title appears in: RCa(II-734).
   Servile State, The.   RCa(II-754).
Bellonci, Maria
   Life and Times of Lucrezia Borgia, The.   SCL12(VII-4308),
   SCL7(IV-2638),   A54(147).
Bellow, Saul
   Adventures of Augie March, The.   MP12(I-43),   MP8(I-33),
   MP4(I-1),   MWL4(1).
   Henderson the Rain King.   MP12(V-2547),   MP8(III-1979),
   MP4(I-408),   MWL4(408),   SCL12(V-3339),   SCL7(III-1987),
   A60(94).
   Herzog.   SCL12(V-3404),   SCL7(III-2025),   A65(127).
   Humboldt's Gift.   SCL12(V-3569),   A76(136).
   Last Analysis, The.   SCL12(VI-4099),   SCL7(IV-2498),   A66(138).
   Mr. Sammler's Planet.   SCL12(VIII-5037),   A71(208).
   Mosby's Memoirs and Other Stories.   SCL12(VIII-5086),
   SCL7(V-3091),   A69(234).
   Seize the Day.   SCL12(X-6756),   SCLs(254).
   To Jerusalem and Back.   LA77(II-828).
   Victim, The.   MP12(XII-6911),   MP8(VIII-5472),   MP4(II-1259),
   MWL4(1259).
Bemis, Samuel Flagg
   Diplomacy of the American Revolution, The.   HAmer(I-284).
   Jay's Treaty: A Study in Commerce and Diplomacy.   HAmer(I-391).
   John Quincy Adams and the Foundations of American Foreign Policy.
   HAmer(I-596).
   John Quincy Adams and the Union.   SCL12(VI-3900),
   SCL7(IV-2359),   A57(138),   BMA(268).
   Pinckney's Treaty: A Study of America's Advantages from Europe's

Distresses. HAmer(I-400).

Benavente, Jacinto
  Bonds of Interest, The. MP12(I-589), MPCE(I-217),
  MP8(I-455), MP6(I-307), MPDr(92), MPv3(64), MP2(I-107),
  MWL2(107).
  Passion Flower, The. MP12(VIII-4505), MPCE(III-1679),
  MP8(V-3509), MP6(IV-2255), MPDr(600), MP3(II-718),
  MWL3(718).
Benedict of Nursia, Saint
  Rule of St. Benedict, The. Different analyses on this title appear in:
  RCh(I-172), RCa(I-234).
Benedictus, David
  Fourth of June, The. SCL12(IV-2744), SCL7(III-1639), A63(56).
Benét, Stephen Vincent
  John Brown's Body. MP12(V-3016), MPCE(II-1115),
  MP8(IV-2347), MP6(III-1505), MPPo(144), MP1(I-445),
  MWL1(445).
  Poetry of Stephen Vincent Benét, The. MP12(IX-5159),
  MP8(VI-4105), MP4(II-960), MWL4(960).
Benford, Gregory
  In the Ocean of Night. SF(III-1026).
Benford, Gregory *and* Gordon Eklund
  If the Stars Are Gods. SF(II-1004).
Bengis, Ingrid
  Combat in the Erogenous Zone. SCL12(III-1447), A73(92).
Bengtsson, Frans G.
  Long Ships, The. SCL12(VII-4487), SCL7(IV-2756), A54(159).
Benjamin, Walter
  Reflections: Essays, Aphorisms, Autobiographical Writings.
  LA79(II-575).
Bennet, E. A.
  C. G. Jung. HEur(III-1312).
Bennett, Arnold
  Anna of the Five Towns. MP12(I-233), MPCE(I-82),
  MP8(I-181), MP6(I-114), MPEng(19), MPv4(15), MP2(I-37),
  MWL2(37).
  Clayhanger Trilogy, The. MP12(II-984), MPCE(I-359),
  MP8(II-763), MP6(I-504), MPEng(109), MP1(I-148),
  MWL1(148).
  Old Wives' Tale, The. MP12(VIII-4344), MPCE(III-1623),
  MP8(V-3382), MP6(IV-2175), MPEng(604), MP1(II-684),
  MWL1(684).
  Riceyman Steps. MP12(X-5577), MPCE(III-1907),
  MP8(VII-4444), MP6(V-2645), MPEng(731), MP1(II-823),
  MWL1(823).

Bennett, Edward W.
   German Rearmament and the West, 1932-1933.   LA80(I-344).
Bennett, John Coleman
   Christians and the State.   RCh(II-1175).
Benoist-Méchin, Jacques
   Sixty Days That Shook the West: The Fall of France, 1940.
   HEur(III-1452).
Benson, Mary
   *African Patriots: The Story of the African National Congress of South
   Africa, The.*   HWor(III-1275).
Bentham, Jeremy
   Introduction to the Principles of Morals and Legislation, An.   Ph(I-551).
Berdyaev, Nicolai
   Destiny of Man, The.   Different analyses on this title appear in:
   Ph(II-940),   RCh(II-960).
   Dostoevsky.   MP12(III-1621),   MP8(II-1258),   MP4(I-245),
   MWL4(245).
   Freedom and the Spirit.   RCh(II-929).
Beresford, John Davys
   Hampdenshire Wonder, The.   SF(II-945).
Beresford, John D. *and* Esme Wynne-Tyson
   Riddle of the Tower, The.   SF(IV-1780).
Berg, A. Scott
   Max Perkins: Editor of Genius.   LA79(I-428).
Berger, John A.
   Franciscan Missions of California, The.   HAmer(I-275).
Berger, Raoul
   Executive Privilege: A Constitutional Myth.   SCL12(IV-2353),
   A75(98).
Berger, Thomas
   Crazy in Berlin.   SCL12(III-1605),   SCLs(81).
   Killing Time.   SCL12(VI-4001),   SCL7(IV-2417),   A68(169).
   *Little Big Man.   SCL12(VII-4401),   SCL7(IV-2698),   A65(176).
   Regiment of Women.   SCL12(IX-6314),   A74(328).
   Reinhart in Love.   SCL12(IX-6321),   SCLs(247).
   Sneaky People.   SCL12(X-7038),   A76(298).
   Vital Parts.   SCL12(XII-8021),   A71(338).
   Who Is Teddy Villanova?   LA78(II-899).
Berger, Yves
   Garden, The.   SCL12(IV-2848),   SCL7(III-1696),   A64(102).
Bergin, Thomas G.
   Dante.   SCL12(III-1699),   SCL7(II-1001),   A66(56). A different
   analysis on this title appears in: HAnc(III-1601).
Bergson, Henri
   Creative Evolution.   Ph(II-767).

Hitler Among the Germans.   LA77(I-357).
Binkley, William C.
    Texas Revolution, The.   HAmer(II-738).
Bion
    Poetry of Bion, The.   MP12(VIII-4825),   MP8(VI-3771),
    MP4(II-729),   MWL4(729).
Bird, Anthony
    Motor Car, 1765-1914, The.   HEur(II-1034).
Bird, Caroline
    Invisible Scar, The.   HAmer(III-1585).
Bird, Robert Montgomery
    Nick of the Woods.   MP12(VII-4199),   MPCE(III-1569),
    MP8(V-3270),   MP6(IV-2101),   MPAm(442),
    MPv4(365),   MP2(II-737),   MWL2(737).
Birley, A. R.
    Marcus Aurelius.   HAnc(II-728).
Birnbaum, Karl E.
    East and West Germany: A Modus Vivendi.   HWor(III-1170).
    "Human Rights and East-West Relations," in Foreign Affairs.
    HWor(III-1261).
Bishop, Elizabeth
    Complete Poems.   SCL12(III-1490),   A70(86).
    Geography III.   LA77(I-326).
    Questions of Travel.   SCL12(IX-6201),   SCL7(VI-3795),   A66(263).
Bishop, James, Jr. *and* Henry Hubbard
    Let the Seller Beware.   HWor(II-862).
Bishop, Jim
    Day Lincoln Was Shot, The.   SCL12(III-1758),   SCL7(II-1058),
    A55(81). A different analysis on this title appears in: HAmer (II-1017).
    FDR's Last Year.   SCL12(IV-2516),   A75(107).
Bissell, Richard
    High Water.   SCL12(V-3434),   SCL7(III-2046),   A54(111).
Bjarnhof, Karl
    Good Light, The.   SCL12(V-3033),   SCL7(III-1812),   A61(104).
Björnson, Björnstjerne
    Arne.   MP12(I-310),   MPCE(I-112),   MP8(I-239),   MP6(I-160),
    MPEur(37),   MP1(I-42),   MWL1(42).
    Beyond Human Power, II.   MP12(I-523),   MPCE(I-191),
    MP8(I-404),   MP6(I-272),   MPDr(77),   MPv4(34),   MP2(I-90),
    MWL2(90).
    Fisher Maiden, The.   MP12(IV-2079),   MPCE(II-750),
    MP8(III-1618),   MP6(II-1022),   MPEur(302),   MPv3(170),
    MP2(I-330),   MWL2(330).
Black, Charles L., Jr.
    Capital Punishment.   SCL12(II-1073),   A75(44). A different analysis

on this title appears in: HWor(III-1284).
Black, Robert C., III
    Younger John Winthrop, The.   HAmer(I-95).
Blackmore, R. D.
    Lorna Doone.   MP12(VI-3508),   MPCE(II-1278),   MP8(IV-2750),
    MP6(III-1733),   MPEng(450),   MP1(I-524),   MWL1(524).
Blair, Anna Lou
    Henry Barnard, School Administrator.   HAmer(II-1034).
Blair, Walter
    Mark Twain and Huck Finn.   HAmer(II-1148).
Blais, Marie-Claire
    Day Is Dark and *Three Travelers, The.*   SCL12(III-1754),
    SCL7(II-1054),   A68(63).
Blake, Robert
    Disraeli.   HEur(II-1000).
Blake, William
    *Poetry of Blake, The.   MP12(VIII-4827),   MP8(VI-3773),
    MP6(V-2416),   MPPo(234),   MP3(II-781),   MWL3(781).
    Songs of Innocence and of Experience.   RCh(II-623).
Blanchard, Paula
    Margaret Fuller: From Transcendentalism to Revolution.
    LA79(I-422).
Blank, Sheldon H.
    Jeremiah, Man and Prophet.   HAnc(I-151).
    Prophetic Faith in Israel.   HAnc(I-185).
Blankfort, Michael
    Take the A Train.   LA79(II-737).
Blanshard, Brand
    Nature of Thought, The.   Ph(II-1040).
Blaustein, Albert P. *and* Clarence C. Ferguson, Jr.
    Desegregation and the Law: The Meaning and Effect of the School
    Segregation Cases.   HAmer(III-1852).
Bleich, Alan R.
    Story of X-Rays from Roentgen to Isotopes, The.   HEur(II-1087).
Blinzler, Josef
    Trial of Jesus, The.   HAnc(II-603).
Blish, James
    Black Easter.   SF(I-233).
    Case of Conscience, A.   SF(I-303).
    Cities in Flight.   SF(I-358).
    Day After Judgment, The.   SF(I-497).
    Doctor Mirabilis.   SF(II-569).
    Seedling Stars, The.   SF(IV-1888).
Blok, Aleksandr
    Poetry of Blok, The.   MP12(VIII-4830),   MP8(VI-3776),

MP4(II-731),   MWL4(731).

Blond, Georges
   Verdun.   HEur(III-1265).

Blondel, Maurice
   Action, L'.   RCa(II-706).

Bloom, Harold
   Anxiety of Influence, The.   SCL12(I-342),   A74(10).
   Poetry and Repression.   LA77(II-627).
   William Butler Yeats.   SCL12(XII-8282),   A71(349).

Bloomfield, Lincoln P.
   Outer Space: Prospects for Man and Society.   HEur(III-1620).

Bloomfield, Morton W. *and* Leonard Newmark
   Linguistic Introduction to the History of English, A.
   HAnc(III-1289).

Bloss, Roy S.
   Pony Express: The Great Gamble.   HAmer(II-928).

Blossom, Virgil T.
   It Has Happened Here.   HWor(II-773).

Blotner, Joseph
   Faulkner: A Biography.   SCL12(IV-2503),   A75(101).

Bloy, Léon
   Woman Who Was Poor, The.   RCa(II-726).

Blum, Jerome
   End of the Old Order in Rural Europe, The.   LA79(I-188).
   Lord and Peasant in Russia from the Ninth to the Nineteenth Centuries.
   HEur(II-868).

Blum, John Morton
   Republican Roosevelt, The.   HAmer(II-1327).
   V Was for Victory.   LA77(II-880).

Blumberg, Stanley A. *and* Gwinn Owens
   Energy and Conflict: The Life and
   Times of Edward Teller.   HWor(II-686).

Blunden, Edmund Charles
   Poetry of Blunden, The.   MP12(VIII-4833),   MP8(VI-3779),
   MP4(II-733),   MWL4(733).

Bly, Robert
   *Light Around the Body, The.   SCL12(VII-4365),   SCL7(IV-2665),
   A68(176).
   *Silence in the Snowy Fields.   SCL12(X-6962),   SCL7(VI-4282),
   A63(247).
   Sleepers Joining Hands.   SCL12(X-7027),   A74(361).

Blythe, Ronald
   Akenfield.   SCL12(I-169),   A70(7).

Boas, Franz
   Mind of Primitive Man, The.   MP12(VII-3906),   MP8(V-3056),

Bourne, Edward G. *and* A. N. Bourne, *eds.*
Voyages and Explorations of Samuel De Champlain, 1604-1616, Narrated by Himself, The. HAmer(I-55).
Bourne, Frank C.
"Roman Alimentary Program and Italian Agriculture, The," in *Transactions and Proceedings of the American Philological Association.* HAnc(II-678).
Bouyer, Louis
Christian Humanism. RCa(II-1058).
Liturgical Piety. RCa(II-1014).
Seat of Wisdom, The. RCa(II-1037).
Bova, Ben
In Quest of Quasars: An Introduction to Stars and Starlike Objects. HWor(II-901).
Bowen, Catherine Drinker
Francis Bacon. SCL12(IV-2760), SCL7(III-1648), A64(99).
Lion and the Throne, The. SCL12(VII-4395), SCL7(IV-2692), A58(150), BMA(344).
Bowen, Elizabeth
*Death of the Heart, The. MP12(III-1381), MPCE(I-509), MP8(II-1066), MP6(II-699), MPEng(142), MPv4(110), MP2(I-228), MWL2(228).
Eva Trout. SCL12(IV-2340), SCL7(II-1392), A69(119).
*Heat of the Day, The. MP12(V-2523), MPCE(II-923), MP8(III-1964), MP6(III-1246), MPEng(289), MPv4(213), MP2(I-420), MWL2(420).
*House in Paris, The. MP12(V-2714), MPCE(II-988), MP8(III-2118), MP6(III-1350), MPEng(318), MPv4(231), MP2(I-463), MWL2(463).
Little Girls, The. SCL12(VII-4408), SCL7(IV-2705), A64(160).
Time in Rome, A. SCL12(XI-7647), SCL7(VII-4668), A61(258).
World of Love, A. SCL12(XII-8414), SCL7(VII-5148), A55(296).
Bowers, Claude G.
Jefferson and Hamilton: The Struggle for Democracy in America. MP12(V-2993), MP8(IV-2330), MP4(I-462), MWL4(462).
Bowles, Jane
Collected Works of Jane Bowles, The. SCL12(III-1431), SCL7(II-841), A67(41).
Bowles, Paul
Collected Stories, 1939-1976. LA80(I-151).
Spider's House, The. SCL12(XI-7177), SCL7(VI-4408), A55(243).
Time of Friendship, The. SCL12(XI-7649), SCL7(VII-4670), A68(331).
Bowne, Borden Parker
Personalism. RCh(II-851).

Bowra, C. M.
   Tradition and Design in the Iliad.   HAnc(I-112).
Boyd, James
   Drums.   MP12(III-1656),   MP8(II-1288),   MP6(II-831),
   MPAm(157),   MP1(I-228),   MWL1(228).
   Marching On.   MP12(VII-3714),   MPCE(III-1356),   MP8(IV-2912),
   MP6(IV-1840),   MPAm(390),   MP1(I-566),   MWL1(566).
Boyd, John
   Last Starship from Earth, The.   SF(III-1156).
   Pollinators of Eden, The.   SF(IV-1705).
   Rakehells of Heaven, The.   SF(IV-1746).
Boyd, Julian P.
   *Anglo-American Union: Joseph Galloway's Plans to Preserve the British
   Empire, 1774-1788.*   HAmer(I-248).
Boye, Karin
   Kallocain.   SF(III-1110).
Boyer, Paul *and* Stephen Nissenbaum
   Salem Possessed.   SCL12(X-6610),   A75(276).
Boyers, Robert, *ed.*
   Legacy of the German Refugee Intellectuals, The.   HWor(I-299).
Boyle, Kay
   Nothing Ever Breaks Except the Heart.   SCL12(VIII-5428),
   SCL7(V-3320),   A67(246).
Bozell, L. Brent *and* William F. Buckley
   McCarthy and His Enemies: The Record and Its Meaning.
   HAmer(III-1820).
Brabant, Frank H.
   *Beginning of the Third Republic in France: A History of the National
   Assembly (February-September 1871), The.*   HEur(II-976).
Brace, Gerald Warner
   Winter Solstice.   SCL12(XII-8347),   SCL7(VII-5112),   A61(307).
Bracher, Karl Dietrich
   "Technique of Nationalist Socialist Seizure of Power, The," in
   Eschenburg's *The Path to Dictatorship, 1918-1933.*   HEur(III-1384).
Brackenridge, Hugh Henry
   *Modern Chivalry.   MP12(VII-4001),   MPCE(III-1479),
   MP8(V-3125),   MP6(IV-1996),   MPAm(419),   MPv4(345),
   MP2(II-693),   MWL2(693).
Brackett, Leigh
   Long Tomorrow, The.   SF(III-1242).
   Sword of Rhiannon, The.   SF(V-2201).
Bradbury, Ray
   Fahrenheit 451.   SF(II-749).
   Illustrated Man, The.   SF(II-1008).
   Martian Chronicles, The.   SF(III-1348).

MP4(II-1195), MWL4(1195).

Bridenbaugh, Carl
Myths and Realities: Societies of the Colonial South. HAmer(I-215).

Bridge, John S. C.
History of France from the Death of Louis XI, A. Different analyses on this title appear in: HEur(I-22; I-32).

Bridges, J. H.
Life and Works of Roger Bacon, The. HAnc(III-1541).

Bridgman, Percy Williams
Logic of Modern Physics, The. Ph(II-880).

Briggs, Asa
Chartist Studies. HEur(II-744).
Victorian Cities. HEur(II-738).

Brightman, Edgar Sheffield
Philosophy of Religion, A. RCh(II-1047).

Bring, Ragnar
Commentary on Galatians. RCh(II-1180).

Bringsvœrd, Tor Age
Karavane. SF(III-1114).

Brinkley, B. R. *and* Keith Porter, *eds.*
International Cell Biology, 1976-1977. HWor(I-506).

Brinkley, George A.
Volunteer Army and the Allied Intervention in South Russia, 1917-1921, The. HWor(I-154).

Brinkley, William
Don't Go Near the Water. SCL12(III-2028), SCL7(II-1215), A57(58).

Broad, Charlie Dunbar
Mind and Its Place in Nature, The. Ph(II-862).

Broch, Hermann
Death of Virgil, The. MP12(III-1385), MPCE(I-511), MP8(II-1069), MP6(II-701), MPEur(213), MP3(I-258), MWL3(258).
Sleepwalkers, The. MP12(X-6089), MPCE(IV-2095), MP8(VII-4854), MP6(V-2898), MPEur(685), MPv4(483), MP2(II-970), MWL2(970).

Brock, William R.
American Crisis: Congress and Reconstruction, 1865-1867, An. HAmer(II-1007).

Brodeur, Paul
Sick Fox, The. SCL12(X-6947), SCL7(VI-4273), A64(241).

Brodie, Fawn M.
Devil Drives, The. SCL12(III-1908), SCL7(II-1145), A68(79).
Thaddeus Stevens: Scourge of the South. SCL12(XI-7496), SCLs(315).
A different analysis on this title appears in: HAmer(II-1029).

Brodrick, James, S. J.
Origin of the Jesuits, The. Different analyses on this title appear in: RCa(II-868), HEur(I-100).
Saint Francis Xavier. RCa(II-990),
Brodsky, Joseph
Selected Poems. SCL12(X-6790), A75(284).
Brogan, Denis W.
France Under the Republic: The Development of Modern France, 1870-1939, Book IV: The Republic in Danger. HEur(II-1055).
France Under the Republic: The Development of Modern France, 1870-1939, Book VI: The Republic Saved. Different analyses on this title appear in: HEur(II-975; II-1068; III-1144).
Brombert, Victor
Novels of Flaubert: A Study of Themes and Techniques, The. HEur(II-832).
Brome, Richard
Jovial Crew, A. MP12(VI-3075), MPCE(II-1131), MP8(IV-2400), MP6(III-1526), MPDr(400), MP3(I-531), MWL3(531).
Northern Lass, The. MP12(VII-4243), MPCE(III-1586), MP8(V-3305), MP6(IV-2126), MPDr(574), MP3(II-689), MWL3(689).
Bromfield, Louis
Green Bay Tree, The. MP12(IV-2378), MPCE(II-866), MP8(III-1849), MP6(II-1161), MPAm(237), MP1(I-331), MWL1(331).
Bromhead, C. N., R. J. Forbes, H. H. Coghlan, Herbert Maryon *and* H. J. Plenderleith
History of Technology, Vol. I: From Early Times to the Fall of the Ancient Empires, A. HAnc(I-17).
Brontë, Anne
Agnes Grey. MP12(I-73), MPCE(I-24), MP8(I-59), MP6(I-38), MPEng(7), MP3(I-16), MWL3(16).
Tenant of Wildfell Hall, The. MP12(XI-6442), MPCE(IV-2222), MP8(VIII-5130), MP6(VI-3076), MPEng(825), MP1(II-963), MWL1(963).
Brontë, Charlotte
Jane Eyre. MP12(V-2976), MPCE(II-1095), MP8(IV-2319), MP6(III-1485), MPEng(367), MP1(I-432), MWL1(432).
Professor, The. MP12(IX-5353), MPCE(III-1819), MP8(VI-4274), MP6(V-2536), MPEng(705), MPv3(429), MP2(II-864), MWL2(864).
Shirley. MP12(X-5985), MPCE(IV-2064), MP8(VII-4769), MP6(V-2855), MPEng(790), MP3(II-968), MWL3(968).
Villette. MP12(XII-6929), MPCE(IV-2425), MP8(VIII-5486), MP6(VI-3316), MPEng(924), MPv3(537), MP2(II-1108),

MWL2(1108).

Brontë, Emily
Poetry of Emily Brontë, The. MP12(IX-4932), MP8(VI-3878), MP4(II-803), MWL4(803).
Wuthering Heights. MP12(XII-7281), MPCE(IV-2555), MP8(VIII-5754), MP6(VI-3497), MPEng(976), MP1(II-1137), MWL1(1137).

Brooke, Henry
Fool of Quality, The. MP12(IV-2107), MPCE(II-755), MP8(III-1643), MP6(II-1030), MPEng(216), MPv4(164), MP2(I-333), MWL2(333).

Brooke, John *and* Lewis B. Namier
Charles Townshend. HAmer(I-229).

Brooke, Rupert
Letters of Rupert Brooke, The. SCL12(VI-4258), SCL7(IV-2608), A69(196).
Poetry of Brooke, The. MP12(VIII-4838), MP8(VI-3784), MP4(II-737), MWL4(737).

Brooke, Zachery N.
"Lay Investiture and Its Relation to the Conflict of Empire and Papacy," in *Proceedings of the British Academy.* HAnc(III-1320).

Brooks, Cleanth
William Faulkner: The Yoknapatawpha Country. SCL12(XII-8288), SCL7(VII-5070), A64(299). A different analysis on this title appears in: HAmer(III-1573).
William Faulkner: Toward Yoknapatawpha and Beyond. LA79(II-874).

Brooks, Gwendolyn
Selected Poems: 1944-1970. SCL12(X-6822), SCLs(266).

Brooks, John
Go-Go Years, The. SCL12(V-2998), A74(157).
Telephone: The First Hundred Years. HWor(II-616).

Brooks, Phillips
Lectures on Preaching. RCh(II-778).

Brooks, Van Wyck
America's Coming-of-Age. MP12(I-179), MP8(I-140), MP4(I-38), MWL4(38).
Days of the Phoenix. SCL12(III-1786), SCL7(II-1076), A58(66).
Dream of Arcadia, The. SCL12(III-2059), SCL7(II-1233), A59(62).
World of Washington Irving, The. HAmer(I-483).

Brook-Shepherd, Gordon
Anschluss: The Rape of Austria. HEur(III-1426).
Prelude to Infamy: The Story of Chancellor Dollfuss of Austria. HEur(III-1397).
Uncle of Europe. LA77(II-861).

Broome, J. H.

Christian Theology in Outline. RCh(II-840).
Brown, William, Herman Kahn| *and* Leon Martel
 Next 200 Years: A Scenario for America and the World, The. Different
 analyses on this title appear in: LA77(II-559), HWor(II-547).
Browne, Robert
 Treatise of Reformation Without Tarrying for Any. RCh(I-400).
Browne, Sir Thomas
 Hydriotaphia: Urn-Burial. MP12(V-2791), MP8(III-2171),
 MP4(I-432), MWL4(432).
 Religio medici. RCh(I-450).
Browning, Elizabeth Barrett
 Sonnets from the Portuguese. MP12(XI-6168), MP8(VII-4916),
 MP6(V-2939), MPPo(348), MP3(II-1007), MWL3(1007).
Browning, Robert
 Blot in the 'Scutcheon, A. MP12(I-578), MPCE(I-213),
 MP8(I-446), MP6(I-299), MPDr(86), MPv3(62), MP2(I-102),
 MWL2(102).
 Dramatic Monologues and Lyrics of Browning. MP12(III-1641),
 MP8(II-1274), MP4(I-247), MWL4(247).
 Dramatis Personae. MP12(III-1644), MP8(II-1277), MP4(I-250),
 MWL4(250).
 Men and Women. MP12(VII-3846), MP8(V-3012), MP4(I-603),
 MWL4(603).
 Ring and the Book, The. MP12(X-5603), MPCE(III-1919),
 MP8(VII-4463), MP6(V-2658), MPPo(320), MP1(II-826),
 MWL1(826).
Brownmiller, Susan
 Against Our Will. SCL12(I-125), A76(8).
Brownson, Orestes Augustus
 American Republic, The. RCa(II-667).
Brubacher, John S. *and* Willis Rudy
 *Higher Education in Transition: A History of American Colleges and
 Universities, 1936-1968.* HAmer(I-315).
Bruce-Boswell, Alexander
 "Poland and Lithuania in the Fourteenth and Fifteenth Centuries," in *Vol.
 VIII of The Cambridge Medieval History.* HAnc(III-1652).
Bruckberger, R. L.
 History of Jesus Christ, The. HAnc(I-570).
 Image of America. SCL12(VI-3618), SCL7(III-2162), A60(99).
Brunner, Emil
 Divine Imperative, The. RCh(II-986).
 Dogmatics. RCh(II-1076).
 Revelation and Reason. Ph(II-1058).
Brunner, John
 Jagged Orbit, The. SF(III-1094).

Force and Matter. Ph(II-633).

Büchner, Georg

Woyzeck. MP12(XII-7275), MPCE(IV-2553), MP8(VIII-5749), MP6(VI-3493), MPDr(952), MPv4(603), MP2(II-1163), MWL2(1163).

Buck, Pearl S.

*Dragon Seed. MP12(III-1638), MPCE(I-604), MP8(II-1271), MP6(II-824), MPAm(154), MP1(I-226), MWL1(226).

*Good Earth, The. MP12(IV-2319), MPCE (II-839), MP8(III-1806), MP6(II-1133), MPAm(217), MP1(I-313), MWL1(313).

Imperial Woman. SCL12(VI-3635), SCL7(III-2169), A57(130).

My Several Worlds. SCL12(VIII-5194), SCL7(V-3160), A54(186).

Buck, Solon J.

Granger Movement: A Study of Agricultural Organization and Its Political, Economic, and Social Manifestations, 1870-1880, The. HAmer(II-1045).

Buckle, George E.

Life of Benjamin Disraeli, Earl of Beaconsfield, Vol. V: 1868-1876, The. HEur(II-1001).

Buckle, Richard

Nijinsky. SCL12(VIII-5351), A73(275).

Buckley, William F. *and* L. Brent Bozell

McCarthy and His Enemies: The Record and Its Meaning. HAmer(III-1820).

Buckman, Peter

Lafayette: A Biography. LA78(II-495).

Buder, Stanley

Pullman: An Experiment in Industrial Order and Community Planning, 1880-1930. HAmer(II-1239).

Budgell, Eustace, Joseph Addison *and* Sir Richard Steele

*Sir Roger de Coverley Papers, The. MP12(X-6067), MP8(VII-4840), MP6(V-2887), MPNf(288), MP3(II-988), MWL3(988).

Budrys, Algis

Michaelmas. SF(III-1387).

Rogue Moon. SF(IV-1821).

Who? SF(V-2474).

Buechner, Frederick

Entrance to Porlock, The. SCL12(IV-2286), A72(124).

Bueler, William M.

U.S. China Policy and the Problem of Taiwan. HWor(II-712).

Bulatovic, Miodrag

Red Cock Flies to Heaven, The. SCL12(IX-6291), SCL7(VI-3852), A63(208).

Buley, R. Carlyle
  Old Northwest: Pioneer Period, 1815-1840, The.   HAmer(I-530).
Bulgakov, Michail
  Heart of a Dog, The.   SF(II-956).
Bulgakov, Sergius
  Wisdom of God, The.   RCh(II-1035).
Bullen, Frank T.
  Cruise of the Cachalot, The.   MP12(III-1232),   MPCE(I-452),
  MP8(II-955),   MP6(II-632),   MPEng(131),   MP1(I-178),
  MWL1(178).
Bullinger, Johann Heinrich
  Decades, The.   RCh(I-381).
Bullock, Alan L. C.
  Hitler: A Study in Tyranny.   SCL12(V-3462),   SCL7(III-2064),
  A65(130). Different analyses on this title appear in: HEur(III-1392;
  III-1442).
Bultmann, Rudolf
  Jesus and the Word.   HAnc(II-591).
  Theology of the New Testament.   RCh(II-1097).
Bulwer-Lytton, Edward George Earle
  Coming Race, The.   SF(I-418).
  Eugene Aram.   MP12(IV-1879),   MPCE(II-665),   MP8(III-1476),
  MP6(II-933),   MPEng(187),   MPv3(148),   MP2(I-297),   MWL2(297).
  Last Days of Pompeii, The.   MP12(VI-3249),   MPCE(II-1203),
  MP8(IV-2533),   MP6(III-1617),   MPEng(420),   MP1(I-490),
  MWL1(490).
  Last of the Barons, The.   MP12(VI-3257),   MPCE(II-1207),
  MP8(IV-2538),   MP6(III-1622),   MPEng(425),   MP1(I-492),
  MWL1(492).
Bulychev, Kirill
  Short Fiction of Kirill Bulychev, The.   SF(IV-2019).
Bunin, Ivan Alexeyevich
  *Village, The.   MP12(XII-6922),   MPCE(IV-2422),
  MP8(VIII-5481),   MP6(VI-3312),   MPEur(791),   MPv3(534),
  MP2(II-1105),   MWL2(1105).
Bunker, Gerald E.
  Peace Conspiracy: Wang Ching-wei and the China War, 1937-1941, The.
  HWor(I-365).
Bunting, Basil
  Collected Poems.   LA79(I-119).
Bunyan, John
  Grace Abounding to the Chief of Sinners.   RCh(I-506).
  *Life and Death of Mr. Badman, The.   MP12(VI-3392),
  MP8(IV-2656),   MP6(III-1675),   MPEng(431),   MP3(II-575),
  MWL3(575).

Pilgrim's Progress, The. MP12(VIII-4705), MPCE(III-1747), MP8(VI-3672), MP6(V-2369), MPEng(678), MP1(II-748), MWL1(748). A different analysis on this title appears in: RCh(I-530).

Buranelli, Vincent
Louis XIV. HEur(I-348).
Trial of Peter Zenger, The. HAmer(I-190).

Burchard, John *and* Albert Bush-Brown
Architecture of America: A Social and Cultural History, The. HAmer(II-1233).

Burchett, Wilfred
Grasshoppers and Elephants: Why Vietnam Fell. HWor(III-1164).

Burckhardt, Carl J.
Richelieu: His Rise to Power. HEur(I-282).

Burckhardt, Jacob
Age of Constantine the Great, The. HAnc(II-848).

Burdick, Eugene
Ninth Wave, The. SCL12(VIII-5376), SCL7(V-3279), A57(191).

Burgess, Anthony
Beard's Roman Women. LA77(I-81).
Clockwork Orange, A. SF(I-396).
Enderby. SCL12(IV-2255), SCL7(II-1356), A69(115).
Ernest Hemingway and His World. LA79(I-196).
MF. SCL12(VII-4963), A72(223).
Napoleon Symphony. LA77(II-525).
1985. LA79(II-484).
Nothing Like the Sun. SCL12(VIII-5431), SCL7(V-3323), A65(215).
Wanting Seed, The. SF(V-2402).

Burke, Edmund
Vindication of Natural Society, A. MP12(XII-6934), MP8(VIII-5489), MP6(VI-3319), MPNf(315), MP3(II-1099), MWL3(1099).

Burkitt, F. C.
Religion of the Manichees, The. HAnc(II-809).

Burl, Aubrey
Prehistoric Avebury. LA80(II-688).

Burlingame, Roger
March of the Iron Men: A Social History of Union Through Invention. HAmer(II-841).

Burner, David
Herbert Hoover: A Public Life. LA80(I-400).

Burnet, John
Early Greek Philosophy. HAnc(I-272).

Burnett, Edmund C.
Continental Congress, The. HAmer(I-258).

Burney, Fanny
> *Cecilia.* MP12(II-861), MPCE(I-318), MP8(I-664), MP6(I-438), MPEng(92), MP3(I-163), MWL3(163).
> *Diary and Letters of Mme. D'Arblay, The.* MP12(III-1499), MP8(II-1163), MP4(I-226), MWL4(226).
> *Evelina.* MP12(IV-1913), MPCE(II-682), MP8(III-1500), MP6(II-953), MPEng(198), MPv3(153), MP2(I-306), MWL2(306).

Burns, James MacGregor
> *Roosevelt: The Lion and the Fox.* SCL12(X-6489), SCL7(VI-3993), A57(224). A different analysis on this title appears in: HAmer(III-1671).
> *Roosevelt: The Soldier of Freedom.* SCL12(X-6492), A71(276).

Burns, Robert
> *Poems, Chiefly in the Scottish Dialect.* MP12(VIII-4783), MP8(VI-3729), MP6(V-2403), MPPo(222), MP3(II-769), MWL3(769).

Burr, Robert N.
> *Our Troubled Hemisphere: Perspectives on United States-Latin American Relations.* HWor(I-266).

Burrell, Michael *and* Abbas Kelidar
> *Lebanon: The Collapse of a State.* HWor(III-1241).

Burroughs, Betty
> *Vasari's Lives of the Artists.* HAnc(III-1589).

Burroughs, Edgar Rice
> *At the Earth's Core.* SF(I-93).
> *Carson of Venus.* SF(I-298).
> *Land That Time Forgot, The.* SF(III-1130).
> *Pellucidar.* SF(IV-1665).
> *Princess of Mars, A.* SF(IV-1720).
> *Tarzan of the Apes.* SF(V-2229).

Burroughs, William S.
> *Nova Express.* SF(IV-1566).

Burrows, Millar
> *Dead Sea Scrolls, The.* HWor(II-601).

Burton, Robert
> *Anatomy of Melancholy, The.* MP12(I-200), MP8(I-160), MP6(I-95), MPNf(11), MP3(I-39), MWL3(39).

Bury, J. B.
> *History of the Papacy in the Nineteenth Century.* HEur(II-906).
> *Invasion of Europe by the Barbarians, The.* HAnc(II-961).

Bush, Clive
> *Dream of Reason: American Consciousness and Cultural Achievement from Independence to the Civil War, The.* LA79(I-165).

Bushman, Richard L.
> *From Puritan to Yankee: Character and Social Order in Connecticut,*

MP2(I-403),   MWL2(403).
Messer Marco Polo.   MP12(VII-3863),   MPCE(III-1417),
MP8(V-3026),   MP6(IV-1921),   MPEng(502),   MP1(II-584),
MWL1(584).

Byron, George Gordon, Lord
*Cain.   MP12(II-734),   MPCE(I-269),   MP8(I-570),   MP6(I-378),
MPDr(121),   MPv3(66),   MP2(I-127),   MWL2(127).
*Childe Harold's Pilgrimage.   MP12(II-921),   MP8(I-709),
MP4(I-127),   MWL4(127).
*Don Juan.   MP12(III-1590),   MPCE(I-580),   MP8(II-1237),
MP6(II-798),   MPPo(66),   MP1(I-217),   MWL1(217).
Lyric Poetry of Byron, The.   MP12(VI-3562),   MP8(IV-2793),
MP4(I-571),   MWL4(571).
*Manfred.   MP12(VII-3690),   MPCE(III-1346),   MP8(IV-2893),
MP6(IV-1827),   MPPo(179),   MPv3(312),   MP2(II-621),
MWL2(621).

Byron, William
Cervantes: A Biography.   LA79(I-84).

Cabell, James Branch
*Cream of the Jest, The.   MP12(II-1194),   MPCE(I-438),
MP8(II-927),   MP6(II-611),   MPAm(110),   MP1(I-168),
MWL1(168).
Jurgen.   MP12(VI-3105),   MPCE(II-1147),   MP8(IV-2418),
MP6(III-1541),   MPAm(317),   MP1(I-464),   MWL1(464).
Rivet in Grandfather's Neck, The.   MP12(X-5632),   MPCE(III-1931),
MP8(VII-4484),   MP6(V-2671),   MPAm(541),   MP3(II-898),
MWL3(898).

Cable, George W.
Grandissimes, The.   MP12(IV-2338),   MPCE(II-849),
MP8(III-1819),   MP6(II-1141),   MPAm(220),   MP1(I-320),
MWL1(320).

Caesar (Gaius Julius Caesar)
Commentaries.   MP12(II-1040),   MP8(II-808),   MP6(I-530),
MPNf(53),   MP3(I-204),   MWL3(204).

Caidin, Martin
Red Star in Space.   HWor(II-780).

Cain, James M.
Postman Always Rings Twice, The.   MP12(IX-5270),
MP8(VI-4203),   MP4(II-1021),   MWL4(1021).

Cajetan, Saint
Commentary on the Summa theologica *of Saint Thomas.*   RCa(I-516).

Cajori, Florian
History of Mathematical Notations, A.   HAnc(III-1284).
History of Mathematics, A.   HAnc(III-1285).

Calderón de la Barca, Pedro
   Devotion of the Cross, The. MP12(III-1471), MPCE(I-537), MP8(II-1139), MP6(II-736), MPDr(208), MP3(I-270), MWL3(270).
   It Is Better than It Was. MP12(V-2942), MPCE(II-1081), MP8(IV-2294), MP6(III-1464), MPDr(389), MP3(I-517), MWL3(517).
   It Is Worse than It Was. MP12(V-2945), MPCE(II-1082), MP8(IV-2296), MP6(III-1466), MPDr(391), MP3(I-519), MWL3(519).
   Life Is a Dream. MP12(VI-3398), MPCE(II-1241), MP8(IV-2661), MP6(III-1679), MPDr(441), MPv3(292), MP2(II-580), MWL2(580).
   Mayor of Zalamea, The. MP12(VII-3788), MPCE(III-1384), MP8(V-2972), MP6(IV-1882), MPDr(503), MPv4(317), MP2(II-645), MWL2(645).
   Mock Astrologer, The. MP12(VII-3998), MPCE(III-1477), MP8(V-3123), MP6(IV-1994), MPDr(551), MP3(II-669), MWL3(669).
Caldwell, Erskine
   Tobacco Road. MP12(XI-6578), MPCE(IV-2278), MP8(VIII-5231), MP6(VI-3144), MPAm(653), MP1(II-996), MWL1(996).
Calisher, Hortense
   Collected Stories of Hortense Calisher, The. SCL12(III-1413), A76(54).
   On Keeping Women. LA78(II-613).
   Tale for the Mirror. SCL12(XI-7386), SCL7(VII-4511), A63(262).
Callado, Antonio
   Quarup. SCL12(IX-6156), SCLs(238).
Callahan, Daniel
   Abortion: Law, Choice and Morality. HWor(III-1158).
Callahan, North
   Henry Knox. SCL12(V-3371), SCLs(128).
Calvin, John
   Institutes of the Christian Religion, The. RCh(I-358).
   Necessity of Reforming the Church, The. RCh(I-371).
Calvino, Italo
   Cosmicomics. SF(I-438).
   t zero. SF(V-2223).
Cameron, E. H.
   Samuel Slater, Father of American Manufactures. HAmer(I-365).
Camoëns, Luis Vaz de
   Lusiads, The. MP12(VI-3557), MPCE(II-1299), MP8(IV-2790), MP6(III-1761), MPPo(167), MPv3(306), MP2(II-608),

MWL2(608).

Campbell, Alexander
Christian System, The. RCh(II-672).

Campbell, Anna M.
Black Death and Men of Learning, The. HAnc(III-1629).

Campbell, G. A. *and* T. F. West
DDT: And Newer Persistent Insecticides. HWor(I-427).

Campbell, John C.
Tito's Separate Road: America and Yugoslavia in World Politics.
HWor(II-644).

Campbell, John McLeod
Nature of the Atonement, The. RCh(II-731).

Campbell, John W., Jr.
Mightiest Machine, The. SF(III-1396).
Moon Is Hell, The. SF(III-1444).
Short Fiction of John W. Campbell, Jr., The. SF(IV-2003).

Campbell, Thomas L.
Dionysius the Pseudo-Areopagite: The Ecclesiastical Hierarchy.
HAnc(II-1014).

Campenhausen, Hans von
Fathers of the Greek Church, The.   Different analyses on this title
appear in: HAnc(II-775; II-803; II-896).

Campion, Thomas
*"Obseruations in the Art of English Poesie," in Elizabethan and Jacobean
Quartos.* HAnc(III-1350).
Poetry of Campion, The. MP12(VIII-4844),   MP8(VI-3790),
MP4(II-740),   MWL4(740).

Camps, Miriam
Britain and the European Community, 1955-1963.   HWor(III-1149).

Camus, Albert
Exile and the Kingdom. MP12(IV-1936),   MP8(III-1515),
MP4(I-311),   MWL4(311),   SCL12(IV-2356),   SCL7(II-1404),
A59(78),   BMA(172).
*Fall, The. MP12(IV-1965),   MP8(III-1537),   MP4(I-316),
MWL4(316). A different analysis on this title appears in:
SCL12(IV-2418),   SCL7(II-1440),   A58(83),   BMA(180).
Lyrical and Critical Essays. SCL12(VII-4616),   SCL7(IV-2813),
A69(215).
*Myth of Sisyphus, The. MP12(VII-4128),   MP8(V-3216),
MP4(I-624),   MWL4(624).
Notebooks: 1935-1942. SCL12(VIII-5418),   SCL7(V-3312),
A64(194).
Notebooks: 1942-1951. SCL12(VIII-5421),   SCL7(V-3314),
A66(203).
*Plague, The. MP12(VIII-4734),   MPCE(III-1764),

MP8(VI-3692), MP6(V-2383), MPEur(587), MPv4(419), MP2(II-836), MWL2(836).
Rebel, The. SCL12(IX-6272), SCL7(VI-3843), A54(228). A different analysis on this title appears in: Ph(II-1127).
Resistance, Rebellion, and Death. SCL12(IX-6375), SCL7(VI-3901), A62(243).
Stranger, The. MP12(XI-6301), MP8(VII-5018), MP4(II-1187), MWL4(1187).

Camus, Jean Pierre
Spirit of Saint Francis of Sales, The. RCa(II-597).

Canfield, Leon H.
Early Persecutions of the Christians, The. HAnc(II-694).

Cantimori, Delio
"Italy in 1848" in François Fejto's *The Opening Of an Era, 1848.* HEur(II-779).

Cantor, Milton
Divided Left: American Radicalism, 1900-1975, The. LA79(I-157).

Čapek, Karel
Absolute at Large, The. SF(I-6).
R.U.R. MP12(X-5736), MPCE(IV-1979), MP8(VII-4563), MP6(V-2729), MPDr(720), MPv4(464), MP2(II-927), MWL2(927). A different analysis on this title appears in: SF(IV-1837).
War with the Newts. SF(V-2424).

Capers, Gerald M.
Stephen A. Douglas. SCL12(XI-7216), SCL7(VI-4434), A60(253).

Capes, William W.
English Church in the Fourteenth and Fifteenth Centuries, The. HAnc(III-1632).

Capote, Truman
Breakfast at Tiffany's. SCL12(II-898), SCLs(49).
In Cold Blood. SCL12(VI-3645), SCL7(III-2175), A67(158).

Cardozo, Nancy
Lucky Eyes and a High Heart: The Biography of Maud Gonne. LA79(I-409).

Carducci, Giosuè
Poetry of Carducci, The. MP12(VIII-4847), MP8(VI-3793), MP6(V-2421), MPPo(240), MP3(II-787), MWL3(787).

Carell, Paul
Hitler Moves East, 1941-1943. HEur(III-1474).

Carew, Thomas
Poetry of Carew, The. MP12(VIII-4850), MP8(VI-3796), MP4(II-743), MWL4(743).

Carleton, William
Emigrants of Ahadarra, The. MP12(III-1752), MPCE(I-640), MP8(II-1364), MP6(II-876), MPEng(177), MP3(I-328), MWL3(328).

Carlson, Elof Axel
  Gene: A Critical History, The.   HWor(I-10).
Carlson, Oliver
  Man Who Made News, James Gordon Bennett, The.   HAmer(II-715).
Carlyle, R. W.
  History of Medieval Political Theory in the West, A.   HAnc(II-1089).
Carlyle, Thomas
  *French Revolution, The.   MP12(IV-2169),   MP8(III-1690),
  MP6(II-1060),   MPNf(128),   MP3(I-404),   MWL3(404).
  *History of Frederick II of Prussia.   MP12(V-2634),   MP8(III-2048),
  MP4(I-415),   MWL4(415).
  *On Heroes, Hero-Worship and the Heroic in History.
  MP12(VIII-4368),   MP8(V-3399),   MP4(I-646),   MWL4(646).
  *Sartor Resartus.   MP12(X-5799),   MP8(VII-4617),   MP6(V-2761),
  MPNf(271),   MP3(II-925),   MWL3(925).
Carnap, Rudolf
  Introduction to Semantics.   Ph(II-1075).
  Philosophy and Logical Syntax.   Ph(II-997).
Caro, Robert A.
  Power Broker: Robert Moses and the Fall of New York, The.
  SCL12(IX-5996),   A75(243).
Carpenter, Humphrey
  Tolkien: A Biography.   LA78(II-851).
Carpentier, Alejo
  Kingdom of This World, The.   SCL12(VI-4033),   SCL7(IV-2445),
  A58(130).
Carr, Edward Hallett
  *History of Soviet Russia, Vol. I-III: The Bolshevik Revolution, 1917-1923,
  A.*   HWor(I-322).
Carr, Raymond
  Spain, 1808-1939.   Different analyses on this title appear in:
  HEur(I-444; II-582; II-595; II-635; II-727; II-946; II-1005; III-1260).
Carr, Virginia Spencer
  Lonely Hunter, The.   SCL12(VII-4461),   A76(185).
Carroll, E. Malcolm
  Origins of the Whig Party.   HAmer(II-692).
Carroll, James
  Mortal Friends.   LA79(II-462).
Carroll, Lewis
  *Alice's Adventures in Wonderland.   MP12(I-107),   MPCE(I-36),
  MP8(I-85),   MP6(I-53),   MPEng(10),   MP1(I-21),   MWL1(21).
  Letters of Lewis Carroll, Vol. One: ca. 1837-1885, The.   LA80(II-474).
  *Through the Looking Glass.   MP12(XI-6526),   MPCE(IV-2257),
  MP8(VIII-5191),   MP6(VI-3115),   MPEng(841),   MPv4(512),
  MP2(II-1023),   MWL2(1023). A different analysis on this title appears

in: SF(V-2278).
Carsac, Francis
Ce Monde est nôtre. SF(III-1435).
Carson, Rachel
Edge of the Sea, The. SCL12(III-2130), SCL7(II-1279), A55(89), BMA(145).
Silent Spring. SCL12(X-6968), SCL7(VI-4288), A63(249). A different analysis on this title appears in: HWor(I-428).
Carter, Charles Howard
Secret Diplomacy of the Habsburgs, 1598-1625, The. HEur(I-222).
Carter, Dan T.
Scottsboro. SCL12(X-6663), A70(269). A different analysis on this title appears in: HAmer(1590).
Carter, Jesse Benedict
Religion of Numa and Other Essays on the Religion of Ancient Rome, The. HAnc(I-202).
Carter, Jimmy
Why Not the Best?. LA77(II-906).
Carter, John Stewart
Full Fathom Five. SCL12(IV-2813), SCL7(III-1676), A66(109).
Carter III, Samuel
Cyrus Field: Man of Two Worlds. HEur(II-835).
Caruso, John Anthony
Great Lakes Frontier: An Epic of the Old Northwest, The. HAmer(I-529).
Carver, General Michael
Alamein, El. HEur(III-1468).
Carver, Raymond
Will You Please Be Quiet, Please? LA77(II-914).
Cary, Joyce
*African Witch, The. SCL12(I-86), SCL7(I-68), A63(1).
*American Visitor, An. SCL12(I-269), SCL7(I-154), A62(19).
Captive and the Free, The. SCL12(II-1085), SCL7(I-626), A60(33).
*Charley Is My Darling. SCL12(II-1198), SCL7(I-690), A61(38).
*Herself Surprised. MP12(V-2603), MPCE(II-959), MP8(III-2021), MP6(III-1288), MPEng(298), MP3(I-459), MWL3(459).
*Horse's Mouth, The. MP12(V-2699), MPCE(II-981), MP8(III-2106), MP6(III-1341), MPEng(312), MPv4(227), MP2(I-456), MWL2(456).
*Not Honour More. SCL12(VIII-5406), SCL7(V-3305), A55(187).
To Be a Pilgrim. MP12(XI-6570), MPCE(IV-2274), MP8(VIII-5225), MP6(VI-3140), MPEng(847), MP3(II-1072),

MWL3(1072).

Casanova de Seingalt, Giovanni Jacopo
    Memoirs.   MP12(VII-3823),   MP8(V-2994),   MP6(IV-1897),
    MPNf(203),   MP3(II-646),   MWL3(646).

Case, Josephine Young
    At Midnight on the 31st of March.   SF(I-89).

Casey, John
    Testimony and Demeanor.   LA80(II-811).

Casey, Michael
    Obscenities.   SCL12(VIII-5470),   A73(283).

Caspar, Max
    Kepler, 1571-1630.   HEur(I-238).

Cassian, John
    Institutes of the Monastic Life, The.   RCa(I-193).

Cassill, R. V.
    Father, The.   SCL12(IV-2485),   SCL7(III-1481),   A66(106).
    Happy Marriage, The.   SCL12(V-3245),   SCL7(III-1921),   A67(133).
    President, The.   SCL12(IX-6034),   SCL7(V-3677),   A65(226).

Cassirer, Ernst
    Philosophy of Symbolic Forms, The.   Ph(II-850).

Cassola, Carlo
    Fausto and Anna.   SCL12(IV-2509),   SCL7(III-1495),   A61(75).

Castaneda, Carlos
    Journey to Ixtlan.   SCL12(VI-3934),   A73(205).
    Separate Reality, A.   SCL12(X-6851),   A72(294).

Castelot, André
    King of Rome, The.   SCL12(VI-4022),   SCL7(IV-2434),   A61(143),
    BMA(287).
    Queen of France.   SCL12(IX-6174),   SCL7(VI-3773),   A58(204).

Castiglione, Baldassare
    Book of the Courtier, The.   MP12(I-596),   MP8(I-461),
    MP4(I-77),   MWL4(77).

Castillo, Michel del
    Child of Our Time.   SCL12(II-1222),   SCL7(I-709),   A59(31).

Cate, James Lea *and* Wesley Frank Craven, *eds.*
    Army Air Forces in World War II, Vol. V: The Pacific: Matterhorn to
    Nagasaki, June 1944 to August 1945, The.   HWor(I-489).

Cater, Douglass *and* Richard Adler, *eds.*
    Television as a Cultural Force.   HWor(II-673).

Cather, Willa
    Death Comes for the Archbishop.   MP12(III-1349),   MPCE(I-495),
    MP8(II-1043),   MP6(II-685),   MPAm(133),   MP1(I-199),
    MWL1(199).
    Lost Lady, A.   MP12(VI-3521),   MPCE(II-1285),   MP8(IV-2759),
    MP6(III-1740),   MPAm(359),   MP1(I-529),   MWL1(529).

My Ántonia. MP12(VII-4103), MPCE(III-1526), MP8(V-3198), MP6(IV-2046), MPAm(430), MP1(II-630), MWL1(630).
O Pioneers! MP12(VII-4265), MPCE(III-1591), MP8(V-3324), MP6(IV-2134), MPAm(447), MP1(II-663), MWL1(663).
Professor's House, The. MP12(IX-5357), MPCE(III-1821), MP8(VI-4277), MP6(V-2539), MPAm(509), MPv3(431), MP2(II-867), MWL2(867).
Shadows on the Rock. MP12(X-5948), MPCE(IV-2053), MP8(VII-4738), MP6(V-2841), MPAm(572), MP1(II-884), MWL1(884).
Song of the Lark, The. MP12(XI-6159), MPCE(IV-2122), MP8(VII-4910), MP6(V-2934), MPAm(586), MPv3(497), MP2(II-981), MWL2(981).
Catherine of Genoa, Saint
   Dialogue Between the Soul and the Body, The. RCa(I-530).
Catherine of Siena, Saint
   Dialogue of Saint Catherine of Siena, The. Different analyses on this title appear in: RCh(I-280), RCa(I-473).
Catton, Bruce
   Coming Fury, The. SCL12(III-1470), SCL7(II-858), A62(78).
   Grant Moves South. SCL12(V-3083), SCL7(III-1849), A61(109), BMA(208).
   Never Call Retreat. SCL12(VIII-5247), SCL7(V-3197), A66(189). A different analysis on this title appears in: HAmer(II-1013).
   This Hallowed Ground. SCL12(XI-7558), SCL7(VII-4607), A57(269), BMA(544).
   War Lords of Washington, The. HAmer(III-1684).
Catullus (Gaius Valerius Catullus)
   Carmina. MP12(II-806), MP8(I-625), MP6(I-413), MPPo(41), MP3(I-156), MWL3(156).
Cau, Jean
   Mercy of God, The. SCL12(VII-4942), SCL7(V-3000), A64(175).
Caudill, Harry M.
   Night Comes to the Cumberlands. SCL12(VIII-5313), SCL7(V-3229), A64(188).
   Watches of the Night, The. LA77(II-896).
Caughey, John W.
   Gold Is the Cornerstone. HAmer(II-846).
Caute, David
   Great Fear: The Anti-Communist Purge Under Truman and Eisenhower, The. LA79(I-255).
Cavafy, Constantine P.
   Complete Poems of Cavafy, The. SCL12(III-1499), SCL7(II-874), A62(84).
   Passions and Ancient Days. SCL12(IX-5760), A72(250).

Shadow of Night, The. MP12(X-5945), MP8(VII-4735), MP4(II-1110), MWL4(1110).
Chapman, George *with* Ben Jonson *and* John Marston
  Eastward Ho! MP12(III-1693), MPCE(I-622), MP8(II-1316), MP6(II-850), MPDr(234), MP3(I-317), MWL3(317).
Chapman, Guy
  Dreyfus Case: A Reassessment, The. HEur(II-1077).
  Third Republic of France: The First Phase, 1871-1894, The. Different analyses on this title appear in: HEur(II-1054; II-1067).
Chapman, Maybelle K.
  Great Britain and the Bagdad Railway, 1888-1914. HEur(II-1136).
Chappell, Fred
  Bloodfire. LA79(I-60).
  Dagon. SCL12(III-1680), SCL7(II-986), A69(82).
  Gaudy Place, The. SCL12(V-2868), A74(144).
  Inkling, The. SCL12(VI-3723), SCL7(IV-2233), A66(132).
  Wind Mountain. LA80(II-877).
Charnock, Stephen
  Discourses Upon the Existence and Attributes of God. RCh(I-539).
Charques, Richard
  Twilight of Imperial Russia, The. HWor(I-105).
Charrière, Henri
  Papillon. SCL12(IX-5720), A71(245).
Chase, Mary Ellen
  Edge of Darkness, The. SCL12(III-2119), SCL7(II-1268), A58(80).
  Lovely Ambition, The. SCL12(VII-4591), SCL7(IV-2800), A61(168).
Chase, Richard, *ed.*
  Melville: A Collection of Critical Essays. HAmer(II-851).
Chateaubriand, François René de
  Atala. MP12(I-349), MPCE(I-129), MP8(I-267), MP6(I-182), MPEur(51), MPv4(29), MP2(I-59), MWL2(59).
Chatelain, Verne E.
  Defenses of Spanish Florida, 1565-1763, The. HAmer(I-37).
Chatterton, Thomas
  Poetry of Chatterton, The. MP12(VIII-4857), MP8(VI-3803), MP4(II-748), MWL4(748).
Chaucer, Geoffrey
  *Canterbury Tales, The (Selections). MP12(II-769), MPCE(I-281), MP8(I-598), MP6(I-393), MPPo(33), MPv4(62), MP2(I-129), MWL2(129).
  Legend of Good Women, The. MP12(VI-3311), MP8(IV-2580), MP6(III-1649), MPPo(164), MP3(I-557), MWL3(557).
  Parliament of Fowls, The. MP12(VIII-4493), MP8(V-3501), MP6(IV-2248), MPPo(207), MP3(II-716), MWL3(716).
  *Troilus and Criseyde. MP12(XI-6725), MPCE(IV-2342),

MP8(VIII-5337), MP6(VI-3220), MPPo(367), MP1(II-1030), MWL1(1030).

Chauncy, Charles
Seasonable Thoughts on the State of Religion in New England. RCh(II-586).

Cheever, John
Brigadier and the Golf Widow, The. SCL12(II-929), SCL7(I-528), A65(16).
Bullet Park. SCL12(II-964), A70(63).
Falconer. LA78(I-309).
Housebreaker of Shady Hill, The. SCL12(V-3557), SCL7(III-2134), A59(122).
Short Stories of John Cheever, The. MP12(X-6011), MP8(VII-4793), MP4(II-1139), MWL4(1139).
Stories of John Cheever, The. LA79(II-713).
Wapshot Chronicle, The. MP12(XII-7020), MP8(VIII-5553), MP4(II-1268), MWL4(1268), SCL12(XII-8076), SCL7(VII-4942), A58(264), BMA(586).
Wapshot Scandal, The. MP12(XII-7024), MP8(VIII-5557), MP4(II-1271), MWL4(1271). A different analysis on this title appears in: SCL12(XII-8080), SCL7(VII-4946), A64(290).
World of Apples, The. SCL12(XII-8407), A74(416).

Chekhov, Anton
Cherry Orchard, The. MP12(II-908), MPCE(I-335), MP8(I-700), MP6(I-465), MPDr(146), MPv3(73), MP2(I-144), MWL2(144).
Letters of Anton Chekhov. SCL12(VI-4215), A74(221).
Seagull, The. MP12(X-5868), MPCE(IV-2025), MP8(VII-4673), MP6(V-2797), MPDr(747), MPv3(474), MP2(II-945), MWL2(945).
Three Sisters, The. MP12(XI-6518), MPCE(IV-2253), MP8(VIII-5185), MP6(VI-3110), MPDr(844), MPv4(509), MP2(II-1020), MWL2(1020).
Uncle Vanya. MP12(XII-6818), MPCE(IV-2383), MP8(VIII-5401), MP6(VI-3260), MPDr(891), MPv4(557), MP2(II-1082), MWL2(1082).

Chennault, Claire Lee
Way of a Fighter. HWor(I-491).

Chenu, O.D, M.D.
Toward Understanding Saint Thomas. HAnc(III-1546).

Cherniavsky, Michael
Tsar and Empire: Studies in Russian Myths. HEur(I-234).

Cherry, Kelly
Lovers & Agnostics. SCL12(VII-4594), A76(195).
Relativity: A Point of View. LA78(II-700).

Apology for the Life of Colley Cibber, Comedian, An.   MP12(I-266),
MP8(I-208),   MP6(I-135),   MPNf(23),   MP3(I-52),   MWL3(52).
Cicchetti, Charles J.
  Alaskan Oil: Alternative Routes and Markets.   HWor(II-1025).
Cicero (Marcus Tullius Cicero)
  Cicero's Orations.   MP12(II-959),   MP8(II-745),   MP6(I-488),
  MPNf(51),   MP3(I-188),   MWL3(188).
  On the Commonwealth of Marcus Tullius Cicero.   HAnc(I-527).
  Treatises of Cicero, The.   MP12(XI-6669),   MP8(VIII-5295),
  MP4(II-1229),   MWL4(1229).
Cipolla, Carlo M.
  Guns, Sails, and Empires.   HAnc(III-1511).
Clagett, Marshall
  Science of Mechanics in the Middle Ages, The.   HAnc(III-1616).
Clapesattle, Helen
  Doctors Mayo, The.   HAmer(II-1181).
Clapham, J. H.
  Economic Development of France and Germany, 1815-1914, The.
  HEur(II-1046).
Clare, John
  Poetry of Clare, The.   MP12(VIII-4863),   MP8(VI-3809),
  MP4(II-751),   MWL4(751).
Clark, Alan
  Barbarossa; The Russian-German Conflict, 1941-1945.   HEur(III-1474).
Clark, Arthur H.
  Clipper Ship Era, The.   HAmer(II-809).
Clark, Eleanor
  Baldur's Gate.   SCL12(I-527),   A71(14).
  Oysters of Locmariaquer, The.   SCL12(IX-5696),   SCLs(213).
Clark, General Mark W.
  From the Danube to the Yalu.   SCL12(IV-2798),   SCL7(III-1664),
  A54(86),   BMA(202).
Clark, G. N.
  "Origin of the Cambridge Modern History, The," in *The Cambridge
  Historical Journal.*   HWor(I-27).
Clark, Kenneth
  Leonardo da Vinci: An Account of His Development As an Artist.
  HAnc(III-1762).
Clark, Kenneth B.
  Pathos of Power.   SCL12(IX-5769),   A75(227).
Clark, Ronald W.
  Edison: The Man Who Made the Future.   LA78(I-284).
  Einstein: The Life and Times.   SCL12(IV-2168),   A72(110).
  Life of Bertrand Russell, The.   LA77(I-423).
Clark, Thomas D.

Emerging South, The. SCL12(IV-2212), SCL7(II-1323), A62(106), BMA(163).

Clark, Walter Van Tilburg

Ox-Bow Incident, The. MP12(VIII-4457), MPCE(III-1663), MP8(V-3473), MP6(IV-2233), MPAm(470), MP1(II-706), MWL1(706).

*Track of the Cat, The. MP12(XI-6633), MPCE(IV-2305), MP8(VIII-5268), MP6(VI-3176), MPAm(664), MPv4(535), MP2(II-1051), MWL2(1051).

Clark, William *and* Meriwether Lewis

Journals of Lewis and Clark, The. MP12(VI-3065), MP8(IV-2392), MP4(I-484), MWL4(484).

Clarke, Arthur C.

Childhood's End. SF(I-337).

City and the Stars, The. SF(I-374).

Imperial Earth. SF(III-1019).

Promise of Space, The. HWor(II-754).

Rendezvous with Rama. SF(IV-1759).

Short Fiction of Arthur C. Clarke, The. SF(IV-1926).

2001: A Space Odyssey. SF(V-2343).

Clarke, Austin

Selected Poems. LA77(II-715).

Clarke, Dwight L.

Stephen Watts Kearny, Soldier of the West. HAmer(II-822).

Clarke, Jack Alden

Huguenot Warrior: The Life and Times of Henri de Rohan, 1579-1638. HEur(I-260).

Clarke, Samuel

Scripture-Doctrine of the Trinity, The. RCh(II-562).

Clarke, W. K. Lowther

First Epistle of Clement to the Corinthians, The. HAnc(II-671).

Clarkson, Grosvenor B.

Industrial America in the World War. HAmer(III-1462).

Claude, Inis L., Jr.

Swords into Plowshares: The Problems and Progress of International Organization. Different analyses on this title appear in: HEur(III-1510), HAmer(III-1745).

Claude, Richard

Supreme Court and the Electoral Process, The. HAmer(III-1885).

Claudel, Paul

Poetry of Claudel, The. MP12(VIII-4866), MP8(VI-3812), MP4(II-754), MWL4(754).

Clavell, James

Shogun. SCL12(X-6926), A76(287).

Clay, Lucius D.

Decision in Germany.   HEur(III-1548).
Clay, Reginald S. *and* Thomas H. Court
    History of the Microscope, The.   HAnc(III-1557).
Cleaver, Eldridge
    Soul on Ice.   SCL12(XI-7135),   SCL7(VI-4380),   A68(301).
Cleaves, Freeman
    Old Tippecanoe: William Henry Harrison and His Time.   HAmer(II-763).
Clemens, Diane Shaver
    Yalta.   HAmer(III-1738).
Clemens, Samuel Langhorne
    Autobiography of Mark Twain, The.   SCL12(I-485),   SCL7(I-278),
    A60(19).
Clement, Hal
    Mission of Gravity.   SF(III-1424).
    Needle.   SF(III-1505).
Clement of Alexandria, Saint
    Stromata, or Miscellanies, The.   Different analyses on this title appear
    in: RCh(I-43),   RCa(I-44).
Clement I, Saint.
    First Epistle of Clement to the Corinthians, The.   RCh(I-1).
    Letter of the Church of Rome to the Church of Corinth, The.   RCa(I-4).
Clements, Frank
    Rhodesia: A Study of the Deterioration of a White Society.
    HEur(III-1644).
Clements, R. E.
    God and Temple; the Presence of God in Israel's Worship.
    HAnc(I-102).
Clendennen, Clarence C.
    United States and Pancho Villa: A Study in Unconventional Diplomacy,
    The.   HAmer(III-1441).
Clifford, James L.
    Young Sam Johnson.   SCL12(XII-8494),   SCL7(VII-5192),
    A55(302),   BMA(623).
Clifton, Lucille
    Generations.   LA77(I-318).
    Ordinary Woman, An.   SCL12(VIII-5642),   A75(221).
Clifton, Mark
    They'd Rather Be Right.   SF(V-2255).
Clive, John
    Macaulay: The Shaping of the Historian.   SCL12(VII-4624),
    A74(246).
Clubb, Oliver Edmund, Jr.
    United States and the Sino-Soviet Bloc in Southeast Asia, The.
    HWor(II-707).
Coates, Robert M.

Poetry of Coleridge, The.   MP12(VIII-4869),   MP8(VI-3815),
MP4(II-756),   MWL4(756).
*Rime of the Ancient Mariner, The.   MP12(X-5600),
MPCE(III-1916),   MP8(VII-4461),   MP6(V-2656),   MPPo(318),
MP1(II-825),   MWL1(825).

Coles, Robert
William Carlos Williams: The Knack of Survival in America.
SCL12(XII-8285),   A76(363).

Colette, Sidonie Gabrielle Claudine
*Chéri.   MP12(II-905),   MPCE(I-334),   MP8(I-697),
MP6(I-463),   MPEur(131),   MP3(I-176),
MWL3(176).
Other One, The.   MP12(VIII-4436),   MPCE(III-1654),
MP8(V-3455),   MP6(IV-2221),   MPEur(557),   MP3(II-709),
MWL3(709).
*Pure and the Impure, The.   SCL12(IX-6128),   SCL7(VI-3750),
A68(257).

Colin, Vladimir
Zecea Lume, A.   SF(V-2534).

Colinvaux, Paul
Why Big Fierce Animals Are Rare: An Ecologist's Perspective.
LA79(II-857).

Collier, Richard
Sands of Dunkirk, The.   SCL12(X-6626),   SCL7(VI-4070),
A62(258).

Collinder, Per
History of Marine Navigation, A.   HAnc(III-1507).

Collingwood, R. G. *and* J. N. L Myers
Roman Britain and the English Settlements.   HAnc(II-619).

Collins, James D.
God in Modern Philosophy.   RCa(II-1071).

Collins, Michael
Carrying the Fire: An Astronaut's Journeys.   SCL12(II-1098),
A75(47).

Collins, Wilkie
*Moonstone, The.   MP12(VII-4059),   MPCE(III-1505),
MP8(V-3167),   MP6(IV-2027),   MPEng(546),   MP1(II-623),
MWL1(623).
No Name.   MP12(VII-4227),   MPCE(III-1579),
MP8(V-3294),   MP6(IV-2117),   MPEng(581),   MP1(II-659),
MWL1(659).
*Woman in White, The.   MP12(XII-7211),   MPCE(IV-2525),
MP8(VIII-5702),   MP6(VI-3457),   MPEng(965),   MP1(II-1125),
MWL1(1125).

Collins, William

MP6(V-2763), MPAm(553), MP3(II-927), MWL3(927).
Spy, The. MP12(XI-6236), MPCE(IV-2149), MP8(VII-4971),
MP6(VI-2965), MPAm(598), MP1(II-921), MWL1(921).
Cooper, John Milton, Jr.
Walter Hines Page: The Southerner as American, 1855-1918.
LA78(II-888).
Cooper, Matthew
German Army, 1933-1945: Its Political and Military Failure, The.
LA79(I-245).
Nazi War Against Soviet Partisans, 1941-1944, The. LA80(II-577).
Cooper, Earl of Shaftesbury, Anthony Ashley
Characteristics. Ph(I-459).
Coover, Robert
Origin of the Brunists, The. SCL12(VIII-5652), SCL7(V-3462),
A67(255).
Pricksongs & Descants. SCL12(IX-6050), A70(250).
Universal Baseball Association, Inc. J. Henry Waugh, Prop., The.
SCL12(XII-7908), SCL7(VII-4834), A69(327).
Copleston, Frederick, S. J.
Friedrich Nietzsche, Philosopher of Culture. HEur(II-1026).
"Kant," in A History of Philosophy, Vol. VI: Wolff to Kant.
HEur(I-493).
Medieval Philosophy. HAnc(II-836).
"Nicholas of Cusa," in Vol. III of A History of Philosophy.
HAnc(III-1711).
Copp, Anthony R.
Regulating Competition in Oil. HWor(II-915).
Coppard, A. E.
Short Stories of A. E. Coppard, The. MP12(X-5993),
MP8(VII-4775), MP4(II-1123), MWL4(1123).
Corbière, Tristan
Poetry of Corbière, The. MP12(VIII-4876), MP8(VI-3822),
MP4(II-763), MWL4(763).
Cordell, Alexander
Rape of the Fair Country, The. SCL12(IX-6252), SCL7(VI-3834),
A60(218).
Corey, Albert B.
Crisis of 1830-1842 in Canadian-American Relations, The.
HAmer(II-803).
Corneille, Pierre
Cid, The. MP12(II-961), MPCE(I-349), MP8(II-747),
MP6(I-490), MPDr(150), MP1(I-142), MWL1(142).
Cinna. MP12(II-966), MPCE(I-352), MP8(II-749),
MP6(I-492), MPDr(152), MP3(I-190), MWL3(190).
Horace. MP12(V-2695), MPCE(II-978), MP8(III-2104),

MP6(III-1339),   MPDr(361),   MP3(I-490),   MWL3(490).
*Menteur, Le.   MP12(VII-3852),   MPCE(III-1412),
MP8(V-3017),   MP6(IV-1914),   MPDr(513),   MP3(II-656),
MWL3(656).
*Polyeucte.   MP12(IX-5231),   MPCE(III-1780),   MP8(VI-4176),
MP6(V-2476),   MPDr(650),   MP3(II-839),   MWL3(839).
Cornelisen, Ann
  Women of the Shadows.   LA77(II-937).
Cornell, Robert J.
  Anthracite Coal Strike of 1902, The.   HAmer(II-1331).
Cornford, Francis Macdonald
  Principium Sapientiae: The Origins of Greek Philosophical Thought.
  HAnc(I-175).
Corrington, John William
  Lonesome Traveler and Other Stories, The.   SCL12(VII-4469),
  SCL7(IV-2742),   A69(200).
Cortázar, Julio
  Hopscotch.   SCL12(V-3515),   SCL7(III-2097),   A67(146).
  Manual for Manuel, A.   LA79(I-418).
  Winners, The.   SCL12(XII-8321),   SCL7(VII-5095),   A66(341).
Corti, Egon Caesar
  Maximilian and Charlotte of Mexico.   HEur(II-877).
Corwin, Edward S.
  Court Over Constitution: A Study of Judicial Review as an Instrument of
  Popular Government.   HAmer(I-439).
  Doctrine of Judicial Review: Its Legal and Historical Basis and Other
  Essays, The.   HAmer(I-439).
Corwin, Virginia
  Saint Ignatius and Christianity in Antioch.   HAnc(II-698).
Costain, Thomas B.
  Chord of Steel, The.   HAmer(II-1090).
Coster, Charles de
  Legend of Tyl Ulenspiegel, The.   MP12(VI-3321),   MPCE(II-1233),
  MP8(IV-2588),   MP6(III-1656),   MPEur(439),   MPv3(287),
  MP2(II-573),   MWL2(573).
Cott, Jonathan
  Forever Young.   LA79(I-231).
Cotton, John
  Keys of the Kingdom of Heaven, The.   RCh(I-458).
Coudert, Frederic R., Jr.
  "Evolution of the Doctrine of Territorial Incorporation, The" in The
  American Law Review.   HAmer(II-1322).
Coulter, E. Merton
  Georgia: A Short History.   HAmer(I-184).
Coulton, George G.

Morning Noon and Night.   SCL12(VIII-5075),   SCL7(V-3083),
A69(231).
Crabbe, George
   Borough: A Poem in Twenty-Four Letters, The.   MP12(I-602),
   MP8(I-467),   MP4(I-79),   MWL4(79).
   Village, The.   MP12(XII-6927),   MP8(VIII-5484),   MP6(VI-3314),
   MPPo(371),   MP3(II-1097),   MWL3(1097).
Craft, Robert
   Stravinsky.   SCL12(XI-7283),   A73(345).
Craig, Gordon A.
   Battle of Königgrätz, The.   HEur(II-915).
   Germany 1866-1945.   LA79(I-249).
   Politics of the Prussian Army, 1640-1945, The.   HEur(II-792).
Crandall, Andrew W.
   Early History of the Republican Party, 1854-1856, The.   HAmer(II-881).
Crane, Hart
   *Bridge, The.   MP12(II-649),   MP8(I-501),   MP6(I-335),
   MPPo(28),   MP3(I-131),   MWL3(131).
Crane, Philip M.
   Surrender in Panama: The Case Against the Treaty.   HWor(III-1335).
Crane, Stephen
   *Maggie: A Girl of the Streets.   MP12(VI-3614),   MPCE(III-1319),
   MP8(IV-2831),   MP6(III-1782),   MPAm(370),   MP1(I-543),
   MWL1(543).
   *Red Badge of Courage, The.   MP12(IX-5468),   MPCE(III-1869),
   MP8(VI-4357),   MP6(V-2593),   MPAm(515),   MP1(II-811),
   MWL1(811).
Crankshaw, Edward
   Fall of the House of Habsburg, The.   SCL12(IV-2432),
   SCL7(II-1453),   A64(77).
   Shadow of the Winter Palace, The.   LA77(II-730).
Cranmer, Thomas
   Defense of the True and Catholic Doctrine of the Sacrament, A.
   RCh(I-385).
Cranshaw, Edward
   Khrushchev: A Career.   HWor(II-739).
Crashaw, Richard
   Carmen Deo nostro.   RCa(II-600).
   *Poetry of Crashaw, The.   MP12(VIII-4883),   MP8(VI-3829),
   MP4(II-768),   MWL4(768).
Craven, Avery O.
   Growth of Southern Nationalism, 1848-1861, The.   HAmer(II-856).
   *Soil Exhaustion as a Factor in the Agricultural History of Virginia an l
   Maryland, 1606-1860.*   HAmer(I-374).
Craven, Wesley F.

Dissolution of the Virginia Company: The Failure of a Colonial Experiment, The. HAmer(I-67).
Southern Colonies in the Seventeenth Century, 1607-1689, The. HAmer(I-61).
Craven, Wesley Frank *and* James Lea Cate, *eds.*
Army Air Forces in World War II, Vol. V: The Pacific: Matterhorn to Nagasaki, June 1944 to August 1945, The. HWor(I-489).
Crawford, Joanna
Birch Interval. SCL12(II-716), SCL7(I-405), A65(11).
Creasy, Sir Edward S. *and* Lt. Col. Joseph B. Mitchell
Twenty Decisive Battles of the World. Different analyses on this title appear in: HAnc(II-581; II-1118).
Crébillon, Prosper Jolyot de
Rhadamistus and Zenobia. MP12(X-5570), MPCE(III-1905), MP8(VII-4438), MP6(V-2643), MPDr(688), MP3(II-888), MWL3(888).
Creeley, Robert
Island, The. SCL12(VI-3775), SCL7(IV-2272), A64(138).
Creighton, Mandell
History of the Papacy from the Great Schism to the Sack of Rome, A. Different analyses on this title appear in: HAnc(III-1595), HEur(I-29; I-47).
Cremin, Lawrence A.
American Common School: An Historic Conception, The. HAmer(I-578).
Transformation of the School: Progressivism in American Education, 1876-1957, The. HAmer(II-1303).
Cremona, P. *and* M. H. H. Macartney
Italy's Foreign and Colonial Policy, 1914-1937. HEur(III-1404).
Crévecœur, Michel-Guillaume Jean de
Letters from an American Farmer. MP12(VI-3333), MP8(IV-2600), MP6(III-1658), MPNf(169), MP3(I-560), MWL3(560).
Crichton, Michael
Andromeda Strain, The. SCL12(I-304), A70(24). A different analysis on this title appears in: SF(I-63).
Cristofer, Michael
Shadow Box, The. LA78(II-762).
Croce, Benedetto
Aesthetic. MP12(I-53), MP8(I-41), MP4(I-3), MWL4(3). A different analysis on this title appears in: Ph(II-745).
Crockett, David
Narrative of the Life of David Crockett, A. MP12(VII-4146), MPCE(III-1545), MP8(V-3231), MP6(IV-2071), MPNf(209), MPv3(363), MP2(II-724), MWL2(724).
Cromwell, Oliver

Oliver Cromwell's Letters and Speeches.   RCh(I-493).

Cronin, Vincent
   Catherine, Empress of All the Russias.   LA79(I-80).
   Napoleon Bonaparte.   SCL12(VIII-5219),   A73(265).

Cronon, E. David
   Black Moses: The Story of Marcus Garvey and the Universal Negro Improvement Association.   HAmer(III-1447).

Cross, Whitney R.
   Burned-Over District: The Social and Intellectual History of Enthusiastic Religion in Western New York, 1800-1850, The.   Different analyses on this title appear in: HAmer(I-423; I-644).

Crosskey, William W.
   Politics and the Constitution in the History of the United States. HAmer(I-605).

Crossman, Richard
   Diaries of a Cabinet Minister, The.   LA77(I-211).

Crowell, Benedict
   How American Went to War, Vol. V: Demobilization: Our Industrial and Military Demobilization After the Armistice, 1918-1920. HAmer(III-1481).

Crowley, John
   Beasts.   SF(I-133).
   Engine Summer.   SF(II-721).

Crowley, Mart
   Boys in the Band, The.   SCL12(II-876),   SCL7(I-509),   A69(51).

Crowther, James G.
   British Scientists of the Nineteenth Century.   HEur(II-561).

Crozier, Brian
   South-East Asia in Turmoil.   HWor(II-705).

Crumley, James
   One to Count Cadence.   SCL12(VIII-5600),   A70(231).

Cruz, Sor Juana Inés de la
   Poetry of Sor Juana Inés de la Cruz, The.   MP12(IX-5149), MP8(VI-4095),   MP4(II-958),   MWL4(958).

Cudworth, Ralph
   True Intellectual System of the Universe, The.   RCh(I-534).

Culler, A. Dwight
   *Poetry of Tennyson, The.   LA78(II-665).

Cullmann, Oscar
   Christ and Time.   RCh(II-1072).
   "Origin of Christmas, The," in *The Early Church, Studies in Early Christian History and Theology.*   HAnc(II-885).
   Peter, Disciple, Apostle, Martyr.   HAnc(II-644).

Cumberland, Charles Curtis
   Mexican Revolution: The Constitutionalist Years.   HWor(I-74).

Cummings, E. E.
> *Enormous Room, The.* MP12(III-1789), MPCE(I-652),
> MP8(II-1394), MP6(II-895), MPAm(166), MP1(I-250),
> MWL1(250).
> Poems: 1923-1954. SCL12(IX-5931), SCL7(V-3635), A54(210),
> BMA(439).
> *Poetry of Cummings, The.* MP12(VIII-4887), MP8(VI-3833),
> MP4(II-772), MWL4(772).
> 95 Poems. SCL12(VIII-5369), SCL7(V-3276), A59(177),
> BMA(395).
> 73 Poems. SCL12(X-6877), SCL7(VI-4230), A64(236).

Cummings, Ray
> Girl in the Golden Atom, The. SF(II-878).

Cumont, Franz
> Oriental Religions in Roman Paganism, The. HAnc(I-435).

Cunha, Fausto
> noites marcianas, As. SF(IV-1545).

Cunliffe, Marcus
> Soldiers and Civilians.· SCL12(XI-7073), SCL7(VI-4343), A69(291).

Cunningham, J. V.
> Collected Poems and Epigrams of J. V. Cunningham, The.
> SCL12(II-1394), A72(67).

Cunningham, Noble E., Jr.
> Jeffersonian Republicans: The Formation of Party Organization,
> 1789-1801, The. HAmer(I-352).

Curran, Charles E.
> Contraception: Authority and Dissent. HEur(III-1663).

Current, Richard N.
> Daniel Webster and the Rise of National Conservatism. HAmer(II-805).
> Lincoln and the First Shot. HAmer(II-949).
> Secretary Stimson: A Study in Statecraft. HAmer(III-1602).

Current, Richard N. *and* James G. Randall
> Lincoln the President, Vol. IV: Last Full Measure. SCL12(VII-4389),
> SCL7(IV-2686), A55(147), BMA(340).

Curtis, D.
> "Roman Monumental Arches," in Supplementary Papers of the American
> School of Classical Studies in Rome. HAnc(I-504).

Curtis, James C.
> Fox at Bay: Martin Van Buren and the Presidency, 1837-1841, The.
> HAmer(II-750).

Cyprian of Carthage, Saint
> On the Unity of the Catholic Church. Different analyses on this title
> appear in: RCh(I-73), RCa(I-75).

Cyril, Bishop of Jerusalem, Saint
> Catechetical Lectures, The. Different analyses on this title appear in:

RCh(I-92),   RCa(I-90).

Dabbs, James McBride
  Southern Heritage, The.   SCL12(XI-7150),   SCLs(288).
Dahl, Roald
  Kiss Kiss.   SCL12(VI-4042),   SCL7(IV-2451),   A61(147).
Dahlberg, Edward
  Confessions of Edward Dahlberg, The.   SCL12(III-1521),   A72(82).
Daiches, David
  King James Version of the English Bible, The.   HEur(I-243).
Dallek, Robert
  Franklin D. Roosevelt and American Foreign Policy, 1932-1945.
  LA80(I-328).
Daly, Lowrie J., S. J.
  Medieval University, The.   HAnc(III-1481).
Damian, Saint Peter
  Selected Writings on the Spiritual Life.   RCh(I-190).
Dana, Richard Henry, Jr.
  Two Years Before the Mast.   MP12(XII-6785),   MPCE(IV-2366),
  MP8(VIII-5379),   MP6(VI-3243),   MPNf(309),   MP1(II-1033),
  MWL1(1033).
Dane, Clemence
  Flower Girls, The.   SCL12(IV-2689),   SCL7(III-1593),   A55(98).
Dangerfield, George
  Damnable Question, The.   LA77(I-188).
  Era of Good Feelings, The.   Different analyses on this title appear in:
  HAmer(I-520; I-560; I-611).
Daniel, Samuel
  "Defence of Rhyme, A," in Elizabethan and Jacobean Quartos.
  HAnc(III-1352).
  Poetry of Daniel, The.   MP12(VIII-4889),   MP8(VI-3835),
  MP4(II-774),   MWL4(774).
Daniélou, Jean, S. J.
  Lord of History, The.   RCa(II-997).
  Origen.   Different analyses on this title appear in: HAnc(II-777; II-798).
Daniel-Rops, Henri
  Jesus and His Times.   RCa(II-1006).
Daniels, Pamela *and* Sara Ruddick, *eds.*
  Working It Out.   LA78(II-937).
D'Annunzio, Gabriele
  Triumph of Death, The.   MP12(XI-6717),   MPCE(IV-2338),
  MP8(VIII-5332),   MP6(VI-3215),   MPEur(767),   MPv4(546),
  MP2(II-1061),   MWL2(1061).
Dansette, Adrien
  Religious History of Modern France, Vol. I: From the Revolution to the

Davenport, Guy
   Da Vinci's Bicycle.   LA80(I-195).
Davenport, John *and* Dylan Thomas
   Death of the King's Canary, The.   LA78(I-238).
Davenport, Russell W.
   Dignity of Man, The.   SCL12(III-1958),   SCL7(II-1176),   A55(83).
Davenport, T. R. H.
   South Africa: A Modern History.   HWor(III-1276).
Davidson, Avram
   Short Fiction of Avram Davidson, The.   SF(IV-1930).
Davidson, Donald
   Long Street, The.   SCL12(VII-4490),   SCL7(IV-2759),   A62(192),
   BMA(350).
Davidson, Eugene
   Making of Adolf Hitler: The Birth and Rise of Nazism, The.
   LA78(II-552).
   *Trial of the Germans: An Account of the Twenty-Two Defendants Before
   the International Military Tribunal at Nuremburg, The.*   HEur(III-1524).
Davidson, Walter Phillips
   Berlin Blockade: A Study in Cold War Politics, The.   Different analyses
   on this title appear in: HEur(III-1546),   HAmer(III-1798).
Davies, D. W.
   Primer of Dutch Seventeenth Century Overseas Trade, A.   HAmer(I-83).
Davies, Godfrey
   Restoration of Charles II, 1658-1660, The.   HEur(I-338).
Davies, John Paton, Jr.
   *Dragon by the Tail: American, British, Japanese, and Russian Encounters
   with China and One Another.*   HWor(II-660).
Davies, R. Trevor
   Spain in Decline, 1621-1700.   Different analyses on this title appear in:
   HEur(I-302; I-342).
Davies, Robertson
   World of Wonders.   LA77(II-952).
Davies, Rupert E.
   Methodism.   HEur(I-412).
Davis, Burke
   Gray Fox.   SCL12(V-3092),   SCL7(III-1853),   A57(93).
   Jeb Stuart: The Last Cavalier.   SCL12(VI-3827),   SCL7(IV-2313),
   A58(120).
   They Called Him Stonewall.   SCL12(XI-7533),   SCL7(VII-4583),
   A54(279).
   To Appomattox.   SCL12(XI-7672),   SCL7(VII-4689),   A60(275).
Davis, Calvin de Armond
   United States and the First Hague Conference, The.   HEur(II-1125).
Davis, David Brion

Hard Times.　MP12(V-2477),　MPCE(II-904),　MP8(III-1928),
MP6(III-1217),　MPEng(275),　MPv3(203),　MP2(I-405),
MWL2(405).
Little Dorrit.　MP12(VI-3448),　MPCE(II-1260),　MP8(IV-2699),
MP6(III-1704),　MPEng(436),　MPv3(295),　MP2(II-585),
MWL2(585).
Martin Chuzzlewit.　MP12(VII-3751),　MPCE(III-1372),
MP8(V-2943),　MP6(IV-1863),　MPEng(478),　MPv3(324),
MP2(II-640),　MWL2(640).
Mystery of Edwin Drood, The.　MP12(VII-4125),
MPCE(III-1537),　MP8(V-3213),　MP6(IV-2059),　MPEng(555),
MPv3(358),　MP2(II-717),　MWL2(717).
Nicholas Nickleby.　MP12(VII-4195),　MPCE(III-1567),
MP8(V-3267),　MP6(IV-2098),　MPEng(570),　MPv3(371),
MP2(II-734),　MWL2(734).
Old Curiosity Shop, The.　MP12(VIII-4316),　MPCE(III-1614),
MP8(V-3358),　MP6(IV-2158),　MPEng(595),　MPv3(389),
MP2(II-761),　MWL2(761).
Oliver Twist.　MP12(VIII-4358),　MPCE(III-1628),　MP8(V-3392),
MP6(IV-2183),　MPEng(607),　MP1(II-686),　MWL1(686).
Our Mutual Friend.　MP12(VIII-4440),　MPCE(III-1656),
MP8(V-3458),　MP6(IV-2224),　MPEng(625),　MPv3(400),
MP2(II-785),　MWL2(785).
Pickwick Papers.　MP12(VIII-4680),　MPCE(III-1739),
MP8(VI-3652),　MP6(IV-2354),　MPEng(667),　MP1(II-743),
MWL1(743).
Tale of Two Cities, A.　MP12(XI-6373),　MPCE(IV-2197),
MP8(VII-5075),　MP6(VI-3033),　MPEng(816),　MP1(II-945),
MWL1(945).
Dickerson, Oliver M.
Navigation Acts and the American Revolution, The.　HAmer(I-234).
Dickey, James
Buckdancer's Choice.　SCL12(II-949),　SCL7(I-544),　A66(38).
Deliverance.　SCL12(III-1866),　A71(58).
Drowning with Others.　SCL12(III-2077),　SCL7(II-1251),　A63(44).
Eye-Beaters, Blood, Victory, Madness, Buckhead and Mercy, The.
SCL12(IV-2383),　A71(69).
Helmets.　SCL12(V-3336),　SCL7(III-1984),　A65(121).
Poems: 1957-1967.　SCL12(IX-5927),　SCL7(V-3631),　A68(247).
Poetry of Dickey, The.　MP12(VIII-4896),　MP8(VI-3842),
MP4(II-778),　MWL4(778).
Strength of Fields, The.　LA80(II-794).
Dickey, William
Rainbow Grocery, The.　LA79(II-570).
Dickinson, Emily

Martin Luther: A Selection from His Writings.   HEur(I-56).
Dillon, Merton L.
  Benjamin Lundy and the Struggle for Negro Freedom.   HAmer(II-721).
Dillon, Richard
  Meriwether Lewis: A Biography.   SCL12(VII-4944),   SCL7(V-3003),
  A66(182). A different analysis on this title appears in: HAmer(I-453).
Dinesen, Isak
  Anecdotes of Destiny.   SCL12(I-308),   SCL7(I-181),   A59(11).
  Carnival: Entertainments and Posthumous Tales.   LA78(I-150).
  Daguerreotypes and Other Essays.   LA80(I-180).
  Last Tales.   SCL12(VI-4135),   SCL7(IV-2530),   A58(138).
  Seven Gothic Tales.   MP12(X-5926),   MP8(VII-4719),
  MP6(V-2827),   MPEur(674),   MP3(II-958),   MWL3(958).
  Shadows on the Grass.   SCL12(X-6900),   SCL7(VI-4239),   A62(269).
Dionysius of Alexandria, Saint
  Extant Fragments of the Works of Dionysius.   RCh(I-77).
  Treatise on the Promises.   RCa(I-78).
Dionysius, the Pseudo-Areopagite
  Divine Names, The.   RCh(I-165).
  Mystical Theology, The.   RCa(I-218).
  On the Divine Names.   RCa(I-215).
Diringer, David
  Alphabet, The.   HAnc(I-82).
Disch, Thomas M.
  Camp Concentration.   SF(I-277).
  Short Fiction of Thomas M. Disch, The.   SF(V-2059).
  334.   SF(V-2274).
Disraeli, Benjamin
  Coningsby.   MP12(II-1077),   MPCE(I-387),   MP8(II-841),
  MP6(I-553),   MPEng(118),   MPv3(86),   MP2(I-170),   MWL2(170).
  Vivian Grey.   MP12(XII-6971),   MPCE(IV-2440),
  MP8(VIII-5519),   MP6(VI-3341),   MPEng(930),   MPv4(577),
  MP2(II-1115),   MWL2(1115).
Divine, David
  Broken Wing: A Study in the British Exercise of Air Power, The.
  HEur(III-1464).
Divine, Robert A.
  Reluctant Belligerent: American Entry into World War II, The.   Different
  analyses on this title appear in: HAmer(III-1651),   HWor(I-467).
Dix, Dom Gregory, O. S. B.
  Shape of the Liturgy, The.   Different analyses on this title appear in:
  HAnc(II-881; II-1096).
Dixon, Robert A., Jr.
  Democratic Representation: Reapportionment in Law and Politics.
  HAmer(III-1886).

Djilas, Milovan
   Land Without Justice.   SCL12(VI-4093),   SCL7(IV-2492),   A59(137).
   New Class, The.   SCL12(VIII-5259),   SCL7(V-3202),   A58(169).
   Unperfect Society, The.   SCL12(XII-7924),   A70(326).
   Wartime.   LA78(II-894).
Dobb, Maurice
   Soviet Economic Development Since 1917.   HEur(III-1305).
Döblin, Alfred
   Berge, Meere und Giganten.   SF(I-163).
Doctorow, E. L.
   Book of Daniel, The.   SCL12(II-831),   A72(39).
   Ragtime.   SCL12(IX-6227), A76(256).
Dodd, Charles Harold
   Apostolic Preaching and Its Developments, The.   HAnc(II-609).
   Epistle of Paul to the Romans, The.   HAnc(II-635).
   Parables of the Kingdom, The.   RCh(II-1012).
Doderer, Heimito von
   Demons, The.   SCL12(III-1877),   SCL7(II-1124),   A62(100).
Dodge, T. A.
   Hannibal.   HAnc(I-440).
Dodson, Kenneth
   Away All Boats.   SCL12(I-500),   SCL7(I-285),   A54(7).
Dollfus, Charles
   Orion Book of Balloons, The.   HEur(I-500).
Dominik, Hans
   Macht der drei, Die.   SF(III-1304).
Donald, David
   Charles Sumner and the Coming of the Civil War.   SCL12(II-1195),
   SCL7(I-687),   A61(36),   BMA(69).
   Politics of Reconstruction, 1863-1867, The.   HAmer(II-1108).
Dondeyne, Albert
   Contemporary European Thought and Christian Faith.   RCa(II-1061).
Donleavy, J. P.
   *Beastly Beatitudes of Balthazar B, The.   SCL12(I-573),
   SCL7(I-340),   A69(30).
   Destinies of Darcy Dancer, Gentleman, The.   LA78(I-254).
   *Ginger Man, The.   SCL12(V-2946),   SCL7(III-1757),   A59(98).
Donne, John
   Death's Duell.   MP12(III-1391),   MP8(II-1075),   MP4(I-202),
   MWL4(202).
   Devotions Upon Emergent Occasions.   RCh(I-441).
   Ignatius His Conclave.   MP12(V-2834),   MP8(IV-2206),
   MP4(I-437),   MWL4(437).
   Poetry of Donne, The.   MP12(VIII-4900),   MP8(VI-3846),
   MP6(V-2428),   MPPo(249),   MP3(II-793),   MWL3(793).

Donnelly, Ignatius
    Caesar's Column.   SF(I-272).
Donohue, Agnes McNeill, *ed.*
    Casebook on The Grapes of Wrath, *A.*   HWor(I-421).
Donoso Cortés, Juan Francisco Maria de la Saludad
    Essay on Catholicism, Liberalism, and Socialism.   RCa(II-650).
Donovan, Robert J.
    Conflict and Crisis: The Presidency of Harry S Truman, 1945-1948.
    LA78(I-210).
Doolin, Paul Rice
    Fronde, *The.*   HEur(I-325).
Doolittle, Hilda
    Bid Me to Live.   SCL12(II-699),   SCL7(I-396),   A61(21).
    End to Torment: A Memoir of Ezra Pound by H. D.   LA80(I-290).
    *Poetry of H. D., The.   MP12(IX-4979),   MP8(VI-3925),
    MP4(II-834),   MWL4(834).
Dooyeweerd, Herman
    New Critique of Theoretical Thought, A.   RCh(II-1016).
Doran, Charles F.
    Myth, Oil, and Politics: Introduction to the Political Economy of
    Petroleum.   HWor(III-1142).
Dorner, Isaac August
    History of the Development of the Doctrine of the Person of Christ.
    RCh(II-692).
Dos Passos, John
    *Manhattan Transfer.   MP12(VII-3693),   MPCE(III-1347),
    MP8(IV-2895),   MP6(IV-1829),   MPAm(385),   MP1(I-555),
    MWL1(555).
    *Midcentury.   SCL12(VII-4966),   SCL7(V-3018),   A62(205).
    Most Likely to Succeed.   SCL12(VIII-5098),   SCL7(V-3103),
    A54(180).
    *Three Soldiers.   MP12(XI-6522),   MPCE(IV-2255),
    MP8(VIII-5188),   MP6(VI-3113),   MPAm(644),   MP1(II-984),
    MWL1(984).
    *U.S.A.   MP12(XII-6863),   MPCE(IV-2399),   MP8(VIII-5436),
    MP6(VI-3280),   MPAm(685),   MP1(II-1051),
    MWL1(1051).
Dossi, Carlo
    Colonia Felice, La.   SF(I-406).
Dostoevski, Fyodor
    *Brothers Karamazov, The.   MP12(II-688),   MPCE(I-251),
    MP8(I-534),   MP6(I-351),   MPEur(89),   MP1(I-88),   MWL1(88).
    *Crime and Punishment.   MP12(II-1197),   MPCE(I-440),
    MP8(II-929),   MP6(II-613),   MPEur(179),   MP1(I-170),
    MWL1(170).

Dowdey, Clifford
    Land They Fought For, The. SCL12(VI-4089), SCL7(IV-2488),
    A55(137).
Downes, Randolph C.
    *Council Fires on the Upper Ohio: A Narrative of Indian Affairs in the Upper
    Ohio Valley Until 1795.* HAmer(I-385).
Dowson, Ernest Christopher
    Poetry of Dowson, The. MP12(VIII-4903), MP8(VI-3849), MP4(II-781),
    MWL4(781). A different analysis on this title appears in: RCa(II-720).
Doyle, Arthur Conan
    Lost World, The. SF(III-1270).
    Micah Clarke. MP12(VII-3869),   MPCE(III-1418),   MP8(V-3031),
    MP6(IV-1925),   MPEng(504),   MP1(II-585),   MWL1(585).
    Poison Belt, The. SF(IV-1702).
    Sign of Four, The. MP12(X-6037), MPCE(IV-2069), MP8(VII-4819),
    MP6(V-2870), MPEng(796), MPv4(479), MP2(II-964), MWL2(964).
    Study in Scarlet, A. MP12(XI-6322), MPCE(IV-2180), MP8(VII-5036)
    MP6(VI-3005), MPEng(813), MP1(II-938), MWL1(938).
    White Company, The. MP12(XII-7111), MPCE(IV-2495),
    MP8(VIII-5623), MP6(VI-3408), MPEng(952), MP1(II-1108),
    MWL1(1108).
Drabble, Margaret
    Arnold Bennett: A Biography. SCL12(I-385),   A75(22).
    Ice Age, The. LA78(I-431).
    Realms of Gold, The. SCL12(IX-6265),   A76(261).
Drachmann, A. B.
    Atheism in Pagan Antiquity. HAnc(I-381).
Drago, Harry Sinclair
    Great American Cattle Trails. HAmer(II-1023).
Drake, William
    Sara Teasdale: Woman & Poet. LA80(II-741).
Draper, Theodore
    Abuse of Power. SCL12(I-17),   SCL7(I-12),   A68(4).
    Roots of American Communism, The. SCL12(X-6496), SCL7(VI-3996),
    A58(217). A different analysis on this title appears in: HAmer(III-1495).
Drayton, Michael
    Poetry of Drayton, The. MP12(VIII-4906),   MP8(VI-3852),
    MP6(V-2431), MPPo(252), MP3(II-796), MWL3(796).
Dreiser, Theodore
    American Tragedy, An. MP12(I-175),   MPCE(I-59),   MP8(I-138),
    MP6(I-82), MPAm(23), MP1(I-29), MWL1(29).
    Bulwark, The. MP12(II-707), MPCE(I-259), MP8(I-548),
    MP6(I-362), MPAm(75), MP3(I-142), MWL3(142).
    Financier, The. MP12(IV-2067), MPCE(II-745), MP8(III-1610),
    MP6(II-1015), MPAm(184), MP1(I-280), MWL1(280).

"Genius," The.   MP12(IV-2221),   MPCE(II-803),   MP8(III-1729),
MP6(II-1084),   MPAm(192),   MP3(I-409),   MWL3(409).
*Jennie Gerhardt.   MP12(V-2996),   MPCE(II-1105),   MP8(IV-2333),
MP6(III-1494),   MPAm(312),   MP3(I-526),   MWL3(526).
*Sister Carrie.   MP12(X-6070),   MPCE(IV-2084),   MP8(VII-4843),
MP6(V-2889),   MPAm(581),   MP1(II-895),   MWL1(895).
*Stoic, The.   MP12(XI-6255),   MPCE(IV-2160),   MP8(VII-4982),
MP6(VI-2975),   MPAm(604),   MP3(II-1020),   MWL3(1020).
*Titan, The.   MP12(XI-6560),   MPCE(IV-2269),   MP8(VIII-5218),
MP6(VI-3133),   MPAm(650),   MP1(II-991),   MWL1(991).
Drew, Elizabeth
Washington Journal: A Diary of the Events of 1973-1974.
SCL12(XII-8124),   A76(348).
Dreyer, J. L. E.
History of Astronomy from Thales to Kepler, A (formerly entitled *History of
the Planetary Systems from Thales to Kepler).* HAnc(II-714).
Dreyfuss, Joel *and* Charles Lawrence III
Bakke Case: The Politics of Inequality, The.   LA80(I-45).
Drinkwater, John
Shakespeare.   HEur(I-211).
Driver, G. R. *and* John C. Miles
Babylonian Laws, The.   HAnc(I-47).
Drucker, Peter F.
Age of Discontinuity, The.   SCL12(I-132),   A71(7).
Unseen Revolution, The.   LA77(II-872).
Drummond, Henry
Ascent of Man, The.   RCh(II-805).
Drury, Allen
Advise and Consent.   SCL12(I-72),   SCL7(I-56),   A60(3).
Capable of Honor.   SCL12(II-1067),   SCL7(I-615),   A67(35).
God Against the Gods, A.   LA77(I-332).
Return to Thebes.   LA78(II-708).
Dry, Avis M.
Psychology of Jung: A Critical Interpretation, The.   HEur(III-1311).
Dryden, John
*Absalom and Achitophel.   MP12(I-19),   MP8(I-15),   MP6(I-12),
MPPo(1),   MP3(I-5),   MWL3(5).
*All for Love.   MP12(I-117),   MPCE(I-40),   MP8(I-92),
MP6(I-57),   MPDr(19),   MPv3(5),   MP2(I-11),   MWL2(11).
*Essay of Dramatic Poesy, An.   MP12(III-1831),   MP8(II-1429),
MP4(I-285),   MWL4(285).
Hind and the Panther, The.   RCa(II-611).
*Marriage à la Mode. MP12(VII-3742),   MPCE(III-1367),   MP8(V-2937),
MP6(IV-1858),   MPDr(497),   MP3(II-634),   MWL3(634).
*Poetry of Dryden, The.   MP12(IX-4909),   MP8(VI-3855),

MP4(II-784),   MWL4(784).

Spanish Friar, The. MP12(XI-6205), MPCE(IV-2138),
MP8(VII-4946), MP6(V-2952), MPDr(797), MP3(II-1009),
MWL3(1009).

Duberman, Martin
  Charles Francis Adams, 1807-1886. SCL12(II-1187),   SCL7(I-683),
  A62(48). A different analysis on this title appears in: HAmer(II-1075).
  James Russell Lowell. SCL12(VI-3813),   SCL7(IV-2300),   A67(171).
  Uncompleted Past, The. SCL12(XII-7865),   A70(315).
  Visions of Kerouac. LA78(II-878).

Dubofsky, Melvyn *and* Warren Van Tine
  John L. Lewis: A Biography. LA78(II-478).

Dubos, René
  So Human an Animal. SCL12(X-7052),   SCLs(285).

Dubos, René *and* Barbara Ward
  Only One Earth: The Care and Maintenance of a Small Planet.
  HWor(II-1074).

Ducasse, Curt John
  Nature, Mind, and Death. Ph(II-1132).

Duchesne, Louis
  "Christian Festivals (Christmas and Epiphany), The," in *Christian Worship,
  Its Origin and Evolution.* HAnc(II-886).

Duchesne-Guillemin, Jacques
  Symbols and Values in Zoroastrianism. HAnc(I-166).

Dudden, Frederick Homes
  Gregory the Great: His Place in History and Thought. HAnc(II-1066).
  Life and Times of St. Ambrose, The. HAnc(II-921).

Dudintsev, Vladimir
  Not by Bread Alone. SCL12(VIII-5398),   SCL7(V-3297),   A58(172).

Duerrenmatt, Friedrich
  Pledge, The. SCL12(IX-5892),   SCL7(V-3600),   A60(195).

Duff, A. M.
  Freedmen in the Early Roman Empire. HAnc(II-624).

Duff, J. Wight
  *Literary History of Rome from the Origins to the Close of the Golden Age,
  A.* Different analyses on this title appear in: HAnc(I-468; I-524; I-533).
  Literary History of Rome in the Silver Age from Tiberius to Hadrian, A.
  Different analyses on this title appear in: HAnc(I-533; I-654).

Duffus, Robert L.
  Santa Fe Trail, The. HAmer(I-590).

Duffy, James E.
  Portuguese Africa. HEur(III-1675).

Dugan, Alan
  Poems 2. SCL12(IX-5941),   SCLs(225).

Dugan, James *and* Carroll Stewart
  Ploesti. SCL12(IX-5896), SCL7(V-3604), A63(186).

Duggan, Alfred

Cunning of the Dove, The. SCL12(III-1672), SCL7(II-979), A61(51).
King of Pontus. SCL12(VI-4019), SCL7(IV-2431), A60(121).
Lady for Ransom, The. MP12(VI-3203), MP8(IV-2494),
MP4(I-492), MWL4(492), SCL12(VI-4070), SCL7(IV-2473),
A54(135).
Leopards and Lilies. MP12(VI-3327), MP8(IV-2594), MP4(I-512),
MWL4(512), SCL12(VI-4184), SCL7(IV-2563), A54(144).
My Life for My Sheep. SCL12(VIII-5187), SCL7(V-3157), A55(166).
Three's Company. SCL12(XI-7616), SCL7(VII-4640), A59(244).
Winter Quarters. SCL12(XII-8343), SCL7(VII-5108), A57(287).

Duggan, Charles

Twelfth-century Decretal Collection. HAnc(II-916).

Duke, John A.

Columban Church, The. HAnc(II-1084).

Duke, Paul

Catherine the Great and the Russian Nobility. HEur(I-467).

Dumas, Alexandre, (fils)

Camille. MP12(II-751), MPCE(I-276), MP8(I-584), MP6(I-386),
MPDr(124), MP1(I-105), MWL1(105).

Dumas, Alexandre, (père)

Chevalier of the Maison Rouge, The. MP12(II-912), MPCE(I-338),
MP8(I-702), MP6(I-467), MPEur(134,) MP3(I-179), MWL3(179).
Corsican Brothers, The. MP12(II-1124), MPCE(I-401), MP8(II-881),
MP6(I-574), MPEur(156), MPv3(93), MP2(I-179), MWL2(179).
Count of Monte-Cristo, The. MP12(II-1136), MPCE(I-406),
MP8(II-889), MP6(I-578), MPEur(161), MP1(I-158), MWL1(158).
Countess de Charny, The. MP12(II-1146), MPCE(I-413),
MP8(II-895), MP6(I-583), MPEur(167), MP3(I-230), MWL3(230).
Memoirs of a Physician. MP12(VII-3836), MPCE(III-1406),
MP8(V-3005), MP6(IV-1907), MPEur(491), MP3(II-651), MWL3(651).
Queen's Necklace, The. MP12(IX-5394), MPCE(III-1836),
MP8(VI-4304), MP6(V-2557), MPEur(610), MPv3(436),
MP2(II-871), MWL7(871).
Three Musketeers, The. MP12(XI-6511), MPCE(IV-2250),
MP8(VIII-5181), MP6(VI-3107), MPEur(754), MP1(II-981),
MWL1(981).
Twenty Years After. MP12(XII-6762), MPCE(IV-2361),
MP8(VIII-5360), MP6(VI-3236), MPEur(773), MPv3(522),
MP2(II-1071), MWL2(1071).
Vicomte de Bragelonne, The. MP12(XII-6904), MPCE(IV-2417),
MP8(VIII-5468), MP6(VI-3303), MPEur(787), MP1(II-1063),
MWL1(1063).

Dumitriu, Petru

Extreme Occident, The. SCL12(IV-2375), SCL7(II-1419), A67(104).

Incognito. MP12(V-2868), MP8(IV-2235), MP4(I-446), MWL4(446).
A different analysis on this title appears in: SCL12(VI-3700),
SCL7(IV-2215), A65(139).

Dunbabin, T. J.
Western Greeks, The. HAnc(I-130).

Duncan, John
Colloquia Peripatetica. RCh(II-762).

Duncum, Barbara M.
*Development of Inhalation Anaesthesia with Special Reference to the Years,
1846-1900, The*. HAmer(II-793).

Dunlap, Orrin E., Jr.
Marconi: The Man and His Wireless. HEur(II-1082).

Dunn, L. C.
Short History of Genetics, A. HEur(II-910).

Dunne, Gerald T.
Hugo Black and the Judicial Revolution. LA78(I-418).

Duns Scotus, John
Opus Oxoniense. RCa(I-427).
Ordinatio: Oxford Commentary on the Sentences of Peter Lombard.
RCh(I-251).

DuPuy, Ernest R.
*Men of West Point: The First 150 Years of the United States Military
Academy*. HAmer(I-435).

Dupuy, T. N.
Genius for War: The German Army and General Staff, 1807-1945, A.
LA78(I-332).

Durant, Will
Reformation, The. SCL12(IV-6307), SCL7(VI-3864), A58(209),
BMA(473).

Durant, Will *and* Ariel Durant
Age of Louis XIV, The. SCL12(I-136), SCL7(I-92), A64(6).
Age of Napoleon, The. LA77(I-33).
Age of Reason Begins, The. SCL12(I-140), SCL7(I-96), A62(15),
BMA(14).
Age of Voltaire, The. SCL12(I-165), SCL7(I-115), A66(5).
Dual Autobiography, A. LA78(I-280).
Rousseau and Revolution. SCL12(X-6513), SCL7(VI-4010), A68(279).

Durden, Robert F.
Climax of Populism: The Election of 1896, The. HAmer(II-1271).

Durrell, Gerald, M.
Birds, Beasts, and Relatives. SCL12(II-719), A70(53).
Three Tickets to Adventure. SCL12(XI-7610), SCL7(VII-4637),
A55(259).
Whispering Land, The. SCL12(XII-8244), SCL7(VII-5043), A63(295).

Durrell, Lawrence
  Acte. SCL12(I-36), SCL7(I-31), A67(1).
  Alexandria Quartet, The. MP12(I-96), MP8(I-75), MP4(I-14), MWL4(14).
  *Balthazar. SCL12(I-538), SCL7(I-313), A59(20), BMA(31).
  *Bitter Lemons. SCL12(II-745), SCL7(I-428), A59(26).
  *Clea. SCL12(II-1308), SCL7(II-765), A61(44), BMA(83).
  Collected Poems. SCL12(II-1365), SCL7(II-798), A61(49).
  *Dark Labyrinth, The. SCL12(III-1716), SCL7(II-1017), A63(35).
  *Justine. SCL12(VI-3967), SCL7(IV-2395), A58(125), BMA(282).
  *Mountolive. SCL12(VIII-5114), SCL7(V-3112), A60(174), BMA(381).
  Nunquam. SCL12(VIII-5446), A71(232).
  Sicilian Carousel. LA78(II-771).
  Tunc. SCL12(XII-7810), SCL7(VII-4783), A69(324).
  Tunc and *Nunquam.* SF(V-2311).
Duun, Olav
  People of Juvik, The. MP12(VIII-4587), MPCE(III-1710), MP8(V-3572), MP6(IV-2298), MPEur(579), MPv4(401), MP2(II-809), MWL2(809).
Dvornik, Francis
  Byzantine Missions Among the Slavs. HAnc(II-1176).
  Byzantium and the Roman Primacy. HAnc(III-1239).
  Slavs, Their Early History and Civilization, The. HAnc(III-1208).

Earl, Lawrence
  Crocodile Fever. SCL12(III-1627), SCL7(II-951), A54(46).
Earle, Edward M.
  Turkey, the Great Powers, and the Bagdad Railway. HEur(II-1135).
Eastlake, William
  Bamboo Bed, The. SCL12(I-542), A70(49).
  Castle Keep. SCL12(II-1107), SCL7(I-635), A66(46).
  Three by Eastlake. SCL12(XI-7596), A71(318).
Eaton, Clement
  History of the Southern Confederacy, A. HAmer(II-944).
  Jefferson Davis: The Sphinx of the Confederacy. LA78(II-464).
Eaton, Quaintaince
  Miracle of the Met: An Informal History of the Metropolitan Opera, 1883-1967, The. HAmer(II-1138).
Ebeling, Gerhard
  Nature of Faith, The. RCh(II-1184).
Eben, Abba
  Abba Eben: An Autobiography. LA78(I-1).
Eberhart, Richard
  Of Poetry and Poets. LA80(II-610).
  *Poetry of Eberhart, The. MP12(IX-4918), MP8(VI-3864),

Eisenschiml, Otto
>*Why Was Lincoln Murdered?*   HAmer(II-1016).

Eklund, Gordon *and* Gregory Benford
>*If the Stars Are Gods.*   SF(II-1004).

Elder III, Lonne
>**Ceremonies in Dark Old Men.*   SCL12(II-1165),   A70(72).

Eliot, George
>**Adam Bede.*   MP12(I-29),   MPCE(I-11),   MP8(I-23),   MP6(I-19),
>MPEng(5),   MP1(I-8),   MWL1(8).
>**Daniel Deronda.*   MP12(III-1304),   MPCE(I-477),   MP8(II-1009),
>MP6(II-660),   MPEng(133),   MP3(I-249),   MWL3(249).
>**Felix Holt, Radical.*   MP12(IV-2029),   MPCE(II-733),
>MP8(III-1581),   MP6(II-1006),   MPEng(207),   MP3(I-388),
>MWL3(388).
>*Lifted Veil, The.*   SF(III-1213).
>**Middlemarch.*   MP12(VII-3879),   MPCE(III-1422),   MP8(V-3039),
>MP6(IV-1932),   MPEng(507),   MP1(II-588),   MWL1(588).
>**Mill on the Floss, The.*   MP12(VII-3896),   MPCE(III-1429),
>MP8(V-3050),   MP6(IV-1939),   MPEng(510),   MP1(II-593),
>MWL1(593).
>**Romola.*   MP12(X-5705),   MPCE(IV-1966),   MP8(VII-4538),
>MP6(V-2712),   MPEng(756),   MP1(II-856),   MWL1(856).
>**Silas Marner.*   MP12(X-6043),   MPCE(IV-2073),   MP8(VII-4821),
>MP6(V-2872),   MPEng(798),   MP1(II-893),   MWL1(893).

Eliot, T. S.
>*After Strange Gods.*   MP12(I-60),   MP8(I-48),   MP4(I-9),   MWL4(9).
>**Ash Wednesday.*   MP12(I-339),   MP8(I-259),   MP6(I-175),
>MPPo(12),   MP3(I-72),   MWL3(72).
>**Cocktail Party, The.*   MP12(II-1010),   MPCE(I-372),   MP8(II-781),
>MP6(I-515),   MPDr(160),   MPv3(81),   MP2(I-158),   MWL2(158).
>**Confidential Clerk, The.*   MP12(II-1074),   MP8(II-838),   MP4(I-150),
>MWL4(150),   SCL12(III-1533),   SCL7(II-897),   A54(34),   BMA(11).
>*Dante.*   MP12(III-1308),   MP8(II-1012),   MP4(I-188),   MWL4(188).
>**Elder Statesman, The.*   MP12(III-1728),   MP8(II-1344),   MP4(I-262),
>MWL4(262),   SCL12(IV-2173),   SCL7(II-1297),   A60(67),
>BMA(152).
>**Family Reunion, The.*   MP12(IV-1983),   MPCE(II-710),
>MP8(III-1551),   MP6(II-984),   MPDr(272),   MPv4(157),
>MP2(I-321),   MWL2(321).
>**Four Quartets.*   MP12(IV-2148),   MP8(III-1672),   MP6(II-1051),
>MPPo(106),   MP3(I-401),   MWL3(401).
>*Idea of a Christian Society, The.*   RCh(II-1043).
>*John Dryden: The Poet, The Dramatist, The Critic.*   MP12(V-3020),
>MP8(IV-2350),   MP4(I-465),   MWL4(465).
>**Murder in the Cathedral.*   MP12(VII-4094),   MPCE(III-1521),

Else, G. F.
   Origin and Form of Early Greek Tragedy, The.   HAnc(I-251).
Elsner, Gisela
   Giant Dwarfs, The.   SCL12(V-2928),   SCL7(III-1740),   A66(118).
Elting, John Robert *and* Vincent J. Esposito
   Military History and Atlas of the Napoleonic Wars, A.   HEur(II-571).
Elton, Geoffrey Rudolph
   History of England, Vol. IV: England Under the Tudors, A.
   HEur(I-7).
   Reformation Europe, 1517-1559.   HEur(I-155).
Elwin, Malcolm
   Lord Byron's Wife.   SCL12(VII-4527),   SCL7(IV-2777),
   A64(165).
Embree, George Daniel
   Soviet Union Between the 19th and 20th Party Congresses, 1952-1956, The.
   HEur(III-1567).
Emerson, Ralph Waldo
   Divinity School Address, The.   RCh(II-684).
   Essays: First and Second Series.   MP12(IV-1845),   MP8(II-1443),
   MP6(II-922),   MPNf(113),   MP3(I-359),   MWL3(359).
   *Poetry of Emerson, The.   MP12(IX-4928),   MP8(VI-3874),
   MP4(II-800),   MWL4(800).
   Representative Men.   MP12(IX-5518),   MP8(VII-4398),
   MP4(II-1054),   MWL4(1054).
   Society and Solitude.   MP12(X-6122),   MP8(VII-4881),
   MP4(II-1156),   MWL4(1156).
Emerton, Ephraim
   *Correspondence of Pope Gregory VII: Selected Letters from the Registrum,
   The.*   HAnc(III-1265).
   Defensor Pacis of Marsiglio of Padua: A Critical Study, The.
   HAnc(III-1610).
Emmerson, James Thomas
   Rhineland Crisis: A Study in Multilateral Diplomacy, The.   Different
   analyses on this title appear in: LA78(II-712),   HWor(I-350).
Empedocles of Acragas
   Empedocles: Fragments.   Ph(I-26).
Empiricus, Sextus
   Outlines of Pyrrhonism.   Ph(I-234).
Emtsev, Mikhail *and* Eremei Parnov
   World Soul.   SF(V-2506).
Engels, John
   Blood Mountain.   LA78(I-117).
   Signals from the Safety Coffin.   SCL12(X-6959),   A76(291).
England, Barry
   Figures in a Landscape.   SCL12(IV-2577),

SCL7(III-1528), A68(108).
England, George A.
Darkness and Dawn. SF(I-484).
Engleman, Fred L.
Peace of Christmas Eve, The. HAmer(I-525).
Ensor, R. C. K.
England, 1870-1914. HEur(II-1061).
Ensslin, W.
"Reforms of Diocletian, The," in *Vol. XII* of *The Cambridge Ancient History.* HAnc(II-831).
Ephraem the Syrian
Hymns of Ephraem the Syrian, The. RCh(I-103).
Ephron, Nora
Crazy Salad. SCL12(III-1609), A76(60).
Epictetus
Discourses and Manual. Ph(I-224).
Epicurus
Principal Doctrines and Letter to Menoeceus. Ph(I-191).
Epiphanius of Salamis, Saint
Panarion. RCh(I-111).
Epstein, Jason
Great Conspiracy Trial, The. SCL12(V-3105), A71(105).
Epstein, Joseph
Familiar Territory: Observations on American Life. LA80(I-310).
Epstein, Leslie
King of the Jews. LA80(II-458).
Epstein, Seymour
Caught in That Music. SCL12(II-1138), SCL7(I-651), A68(37).
Epstein, William
Last Chance: Nuclear Proliferation and Arms Control, The. HWor(II-567).
Erasmus, Desiderius
Enchiridion militis Christiani. Different analyses on this title appear in: RCh(I-321), RCa(I-498).
Paraclesis, The. RCa(I-505).
*Praise of Folly, The. MP12(IX-5294), MP8(VI-4223), MP6(V-2506), MPNf(254), MP3(II-846), MWL3(846). Different analyses on this title appear in: RCh(I-326), RCa(I-501).
Erastus, Thomas
Treatise of Excommunication, A. RCh(I-414).
Ergang, Robert Reinhold
Potsdam Führer: Frederick William I, Father of Prussian Militarism, The. HEur(I-398).
Erickson, Caroly
Bloody Mary. LA79(I-64).
Erigena, Johannes Scotus

Caravan Merchants and the Fairs of Champagne, The.   HAnc(III-1424).
Fagen, M. D., *ed.*
  History of Engineering and Science in the Bell System: The Early Years,
  1875-1925, A.   HWor(I-4).
Fairbairn, Ann
  Five Smooth Stones.   SCL12(IV-2651),   SCL7(III-1568),   A67(115).
Falk, Richard A.
  This Endangered Planet: Prospects and Proposals for Human Survival.
  HWor(II-1072).
Falkner, Murry C.
  Falkners of Mississippi: A Memoir, The.   SCL12(IV-2415),
  SCL7(II-1437),   A68(97).
Fall, Bernard B.
  Hell in a Very Small Place: The Siege of Dien Bien Phu, in *Great Battles*
  of History series.   HEur(III-1581).
Farago, Ladislas
  Broken Seal: "Operation Magic" and the Secret Road to Pearl Harbor,
  The.   HAmer(III-1701).
Faris, Robert E.
  Chicago Sociology, 1920-1932.   HAmer(III-1361).
Farmer, Philip José
  Lovers, The.   SF(III-1289).
  Riverworld Series.   SF(IV-1809).
  Strange Relations.   SF(V-2190).
Farquhar, George
  *Beaux' Stratagem, The.   MP12(I-464),   MPCE(I-163),
  MP8(I-362),   MP6(I-240),   MPDr(63),   MPv3(53),   MP2(I-86),
  MWL2(86).
  *Recruiting Officer, The.   MP12(IX-5459),   MPCE(III-1865),
  MP8(VI-4351),   MP6(V-2588),   MPDr(676),   MPv4(442),
  MP2(II-882),   MWL2(882).
Farquharson, A. S. L.
  Marcus Aurelius: His Life and His World.   HAnc(II-727).
Farrar, F. W.
  Lives of the Fathers.   HAnc(II-931).
Farrar, Victor J.
  Annexation of Russian America to the United States, The.
  HAmer(II-1039).
Farrell, James T.
  *Studs Lonigan: A Trilogy.   MP12(XI-6320),   MP8(VII-5034),
  MP6(VI-3003),   MPAm(616),   MP3(II-1028),   MWL3(1028).
Farrell, Michael
  Thy Tears Might Cease.   SCL12(XI-7626),   SCL7(VII-4650),
  A65(293).
Farrington, Benjamin

SCL7(VII-4726), A58(245), BMA(561).
Uncollected Stories of William Faulkner. LA80(II-838).
*Unvanquished, The. MP12(XII-6860), MP8(VIII-5433), MP4(II-1253), MWL4(1253).
*Wild Palms, The. MP12(XII-7142), MP8(VIII-5647), MP4(II-1287), MWL4(1287).

Faust, Irvin
File on Stanley Patton Buchta, The. SCL12(IV-2580), SCLs(102).
Roar Lion Roar. SCL12(X-6439), SCL7(VI-3951), A66(269).
Steagle, The. SCL12(XI-7214), SCL7(VI-4432), A67(308).

Fawcett, Edgar
Ghost of Guy Thyrle, The. SF(II-869).

Fawtier, Robert
Capetian Kings of France: Monarchy and Nation (987-1328), The. HAnc(III-1202).

Fay, C. R.
Adam Smith and the Scotland of His Day. HEur(I-487).
Palace of Industry, 1851: A Study of the Great Exhibition and Its Fruits. HEur(II-801).

Fay, Sidney B.
Origins of the World War, Vol. I: Before Sarajevo, The. Different analyses on this title appear in: HEur(II-1073; III-1154; III-1195).
Origins of the World War, Vol. II: After Sarajevo, The. HEur(III-1245).
Rise of Brandenburg-Prussia to 1786, The. HEur(I-399).

Feather, Norman *and* Harrie Massey
"James Chadwick," in Biographical Memoirs of Fellows of the Royal Society. HWor(I-287).

Federal Reserve System Board of Governors
Federal Reserve System: Purpose and Function, The. HAmer(III-1434).

Fedotov, George P.
Russian Religion Mind: Kievan Christianity: The Tenth to the Thirteenth Centuries, The. HAnc(III-1207).

Fehrenbacher, Don E.
Prelude to Greatness: Lincoln in the 1850's. HAmer(II-908).

Fei, Han
Han Fei Tzu. Ph(I-201).

Feibleman, Peter S.
Strangers and Graves. SCL12(XI-7280), SCL7(VII-4473), A67(311).

Fein, Helen
Accounting for Genocide. LA80(I-10).

Feis, Herbert
Atomic Bomb and the End of World War II, The. HAmer(III-1755).
Between War and Peace: The Potsdam Conference. HEur(III-1514).

Churchill, Roosevelt, Stalin. Different analyses on this title appear in: HEur(III-1480; III-1503).
Road to Pearl Harbor, The. HWor(I-440).
Feldman, Irving
Leaping Clear. LA77(I-408).
New and Selected Poems. LA80(II-580).
Feng Meng-lung
Lieh Kuo Chih. MP12(VI-3385), MPCE(II-1238), MP8(IV-2650), MP6(III-1673), MPEur(445), MP3(I-572), MWL3(572).
Fennell, J. L. I.
Ivan the Great of Moscow. Different analyses on this title appear in: HAnc(III-1739; III-1743).
Fensch, Thomas
Steinbeck and Covici: The Story of a Friendship. LA80(II-780).
Fenton, Mildred Adams *and* Carroll Lane
Giants of Geology. HEur(II-681).
Ferber, Edna
So Big. MP12(X-6115), MP8(VII-4875), MP4(II-1153), MWL4(1153).
Ferguson, Charles W.
Naked to Mine Enemies. SCL12(VIII-5209), SCL7(V-3168), A59(174).
Ferguson, Clarence C., Jr. *and* Albert P. Blaustein
Desegregation and the Law: The Meaning and Effect of the School Segregation Cases. HAmer(III-1852).
Ferguson, John
Pelagius. HAnc(II-949).
Ferguson, W. S.
"Athenian Expedition to Sicily, The," in *Vol. V* of *The Cambridge Ancient History.* HAnc(I-310).
"Fall of the Athenian Empire, The," in *Vol. V* of *The Cambridge Ancient History.* HAnc(I-310).
"Leading Ideas of the New Period, The," in *Vol. V* of *The Cambridge Ancient History.* HAnc(I-405).
"Oligarchic Movement in Athens, The," in *Vol. V* of *The Cambridge Ancient History.* HAnc(I-310).
Fermor, Patrick Leigh
Mani. SCL12(VII-4746), SCL7(IV-2891), A61(173).
Fernández de Lizardi, José Joaquín
Itching Parrot, The. MP12(V-2955), MPCE(II-1085), MP8(IV-2304), MP6(III-1473), MPAm(303), MPv3(251), MP2(I-499), MWL2(499).
Ferrara, Orestes
Borgia Pope: Alexander the Sixth, The. HEur(I-28).

Ferré, Nels
    Christian Understanding of God, The.   RCh(II-1124).
Ferreira, António
    Inês de Castro.   MP12(V-2883),   MPCE(II-1059),   MP8(IV-2247),
    MP6(III-1438),   MPDr(374),   MP3(I-506),   MWL3(506).
Ferreira de Castro, José Maria
    Emigrants, The.   SCL12(IV-2216),   SCL7(II-1327),   A63(51).
Ferrell, Robert H.
    *American Diplomacy in the Great Depression: Hoover-Stimson Foreign
    Policy, 1929-1933.*   HAmer(III-1601).
    "Truman Foreign Policy: A Traditional View," in *The Truman Period as a
    Research Field: A Reappraisal.*   HWor(II-665).
Ferrell, Robert H., *ed.*
    George C. Marshall.   HAmer(III-1796).
Ferris, Timothy
    "Seeking an End to Cosmic Loneliness," in *New York Times.*
    HWor(II-831).
Feuchtwanger, Lion
    Oppermanns, The.   HWor(I-244).
    *Power.   MP12(IX-5277),   MPCE(III-1797),   MP8(VI-4208),
    MP6(V-2494),   MPEur(599),   MP1(II-773),   MWL1(773).
    Ugly Duchess, The.   MP12(XII-6796),   MPCE(IV-2373),
    MP8(VIII-5385),   MP6(VI-3247),   MPEur(776),   MP1(II-1037),
    MWL1(1037).
Feuerbach, Ludwig
    Essence of Christianity, The.   RCh(II-697).
Feuerlicht, Roberta Strauss
    Justice Crucified: The Story of Sacco and Vanzetti.   LA78(II-487).
Fichte, Johann Gottlieb
    Addresses to the German Nation.   HAnc(II-587).
Fichtenau, Heinrich
    Carolingian Empire, The.   HAnc(II-1149).
Fiedler, Leslie
    Freaks: Myths and Images of the Secret Self.   LA79(I-235).
Field, Andrew
    Nabokov: His Life in Part.   LA78(II-590).
Field, Edward
    Stand Up, Friend, with Me.   SCL12(XI-7208),   SCL7(VI-4426),
    A64(252).
    Variety Photoplays.   SCL12(XII-7968),   SCL7(VII-4870),   A68(343).
Fieldhouse, D. K.
    "Imperialism: An Historiographical Revision," in *The Economic History
    Review.*   HWor(I-35).
Fielding, Gabriel
    Birthday King, The.   SCL12(II-732),   SCL7(I-415),   A64(22).

Brotherly Love. SCL12(II-943), SCL7(I-538), A62(33).
In the Time of Greenbloom. SCL12(VI-3688), SCL7(III-2202), A58(111).
Through Streets Broad and Narrow. SCL12(XI-7623), SCL7(VII-4647), A61(255).

Fielding, Henry
*Amelia. MP12(I-161), MPCE(I-56), MP8(I-127), MP6(I-77), MPEng(16), MP1(I-24), MWL1(24).
*Jonathan Wild. MP12(V-3030), MPCE(II-1121), MP8(IV-2359), MP6(III-1512), MPEng(379), MPv3(259), MP2(I-516), MWL2(516).
*Joseph Andrews. MP12(V-3036), MPCE(II-1124), MP8(IV-2365), MP6(III-1517), MPEng(385), MP1(I-448), MWL1(448).
Temple Beau, The. MP12(XI-6435), MPCE(IV-2220), MP8(VIII-5124), MP6(VI-3071), MPDr(836), MPv4(504), MP2(II-1013), MWL2(1013).
*Tom Jones. MP12(XI-6598), MPCE(IV-2285), MP8(VIII-5246), MP6(VI-3158), MPEng(863), MP1(II-1000), MWL1(1000).
Tom Thumb the Great. MP12(XI-6609), MPCE(IV-2291), MP8(VIII-5253), MP6(VI-3164), MPDr(860), MPv4(531), MP2(II-1046), MWL2(1046).

Figgis, John Neville
Political Aspects of St. Augustine's "City of God," The. HAnc(II-942).

Filas, Francis L., S. J.
Joseph: The Man Closest to Jesus. RCa(II-1115).

Filler, Louis
Crusaders for American Liberalism. HAmer(III-1355).

Findlay James F., Jr.
Dwight L. Moody: American Evangelist, 1837-1899. HAmer(II-1175).
"Moody, 'Gapman,' and the Gospel: The Early Days of Moody Bible Institute," in Church History. HAmer(II-1175).

Findley, Timothy
Last of the Crazy People, The. SCL12(VI-4122), SCL7(IV-2521), A68(173).

Finer, Herman
Mussolini's Italy. HEur(III-1300)

Finkelstein, Louis
Pharisees, The. HAnc(I-478).

Finlay, Carlos E.
Carlos Finlay and Yellow Fever. HAmer(II-1315).

Finney, Brian
Christopher Isherwood: A Critical Biography. LA80(I-145).

Finney, Charles Grandison
Lectures on Revivals of Religion. RCh(II-675).

Finney, Jack
    Time and Again. SCL12(XI-7644), A71(324). A different analysis on this title appears in: SF(V-2283).
Firbank, Arthur Annesley Ronald
    Complete Ronald Firbank, The. SCL12(III-1502), SCL7(II-877), A62(87).
Fischer, Fritz
    War of Illusions: German Policies from 1911 to 1914. Different analyses on this title appear in: HWor(I-51; II-923).
    World Power or Decline: The Controversy over Germany's Aims in the First World War. HWor(II-921).
Fischer, Louis
    Life of Lenin, The. SCL12(VII-4347), SCL7(IV-2654), A65(170).
Fisher, Vardis
    Children of God. MP12(II-927), MPCE(I-341), MP8(I-715), MP6(I-470), MPAm(89), MP1(I-137), MWL1(137).
FitzGerald, Edward
    Rubáiyát of Omar Khayyám, The. MP12(X-5730), MP8(VII-4558), MP6(V-2725), MPPo(325), MP3(II-907), MWL3(907).
Fitzgerald, F. Scott
    Afternoon of an Author. SCL12(I-115), SCL7(I-81), A59(3).
    Great Gatsby, The. MP12(IV-2358), MPCE(II-860), MP8(III-1832), MP6(II-1152), MPAm(228), MP1(I-329), MWL1(329).
    Last Tycoon, The. MP12(VI-3277), MPCE(II-1216), MP8(IV-2553), MP6(III-1631), MPAm(330), MP3(I-552), MWL3(552).
    Letters of F. Scott Fitzgerald, The. MP12(VI-3347), MP8(IV-2612), MP4(I-523), MWL4(523), SCL12(VI-4237), SCL7(IV-2589), A64(149).
    Price Was High: The Last Uncollected Stories of F. Scott Fitzgerald, The. LA80(II-693).
    Tender Is the Night. MP12(XI-6448), MPCE(IV-2223), MP8(VIII-5135), MP6(VI-3078), MPAm(635), MPv3(511), MP2(II-1016), MWL2(1016).
FitzGerald, Frances
    Fire in the Lake. SCL12(IV-2605), A73(166).
Fitzgerald, Robert
    In the Rose of Time. SCL12(VI-3686), SCL7(III-2200), A58(109).
FitzGibbon, Constantine
    Life of Dylan Thomas, The. SCL12(VII-4327), SCL7(IV-2647), A66(148).
    When the Kissing Had to Stop. SCL12(XII-8225), SCL7(VII-5028), A61(296).

Fitzhugh, George
Cannibals All: Or, Slaves Without Masters. HAmer(I-651).
Flacius (and others), Matthias
Magdeburg Centuries, The. RCh(I-388).
Flammarion, Camille
Lumen. SF(III-1294).
Omega: The Last Days of the World. SF(IV-1592).
Flanagan, Thomas
Year of the French, The. LA80(II-880).
Flaubert, Gustave
*Bouvard and Pécuchet. MP12(II-615), MPCE(I-222),
MP8(I-478), MP6(I-316), MPEur(80), MP3(I-121), MWL3(121).
*Madame Bovary. MP12(VI-3599), MPCE(III-1312),
MP8(IV-2821), MP6(III-1774), MPEur(461), MP1(I-539),
MWL1(539).
*Salammbô. MP12(X-5769), MPCE(IV-1988), MP8(VII-4592),
MP6(V-2744), MPEur(657), MP1(II-860), MWL1(860).
*Sentimental Education, A. MP12(X-5909), MPCE(IV-2039),
MP8(VII-4707), MP6(V-2820), MPEur(671), MP1(II-876),
MWL1(876).
*Temptation of Saint Anthony, The. MP12(XI-6438),
MPCE(IV-2221), MP8(VIII-5127), MP6(VI-3073), MPEur(746),
MP3(II-1059), MWL3(1059).
Flecker, James Elroy
Poetry of Flecker, The. MP12(IX-4941), MP8(VI-3887),
MP4(II-808), MWL4(808).
Fleming, D. F.
Cold War and Its Origins, Vol. I: 1917-1950, The. Different analyses on
this title appear in: HEur(III-1558), HAmer(III-1780).
Cold War and Its Origins, Vol. II: 1950-1960, The. HEur(III-1558).
Fleming, Donald *and* Bernard Bailyn, *eds.*
Intellectual Migration: Europe and America, 1930-1960, The.
HWor(I-297).
Fleming, John Dick
Israel's Golden Age: The Story of the United Kingdom. HAnc(I-108).
Fleming, Peter
Siege of Peking, The. SCL12(X-6953), SCL7(VI-4279), A60(242).
Flenley, Ralph
Modern German History. HEur(II-606).
Fletcher, C. R. L.
Gustavus Adolphus and The Thirty Years War. HEur(I-276).
Fletcher, John
*Faithful Shepherdess, The. MP12(IV-1962), MPCE(II-703),
MP8(III-1535), MP6(II-978), MPDr(270), MP3(I-383),
MWL3(383).

Rule a Wife and Have a Wife. MP12(X-5732), MPCE(IV-1977), MP8(VII-4560), MP6(V-2727), MPDr(717), MP3(II-909), MWL3(909).

Woman's Prize, The. MP12(XII-7229), MPCE(IV-2535), MP8(VIII-5714), MP6(VI-3467), MPDr(943), MP3(II-1141), MWL3(1141).

Fletcher, John *and* Francis Beaumont

Coxcomb, The. MP12(II-1185), MPCE(I-435), MP8(II-919), MP6(I-603), MPDr(181), MP3(I-236), MWL3(236).

King and No King, A. MP12(VI-3133), MPCE(II-1158), MP8(IV-2441), MP6(III-1558), MPDr(409), MP3(I-541), MWL3(541).

Maid's Tragedy, The. MP12(VI-3638), MPCE(III-1331), MP8(IV-2848), MP6(IV-1795), MPDr(480), MPv4(304), MP2(II-612), MWL2(612).

Philaster. MP12(VIII-4639), MPCE(III-1727), MP8(V-3616), MP6(IV-2331), MPDr(622), MPv3(411), MP2(II-825), MWL2(825).

Scornful Lady, The. MP12(X-5848), MPCE(IV-2019), MP8(VII-4655), MP6(V-2785), MPDr(744), MP3(II-940), MWL3(940).

Woman Hater, The. MP12(XII-7207), MPCE(IV-2524), MP8(VIII-5699), MP6(VI-3454), MPDr(937), MP3(II-1138), MWL3(1138).

Fletcher, John *and* Philip Massinger

Beggars' Bush, The. MP12(I-472), MPCE(I-167), MP8(I-368), MP6(I-245), MPDr(69), MP3(I-96), MWL3(96).

Sir John van Olden Barnavelt. MP12(X-6063), MPCE(IV-2082), MP8(VII-4837), MP6(V-2884), MPDr(780), MP3(II-985), MWL3(985).

Fletcher, John *and* William Shakespeare

Two Noble Kinsmen, The. MP12(XII-6775), MPCE(IV-2363), MP8(VIII-5371), MP6(VI-3241), MPDr(889), MPv.4(551), MP2(II-1076), MWL2(1076).

Fletcher, Robert S.

History of Oberlin College: From Its Foundation Through the Civil War, A. HAmer(II-710).

Fletcher, Sir Banister

History of Architecture on the Comparative Method. HAnc(III-1418).

Flexner, Abraham

Daniel Coit Gilman: Creator of the American Type of University. HAmer(II-1080).

Flexner, Eleanor

Mary Wollstonecraft. SCL12(VII-4806), A73(238).

Flexner, James Thomas

MWL2(57).

Crime of Sylvestre Bonnard, The. MP12(II-1202), MPCE(I-443), MP8(II-932), MP6(II-615), MPEur(182), MPv3(108), MP2(I-196), MWL2(196).

Gods Are Athirst, The. MP12(IV-2282), MPCE(II-826), MP8(II-1776), MP6(II-1115), MPEur(329), MP3(I-420), MWL3(420).

Penguin Island. MP12(VIII-4579), MPCE(III-1707), MP8(V-3566), MP6(IV-2294), MPEur(576), MP1(II-729), MWL1(729).

Revolt of the Angels, The. MP12(X-5558), MPCE(III-1900), MP8(VII-4429), MP6(V-2636), MPEur(637), MP1(II-821), MWL1(821).

France, Marie de
Lais of Marie de France, The. MP12(VI-3230), MPCE(II-1196), MP8(IV-2516), MP4(I-497), MWL4(497).

Francis, Robert
Come Out into the Sun. SCL12(III-1461), SCL7(II-849), A67(45).

Francis of Assisi, Saint
Extant Writings of Saint Francis of Assisi, The. RCa(I-349).

Francis of Sales, Saint
Introduction to the Devout Life. Different analyses on this title appear in: RCh(I-428), RCa(I-568).
Love of God, The. RCa(II-584).

Francis, Thomas F., Jr.
Evaluation of the 1954 Field Trail of Poliomyelitis Vaccine: Final Report. HAmer(III-1839).

Franck, Thomas M. and Edward Weisband
Resignation in Protest. SCL12(IX-6371), A76(265).

Frank, Joseph
Dostoevsky. LA77(I-236).

Frank, Pat
Alas, Babylon. SF(I-38).

Franke, Herbert W.
Zone Null. SF(V-2538).

Frankfort, H.
Ancient Egyptian Religion: An Interpretation. HAnc(I-54).
"Egyptian Way of Life, The," in Ancient Egyptian Religion: An Interpretation. HAnc(I-38).

Frankland, Noble and Sir Charles Webster
Strategic Air Offensive Against Germany, 1939-1945, The. HEur(III-1463).

Franklin, Benjamin
Autobiography of Benjamin Franklin, The. MP12(I-362), MP8(I-278), MP6(I-188), MPNf(29), MP3(I-74), MWL3(74). A

different analysis on this title appears in: HAmer(I-238).
Benjamin Franklin: A Biography in His Own Words. SCL12(I-643),
A73(32).
Franklin, John Hope
Emancipation Proclamation, The. HAmer(II-982).
Fraser, George McDonald
Royal Flash. SCL12(X-6517), A71(280).
Fraser, Lady Antonia
Mary Queen of Scots. SCL12(VII-4800), A70(198).
Royal Charles: Charles II and the Restoration. LA80(II-732).
Fraser, Ronald
In Hiding. SCL12(VI-3650), A73(201).
Frayn, Michael
Very Private Life, A. SCL12(XII-7986), SCL7(VII-4884),
A69(334).
Frazer, Sir James George
Golden Bough, The. MP12(IV-2296), MP8(III-1787),
MP4(I-384), MWL4(384).
Frederic, Harold
Copperhead, The. MP12(II-1113), MPCE(I-397), MP8(II-872),
MP6(I-569), MPAm(103), MP3(I-227), MWL3(227).
*Damnation of Theron Ware, The. MP12(III-1279), MPCE(I-470),
MP8(II-989), MP6(II-653), MPAm(122), MPv4(99),
MP2(I-214), MWL2(214).
Freehling, William W.
*Prelude to Civil War: The Nullification Controversy in South Carolina,
1816-1836.* HAmer(II-705).
Freeman, Douglas Southall
George Washington: A Biography, Vol. VI: Patriot and President.
HAmer(I-343).
*Lee's Lieutenants: A Multiple Biography of the Military Leaders in Lee's
Command During the Civil War, Vol. I: Manassas to Malvern Hill.*
HAmer(II-955).
*Lee's Lieutenants: A Multiple Biography of the Military Leaders in Lee's
Command During the Civil War, Vol. II: Cedar Mountain to
Chancellorville.* HAmer(II-955).
*Lee's Lieutenants: A Multiple Biography of the Military Leaders in Lee's
Command During the Civil War, Vol. III: Gettysburg to Appomattox.*
HAmer(II-955).
R. E. Lee. MP12(IX-5497), MP8(VII-4381), MP6(V-2608),
MPNf(261), MP3(II-874), MWL3(874). A different analysis on this
title appears in: HAmer(II-999).
Freidel, Frank
Franklin D. Roosevelt, Vol. III: The Triumph. HAmer(III-1611).
Franklin D. Roosevelt: Launching the New Deal. SCL12(IV-2764),

A74(137).

Splendid Little War, The.   HAmer(II-1287).

Freksa, Friedrich

Druso.   SF(II-639).

Frémont, John Charles

Narratives of Exploration and Adventure.   SCL12(VIII-5223),
SCL7(V-3178),   A57(185).

French, A.

Growth of the Athenian Economy, The.   HAnc(I-171).

French, Allen

Day of Concord and Lexington: Nineteenth of April, 1775, The. HAmer(I-254).

Frend, W. H. C.

Martyrdom and Persecution in the Early Church.   Different analyses on
this title appear in: HAnc(II-639; II-814).

Freneau, Philip

Poetry of Freneau, The.   MP12(IX-4943),   MP8(VI-3889),
MP6(V-2436),   MPPo(258),   MP3(II-801),   MWL3(801).

Frere, Sheppard

Britannia: A History of Roman Britain.   HAnc(II-618).

Freud, Sigmund

General Introduction to Psychoanalysis, A.   MP12(IV-2218),
MP8(III-1726),   MP4(I-371),   MWL4(371).

Interpretation of Dreams, The.   MP12(V-2908),   MP8(IV-2267),
MP6(III-1447),   MPNf(163),   MP3(I-508),   MWL3(508).

Freud, Sigmund *and* Josef Breuer

Studies on Hysteria.   MP12(XI-6317),   MP8(VII-5031),
MP4(II-1195),   MWL4(1195).

Freud's "Wolf-Man"

Wolf-Man, The.   SCL12(XII-8362),   A72(349).

Freytag, Gustav

Debit and Credit.   MP12(III-1393),   MPCE(I-512),   MP8(II-1077),
MP6(II-703),   MPEur(216),   MP3(I-261),   MWL3(261).

Friedenthal, Richard

Goethe.   SCL12(V-2990),   SCL7(III-1780),   A66(120).

Friedjung, Heinrich

Struggle for Supremacy in Germany, 1859-1866, The.   HEur(II-915).

Friedlander, Paul

Plato, an Introduction.   HAnc(I-325).

Friedman, Alan

Hermaphrodeity.   SCL12(V-3393),   A73(199).

Friedman, Bruce Jay

Dick, The.   SCL12(III-1943),   A71(61).

Mother's Kisses, A.   SCL12(VIII-5111),   SCL7(V-3109),   A65(205).

Stern.   SCL12(XI-7227),   SCLs(292).

Friedman, Herbert

Fuchida, Mitsuo *and* Masatake Okumiya
  Midway: The Battle That Doomed Japan.   SCL12(VIII-4987),
  SCL7(V-3029),   A55(160). A different analysis on this title appears in:
  HWor(I-476).
Fuchs, Victor R.
  Who Shall Live?   SCL12(XII-8254),   A76(359).
Fuentes, Carlos
  *Change of Skin, A.   SCL12(II-1175),   SCL7(I-676),   A69(65).
  *Death of Artemio Cruz, The.   MP12(III-1369),   MP8(II-1057),
  MP4(I-195),   MWL4(195),   SCL12(III-1821),   SCL7(1096),   A65(63).
  Terra Nostra.   LA77(II-807).
  *Where the Air Is Clear.   MP12(XII-7107),   MP8(VIII-5619),
  MP4(II-1279),   MWL4(1279). A different analysis on this title appears
  in: SCL12(XII-8235),   SCL7(VII-5034),   A61(300).
Fuess, Claude M.
  Daniel Webster.   HAmer(I-662).
Fuller, John F. C.
  Julius Caesar, Man, Soldier, and Tyrant.   HAnc(I-518).
  *Military History of the Western World, Vol. I: From the Earliest Times to
  the Battle of Lepanto, A.*   Different analyses on this title appear in:
  HAnc(II-580; II-978; II-1119).
  *Military History of the Western World, Vol. II: From the Defeat of the
  Spanish Armada, 1588, to the Battle of Waterloo, A.*   HEur(I-315).
Fuller, Reginald H.
  Mission and Achievement of Jesus, The.   HAnc(II-592).
Fuller, Thomas
  Holy State and the Profane State, The.   MP12(V-2672),
  MP8(III-2084),   MP4(I-428),   MWL4(428).
Fülöp-Miller, René
  Jesuits: A History of the Society of Jesus, The.   HEur(I-101).
  Night of Time, The.   SCL12(VIII-5327),   SCL7(V-3242),   A55(175).
Furbank, P. N.
  E. M. Forster: A Life.   LA79(I-183).
Furnas, Joseph Chamberlain
  Goodbye to Uncle Tom.   SCL12(V-3058),   SCL7(III-1830),   A57(87).
  Road to Harpers Ferry, The.   HAmer(II-922).
Fussell, Edwin
  Lucifer in Harness.   SCL12(VII-4607),   A74(242).
Fussell, George E.
  Farming Techniques from Prehistoric to Modern Times.   HAnc(II-1171).
Fussell, Paul
  Great War and Modern Memory, The.   SCL12(V-3132),   A76(114).

Gaboriau, Émile
  File No. 113.   MP12(IV-2058),   MPCE(II-740),   MP8(III-1604),

MP6(II-1013),   MPEur(299),   MP1(I-278),   MWL1(278).
Monsieur Lecoq.   MP12(VII-4040),   MPCE(III-1498),
MP8(V-3152),   MP6(IV-2017),   MPEur(508),   MPv4(351),
MP2(II-703),   MWL2(703).

Gabrieli, Francesco
"Transmission of Learning and Literary Influences to Western Europe," in
Vol. II of *The Cambridge History of Islam.*   HAnc(II-1192).

Gaddis, William
J R.   SCL12(VI-3946),   A76(151).
Recognitions, The.   SCL12(IX-6275),   SCLs(243).

Gade, John A.
*Hanseatic Control of Norwegian Commerce During the Late Middle Ages,
The.*   HAnc(III-1433).

Gail, Otto Willi
Shot into Infinity, The.   SF(V-2070).

Gaillard, Frye
Watermelon Wine: The Spirit of Country Music.   LA79(II-835).

Gaines, Ernest J.
*Autobiography of Miss Jane Pittman, The.   SCL12(I-489),   A72(15).
*Bloodline.   SCL12(II-797),   SCL7(I-452),   A69(41).
Catherine Carmier.   SCL12(II-1130),   SCLs(61).
In My Father's House.   LA79(I-311).

Galbraith, John Kenneth
Affluent Society, The.   SCL12(I-83),   SCL7(I-65),   A59(1).
Age of Uncertainty, The.   LA78(I-23).
Ambassador's Journal.   SCL12(I-248),   A70(18).
Economics and the Public Purpose.   SCL12(III-2115),   A74(109).
Great Crash, 1929, The.   HAmer(III-1579).
Money: Whence It Came, Where It Went.   SCL12(VIII-5052),
A76(230).

Galdós, Benito Pérez
*Doña Perfecta.   MP12(III-1618),   MPCE(I-596),   MP8(II-1256),
MP6(II-813),   MPEur(256),   MP3(I-298),   MWL3(298).
Saragossa.   MP12(X-5796),   MPCE(IV-2000),   MP8(VII-4614),
MP6(V-2759),   MPEur(665),   MPv4(471),   MP2(II-935),
MWL2(935).

Galenson, Walter
*CIO Challenge to the AFL: A History of the American Labor Movement,
1935-1941, The.*   HAmer(III-1658).

Galilei, Galileo
Dialogue Concerning the Two Chief World Systems.   RCa(II-593).
Letter to the Grand Duchess Christina.   RCa(II-579).

Gallagher, John *and* Ronald Robinson, *with* Alice Denny
Africa and the Victorians.   HEur(II-1051).

Gallant, Mavis

Fairly Good Time, A. SCL12(IV-2408), SCLs(91).
Gallegos, Rómulo
  Doña Bárbara. MP12(III-1614), MPCE(I-593), MP8(II-1253),
  MP6(II-811), MPAm(151), MPv4(146), MP2(I-279),
  MWL2(279).
Gallo, Max
  Spain Under Franco: A History. HWor(II-1045).
Galloway, David Darryl
  Family Album, A. LA79(I-204).
Galouye, Daniel F.
  Dark Universe. SF(I-474).
Galsworthy, John
  Country House, The. MP12(II-1155), MPCE(I-416),
  MP8(II-903), MP6(I-589), MPEng(121), MP3(I-232),
  MWL3(232).
  *Forsyte Saga, The. MP12(IV-2119), MPCE(II-761),
  MP8(III-1652), MP6(II-1034), MPEng(219), MP1(I-284),
  MWL(284).
  Fraternity. MP12(IV-2159), MPCE(II-780), MP8(III-1681),
  MP6(II-1058), MPEng(237), MPv4(171), MP2(I-343),
  MWL2(343).
  Justice. MP12(VI-3108), MPCE(II-1148), MP8(IV-2421),
  MP6(III-1543), MPDr(407), MP1(I-466), MWL1(466).
  Loyalties. MP12(VI-3544), MPCE(II-1295), MP8(IV-2779),
  MP6(III-1754), MPDr(465), MP1(I-533), MWL1(533).
  Modern Comedy, A. MP12(VII-4005), MPCE(III-1481),
  MP8(V-3128), MP6(IV-1998), MPEng(536), MP1(II-612),
  MWL1(612).
  Patrician, The. MP12(VIII-4531), MPCE(III-1685),
  MP8(V-3530), MP6(IV-2265), MPEng(641), MP3(II-724),
  MWL3(724).
  Strife. MP12(XI-6311), MPCE(IV-2178), MP8(VII-5026),
  MP6(VI-3001), MPDr(813), MP1(II-936), MWL1(936).
Galt, John
  Annals of the Parish. MP12(I-240), MPCE(I-83), MP8(I-188),
  MP6(I-120), MPEng(22), MPv4(17), MP2(I-39), MWL2(39).
Galvao, Henrique
  Santa Maria: My Crusade for Portugal. HEur(III-1676).
Gamow, George
  Thirty Years That Shook Physics. HWor(I-169).
Gans, Herbert J.
  Levittowners, The. HWor(II-552).
García Márquez, Gabriel
  Autumn of the Patriarch, The. LA77(I-77).
  In Evil Hour. LA80(I-421).

MP4(II-812),   MWL4(812).
Garvey, Amy-Jacques
    Garvey and Garveyism.   HAmer(III-1446).
Garvin, James L.
    Life of Joseph Chamberlain, Vol. I: 1836-1885, The.   HEur(II-1042).
Gary, Romain
    Roots of Heaven, The.   SCL12(X-6499),   SCL7(VI-3999),   A59(212).
Gascar, Pierre
    Beasts and Men.   SCL12(I-576),   SCL7(I-343),   A57(20).
    Seed, The.   SCL12(X-6735),   SCL7(VI-4138),   A60(235).
Gascoigne, George
    Poetry of Gascoigne, The.   MP12(IX-4955),   MP8(VI-3901),
    MP4(II-814),   MWL4(814).
Gaskell, Mrs. Elizabeth
    Cranford.   MP12(II-1191),   MPCE(I-437),   MP8(II-925),
    MP6(II-609),   MPEng(123),   MPv3(106),   MP2(I-194),
    MWL2(194).
    Mary Barton.   MP12(VII-3756),   MP8(V-2947),   MP4(I-594),
    MWL4(594).
Gasquet, Francis Neil Aidan Cardinal
    Parish Life in Mediaeval England.   RCa(II-736).
Gass, William Howard
    In the Heart of the Heart of the Country.   SCL12(VI-3682),
    SCL7(III-2196),   A69(164).
    Omensetter's Luck.   SCL12(VIII-5535),   SCLs(209).
    On Being Blue.   LA77(II-594).
    World Within the Word, The.   LA79(II-913).
Gassendi, Pierre
    Syntagma Philosophicum.   Ph(I-404).
Gaston, Paul M.
    New South Creed, The.   SCL12(VIII-5283),   A71(225).
Gates, John D.
    du Pont Family, The.   LA80(I-240).
Gates, Paul W.
    *Economic History of the United States, Vol. III: The Farmer's Age:
    Agriculture, 1815-1860, The.*   HAmer(II-682).
Gatland, Kenneth
    Manned Spacecraft.   HWor(II-939).
Gaustad, Edwin Scott
    Religious History of America, A.   HWor(I-509).
Gautier, Théophile
    Mademoiselle de Maupin.   MP12(VI-3604),   MPCE(III-1315),
    MP8(IV-2824),   MP6(III-1776),   MPEur(464),   MP1(I-542),
    MWL1(542).
    Poetry of Gautier, The.   MP12(IX-4961),   MP8(VI-3907),

When Harlie Was One.   SF(V-2455).

Gershoy, Leo
French Revolution and Napoleon, The.   Different analyses on this title
appear in: HEur(I-549; II-600).

Gerson, John
On Ecclesiastical Unity.   RCh(I-299).

Gerson, Louis L.
*American Secretaries of State and Their Diplomacy, Vol. XVII: John
Foster Dulles, The.*   HWor(II-694).

Geston, Mark S.
Lords of the Starship.   SF(III-1261).

Gewirth, Alan
*Marsilius of Padua: The Defender of Peace, Vol. I: Marsilius of Padua
and Medieval Political Philosophy.*   HAnc(III-1611).

Geyl, Pieter
Debates with Historians.   HWor(I-331).

Geymonat, Ludovico
Galileo Galilei.   HEur(I-288).

Ghiselin, Brewster
Country of the Minotaur.   SCL12(III-1598),   A71(51).

Gibbon, Edward
*History of the Decline and Fall of the Roman Empire, The.
MP12(V-2649),   MP8(III-2062),   MP6(III-1317),   MPNf(146),
MP3(I-474),   MWL3(474). A different analysis on this title appears in:
HAnc(II-983).

Gibbons, Reginald, *ed.*
*Poet's Work: 29 Masters of 20th Century Poetry on the Origins and
Practice of Their Art, The.*   LA80(II-668).

Gibbons, Stella
Cold Comfort Farm.   MP12(II-1016),   MP8(II-784),   MP4(I-139),
MWL4(139).

Gibney, Frank
Operators, The.   SCL12(VIII-5624),   SCL7(V-3441),   A61(191).

Gibran, Kahlil
Prophet, The.   MP12(IX-5372),   MP8(VI-4287),   MP4(II-1036),
MWL4(1036).

Gibson, Ian
Death of Lorca, The.   SCL12(III-1827),   A74(69).

Gibson, John M.
Physician to the World.   HAmer(II-1316).

Gibson, William
Mass for the Dead, A.   SCL12(VII-4810),   SCL7(IV-2927),
A69(222).

Giddens, Paul H.
Birth of the Oil Industry, The.   HAmer(II-914).

Gide, André
Counterfeiters, The. MP12(II-1140), MPCE(I-409),
MP8(II-892), MP6(I-580), MPEur(164), MP1(I-160),
MWL1(160).
Journals of André Gide, The. MP12(VI-3059), MP8(IV-2386),
MP4(I-478), MWL4(478).
Gierke, Otto
Political Theories of the Middle Ages. HAnc(II-786).
Gilbert, Felix
To the Farewell Address: Ideas of Early American Foreign Policy.
Different analyses on this title appear in: HAmer(I-286; I-406).
Gilbert, G. M.
Nuremberg Diary. HEur(III-1524).
Gilbert, Martin, *ed.*
Winston S. Churchill: The Prophet of Truth, Vol. V: 1922-1939.
LA78(II-917).
Gilbert, Sandra M. *and* Susan Gubar
*Madwoman in the Attic: The Woman Writer and the Nineteenth-Century
Literary Imagination, The.* LA80(II-512).
Gilbert, W. S.
Gondoliers, The. MP12(IV-2310), MPCE(II-836),
MP8(III-1798), MP6(II-1126), MPDr(307), MPv4(188),
MP2(I-377), MWL2(377).
H.M.S. Pinafore. MP12(V-2669), MPCE(II-968),
MP8(III-2082), MP6(III-1325), MPDr(353), MP1(I-370),
MWL1(370).
Iolanthe. MP12(V-2922), MPCE(II-1072), MP8(IV-2278),
MP6(III-1454), MPDr(379), MPv4(247), MP2(I-493),
MWL2(493).
Mikado, The. MP12(VII-3893), MPCE(III-1428), MP8(V-3048),
MP6(IV-1937), MPDr(530), MP1(II-591), MWL1(591).
Patience. MP12(VIII-4528), MPCE(III-1684), MP8(V-3528),
MP6(IV-2263), MPDr(603), MPv4(393), MP2(II-798),
MWL2(798).
Pirates of Penzance, The. MP12(VIII-4726), MPCE(III-1756),
MP8(VI-3687), MP6(V-2379), MPDr(636), MPv4(418),
MP2(II-834), MWL2(834).
Trial by Jury. MP12(XI-6692), MPCE(IV-2325),
MP8(VIII-5313), MP6(VI-3200), MPDr(866), MPv4(542),
MP2(II-1058), MWL2(1058).
Gildner, Gary
Runner, The. LA79(II-613).
Gill, Brendan
Day the Money Stopped, The. SCL12(III-1773), SCL7(II-1067),
A58(63).

Here at the New Yorker.   SCL12(V-3383),   A76(125).

Gill, Richard
   Happy Rural Seat.   SCL12(V-3249),   A73(191).

Gillispie, Charles Coulston
   Diderot Pictorial Encyclopedia of Trades and Industry, A.   HEur(I-430).

Gilman, Richard
   Decadence: The Strange Life of an Epithet.   LA80(I-210).

Gilmore, Susan *and* Michael V. Miller, *eds.*
   Revolution at Berkeley.   HAmer(III-1915).

Gilroy, Frank D.
   Subject Was Roses, The.   SCL12(XI-7315),   SCLs(300).

Gilson, Étienne
   Christian Philosophy of St. Thomas Aquinas, The.   HAnc(III-1547).
   History of Christian Philosophy in the Middle Ages.   HAnc(II-836).
   Mystical Theology of Saint Bernard, The.   HAnc(III-1332).
   Philosopher and Theology, The.   RCa(II-1088).
   Reason and Revelation in the Middle Ages.   Different analyses on this
   title appear in: HAnc(III-1397; III-1566).
   Spirit of Mediaeval Philosophy, The.   Different analyses on this title
   appear in: Ph(II-946),   RCa(II-816).
   Unity of Philosophical Experience, The.   RCa(II-845).

Gimbel, John
   *American Occupation of Germany: Politics and the Military, 1945-1949,
   The.*   HWor(II-650).

Ginger, Ray
   Six Days or Forever: Tennessee Versus John Thomas Scopes.
   HAmer(III-1553).

Ginsberg, Allen
   Journals: Early Fifties Early Sixties.   LA78(II-483).

Giono, Jean
   *Horseman on the Roof, The.   SCL12(V-3528),   SCL7(III-2112),
   A54(114).
   *Song of the World.   MP12(XI-6163),   MPCE(IV-2124),
   MP8(VII-4913),   MP6(V-2936),   MPEur(709),   MPv4(486),
   MP2(II-983),   MWL2(983).

Gipson, Lawrence H.
   *British Empire Before the American Revolution, Vol. III: The Victorious
   Years, 1758-1760: The Great War for the Empire, The.*   HAmer(I-204).
   *British Empire Before the American Revolution, Vol. VI: The Years of
   Defeat, 1754-1757: The Great War for the Empire, The.*
   HAmer(I-204).

Giraudoux, Jean
   *Amphitryon 38.   MP12(I-189),   MP8(I-149),   MP6(I-86),
   MPDr(28),   MP3(I-30),   MWL3(30).
   *Madwoman of Chaillot, The.   MP12(VI-3611),   MP8(IV-2828),

Introduction to Descriptive Linguistics, An. HAnc(I-13).
Gleason, S. Everett *and* William L. Langer
   Undeclared War, 1940-1941, The. HAmer(III-1689).
Glendinning, Victoria
   Elizabeth Bowen. LA79(I-179).
Glubb, General Sir John Bagot
   Lost Centuries, The. HAnc(III-1578).
   Soldier with the Arabs, A. SCL12(X-7070), SCL7(VI-4340),
   A59(226).
Godden, Jon
   Seven Islands, The. SCL12(X-6859), SCL7(VI-4215), A57(238).
Godden, Jon *and* Rumer Godden
   Two Under the Indian Sun. SCL12(XII-7847), SCL7(VII-4809),
   A67(333).
Godden, Rumer
   Episode of Sparrows, An. SCL12(IV-2290), SCL7(II-1367),
   A55(95).
   Five for Sorrow, Ten for Joy. LA80(I-325).
   Greengage Summer, The. SCL12(V-3158), SCL7(III-1880),
   A59(106).
   Peacock Spring, The. LA77(II-614).
Godfrey, John
   Church in Anglo-Saxon England, The. Different analyses on this title
   appear in: HAnc(II-1060; II-1083; II-1128).
Godlee, Rickman John
   Lord Lister. HEur(II-936).
Godwin, Gail
   Odd Woman, The. SCL12(VIII-5473), A75(218).
Godwin, William
   Caleb Williams. MP12(II-740), MPCE(I-272), MP8(I-575),
   MP6(I-382), MPEng(75), MP1(I-101), MWL1(101).
   Inquiry Concerning Political Justice, An. MP12(V-2901),
   MP8(IV-2261), MP4(I-454), MWL4(454).
Goebbels, Joseph
   Final Entries, 1945: The Diaries of Joseph Goebbels. LA79(I-212).
Goethe, Johann Wolfgang von
   Egmont. MP12(III-1719), MPCE(I-631), MP8(II-1337),
   MP6(II-866), MPDr(242), MPv3(142), MP2(I-288), MWL2(288).
   Elective Affinities. MP12(III-1731), MPCE(I-634),
   MP8(II-1347), MP6(II-870), MPEur(276), MP3(I-326),
   MWL3(326).
   Faust. MP12(IV-2020), MPCE(II-730), MP8(III-1574),
   MP6(II-1000), MPDr(278), MP1(I-276), MWL1(276).
   Poetry and Truth from My Own Life. MP12(VIII-4792),
   MP8(VI-3738), MP4(II-706), MWL4(706).

Sorrows of Young Werther, The. MP12(XI-6182),
MPCE(IV-2129), MP8(VII-4928), MP6(V-2943), MPEur(712),
MP1(II-915), MWL1(915).
Wilhelm Meister's Apprenticeship. MP12(XII-7148),
MPCE(IV-2504), MP8(VIII-5653), MP6(VI-3424), MPEur(816),
MPv3(546), MP2(II-1136), MWL2(1136).
Wilhelm Meister's Travels. MP12(XII-7152), MPCE(IV-2505),
MP8(VIII-5656), MP6(VI-3427), MPEur(819), MPv3(549),
MP2(II-1139), MWL2(1139).
Goetzmann, William H.
Exploration and Empire. SCL12(IV-2372), SCL7(II-1416),
A67(101). A different analysis on this title appears in: HAmer(II-797).
Gogarten, Friedrich
Reality of Faith, The. RCh(II-1167).
Gogol, Nikolai V.
Dead Souls. MP12(III-1342), MPCE(I-491), MP8(II-1038),
MP6(II-681), MPEur(202), MP1(I-194), MWL1(194).
Inspector General, The. MP12(V-2904), MPCE(II-1065),
MP8(IV-2264), MP6(III-1444), MPDr(376), MPv3(245),
MP2(I-491), MWL2(491).
Overcoat, The. MP12(VIII-4452), MPCE(III-1660),
MP8(V-3470), MP6(IV-2230), MPEur(560), MPv4(387),
MP2(II-790), MWL2(790).
Taras Bulba. MP12(XI-6408), MPCE(IV-2211),
MP8(VII-5101), MP6(VI-3054), MPEur(740), MP1(II-954),
MWL1(954).
Goitein, S. D.
Jews and Arabs: Their Contacts Through the Ages. HWor(I-414).
Golan, Matti
Secret Conversations of Henry Kissinger, The. LA77(II-709).
Gold, Herbert
Fathers. SCL12(IV-2492), SCL7(III-1488), A68(105).
Great American Jackpot, The. SCL12(V-3095), A70(143).
Magis Will, The. SCL12(VII-4640), A72(208).
Therefore Be Bold. SCL12(XI-7523), SCL7(VII-4574), A61(248).
Gold, Ivan
Nickel Miseries. SCL12(VIII-5301), SCLs(202).
Goldberg, Arthur J.
AFL-CIO: Labor United. HWor(II-732).
Golden, Harry
Only in America. SCL12(VIII-5617), SCL7(V-3435), A59(190).
Golding, William
Darkness Visible. LA80(I-184).
Free Fall. MP12(IV-2163), MP8(III-1684), MP4(I-361),
MWL4(361), SCL12(IV-2770), SCL7(III-1654), A61(94),

BMA(198).

Inheritors, The. MP12(V-2894), MP8(IV-2255), MP4(I-452), MWL4(452), SCL12(VI-3719), SCL7(IV-2229), A63(101). A different analysis on this title appears in: SF(III-1063).

Lord of the Flies. MP12(VI-3505), MP8(IV-2747), MP4(I-566), MWL4(566). A different analysis on this title appears in : SF(III-1257).

Pyramid, The. SCL12(IX-6146), SCL7(VI-3760), A68(264).

Spire, The. SCL12(XI-7186), SCL7(VI-4417), A65(287).

Goldman, Eric G.

Crucial Decade, The. SCL12(III-1654), SCL7(II-965), A57(51).

Goldmark, Josephine

Impatient Crusader: Florence Kelley's Life Story. HAmer(III-1372).

Goldoni, Carlo

Mistress of the Inn, The. MP12(VII-3982), MPCE(III-1468), MP8(V-3114), MP6(IV-1986), MPDr(545), MPv4(343), MP2(II-691), MWL2(691).

Goldsmith, Oliver

Poetry of Goldsmith, The. MP12(IX-4964), MP8(VI-3910), MP4(II-823), MWL4(823).

She Stoops to Conquer. MP12(X-5957), MPCE(IV-2058), MP8(VII-4744), MP6(V-2846), MPDr(766), MP1(II-889), MWL1(889).

Vicar of Wakefield, The. MP12(XII-6901), MPCE(IV-2416), MP8(VIII-5465), MP6(VI-3301), MPEng(915), MP1(II-1061), MWL1(1061).

Gomme, A. W.

Historical Commentary on Thucydides, A. HAnc(I-293).

Gompers, Samuel

Seventy Years of Life and Labour. HAmer(II-1154).

Gomperz, Theodor

Greek Thinkers: A History of Ancient Philosophy. HAnc(I-288).

Goncharov, Ivan Alexandrovich

Oblomov. MP12(VII-4270), MPCE(III-1594), MP8(V-3326), MP6(IV-2136), MPEur(549), MPv3(383), MP2(II-755), MWL2(755).

Goncourt, Edmond *and* Jules de Goncourt

Charles Demailly. MP12(II-888), MPCE(I-326), MP8(I-686), MP6(I-454), MPEur(126), MP3(I-171), MWL3(171).

Germinie Lacerteux. MP12(IV-2242), MPCE(II-809), MP8(III-1746), MP6(II-1096), MPEur(324), MPv4(180), MP2(I-363), MWL2(363).

Goncourt Journals, The. MP12(IV-2307), MP8(III-1795), MP4(I-387), MWL4(387).

Manette Salomon. MP12(VII-3686), MPCE(III-1345), MP8(IV-2890), MP6(IV-1824), MPEur(469), MP3(II-628),

MWL3(628).

Renée Mauperin.   MP12(IX-5514),   MPCE(III-1885),
MP8(VII-4395),   MP6(V-2618),   MPEur(631),   MPv4(447),
MP2(II-894),   MWL2(894).

Sister Philomène.   MP12(X-6075),   MPCE(IV-2087),
MP8(VII-4845),   MP6(V-2891),   MPEur(682),   MP3(II-990),
MWL3(990).

Gonzalez, Edward
  Cuba Under Castro: The Limits of Charisma.   HWor(II-747).
Gooch, Brison D.
  *New Bonapartist Generals in the Crimean War: Distrust and
  Decision-Making in the Anglo-French Alliance, The.*   HEur(II-815).
Gooch, G. P.
  Before the War.   HEur(II-1115).
  Frederick the Great: The Ruler, the Writer, the Man.   HEur(I-417).
Goodall, Norman
  Ecumenical Movement: What It Is and What It Does, The.
  HEur(III-1553).
Goodenough, Erwin R.
  Introduction to Philo Judaeus, An.   HAnc(II-614).
Goodman, Mitchell
  End of It, The.   SCL12(IV-2236),   SCL7(II-1343),   A62(112).
Goodman, Paul
  New Reformation.   SCL12(VIII-5280),   A71(223).
Goodspeed, Edgar Johnson
  History of Early Christian Literature, A.   HAnc(II-699).
  New Solutions of New Testament Problems.   HAnc(II-782).
  Story of the Apocrypha, The.   HAnc(I-445).
Goodwin, Richard N.
  Triumph or Tragedy: Reflections on Vietnam.   SCL12(XI-7790),
  SCL7(VII-4770),   A67(328).
Gor, Gennadiy Samoilovich
  Short Fiction of Gennadiy Samoilovich Gor, The.   SF(IV-1963).
Gordimer, Nadine
  Burger's Daughter.   LA80(I-123).
  Conservationist, The.   SCL12(III-1555),   A76(57).
  Livingston's Companions.   SCL12(VII-4440),   A72(198).
  Not for Publication.   SCL12(VIII-5402),   SCL7(V-3301),   A66(200).
  Selected Stories.   LA77(II-725).
  World of Strangers, A.   SCL12(XII-8420),   SCL7(VII-5154),
  A59(283).
Gordon, Caroline
  *Aleck Maury, Sportsman.   MP12(I-93),   MPCE(I-34),   MP8(I-72),
  MP6(I-49),   MPAm(10),   MP1(I-17),   MWL1(17).
  *Malefactors, The.   SCL12(VII-4688),   SCLs(176).

Old Red and Other Stories.   SCL12(VIII-5523),   SCL7(V-3376),
A64(198).

Gordon, David C.
Passing of French Algeria, The.   HEur(III-1631).

Gordon, Mary
Final Payments.   LA79(I-218).

Gordon, Rex
First on Mars.   SF(II-787).

Gordon, Suzanne
Lonely in America.   LA77(I-445).

Gore, Charles
Christ and Society.   RCh(II-942).

Gorky, Maxim
Artamonov Business, The.   MP12(I-326),   MPCE(I-118),
MP8(I-252),   MP6(I-169),   MPEur(42),   MP3(I-69),   MWL3(69).
Foma Gordyeeff.   MP12(IV-2100),   MPCE(II-753),
MP8(III-1637),   MP6(II-1027),   MPEur(306),   MPv4(I-161),
MP2(I-331),   MWL2(331).
Lower Depths, The.   MP12(VI-3540),   MPCE(II-1293),
MP8(IV-2776),   MP6(III-1752),   MPDr(462),   MPv3(303),
MP2(II-604),   MWL2(604).
Mother.   MP12(VII-4072),   MP8(V-3176),   MP6(IV-2034),
MPEur(517),   MP3(II-676),   MWL3(676).

Gornick, Vivian
Essays in Feminism.   LA80(I-302).

Gossage, A. J.
"Plutarch," in Latin Biography.   HAnc(II-689).

GottliebFichte, Johann
Vocation of Man, The.   Ph(I-570).

Gottmann, Jean
Megalopolis: The Urbanized Northeastern Seaboard of the United States.
HAmer(III-1815).

Goudge, Elizabeth
My God and My All: The Life of St. Francis of Assisi.   HAnc(III-1449).

Goulden, Joseph C.
*Meany: A Biography of the Unchallenged Strong Man of American
Labor.*   HWor(II-733).

Gourmont, Remy de
Night in the Luxembourg, A.   MP12(VII-4215),   MPCE(III-1575),
MP8(V-3284),   MP6(IV-2112),   MPEur(547),   MP1(II-655),
MWL1(655).

Gouzenko, Igor
Fall of a Titan, The.   SCL12(IV-2425),   SCL7(II-1446),   A54(68).

Govan, Thomas P.
Nicholas Biddle: Nationalist and Public Banker, 1786-1844.

HAmer(I-542).

Goyen, William
Fair Sister, The. SCL12(IV-2405), SCL7(II-1434), A64(75).

Goytisolo, Juan
Fiestas. SCL12(IV-2559), SCL7(III-1514), A61(77).

Graber, Doris A.
"Truman and Eisenhower Doctrines in the Light of the Doctrine of Non-Intervention, The," in *Political Science Quarterly.* HWor(II-761).

Grabill, Joseph L.
Protestant Diplomacy and the Near East: Missionary Influence on American Policy, 1810-1927. HWor(I-114).

Graebner, Norman A.
Empire on the Pacific: A Study in American Continental Expansion. HAmer(II-782).

Graham, A. J.
Colony and Mother City in Ancient Greece. HAnc(I-132).

Graham, Dom Aelred, O.S.B
Zen Catholicism. RCa(II-1124).

Grahame, Kenneth
Wind in the Willows, The. MP12(XII-7159), MPCE(IV-2507), MP8(VIII-5662), MP6(VI-3431), MPEng(955), MPv4(591), MP2(II-1141), MWL2(1141).

Grandville, J. J. *and* Taxile Delord
autre monde, Un. SF(I-105).

Granger, Bruce I.
Benjamin Franklin: An American Man of Letters. HAmer(I-239).

Granville-Barker, Harley
Madras House, The. MP12(VI-3607), MPCE(III-1317), MP8(IV-2826), MP6(III-1778), MPDr(472), MP3(II-604), MWL3(604).

Grass, Günter
*Cat and Mouse. MP12(II-842), MP8(I-647), MP4(I-113), MWL4(113), SCL12(II-1114), SCL7(I-641), A64(46).
Dog Years. SCL12(III-2005), SCL7(II-1202), A66(78).
Flounder, The. LA79(I-226).
From the Diary of a Snail. SCL12(IV-2801), A74(140).
Local Anaesthetic. SCL12(VII-4450), A71(170).
*Tin Drum, The. MP12(XI-6553), MP8(VIII-5211), MP4(II-1220), MWL4(1220), SCL12(XI-7662), SCL7(VII-4679), A64(269).

Gratian, Johannes
Decretum Gratiani. RCa(I-324).

Grau, Shirley Ann
Black Prince, The. SCL12(II-761), SCL7(I-436), A55(26).
Condor Passes, The. SCL12(III-1513), A72(78).

Quiet American, The. SCL12(IX-6204), SCL7(VI-3798), A57(215).
Sense of Reality, A. SCL12(X-6845), SCL7(VI-4206), A64(234).
Sort of Life, A. SCL12(XI-7124), A72(297).
Travels with My Aunt. SCL12(XI-7765), A71(332).
Greene, John C.
    Darwin and the Modern World View. HEur(II-858).
Greene, Lorenzo J.
    Negro in Colonial New England, The. HAmer(I-72).
Greene, Robert
    Friar Bacon and Friar Bungay. MP12(IV-2172), MPCE(II-782), MP8(III-1693), MP6(II-1062), MPDr(281), MPv4(173), MP2(I-345), MWL2(345).
    Greene's Groatsworth of Wit Bought with a Million of Repentance. MP12(IV-2394), MP8(III-1862), MP4(I-397), MWL4(397).
Greenfield, Kent Roberts
    Command Decisions. HAmer(III-1723).
Greenidge, Abel H. J.
    Roman Political Life. HAnc(I-451).
    Roman Public Life. HAnc(I-222).
Greenslade, S. L.
    Church and State from Constantine to Theodosius. HAnc(II-855).
Greenwood, Ernest
    Amber to Amperes. HEur(II-562).
Greer, Ben
    Slammer. SCL12(X-7011), A76(294).
Greer, Germaine
    Female Eunuch, The. SCL12(IV-2537), A72(138).
    Obstacle Race: The Fortunes of Women Painters and Their Work, The. LA80(II-600).
Greg, Percy
    Across the Zodiac. SF(I-11).
Gregg, Josiah
    Commerce of the Prairies, The. HAmer(I-590).
Gregor-Dellin, Martin
    Lamp Post, The. SCL12(VI-4082), SCL7(IV-2485), A65(167).
Gregory, Horace
    Collected Poems. SCL12(II-1368), SCL7(II-801), A65(50).
Gregory, Horace *and* Marya A. Zaturenska
    History of American Poetry, 1900-1940, A. HAmer(III-1403).
Gregory, Lady
    Seven Short Plays. MP12(X-5932), MP8(VII-4725), MP6(V-2832), MPDr(764), MP3(II-963), MWL3(963).
Gregory of Nazianzus, Saint
    Five Theological Orations. RCh(I-113), RCa(I-116).

Gregory of Nyssa, Saint
    Great Catechism, The.   Different analyses on this title appear in:
    RCh(I-125),   RCa(I-120).
    Lord's Prayer, The.   RCa(I-136).
Gregory Thaumaturgus, Saint
    Oration and Panegyric Addressed to Origen, The.   RCa(I-69).
Gregory the Great, Saint
    Dialogues.   RCa(I-241).
    Pastoral Care.   Different analyses on this title appear in: RCh(I-176),
    RCa(I-237).
Gregory, Bishop of Tours, Saint
    History of the Franks.   Different analyses on this title appear in:
    RCa(I-244),   HAnc(II-997).
Griffin, Clifford S.
    Their Brothers' Keepers: Moral Stewardship in the United States,
    1800-1865.   HAmer(I-645).
Griffin, Gerald
    Collegians, The.   MP12(II-1028),   MPCE(I-376),   MP8(II-796),
    MP6(I-523),   MPEng(115),   MPv4(77),   MP2(I-160),   MWL2(160).
Griffin, John Howard
    Black Like Me.   SCL12(II-754),   SCLs(34).
    Devil Rides Outside, The.   SCL12(III-1913),   SCLs(88).
Griffith, George
    Angel of the Revolution, The.   SF(I-67).
Griffith, G. T. *and* Sir William W. Tarn
    Hellenistic Civilization.   HAnc(I-341).
Griffiths, Trevor
    Comedians.   LA77(I-174).
Grifoni, Ulisse
    Dalla Terra alle stelle.   SF(I-465).
Grillmeier, Aloys, S. J.
    Christ in Christian Tradition: From the Apostolic Age to Chalcedon.
    HAnc(II-965).
Grillparzer, Franz
    Jewess of Toledo, The.   MP12(V-3008),   MPCE(II-1112),
    MP8(IV-2341),   MP6(III-1500),   MPDr(395),   MP3(I-528),
    MWL3(528).
    Sappho.   MP12(X-5793),   MPCE(IV-1999),   MP8(VII-4611),
    MP6(V-2757),   MPDr(730),   MP3(II-923),   MWL3(923).
Grimm, Harold J.
    Reformation Era, 1500-1650, The.   Different analyses on this title
    appear in: HEur(I-94; I-151).
Grimmelshausen, H. J. C. von
    Simplicissimus the Vagabond.   MP12(X-6053),   MPCE(IV-2077),
    MP8(VII-4829),   MP6(V-2877),   MPEur(679),   MPv4(481),

MP2(II-966),   MWL2(966).
Grindrod, Muriel
Rebuilding of Italy, The.   HEur(III-1541).
Groc, Leon *and* Jacqueline Zorn
Univers Vagabond, L'.   SF(V-2362).
Groote, Gerhard (Geert de)
Following of Christ, The.   RCh(I-291).
Grosser, Alfred
French Foreign Policy Under De Gaulle.   HEur(III-1651).
Grotius, Hugo
On the Law of War and Peace.   MP12(VIII-4373),   MP8(V-3404),
MP4(I-648),   MWL4(648).
Truth of the Christian Religion, The.   RCh(I-432).
Grubb, Davis
Dream of Kings, A.   SCL12(III-2063),   SCL7(II-1237),   A55(86).
Night of the Hunter, The.   SCL12(VIII-5320),   SCL7(V-3236),
A54(192).
Voices of Glory, The.   SCL12(XII-8039),   SCL7(VII-4919),
A63(282).
Gruening, Ernest
Battle for Alaska Statehood, The.   HWor(II-795).
Guardini, Romano
Humanity of Christ, The.   RCa(II-1064).
Lord, The.   RCa(II-849).
Guarducci, Margherita
*Tomb of St. Peter—New Discoveries in the Sacred Grottoes of the Vatican,
The*.   HAnc(II-645).
Gubar, Susan *and* Sandra M. Gilbert
*Madwoman in the Attic: The Woman Writer and the Nineteenth-Century
Literary Imagination, The*.   LA80(II-512).
Guderian, Heinz
Panzer Leader.   HWor(I-484).
Guérard, Albert
France: A Modern History.   HAnc(III-1705).
Triumph of the Novel, The.   LA77(II-847).
Guérdan, René
Byzantium: Its Triumphs and Tragedy.   HAnc(III-1720).
Guest, Barbara
Poems.   SCL12(IX-5906),   SCL7(V-3614),   A63(189).
Guest, Judith
Ordinary People.   LA77(II-597).
Guillén, Jorge
Cántico.   SCL12(II-1064),   SCL7(I-612),   A66(43).
Guillermaz, Jacques
Chinese Communist Party in Power, 1949-1976, The.   LA78(I-174).

Güiraldes, Ricardo
  Don Segundo Sombra.   MP12(III-1609),   MPCE(I-590),
  MP8(II-1250),   MP6(II-809),   MPAm(148),   MPv4(143),
  MP2(I-277),   MWL2(277).
Guitton, Jean
  Essay on Human Love.   RCa(II-923).
Gunderson, Robert G.
  Log-Cabin Campaign, The.   HAmer(II-762).
Gunkel, Hermann
  Legends of Genesis: The Biblical Saga and History, The.   HAnc(I-98).
Gunn, James E.
  Immortals, The.   SF(II-1014).
  Listeners, The.   SF(III-1226).
Gunn, Thom
  Selected Poems, 1950-1975.   LA80(II-750).
  Touch.   SCL12(XI-7713),   SCL7(VII-4717),   A69(315).
Gunnarsson, Gunnar
  Guest the One-Eyed.   MP12(IV-2416),   MP8(III-1878),
  MP6(III-1185),   MPEur(347),   MP3(I-437),   MWL3(437).
Gunther, John
  Inside Africa.   SCL12(VI-3737),   SCL7(IV-2243),   A55(131).
  Inside Russia Today.   SCL12(VI-3740),   SCL7(IV-2246),   A59(125).
Gurley, John G.
  China's Economy and the Maoist Strategy.   HWor(II-561).
Guthrie, A. B., Jr.
  *Big Sky, The.   MP12(I-531),   MPCE(I-193),   MP8(I-410),
  MP6(I-275),   MPAm(57),   MP1(I-70),   MWL1(70).
  Last Valley, The.   SCL12(VI-4151),   A76(161).
  These Thousand Hills.   SCL12(XI-7529),   SCL7(VII-4580),
  A57(263).
Guthrie, W. K. C.
  Greeks and Their Gods, The.   HAnc(I-161).
Gutman, Herbert G
  Black Family in Slavery and Freedom, 1750-1925, The.   LA77(I-87).
Gutman, Robert W.
  Richard Wagner.   SCL12(X-6406),   SCL7(VI-3925),   A69(280).
Guttmann, Allen
  Wound in the Heart: America and the Spanish Civil War, The.
  HAmer(III-1664).
Guzmán, Martin Luis
  *Eagle and the Serpent, The.   MP12(III-1679),   MP8(II-1305),
  MP4(I-253),   MWL4(253).
Gwatkin, Henry Melvill *and* J. P. Whitney, *eds.*
  *Cambridge Medieval History, Vol. I: The Christian Roman Empire and
  the Foundation of the Teutonic Kingdoms, The.*   HAnc(II-959).

Gwynn, Denis
    Daniel O'Connell, the Irish Liberator.   HEur(II-672).
    History of Partition, 1912-1925, The.   HEur(III-1237).
    Struggle for Catholic Emancipation, The.   HEur(II-672).
Gwyther, John
    Captain Cook and the South Pacific.   SCL12(II-1080),   SCL7(I-621),
    A55(41).

Hachiya, Michihiko
    Hiroshima Diary.   SCL12(V-3443),   SCL7(III-2052),   A55(121),
    BMA(234).
Hacker, Andrew
    End of the American Era, The.   HWor(I-531).
Hacker, Marilyn
    Presentation Piece.   SCL12(IX-6030),   A75(250).
Hackett, Francis
    Francis the First.   HEur(I-85).
Hadas, Moses
    History of Greek Literature, A.   Different analyses on this title appear
    in: HAnc(I-113; I-262).
    History of Latin Literature, A.   HAnc(I-534).
Hadley, Charles D. *and* Everett Carll Ladd, Jr.
    *Transformations of the American Party System: Political Coalitions from
    the New Deal to the 1970s.*   HWor(III-1307).
Hadzsits, George Depue
    Lucretius and His Influence.   HAnc(I-514).
Haeckel, Ernst Heinrich
    Riddle of the Universe, The.   Ph(II-734).
Hafen, LeRoy R. *and* Ann W. Hafen
    *Handcarts to Zion: The Story of a Unique Western Migration, 1856-1860
    .*   HAmer(II-816).
Haffner, Sebastian
    Meaning of Hitler, The.   LA80(II-528).
Hāfiz
    Divan, The.   MP12(III-1527),   MP8(II-1190),   MP6(II-761),
    MPPo(61),   MP3(I-285),   MWL3(285).
Hagedorn, Hermann
    Roosevelt Family of Sagamore Hill, The.   SCL12(X-6483),
    SCL7(VI-3987),   A54(240).
Haggard, H. Rider
    King Solomon's Mines.   MP12(VI-3163),   MPCE(II-1169),
    MP8(IV-2465),   MP6(III-1574),   MPEng(410),   MP1(I-475),
    MWL1(475).
    She.   MP12(X-5952),   MPCE(IV-2055),   MP8(VII-4741),
    MP6(V-2843),   MPEng(787),   MP1(II-886),   MWL1(886). A

different analysis on this title appears in: SF(IV-1908).

Haight, Gordon S.
George Eliot: A Biography. SCL12(V-2895), SCL7(III-1729),
A69(130).

Haines, Charles G.
*Role of the Supreme Court in American Government and Politics,
1789-1835, The.* HAmer(I-347).

Haines, John
Stone Harp, The. SCL12(XI-7237), A72(305).
Winter News. SCL12(XII-8336), SCL7(VII-5101), A67(344).

Hakluyt, Richard
Hakluyt's Voyages. MP12(V-2450), MPCE(II-894),
MP8(III-1906), MP6(III-1201), MPNf(131), MP1(I-346),
MWL1(346).

Halasz, Nicholas
Captain Dreyfus: The Story of a Mass Hysteria. HEur(II-1078).

Halberstam, David
Best and the Brightest, The. SCL12(I-673), A73(42).
Powers That Be, The. LA80(II-684).

Haldeman, Joe
Forever War, The. SF(II-813).
Mindbridge. SF(III-1407).

Hale, Edward Everett
*Man Without a Country, The. MP12(VII-3683), MPCE(III-1343),
MP8(IV-2888), MP6(IV-1822), MPAm(383), MP1(I-553),
MWL1(553).

Hale, Oron J.
*Publicity and Diplomacy: With Special Reference to England and
Germany, 1890-1914.* HEur(III-1212).

Hale, Richard W., Jr. *and* Robert B.
Britain, Her Peoples, and the Commonwealth. HEur(III-1375).

Halecki, Oscar
*"From the Union with Hungary to the Union with Lithuania: Jadwiga
1374-99,"* in *The Cambridge History of Poland. From the Origins to
Sobieski (to 1696).* HAnc(III-1653).
Millennium of Europe, The. RCa(II-1128).

Hales, Edward E.
Mazzini and the Secret Societies. HEur(II-700).
*Pio Nono: A Study in European Politics and Religion in the Nineteenth
Century.* Different analyses on this title appear in: HEur(II-773; II-905;
II-981).

Halévy, Elie
Growth of Philosophic Radicalism, The. Different analyses on this title
appear in: HEur(I-536; II-631).
"Rule of Democracy 1905-1914, The," in *A History of the English People*

in the Nineteenth Century.   HEur(III-1217).
Halévy, Ludovic
   Abbé Constantin, The.   MP12(I-1),   MPCE(I-1),   MP8(I-1),
   MP6(I-1),   MPEur(1),   MP1(I-1),   MWL1(1).
Haley, Alex
   Roots.   LA77(II-690).
Hall, A. R.
   Scientific Revolution, 1500-1800, The.   HEur(I-136).
Hall, Donald
   Alligator Bride, The.   SCL12(I-237),   SCLs(5).
   *Poetry of Hall, The.   MP12(IX-4973),   MP8(VI-3919),
   MP4(II-829),   MWL4(829).
   Remembering Poets: Reminiscences and Opinions.   LA79(II-584).
   Roof of Tiger Lilies, A.   SCL12(X-6475),   SCL7(VI-3980),
   A65(252).
   String Too Short to Be Saved.   SCL12(XI-7302),   SCL7(VII-4479),
   A62(2906).
Hall, James B.
   Us He Devours.   SCL12(XII-7949),   SCL7(VII-4858),   A65(299).
Hall, James Norman *and* Charles Nordhoff
   Mutiny on the Bounty.   MP12(VII-4099),   MPCE(III-1524),
   MP8(V-3195),   MP6(IV-2044),   MPAm(427),   MP1(II-628),
   MWL1(628).
Hall, Lawrence Sargent
   Stowaway.   SCL12(XI-7271),   SCL7(VII-4464),   A62(288).
Hall, Oakley
   Bad Lands, The.   LA79(I-47).
Hallberg, Charles
   Suez Canal: Its History and Diplomatic Importance, The.   HEur(II-820).
Halle, Louis J.
   Cold War as History, The.   HEur(III-1536).
   Out of Chaos.   LA78(II-626).
Halperin, S. William
   Germany Tried Democracy.   HEur(III-1297).
   Italy and the Vatican at War.   Different analyses on this title appear in:
   HEur(II-960; II-980).
Halpern, Ben
   Idea of the Jewish State, The.   HWor(II-637).
Halpern, Martin
   Two Sides of an Island.   SCL2(XII-7841),   SCL7(VII-4803),
   A64(278).
Halsband, Robert
   Life of Lady Mary Wortley Montagu, The.   SCL12(VII-4344),
   SCL7(IV-2651),   A58(147).
Hamarneh, Sami K.

"Arabic Historiography as Related to the Health Professions in Medieval Islam," in *Medical History.*   HAnc(III-1228).

"Climax of Chemical Therapy in the 10th Century Arabic Medicine, The," in *Der Islam.*   HAnc(II-1181).

"Climax of Medieval Arabic Professional Pharmacy, The," in *Bulletin of the History of Medicine.*   Different analyses on this title appear in: HAnc(II-1181; III-1228).

Index of Arabic Manuscripts on Medicine and Pharmacy at the National Library of Cairo.   HAnc(III-1228).

"Medical Education and Practice in Medieval Islam," in O'Malley's *The History of Medical Education.*   Different analyses on this title appear in: HAnc(II-1181; III-1228).

"Sources and Development of Arabic Medical Therapy and Pharmacology," in *Sudhoffs Archiv.*   Different analyses on this title appear in: HAnc(II-1181; III-1228).

"Surgical Developments in Medieval Arabic Medicine," in *Viewpoints: American Friends of the Middle East.*   HAnc(III-1228).

Hamerow, Theodore S.
Restoration, Revolution, Reaction: Economics and Politics in Germany, 1815-1871.   Different analyses on this title appear in: HEur(II-791; II-884).

Hamilton, Alexander, James Madison *and* John Jay
Federalist, The.   MP12(IV-2025),   MP8(III-1577),   MP6(II-1002), MPNf(124),   MP3(I-384),   MWL3(384).

Hamilton, Edith
"Pindar: The Last Greek Aristocrat," in *The Great Way to Western Civilization.*   HAnc(I-218).

Hamilton, Edmond
Short Fiction of Edmond Hamilton, The.   SF(IV-1939).

Hamilton, Holman
Prologue to Conflict: The Crisis and Compromise of 1850. HAmer(II-857).

Hamilton, Nigel
Brothers Mann: The Lives of Heinrich and Thomas Mann, 1871-1950 and 1875-1955, The.   LA80(I-119).

Hammar, George
Christian Realism in Contemporary American Theology. HAmer(III-1606).

Hammarskjöld, Dag
Markings.   SCL12(VII-4775),   SCL7(IV-2910),   A65(195).

Hammer, Ellen Joy
Struggle for Indochina, The.   HWor(II-700).

Hammett, Dashiell
Glass Key, The.   MP12(IV-2267),   MPCE(II-823),   MP8(III-1762), MP6(II-1110),   MPAm(207),   MP1(I-307),   MWL1(307).

Maltese Falcon, The. MP12(VI-3661), MPCE(III-1337),
MP8(IV-2868), MP6(IV-1806), MPAm(380), MP1(I-551),
MWL1(551).
Thin Man, The. MP12(XI-6489), MPCE(IV-2240),
MP8(VIII-5164), MP6(VI-3093), MPAm(638), MP1(II-970),
MWL1(970).
Hammond, Barbara *and* John L. Hammond
Age of the Chartists. HEur(II-735).
Hammond, B. G. L.
History of Greece to 322 B.C., A. HAnc(I-340).
Hammond, Bray
Banks and Politics in America, from the Revolution to the Civil War.
Different analyses on this title appear in: HAmer(I-568; II-699).
Hammond, George P.
Don Juan de Oñate and the Founding of New Mexico.
HAmer(I-44).
Hammond, John L. *and* Barbara Hammond
Age of the Chartists. HEur(II-735).
Hammond, Mason
*Augustan Principate in Theory and Practice During the Julio-Claudian
Period, The.* HAnc(I-564).
City-State and World State. HAnc(I-509).
Hamsun, Knut
Growth of the Soil. MP12(IV-2404), MPCE(II-878),
MP8(III-1870), MP6(II-1177), MPEur(341), MP1(I-338),
MWL1(338).
Hunger. MP12(V-2780), MPCE(II-1024), MP8(III-2163),
MP6(III-1386), MPEur(380), MP1(I-400), MWL1(400). A different
analysis on this title appears in: SCL12(V-3573), SCL7(III-2141),
A68(160).
Hancock, W. K.
*Survey of British Commonwealth Affairs, Vol. I: Problems of Nationality,
1918-1936.* HEur(III-1316).
Handke, Peter
Left-Handed Woman, The. LA79(I-363).
Moment of True Feeling, A. LA78(II-585).
Short Letter, Long Farewell. SCL12(X-6936), A75(296).
Sorrow Beyond Dreams, A. SCL12(XI-7120), A76(302).
Hanke, Lewis
Spanish Struggle for Justice in the Conquest of America, The.
HEur(I-131).
Hanmura, Ryo
Sanreizan Hiroku. SF(IV-1854).
Hannah, Barry
Airships. LA79(I-5).

MP4(II-831),   MWL4(831).
*Return of the Native, The.   MP12(X-5545),   MPCE(III-1894),
MP8(VII-4420),   MP6(V-2628),   MPEng(728),   MP1(II-818),
MWL1(818).
*Tess of the D'Urbervilles.   MP12(XI-6457),   MPCE(IV-2228),
MP8(VIII-5141),   MP6(VI-3080),   MPEng(827),   MP1(II-965),
MWL1(965).
*Under the Greenwood Tree.   MP12(XII-6829),   MPCE(IV-2386),
MP8(VIII-5411),   MP6(VI-3265),   MPEng(892),   MPv4(559),
MP2(II-1084),   MWL2(1084).
*Woodlanders, The.   MP12(XII-7247),   MPCE(IV-2543),
MP8(VIII-5726),   MP6(VI-3474),   MPEng(968),   MPv4(598),
MP2(II-1156),   MWL2(1156).
Hare, Christopher
   Charles de Bourbon: High Constable of France.   HEur(I-84).
Hargreaves, John D.
   Prelude to the Partition of West Africa.   HEur(II-1050).
Harkness, Georgia
   John Calvin: The Man and His Ethics.   HEur(I-120).
Harlan, Louis R.
   Booker T. Washington: The Making of a Black Leader, 1856-1901.
   HAmer(II-1252).
Harnack, Adolf
   History of Dogma, The.   HAnc(II-869).
   Origin of the New Testament, The.   HAnc(II-781).
   What Is Christianity?   RCh(II-823).
Harness, Charles L.
   Paradox Men, The.   SF(IV-1641).
   Rose, The.   SF(IV-1832).
Harper, Lawrence A.
   English Navigation Laws, The.   HAmer(I-125).
Harper, Vincent
   Mortgage on the Brain, The.   SF(III-1459).
Harrer, Heinrich
   Seven Years in Tibet.   SCL12(X-6868),   SCL7(VI-4224),   A54(252).
Harriman, W. Averell and Elie Abel
   Special Envoy to Churchill and Stalin, 1941-1946.   SCL12(XI-7165),
   A76(306).
Harrington, Michael
   Other America: Poverty in the United States, The.   HAmer(III-1867).
   Socialism.   SCL12(X-7063),   A73(328).
   Twilight of Capitalism, The.   LA77(II-857).
Harris, H. A.
   Greek Athletes and Athletics.   HAnc(I-118).
Harris, Joel Chandler

Short Fiction of Nathaniel Hawthorne, The.   SF(IV-2035).
Hayden, Robert
　　Angle of Ascent.   LA77(I-48).
Haydn, Richard
　　Journal of Edwin Carp, The.   SCL12(VI-3909),   SCL7(IV-2368),
　　A54(123).
Haydon, Benjamin Robert
　　Autobiography of Benjamin Robert Haydon, The.   MP12(I-365),
　　MP8(I-281),   MP4(I-48),   MWL4(48).
Hayes , Carlton J. H.
　　Generation of Materialism, 1871-1900, A. Vol. XVI of *The Rise of*
　　Modern Europe series.   HEur(II-991).
　　Nationalism: A Religion.   RCa(II-1091).
Hays, Samuel P.
　　Conservation and the Gospel of Efficiency: The Progressive Conservation
　　Movement, 1890-1920.   HAmer(III-1376).
Hazel, Robert
　　American Elegies.   SCL12(I-259),   A70(21).
　　Poems/1951-1961.   SCL12(IX-5924),   SCL7(V-3628),   A62(229),
　　BMA(442).
Hazeltine, Harold Dexter
　　"Roman and Canon Law in the Middle Ages," in *Vol. V.* of *The*
　　Cambridge Medieval History.   HAnc(III-1494).
Hazlitt, William
　　Critical Essays of William Hazlitt.   MP12(II-1217),   MP8(II-943),
　　MP4(I-166),   MWL4(166).
　　Familiar Essays of William Hazlitt, The.   MP12(IV-1974),
　　MP8(III-1542),   MP4(I-319),   MWL4(319).
　　*Liber Amoris.   MP12(VI-3379),   MP8(IV-2644),   MP6(III-1670),
　　MPNf(180),   MP3(I-570),   MWL3(570).
Hazo, Samuel
　　Once for the Last Bandit.   SCL12(VIII-5565),   A73(289).
Hazzard, Shirley
　　Bay of Noon, The.   SCL12(I-562),   A71(17).
　　Evening of the Holiday, The.   SCL12(IV-2343),   SCL7(II-1395),
　　A67(98).
H. D. *See* Doolittle, Hilda.
Head, Barclay V.
　　Historia Numorum.   HAnc(I-145).
Heaney, Seamus
　　Field Work.   LA80(I-315).
Hearn, Lafcadio
　　*Chita.   MP12(II-940),   MPCE(I-345),   MP8(II-727),
　　MP6(I-477),   MPAm(92),   MPv3(75),   MP2(I-149),   MWL2(149).
　　Youma.   MP12(XII-7306),   MPCE(IV-2569),   MP8(VIII-5771),

Religion and the American Mind. SCL12(IX-6334),
SCL7(VI-3876), A67(283). A different analysis on this title appears in:
HAmer(I-178).

Heine, Heinrich
Book of Songs. MP12(I-593), MP8(I-458), MP6(I-309),
MPPo(25), MP3(I-118), MWL3(118).

Heinlein, Robert A.
Beyond This Horizon. SF(I-207).
Citizen of the Galaxy. SF(I-363).
Double Star. SF(II-587).
Moon Is a Harsh Mistress, The. SF(III-1439).
Past Through Tomorrow, The. SF(IV-1645).
Puppet Masters, The. SF(IV-1730).
Starship Troopers. SF(V-2173).
Stranger in a Strange Land. SF(V-2195).

Heinrich, Willi
Cross of Iron, The. SCL12(III-1630), SCL7(II-954), A57(48).

Heisenberg, Werner
Physics and Beyond: Encounters and Conversations. HWor(I-249).

Heller, Joseph
*Catch-22. MP12(II-848), MP8(I-653), MP4(I-117),
MWL4(117), SCL12(II-1125), SCL7(I-647), A62(44).
Good as Gold. LA80(I-372).
*Something Happened. SCL12(XI-7101), A75(303).
*We Bombed in New Haven. SCL12(XII-8156), SCL7(VII-4989),
A69(340).
Zionist Idea, The. HEur(II-1092).

Hellman, Lillian
Collected Plays, The. SCL12(II-1355), A73(83).
*Little Foxes, The. MP12(VI-3451), MPCE(II-1261),
MP8(IV-2702), MP6(III-1706), MPDr(451), MP3(II-588),
MWL3(588).
*Pentimento. SCL12(IX-5805), A74(303).
Scoundrel Time. LA77(II-702).
*Toys in the Attic. SCL12(XI-7275), SCL7(VII-4729), A61(263).
*Unfinished Woman, An. SCL12(XII-7898), A70(322).

Helmreich, Ernst C.
Diplomacy of the Balkan Wars, 1912-1913, The. HEur(III-1242).

Hemenway, Robert
Girl Who Sang with the Beatles and Other Stories, The.
SCL12(V-2952), A71(99).

Hemingway, Ernest
Farewell to Arms, A. MP12(IV-1995), MPCE(II-716),
MP8(III-1560), MP6(II-991), MPAm(179), MP1(I-269),
MWL1(269).

Fifth Column, The. SCL12(IV-2563), A70(125).
*For Whom the Bell Tolls. MP12(IV-2114), MPCE(II-758),
MP8(III-1649), MP6(II-1032), MPAm(186), MP1(I-282),
MWL1(282).
*Islands in the Stream. SCL12(VI-3781), A71(135).
*Moveable Feast, A. MP12(VII-4087), MP8(V-3187),
MP4(I-621), MWL4(621). A different analysis on this title appears in:
SCL12(VIII-5119), SCL7(V-3116), A65(208). A different analysis on
this title appears in: HAmer(III-1563).
*Old Man and the Sea, The. MP12(VIII-4325), MPCE(III-1617),
MP8(V-3367), MP6(IV-2165), MPAm(457), MPv4(374),
MP2(II-764), MWL2(764).
Short Stories of Ernest Hemingway, The. MP12(X-6002),
MP8(VII-4784), MP4(II-1130), MWL4(1130).
*Sun Also Rises, The. MP12(XI-6335), MPCE(IV-2181),
MP8(VII-5048), MP6(VI-3012), MPAm(618), MP1(II-941),
MWL1(941).
Hemingway, Mary Welsh
How It Was. LA77(I-362).
Hemming, John
Conquest of the Incas, The. SCL12(III-1544), A72(85).
Hémon, Louis
Maria Chapdelaine. MP12(VII-3721), MPCE(III-1359),
MP8(V-2919), MP6(IV-1844), MPAm(396), MPv3(316),
MP2(II-626), MWL2(626).
Henderson, Archibald
George Bernard Shaw. SCL12(V-2878), SCL7(III-1718), A57(84).
Henderson, Bernard W.
Five Roman Emperors. HAnc(II-677).
Henderson, Bill, *ed.*
Pushcart Prize, III: Best of the Small Presses, The. LA79(II-565).
Henderson, Nicholas
Prince Eugen of Savoy. SCL12(IX-6059), SCL7(V-3692),
A66(242).
Henderson, Philip
William Morris. SCL12(XII-8301), SCL7(VII-5081), A68(353).
Henderson, William Otto
Zollverein, The. HEur(II-712).
Henderson, Zenna
Pilgrimage: The Book of the People and *The People: No Different
Flesh.* SF(IV-1682).
Hendrick, Burton J.
Life of Andrew Carnegie, The. HAmer(II-1169).
Henley, William Ernest
Poetry of Henley, The. MP12(IX-4982), MP8(VI-3928),

Somewhere Is Such a Kingdom.   LA77(II-758).

Hill, Melvyn A., *ed.*
    Hannah Arendt: The Recovery of the Public World.
    LA80(I-395).

Hilton, James
    *Goodbye, Mr. Chips.   MP12(IV-2328),   MPCE(II-844),
    MP8(III-1812),   MP6(II-1135),   MPEng(246),   MP1(I-316),
    MWL1(316).
    *Lost Horizon.   MP12(VI-3512),   MPCE(II-1280),   MP8(IV-2753),
    MP6(III-1735),   MPEng(453),   MP1(I-527),   MWL1(527). A
    different analysis on this title appears in: SF(III-1265).

Hilton, Walter
    Ladder of Perfection, The.   Different analyses on this title appear in:
    RCh(I-316),   RCa(I-494).

Himmelfarb, Gertrude
    Darwin and the Darwinian Revolution.   SCL12(III-1719),
    SCL7(II-1020),   A60(51).

Hingley, Ronald
    New Life of Anton Chekhov, A.   LA77(II-543).

Hinsley, F. H.
    *"British Foreign Policy and Colonial Questions, 1895-1904," in The
    Cambridge History of the British Empire.*   HEur(III-1154).
    *"Great Britain and the Powers, 1904-1914," in The Cambridge History of
    the British Empire.*   HEur(III-1200).

Hippolytus, Saint
    Apostolic Tradition, The.   RCh(I-54).
    Refutation of All Heresies.   RCa(I-58).

Hirmer, Max *and* C. M. Kraay
    Greek Coins.   HAnc(I-147).

Hirmer, M. *and* K. Lange
    Egypt. Architecture, Sculpture, Painting in Three Thousand Years.
    HAnc(I-28).

Hirmer, M. *and* R. Lullies
    Greek Sculpture.   HAnc(I-278).

Hirst, Leonard B.
    Conquest of Plague, The.   HAnc(III-1627).

Hitti, Philip K.
    History of the Arabs.   Different analyses on this title appear in:
    HAnc(II-1077; II-1107).

Hjortsberg, William
    Alp.   SCL12(I-241),   A70(14).
    Gray Matters.   SF(II-921).
    Toro! Toro! Toro!   SCL12(XI-7711),   A75(329).

Hoagland, Edward
    Edward Hoagland Reader, The.   LA80(I-260).

Red Wolves and Black Bears. LA77(II-658).
Hoban, Russell
Turtle Diary. LA77(II-852).
Hobbes, Thomas
De Corpore. Ph(I-399).
Leviathan. MP12(VI-3376), MP8(IV-2641), MP6(III-1667),
MPNf(177), MP3(I-567), MWL3(567). A different analysis on this
title appears in: Ph(I-392).
Hobhouse, Christopher
1851 and the Crystal Palace. HEur(II-800).
Hochhuth, Rolf
Deputy, The. SCL12(III-1883), SCL7(II-1127), A65(71).
Hocking, William Ernest
Meaning of God in Human Experience, The. RCh(II-869).
Hodge, Charles
Systematic Theology. RCh(II-766).
Hodgson, Ralph
Poetry of Hodgson, The. MP12(IX-4986), MP8(VI-3932),
MP4(II-840), MWL4(840).
Skylark, The. SCL12(X-7008), SCL7(VI-4319), A61(235).
Hodgson, William Hope
Deep Waters. SF(II-524).
Hoepffner, Ernest
Troubadours dans leur vie et dans leurs oeuvres, Les. HAnc(III-1300).
Hoepli, Nancy L., *ed.*
Common Market, The. HWor(III-1151).
Höffding, Harald
Philosophy of Religion, The. RCh(II-828).
Hoffer, Eric
Temper of Our Time, The. SCL12(XI-7434), SCL7(VII-4537),
A67(316).
Hoffman, Banesh
Albert Einstein. SCL12(I-176), A73(7).
Hoffman, Frederick J.
Twenties: American Writing in the Postwar Decade, The.
HAmer(III-1562).
Hoffman, William
Days in the Yellow Leaf. SCL12(III-1780), SCL7(II-1070),
A59(50).
Hoffmann, E. T. A.
Devil's Elixir, The. MP12(III-1467), MPCE(I-536),
MP8(II-1136), MP6(II-734), MPEur(227), MP3(I-267),
MWL3(267).
"Sandman, The." SF(IV-1848).
Hoffmann, Peter

History of the German Resistance, 1933-1945, The. LA78(I-388).
Hoffmann, Stanley
 Primacy or World Order: American Foreign Policy Since the Cold War. LA79(II-551).
Hofmannsthal, Hugo von
 Poetry of Hofmannsthal, The. MP12(IX-4988), MP8(VI-3934), MP4(II-842), MWL4(842).
Hofstadter, Douglas R.
 Gödel, Escher, Bach: An Eternal Golden Braid. LA80(I-367).
Hofstadter, Richard
 Age of Reform, The. SCL12(I-144), SCLs(1). A different analysis on this title appears in: HAmer(II-1228).
 Anti-Intellectualism in American Life. SCL12(I-330), SCLs(11). A different analysis on this title appears in: HAmer(II-1304).
 Progressive Historians: Turner, Beard, Parrington, The. HWor(I-207).
Höhne, Heinz
 Canaris: Hitler's Master Spy. LA80(I-125).
Holborn, Hajo
 History of Modern Germany, Vol. I: The Reformation, A. Different analyses on this title appear in: HEur(I-79; I-89; I-93; I-150; I-292).
 History of Modern Germany, Vol. II: 1648-1840, A. Different analyses on this title appear in: HEur(I-379; I-483).
Hölderlin, Johann Christian Friedrich
 Poetry of Hölderlin, The. MP12(IX-4991), MP8(VI-3937), MP4(II-845), MWL4(845).
Holland, Cecelia
 Rakóssy. SCL12(IX-6245), SCL7(VI-3827), A67(280).
Holland, D. Larrimore
 "Earliest Text of the Old Roman Symbol: A Debate with Hans Leitzmann and J. N. D. Kelly, The," in Church History. HAnc(II-755).
Hollander, John
 Blue Wine and Other Poems. LA80(I-94).
 Spectral Emanations: New and Selected Poems. LA79(II-699).
Hollon, W. Eugene
 Lost Pathfinder, Zebulon Montgomery Pike, The. HAmer(I-469).
Holm, Sven
 Termush, Atlanterhavskysten. SF(V-2245).
Holmes, Oliver Wendell
 Autocrat of the Breakfast Table, The. MP12(I-379), MP8(I-293), MP6(I-193), MPNf(35), MP3(I-76), MWL3(76).
Holmes, Thomas Rice
 Caesar's Conquest of Gaul. HAnc(I-518).
Holroyd, Michael
 Lytton Strachey. SCL12(VII-4620), SCL7(IV-2817), A69(218).
Holst, Spencer

Spencer Holst Stories. LA77(II-780).
Holt, Edgar
Boer War, The. HEur(II-1130).
Holt, J. C.
Magna Carta. HAnc(III-1453).
Homer
*Iliad, The. MP12(V-2837), MPCE(II-1046), MP8(IV-2209),
MP6(III-1415), MPPo(138), MP1(I-423), MWL1(423).
*Odyssey, The. MP12(VII-4275), MPCE(III-1595),
MP8(V-3331), MP6(IV-2140), MPPo(191), MP1(II-665),
MWL1(665).
Honour, Hugh
New Golden Land, The. LA77(II-538).
Hoogenboom, Ari
*Outlawing the Spoils: A History of the Civil Service Reform Movement,
1865-1883.* HAmer(II-1131).
Hook, Sidney
Quest for Being, The. SCL12(IX-6194), SCL7(VI-3788), A62(235).
Hooker, Richard
Treatise on the Laws of Ecclesiastical Polity. RCh(I-418).
Hooper, Walter *and* Roger Lancelyn Green
C. S. Lewis: A Biography. SCL12(III-1666), A74(66).
Hooper, William Davis
*Marcus Porcius Cato, On Agriculture; Marcus Terentius Varro, On
Agriculture.* HAnc(I-467).
Hoopes, Townsend Walter
Devil and John Foster Dulles, The. SCL12(III-1905), A74(80). A
different analysis on this title appears in: HWor(II-693).
Hoover, J. Edgar
Masters of Deceit. SCL12(VII-4824), SCL7(IV-2937), A59(158).
Hope, A. D.
New Poems: 1965-1969. SCL12(VIII-5276), A71(220).
Poems. SCL12(IX-5909), SCL7(V-3617), A63(191).
Hope, Anthony
Prisoner of Zenda, The. MP12(IX-5340), MPCE(III-1814),
MP8(VI-4263), MP6(V-2528), MPEng(699), MP1(II-784),
MWL1(784).
Hopkins, C. Howard
Rise of the Social Gospel in American Protestantism, 1865-1915, The.
HAmer(II-1198).
Hopkins, Gerard Manley
Poetry of Hopkins, The. MP12(IX-4994), MP8(VI-3940),
MP6(V-2442), MPPo(266), MP3(II-807), MWL3(807). A different
analysis on this title appears in: RCa(II-760).
Hopkins, Samuel

System of Doctrines. RCh(II-629).
Hopkins, Vincent J.
    Dred Scott's Case. HAmer(II-902).
Horace (Quintus Horatius Flaccus)
    *Ars Poetica. MP12(I-319), MP8(I-246), MP6(I-164),
    MPNf(26), MP3(I-65), MWL3(65).
    Epistles of Horace, The. MP12(III-1808), MP8(II-1411),
    MP4(I-282), MWL4(282).
    Poetry of Horace, The. MP12(IX-4997), MP8(VI-3943),
    MP6(V-2445), MPPo(269), MP3(II-810), MWL3(810).
Horgan, Paul
    Centuries of Santa Fe, The. SCL12(II-1161), SCL7(I-666), A57(39).
    Great River. SCL12(V-3121), SCL7(III-1866), A54(98),
    BMA(216).
    Lamy of Santa Fe. SCL12(VI-4085), A76(157).
    Thin Mountain Air, The. LA78(II-821).
Horn, David Bayne
    "Diplomatic Revolution, The" in *The New Cambridge Modern History.*
    HEur(I-440).
Horne, Alistair
    Fall of Paris, The. SCL12(IV-2428), SCL7(II-1449), A67(107).
    Price of Glory: Verdun, 1916, The. SCL12(IX-6047),
    SCL7(V-3686), A64(215). A different analysis on this title appears in:
    HEur(III-1264).
Horsman, Reginald
    *Matthew Elliott, British Indian Agent: A Study of British Indian Policy in the
    Old Northwest.* HAmer(I-387).
Horton, Walter Marshall
    Christian Theology: An Ecumenical Approach. RCh(II-1148).
Hosford, Frances J.
    *Father Shipherd's Magna Charta: A Century of Coeducation in Oberlin
    College.* HAmer(II-711).
Hoskyns, Catherine
    Congo Since Independence: January, 1960-December, 1961, The.
    HEur(III-1615).
Hotchner, A. E.
    Papa Hemingway. SCL12(IX-5710), SCL7(V-3501), A67(259).
House, Lolabel
    *Study of the Twelfth Amendment of the Constitution of the United States,
    A.* HAmer(I-458).
Houseman, John
    Run-Through. SCL12(X-6535), A73(308).
Houser, George, Jennifer Davis, Herbert Shore *and* Susan Rogers
    No One Can Stop the Rain. HWor(III-1223).
Housman, A. E.

Shropshire Lad, A. MP12(X-6030), MP8(VII-4812),
MP6(V-2864), MPPo(338), MP3(II-974), MWL3(974).
Hovell, Mark
Chartist Movement, The. HEur(II-743).
How, W. W.
"Cicero's Ideal in His De Republica," in *Journal of Roman Studies*.
HAnc(I-529).
Howard, A. Dick
Criminal Justice in Our Time. HAmer(III-1896).
Howard, Donald S.
W. P. A. and Federal Relief Policy, The. HAmer(III-1635).
Howard, Henry, Earl of Surrey *and* Sir Thomas Wyatt
Poetry of Wyatt and Surrey, The. MP12(IX-5219), MP8(VI-4165),
MP4(II-1010), MWL4(1010).
Howard, Jane
Different Woman, A. SCL12(III-1954), A74(84).
Howard, Leon
Connecticut Wits, The. HAmer(I-639).
Howard, Maureen
Before My Time. SCL12(I-605), A76(25).
Howard, Michael
Franco-Prussian War: The German Invasion of France, 1870-1871, The.
HEur(II-955).
Howard, Richard
Preferences. SCL12(IX-6012), A75(247).
Two-Part Inventions. SCL12(XII-7858), A75(337).
Howard, Ted *and* Jeremy Rifkin
*Who Should Play God? The Artificial Creation of Life and What It Means
for the Future of the Human Race*. HWor(III-1326).
Howarth, David
Waterloo: Day of Battle. SCL12(XII-8141), SCL7(VII-4982),
A69(337).
Howe, Edgar Watson
Story of a Country Town, The. MP12(XI-6268), MPCE(IV-2164),
MP8(VII-4994), MP6(VI-2982), MPAm(613), MP1(II-929),
MWL1(929).
Howe, Irving
*Celebrations and Attacks: Thirty Years of Literary and Cultural
Commentary*. LA80(I-136).
Critical Point, The. SCL12(III-1623), A74(56).
Leon Trotsky. LA79(I-368).
World of Our Fathers. LA77(II-947).
Howe, Mark DeWolfe
Justice Oliver Wendell Holmes. SCL12(VI-3963), SCL7(IV-2391),
A58(122), BMA(278).

Howell, Roger, Jr.
    Cromwell. LA78(I-219).
Howells, William Dean
    *Hazard of New Fortunes, A. MP12(V-2495), MPCE(II-910),
    MP8(III-1944), MP6(III-1230), MPAm(252), MPv4(206),
    MP2(I-412), MWL2(412).
    *Indian Summer. MP12(V-2877), MPCE(II-1056), MP8(IV-2242),
    MP6(III-1434), MPAm(295), MPv4(240), MP2(I-482),
    MWL2(482).
    *Modern Instance, A. MP12(VII-4010), MP8(V-3130),
    MP6(IV-2000), MPAm(422), MPv3(350), MP2(II-695),
    MWL2(695).
    *Rise of Silas Lapham, The. MP12(X-5618), MPCE(III-1924),
    MP8(VII-4475), MP6(V-2664), MPAm(535), MP1(II-828),
    MWL1(828).
Howes, Barbara
    Blue Garden, The. SCL12(II-810), A73(59).
    Looking Up at Leaves. SCL12(VII-4520), SCL7(IV-2773),
    A67(201).
Hoyle, Fred
    Black Cloud, The. SF(I-228).
    October the First Is Too Late. SF(IV-1574).
Hoyt, Edwin P.
    Improper Bostonian: Dr. Oliver Wendell Holmes, The. LA80(I-414).
Hubbard, Henry *and* James Bishop, Jr.
    Let the Seller Beware. HWor(II-862).
Hubbard, L. Ron
    Fear and *Typewriter in the Sky.* SF(II-761).
Hudson, W. H.
    Crystal Age, A. SF(I-449).
    *Far Away and Long Ago. MP12(IV-1986), MPCE(II-711),
    MP8(III-1554), MP6(II-986), MPNf(121), MPv3(165),
    MP2(I-323), MWL2(323).
    *Green Mansions. MP12(IV-2386), MPCE(II-870), MP8(III-1855),
    MP6(II-1165), MPEng(251), MP1(I-333), MWL1(333).
    *Hampshire Days. MP12(V-2462), MP8(III-1914), MP4(I-406),
    MWL4(406).
    *Purple Land, The. MP12(IX-5382), MPCE(III-1834),
    MP8(VI-4294), MP6(V-2551), MPEng(708), MP1(II-791),
    MWL1(791).
Huff, Robert
    Ventriloquist, The. LA78(II-873).
Hügel, Baron Friedrich John von
    Mystical Element of Religion, The. RCa(II-749).
    Selected Letters. RCh(II-938).

Huie, William Bradford
   He Slew the Dreamer: My Search for the Truth About James Earl Ray and the Murder of Martin Luther King. HAmer(III-1929).
Huizinga, Johan
   Waning of the Middle Ages, The. MP12(XII-7017), MP8(VIII-5550), MP4(II-1266), MWL4(1266).
Hulbert, Archer B.
   Historic Highways of America, Vol. X: The Cumberland Road. HAmer(I-494).
Hulme, Harold
   Life of Sir John Eliot, The. HEur(I-266).
Hulme, Kathryn
   Nun's Story, The. SCL12(VIII-5449), SCL7(V-3334), A57(195).
Hume, David
   *Dialogues Concerning Natural Religion. Different analyses on this title appear in: Ph(I-525), RCh(II-615).
   Enquiry Concerning Human Understanding, An. MP12(III-1793), MP8(II-1397), MP6(II-897), MPNf(101), MP3(I-399), MWL3(339).
   Enquiry Concerning the Principles of Morals, An. Ph(I-488).
   *Treatise of Human Nature (Book I), A. Ph(I-471).
Hume, Martin
   Court of Philip IV, The. HEur(I-302).
Humes, H. L.
   Men Die. SCL12(VII-4929), SCL7(V-2994), A60(165).
Humphrey, William
   Home from the Hill. SCL12(V-3494), SCL7(III-2087), A59(119).
   Ordways, The. SCL12(VIII-5645), SCL7(V-3456), A66(221).
   Time and a Place, A. SCL12(XI-7641), SCL7(VII-4665), A69(309).
Hungerford, Edward
   Story of the Baltimore and Ohio Railroad, The. HAmer(I-627).
Hunt, H. A. K.
   Humanism of Cicero, The. HAnc(I-543).
Hunt, John
   Conquest of Everest, The. SCL12(III-1541), SCL7(II-900), A54(37).
Hunt, Leigh
   Autobiography of Leigh Hunt, The. MP12(I-373), MP8(I-287), MP4(I-51), MWL4(51).
Hunt, Richard W.
   "Studies on Priscian in the Twelfth Century: The School of Ralph of Beauvais," in Medieval and Renaissance Studies. HAnc(II-1026).
Hunter, Louis C.
   Steamboats on the Western Rivers: An Economic and Technological History. HAmer(I-474).
Huss, John

Physical Basis of Life, The.   MP12(VIII-4677),
MP8(VI-3649),   MP6(IV-2351),   MPNf(245),   MP3(II-754),
MWL3(754).
Huysmans, Joris Karl
   *Against the Grain.   MP12(I-62),   MPCE(I-20),   MP8(I-50),
   MP6(I-33),   MPEur(9),   MPv4(4),   MP2(I-4),   MWL2(4).
   *Down There.   MP12(III-1627),   MP8(II-1263),   MP6(II-817),
   MPEur(258),   MP3(I-300),   MWL3(300).
   *En Route.   RCa(II-716).
Hyatt, J. Philip
   Jeremiah: Prophet of Courage and Hope.   HAnc(I-151).
Hyde, Earl of Clarendon, Edward
   History of the Rebellion and Civil Wars in England.   MP12(V-2658),
   MP8(III-2071),   MP4(I-420),   MWL4(420).
Hyland, William *and* Richard Wallace Shryock
   Fall of Khrushchev, The.   HWor(II-978).
Hyman, Mac
   No Time for Sergeants.   SCL12(VIII-5388),   SCL7(V-3287),
   A54(195).

Ibáñez, Vicente Blasco
   Cabin, The.   MP12(II-722),   MPCE(I-265),   MP8(I-559),
   MP6(I-369),   MPEur(95),   MPv4(59),   MP2(I-125),   MWL2(125).
Ibsen, Henrik
   *Brand.   MP12(II-627),   MPCE(I-227),   MP8(I-487),   MP6(I-323),
   MPDr(103),   MP3(I-126),   MWL3(126).
   *Doll's House, A.   MP12(III-1570),   MPCE(I-568),   MP8(II-1223),
   MP6(II-787),   MPDr(216),   MP1(I-216),   MWL1(216).
   *Enemy of the People, An.   MP12(III-1777),   MPCE(I-649),
   MP8(II-1383),   MP6(II-891),   MPDr(253),   MPv3(146),
   MP2(I-292),   MWL2(292).
   *Ghosts.   MP12(IV-2250),   MPCE(II-813),   MP8(III-1752),
   MP6(II-1101),   MPDr(298),   MP1(I-301),   MWL1(301).
   *Hedda Gabler.   MP12(V-2532),   MPCE(II-928),   MP8(III-1970),
   MP6(III-1251),   MPDr(324),   MP1(I-359),   MWL1(359).
   *Lady from the Sea.   MP12(VI-3206),   MPCE(II-1188),
   MP8(IV-2497),   MP6(III-1596),   MPDr(431),   MPv3(277),
   MP2(I-544),   MWL2(544).
   *Master Builder, The.   MP12(VII-3759),   MPCE(III-1373),
   MP8(V-2950),   MP6(IV-1866),   MPDr(501),   MPv3(328),
   MP2(II-643),   MWL2(643).
   *Peer Gynt.   MP12(VIII-4559),   MPCE(III-1696),   MP8(V-3551),
   MP6(IV-2280),   MPDr(607),   MP1(II-722),   MWL1(722).
   *Pillars of Society, The.   MP12(VIII-4710),   MPCE(III-1750),
   MP8(VI-3675),   MP6(V-2371),   MPDr(633),   MPv3(416),

MP2(II-831), MWL2(831).
Rosmersholm. MP12(X-5718), MPCE(IV-1970),
MP8(VII-4550), MP6(V-2719), MPDr(714), MPv3(460),
MP2(II-922), MWL2(922).
When We Dead Awaken. MP12(XII-7100), MPCE(IV-2492),
MP8(VIII-5614), MP6(VI-3403), MPDr(918), MP3(II-1127),
MWL3(1127).
Wild Duck, The. MP12(XII-7137), MPCE(IV-2501),
MP8(VIII-5645), MP6(VI-3422), MPDr(923), MP1(II-1113),
MWL1(1113).
Icaza, Jorge
    Huasipungo. MP12(V-2750), MPCE(II-1009), MP8(III-2142),
    MP6(III-1368), MPAm(279), MPv4(238), MP2(I-472), MWL2(472).
Ickes, Harold L.
    Secret Diary of Harold L. Ickes: Volume II, The. SCL12(X-6724),
    SCL7(VI-4132), A54(249).
Ienaga, Saburō
    Pacific War: World War II and the Japanese, 1931-1945, The.
    LA79(II-520).
Ignatius, Bishop of Antioch, Saint
    Epistles of Saint Ignatius of Antioch, The. RCa(I-7).
    Seven Epistles of Ignatius, The. RCh(I-7).
Ignatius Loyola, Saint
    Spiritual Exercises. RCa(II-534).
Ignatow, David
    Rescue the Dead. SCL12(IX-6368), SCL7(VI-3898), A69(277).
    Tread the Dark: New Poems. LA79(II-777).
Ikku, Jippensha
    Hiza-Kurige. MP12(V-2667), MP8(III-2080), MP6(III-1324),
    MPEur(365), MP3(I-481), MWL3(481).
Illich, Ivan D.
    Medical Nemesis. LA77(II-489).
Iltis, Hugo
    Life of Mendel. HEur(II-909).
Inge, William
    Bus Stop. SCL12(II-998), SCLs(52).
    Dark at the Top of the Stairs, The. SCL12(III-1710), SCL7(II-1011),
    A59(48).
Inge, William Ralph
    Christian Mysticism. RCh(II-816).
Ingoldsby, Thomas
    Ingoldsby Legends, The. MP12(V-2891), MP8(IV-2252),
    MP4(I-449), MWL4(449).
Ingrao, Charles W.
    In Quest and Crisis: Emperor Joseph I and the Habsburg Monarchy.

LA80(I-426).

Ingstad, Helge
  Westward to Vinland: The Discovery of Pre-Columbian Norse House-Sites in North America. HAmer(I-15).

Innocent III, Pope
  De contemptu mundi. RCa(I-342).
  De sacro altaris mysterio. RCa(I-345).

Insight Team of the London Sunday *Times*, The
  Yom Kippur War, The. HWor(III-1184).

Ionesco, Eugène
  Rhinoceros. MP12(X-5574), MP8(VII-4441), MP4(II-1066), MWL4(1066).

Irenaeus, Saint
  Against Heresies. Different analyses on this title appear in: RCh(I-35), RCa(I-37).
  Demonstration of Apostolic Teaching, The. RCa(I-47).

Irvine, William
  Apes, Angels, and Victorians. SCL12(I-346), SCL7(I-199), A55(11), BMA(22).

Irving, David
  Hitler's War. LA78(I-398).
  Trail of the Fox, The. LA78(II-856).
  War Path: Hitler's Germany in the Years 1933-1939, The. LA79(II-819).

Irving, John
  World According to Garp, The. LA79(II-908).

Irving, Washington
  Chronicle of the Conquest of Granada, A. MP12(II-950), MP8(II-736), MP6(I-483), MPNf(45), MP3(I-183), MWL3(183). A different analysis on this title appears in: HAnc(III-1750).
  History of New York, by Diedrich Knickerbocker, A. MP12(V-2643), MP8(III-2056), MP6(III-1312), MPNf(140), MP3(I-469), MWL3(469).
  Legend of Sleepy Hollow, The. MP12(VI-3314), MPCE(II-1229), MP8(IV-2583), MP6(III-1651), MPAm(335), MPv4(283), MP2(II-569), MWL2(569).
  Legend of the Moor's Legacy. MP12(VI-3317), MPCE(II-1231), MP8(IV-2585), MP6(III-1653), MPAm(337), MPv4(285), MP2(II-571), MWL2(571).
  Rip Van Winkle. MP12(X-5611), MPCE(III-1922), MP8(VII-4469), MP6(V-2662), MPAm(533), MPv4(454), MP2(II-905), MWL2(905).

Isherwood, Christopher
  Berlin Stories, The. SCL12(I-651), SCL7(I-374), A54(13).
  Christopher and His Kind, 1929-1939. LA77(I-158).
  Kathleen and Frank. SCL12(VI-3976), A73(210).

Isidore of Seville, Saint
Etymologies, The. RCa(I-248).
Isselin, Henri
Battle of the Marne, The. HEur(III-1252).

Jackson, Charles
Lost Weekend, The. MP12(VI-3524), MPCE(II-1286),
MP8(IV-2762), MP6(III-1742), MPAm(362), MP1(I-531),
MWL1(531).
Jackson, David K.
*Contributors and Contributions to the Southern Literary Messenger,
1834-1864, The.* HAmer(II-727).
Jackson, Gabriel
Spanish Republic and the Civil War, 1931-1939, The. Different analyses on
this title appear in: HEur(III-1370; III-1418).
Jackson, George L.
Blood in My Eye. SCL12(II-789), A73(55).
Jackson, Robert H.
Struggle for Judicial Supremacy, The. HAmer(III-1669).
Jackson, Robert Victor
*South Asian Crisis: India, Pakistan and Bangladesh: A Political and
Historical Analysis of the 1971 War.* HWor(II-1095).
Jackson, Shirley
We Have Always Lived in the Castle. SCL12(XII-8159),
SCL7(VII-4992), A63(288).
Jackson, W. G. F.
Battle for Italy, The. HEur(II-1488).
Jacobs, E. F.
"Innocent III," in *Vol. VI* of *The Cambridge Medieval History.*
HAnc(III-1459).
Jacobs, Paul
Prelude to Riot: A View of Urban America from the Bottom.
HAmer(III-1926).
Jacobsen, H. A. *and* J. Rohwer, *eds.*
Decsive Battles of World War II: The German View. Different analyses on
this title appear in: HEur(III-1469; III-1475; III-1494).
Jacobsen, Jens Peter
Niels Lyhne. MP12(VII-4205), MPCE(III-1571), MP8(V-3275),
MP6(IV-2105), MPEur(541), MPv3(374), MP2(II-741),
MWL2(741).
Jacobsen, Josephine
Shade-Seller: New and Selected Poems, The. SCL12(X-6889),
A75(293).
Jacobson, Dan
Beginners, The. SCL12(I-612), SCL7(I-355), A67(28).

History of the Council of Trent, A. HEur(I-145).
Jeffers, Robinson
    Cawdor. MP12(II-858), MPCE(I-316), MP8(I-662), MP6(I-437),
    MPPo(44), MP1(I-130), MWL1(130).
    Hungerfield and Other Poems. SCL12(V-3577), SCLs(130).
    *Poetry of Jeffers, The. MP12(IX-5006), MP8(VI-3952),
    MP4(II-853), MWL4(853).
    *Roan Stallion. MP12(X-5636), MPCE(III-1932), MP8(VII-4487),
    MP6(V-2673), MPPo(323), MP1(II-835), MWL1(835).
    Tamar. MP12(XI-6393), MPCE(IV-2204), MP8(VII-5090),
    MP6(VI-3045), MPPo(353), MP1(II-948), MWL1(948).
Jefferson, Thomas
    Notes on the State of Virginia. MP12(VII-4260), MP8(V-3319),
    MP6(IV-2131), MPNf(214), MP3(II-692), MWL3(692).
Jellinek, Frank
    Paris Commune of 1871, The. HEur(II-985).
Jenkins, Elizabeth
    Elizabeth the Great. SCL12(IV-2193), SCL7(II-1305), A60(70),
    BMA(156).
Jenkins, Romilly
    Byzantium: The Imperial Centuries, A.D. 610-1071. HAnc(III-1217).
Jenkins, Roy
    Asquith. SCL12(I-410), SCL7(I-235), A66(12).
    Mr. Balfour's Poodle. HEur(III-1216).
Jenkins, William S.
    Pro-Slavery Thought in the Old South. HAmer(I-650).
Jenks, Christopher *and* David Riesman
    Academic Revolution, The. HWor(I-517).
Jennings, Jesse D.
    Prehistory of North America. HAmer(I-3).
Jensen, Axel
    Epp. SF(II-725).
Jensen, De Lamar
    *Diplomacy and Dogmatism: Bernardino de Mendoza and the French
    Catholic League.* HEur(I-221).
Jensen, Johannes V.
    *Long Journey, The. MP12(VI-3477), MPCE(II-1268), MP8(IV-2724),
    MP6(III-1718), MPEur(451), MPv4(294), MP2(II-589), MWL2(589).
Jensen, Merrill
    *Articles of Confederation: An Interpretation of the Social Constitutional
    History of the American Revolution, 1774-1781, The.* HAmer(I-290).
    *New Nation: A History of the United States During the Confederation,
    1781-1789, The.* Different analyses on this title appear in: HAmer(I-290;
    I-327).
Jerimias, Joachim

Eucharistic Words of Jesus, The.   HAnc(II-599).
Jerome, Jerome K.
  Three Men in a Boat.   MP12(XI-6508),   MPCE(IV-2249),
  MP8(VIII-5178),   MP6(VI-3104),   MPEng(838),   MPv4(507),
  MP2(II-1018),   MWL2(1018).
Jerome, Saint
  De viris illustribus.   RCa(I-148).
  Letters of St. Jerome, The.   Different analyses on this title appear in:
  RCh(I-108),   RCa(I-180).
Jervey, Theodore D.
  Robert Y. Hayne and His Times.   HAmer(I-663).
Jewett, Sarah Orne
  *Country Doctor, A.   MP12(II-1149),   MPCE(I-414),   MP8(II-898),
  MP6(I-585),   MPAm(106),   MPv3(97),   MP2(I-183),   MWL2(183).
  *Country of the Pointed Firs, The.   MP12(II-1158),   MPCE(I-418),
  MP8(II-905),   MP6(I-591),   MPAm(108),   MP1(I-163),   MWL1(163).
  *Deephaven.   MP12(III-1409),   MPCE(I-520),   MP8(II-1088),
  MP6(II-714),   MPAm(136),   MPv4(120),   MP2(I-238),   MWL2(238).
Jhabvala, Ruth Prawer
  Amrita.   SCL12(I-287),   SCL7(I-164),   A57(4).
  Heat and Dust.   LA77(I-352).
  Nature of Passion, The.   SCL12(VIII-5230),   SCL7(V-3181),   A58(166).
  Travelers.   SCL12(XI-7748),   A74(394).
Jiménez, Juan Ramón
  *Platero and I.   MP12(VIII-4752),   MP8(VI-3704),   MP6(V-2390),
  MPEur(590),   MP3(II-764),   MWL3(764). A different analysis on this
  title appears in: SCL12(IX-5882),   SCL7(V-3595),   A58(188),   BMA(436).
  *Poetry of Jiménez, The.   MP12(IX-5009),   MP8(VI-3955),
  MP4(II-856),   MWL4(856).
Joachim, Harold Henry
  Nature of Truth, The.   Ph(II-773).
Joachim of Fiore
  Treatise on the Four Gospels.   RCh(I-224).
Johannesson, Olof
  Sagan om den stora datamaskine.   SF(IV-1844).
Johannis, L. R.
  C'era una volta un planeta.   SF(I-322).
John Chrysostom, Saint
  Discourse on the Priesthood.   RCa(I-123).
  Homilies of Saint John Chrysostom.   RCa(I-154).
  Homilies on the Statues.   RCh(I-117).
John Climacus, Saint
  Ladder of Devine Ascent, The.   Different analyses on this title appear
  in: RCh(I-179),   RCa(I-254).
John of Damascus, Saint

Fountain of Wisdom, The. RCh(I-186).
Writings. HAnc(II-1113).
John of Paris
De potestate regia et papali. RCa(I-432).
John of Ruysbroeck
Adornment of the Spiritual Marriage, The. RCh(I-272).
John of Salisbury
Policraticus. RCh(I-216).
Policraticus and *Metalogicon.* RCa(I-335).
John of St. Thomas
Ars logica. RCa(II-589).
Cursus theologicus. RCa(II-605).
John of the Cross, Saint
Ascent of Mount Carmel and *The Dark Night of the Soul, The.*
RCa(I-204).
Dark Night of the Soul, The. RCh(I-406).
John XXIII, Pope
Mater et magistra. RCa(II-1106).
Pacem in terris. RCa(II-1131).
Johnson, Chalmers A.
*Peasant Nationalism and Communist Power: The Emergence of
Revolutionary China, 1937-1945.* Different analyses on this title appear
in: HWor(I-214; I-363).
Johnson, Charles A.
Frontier Camp Meeting: Religion's Harvest Time, The. HAmer(I-422).
Johnson, Haynes
Bay of Pigs: The Leaders' Story of Brigade 2506, The. HWor(II-929).
Johnson, James Weldon
Autobiography of an Ex-Coloured Man, The. SCL12(I-463),
SCLs(14).
Johnson, Lyndon B.
Vantage Point, The. SCL12(XII-7964), A72(339).
Johnson, Pamela Hansford
Unspeakable Skipton, The. SCL12(XII-7930), SCL7(VII-4848),
A60(284).
Johnson, Samuel
Idler, The. MP12(V-2822), MP8(IV-2196), MP4(I-434),
MWL4(434).
Life of Richard Savage. MP12(VI-3406), MP8(IV-2667),
MP4(I-549), MWL4(549).
Lives of the Poets. MP12(VI-3468), MP8(IV-2716), MP4(I-558),
MWL4(588).
Poetry of Johnson, The. MP12(IX-5011), MP8(VI-3957),
MP4(II-857), MWL4(857).
Preface to Shakespeare. MP12(IX-5299),

MP8(VI-4228),   MP4(II-1024),   MWL4(1024).
*Rambler, The.   MP12(IX-5426),   MP8(VI-4327),   MP4(II-1044),
MWL4(1044).
*Rasselas.   MP12(IX-5441),   MPCE(III-1857),   MP8(VI-4337),
MP6(V-2579),   MPEng(716),   MP1(II-804),   MWL1(804).
Johnson, Thomas H.
    Emily Dickinson.   SCL12(IV-2219),   SCL7(II-1330),   A55(92).
Johnson, Uwe
    Anniversaries: From the Life of Gesine Cresspahl.   SCL12(I-321),
    A76(14).
    Speculations About Jakob.   MP12(XI-6219),   MP8(VII-4956),
    MP4(II-1176),   MWL4(1176),   SCL12(XI-7171),   SCL7(VI-4402),
    A64(247).
    Third Book About Achim, The.   SCL12(XI-7549),   SCL7(VII-4598),
    A68(318).
Johnson, Vance
    Heaven's Tableland: The Dust Bowl Story.   HAmer(III-1630).
Johnson, William H. E.
    Russia's Education Heritage.   HEur(I-434).
Johnston, Denis
    Nine Rivers from Jordan.   SCL12(VIII-5363),   SCL7(V-3270),
    A55(184).
Johnston, Mary
    Great Valley, The.   MP12(IV-2372),   MPCE(II-865),
    MP8(III-1843),   MP6(II-1159),   MPAm(234),   MP3(I-428),
    MWL3(428).
Johnston, William B., Sar A. Levitan and Robert Taggart
    Still A Dream.   HWor(II-811).
Johnstone, Robert M., Jr.
    Jefferson and the Presidency: Leadership in the Young Republic.
    LA79(I-331).
Join-Lambert, Michel
    Jerusalem.   HAnc(I-103).
Joinville, Jean de
    Life of Saint Louis, The.   RCa(I-435).
Jókai, Maurus
    Modern Midas, A.   MP12(VII-4015),   MPCE(III-1484),
    MP8(V-3133),   MP6(IV-2002),   MPEur(501),   MPv4(348),
    MP2(II-697),   MWL2(697).
Jolowicz, H. F.
    Historical Introduction to the Study of Roman Law.   Different analyses
    on this title appear in: HAnc(I-256; I-493).
Jonas, Manfred
    Isolationism in America, 1935-1941.   HAmer(III-1652).
Jones, A. H. M.

Athenian Democracy.   HAnc(I-208).
Constantine and the Conversion of Europe.   HAnc(II-849).
Greek City from Alexander to Justinian, The.   HAnc(I-355).
*Later Roman Empire 284-602—A Social, Economic, and Administrative
Survey, The.*   HAnc(II-936).
Jones, Bessie Zaban
Lighthouse of the Skies.   HAmer(II-833).
Jones, David
In Parenthesis.   SCL12(VI-3657),   SCL7(III-2182),   A63(93).
Jones, D. F.
Colossus.   SF(I-409).
Jones, Douglas C.
Arrest Sitting Bull.   LA78(I-72).
Jones, Ernest
Life and Works of Sigmund Freud, The.   SCL12(VII-4312),
SCL7(IV-2641),   A58(144). A different analysis on this title appears in:
HEur(III-1141).
Jones, G. F.
Ethos of the Song of Roland, The.   HAnc(III-1310).
Jones, Henry Arthur
Michael and His Lost Angel.   MP12(VII-3873),   MPCE(III-1420),
MP8(V-3034),   MP6(IV-1928),   MPDr(522),   MPv4(325),
MP2(II-660),   MWL2(660).
Mrs. Dane's Defence.   MP12(VII-3978),   MPCE(III-1466),
MP8(V-3111),   MP6(IV-1984),   MPDr(542),   MPv4(341),
MP2(II-688),   MWL2(688).
Jones, H. Stuart
*Cambridge Ancient History, Vol. VII: The Primitive Institutions of Rome,
The.*   HAnc(I-284).
Jones, James
Thin Red Line, The.   SCL12(XI-7543), SCL7(VII-4592),   A63(265).
Jones, James
Whistle.   LA79(II-843).
Jones, Joseph M.
Fifteen Weeks, The.   HAmer(III-1779).
Jones, LeRoi
Tales.   SCL12(XI-7392),   SCLs(310).
Jones, Leslie Webber
*Introduction to Divine and Human Readings by Cassiodorus Senator,
An.*   HAnc(II-1048).
Jones, Madison
Buried Land, A.   SCL12(II-973),   SCL7(I-554),   A64(39).
Jones, Madison
Forest of the Night.   SCL12(IV-2724),   SCL7(III-1628),   A61(87).
Innocent, The.   SCL12(VI-3727),   SCL7(IV-2237),   A58(114).

Good News Yesterday and Today, The. RCa(II-843).

Mass of the Roman Rite, The. Different analyses on this title appear in: RCa(II-949), HAnc(II-1071).

Just, Ward

Stringer. SCL12(XI-7305), A75(315).

Justice, Donald

Departures. SCL12(II-1880), A74(77).

Night Light. SCL12(VIII-5317), SCL7(V-3233), A68(221).

Justin Martyr, Saint

First Apology and *The Second Apology, The.* Different analyses on the title appear in: RCh(I-19), RCa(I-19).

Juvenal (Decimus Junius Juvenalis)

*Satires. MP12(X-5812), MP8(VII-4630), MP6(V-2767), MPPo(327), MP3(II-931), MWL3(931).

Kael, Pauline

Deeper into Movies. SCL12(III-1855), A74(73).

Reeling. LA77(II-662).

Kael, Pauline, Herman J. Mankiewicz *and* Orson Welles

Citizen Kane Book, The. SCL12(II-1283), A72(59).

Kafka, Franz

*Castle, The. MP12(II-820), MPCE(I-301), MP8(I-636), MP6(I-422), MPEur(113), MP1(I-122), MWL1(122).

Diaries of Kafka: 1910-1923, The. MP12(III-1491), MP8(II-1155), MP4(I-224), MWL4(224).

Letters to Felice. SCL12(VI-4280), A74(226).

Letters to Friends, Family, and Editors. LA78(II-526).

*Trial, The. MP12(XI-6687), MPCE(IV-2322), MP8(VIII-5310), MP6(VI-3197), MPEur(764), MP1(II-1020), MWL1(1020).

Kafker, Frank A. *and* James M. Laux

French Revolution: Conflicting Interpretations, The. HEur(I-517).

Kagawa, Toyohiko

Love, the Law of Life. RCh(II-921).

Kahin, George M. *and* John W. Lewis

United States in Vietnam, The. HAmer(III-1909).

Kähler, Heinz

Hagia Sophia. HAnc(II-1043).

Kahn, David

Hitler's Spies: German Military Intelligence in World War II. LA79(I-281).

Kahn, Frenz D. *and* Henry P. Palmer

Quasars, Their Importance in Astronomy and Physics. HWor(II-902).

Kahn, Herman, William Brown *and* Leon Martel

Next 200 Years: A Scenario for America and the World, The. Different analyses on this title appear in: LA77(II-559), HWor(II-547).

Kaiser, Robert Blair

RFK Must Die: The History of the Robert Kennedy Assassination and Its Aftermath. HAmer(III-1930).

Kai-yu Hsu
Chou En-lai: China's Gray Eminence. HWor(III-1268).

Kalidasa
Sakuntala. MP12(X-5765), MPCE(IV-1986), MP8(VII-4589), MP6(V-2742), MPDr(725), MPv3(464), MP2(II-931), MWL2(931).

Kalmer, Joseph *and* Paul Roubiczek
Warrior of God. HAnc(III-1677).

Kalven, Harry, Jr.
"Metaphysics of the Law of Obscenity, The," in *The Supreme Court and the Constitution.* HWor(III-1178).

Kandel, Isaac L.
Impact of the War upon American Education, The. HAmer(III-1727).

Kaneko, Hisakazu
Manjiro. SCL12(VII-4749), SCL7(IV-2894), A57(168).

Kann, Robert
Multinational Empire: Nationalism and National Reform in the Habsburg Monarchy, 1848-1918, Vol. I: Empire and Nationalities, The. Different analyses on this title appear in: HEur(I-482; II-941).
Study in Austrian Intellectual History: From Late Baroque to Romanticism, A. HEur(I-482).

Kant, Immanuel
Critique of Judgment. Ph(I-556).
Critique of Practical Reason. Ph(I-545).
Critique of Pure Reason. MP12(II-1220), MP8(II-946), MP6(II-624), MPNf(72), MP3(I-240), MWL3(240). A different analysis on this title appears in: Ph(I-531).
Religion Within the Limits of Reason Alone. RCh(II-626).

Kantor, MacKinlay
*Andersonville. SCL12(I-300), SCL7(I-177), A55(7).

Kantorowicz, Ernst
King's Two Bodies, The. HAnc(III-1345).

Kao Tse-ch'eng
Story of the Guitar. MP12(XI-6288), MPCE(IV-2171), MP8(VII-5008), MP6(VI-2992), MPDr(806), MP3(II-1022), MWL3(1022).

Kapelrud, A. S.
Central Ideas in Amos. HAnc(I-126).

Kaplan, Barry Jay *and* Nicholas Meyer
Black Orchid. LA78(I-100).

Kaplan, Herbert H.
First Partition of Poland, The. HEur(I-473).

Kaplan, Justin

Kearns, Doris
  Lyndon Johnson and the American Dream.   LA77(II-465).
Keats, John
  Eve of St. Agnes, The.   MP12(IV-1909),   MPCE(II-679),
  MP8(III-1498),   MP6(II-951),   MPPo(95),   MP1(I-263),
  MWL1(263).
  Insolent Chariots, The.   SCL12(VI-3755),   SCL7(IV-2253),
  A59(128),   BMA(252).
  Letters of John Keats, The.   MP12(VI-3350),   MP8(IV-2615),
  MP4(I-525),   MWL4(525).
  You Might as Well Live.   SCL12(XII-8486),   A71(368).
Keegan, John
  Face of Battle, The.   LA78(I-305).
Keeling, S. V.
  Descartes.   HEur(I-296).
Keene, Donald, *ed.*
  Old Woman, the Wife, and the Archer, The.   SCL12(VIII-5528),
  SCL7(V-3381),   A62(224).
Keesler, Henry H. *and* Eugene Rachlis
  Peter Stuyvesant and His New York.   HAmer(I-141).
Kelidar, Abbas *and* Michael Burrell
  Lebanon: The Collapse of a State.   HWor(III-1241).
Keller, Gottfried
  Grüne Heinrich, Der.   MP12(IV-2408),   MPCE(II-880),
  MP8(III-1873),   MP6(II-1179),   MPEur(344),   MP3(I-432),
  MWL3(432).
Kellermann, Bernhard
  Tunnel, The.   SF(V-2316).
Kellogg, Charles Flint
  *NAACP: A History of the National Association for the Advancement of
  Colored People, Vol. 1: 1909-1920.*   HAmer(III-1386).
Kellogg, Marjorie
  Tell Me That You Love Me, Junie Moon.   SCL12(XI-7430),
  SCL7(VII-4533),   A69(305).
Kelly, Fred C.
  Wright Brothers: A Biography Authorized by Orville Wright, The.
  HAmer(II-1348).
Kelly, J. N. D.
  Early Christian Creeds.   Different analyses on this title appear in:
  HAnc(II-753; II-870).
  Early Christian Doctrines.   HAnc(II-750).
Kelly, Laurence
  Lermontov: Tragedy in the Caucasus.   LA79(I-373).
Kemal, Yashar
  Memed, My Hawk.   SCL12(VII-4877),   SCL7(V-2964),   A62(202).

Kenner, Hugh
    Bucky. SCL12(II-955), A74(34).
    Homemade World, A. SCL12(V-3504), A76(132).
    Joyce's Voices. LA79(I-340).
Kerouac, Jack
    On the Road. SCL12(VIII-5556), SCL7(V-3398), A58(179).
Kesey, Ken
    One Flew Over the Cuckoo's Nest. SCL12(VIII-5587),
    SCL7(V-3423), A63(160).
    Sometimes a Great Notion. SCL12(XI-7105), SCL7(VI-4361),
    A65(283).
Keyes, Daniel
    Flowers for Algernon. SF(II-802).
Keyes, G. L.
    Christian Faith and the Interpretation of History. HAnc(II-944).
Keys, Thomas E.
    History of Surgical Anesthesia, The. HAmer(II-793).
Kidd, B. J.
    Counter-Reformation, 1550-1600, The. HEur(I-146).
Kierkegaard, Søren
    Attack on Christendom. RCh(II-728).
    Christian Discourses. RCh(II-709).
    Concluding Unscientific Postscript. Different analyses on this title
    appear in: Ph(II-626), RCh(II-704).
    Either/Or. Ph(II-612).
    Philosophical Fragments. Ph(II-619).
    Sickness unto Death, The. MP12(X-6032), MP8(VII-4814),
    MP6(V-2866), MPNf(285), MP3(II-976), MWL3(976).
    Training in Christianity. RCh(II-720).
Kim, Richard E.
    Martyred, The. SCL12(VII-4793), SCL7(IV-2924), A65(199).
King, Bolton *and* Thomas Okey
    Italy Today. HEur(II-1112).
King, N. Q.
    Emperor Theodosius and the Establishment of Christianity, The.
    HAnc(II-906).
King, Stephen
    Dead Zone, The. LA80(I-205).
Kingsley, Amis
    That Uncertain Feeling. MP12(XI-6466), MP8(VIII-5147),
    MP4(II-1210), MWL4(1210).
Kingsley, Charles
    Hereward the Wake. MP12(V-2591), MPCE(II-956),
    MP8(III-2009), MP6(III-1282), MPEng(295), MP1(I-367),
    MWL1(367).

Hypatia. MP12(V-2794), MPCE(II-1029), MP8(III-2174), MP6(III-1393), MPEng(333), MP1(I-402), MWL1(402).
Westward Ho! MP12(XII-7084), MPCE(IV-2484), MP8(VIII-5603), MP6(VI-3395), MPEng(946), MP1(II-1103), MWL1(1103).
Kingsley, Henry
Ravenshoe. MP12(IX-5446), MPCE(III-1860), MP8(VI-4340), MP6(V-2581), MPEng(719), MPv4(440), MP2(II-880), MWL2(880).
Kingston, Maxine Hong
Woman Warrior, The. LA77(II-932).
Kinnell, Galway
Body Rags. SCL12(II-822), SCL7(I-470), A68(31).
Flower Herding on Mount Monadnock. SCL12(IV-2692), SCL7(III-1596), A65(101).
Kinross, Patrick Balfour Lord
Ataturk. SCL12(I-434), SCL7(I-255), A66(21).
Kinsella, Thomas
Nightwalker and Other Poems. SCL12(VIII-5345), SCL7(V-3261), A69(243).
Kipling, Rudyard
Broshwood Boy, The. MP12(II-696), MPCE(I-254), MP8(I-540), MP6(I-354), MPEng(71), MPv4(55), MP2(I-120), MWL2(120).
Captains Courageous. MP12(II-787), MPCE(I-288), MP8(I-612), MP6(I-405), MPEng(83), MP1(I-111), MWL1(111).
Jungle Books, The. MP12(VI-3097), MPCE(II-1143), MP8(IV-2413), MP6(III-1537), MPEng(397), MP1(I-461), MWL1(461).
Kim. MP12(VI-3130), MPCE(II-1156), MP8(IV-2438), MP6(III-1556), MPEng(404), MP1(I-473), MWL1(473).
Poetry of Kipling, The. MP12(IX-5019), MP8(VI-3965), MP4(II-865), MWL4(865).
Short Fiction of Rudyard Kipling, The. SF(V-2051).
Kirby, S. Woodburn
Singapore: The Chain of Disaster. HWor(I-460).
Kirk, G. S.
Heraclitus, the Cosmic Fragments. HAnc(I-212).
Kirk, G. S. *and* J. E. Raven
Presocratic Philosopher: A Critical History with a Selection of Texts, The. HAnc(I-267).
Kirk, Kenneth E.
Vision of God: The Christian Doctrine of the Summum Bonum, *The.* RCh(II-977).
Kirkland, Edward Chase

Industry Comes of Age: Business, Labor, and Public Policy, 1860-1897.
HAmer(II-1159).

Kirkwood, James
  Good Times/Bad Times.   SCL12(V-3045),   SCL7(III-1821),
  A69(138).

Kirst, Hans Hellmut
  Revolt of Gunner Asch, The.   SCL12(X-6400),   SCL7(VI-3919),
  A57(221).

Kissinger, Henry A.
  White House Years.   LA80(II-866).

Kitch, M. J.
  Capitalism and the Reformation.   HAnc(III-1522).

Kittredge, George Lyman
  Witchcraft in Old and New England.   HAmer(I-173).

Klein-Haparash, J.
  He Who Flees the Lion.   SCL12(V-3305),   SCL7(III-1960),
  A64(124).

Kleist, Heinrich von
  Broken Jug, The.   MP12(II-671),   MPCE(I-247),   MP8(I-518),
  MP6(I-345),   MPDr(109),   MP3(I-135),   MWL3(135).
  Prince of Homburg, The.   MP12(IX-5321),   MPCE(III-1810),
  MP8(VI-4246),   MP6(V-2523),   MPDr(658),   MP3(II-854),
  MWL3(854).

Klingberg, Frank J.
  *Anti-Slavery Movement in England: A Study in English Humanitarianism,
  The.*   HEur(II-718).

Kluchevsky, Vasily O.
  History of Russia, A.   Different analyses on this title appear in:
  HEur(I-248; I-466).

Kluger, Richard
  Simple Justice.   LA77(II-735).

Knapton, Ernest John
  Empress Josephine.   SCL12(IV-2226),   SCL7(II-1337),   A65(80).

Knauth, Percy
  Season in Hell, A.   SCL12(X-6701),   A76(276).

Knight, Damon
  Analogue Men.   SF(I-48).

Knight, Eric
  This Above All.   MP12(XI-6497),   MPCE(IV-2244),
  MP8(VIII-5170),   MP6(VI-3098),   MPEng(836),   MP1(II-974),
  MWL1(974).

Knollenberg, Bernhard
  Origins of the American Revolution, 1759-1766.   HAmer(I-223).

Knott, Bill
  Selected and Collected Poems.   LA78(II-748).

Knowles, David
  Evolution of Medieval Thought, The. HAnc(III-1526).
Knowles, John
  Morning in Antibes. SCL12(VIII-5072), SCL7(V-3080), A63(148).
  Paragon, The. SCL12(IX-5734), A72(246).
  *Separate Peace, A. SCL12(X-6847), SCL7(VI-4208), A61(225).
  Spreading Fires. SCL12(XI-7189), A75(307).
Knowles, Dom David, O. S. B.
  Monastic Order in England, The. RCa(II-870).
  Religious Orders in England, The. HEur(I-113).
Knox, John
  History of the Reformation in Scotland. RCh(I-409).
Knox, Ronald
  Enthusiasm. RCa(II-961).
Knudsen, John I.
  History of the League of Nations, A. HEur(III-1293).
Koch, Adrienne
  Power, Morals and the Founding Fathers: Essays in the Interpretation of the American Enlightenment. HAmer(I-198).
Koenigsberger, H. G.
  "Western Europe and the Power of Spain," in The New Cambridge Modern History. HEur(I-159).
Koestler, Arthur
  *Act of Creation, The. SCL12(I-24), SCL7(I-19), A65(1).
  *Darkness at Noon. MP12(III-1321), MPCE(I-485), MP8(II-1021), MP6(II-669), MPEur(200), MP1(I-187), MWL1(187).
  Invisible Writing, The. SCL12(VI-3763), SCL7(IV-2261), A54(117).
  Janus: A Summing Up. LA79(I-326).
  *Sleepwalkers, The. SCL12(X-7034), SCL7(VI-4325), A60(245).
  Thirteenth Tribe, The. LA77(II-817).
Kohn, Hans
  Nationalism and Liberty: The Swiss Example. HAnc(III-1606).
Kolko, Gabriel
  Railroads and Regulation, 1877-1916. HAmer(II-1160).
  Triumph of Conservatism: A Reinterpretation of American History, 1900-1916, The. HAmer(III-1435).
Kolodin, Irving
  Metropolitan Opera, The. HAmer(II-1137).
Komatsu, Sakyo
  Death of the Dragon, The. SF(I-508).
Konvitz, Milton R. *and* Stephen E. Whicher, *eds.*
  Emerson: A Collection of Critical Essays. HAmer (II-851).
Kopit, Arthur
  Indians. SCL12(VI-3708), A70(177).

Korda, Michael
    Charmed Lives: A Family Romance.   LA80(I-141).
Kornbluth, Cyril M.
    Best of C. M. Kornbluth, The.   SF(I-178).
    Syndic, The.   SF(V-2211).
Kornbluth, Cyril M. *and* Frederik Pohl
    Gladiator-at-Law.   SF(II-894).
    Space Merchants, The.   SF(V-2127).
Kosinski, Jerzy
    *Being There.   SCL12(I-619),   A72(21).
    Blind Date.   LA78(I-104).
    *Cockpit.   SCL12(II-1334),   A76(50).
    *Painted Bird, The.   SCL12(IX-5699),   SCL7(V-3491),   A66(224).
    Passion Play.   LA80(II-649).
    *Steps.   SCL12(XI-7224),   SCL7(VI-4442),   A69(302).
Koskoff, David E.
    Mellons: The Chronicle of America's Richest Family, The.   LA79(I-434).
Kovic, Ron
    Born on the Fourth of July.   LA77(I-115).
Kovrig, Bennett
    Myth of Liberation, The.   HWor(II-595).
Kozol, Jonathan
    Death at an Early Age.   SCL12(III-1792),   SCL7(II-1079),   A68(67).
Kraay, C. M. *and* Max Hirmer
    Greek Coins.   HAnc(I-147).
Kraditor, Aileen S.
    Means and Ends in American Abolitionism: Garrison and His Critics on Strategy and Tactics, 1834-1850.   HAmer(II-722).
Kraemer, Hendrik
    Christian Message in a Non-Christian World, The.   RCh(II-1038).
Kramish, Arnold
    Atomic Energy in the Soviet Union.   HEur(III-1563).
Krammer, Arnold
    Nazi Prisoners of War in America.   LA80(II-573).
Kramnick, Isaac
    Rage of Edmund Burke: Portrait of an Ambivalent Conservative, The.   LA78(II-686).
Krausnick, Helmut
    "Stages of 'Co-ordination,' " in Eschenburg's *The Path to Dictatorship, 1918-1933.*   HEur(III-1383).
Krieger, Leonard
    Ranke: The Meaning of History.   LA78(II-690).
Kristeller, Paul Oscar
    Philosophy of Marsilio Ficino, The.   HAnc(III-1725).
Kronenberger, Louis

Kuyper, Abraham
Lectures on Calvinism.   RCh(II-969).
Kyd, Thomas
*Spanish Tragedy, The.   MP12(XI-6211),   MPCE(IV-2141),
MP8(VII-4951),   MP6(VI-2956),   MPDr(802),   MPv3(499),
MP2(II-990),   MWL2(990).
Kyôden, Santô
Inazuma-byôshi.   MP12(V-2864),   MPCE(II-1052),   MP8(IV-2232),
MP6(III-1429),   MPEur(394),   MP3(I-503),   MWL3(503).

Labaree, Benjamin W.
Boston Tea Party, The.   HAmer(I-243).
Labaree, Leonard W. *and* Whitfield J. Bell, Jr., *eds.*
Papers of Benjamin Franklin, The.   SCL12(IX-5717),
SCL7(V-3507),   A60(184).
Labarge, Margaret Wade
Simon de Montfort.   HAnc(III-1530).
Laclos, Pierre Choderlos de
Dangerous Acquaintances.   MP12(III-1299),   MPCE(I-475),
MP8(II-1006),   MP6(II-658),   MPEur(192),   MP3(I-246),
MWL3(246).
Lacouture, Jean
André Malraux.   LA77(I-43).
Ho Chi Minh: A Political Biography.   HWor(II-698).
Lactantius, Lucius Caecilius Firmianus
Divine Institutes, The.   Different analyses on this title appear in:
RCh(I-79),   RCa(I-81).
Ladd, Everett Carll, Jr. *and* Charles D. Hadley
*Transformations of the American Party System: Political Coalitions from
the New Deal to the 1970s.*   HWor(III-1307).
Lader, Lawrence
Power on the Left: American Radical Movements Since 1946.
LA80(II-680).
LaFarge, John, S. J.
Manner Is Ordinary, The.   RCa(II-1010).
La Fayette, Madame Marie de
Princess of Clèves, The.   MP12(IX-5330),   MPCE(III-1812),
MP8(VI-4254),   MP6(V-2525),   MPEur(602),   MPv4(429),
MP2(II-856),   MWL2(856).
La Feber, Walter
America, Russia, and the Cold War, 1945-1971.   Different analyses on
this title appear in: HAmer(III-1808),   HWor(II-1052).
Lafferty, R. A.
Does Anyone Else Have Something Further to Add?   SF(II-574).
La Fontaine, Jean de

La Nauze, John Andrew
  Making of the Australian Constitution, The.   HWor(I-20).
Lanchester, H. C. O.
  "Sibylline Oracles," in *Encyclopaedia of Religion and Ethics.*
  HAnc(I-203).
Landor, Walter Savage
  Imaginary Conversations.   MP12(V-2842),   MP8(IV-2212),
  MP6(III-1418),   MPNf(158),   MP3(I-499),   MWL3(499).
  Poetry of Landor, The.   MP12(IX-5028),   MP8(VI-3974),
  MP4(II-873),   MWL4(873).
Lane, Carroll *and* Mildred Adams Fenton
  Giants of Geology.   HEur(II-681).
Lane, Frederic C.
  "Andrea Barbarigo Merchant of Venice 1418-1449" in *Johns Hopkins
  University Studies in Historical and Political Science.*   HAnc(III-1355).
Lane, Harlan
  Wild Boy of Aveyron, The.   LA77(II-910).
Lane, Margaret
  Night at Sea, A.   SCL12(VIII-5309),   SCL7(V-3225),   A66(196).
Lanfranc
  Liber de Corpore et Sanguine Domini.   RCa(I-283).
Lang, Jochen von
  Secretary, Martin Bormann: The Man Who Manipulated Hitler, The.
  LA80(II-746).
Langdon-Davies, John
  Carlos: The King Who Would Not Die.   HEur(I-374).
Lange, K. *and* M. Hirmer
  Egypt. Architecture, Sculpture, Painting in Three Thousand Years.
  HAnc(I-28).
Langer, Lawrence L.
  Holocaust and the Literary Imagination, The.   SCL12(V-3481),
  A76(128).
Langer, William L.
  Diplomacy of Imperialism, 1890-1902, The.   HEur(II-1116).
  European Alliances and Alignments, 1871-1890.   Different analyses on
  this title appear in: HEur(II-989; II-1010).
  Franco-Russian Alliance, 1890-1914, The.   HEur(II-1072).
Langer, William L. *and* S. Everett Gleason
  Undeclared War, 1940-1941, The.   HAmer(III-1689).
Langland, William
  Vision of William, Concerning Piers the Plowman, The.
  MP12(XII-6965),   MP8(VIII-5513),   MP6(VI-3336),   MPPo(373),
  MP3(II-1105),   MWL3(1105).
Lanier, Sidney
  Poetry of Lanier, The.   MP12(IX-5032),   MP8(VI-3978),

MP6(V-2447), MPPo(272), MP3(II-812), MWL3(812).

Lao She
Mao ch'eng chi. SF(III-1344).

Lapp, Ralph E.
Voyage of the Lucky Dragon, The. SCL12(XII-8056),
SCL7(VII-4930), A59(268).

Laqueur, Walter Ze'ev
History of Zionism, A. HWor(I-239).
Israel-Arab Reader, The. HWor(I-413).
Terrorism. HWor(II-1034).

Lardner, Ring
You Know Me Al. MP12(XII-7303), MPCE(IV-2567),
MP8(VIII-5769), MP6(VI-3510), MPAm(735), MP3(II-1159),
MWL3(1159).

Lardner, Ring, Jr.
Lardners, The. LA77(I-404).

Larionova, Olga
Leopard's vershini Kilimandzharo. SF(III-1188).

Larkin, Oliver W.
Daumier: Man of His Time. SCL12(III-1738), SCL7(II-1038),
A67(66).

Larkin, Philip
*Girl in Winter, A. SCL12(V-2949), SCL7(III-1760), A63(67).
*High Windows. SCL12(V-3440), A75(151).
*Poetry of Larkin, The. MP12(IX-5035), MP8(VI-3981),
MP4(II-876), MWL4(876).
*Whitsun Weddings, The. SCL12(XII-8249), SCL7(VII-5048),
A66(333).

La Rochefoucauld, François, Duc de
Maxims, The. MP12(VII-3782), MP8(V-2967), MP6(IV-1877),
MPNf(199), MP3(II-642), MWL3(642).

Larsen, Karen
History of Norway, A. HEur(III-1167).

Larson, Cedric and James R. Mock
Words That Won the War. HAmer(III-1456).

Larson, Henrietta M.
Jay Cooke, Private Banker. HAmer(II-988).

Lasch, Christopher
Culture of Narcissism: American Life in an Age of Diminishing
Expectations, The. LA80(I-175).

Lash, Joseph P.
Eleanor: The Years Alone. SCL12(IV-2181), A73(143).
Eleanor and Franklin. SCL12(IV-2177), A72(115).
Roosevelt and Churchill, 1939-1941. LA77(II-685).

Lasswell, Harold D.

Propaganda Technique in World War I.   HAmer(III-1458).
Lasswitz, Kurd
   Two Planets.   SF(V-2334).
Last, Hugh
   "Tiberius Gracchus," in Vol. IX of The Cambridge Ancient History.
   HAnc(I-483).
Laswell, Harold D. *and* Lung-chu Chen
   Formosa, China, and the United Nations: Formosa in the World
   Community.   HWor(III-1114).
Latter, Albert L. *and* Edward Teller
   Our Nuclear Future.   SCL12(VIII-5673),   SCL7(V-3472),   A59(198).
Laumer, Keith
   Plague of Demons, A.   SF(IV-1687).
   Retief: Ambassador to Space.   SF(IV-1775).
   Worlds of the Imperium.   SF(V-2511).
Laurence, Margaret
   Stone Angel, The.   SCL12(XI-7234),   SCL7(VI-4445),   A65(290).
Laux, James M. *and* Frank A. Kafker
   French Revolution: Conflicting Interpretations, The.   HEur(I-517).
Lavender, David
   First in the Wilderness, The.   HAmer(I-478).
Law, William
   Serious Call to a Devout and Holy Life, A.   RCh(II-566).
Lawrence, D. H.
   Collected Letters of D. H. Lawrence, The.   MP12(II-1019),
   MP8(II-787),   MP4(I-141),   MWL4(141). A different analysis on this
   title appears in: SCL12(II-1352),   SCL7(II-791),   A63(26).
   Lady Chatterley's Lover.   SCL12(VI-4064),   SCL7(IV-2468),
   A60(129).
   Letters of D. H. Lawrence, Vol. I: September 1901-May 1913, The.
   LA80(II-469).
   Plumed Serpent, The.   MP12(VIII-4765),   MPCE(III-1773),
   MP8(VI-3715),   MP6(V-2396),   MPEng(681),   MPv4(424),
   MP2(II-843),   MWL2(843).
   Poetry of Lawrence, The.   MP12(IX-5037),   MP8(VI-3983),
   MP4(II-877),   MWL4(877).
   Rainbow, The.   MP12(IX-5410),   MPCE(III-1842),
   MP8(VI-4316),   MP6(V-2564),   MPEng(713),   MP1(II-800),
   MWL1(800).
   Short Stories of D. H. Lawrence.   MP12(X-5995),   MP8(VII-4777),
   MP4(II-1125),   MWL4(1125).
   Sons and Lovers.   MP12(XI-6177),   MPCE(IV-2126),
   MP8(VII-4925),   MP6(V-2941),   MPEng(807),   MP1(II-913),
   MWL1(913).
   Studies in Classic American Literature.   MP12(XI-6314),

MP8(VII-5028), MP4(II-1192), MWL4(1192).
Twilight in Italy. MP12(XII-6766), MP8(VIII-5363),
MP4(II-1238), MWL4(1238).
Women in Love. MP12(XII-7239), MP8(VIII-5720),
MP4(II-1298), MWL4(1298).
Lawrence, T. E.
Seven Pillars of Wisdom. MP12(X-5929), MP8(VII-4722),
MP6(V-2830), MPNf(282), MP3(II-961), MWL3(961).
Lawrence, Charles, III *and* Joel Dreyfuss
Bakke Case: The Politics of Inequality, The. LA80(I-45).
Lawrence (Nicholas Herman), Brother
Practice of the Presence of God, The. RCh(I-543).
Lawson, John
Biblical Theology of Saint Irenaeus, The. HAnc(II-749).
Laxness, Halldór
Independent People. MP12(V-2872), MPCE(II-1053),
MP8(IV-2239), MP6(III-1432), MPEur(397), MP1(I-425),
MWL1(425).
Paradise Reclaimed. SCL12(IX-5730), SCL7(V-3509), A63(171).
Layamon
Brut, The. MP12(II-699), MP8(I-542), MP6(I-356),
MPPo(30), MP3(I-140), MWL3(140).
Lea, Henry Charles
History of Sacerdotal Celibacy in the Christian Church. HAnc(III-1259).
History of the Inquisition of the Middle Ages, The. HAnc(III-1486).
Lea, Tom
King Ranch, The. SCL12(VI-4030), SCL7(IV-2442), A58(127).
Leakey, Richard E. *and* Roger Lewin
Origins. HWor(I-222).
People of the Lake: Mankind and Its Beginnings. LA79(II-535).
Learsi (Israel Goldberg), Rufus
Fulfillment: The Epic Story of Zionism. HEur(II-1091).
Leasor, James
Red Fort, The. SCL12(IX-6294), SCL7(VI-3855), A58(206).
Léautaud, Paul
Child of Montmartre, The. SCL12(II-1219), SCL7(I-706), A60(39).
Lebra, Joyce C.
Japanese-Trained Armies in Southeast Asia: Independence and Volunteer Forces in World War II. HWor(I-461).
Lechler, Gotthard
John Wycliffe and His English Precursors. HAnc(III-1642).
Leckie, Robert
Conflict: The History of the Korean War, 1950-1953. HWor(II-678).
Lecky, William Edward Hartpole
History of Ireland in the Eighteenth Century, A. HEur(II-553).

Lecler, Joseph, S. J.
    Toleration and the Reformation.   HEur(I-217).
Leclerq, Jean
    Love of Learning and the Desire for God, The.   HAnc(II-1049).
Lee, Harper
    To Kill a Mockingbird.   SCL12(XI-7679),   SCL7(VII-4696),
    A61(260),   BMA(555).
Lee, Laurie
    As I Walked Out One Midsummer Morning.   SCL12(I-398),   A70(34).
    Edge of Day, The.   SCL12(III-2122),   SCL7(II-1271),   A61(67).
Leech, Margaret
    In the Days of McKinley.   SCL12(VI-3674),   SCL7(III-2192),
    A60(102).
Le Fanu, Joseph Sheridan
    House by the Churchyard, The.   MP12(V-2705),   MPCE(II-983),
    MP8(III-2112),   MP6(III-1345),   MPEng(315),   MPv4(229),
    MP2(I-458),   MWL2(458).
    Uncle Silas.   MP12(XII-6808),   MPCE(IV-2379),   MP8(VIII-5394),
    MP6(VI-3254),   MPEng(888),   MPv4(553),   MP2(II-1078),
    MWL2(1078).
Le Faure, Georges *and* Henri De Graffigny
    Aventures extraordinaires d'un savant russe.   SF(I-109).
Lefebvre, Georges
    Coming of the French Revolution, The.   Different analyses on this title
    appear in: HEur(I-508; I-513).
    French Revolution: From Its Origins to 1793, The.   Different analyses on
    this title appear in: HEur(I-504; I-522).
    Napoleon: From 18 Brumaire to Tilsit, 1799-1807.   Different analyses on
    this title appear in: HEur(I-548; II-558; II-565).
Leff, Gordon
    Heresy in the Later Middle Ages.   HAnc(III-1384).
Lefler, Hugh T. *and* Albert R. Newsome
    North Carolina: The History of a Southern State.   HAmer(I-136).
Leggett, John
    Ross and Tom.   SCL12(X-6506),   A75(262).
    Who Took the Gold Away.   SCL12(XII-8258),   A70(348).
Le Guin, Ursula K.
    Dispossessed, The.   SF(II-548).
    Early Hainish Novels, The.   SF(II-681).
    Earthsea Trilogy, The.   SF(II-692).
    Lathe of Heaven, The.   SF(III-1161).
    Left Hand of Darkness, The.   SF(III-1171).
    Orsinian Tales.   LA77(II-601).
    Word for World Is Forest, The.   SF(V-2492).
Lehman, Milton

Liroff, Richard A.
   National Policy for the Environment: NEPA and Its Aftermath, A.
   HWor(II-876).
Littleton, Taylor, *ed.*
   Time to Hear and Answer: Essays for the Bicentennial Season, A.
   LA78(II-841).
Litwack, Leon F.
   Been in the Storm So Long: The Aftermath of Slavery.   LA80(I-65).
Liu, Wu-chi *and* Irving Yucheng Lo, *eds.*
   Sunflower Splendor.   LA77(II-792).
Livermore, Harold V.
   New History of Portugal, A.   Different analyses on this title appear in
   HEur(I-306; II-646; II-676; II-723; III-1220).
Livermore, Seward W.
   Politics Is Adjourned: Woodrow Wilson and the War Congress,
   1916-1918.   HAmer(III-1474).
Livermore, Shaw, Jr.
   Twilight of Federalism: The Disintegration of the Federalist Party,
   1815-1830, The.   HAmer(I-609).
Livesay, Harold C.
   Samuel Gompers and Organized Labor in America.   LA79(II-641).
Livezey, William E.
   Mahan on Sea Power.   HAmer(II-1204).
Livy (Titus Livius)
   Annals of the Roman People.   MP12(I-243),   MP8(I-191),
   MP6(I-122),   MPNf(17),   MP3(I-47),   MWL3(47).
Llerena, Mario
   Unsuspected Revolution: The Birth and Rise of Castroism, The.
   LA79(II-799).
Llewellyn, Richard
   How Green Was My Valley.   MP12(V-2742),   MPCE(II-1005),
   MP8(III-2136),   MP6(III-1364),   MPEng(324),   MP1(I-385),
   MWL1(385).
Lo, Irving Yucheng *and* Wu-chi Liu, *eds.*
   Sunflower Splendor.   LA77(II-792).
Lo Kuan-chung
   Romance of the Three Kingdoms.   MP12(X-5681),   MPCE(III-1952),
   MP8(VII-4522),   MP6(V-2698),   MPEur(649),   MP3(II-903),
   MWL3(903).
Lobeira, Vasco de
   *Amadis de Gaul.   MP12(I-152),   MPCE(I-51),   MP8(I-121),
   MP6(I-72),   MPEur(18),   MP3(I-27),   MWL3(27).
Locke, John
   Essay Concerning Human Understanding, An.   MP12(III-1828),
   MP8(II-1426),   MP6(II-917),   MPNf(107),   MP3(I-354),

MWL3(354). A different analysis on this title appears in: Ph(I-428).
Of Civil Government: The Second Treatise. Ph(I-436).
Reasonableness of Christianity, The. RCh(II-551).

Locke, Raymond Friday, *ed.*
"History, Red Power and the New Indian," in *The American Indian.*
HWor(II-868).

Lockridge, Ross, Jr.
Raintree County. MP12(IX-5415), MPCE(III-1845)),
MP8(VI-4319), MP6(V-2566), MPAm(512), MPv4(437),
MP2(II-874), MWL2(874).

Lods, Adolphe
Israel from Its Beginnings to the Middle of the Eighth Century.
HAnc(I-107).

Lofts, Norah
Bless This House. SCL12(II-785), SCL7(I-448), A54(22).

Logan, John
Spring of the Thief. SCL12(XI-7193), SCL7(VI-4420), A64(250).

Loisy, Alfred
Gospel and the Church, The. RCh(II-832).

Lomack, Milton
Aaron Burr: The Years from Princeton to Vice President, 1756-1805.
LA80(I-6).

Lombard, Peter
Book of Sentences, The. RCa(I-328).

London, Jack
Before Adam. SF(I-144).

London, Jack
Call of the Wild, The. MP12(II-748), MPCE(I-274),
MP8(I-581), MP6(I-384), MPAm(80), MP1(I-103), MWL1(103).
Iron Heel, The. SF(III-1068).
Sea Wolf, The. MP12(X-5865), MPCE(IV-2024),
MP8(VII-4670), MP6(V-2795), MPAm(563), MP1(II-874),
MWL1(874).
Star Rover. SF(V-2159).

London, Joan and Henry Anderson
So Shall Ye Reap. HWor(II-845).

Lonergan, Bernard J. F., S. J.
Insight. RCa(II-1043).

Long, Herbert S.
"Unity of Empedocles Thought, The," in *American Journal of Philology.* HAnc(I-273).

Longfellow, Henry Wadsworth
Courtship of Miles Standish, The. MP12(II-1172), MPCE(I-427),
MP8(II-911), MP6(I-597), MPPo(59), MP1(I-165), MWL1(165).
Evangeline. MP12(IV-1906), MPCE(II-677), MP8(III-1495),

Lucretius (Titus Lucretius Carus)
De Rerum Natura. MP12(III-1337), MP8(II-1033), MP6(II-676), MPNf(75), MP3(I-252), MWL3(252). A different analysis on this title appears in: Ph(I-218).
Ludovici, L. J.
Fleming: Discoverer of Penicillin. HEur(III-1338).
Lukacs, John
1945: Year Zero. LA79(II-490).
Lukas, J. Anthony
Nightmare. LA77(II-565).
Luke, Peter
Hadrian VII. SCL12(V-3209), A70(161).
Lullies, R. and M. Hirmer
Greek Sculpture. HAnc(I-278).
Lundin, Claës
Oxygen och Aromasia. SF(IV-1637).
Lundwall, Sam J.
2018 A.D. or The King Kong Blues. SF(V-2339).
Lung-chu Chen and Harold D. Laswell
Formosa, China and the United Nations: Formosa in the World Community. HWor(III-1114).
Lunts, Lev
City of Truth, The. SF(I-378).
Vosstanie veshchei. SF(V-2373).
Lupton, Kenneth
Mungo Park the African Traveler. LA80(II-550).
Lurie, Alison
War Between the Tates, The. SCL12(XII-8091), A75(347).
Lustig, Arnost
Prayer for Katerina Horovitzova, A. SCL12(IX-6008), A74(320).
Luther, Martin
Babylonian Captivity of the Church, The. RCh(I-334).
Bondage of the Will, The. RCh(I-347).
Open Letter to the Christian Nobility of the German Nation, An. RCh(I-330).
Treatise on Christian Liberty, A. RCh(I-339).
Luthin, Reinhard H.
First Lincoln Campaign, The. HAmer(II-937).
Luttichau, Charles V. P. von
"German Counteroffensive in the Ardennes, The," in Command Decisions. HEur(III-1499).
Lutz, Harley Leist
Public Finance. HAmer(III-1418).
Lutzow, Count
Life and Times of Master John Hus, The. HAnc(III-1678).

Lyly, John
Campaspe. MP12(II-754), MPCE(I-277), MP8(I-586),
MP6(I-388), MPDr(126), MP3(I-148), MWL3(148).
Endymion. MP12(III-1774), MPCE(I-647), MP8(II-1381),
MP6(II-889), MPDr(251), MP3(I-337), MWL3(337).
Euphues and His England. MP12(IV-1894), MPCE(II-671),
MP8(III-1487), MP6(II-942), MPEng(190), MP3(I-366),
MWL3(366).
Euphues, the Anatomy of Wit. MP12(IV-1898), MPCE(II-674),
MP8(III-1489), MP6(II-944), MPEng(192), MP3(I-368),
MWL3(368).
Lynch, John
Spain Under the Habsburgs, Vol. I: Empire and Absolutism, 1516-1598.
Different analyses on this title appear in: HEur(I-42; I-190).
Lyon, Bryce
Constitutional and Legal History of Medieval England, A. Different
analyses on this title appear in: HAnc(III-1531; III-1572).
Lyon, E. Wilson
Louisiana in French Diplomacy, 1759-1804. HAmer(I-447).
Man Who Sold Louisiana: The Career of Francois Barbé-Marbois, The.
HAmer(I-447).
Lyons, F. S. L.
Charles Stewart Parnell. LA78(I-169).
Lytle, Andrew
Bedford Forrest and His Critter Company. SCL12(I-602),
SCL7(I-349), A61(16).
Long Night, The. MP12(VI-3483), MPCE(II-1271),
MP8(IV-2728), MP6(III-1722), MPAm(350), MPv4(298),
MP2(II-593), MWL2(593).
Novel, A Novella and Four Stories, A. SCL12(VIII-5438),
SCL7(V-3330), A59(179).
Velvet Horn, The. MP12(XII-6884), MP8(VIII-5451),
MP4(II-1256), MWL4(1256). A different analysis on this title appears
in: SCL12(XII-7971), SCL7(VII-4873), A58(255), BMA(573).

Mabee, Carleton
American Leonardo: A Life of Samuel F. B. Morse, The.
HAmer(II-745).
McArthur, A. Allan
Evolution of the Christian Year, The. Different analyses on this title
appear in: HAnc(II-880; II-1095).
MacArthur, Douglas
Reminiscenses. SCL12(IX-6350), SCL7(VI-3884), A65(243). A
different analysis on this title appears in: HAmer(III-1833).
Macartney, Carlile Aylmer

Hungary and Her Successors: The Treaty of Trianon and Its Consequences, 1919-1937. HWor(I-185).

Macartney, M. H. H. *and* P. Cremona
Italy's Foreign and Colonial Policy, 1914-1937. HEur(III-1404).

Macaulay, Rose
Towers of Trebizond, The. SCL12(XI-7719), SCL7(VII-4723), A58(242).

Macaulay, Thomas Babington
*History of England, The. MP12(V-2631), MP8(III-2045), MP6(III-1307), MPNf(137), MP3(I-466), MWL3(466).

McAuliffe, Mary Sperling
Crisis on the Left: Cold War Politics and American Liberals, 1947-1954. LA79(I-138).

McCaffrey, Anne
Dragonflight. SF(II-605).
Ship Who Sang, The. SF(IV-1917).

McCagg, William O., Jr.
Stalin Embattled, 1943-1948. LA79(II-702).

McCague, James
Moguls and Iron Men: The Story of the First Transcontinental Railroad. HAmer(II-971).

McCaleb, Walter F.
Aaron Burr Conspiracy, The. HAmer(I-464).

McCarthy, Abigail
Circles: A Washington Story. LA78(I-179).

McCarthy, Cormac
Orchard Keeper, The. SCL12(VIII-5634), SCL7(V-3448), A66(218).
Outer Dark. SCL12(VIII-5685), SCL7(V-3484), A69(258).

McCarthy, Joseph R.
America's Retreat from Victory: The Story of George Catlett Marshall. HAmer(III-1767).

McCarthy, Mary
*Birds of America. SCL12(II-726), A72(33).
Cannibals and Missionaries. LA80(I-133).
*Charmed Life, A. SCL12(II-1201), SCL7(I-693), A55(50).
*Group, The. SCL12(V-3169), SCL7(III-1887), A64(119).
*Memories of a Catholic Girlhood. SCL12(VII-4926), SCL7(V-2991), A58(158).

McCarthy, Patrick
Céline. LA77(I-134).

McCleery, William *and* Thomas C. Southerland, Jr.
Way to Go: The Coming Revival of U.S. Rail Passenger Service, The. HWor(I-524).

McCloskey, Robert G.

American Conservatism in the Age of Enterprise, 1865-1910. A Study of William Graham Sumner, Stephen J. Field, and Andrew Carnegie. HAmer(II-1170).

McConkey, James
Crossroads. SCL12(III-1638), SCL7(II-962), A68(60).

McCord, Norman
Anti-Corn Law League, 1838-1846, The. HEur(II-767).

McCormick, Richard P.
Second American Party System, The. HAmer(II-693).

McCormick, Thomas J.
China Market: America's Quest for Informal Empire, 1893-1901. HAmer(II-1299).

McCoy, Horace
They Shoot Horses, Don't They? MP12(XI-6486), MP8(VIII-5161), MP4(II-1214), MWL4(1214).

McCullers, Carson
*Clock Without Hands. SCL12(II-1314), SCL7(II-771), A62(67).
*Heart Is a Lonely Hunter, The. MP12(V-2501), MPCE(II-912), MP8(III-1949), MP6(III-1234), MPAm(255), MPv4(210), MP2(I-416), MWL2(416).
*Member of the Wedding, The. MP12(VII-3815), MPCE(III-1400), MP8(V-2988), MP6(IV-1895), MPAm(401), MPv4(322), MP2(II-655), MWL2(655).
*Mortgaged Heart, The. SCL12(VIII-5083), A72(225).

McCullough, Colleen
Thorn Birds, The. LA78(II-831).

McCullough, David
Path Between the Seas: The Creation of the Panama Canal, 1870-1914, The. LA78(II-636).

MacDonald, Dwight
Against the American Grain. SCL12(I-128), SCL7(I-88), A63(3).

McDonald, Forrest
Alexander Hamilton: A Biography. LA80(I-23).
We the People: The Economic Origins of the Constitution. HAmer(III-1428).

MacDonald, John D.
Girl, the Gold Watch, & Everything, The. SF(II-883).

McDonald, Philip B.
Saga of the Seas: The Story of Cyrus W. Field and the Laying of the First Atlantic Cable, A. Different analyses on this title appear in: HEur(II-836), HAmer(II-898).

Macdonald, Robert W.
League of Arab States: A Study in the Dynamics of Regional Organization, The. HWor(I-498).

Macdonald, Ross

Machen, John Gresham
   Christianity and Liberalism.   RCh(II-908).
Machiavelli, Niccolò
   *Prince, The.   MP12(IX-5314),   MP8(VI-4240),   MP6(V-2518),
   MPNf(258),   MP3(II-852),   MWL3(852). Different analyses on this
   title appear in: Ph(I-354),   RCa(I-523).
Machin, G. I. T.
   Catholic Question in English Politics, 1820-1830, The.   HEur(II-673).
McHugh, Vincent
   I Am Thinking of My Darling.   SF(II-991).
McIlwain, Charles Howard
   Constitutionalism: Ancient and Modern.   Different analyses on this title
   appear in: HAnc(II-787); III-1387).
MacInnes, Colin
   Three Years to Play.   SCL12(XI-7613),   A72(322).
Macintosh, Douglas Clyde
   Theology as an Empirical Science.   RCh(II-899).
McIntosh, Thomas P.
   Potato, Its History, Varieties, Culture, and Diseases, The.   HEur(I-427).
Macintyre, Captain Donald
   Battle of the Atlantic, The.   HEur(III-1257).
McIntyre, Vonda
   Exile Waiting, The.   SF(II-739).
Mack, Gerstle
   *Land Divided: A History of the Panama Canal and Other Isthmian Canal
   Projects, The.*   HAmer(II-1343).
Mack, John E.
   Prince of Our Disorder, A.   LA77(II-637).
Mack Smith, Denis
   Cavour and Garibaldi.   HEur(II-873).
   Italy: A Modern History.   Different analyses on this title appear in:
   HEur(II-960; II-1097; II-1111).
McKay, Donald Cope
   National Workshops: A Study in the French Revolution of 1848, The.
   HEur(II-787).
McKelvey, Blake
   American Prisons: A History of Good Intentions.   HWor(II-888).
MacKendrick, Paul
   Greek Stones Speak: The Story of Archaeology in Greek Lands, The.
   HAnc(I-300).
McKenna, Richard
   Casey Agonistes and Other Science Fiction and Fantasy Stories.
   SF(I-308).
   Sand Pebbles, The.   SCL12(X-6623),   SCL7(VI-4067),   A64(226).
Mackenzie, Henry

Man of Feeling, The. MP12(VII-3669), MPCE(III-1338), MP8(IV-2876), MP6(IV-1813), MPEng(463), MPv4(307), MP2(II-615), MWL2(615).

MacKenzie, Jeanne *and* Norman MacKenzie
  Fabians, The. LA78(I-300).
  H. G. Wells. SCL12(V-3413), A74(190).

McKenzie, John L., S. J.
  "Gospel According to Matthew, The," in *The Jerome Biblical Commentary.* HAnc(I-569).
  Two-Edged Sword, The. RCa(II-1028).

MacKenzie, Rachel
  Wine of Astonishment, The. SCL12(XII-8317), A75(360).

MacKinney, Loren C.
  Bishop Fulbert and Education at the School of Chartres. HAnc(III-1234).

McKitrick, Eric L.
  Andrew Johnson and Reconstruction. Different analyses on this title appear in: HAmer(II-1029; II-1052).

Maclean, John, *et al,*
  "How America Stumbled in Iran," in *Chicago Tribune.* HWor(III-1344).

Maclaurin, W. Rupert
  Invention and Innovation in the Radio Industry: Massachusetts Institute of Technology Studies of Innovation. HAmer(III-1523).

MacLeish, Archibald
  *Conquistador. MP12(II-1088), MP8(II-850), MP6(I-560), MPPo(56), MP3(I-223), MWL3(223).
  Herakles. SCL12(V-3374), SCL7(III-2005), A68(152).
  *J. B. SCL12(VI-3820), SCL7(IV-2307), A59(131), BMA(255).
  New & Collected Poems, 1917-1976. LA77(II-534).
  *Poetry of MacLeish, The. MP12(IX-5054), MP8(VI-4000), MP4(II-885), MWL4(885).
  Riders on the Earth. LA79(II-601).
  Songs for Eve. SCL12(XI-7113), SCL7(VI-4369), A54(255), BMA(519).
  "Wild Old Wicked Man" and Other Poems, The. SCL12(XII-8275), SCL7(VII-5064), A69(346).

McLellan, David S.
  Dean Acheson. LA77(I-197).

McLoughlin, William G.
  Modern Revivalism: Charles Grandison Finney to Billy Graham. HAmer(II-1176).

McLoughlin, William G. *and* Robert N. Bellah, *eds.*
  Religion in America. HWor(I-511).

McMillan, George
  Making of an Assassin, The. LA77(II-470).

Macmillan, Harold
  Blast of War, The. SCL12(II-775), SCL7(I-442), A69(36).
  Past Masters, The. LA77(II-610).

*New Life, A.   SCL12(VIII-5264),   SCL7(V-3207),   A62(217).
*Pictures of Fidelman.   SCL12(IX-5852),   A70(238).
Rembrandt's Hat.   SCL12(IX-6339),   A74(332).
*Tenants, The.   SCL12(XI-7463),   A72(313).
Malcolm X,
    Autobiography of Malcolm X, The.   SCL12(I-481),   SCLs(17).
Malebranche, Nicolas de
    Dialogues on Metaphysics and on Religion.   Ph(I-422).
    Treatise Concerning the Search After Truth.   RCh(I-522).
Malin, James C.
    John Brown and the Legend of Fifty-Six.   HAmer(II-893).
    Nebraska Question, 1852-1854, The.   HAmer(II-873).
Mallarmé, Stéphane
    *Poetry of Mallarmé, The.   MP12(IX-5059),   MP8(VI-4005),
    MP6(V-2456),   MPPo(283),   MP3(II-821),   MWL3(821).
Mallea, Eduardo
    *All Green Shall Perish.   SCL12(I-211),   SCL7(I-138),   A67(8).
    *Bay of Silence, The.   MP12(I-454),   MP8(I-354),   MP6(I-233),
    MPAm(47),   MP3(I-89),   MWL3(89).
    *Fiesta in November.   MP12(IV-2050),   MPCE(II-737),
    MP8(III-1598),   MP4(I-335),   MWL4(335).
Mallet-Joris, Françoise
    House of Lies.   SCL12(V-3554),   SCL7(III-2131),   A58(107).
Malliol, William
    Sense of Dark, A.   SCL12(X-6842),   SCL7(VI-4203),   A68(293).
Malloy, James M.
    Bolivia: The Uncompleted Revolution.   HWor(I-291).
Malof, Peter and J. Warren Nystrom
    Common Market: The European Community in Action, The.
    HEur(III-1604).
Malone, Dumas
    Jefferson and His Time, Vol. III: Jefferson and the Ordeal of Liberty.
    HAmer(I-429).
    Jefferson and the Ordeal of Liberty.   SCL12(VI-3830),
    SCL7(IV-2316),   A63(108).
    Jefferson the President: First Term, 1801-1805.   SCL12(VI-3849),
    A71(140).
    Jefferson the President: Second Term, 1805-1809.   SCL12(VI-3854),
    A75(158).
Malory, Sir Thomas
    *Morte d'Arthur, Le.   MP12(VII-4063),   MPCE(III-1507),
    MP8(V-3170),   MP6(IV-2029),   MPEng(549),   MP1(II-625),
    MWL1(625).
Malozemoff, Andrew
    Russian Far Eastern Policy, 1881-1904: With Special Emphasis on the

MP6(II-688),   MPEur(205),   MPv4(103),   MP2(I-221),
MWL2(221).
*Doctor Faustus.   MP12(III-1539),   MPCE(I-553),   MP8(II-1199),
MP6(II-770),   MPEur(240),   MPv4(133),   MP2(I-258),
MWL2(258).
Letters of Thomas Mann, 1889-1955.   SCL12(VI-4262),   A72(190).
*Magic Mountain, The.   MP12(VI-3618),   MPCE(III-1322),
MP8(IV-2833),   MP6(III-1783),   MPEur(466),   MP1(I-545),
MWL1(545).
Mansergh, Nicholas
    Irish Question, 1840-1921, The.   HEur(III-1236).
Mansfield, Katherine
    Short Stories of Katherine Mansfield.   MP12(X-6018),
    MP8(VII-4800),   MP6(V-2860),   MPEng(793),   MP3(II-970),
    MWL3(970).
Manson, Edward and Sir John McDonnell, eds.
    Great Jurists of the World. Vol. II of Continental Legal History series.
    HAnc(II-723).
Mantoux, Paul
    Industrial Revolution in the Eighteenth Century, The.   HEur(I-407).
Manvell, Roger
    Ellen Terry.   SCL12(IV-2198),   SCL7(II-1309),   A69(106).
Manzoni, Alessandro
    *Betrothed, The.   MP12(I-507),   MPCE(I-185),   MP8(I-392),
    MP6(I-262),   MPEur(74),   MPv3(55),   MP2(I-88),   MWL2(88).
Maran, René
    Batouala.   MP12(I-451),   MP8(I-351),   MP6(I-231),   MPEur(68),
    MP3(I-87),   MWL3(87).
Marcel, Gabriel
    Being and Having.   RCh(II-1003).
    Homo Viator.   RCa(II-893).
    Mystery of Being, The.   Different analyses on this title appear in:
    Ph(II-1120),   RCa(II-966).
Marcel, Parcel
    *Remembrance of Things Past.   MP12(IX-5500),   MPCE(III-1880),
    MP8(VII-4384),   MP6(V-2610),   MPEur(628),   MP1(II-815),
    MWL1(815).
Marcellinus, Ammianus
    Histories, The.   HAnc(II-900).
March, William
    Bad Seed, The.   SCL12(I-524),   SCL7(I-302),   A54(10).
Marchand, Leslie A.
    Byron.   SCL12(II-1021),   SCL7(I-583),   A58(47),   BMA(56).
Marchetti, Victor and John D. Marks
    CIA and the Cult of Intelligence, The.   SCL12(II-1271),   A75(54).

Marconi, Degna M.
  My Father, Marconi.   HEur(II-1081).
Marcus, Harold G.
  "Imperialism and Expansionism in Ethiopia from 1865-1900," in
  Colonialism in Africa, 1870-1960, Vol. I: The History and Politics of
  Colonialism, 1870-1914.   HEur(II-1097).
Marcus, Steven
  Representations.   LA77(II-673).
Marcus Aurelius (Marcus Aurelius Antoninus)
  Meditations.   MP12(VII-3802),   MP8(V-2980),   MP6(IV-1888),
  MPNf(201),   MP3(II-644),   MWL3(644). A different analysis on this
  title appears in: Ph(I-229).
Marder, Arthur J.
  Anatomy of British Sea Power: A History of British Naval Policy in the
  Pre-Dreadnought Era, 1880-1905, The.   HEur(II-1059).
  From the Dreadnought to Scapa Flow, Vol. I: The Road to War.
  HEur(III-1189).
  From the Dreadnought to Scapa Flow, Vol. III: Jutland and After.
  HEur(III-1269).
Margaret Mary, Saint
  Autobiography of Saint Margaret Mary Alacoque, The.   RCa(II-615).
Margenau, Henry
  Nature of Physical Reality: Philosophy of Modern Physics, The.
  HWor(I-172).
Mariéjol, Jean H.
  Spain of Ferdinand and Isabella, The.   HEur(I-3).
Maritain, Jacques
  Art and Scholasticism.   RCa(II-766).
  Bergsonian Philosophy and Thomism.   HEur(III-1185).
  Degrees of Knowledge.   Different analyses on this title appear in:
  Ph(II-963),   RCa(II-828).
  Man and the State.   RCa(II-973).
  Moral Philosophy.   RCa(II-1094).
  True Humanism.   RCh(II-1020).
Marius, Richard
  Coming of Rain, The.   SCL12(III-1479),   A70(82).
Marivaux, Pierre de
  Marianne.   MP12(VII-3728),   MPCE(III-1361),   MP8(V-2925),
  MP6(IV-1849),   MPEur(478),   MP3(II-631),   MWL3(631).
Markandaya, Kamala
  Nectar in a Sieve.   SCL12(VIII-5240),   SCL7(V-3190),   A55(169).
  Silence of Desire, A.   SCL12(X-6965),   SCL7(VI-4285),   A61(232).
  Some Inner Fury.   SCL12(XI-7086),   SCL7(VI-4355),   A57(250).
Markfield, Wallace
  Teitelbaum's Window.   SCL12(XI-7413),   A71(311).

Marryat, Frederick
Mr. Midshipman Easy. MP12(VII-3960), MPCE(III-1458),
MP8(V-3096), MP6(IV-1973), MPEng(524), MP1(II-602),
MWL1(602).
Peter Simple. MP12(VIII-4626), MPCE(III-1721), MP8(V-3605),
MP6(IV-2325), MPEng(658), MPv4(413), MP2(II-822),
MWL2(822).
Marshall, Samuel L.
Swift Sword: The Historical Record of Israel's Victory, June, 1967.
HEur(III-1657).
Marshall, Samuel L., *ed.*
Laser Technology and Applications. HWor(II-883).
Marshall-Cornwall, James
Napoleon as Military Commander. Different analyses on this title
appear in: HEur(II-557; II-591).
Marston, John
Malcontent, The. MP12(VI-3658), MPCE(III-1336),
MP8(IV-2865), MP6(IV-1804), MPDr(486), MP3(II-619),
MWL3(619).
Martel, Leon, Herman Kahn, *and* William Brown
Next 200 Years: A Scenario for America and the World, The. Different
analyses on this title appear in: LA77(II-559), HWor(II-547).
Martensen, Hans Lassen
Christian Dogmatics. RCh(II-712).
Martial (Marcus Valerius Martialis)
Epigrams of Martial. MP12(III-1800), MP8(II-1403),
MP6(II-903), MPPo(80), MP3(I-344), MWL3(344).
Martin, George
Verdi. SCL12(XII-7978), SCL7(VII-4880), A64(286).
Martin, John Bartlow
Adlai Stevenson and the World. LA78(I-6).
Adlai Stevenson of Illinois. LA77(I-12).
Martin, Paul E.
"Swiss Confederation in the Middle Ages, The, in *Vol. VII* of *The
Cambridge Medieval History.* HAnc(III-1605).
Martin, Ralph G.
Jennie: The Life of Lady Randolph Churchill, Volume II.
SCL12(VI-3857), A72(186).
Martin du Gard, Roger
Postman, The. SCL12(IX-5986), SCL7(V-3663), A55(208).
World of the Thibaults, The. MP12(XII-7266), MPCE(IV-2548),
MP8(VIII-5743), MP6(VI-3489), MPEur(831), MP1(II-1130),
MWL1(1130).
Martineau, James
Study of Religion, A. RCh(II-802).

Martínez Sierra, Gregorio
　　Kingdom of God, The.　MP12(VI-3173),　MPCE(II-1175),
　　MP8(IV-2471),　MP6(III-1579),　MPDr(423),　MP3(I-545),
　　MWL3(545).
Martins, J. P. Oliveira
　　Golden Age of Prince Henry, the Navigator, The.　HAnc(III-1689).
Martinson, Harry E.
　　Aniara.　SF(I-72).
Marvell, Andrew
　　*Poetry of Marvell, The.　MP12(IX-5067),　MP8(VI-4013),
　　MP6(V-2458),　MPPo(286),　MP3(II-823),　MWL3(823).
Marx, Karl
　　Critique of the Gotha Program.　HEur(II-995).
　　Kapital, Das.　MP12(VI-3117),　MP8(IV-2429),　MP6(III-1548),
　　MPNf(166),　MP3(I-538),　MWL3(538).
Marxsen, W.
　　Introduction to the New Testament.　HAnc(II-634).
Maryon, Herbert, C. N. Bromhead, R. J. Forbes, H. H. Coghlan, *and* H. J.
　　Plenderleith
　　*History of Technology, Vol. I: From Early Times to the Fall of the Ancient
　　Empires, A.*　HAnc(I-17).
Masefield, John
　　Selected Poems.　LA79(II-666).
Maser, Werner
　　Hitler's Mein Kampf*: An Analysis.*　HWor(I-191).
Mason, Alpheus Thomas
　　Brandeis: A Free Man's Life.　HAmer(III-1371).
Mason, Edward S.
　　*Paris Commune: An Episode in the History of the Socialist Movement,
　　The.*　HEur(II-986).
Massey, Harrie *and* Norman Feather
　　*"James Chadwick," in Biographical Memoirs of Fellows of the Royal
　　Society.*　HWor(I-287).
Massie, Robert K.
　　Nicholas and Alexandra.　SCL12(VIII-5296),　SCL7(V-3220),
　　A68(217).
Massie, Suzanne and Robert K. Massie
　　Journey.　SCL12(VI-3912),　A76(147).
Massinger, Philip
　　*Bondman, The.　MP12(I-585),　MPCE(I-215),　MP8(I-452),
　　MP6(I-304),　MPDr(89),　MP3(I-116),　MWL3(116).
　　*Maid of Honour, The.　MP12(VI-3634),　MPCE(III-1329),
　　MP8(IV-2845),　MP6(IV-1793),　MPDr(477),　MP3(II-613),
　　MWL3(613).
　　*New Way to Pay Old Debts, A.　MP12(VII-4180),

MPCE(III-1558), MP8(V-3259), MP6(IV-2090), MPDr(569), MPv3(369), MP2(II-732), MWL2(732).
Roman Actor, The. MP12(X-5665), MPCE(III-1947), MP8(VII-4508), MP6(V-2687), MPDr(706), MP3(II-901), MWL3(901).

Massinger, Philip *and* John Fletcher
Beggars' Bush, The. MP12(I-472), MPCE(I-167), MP8(I-368), MP6(I-245), MPDr(69), MP3(I-96), MWL3(96).
Sir John van Olden Barnavelt. MP12(X-6063), MPCE(IV-2082), MP8(VII-4837), MP6(V-2884), MPDr(780), MP3(II-985), MWL3(985).

Masterman, J. C.
Double-Cross in the War of 1939-1945, The. SCL12(III-2043), A73(126).

Masters, Edgar Lee
Spoon River Anthology. MP12(XI-6233), MP8(VII-4968), MP6(VI-2962), MPPo(350), MP3(II-1015), MWL3(1015).

Masters, John
Bhowani Junction. SCL12(II-696), SCL7(I-393), A54(16).

Materer, Timothy
Vortex: Pound, Eliot, and Lewis. LA80(II-855).

Mather, Cotton
Magnalia Christi Americana. MP12(VI-3623), MP8(IV-2836), MP6(III-1786), MPNf(196), MP3(II-608), MWL3(608). A different analysis on this title appears in: RCh(II-557).

Matheson, Richard
I Am Legend. SF(II-986).

Mathews, Shailer
Growth of the Idea of God, The. RCh(II-965).

Mathiez, Albert
French Revolution, The. HEur(I-530).

Matthews, D. J. A.
Norman Conquest, The. HAnc(III-1251).

Matthews, Herbert Lionel
Yoke and the Arrows, The. SCL12(XII-8476), SCL7(VII-5186), A58(279).

Matthews, Herbert Lionel, *ed.*
United States and Latin America, The. HAmer(III-1791).

Matthews, Jack
Beyond the Bridge. SCL12(II-693), A71(24).
Hanger Stout, Awake! SCL12(V-3232), SCL7(III-1911), A68(137).
Tale of Asa Bean, The. SCL12(XI-7389), A72(310).

Matthiessen, Francis O.
American Renaissance: Art and Expression in the Age of Emerson and Whitman. HAmer (II-850).

Matthiessen, Peter
　　At Play in the Fields of the Lord.　SCL12(I-428),　SCL7(I-249),
　　A66(15).
　　Cloud Forest, The.　MP12(II-1003),　MP8(II-776),　MP4(I-136),
　　MWL4(136),　SCL12(II-1319),　SCL7(II-775),　A62(71),　BMA(89).
　　Far Tortuga.　SCL12(IV-2462),　A76(81).
　　Partisans.　SCL12(IX-5750),　SCLs(216).
　　Raditzer.　SCL12(IX-6222),　SCL7(VI-3810),　A62(239).
　　Sal Si Puedes.　SCL12(X-6606),　A71(283).
　　Snow Leopard, The.　LA79(II-685).
　　Under the Mountain Wall.　SCL12(XII-7874),　SCL7(VII-4824),
　　A63(272).
Mattingly, Garrett
　　Armada, The.　SCL12(I-367),　SCL7(I-217),　A60(13),　BMA(25).
　　A different analysis on this title appears in: HEur(I-195).
　　Renaissance Diplomacy.　HEur(I-24).
Mattingly, Harold B.
　　Imperial Civil Service of Rome, The.　HAnc(II-623).
　　"Imperial Recovery, The," in *Vol. XI* of *The Cambridge Ancient
　　History.*　HAnc(II-831).
Maturin, Charles Robert
　　Melmoth the Wanderer.　MP12(VII-3809),　MPCE(III-1396),
　　MP8(V-2985),　MP6(IV-1893),　MPEng(488),　MPv3(332),
　　MP2(II-653),　MWL2(653).
Maugham, W. Somerset
　　Cakes and Ale.　MP12(II-737),　MPCE(I-270),　MP8(I-573),
　　MP6(I-380),　MPEng(73),　MP1(I-99),　MWL1(99).
　　Liza of Lambeth.　MP12(VI-3471),　MPCE(II-1266),
　　MP8(IV-2719),　MP6(III-1716),　MPEng(442),　MPv4(292),
　　MP2(II-587),　MWL2(587).
　　Moon and Sixpence, The.　MP12(VII-4056),　MPCE(III-1504),
　　MP8(V-3164),　MP6(IV-2025),　MPEng(543),　MP1(II-621),
　　MWL1(621).
　　Of Human Bondage.　MP12(VII-4288),　MPCE(III-1602),
　　MP8(V-3338),　MP6(IV-2146),　MPEng(592),　MP1(II-670),
　　MWL1(670).
　　Summing Up, The.　MP12(XI-6332),　MP8(VII-5045),
　　MP4(II-1198),　MWL4(1198).
Maupassant, Guy de
　　Bel-Ami.　MP12(I-481),　MPCE(I-172),　MP8(I-374),
　　MP6(I-249),　MPEur(71),　MP1(I-62),　MWL1(62).
　　Mont-Oriol.　MP12(VII-4045),　MPCE(III-1501),　MP8(V-3155),
　　MP6(IV-2019),　MPEur(511),　MP1(II-618),　MWL1(618).
　　Woman's Life, A.　MP12(XII-7224),　MPCE(IV-2532),
　　MP8(VIII-5711),　MP6(VI-3464),　MPEur(828),　MP1(II-1127),

May, Henry
    End of American Innocence: A Study of the First Years of Our Own
    Time, 1912-1917, The.   HAmer(III-1401).
May, Rollo
    Love and Will.   SCL12(VII-4570),   A70(187).
Mayakovsky, Vladimir
    Bedbug, The.   SF(I-138).
    Poetry of Mayakovsky, The.   MP12(IX-5070),   MP8(VI-4016),
    MP4(II-893),   MWL4(893).
Mayer, Arno J.
    Politics and Diplomacy of Peacemaking: Containment and
    Counterrevolution at Versailles, 1918-1919.   HEur(III-1287).
Mayfield, Sara
    Constant Circle, The.   SCL12(III-1558),   SCL7(II-909),   A68(57).
Maynard, Theodore
    De Soto and the Conquistadores.   HAmer(I-36).
Mayo Clinic Division of Publications
    Sketch of the History of the Mayo Clinic and the Mayo Foundation.
    HAmer(II-1182).
Mazlish, Bruce
    Kissinger.   HWor(II-1052).
    Riddle of History, The.   HEur(III-1280).
Mazour, Anatole G.
    First Russian Revolution: The Decembrist Revolt, The.   HEur(II-667).
Meacham, Harry
    Caged Panther, The.   SCL12(II-1037),   SCL7(I-595),   A68(34).
Mead, George Herbert
    Mind, Self, and Society.   Ph(II-992).
Mead, Margaret
    Blackberry Winter.   SCL12(II-771),   A73(52).
Mead, Shepherd
    Big Ball of Wax.   SF(I-213).
Mearns, David C.
    Story Up to Now: The Library of Congress, 1800-1946, The.
    HAmer(II-1280).
Mecham, J. Lloyd
    United States and Inter-American Security, 1889-1960, The.
    HAmer(III-1792).
Medlicott, W. N.
    Bismarck and Modern Germany.   HEur(II-920).
    Congress of Berlin and After: A Diplomatic History of the Near Eastern
    Settlement, 1878-1880, The.   HEur(II-1011).
Medvedev, Roy A.
    October Revolution, The.   LA80(II-605).
Mee, Charles L., Jr.

Meeting at Potsdam. SCL12(VII-4870), A76(206).
Mehnert, Klaus
Peking and Moscow. SCL12(IV-5795), SCL7(V-3540), A64(211).
A different analysis on this title appears in: HEur(III-1586).
Meier, August
Negro Thought in America, 1880-1915; Racial Ideologies in the Age of Booker T. Washington. HAmer(II-1251).
Meisler, Stanley
"Spain's New Democracy," in *Foreign Affairs.* HWor(II-1047).
Meisner, Maurice
Mao's China: A History of the People's Republic. Different analyses on this title appear in: LA78(II-557), HWor(II-658).
Melanchthon, Philipp
Loci communes rerum theologicarum. RCh(I-343).
Meleager,
Epigrams of Meleager, The. MP12(III-1802), MP8(II-1405), MP4(I-280), MWL4(280).
Melville, Herman
Benito Cereno. MP12(I-495), MPCE(I-177), MP8(I-385), MP6(I-256), MPAm(54), MP3(I-98), MWL3(98).
Billy Budd, Foretopman. MP12(I-538), MPCE(I-195), MP8(I-416), MP6(I-280), MPAm(60), MPv4(36), MP2(I-92), MWL2(92).
Confidence Man, The. MP12(II-1071), MPCE(I-386), MP8(II-835), MP6(I-551), MPAm(94), MP3(I-221), MWL3(221).
Israel Potter. MP12(V-2938), MPCE(II-1079), MP8(IV-2291), MP6(III-1462), MPAm(300), MP3(I-515), MWL3(515).
Mardi. MP12(VII-3717), MPCE(III-1357), MP8(IV-2915), MP6(IV-1842), MPAm(393), MPv3(314), MP2(II-623), MWL2(623).
Moby Dick. MP12(VII-3992), MPCE(III-1474), MP8(V-3120), MP6(IV-1991), MPAm(416), MP1(II-609), MWL1(609).
Omoo. MP12(VIII-4364), MPCE(III-1631), MP8(V-3396), MP6(IV-2186), MPAm(467), MP1(II-689), MWL1(689).
Pierre. MP12(VIII-4690), MPCE(III-1744), MP8(VI-3659), MP6(IV-2359), MPAm(484), MPv4(415), MP2(II-829), MWL2(829).
Poetry of Melville, The. MP12(IX-5073), MP8(VI-4019), MP4(II-896), MWL4(896).
Redburn. MP12(IX-5481), MPCE(III-1876), MP8(VI-4366), MP6(V-2600), MPAm(521), MPv3(442), MP2(II-885), MWL2(885).
Short Fiction of Herman Melville, The. SF(IV-1989).
Typee. MP12(XII-6791), MPCE(IV-2370), MP8(VIII-5382),

MP6(VI-3245),   MPAm(676),   MP1(II-1035),   MWL1(1035).
*White-Jacket.   MP12(XII-7118),   MPCE(IV-2497),
MP8(VIII-5629),   MP6(VI-3412),   MPAm(709),   MPv3(542),
MP2(II-1128),   MWL2(1128).

Memmi, Albert
    Scorpion, The.   SCL12(X-6656),   A72(285).

Menander
    Arbitration, The.   MP12(I-288),   MPCE(I-103),   MP8(I-224),
    MP6(I-149),   MPDr(44),   MP3(I-54),   MWL3(54).

Mencinger, Janez
    Abadon.   SF(I-1).

Mencius
    Meng Tzu.   Ph(I-180).

Mencken, H. L.
    Prejudices: Six Series.   MP12(IX-5302),   MP8(VI-4231),
    MP6(V-2510),   MPNf(256),   MP3(II-847),   MWL3(847).

Mendenhall, George E.
    Law and Covenant in Israel and in the Ancient Near East.   HAnc(I-86).

Menen, Aubrey
    Fig Tree, The.   SCL12(IV-2571),   SCL7(III-1522),   A60(74).
    Ramayana, The.   SCL12(IX-6249),   SCL7(VI-3831),   A54(222).
    SheLa.   SCL12(X-6906),   SCL7(VI-4245),   A63(237).

Meredith, George
    *Beauchamp's Career.   MP12(I-460),   MPCE(I-161),   MP8(I-359),
    MP6(I-238),   MPEng(48),   MPv3(50),   MP2(I-83),   MWL2(83).
    *Diana of the Crossways.   MP12(III-1486),   MPCE(I-540),
    MP8(II-1152),   MP6(II-748),   MPEng(154),   MP1(I-206),
    MWL1(206).
    *Egoist, The.   MP12(III-1723),   MPCE(I-633),   MP8(II-1340),
    MP6(II-868),   MPEng(175),   MP1(I-241),   MWL1(241).
    *Evan Harrington.   MP12(IV-1902),   MPCE(II-676),
    MP8(III-1492),   MP6(II-946),   MPEng(195),   MPv3(150),
    MP2(I-304),   MWL2(304).
    *Ordeal of Richard Feverel, The.   MP12(VIII-4390),
    MPCE(III-1632),   MP8(V-3421),   MP6(IV-2193),   MPEng(611),
    MP1(II-692),   MWL1(692).
    *Poetry of Meredith, The.   MP12(IX-5077),   MP8(VI-4023),
    MP4(II-899),   MWL4(899).

Meredith, William
    Earth Walk.   SCL12(III-2104),   A71(66).
    Wreck of the Thresher and Other Poems, The.   SCL12(XII-8444),
    SCL7(VII-5167),   A65(324).

Merejkowski, Dmitri
    Death of the Gods, The.   MP12(III-1377),   MPCE(I-507),
    MP8(II-1063),   MP6(II-696),   MPEur(210),   MP1(I-201),

MWL1(201).

Romance of Leonardo da Vinci, The. MP12(X-5672), MPCE(III-1950), MP8(VII-4514), MP6(V-2691), MPEur(646), MPv3(456), MP2(II-911), MWL2(911).

Mérimée, Prosper
Carmen. MP12(II-803), MPCE(I-295), MP8(I-623), MP6(I-411), MPEur(108), MP1(I-116), MWL1(116).
Colomba. MP12(II-1031), MPCE(I-377), MP8(II-799), MP6(I-526), MPEur(147), MPv4(80), MP2(I-162), MWL2(162).

Meritt, Benjamin D., H. T. Wade-Gery *and* M. F. McGregor
Athenian Tribute Lists, The. HAnc(I-245)

Meriwether, James B. *and* Michael Millgate, *eds.*
Lion in the Garden. SCL12(VII-4398), SCL7(IV-2695), A68(179).

Merk, Frederick
History of the Westward Movement. LA79(I-277).
Monroe Doctrine and American Expansionism, 1843-1849, The. SCL12(VIII-5056), SCL7(V-3068), A67(217).
Oregon Question: Essays in Anglo-American Diplomacy and Politics, The. HAmer(II-781).

Merk, Frederick *and* Lois Bannister Merk
Manifest Destiny and Mission in American History: A Reinterpretation. HAmer(II-828).

Merle, Robert
Malevil. SF(III-1317).

Merril, Judith
Short Fiction of Judith Merril, The. SF(IV-2014).

Merrill, James
Braving the Elements. SCL12(II-894), A73(62).
(Diblos) Notebook, The. SCL12(III-1940), SCL7(II-1173), A66(69).
Divine Comedies. LA77(I-222).
Fire Screen, The. SCL12(IV-2614), A71(73).
Mirabell: Books of Number. LA79(I-448).
Nights and Days. SCL12(VIII-5341), SCL7(V-3257), A67(243).

Merriman, Roger B.
Rise of the Spanish Empire in the Old World and in the New, Vol. II: The Catholic Kings, The. HEur(I-3).
Rise of the Spanish Empire in the Old World and in the New, Vol. IV: The Prudent King, The. HEur(I-191).

Merritt, Abraham
Moon Pool, The. SF(III-1449).

Merton, Reginald
Cardinal Jiménes and the Making of Spain. HAnc(III-1730).

Merton, Thomas
Ascent to Truth. RCa(II-979).
Seeds of Contemplation. RCa(II-955).

Michelangelo Buonarroti
Poetry of Michelangelo, The. MP12(IX-5080), MP8(VI-4026), MP4(II-902), MWL4(902).
Michelet, Jules
History of the French Revolution. Different analyses on this title appear in: HEur(I-503; I-508).
Michels, A. K.
Calendar of the Roman Republic, The. HAnc(I-539).
Michener, James A.
Bridge at Andau, The. SCL12(II-914), SCL7(I-519), A58(42).
Centennial. SCL12(II-1157), A75(50).
Chesapeake. LA79(I-99).
Hawaii. SCL12(V-3298), SCL7(III-1956), A60(85).
Presidential Lottery. SCL12(IX-6039), A70(246).
Middleton, Drew
Sky Suspended: The Battle of Britain, The. HWor(I-436).
Middleton, Thomas
*Chaste Maid in Cheapside, A. MP12(II-900), MPCE(I-331), MP8(I-694), MP6(I-460), MPDr(143), MP3(I-174), MWL3(174).
*Spanish Gipsy, The. MP12(XI-6208), MPCE(IV-2140), MP8(VII-4948), MP6(V-2954), MPDr(799), MP3(II-1011), MWL3(1011).
Trick to Catch the Old One, A. MP12(XI-6695), MPCE(IV-2326), MP8(VIII-5315), MP6(VI-3201), MPDr(868), MPv4(544), MP2(II-1059), MWL2(1059).
*Women Beware Women. MP12(XII-7235), MPCE(IV-2538), MP8(VIII-5717), MP6(VI-3470), MPDr(946), MP3(II-1144), MWL3(1144).
Middleton, Thomas *and* William Rowley
*Changeling, The. MP12(II-885), MPCE(I-325), MP8(I-683), MP6(I-451), MPDr(140), MP3(I-169), MWL3(169).
Miers, Earl Schenck
Web of Victory, The. SCL12(XII-8166), SCL7(VII-4999), A55(293), BMA(601).
Miglieruolo, Mauro Antonio
Come ladro di notte. SF(I-415).
Mikdashi, Zuhayr
Community of Oil Exporting Countries, The. HWor(II-914).
Mikszáth, Kálmán
St. Peter's Umbrella. MP12(X-5757), MPCE(IV-1983), MP8(VII-4582), MP6(V-2736), MPEur(654), MP3(II-914), MWL3(914).
Miles, John C. *and* G. R. Driver
Babylonian Laws, The. HAnc(I-47).

Wolf by the Ears: Thomas Jefferson and Slavery, The. LA78(II-928).
Miller, Marshall Lee
    Bulgaria During the Second World War. HWor(I-447).
Miller, Merle
    Day in Late September, A. SCL12(III-1750), SCL7(II-1050),
    A64(61).
    Plain Speaking. SCL12(IX-5874), A75(240).
    Reunion. SCL12(X-6394), SCL7(VI-3913), A54(231).
Miller, Michael V. *and* Susan Gilmore, *eds.*
    Revolution at Berkeley. HAmer(III-1915).
Miller, Nathan
    Roosevelt Chronicles, The. LA80(II-726).
Miller, Perry
    Life of the Mind in America, The. SCL12(VII-4359), SCLs(160).
    New England Mind, Vol. I: The Seventeenth Century, The.
    HAmer(I-129).
    New England Mind, Vol. II: From Colony to Province, The.
    HAmer(I-129).
Miller, Ronald E. *and* Richard J. Barnet
    Global Reach. SCL12(V-2963), A76(103).
Miller, Stuart Creighton
    Unwelcome Immigrant: The American Image of the Chinese, 1785-1882,
    The. HAmer(II-1126).
Miller, Townsend
    Castles and the Crown, The. Different analyses on this title appear in:
    HAnc(III-1749), HEur(I-41).
Miller, Vassar
    My Bones Being Wiser. SCL12(VIII-5156), SCLs(191).
Miller, Walter M., Jr.
    Canticle for Leibowitz, A. SF(I-288).
    Conditionally Human. SF(I-423).
Millett, Kate
    Sexual Politics. SCL12(X-6883), A71(290).
Millgate, Michael *and* James B. Meriwether, *eds.*
    Lion in the Garden. SCL12(VII-4398), SCL7(IV-2695), A68(179).
Millhauser, Steven
    Edwin Mullhouse, The Life and Death of an American Writer 1943-1954
    by Jeffrey Cartwright. SCL12(IV-2147), A73(135).
Millis, Harry A. *and* Emily Clark Brown
    From the Wagner Act to Taft-Hartley: A Study of National Labor Policy
    and Labor Relations. HWor(II-575).
Millis, Walter
    Arms and Men. SCL12(I-380), SCL7(I-225), A57(10).
    Forrestal Diaries, The. HAmer(III-1786).
    *Martial Spirit: A Study of Our War with Spain, The. HAmer(II-1288).

Milosz, Czeslaw
  Bells in Winter.   LA79(I-51).
Milton, David *and* Nancy Dall Milton
  Wind Will Not Subside, The.   LA77(II-918).
Milton, George F.
  Age of Hate: Andrew Jackson and the Radicals, The.   HAmer(II-1028).
Milton, John
  Areopagitica.   MP12(I-299),   MP8(I-230),   MP4(I-42),
  MWL4(42).
  Comus.   MP12(II-1051),   MPCE(I-381),   MP8(II-817),
  MP6(I-537),   MPDr(168),   MP3(I-210),   MWL3(210).
  Lyric Poetry of Milton, The.   MP12(VI-3569),   MP8(IV-2800),
  MP4(I-577),   MWL4(577).
  Paradise Lost.   MP12(VIII-4482),   MPCE(III-1671),
  MP8(V-3493),   MP6(IV-2241),   MPPo(202),   MP1(II-711),
  MWL1(711). A different analysis on this title appears in: RCh(I-511).
  Paradise Regained.   MP12(VIII-4487),   MP8(V-3495),
  MP6(IV-2243),   MPPo(204),   MP3(II-711),   MWL3(711).
  Samson Agonistes.   MP12(X-5776),   MPCE(IV-1990),
  MP8(VII-4598),   MP6(V-2747),   MPDr(728),   MP3(II-920),
  MWL3(920).
Minar, Edwin L.
  Early Pythagorean Politics in Practice and Theory.   HAnc(I-196).
Miner, Dwight C.
  Fight for the Panama Route, The.   HAmer(II-1342).
Minor, Benjamin B.
  Southern Literary Messenger, 1834-1864, The.   HAmer(II-728).
Minucius Felix
  Octavius.   Different analyses on this title appear in: RCh(I-51),
  RCa(I-50).
Mirandola, Giovanni Pico della
  Oration on the Dignity of Man.   MP12(VIII-4385),   MP8(V-3416),
  MP4(II-655),   MWL4(655). A different analysis on this title appears in:
  RCa(I-487).
Mishima, Yukio
  Death in Midsummer and Other Stories.   SCL12(III-1804),
  SCL7(II-1084),   A67(71).
  Decay of the Angel, The.   SCL12(III-1839),   A75(68).
  Runaway Horses.   SCL12(X-6531),   A74(345).
  Sound of Waves, The.   MP12(XI-6199),   MP8(VII-4940),
  MP4(II-1171),   MWL4(1171),   SCL12(XI-7147),   SCL7(VI-4385),
  A57(255).
  Spring Snow.   SCL12(XI-7196),   A73(340).
  Temple of Dawn, The.   SCL12(XI-7438),   A74(381).
  Temple of the Golden Pavilion, The.   SCL12(XI-7443),

SCL7(VII-4541), A60(266).

Mistral, Gabriela
Poetry of Gabriela Mistral, The. MP12(IX-4949), MP8(VI-3895),
MP4(II-810), MWL4(810).

Mitchell, Broadus
Alexander Hamilton, Vol. I: Youth to Maturity, 1755-1788.
SCL12(I-187), SCL7(I-125), A58(14).
*Alexander Hamilton, Vol. I: Youth to Maturity, 1755-1788 and Vol. II:
The National Adventure, 1788-1804.* HAmer(I-359).
Depression Decade: From New Era Through New Deal, 1929-1941.
HAmer(III-1596).

Mitchell, Broadus *and* Louise P. Mitchell
*Biography of the Constitution of the United States: Its Origin, Formation,
Adoption, Interpretation, A.* Different analyses on this title appear in:
HAmer(I-332; I-369).

Mitchell, Lt. Col. Joseph B. *and* Sir Edward S. Creasy
Twenty Decisive Battles of the World. Different analyses on this title
appear in: HAnc(II-581; II-1118).

Mitchell, Margaret
Gone with the Wind. MP12(IV-2313), MP8(III-1800),
MP6(II-1128), MPAm(214), MP3(I-424), MWL3(424).

Mitchell, Silas Weir
Hugh Wynne, Free Quaker. MP12(V-2763), MPCE(II-1016),
MP8(III-2151), MP6(III-1376), MPAm(285), MP1(I-390),
MWL1(390).

Mitford, Jessica
Kind and Usual Punishment. SCL12(VI-4005), A74(217). A different
analysis on this title appears in: HWor(II-889).

Mitford, Mary Russell
Our Village. MP12(VIII-4446), MPCE(III-1659), MP8(V-3464),
MP6(IV-2228), MPEng(628), MPv3(403), MP2(II-788),
MWL2(788).

Mitford, Nancy
Voltaire in Love. SCL12(XII-8043), SCL7(VII-4923), A59(266).

Mitzman, Arthur
Iron Cage: An Historical Interpretation of Max Weber, The.
HWor(I-43).

Mivart, St. George Jackson
On the Genesis of the Species. RCa(II-682).

Mizener, Arthur
Saddest Story, The. SCL12(X-6580), A72(279).

Mo Ti
Mo Tzu. Ph(I-31).

Mock, James R. *and* Cedric Larson
Words That Won the War. HAmer(III-1456).

Moers, Ellen
  Literary Women. LA77(I-439).
Möhler, Johann Adam
  Symbolism. RCa(II-640).
Mojtabai, A. G.
  Stopping Place, A. LA80(II-785).
Moley, Raymond
  After Seven Years. HAmer(III-1618).
Molière (Jean Baptiste Poquelin)
  *Bourgeois Gentleman, The. MP12(II-611), MPCE(I-219),
  MP8(I-476), MP6(I-314), MPDr(98), MPv4(46), MP2(I-111),
  MWL2(111).
  Doctor in Spite of Himself, The. MP12(III-1546), MPCE(I-557),
  MP8(II-1205), MP6(II-775), MPDr(213), MP3(I-289),
  MWL3(289).
  *Don Juan. MP12(III-1595), MPCE(I-583), MP8(II-1240),
  MP6(II-800), MPDr(221), MP3(I-296), MWL3(296).
  *Hypochondriac, The. MP12(V-2798), MPCE(II-1031),
  MP8(III-2178), MP6(III-1396), MPDr(369), MPDr(369),
  MPv3(235), MP2(I-474), MWL2(474).
  *Misanthrope, The. MP12(VII-3921), MPCE(III-1440),
  MP8(V-3068), MP6(IV-1950), MPDr(535), MP1(II-595),
  MWL1(595).
  *Miser, The. MP12(VII-3928), MPCE(III-1443), MP8(V-3072),
  MP6(IV-1954), MPDr(537), MPv3(343), MP2(II-673),
  MWL2(673).
  Romantic Ladies, The. MP12(X-5689), MPCE(III-1957),
  MP8(VII-4527), MP6(V-2702), MPDr(709), MPv3(458),
  MP2(II-918), MWL2(918).
  School for Husbands, The. MP12(X-5834), MPCE(IV-2011),
  MP8(VII-4647), MP6(V-2779), MPDr(736), MP3(II-938),
  MWL3(938).
  School for Wives, The. MP12(X-5843), MPCE(IV-2016),
  MP8(VII-4653), MP6(V-2783), MPDr(742), MPv3(469),
  MP2(II-940), MWL2(940).
  *Tartuffe. MP12(XI-6421), MPCE(IV-2215), MP8(VIII-5113),
  MP6(VI-3061), MPDr(831), MP1(II-959), MWL1(959).
Molland, A. G.
  *"Geometrical Background to the 'Merton School': An Exploration into the
  Application of Mathematics to Natural Philosophy in the Fourteenth
  Century, The,"* in *The British Journal for the History of Science.*
  HAnc(III-1617).
Molland, Einar
  "Irenaeus of Lugdunum and the Apostolic Succession," in *Journal of
  Ecclesiastical History.* HAnc(II-745).

Molmenti, Pompeo
Venice, Its Individual Growth from the Earliest Beginnings to the Fall of the Republic. HAnc(III-1357).
Molnar, Ferenc
Liliom. MP12(VI-3428), MPCE(II-1253), MP8(IV-2684), MP6(III-1695), MPDr(444), MP1(I-511), MWL1(511).
Momaday, N. Scott
*House Made of Dawn. SCL12(V-3542), SCL7(III-2119), A69(156).
Names: A Memoir, The. LA78(II-594).
Way to Rainy Mountain, The. SCL12(XII-8153), A70(335).
Momigliano, Arnaldo
Conflict Between Paganism and Christianity in the Fourth Century, The. HAnc(II-927).
Mommsen, Theodore
History of Rome, The. HAnc(I-283).
Monegal, Emir Rodriguez
Jorge Luis Borges: A Literary Biography. LA80(II-444).
Monsarrat, Nicholas
Tribe That Lost Its Head, The. SCL12(XI-7783), SCL7(VII-4763), A57(275).
Montagu, Ashley, *ed.*
Toynbee and History. HWor(I-333).
Montagu, Ewen
Man Who Never Was, The. SCL12(VII-4721), SCL7(IV-2868), A54(168).
Montaigne, Michel Eyquem de
Apology for Raimond Sebond. Ph(I-359).
Essais. MP12(III-1825), MP8(II-1423), MP6(II-915), MPNf(104), MP3(I-352), MWL3(352).
Montale, Eugenio
New Poems. LA77(II-553).
Montalembert, Charles Forbes Rene
Saint Columban. HAnc(II-1054).
Montanari, Gianni
Daimon. SF(I-462).
Sepoltura, La. SF(IV-1896).
Montesquieu, Charles de
Persian Letters. MP12(VIII-4607), MP8(V-3589), MP6(IV-2313), MPNf(234), MP3(II-736), MWL3(736).
Spirit of the Laws, The. MP12(XI-6222), MP8(VII-4959), MP4(II-1178), MWL4(1178).
Montgomery, Viscount
Memoirs of Field-Marshal Montgomery, The. SCL12(VII-4913),

Mörike, Eduard
> *Poetry of Mörike, The.* MP12(IX-5084), MP8(VI-4030), MP4(II-904), MWL4(904).

Morison, Samuel Eliot
> *Admiral of the Ocean Sea.* Different analyses on this title appear in: HAnc(III-1758), HEur(I-18), HAmer(I-19).
> *Christopher Columbus, Mariner.* SCL12(II-1261), SCL7(II-738), A55(53), BMA(76).
> *European Discovery of America: The Northern Voyages, A.D. 500-1600, The.* SCL12(IV-2329), A72(129). A different analysis on this title appears in: HAmer(I-25).
> *European Discovery of America: The Southern Voyages, 1492-1616, The.* SCL12(IV-2334), A75(92).
> *Founding of Harvard College, The.* HAmer(I-105).
> *Harrison Gray Otis, 1765-1848: The Urbane Federalist.* HAmer(I-519).
> *History of United States Naval Operations in World War II, Vol. I: The Battle of the Atlantic, September 1939-May 1943.* HWor(I-407).
> *History of United States Naval Operations in World War II, Vol. V: The Struggle for Guadalcanal, August, 1942-February, 1943.* HAmer(III-1713).
> *History of United States Naval Operations in World War II, Vol. XII: Leyte: June, 1944-January, 1945.* HAmer(III-1733).
> *Intellectual Life of Colonial New England, The.* HAmer(I-106).
> *John Paul Jones: A Sailor's Biography.* SCL12(VI-3896), SCL7(IV-2355), A60(111), BMA(264).
> *Leyte: June 1944-January 1945.* SCL12(VII-4287), SCL7(IV-2624), A59(147).
> *Old Bruin: Commodore Matthew C. Perry, 1794-1858.* SCL12(VIII-5510), SCL7(V-3366), A68(234). A different analysis on this title appears in: HAmer(II-887).
> *Strategy and Compromise.* HAmer(III-1718).
> *Victory in the Pacific, 1945.* SCL12(XII-7992), SCL7(VII-4890), A61(275).

Morrell, David
> *First Blood.* SCL12(IV-2632), A73(171).

Morris, Charles W.
> *Signs, Language and Behavior.* Ph(II-1102).

Morris, Desmond
> *Naked Ape, The.* SCL12(VIII-5204), SCL7(V-3163), A69(239).

Morris, Donald R.
> *Washing of the Spears, The.* SCL12(XII-8113), SCL7(VII-4970), A66(326).

Morris, Edmund
> *Rise of Theodore Roosevelt, The.* LA80(II-717).

Morris, James

Islam Inflamed.   SCL12(VI-3769),   SCL7(IV-2266),   A58(117).

Pax Britannica.   SCL12(IX-5781),   SCL7(V-3526),   A69(260).

Morris, Richard B.

Peacemakers, The.   SCL12(IX-5785),   SCL7(V-3530),   A66(230). A different analysis on this title appears in HAmer(I-302).

Morris, Roger

Uncertain Greatness: Henry Kissinger and American Foreign Policy. LA78(II-869).

Morris, William

Defence of Guenevere and Other Poems, The.   MP12(III-1417), MP8(II-1094),   MP4(I-204),   MWL4(204).

Earthly Paradise, The.   MP12(III-1687),   MP8(II-1311), MP4(I-255),   MWL4(255).

Morris, William

News from Nowhere.   SF(III-1516).

Morris, Willie

North Toward Home.   SCL12(VIII-5394),   SCL7(V-3293), A68(227).

Yazoo.   SCL12(XII-8456),   A72(354).

Morris, Wright

Cause for Wonder.   SCL12(II-1142),   SCL7(I-655),   A64(49).

*Ceremony in Lone Tree.   MP12(II-872),   MP8(I-672), MP4(I-121),   MWL4(121). A different analysis on this title appears in: SCL12(II-1168),   SCL7(I-670),   A61(33),   BMA(66).

Earthly Delights, Unearthly Adornments: American Writers as Image-Makers.   LA79(I-175).

*Field of Vision, The.   MP12(IV-2042),   MP8(III-1591), MP4(I-331),   MWL4(331). A different analysis on this title appears in: SCL12(IV-2555),   SCLs(98).

Fire Sermon.   SCL12(IV-2618),   A72(145).

Fork River Space Project, The.   LA78(I-319).

Life, A.   SCL12(VII-4304),   A74(229).

One Day.   SCL12(VIII-5575),   SCL7(V-3412),   A66(213).

Real Losses, Imaginary Gains.   LA77(II-652).

What a Way to Go!   SCL12(XII-8189),   SCL7(VII-5008),   A63(290).

Morrison, Karl Frederick

"Canossa: A Revision," in Traditio.   HAnc(III-1271).

Rome and The City of God.   HAnc(II-854).

Morrison, Toni

Song of Solomon.   LA78(II-789).

*Sula.   SCL12(XI-7322),   A75(318).

Morse, Arthur D.

While Six Million Died: A Chronicle of American Apathy. HWor(I-306).

Morton, Frederic

Rothschilds, The. SCL12(X-6509), SCL7(VI-4006), A63(221).
Schatten Affair, The. SCL12(X-6650), SCL7(VI-4086), A66(283).
Morton, Richard L.
Colonial Virginia. HAmer(I-63).
Moschus
Poetry of Moschus, The. MP12(IX-5087), MP8(VI-4033), MP4(II-907), MWL4(907).
Mosley, Leonard
Dulles: A Biography of Eleanor, Allen, and John Foster Dulles and Their Family Network. LA79(I-170).
Lindbergh. LA77(I-433).
On Borrowed Time. SCL12(VIII-5544), A70(228).
Moss, Howard
Notes from the Castle. LA80(II-597).
Mosse, George L.
Toward the Final Solution: A History of European Racism. LA79(II-761).
Mossiker, Frances
Queen's Necklace, The. SCL12(IX-6190), SCL7(VI-3784), A62(232).
Mostert, Noël
Supership. SCL12(XI-7342), A75(322).
Motley, Willard
*Knock on Any Door. SCL12(VI-4048), SCLs(151).
*Let No Man Write My Epitaph. SCL12(VI-4195), SCLs(157).
Motta, Luigi
Tunnel Sottomarino, Il. SF(V-2321).
Moulton, Harold G. *and* Leo Pasvolsky
War Debts and World Prosperity. HAmer(III-1539).
Moulton, J. L.
Norwegian Campaign of 1940, The. HEur(III-1449).
Mounier, Emmanuel
Character of Man, The. RCa(II-902).
Mouroux, Jean
Meaning of Man, The. RCa(II-933).
Mowat, Charles Loch
Britain Between the Wars, 1918-1940. Different analyses on this title appear in: HEur(III-1318; III-1327).
Mowat, Farley
Dog Who Wouldn't Be, The. SCL12(III-2002), SCL7(II-1199), A58(76).
Mowry, Arthur M.
Dorr War: Or, the Constitutional Struggle in Rhode Island, The. HAmer(II-768).
Mowry, George E.

California Progressives, The.   HAmer(II-1310).
Era of Theodore Roosevelt and the Birth of Modern America, 1900-1912, The. New American Nation series.   HAmer(II-1327).
Theodore Roosevelt and the Progressive Movement.   HAmer(III-1393).
Mowshowitz, Abbe
Conquest of Will: Information Processing in Human Affairs, The. HWor(II-538).
Mühlenberg, Henry Melchior
Journals of Henry Melchoir Mühlenberg, The.   RCh(II-620).
Muir, John
Story of My Boyhood and Youth, The.   MP12(XI-6286), MP8(VII-5006),   MP4(II-1183),   MWL4(1183).
Mulder, John M.
Woodrow Wilson: The Years of Preparation.   LA79(II-892).
Mullin, Francis A.
History of the Work of the Cistercians in Yorkshire 1131-1300, A. HAnc(III-1428).
Mulock, Dinah Maria
John Halifax, Gentleman.   MP12(V-3023),   MPCE(II-1117), MP8(IV-2353),   MP6(III-1508),   MPEng(373),   MPv4(256), MP2(I-511),   MWL2(511).
Multatuli
Max Havelaar.   MP12(VII-3778),   MPCE(III-1380),   MP8(V-2964), MP6(IV-1874),   MPEur(485),   MP3(II-639),   MWL3(639).
Mumford, Lewis
Brown Decades, The.   MP12(II-693),   MP8(I-537),   MP4(I-97), MWL4(97).
City in History, The.   SCL12(II-1289),   SCL7(II-756),   A62(64).
Pentagon of Power, The.   SCL12(IX-5799),   A72(253).
Urban Prospect, The.   HWor(II-554).
Mundell, Robert A. *and* Alexander K. Swoboda, *eds.*
Monetary Problems of the International Economy.   HWor(II-1101).
Mundy, John H. *and* Peter Riesenberg
Medieval Town, The.   HAnc(III-1326).
Munro, Dana G.
Intervention and Dollar Diplomacy in the Caribbean, 1900-1921. HAmer(III-1381).
Murdoch, Iris
*Bell, The.   MP12(I-485),   MP8(I-377),   MP4(I-67),   MWL4(67), SCL12(I-628),   SCL7(I-362),   A59(23),   BMA(35).
*Black Prince, The.   SCL12(II-764),   A74(22).
Fairly Honourable Defeat, A.   SCL12(IV-2411),   A72(134).
*Flight from the Enchanter, The.   SCL12(IV-2675),   SCL7(III-1584), A57(70).
Sacred and Profane Love Machine, The.   SCL12(X-6574),   A75(270).

Severed Head, A. SCL12(X-6880), SCL7(VI-4233), A62(266).
Unicorn, The. SCL12(XII-7902), SCL7(VII-4828), A64(281).
Unofficial Rose, An. SCL12(XII-7920), SCL7(VII-4841), A63(276).
Word Child, A. SCL12(XII-8391), A76(366).

Murger, Henri
Bohemians of the Latin Quarter, The. MP12(I-581), MPCE(I-214), MP8(I-449), MP6(I-301), MPEur(77), MPv4(41), MP2(I-104), MWL2(104).

Murphy, William S. *and* Jerry Cohen
Burn, Baby, Burn: The Los Angeles Race Riots, August, 1965. HAmer(III-1925).

Murray, A. Victor
Abélard and St. Bernard: A Study in 12th Century Modernism. HAnc(III-1316).

Murray, Albert
Train Whistle Guitar. SCL12(XI-7733), A75(331).

Murray, John Courtney, S. J.
We Hold These Truths. RCa(II-1098).

Murray, K. M. Elisabeth
Caught in the Web of Words. LA78(I-160).

Murray, Marian
Circus: From Rome to Ringling. HAmer(II-1070).

Murray, Marris
Fire-Raisers, The. SCL12(IV-2623), SCL7(III-1544), A54(74).

Murray, Robert K.
Red Scare: A Study in National Hysteria, 1919-1920, The. HAmer(III-1494).

Muscatine, Charles
Chaucer and the French Tradition. HAnc(III-1658).

Muse, Benjamin
American Negro Revolution from Nonviolence to Black Power, The. HWor(II-808).

Musil, Robert
Man Without Qualities: Volume II, The. SCL12(VII-4724), SCL7(IV-2871), A54(171).

Musset, Alfred de
No Trifling with Love. MP12(VII-4231), MPCE(III-1580), MP8(V-3297), MP6(IV-2120), MPDr(571), MPv4(372), MP2(II-748), MWL2(748).
Poetry of Musset, The. MP12(IX-5089), MP8(VI-4035), MP4(II-908), MWL4(908).

Mustard, Harry S.
Government in Public Health. HAmer (III-1397).

Muther, Jeannette E. *and* Ruth B. Russell

History of the United Nations Charter: The Role of the United States, 1940-1945, A. Different analyses on this title appear in: HEur(III-1509), HAmer(III-1744).

Muzzey, David S.
James G. Blaine: A Political Idol of Other Days. Different analyses on this title appear in: HAmer(II-1144; II-1192).

Mydans, Shelley
Thomas. SCL12(XI-7565), SCL7(VII-4614), A66(309).

Myers, J. N. L. *and* R. G. Collingwood
Roman Britain and the English Settlements. HAnc(II-619).

Myers, John L.
Herodotus, Father of History. HAnc(I-261).

Mylonas, George E.
Eleusis and the Eleusinian Mysteries. HAnc(I-160).

Myrdal, Alva
Game of Disarmament: How the United States and Russia Run the Arms Race, The. Different analyses on this title appear in: HWor(II-569; II-1058).

Myrdal, Jan
Confessions of a Disloyal European. SCL12(III-1517), SCL7(II-885), A69(76).

Myrer, Anton
Last Convertible, The. LA79(I-359).

Myrivilis, Stratis
Mermaid Madonna, The. SCL12(VII-4949), SCL7(V-3008), A60(168).

Nabokov, Vladimir
*Ada or Ardor: A Family Chronicle. SCL12(I-43), A70(1), SF(I-16).
*Defense, The. SCL12(III-1859), SCL7(II-1114), A65(69).
Despair. SCL12(III-1901), SCL7(II-1141), A67(78).
Details of a Sunset and Other Stories. LA77(I-206).
*Gift, The. SCL12(V-2934), SCL7(III-1746), A64(110).
King, Queen, Knave. SCL12(VI-4026), SCL7(IV-2438), A69(181).
*Lolita. SCL12(VII-4455), SCL7(IV-2733), A59(150).
Look at the Harlequins! SCL12(VII-4512), A75(182).
Mary. SCL12(VII-4796), A71(202).
*Pale Fire. MP12(VIII-4462), MP8(V-3476), MP4(II-662), MWL4(662). A different analysis on this title appears in: SCL12(IX-5705), SCL7(V-3497), A63(165), BMA(418).
*Pnin. SCL12(IX-5903), SCL7(V-3611), A58(191).
Poems and Problems. SCL12(IX-5920), A72(258).
*Real Life of Sebastian Knight, The. MP12(IX-5450), MP8(VI-4343), MP4(II-1046), MWL4(1046), SCL12(IX-6258),

SCL7(VI-3837), A60(220).
Russian Beauty and Other Stories, A. SCL12(X-6564), A74(349).
Speak, Memory. SCL12(XI-7161), SCL7(VI-4395), A68(305).
Strong Opinions. LA77(II-789).
Transparent Things. SCL12(XI-7741), A73(364).
Tyrants Destroyed. SCL12(XII-7861), A76(337).
Nabokov, Vladimir *and* Edmund Wilson
Nabokov-Wilson Letters: Correspondence Between Vladimir Nabokov and Edmund Wilson, 1940-1971, The. LA80(II-564).
Nai-an, Shih
All Men Are Brothers. MP12(I-125), MPCE(I-43), MP8(I-98), MP6(I-60), MPEur(12), MP3(I-24), MWL3(24).
Naipaul, V. S.
Bend in the River, A. LA80(I-69).
Guerrillas. SCL12(V-3182), A76(118).
Loss of El Dorado, The. SCL12(VII-4542), A71(178).
Namier, Lewis B.
England in the Age of the American Revolution. HAmer(I-227).
Europe in Decay: A Study of Disintegration, 1936-1940. HEur(III-1443).
Structure of Politics at the Accession of George III, The. HAmer(I-227).
Namier, Lewis B. *and* John Brooke
Charles Townshend. HAmer(I-229).
Narayan, R. K.
Financial Expert, The. SCL12(IV-2586), SCLs(105).
Guide, The. MP12(IV-2418), MP8(III-1880), MP4(I-399), MWL4(399). A different analysis on this title appears in: SCL12(V-3189), SCL7(III-1893), A59(109).
Man-Eater of Malgudi, The. SCL12(VII-4743), SCL7(IV-2888), A62(199).
Painter of Signs, The. LA77(II-605).
Nash, Gerald
"Herbert Hoover and the Origins of the Reconstruction Finance Corporation," in *Mississippi Valley Historical Review.* HAmer(III-1596).
Nash, Thomas
*Unfortunate Traveller, The. MP12(XII-6855), MPCE(IV-2396), MP8(VIII-5430), MP6(VI-3278), MPEng(900), MPv3(528), MP2(II-1092), MWL2(1092).
Nathan, John
Mishima: A Biography. SCL12(VIII-5014), A75(194).
Nathan, Leonard
Day the Perfect Speakers Left, The. SCL12(III-1776), A70(94).
Nathan, Robert
Elixir, The. SCL12(IV-2191), A72(119).

National Organization for Women
> *NOW Origins: A Summary Description of How 28 Women Changed the World by Reviving a Revolution Everyone Thought Was Dead!* HWor(II-1001).

Naumann, Hans
> *"Nibelungenlied: eine stauffische Elegie oder ein Deutsches Nationalepos?, Das," in Dichtung und Volkstum.* HAnc(III-1406).

Nee, Victor G. *and* Bret de Bary Nee
> *Longtime Californ'.* SCL12(VII-4507), A74(237).

Nehls, Edward, *ed.*
> *D. H. Lawrence: A Composite Biography.* SCL12(III-1926), SCL7(II-1159), A60(60), BMA(129).

Neill, Stephen Charles *and* Ruth Rouse, *eds.*
> *History of the Ecumenical Movement, 1517-1948, A.* HEur(III-1552).

Nekrasov, Nikolai
> *Poetry of Nekrasov, The.* MP12(IX-5092), MP8(VI-4038), MP4(II-911), MWL4(911).

Nelles, Walker
> *"Commonwealth v. Hunt," in Columbia Law Review.* HAmer(II-787).

Nelson, Benjamin N.
> *Idea of Usury, The.* HAnc(III-1521).

Nelson, Donald M.
> *Arsenal of Democracy: The Story of American War Production.* HAmer(III-1682).

Nelson, N. E.
> *"Cicero's de Officiis in Christian Thought: 300-1300," in University of Michigan Essays and Studies in English and Comparative Literature.* HAnc(I-544).

Nelson, William H.
> *American Tory, The.* HAmer(I-249).

Nemerov, Howard
> *Collected Poems of Howard Nemerov, The.* LA78(I-200).
> *Figures of Thought: Speculations on the Meaning of Poetry & Other Essays.* LA79(I-209).
> *Gnomes & Occasions.* SCL12(V-2970), A74(153).
> *Mirrors & Windows: Poems.* SCL12(VIII-5012), SCL7(V-3043), A59(164).
> *Reflexions on Poetry & Poetics.* SCL12(IX-6303), A73(304).
> *Western Approaches, The.* SCL12(XII-8186), A76(352).

Neruda, Pablo
> *Heights of Macchu Picchu, The.* SCL12(V-3321), SCL7(III-1974), A68(149).
> *New Poems.* SCL12(VIII-5270), A73(272).
> **Poetry of Neruda, The.* MP12(IX-5095), MP8(VI-4041), MP4(II-913), MWL4(913).

Nerval, Gérard de
Poetry of Nerval, The.   MP12(IX-5098),   MP8(VI-4044),
MP4(II-916),   MWL4(916).
Nestorius
Bazaar of Heraclides, The.   RCh(I-162).
Neugebauer, Otto
Exact Sciences in Antiquity, The.   Different analyses on this title appear
in: HAnc(I-23; II-715).
Neuman, Abraham
Jews in Spain, The.   HAnc(III-1754).
Neville, Leslie E. *and* Nathaniel F. Silsbee
Jet Propulsion Progress: The Development of Aircraft Gas Turbines.
HWor(I-358).
Nevins, Allan
Ford: The Times, the Man, the Company.   SCL12(IV-2721),
SCL7(III-1625),   A54(83). A different analysis on this title appears in:
HAmer(III-1423).
Frémont: Pathmarker of the West.   HAmer(II-798).
Grover Cleveland: A Study in Courage.   HAmer(II-1142).
Ordeal of the Union, Vol. II: A House Dividing, 1852-1857.
HAmer(II-874).
*Ordeal of the Union, Vol. V: The War for the Union, Part I: The
Impoverished War, 1861-1862.*   HAmer(II-960).
*Ordeal of the Union, Vol. VI: The War for the Union, Part II: War
Becomes Revolution, 1862-1863.*   HAmer(II-960).
*Ordeal of the Union, Vol. VII: The War for the Union, Part III: The
Organized War, 1863-1864.*   HAmer(II-960).
*Ordeal of the Union, Vol. VIII: The War for the Union. Part IV: The
Organized War to Victory, 1864-1865.*   HAmer(II-960).
Study in Power: John D. Rockefeller, Industrialist and Philanthropist.
HAmer(II-1119).
War for the Union: Vol. I, The.   SCL12(XII-8095),
SCL7(VII-4953),   A60(286),   BMA(590).
War for the Union: Vol. II, The.   SCL12(XII-8099),
SCL7(VII-4957),   A61(284),   BMA(594).
Nevins, Allan, *ed.*
Leatherstocking Saga, The.   SCL12(VI-4176),   SCL7(IV-2556),
A54(141).
Nevins, Allan *and* Frank Ernest Hill
Ford: Decline and Rebirth, 1933-1962.   SCL12(IV-2715),
SCL7(III-1619),   A64(96).
Ford: Expansion and Challenge, 1915-1933.   SCL12(IV-2718),
SCL7(III-1622),   A58(96).
Newbolt, Henry
Naval Operations.   HEur(III-1255).

Newby, P. H.
Guest and His Going, A. SCL12(V-3186), SCL7(III-1890),
A61(113).
Kith. LA78(II-491).
Picnic at Sakkara, The. SCL12(IX-5842), SCL7(V-3567),
A55(202).
Newfield, Jack
Prophetic Minority, A. HAmer(III-1863).
Newhall, Beaumont
Latent Image: The Discovery of Photography. HEur(II-751).
Newhouse, John
Cold Dawn: The Story of SALT. HWor(II-1059).
Newman, Alfred H.
Assassination of John F. Kennedy: The Reasons Why, The.
HAmer(III-1903).
Newman, Edwin
Strictly Speaking. SCL12(XI-7295), A75(311).
Newman, John Henry Cardinal
Apologia pro Vita Sua. MP12(I-263), MP8(I-205), MP6(I-133),
MPNf(20), MP3(I-49), MWL3(49). Different analyses on this title
appear in: RCh(II-743), RCa(II-661).
Essay on the Development of Christian Doctrine, An. RCa(II-644).
Grammar of Assent, A. Different analyses on this title appear in:
Ph(II-666), RCa(II-678).
Idea of a University, The. RCa(II-653).
Newman, William J.
Balance of Power in the Interwar Years, 1919-1939, The. HWor(I-200).
Newmark, Leonard *and* Morton W. Bloomfield
Linguistic Introduction to the History of English, A. HAnc(III-1289).
Newsome, Albert R. *and* Hugh T. Lefler
North Carolina: The History of a Southern State. HAmer(I-136).
Newton, Sir Isaac
Philosophiae Naturalis Principia Mathematica. MP12(VIII-4653),
MP8(V-3628), MP6(IV-2337), MPNf(239), MP3(II-743),
MWL3(743).
Nexö, Martin Andersen
Pelle the Conqueror. MP12(VIII-4566), MPCE(III-1700),
MP8(V-3555), MP6(IV-2284), MPEur(571), MPv3(407),
MP2(II-804), MWL2(804).
Nicholas, Barry
Introduction to Roman Law, An. HAnc(II-1036).
Nicholas of Cusa (Nicolas Cusanus)
Of Learned Ignorance. Different analyses on this title appear in:
Ph(I-343), RCh(I-312), RCa(I-482).
Nichols, Roy Franklin

Nin, Anaïs
    Diary of Anaïs Nin, The.   LA77(I-217).
    Diary of Anaïs Nin: 1931-1934, The.   SCL12(III-1933),
    SCL7(II-1166),   A67(84).
    Diary of Anaïs Nin: 1934-1939, The.   SCL12(III-1937),
    SCL7(II-1170),   A68(83).
    Spy in the House of Love, A.   SCL12(XI-7201),   SCL7(VI-4423),
    A54(261).
Nisbet, Robert A.
    Sociology as an Art Form.   LA77(II-753).
    Twilight of Authority.   HWor(II-896).
Nissenbaum, Stephen *and* Paul Boyer
    Salem Possessed.   SCL12(X-6610),   A75(276).
Nitske, W. Robert *and* Charles Marrow Wilson
    Rudolf Diesel: Pioneer of the Age of Power.   HEur(II-1101).
Niven, Larry
    Ringworld.   SF(IV-1799).
    Short Fiction of Larry Niven, The.   SF(IV-2023).
Niven, Larry *and* Jerry Pournelle
    Mote in God's Eye, The.   SF(III-1463).
Nixon, Richard M.
    RN: The Memoirs of Richard Nixon.   Different analyses on this title
    appear in: LA79(II-605),   HWor(III-1191).
Noble, David F.
    *America by Design: Science, Technology, and the Rise of Corporate
    Capitalism.*   HWor(II-614).
Noble, David W.
    *Historians Against History: The Frontier Thesis and the National Covenant
    in American Historical Writing Since 1830.*   HAmer(II-733).
Noble, William *and* James Leo Herlihy
    Blue Denim.   SCL12(II-802),   SCLs(41).
Noggle, Burl
    Teapot Dome: Oil and Politics in the 1920's.   HAmer(III-1528).
Noguères, Henri
    Massacre of St. Bartholomew, The.   HEur(I-188).
Nolte, Ernest
    Three Faces of Fascism.   HEur(III-1302).
Noonan, John T., Jr.
    *Contraception: A History of Its Treatment by the Catholic Theologians and
    Canonists.*   HEur(III-1662).
Nordhoff, Charles *and* James Norman Hall
    Mutiny on the Bounty.   MP12(VII-4099),   MPCE(III-1524),
    MP8(V-3195),   MP6(IV-2044),   MPAm(427),   MP1(II-628),
    MWL1(628).
Norgay, Tenzing

Tiger of the Snows.   SCL12(XI-7634),   SCL7(VII-4658),   A55(265).
Norris, Frank
McTeague.   MP12(VI-3594),   MPCE(III-1309),   MP8(IV-2818),
MP6(III-1771),   MPAm(367),   MP1(I-537),   MWL1(537).
Pit, The.   MP12(VIII-4729),   MPCE(III-1757),   MP8(VI-3689),
MP6(V-2381),   MPAm(493),   MP1(II-756),   MWL1(756).
Responsibilities of the Novelist, The.   MP12(X-5528),
MP8(VII-4408),   MP4(II-1061),   MWL4(1061).
Norris, George W.
Fighting Liberal: The Autobiography of George W. Norris.
HAmer(III-1624).
North, Christopher R.
Suffering Servant in Deutero-Isaiah, The.   HAnc(I-186).
Norton, Andre
Here Abide Monsters.   SF(II-969).
Star Man's Son 2250 A.D.   SF(V-2156).
Norton, Thomas *and* Thomas Sackville
Gorboduc.   MP12(IV-2332),   MPCE(II-846),   MP8(III-1814),
MP6(II-1137),   MPDr(309),   MPv3(189),   MP2(I-379),
MWL2(379).
Norwood, Gilbert
Pindar.   HAnc(I-217).
Noth, Martin
Exodus: A Commentary.   HAnc(I-78).
History of Israel, The.   Different analyses on this title appear in:
HAnc(I-94; I-191).
Nourse, Edwin G.
*Economics in the Public Service: Administrative Aspects of the
Employment Act*.   HAmer(III-1773).
Noüy, Pierre Lecomte du
Human Destiny.   RCa(II-913).
Novak, Barbara
*American Painting of the Nineteenth Century: Realism, Idealism, and the
American Experience*.   HAmer(I-616).
Novak, Robert *and* Rowland Evans
Lyndon B. Johnson: The Exercise of Power.   HAmer(III-1921).
Nove, Alec
Economic Rationality and Soviet Politics.   HEur(III-1331).
Nowell, Charles E.
History of Portugal, A.   Different analyses on this title appear in:
HEur(I-306; II-647; II-677; II-724; III-1221).
Magellan's Voyage Around the World.   HEur(I-71).
Nowell, Elizabeth
Thomas Wolfe.   SCL12(XI-7574),   SCL7(VII-4622),   A61(251),
BMA(547).

Nowlan, Philip Francis
Armageddon 2419 A.D.   SF(I-84).
Nussbaum, G. B.
*Ten Thousand: A Study in Social Organization and Action in Xenophon's
Anabasis, The.*   HAnc(I-316).
Nye, Russel B.
George Bancroft: Brahmin Rebel.   HAmer(II-732).
Midwestern Progressive Politics, 1870-1958.   HAmer(II-1309).
Nygren, Anders
Agape and Eros.   RCh(II-946).
Nystrom, J. Warren *and* Peter Malof
Common Market: The European Community in Action, The.
HEur(III-1604).

Oates, Joyce Carol
Anonymous Sins and Other Poems.   SCL12(I-325),   A70(31).
*Assassins, The.   SCL12(I-413),   A76(18).
By the North Gate.   SCL12(II-1018),   SCL7(I-580),   A64(43).
Childwold.   LA77(I-149).
*Do with Me What You Will.   SCL12(III-1985),   A74(98).
*Expensive People.   SCL12(IV-2364),   SCL7(II-1408),   A69(122).
*Garden of Earthly Delights, A.   SCL12(IV-2854),   SCL7(III-1702),
A68(122).
Goddess and Other Women, The.   SCL12(V-2983),   A75(121).
Love and Its Derangements.   SCL12(VII-4565),   A71(181).
*Marriages and Infidelities.   SCL12(VII-4786),   A73(234).
Night-Side.   LA78(II-608).
Son of the Morning.   LA79(II-693).
*them.   SCL12(XI-7509),   A70(307).
Upon the Sweeping Flood.   SCL12(XII-7940),   SCL7(VII-4854),
A67(336).
Wheel of Love, The.   SCL12(XII-8212),   A71(346).
With Shuddering Fall.   SCL12(XII-8357),   SCL7(VII-5119),
A65(313).
*Wonderland.   SCL12(XII-8381),   A72(352).
Oates, Stephen B.
To Purge This Land with Blood: A Biography of John Brown.
HAmer(II-921).
O'Ballance, Edgar
Algerian Insurrection, 1954-1962, The.   HEur(III-1630).
Oborn, George T.
"Why Did Decius and Valerian Proscribe Christianity?" in *Church
History.*   HAnc(II-815).
O'Brian, Conor Cruise
States of Ireland, The.   HWor(III-1119).

SCL7(VII-4903),   A61(278).
*Wise Blood.   MP12(XII-7192),   MP8(VIII-5687),   MP4(II-1296),
   MWL4(1296).
O'Connor, Frank
   Domestic Relations.   SCL12(III-2022),   SCL7(II-1213),   A58(78).
   My Father's Son.   SCL12(VIII-5169),   A70(215).
   Only Child, An.   SCL12(VIII-5614),   SCL7(V-3432),   A62(227).
O'Connor, James
   Fiscal Crisis of the State, The.   HWor(II-850).
O'Dea, Thomas
   American Catholic Dilemma.   RCa(II-1066).
O'Dea, William T.
   Social History of Lighting, The.   HEur(II-755).
Odets, Clifford
   *Golden Boy.   MP12(IV-2304),   MPCE(II-834),   MP8(III-1793),
   MP6(II-1124),   MPDr(305),   MP3(I-422),   MWL3(422).
Odle, E. V.
   Clockwork Man, The.   SF(I-392).
O'Donnell, Joseph M.
   Canons of the First Council of Arles, 324 A.D., The.   HAnc(II-859).
O'Donnell, Lawrence
   Fury.   SF(II-855).
Oesterley, W. O. E.
   Jewish Background of the Christian Liturgy, The.   HAnc(II-596).
O'Faoláin, Seán
   Finest Stories of Seán O'Faoláin, The.   SCL12(IV-2597),
   SCL7(III-1538),   A58(88).
   I Remember! I Remember!   SCL12(VI-3590),   SCL7(III-2152),
   A63(86).
   Nest of Simple Folk, A.   MP12(VII-4165),   MPCE(III-1554),
   MP8(V-3245),   MP6(IV-2082),   MPEng(561),   MPv4(363),
   MP2(II-728),   MWL2(728).
   *Vive Moi!   SCL12(XII-8029),   SCL7(VII-4910),   A65(305).
Offler, H. S., E. Bonjour and G. R. Potter
   Short History of Switzerland, A.   HEur(II-796).
O'Flaherty, Liam
   *Informer, The.   MP12(V-2886),   MPCE(II-1061),   MP8(IV-2249),
   MP6(III-1440),   MPEng(343),   MPv4(243),   MP2(I-486),
   MWL2(486).
   Stories of Liam O'Flaherty, The.   SCL12(XI-7255),
   SCL7(VII-4458),   A57(258).
Ogata, Sadako N.
   Defiance in Manchuria: The Making of Japanese Foreign Policy,
   1931-1932.   HWor(I-274).
Ogg, David

Tell Me a Riddle.   SCL12(XI-7424),   SCL7(VII-4527),   A62(296).
Yonnondio: From the Thirties.   SCL12(XII-8479),   A75(368).
Olson, Charles
   Archaeologist of Morning.   SCL12(I-355),   A72(9).
O'Malley, C. D.
   Andreas Vesalius of Brussels, 1514-1564.   (HEur(I-134).
O'Meara, Patrick
   Rhodesia: Racial Conflict or Coexistence?   HWor(II-984).
Oman, John Wood
   Natural and the Supernatural, The.   RCh(II-973).
O'Neill, Eugene
   *Anna Christie.   MP12(I-226),   MPCE(I-78),   MP8(I-177),
   MP6(I-110),   MPDr(37),   MPv3(21),   MP2(I-35),   MWL2(35).
   Desire Under the Elms.   MP12(III-1458),   MPCE(I-531),
   MP8(II-1131),   MP6(II-730),   MPDr(206),   MPv3(119),
   MP2(I-247),   MWL2(247).
   *Emperor Jones, The.   MP12(III-1769),   MPCE(I-646),
   MP8(II-1377),   MP6(II-888),   MPDr(249),   MPv3(144),
   MP2(I-291),   MWL2(291).
   *Long Day's Journey into Night.   SCL12(VII-4480),
   SCL7(IV-2753),   A57(162),   BMA(347).
   *Mourning Becomes Electra.   MP12(VII-4081),   MPCE(III-1514),
   MP8(V-3184),   MP6(IV-2037),   MPDr(559),   MPv3(354),
   MP2(II-710),   MWL2(710).
   *Strange Interlude.   MP12(XI-6294),   MPCE(IV-2173),
   MP8(VII-5013),   MP6(VI-2994),   MPDr(808),   MPv3(504),
   MP2(II-1000),   MWL2(1000).
   Touch of the Poet, A.   SCL12(XI-7716),   SCL7(VII-4720),
   A58(239),   BMA(558).
Ong, Walter J., S. J.
   American Catholic Crossroads.   RCa(II-1076).
Ooka, Shohei
   Fires on the Plain.   SCL12(IV-2626),   SCL7(III-1547),   A58(91).
Opie, Redvers, *et al.*
   Search for Peace Settlements, The.   HWor(II-593).
Oppen, George
   Of Being Numerous.   SCL12(VIII-5489),   SCL7(V-3349),   A69(252).
Oppenheim, A. Leo
   Ancient Mesopotamia: Portrait of a Dead Civilization.   HAnc(I-43).
Orfield, Gary
   Reconstruction of Southern Education, The.   HWor(II-968).
Orieux, Jean
   Voltaire.   LA80(II-850).
Origen,
   Contra Celsum.   Different analyses on this title appear in:

RCh(I-66), RCa(I-71).
De Principiis. Ph(I-240).
On First Principles. Different analyses on this title appear in:
RCh(I-57), RCa(I-65).
Orosius, Paulus
Seven Books of History Against the Pagans. Different analyses on this title appear in: RCh(I-145), RCa(I-178).
Ortega y Gasset, José
*Revolt of the Masses, The. MP12(X-5562), MP8(VII-4432),
MP6(V-2638), MPNf(266), MP3(II-886), MWL3(886).
Orwell, George
*Nineteen Eighty-Four. MP12(VII-4224), MPCE(III-1578),
MP8(V-3291), MP6(IV-2115), MPEng(578), MPv4(369),
MP2(II-746), MWL2(746). A different analysis on this title appears in:
SF(III-1531).
Osaragi, Jiro
Journey, The. SCL12(VI-3916), SCL7(IV-2371), A61(137).
Osborne, Charles
W. H. Auden: The Life of a Poet. LA80(II-860).
Osborne, John
*Inadmissible Evidence. SCL12(VI-3691), SCL7(III-2205), A66(129).
*Look Back in Anger. MP12(VI-3490), MP8(IV-2734),
MP4(I-563), MWL4(563). A different analysis on this title appears in:
SCL12(VII-4517), SCL7(IV-2771), A58(153), BMA(354).
Osborne, Milton
*"Kampuchea and Vietnam: A Historical Perspective," in Pacific
Community.* HWor(III-1351).
Osgood, Herbert L.
American Colonies in the Seventeenth Century, The. HAmer(I-113).
Osgood, Robert E.
NATO: The Entangling Alliance. HAmer(III-1809).
O'Shea, Donald C., *et al.*
Introduction to Lasers and Their Applications, An. HWor(II-884).
Oshikawa, Shunro
Kaitei Gunkan. SF(III-1106).
Ostrogorsky, George
History of the Byzantine State. HAnc(II-1155).
Oswald, John Clyde
History of Printing, A. HAnc(III-1716).
Otis, Brooks
Virgil, A Study in Civilized Poetry. HAnc(I-559).
Otis, D. S.
"History of the Allotment Policy," in Readjustment of Indian Affairs.
HAmer(II-1164).
Otloh of St. Emmeram

Ozick, Cynthia
    Bloodshed and Three Novellas. LA77(I-101).

Packard, Vance
    Hidden Persuaders, The. SCL12(V-3416), SCL7(III-2028),
    A58(104), BMA(231).
    Nation of Strangers, A. SCL12(VIII-5227), A73(269).
    People Shapers, The. LA78(II-649).
    Status Seekers, The. SCL12(XI-7211), SCL7(VI-4429), A60(251).
    Waste Makers, The. SCL12(XII-8132), SCL7(VII-4973), A61(287).
Padover, Saul K.
    Karl Marx: An Intimate Biography. LA79(I-349).
    Life and Death of Louis XVI, The. HEur(I-521).
Page, Charles Hunt
    Class and American Sociology: From Ward to Ross. HAmer(III-1359).
Page, Thomas Nelson
    Marse Chan. MP12(VII-3748), MPCE(III-1370), MP8(V-2941),
    MP6(IV-1861), MPAm(399), MPv4(316), MP2(II-638),
    MWL2(638).
Pagels, Elaine
    Gnostic Gospels, The. LA80(I-363).
Paige, Glenn D.
    Korean Decision, June 24-30, 1950, The. HAmer(III-1827).
Pain, Nesta
    King and Becket, The. HAnc(III-1377).
Paine, Thomas
    Age of Reason, The. MP12(I-70), MP8(I-56), MP4(I-11),
    MWL4(11).
    Crisis, The. MP12(II-1211), MP8(II-938), MP6(II-620),
    MPNf(69), MP3(I-238), MWL3(238).
Painter, George D.
    *Chateaubriand: A Biography, Vol. I (1768-93): The Longed-for
    Tempests.* LA79(I-95).
    Proust: The Early Years. SCL12(IX-6105), SCL7(VI-3731),
    A60(206), BMA(459).
    Proust: The Later Years. SCL12(IX-6109), SCL7(VI-3735),
    A66(252).
    William Caxton: A Biography. LA78(II-909).
Painter, Sidney
    Reign of King John, The. HAnc(III-1455).
Pais, Ettore
    Ancient Italy. HAnc(I-255).
Pakenham, Thomas
    Boer War, The. LA80(I-97).
Paley, Grace

A60(199).

Paston Family
Paston Letters A. D. 1422-1509, The.   MP12(VIII-4513),
MP8(V-3515),   MP4(II-673),   MWL4(673).

Pastor, Ludwig von
History of the Popes from the Close of the Middle Ages, The.   Different
analyses on this title appear in: RCa(II-796),   HEur(I-46).

Pasvolsky, Leo *and* Harold G. Moulton
War Debts and World Prosperity.   HAmer(III-1539).

Pater, Walter
Marius the Epicurean.   MP12(VII-3732),   MPCE(III-1363),
MP8(V-2928),   MP6(IV-1851),   MPEng(472),   MPv3(318),
MP2(II-630),   MWL2(630).
Renaissance, The.   MP12(IX-5511),   MP8(VII-4392),
MP4(II-1052),   MWL4(1052).

Paton, Alan
*Cry, the Beloved Country.   MP12(III-1235),   MPCE(I-454),
MP8(II-957),   MP6(II-634),   MPEur(185),   MPv4(91),
MP2(I-202),   MWL2(202).
Knocking on the Door.   LA77(I-396).

Patrick, John
Apology of Origen in Reply to Celsus, The.   HAnc(II-733).
Teahouse of the August Moon, The.   SCL12(XI-7410),
SCL7(VII-4517),   A54(273),   BMA(533).

Patrick, Saint
Writings of Saint Patrick, The.   RCa(I-207).

Pattison, William D.
*Beginnings of the American Rectangular Land Survey System,
1784-1800.*   HAmer(I-310).

Paul, Günter
Satellite Spin-Off: The Achievements of Space Flight, The.
HWor(II-755).

Paul, Rodman W.
California Gold: The Beginning of Mining in the Far West.
HAmer(II-845).

Paul, Sherman, *ed.*
Thoreau: A Collection of Critical Essays.   HAmer(II-851).

Paustovsky, Konstantin
Story of a Life, The.   SCL12(XI-7265),   SCLs(295).

Paxson, Frederic L.
When the West Is Gone.   HAmer(II-1215).

Paz, Octavio
Eagle or Sun?   SCL12(III-2095),   A72(102).
Labyrinth of Solitude, The.   MP12(VI-3200),   MP8(IV-2491),
MP4(I-489),   MWL4(489),   SCL12(VI-4057),   SCL7(IV-2462),

A63(117).

Poetry of Paz, The. MP12(IX-5109), MP8(VI-4055), MP4(II-926), MWL4(926).

Peacock, Thomas Love

Crotchet Castle. MP12(III-1229), MPCE(I-451), MP8(II-953), MP6(II-631), MPEng(129), MPv4(90), MP2(I-201), MWL2(201).

Headlong Hall. MP12(V-2498), MPCE(II-911), MP8(III-1947), MP6(III-1232), MPEng(278), MPv4(209), MP2(I-414), MWL2(414).

Nightmare Abbey. MP12(VII-4221), MPCE(III-1577), MP8(V-3289), MP6(IV-2113), MPEng(576), MP1(II-657), MWL1(657).

Pearce, Roy H.

Whitman: A Collection of Critical Essays. HAmer(II-851).

Peare, Catherine Owens

William Penn. SCL12(XII-8305), SCL7(VII-5085), A58(270).

Pears, Edwin

Destruction of the Greek Empire and the Story of the Capture of Constantinople by the Turks, The. HAnc(III-1720).

Pearson, Hasketh

Merry Monarch. SCL12(VII-4955), SCL7(V-3014), A61(177), BMA(367).

Pearson, John

Sitwells: A Family Biography, The. LA80(II-763).

Peary, Robert Edwin

North Pole, Its Discovery in 1909 Under the Auspices of the Peary Arctic Club, The. HWor(I-65).

Peattie, Donald Culross

Almanac for Moderns, An. MP12(I-146), MP8(I-115), MP4(I-30), MWL4(30).

Peele, George

Old Wives' Tale, The. MP12(VIII-4349), MPCE(III-1626), MP8(V-3385), MP6(IV-2177), MPDr(587), MPv4(379), MP2(II-771), MWL2(771).

Péguy, Charles

Basic Verities. RCa(II-879).

Poetry of Péguy, The. MP12(IX-5112), MP8(VI-4058), MP4(II-928), MWL4(928).

Peirce, Charles Sanders

Collected Papers. Ph(II-952).

Pennell, Elizabeth Robins *and* Joseph Pennell

Lithography and Lithographers. Some Chapters in the History of the Art. HEur(I-545).

Penrose, Boies

Travel and Discovery in the Renaissance, 1420-1620. HEur(I-13).

Pepper, Suzanne
Civil War in China: The Political Struggle, 1945-1949. HWor(I-215).
Pepys, Samuel
*Diary. MP12(III-1497), MP8(II-1161), MP6(II-753),
MPNf(89), MP3(I-283), MWL3(283).
Percy, Walker
Lancelot. LA78(II-501).
*Last Gentleman, The. SCL12(VI-4109), SCL7(IV-2508),
A67(184).
Love in the Ruins. SCL12(VII-4577), A72(205). A different analysis
on this title appears in: SF(III-1278).
Message in the Bottle, The. SCL12(VII-4959), A76(221).
*Moviegoer, The. SCL12(VIII-5122), SCL7(V-3119), A62(212).
Pereda, José María de
Pedro Sánchez. MP12(VIII-4556), MPCE(III-1694),
MP8(V-3549), MP6(IV-2278), MPEur(569), MP3(II-728),
MWL3(728).
Peñas Arriba. MP12(VIII-4572), MPCE(III-1703), MP8(V-3561),
MP6(IV-2289), MPEur(574), MP3(II-730), MWL3(730).
Sotileza. MP12(XI-6186), MPCE(IV-2132), MP8(VII-4930),
MP6(V-2945), MPEur(714), MPv4(488), MP2(II-985),
MWL2(985).
Pérez Galdós, Benito
*Ángel Guerra. MP12(I-223), MPCE(I-76), MP8(I-175),
MP6(I-108), MPEur(28), MP3(I-42), MWL3(42).
*Fortunata and Jacinta. MP12(IV-2132), MPCE(II-768),
MP8(III-1660), MP6(II-1041), MPEur(309), MPv4(166),
MP2(I-336), MWL2(336).
Perkins, Bradford
Castlereagh and Adams: England and the United States, 1812-1823.
HAmer(I-524).
Prologue to War: England and the United States, 1805-1812.
HAmer(I-507).
Perkins, Dexter
History of the Monroe Doctrine, A. HAmer(I-596).
Perkins, Frances
Roosevelt I Knew, The. HAmer(III-1645).
Perowne, John James Stewart
Death of the Roman Republic. HAnc(I-497).
End of the Roman World, The. HAnc(II-938).
Hadrian. HAnc(II-704).
Perrett, Geoffrey
Dream of Greatness: The American People, 1945-1963, A. LA80(I-226).
Perry, Ralph Barton
General Theory of Value. Ph(II-874).

Thought and Character of William James: Briefer Version, The.
HAmer(III-1366).
Perse, St.-John
Anabasis. MP12(I-192), MP8(I-152), MP6(I-88), MPPo(6),
MP3(I-32), MWL3(32).
Chronique. MP12(II-956), MP8(II-742), MP4(I-134),
MWL4(134), SCL12(II-1265), SCL7(II-742), A62(58), BMA(80).
Èloges and Other Poems. MP12(III-1746), MP8(II-1359),
MP4(I-271), MWL4(271), SCL12(IV-2203), SCL7(II-1314),
A57(61), BMA(160).
Seamarks. MP12(X-5874), MP8(VII-4676), MP4(II-1102),
MWL4(1102), SCL12(X-6677), SCL7(VI-4106), A59(216),
BMA(496).
Pershing, John J.
My Experience in the World War. HAmer(III-1470).
Peterson, Donald
Spectral Boy, The. SCL12(XI-7168), SCL7(VI-4399), A66(306).
Peterson, Merril D.
"Parrington and American Liberalism," in *Virginia Quarterly Review.*
HWor(I-209).
Peterson, Robert T.
Art of Ecstasy, The. SCL12(I-391), A72(12).
Petit-Dutaillis, Charles
*Feudal Monarchy in France and England from the Tenth to the Thirteenth
Century, The.* HAnc(III-1203).
"France: Louis XI," in *Vol. VIII* of *The Cambridge Medieval History.*
HAnc(III-1735).
Petrakis, Harry Mark
Dream of Kings, A. SCL12(III-2066), SCL7(II-1240), A68(86).
Pericles on 31st Street. SCL12(IX-5812), SCLs(219).
Petrarch
On His Own Ignorance. RCa(I-469).
Rime of Petrarch, Le. MP12(X-5597), MP8(VII-4458),
MP6(V-2654), MPPo(315), MP3(II-893), MWL3(893).
Petras, James F.
"U.S.-Cuban Policy Debate, The," in *Monthly Review.* HWor(III-1254).
Petrie, Charles
Earlier Diplomatic History, 1492-1713. HEur(I-343).
Petronius (Gaius Petronius Arbiter)
Satyricon, The. MP12(X-5820), MPCE(IV-2005),
MP8(VII-4638), MP6(V-2771), MPEur(668), MPv3(466),
MP2(II-938), MWL2(938).
Pfeiffer, Robert H.
Introduction to the Old Testament. HAnc(II-666).
Pflanze, Otto

Bismarck and the Development of Germany.   HEur(II-921).
Philbrick, Francis S.
    Rise of the West, 1754-1830, The. New American Nation series.
    HAmer(I-326).
Philby, H. St. John
    Harun al-Rashid.   HAnc(II-1144).
Philip, J. A.
    Pythagoras and Early Pythagoreans.   HAnc(I-197).
Philips, C. E. Lucas
    Alamein.   HEur(III-1468).
Philips, C. H. *and* Mary Doreen Wainwright, *eds.*
    Partition of India: Policies and Perspectives, 1935-1947, The.
    HWor(II-607).
Phillips, Cabell
    Truman Presidency: The History of a Triumphant Succession, The.
    HAmer(III-1761).
Phillips, R. Hart
    Cuba: Island of Paradox.   SCL12(III-1669),   SCL7(II-976),   A60(48).
Phillipson, Coleman
    Three Criminal Law Reformers: Beccaria, Bentham, Romilly.
    HEur(I-458).
Phillpotts, Eden
    Saurus.   SF(IV-1866).
Piaget, Jean
    Grasp of Consciousness, The.   LA77(I-341).
Picard, Gilbert Charles *and* Collette Picard
    Life and Death of Carthage, The.   HAnc(I-411).
Picard, Max
    World of Silence, The.   RCa(II-936).
Pick, Robert
    Escape of Socrates, The.   SCL12(IV-2320),   SCL7(II-1386),   A54(58).
Pieper, Josef
    Belief and Faith.   RCa(II-1121).
    End of Time, The.   RCa(II-964).
    Leisure the Basis of Culture.   RCa(II-940).
Pierce, Ovid Williams
    On a Lonesome Porch.   SCL12(VIII-5540),   SCL7(V-3387),
    A61(188).
Piercy, Marge
    Dance the Eagle to Sleep.   SCL12(III-1687),   A71(55).
    Woman on the Edge of Time.   SF(V-2488).
Pigafetta, Antonio
    Voyage of Magellan.   SCL12(XII-8050),   SCLs(328).
Pike, Douglas
    Vietnam-Cambodia Conflict.   HWor(III-1353).

Pike, Zebulon Montgomery
Journals, with Letters and Related Documents. HAmer(I-470).
Pilnyak, Boris
Naked Year, The. MP12(VII-4131), MPCE(III-1538),
MP8(V-3219), MP6(IV-2061), MPEur(526), MPv4(360),
MP2(II-719), MWL2(719).
Pindar
Epinicia, The. MP12(III-1805), MP8(II-1408), MP6(II-905),
MPPo(82), MP3(I-346), MWL3(346).
Pinero, Arthur Wing
Mid-Channel. MP12(VII-3877), MP8(V-3037), MP6(IV-1930),
MPDr(525), MP3(II-661), MWL3(661).
Second Mrs. Tanqueray, The. MP12(X-5882), MPCE(IV-2029),
MP8(VII-4684), MP6(V-2802), MPDr(750), MPv3(476),
MP2(II-947), MWL2(947).
Pinter, Harold
*Caretaker, The. MP12(I-800), MP8(I-620), MP4(I-110),
MWL4(110).
Proust Screenplay, The. LA78(II-673).
Three Plays. SCL12(XI-7604), SCL7(VII-4631), A63(267).
Piper, H. Beam
Little Fuzzy. SF(III-1230).
Pipes, Richard
Russia Under the Old Regime. SCL12(X-6559), A75(265).
Pirajno, Alberto Denti di
Ippolita. SCL12(VI-3767), SCL7(IV-2264), A62(157).
Pirandello, Luigi
Late Mattia Pascal, The. MP12(VI-3285), MPCE(II-1221),
MP8(IV-2558), MP6(III-1636), MPEur(433), MPv4(281),
MP2(I-562), MWL2(562).
Old and the Young, The. MP12(VIII-4305), MPCE(III-1610),
MP8(V-3349), MP6(IV-2153), MPEur(552), MP1(II-676),
MWL1(676).
*Right You Are—If You Think So. MP12(X-5593),
MPCE(III-1914), MP8(VII-4455), MP6(V-2651), MPDr(697),
MP3(II-891), MWL3(891).
Pirandello, Luigi
*Six Characters in Search of an Author. MP12(X-6079),
MPCE(IV-2089), MP8(VII-4848), MP6(V-2893), MPDr(783),
MP3(II-993), MWL3(993).
Pirenne, Henri
"Carolingian Coup d'Etat and the Volte-Face of the Papacy, The," in
Mohammed and Charlemagne. HAnc(II-1133).
Economic and Social History of Medieval Europe. HAnc(III-1362).
Medieval Cities. HAnc(II-1133).

Pitt, Barrie
>   *1918: The Last Act.*   SCL12(VIII-5366),   SCL7(V-3273),   A64(191).
Pius XI, Pope
>   *Atheistic Communism.*   RCa(II-858).
>   *Casti connubii.*   RCa(II-808).
>   *Christian Education of Youth, The.*   RCa(II-801).
>   *Mit brennender Sorge.*   RCa(II-860).
>   *Quadragesimo anno.*   RCa(II-812).
Pius XII, Pope
>   *Divino afflante Spiritu.*   RCa(II-883).
>   *Mediator Dei.*   RCa(II-915).
>   *Mystical Body of Christ, The.*   RCa(II-886).
Plath, Sylvia
>   *Ariel.*   SCL12(I-358),   SCL7(I-208),   A67(17).
>   *Bell Jar, The.*   SCL12(I-632),   A72(25).
>   *Colossus and Other Poems, The.*   SCL12(III-1443),   SCLs(77).
>   *Letters Home.*   SCL12(VI-4211),   A76(164).
>   *Winter Trees.*   SCL12(XII-8350),   A73(383).
Plato
>   *Apology.*   Ph(I-42).
>   *Crito.*   Ph(I-54).
>   *Dialogues of Plato, The.*   MP12(III-1482),   MP8(II-1148),
>   MP6(II-744),   MPNf(82),   MP3(I-277),   MWL3(277).
>   *Euthyphro.*   Ph(I-49).
>   *Gorgias.*   Ph(I-70).
>   *Laws.*   Ph(I-131).
>   *Meno.*   Ph(I-64).
>   *Parmenides.*   Ph(I-106).
>   *Phaedo.*   Ph(I-81).
>   *Phaedrus.*   Ph(I-95).
>   *Philebus.*   Ph(I-120).
>   *Protagoras.*   Ph(I-59).
>   *Republic.*   MP12(IX-5522),   MP8(VII-4402),   MP6(V-2620),
>   MPNf(263),   MP3(II-876),   MWL3(876). A different analysis on this
>   title appears in: Ph(I-88).
>   *Sophist.*   Ph(I-110).
>   *Statesman.*   Ph(I-116).
>   *Symposium.*   Ph(I-74).
>   *Theaetetus.*   Ph(I-98).
>   *Timaeus.*   Ph(I-125).
Plautus (Titus Maccius Plautus)
>   *Amphitryon.*   MP12(I-185),   MPCE(I-62),   MP8(I-146),
>   MP6(I-84),   MPDr(25),   MPv3(15),   MP2(I-24),
>   MWL2(24).

MP4(I-299),　　MWL4(299).

Fall of the House of Usher, The.　MP12(IV-1968),　MPCE(II-705),
MP8(III-1540),　MP6(II-980),　MPAm(177),　MPv4(155),
MP2(I-316),　MWL2(316).

Gold Bug, The.　MP12(IV-2286),　MPCE(II-828),
MP8(III-1779),　MP6(II-1118),　MPAm(209),　MPv4(187),
MP2(I-373),　MWL2(373).

Ligeia.　MP12(VI-3418),　MPCE(II-1247),　MP8(IV-2679),
MP6(III-1691),　MPAm(343),　MPv4(290),　MP2(II-583),
MWL2(583).

Narrative of Arthur Gordon Pym, The.　MP12(VII-4143),
MPCE(III-1544),　MP8(V-2068),　MPAm(433),　MP1(II-640),
MWL1(640). A different analyses on this title appears in: SF(III-1480).

Science Fiction of Edgar Allan Poe, The.　SF(IV-1871).

Pogue, Forrest C.

"Decision to Halt at the Elbe, The," in *Command Decisions.*
HWor(II-582).

George C. Marshall: Education of a General, 1880-1939.
SCL12(V-2882),　SCL7(III-1722),　A64(107).

George C. Marshall: Ordeal and Hope, 1939-1942.　SCL12(V-2885),
SCL7(III-1725),　A67(122). A different analysis on this title appears in:
HAmer(III-1717).

George C. Marshall: Organizer of Victory, 1943-1954.
SCL12(V-2890),　A74(148).

Pohl, Frederik

Gateway.　SF(II-858).

Man Plus.　SF(III-1328).

Short Fiction of Frederik Pohl, The.　SF(IV-1948).

Pohl, Frederik *and* Cyril M. Kornbluth

Gladiator-at-Law.　SF(II-894).

Space Merchants, The.　SF(V-2127).

Poirier, Richard

Robert Frost: The Work of Knowing.　LA78(II-722).

Pois, Robert A.

Friedrich Meinecke and German Politics in the Twentieth Century.
HWor(I-59).

Politian

Orfeo.　MP12(VIII-4398),　MPCE(III-1635),　MP8(V-3428),
MP6(IV-2199),　MPDr(590),　MP3(II-702),　MWL3(702).

Pollack, Jack Harrison

Earl Warren: The Judge Who Changed America.　LA80(I-255).

Pollock, John

Wilberforce.　LA79(II-862).

Pollock, Sir Frederick *and* Frederick William Maitland

History of English Law Before the Time of Edward I, The.

HAnc(III-1389).

Polo, Marco
Travels of Marco Polo, The. MP12(XI-6650), MPCE(IV-2309),
MP8(VIII-5283), MP6(VI-3183), MPNf(303), MP1(II-1011),
MWL1(1011). A different analysis on this title appears in:
HAnc(III-1553).
Epistles and *The Martyrdom of Saint Polycarp, The.* RCa(I-16).

Polycarp of Smyrna, Saint
Epistle to the Philippians. RCh(I-17).

Pomerance, Bernard
Elephant Man, The. LA80(I-280).

Pomerius, Julianus
Contemplative Life, The. RCa(I-220).

Pomper, Gerald M., et al.
Election of 1976: Reports and Interpretations, The. HWor(III-1305).

Ponchaud, François
Cambodia: Year Zero. HWor(III-1216).

Poncins, Gontran de
Ghost Voyage, The. SCL12(V-2925), SCL7(III-1737), A54(89).

Pond, Hugh
Salerno. SCL12(X-6613), SCL7(VI-4061), A63(231).

Pontoppidan, Henrik
Promised Land, The. MP12(IX-5368), MPCE(III-1827),
MP8(VI-4284), MP6(V-2545), MPEur(605), MPv3(434),
MP2(II-869), MWL2(869).

Poole, Peter A.
Expansion of the Vietnam War into Cambodia, The. HWor(II-1086).

Pope, Alexander
Dunciad, The. MP12(III-1672), MP8(II-1299), MP6(II-840),
MPPo(72), MP3(I-310), MWL3(310).
Essay on Criticism. MP12(III-1834), MP8(II-1432),
MP4(II-287), MWL4(287).
Essay on Man. MP12(IV-1837), MP8(II-1435), MP4(I-290),
MWL4(290).
Rape of the Lock, The. MP12(IX-5436), MPCE(III-1853),
MP8(VI-4335), MP6(V-2577), MPPo(313), MP1(II-802),
MWL1(802).

Pope, Dudley
Decision at Trafalgar. SCL12(III-1843), SCL7(II-1102), A61(55),
BMA(121).

Pope, Hugh
English Versions of the Bible. HEur(I-245).

Pope-Hennessy, James
Queen Mary. SCL12(IX-6170), SCL7(VI-3770), A61(200),
BMA(463).

Pope-Hennessy, John
   Italian Renaissance Sculpture.   HAnc(III-1668).
Porath, Yehoshuah
   Emergence of the Palestinian-Arab National Movement, 1918-1929, The.
   HWor(I-237).
Porter, Jane
   Scottish Chiefs, The.   MP12(X-5851),   MPCE(IV-2021),
   MP8(VII-4658),   MP6(V-2788),   MPEng(775),   MPv3(471),
   MP2(II-942),   MWL2(942).
   Thaddeus of Warsaw.   MP12(XI-6462),   MPCE(IV-2231),
   MP8(VIII-5144),   MP6(VI-3083),   MPEng(830),   MP1(II-967),
   MWL1(967).
Porter, Katherine Anne
   Collected Stories of Katherine Anne Porter, The.   SCL12(III-1419),
   SCL7(II-835),   A66(51).
   Old Mortality.   MP12(VIII-4330),   MPCE(III-1620),
   MP8(V-3370),   MP6(IV-2167),   MPAm(460),   MPv4(376),
   MP2(II-766),   MWL2(766).
   Pale Horse, Pale Rider.   MP12(VIII-4465),   MP8(V-3479),
   MP4(II-665),   MWL4(665).
   Ship of Fools.   MP12(X-5979),   MP8(VII-4763),   MP4(II-1118),
   MWL4(1118),   SCL12(X-6915),   SCL7(VI-4254),   A63(240).
Porter, Keith *and* B. R. Brinkley, *eds.*
   International Cell Biology, 1976-1977.   HWor(I-506).
Porter, Kenneth W.
   John Jacob Astor, Business Man.   HAmer(I-479).
Portis, Charles
   True Grit.   SCL12(XII-7796),   SCL7(VII-4773),   A69(321).
Pöschl, Viktor
   Art of Vergil: Image and Symbol in the Aeneid, The.   HAnc(I-558).
Poschmann, Bernhard
   Penance and the Anointing of the Sick.   HAnc(II-765).
Post, Gaines
   Studies in Medieval Legal Thought.   HAnc(III-1346).
Post, L. A.
   From Homer to Menander.   HAnc(I-369).
Postan, M. M.
   *Cambridge Economic History, Vol. I: The Agrarian Life of the Middle
   Ages, The.*   HAnc(III-1325).
Postgate, Raymond *and* G. D. H. Cole
   British Common People, 1746-1946, The.   HEur(II-739).
Postman, Neil *and* Charles Weingartner
   Teaching as a Subversive Activity.   SCL12(XI-7405),   A70(303).
Potok, Chaim
   Chosen, The.   SCL12(II-1254),   SCL7(II-731),   A68(41).

Potter, David M.
  Lincoln and His Party in the Secession Crisis.   HAmer(II-948).
Potter, G. R., E. Bonjour *and* H.S. Offler
  Short History of Switzerland, A.   HEur(II-796).
Pottle, Frederick A.
  James Boswell: The Earlier Years, 1740-1769.   SCL12(VI-3789),
  SCL7(IV-2281),   A67(168).
Potts, Willard, *ed.*
  *Portraits of the Artist in Exile: Recollections of James Joyce by
  Europeans.*   LA80(II-675).
Pound, Ezra
  *Cantos.   MP12(II-776),   MP8(I-603),   MP6(I-398),   MPPo(38),
  MP3(I-151),   MWL3(151).
  Personae.   MP12(VIII-4612),   MP8(V-3593),   MP4(II-681),
  MWL4(681).
Pournelle, Jerry *and* Larry Niven
  Mote in God's Eye, The.   SF(III-1463).
Pourrat, Rev. Pierre
  Christian Spirituality.   HAnc(II-932).
Powell, Anthony
  *Acceptance World, The.   SCL12(I-20),   SCL7(I-15),   A57(1),
  BMA(4).
  *Afternoon Men.   SCL12(I-112),   SCL7(I-78),   A64(4).
  *At Lady Molly's.   SCL12(I-424),   SCL7(I-246),   A59(17),
  BMA(28).
  *Books Do Furnish a Room.   SCL12(II-837),   A72(44).
  *Casanova's Chinese Restaurant.   SCL12(II-1101),   SCL7(I-632),
  A61(30),   BMA(60).
  *Dance to the Music of Time, A.   MP12(III-1288),   MP8(II-995),
  MP4(I-178),   MWL4(178). A different analysis on this title appears in:
  SCL12(III-1690),   SCL7(II-993),   A63(28).
  Dance to the Music of Time: Second Movement, A.   MP12(III-1293),
  MP8(II-1000),   MP4(I-183),   MWL4(183).
  Hearing Secret Harmonies.   LA77(I-347).
  Infants of the Spring.   LA78(I-447).
  *Kindly Ones, The.   SCL12(VI-4009),   SCL7(IV-2421),   A63(115).
  *Military Philosophers, The.   SCL12(VIII-4998),   A70(207).
  *Soldier's Art, The.   SCL12(XI-7076),   SCL7(VI-4346),   A69(294).
  *Temporary Kings.   SCL12(XI-7448),   A74(386).
  *Valley of Bones, The.   SCL12(XII-7958),   SCL7(VII-4864),
  A65(302).
Powell, Dawn
  Golden Spur, The.   SCL12(V-3024),   SCL7(III-1803),   A63(76).
  Wicked Pavilion, The.   SCL12(XII-8269),   SCL7(VII-5058),
  A54(291).

Powell, Sumner Chilton
  Puritan Village.   SCL12(IX-6134),   SCLs(234).
Powers, J. F.
  Morte d'Urban.   SCL12(VIII-5079),   SCL7(V-3087),   A63(151).
  Presence of Grace, The.   SCL12(IX-6017),   SCL7(V-3674),
  A57(209).
Powicke, Frederick M.
  Thirteenth Century, 1216-1307, The.   HAnc(III-1583).
Powys, John Cowper
  Wolf Solent.   MP12(XII-7203),   MPCE(IV-2523),
  MP8(VIII-5696),   MP6(VI-3452),   MPEng(962),   MP3(II-1136),
  MWL3(1136).
Powys, Llewelyn
  Ebony and Ivory.   MP12(III-1697),   MP8(II-1319),   MP6(II-853),
  MPEng(173),   MP3(I-320),   MWL3(320).
Powys, T. F.
  Mr. Weston's Good Wine.   MP12(VII-3970),   MPCE(III-1462),
  MP8(V-3105),   MP6(IV-1980),   MPEng(530),   MPv4(338),
  MP2(II-686),   MWL2(686).
Pratt, Fletcher *and* L. Sprague De Camp
  Incomplete Enchanter, The.   SF(III-1031).
Pratt, James Bissett
  Personal Realism.   Ph(II-1016).
Pratt, Julius W.
  *America's Colonial Experiment: How the United States Gained, Governed,
  and in Part Gave Away a Colonial Empire.*   Different analyses on this
  title appear in: HAmer(II-1294; II-1321).
Prescott, H. F. M.
  Once to Sinai.   SCL12(VIII-5569),   SCL7(V-3406),   A59(187).
  Son of Dust.   SCL12(XI-7110),   SCL7(VI-4366),   A57(252).
Prescott, William Hickling
  History of the Conquest of Mexico.   MP12(V-2646),   MP8(III-2059),
  MP6(III-1314),   MPNf(143),   MP3(I-471),   MWL3(471). A different
  analysis on this title appears in: HEur(I-61).
Previte-Orton, Charles W.
  *Shorter Cambridge Medieval History, Vol. I: The Late Roman Empire to
  the Twelfth Century, The.*   Different analyses on this title appear in:
  HAnc(II-976; II-1160).
Prévost, Abbé
  Manon Lescaut.   MP12(VII-3696),   MPCE(III-1348),
  MP8(IV-2898),   MP6(IV-1831),   MPEur(472),   MP1(I-557),
  MWL1(557).
Price, Arnold H.
  Evolution of the Zollverein, The.   HEur(II-713).
Price, Harry Bayard

Marshall Plan and Its Meaning, The.   HEur(III-1535).
Price, Henry Habberley
   Perception.   Ph(II-968).
Price, Reynolds
   Generous Man, A.   SCL12(V-2872),   SCLs(115).
   Long and Happy Life, A.   MP12(VI-3474),   MP8(IV-2721),
   MP4(I-561),   MWL4(561). A different analysis on this title appears in:
   SCL12(VII-4475),   SCL7(IV-2748),   A63(135).
   Love and Work.   SCL12(VII-4573),   SCL7(IV-2793),   A69(208).
   Names and Faces of Heroes, The.   SCL12(VIII-5213),
   SCL7(V-3172),   A64(185).
   Permanent Errors.   SCL12(IX-5815),   A71(250).
   Surface of Earth, The.   SCL12(XI-7345),   A76(309).
Priest, Christopher
   Darkening Island.   SF(I-480).
   Inverted World.   SF(III-1045).
Priest, Loring B.
   *Uncle Sam's Stepchildren: The Reformation of United States Indian Policy,
   1865-1887.*   HAmer(II-1163).
Priestley, J. B.
   Found, Lost, Found.   LA78(I-325).
   *Good Companions, The.   MP12(IV-2316),   MPCE(II-838),
   MP8(III-1803),   MP6(II-1131),   MPEng(243),   MP1(I-311),
   MWL1(311).
Prior, Matthew
   Poetry of Prior, The.   MP12(IX-5115),   MP8(VI-4061),
   MP4(II-930),   MWL4(930).
Pritchett, V. S.
   Cab at the Door, A.   SCL12(II-1025),   SCL7(I-587),   A69(57).
   Camberwell Beauty and Other Stories, The.   SCL12(II-1053),   A75(41).
   Gentle Barbarian: The Life and Work of Turgenev, The.   LA78(I-340).
   George Meredith and English Comedy.   SCL12(V-2906),   A71(96).
   Midnight Oil.   SCL12(VIII-4978),   A73(254).
   Myth Makers: Literary Essays, The.   LA80(II-560).
   On the Edge of the Cliff.   LA80(II-627).
   Sailor, Sense of Humour, and Other Stories, The.   SCL12(X-6586),
   SCL7(VI-4048),   A57(230).
   Selected Stories.   LA79(II-669).
   When My Girl Comes Home.   SCL12(XII-8216),   SCL7(VII-5019),
   A62(301).
Procter, Evelyn S.
   Alfonso X of Castile, Patron of Literature and Learning.
   HAnc(III-1525).
Prokosch, Frederic
   Missolonghi Manuscript, The.   SCL12(VIII-5021),   SCL7(V-3048),

A69(228).

Seven Who Fled, The. MP12(X-5934), MP8(VII-4727),
MP6(V-2834), MPAm(566), MPv3(483), MP2(II-955),
MWL2(955).

Tale for Midnight, A. SCL12(XI-7383), SCL7(VII-4508),
A55(246).

Propertius (Sextus Propertius)
*Elegies of Propertius, The. MP12(III-173), MP8(II-1352),
MP4(I-265), MWL4(265).

Prosper of Aquitaine
Call of All Nations, The. RCa(I-204).

Prosperi, Piero
Autocrisi. SF(I-102).

Proust, Marcel
*Jean Santeuil. SCL12(VI-3823), SCL7(IV-2310), A57(135).

Provencher, Jean
René Lévesque: Portrait of a Québécois. HWor(II-824).

Pryce-Jones, David
Face of Defeat, The. SCL12(IV-2395), A74(113).
Hungarian Revolution, The. HEur(III-1597).

P'u Sung-ling,
Strange Stories from a Chinese Studio. MP12(XI-6299),
MP8(VII-5016), MP6(VI-2997), MPEur(729), MP3(II-1024),
MWL3(1024).

Puig, Manuel
Buenos Aires Affair, The. LA77(I-129).
Heartbreak Tango. SCL12(V-3315), A74(187).

Puleston, William D.
Mahan: The Life and Work of Captain Alfred Thayer Mahan, U. S. N.
HAmer(II-1203).

Purdy, James
Cabot Wright Begins. SCL12(II-1033), SCL7(I-591), A65(25).
Children Is All. SCL12(II-1228), SCL7(I-715), A63(23).
Color of Darkness. MP12(II-1034), MP8(II-802), MP4(I-144),
MWL4(144). A different analysis on this title appears in:
SCL12(III-1439), SCLs(74).
In a Shallow Grave. LA77(I-380).
Jeremy's Version. SCL12(VI-3862), A71(144).
Malcolm. MP12(VI-3655), MP8(IV-2862), MP4(I-588),
MWL4(588). A different analysis on this title appears in:
SCL12(VII-4680), SCL7 (IV-2847), A60(149).
Nephew, The. SCL12(VIII-5244), SCL7(V-3194), A61(185).

Pusey, Edward B.
Eirenicon, An. RCh(II-751).

Pushkin, Alexander

Boris Godunov. MP12(I-599), MPCE(I-218), MP8(I-464), MP6(I-312), MPDr(95), MPv4(44), MP2(I-109), MWL2(109).
Bronze Horseman: A Petersburg Tale, The. MP12(II-674), MP8(I-521), MP4(I-91), MWL4(91).
Captain's Daughter, The. MP12(II-792), MPCE(I-291), MP8(I-615), MP6(I-407), MPEur(105), MP1(I-113), MWL1(113).
Eugene Onegin. MP12(IV-1883), MPCE(II-666), MP8(III-1479), MP6(II-936), MPPo(89), MPv4(150), MP2(I-299), MWL2(299).
Ruslan and Lyudmila. MP12(X-5740), MP8(VII-4566), MP4(II-1080), MWL4(1080).

Putnam, Carlton
  Theodore Roosevelt: The Formative Years. SCL12(XI-7516), SCL7(VII-4570), A59(237).
Pylyshyn, Zenon W., *ed*.
  Perspectives on the Computer Revolution. HWor(II-540).
Pynchon, Thomas
  Crying of Lot 49, The. SCL12(III-1662), SCL7(II-973), A67(63).
  Gravity's Rainbow. SCL12(V-3087), A74(166). A different analysis on this title appears in: SF(II-915).
  V. SCL12(XII-4955), SCL7(VII-4861), A64(284).

Quandt, William B.
  Decade of Decisions: American Policy Toward the Arab-Israeli Conflict, 1967-1977. LA78(I-243).
Quarles, John
  Cleaning Up America. HWor(II-878).
Qubain, Fahim I.
  Crisis in Lebanon. HWor(II-760).
Queiroz, José Maria Eça de
  Maias, The. SCL12(VII-4646), SCL7(IV-2824), A66(157).
Quennell, Peter
  Alexander Pope. SCL12(I-194), A70(10).
  Hogarth's Progress. SCL12(V-3474), SCL7(III-2072), A55(124).
Quine, Willard Van Orman
  From a Logical Point of View. HAnc(II-837).
Quinn, David B.
  Raleigh and the British Empire. HAmer(I-48).

Râbe, David
  In the Boom Boom Room. SCL12(VI-3664), A76(144).
Rabelais, François
  Gargantua and Pantagruel. MP12(IV-2208), MPCE(II-797), MP8(III-1721), MP6(II-1079), MPEur(318), MP1(I-298),

MWL1(298).

Rabinowitch, Alexander
  Bolsheviks Come to Power, The. LA77(I-109).
Rabinowitz, Dorothy
  New Lives. LA77(II-549).
Rachlis, Eugene *and* Henry H. Keesler
  Peter Stuyvesant and His New York. HAmer(I-141).
Racine, Jean Baptiste
  *Andromache. MP12(I-219), MPCE(I-73), MP8(I-173),
  MP6(I-106), MPDr(35), MPv3(19), MP2(I-33), MWL2(33).
  *Bérœnice. MP12(I-504), MPCE(I-184), MP8(I-390),
  MP6(I-260), MPDr(75), MP3(I-101), MWL3(101).
  *Britannicus. MP12(II-662), MPCE(I-242), MP8(I-512),
  MP6(I-340), MPDr(106), MP3(I-133), MWL3(133).
  *Mithridate. MP12(VII-3987), MPCE(III-1471), MP8(V-3117),
  MP6(IV-1989), MPDr(548), MP3(II-667), MWL3(667).
  *Phèdre. MP12(VIII-4632), MPCE(III-1724), MP8(V-3611),
  MP6(IV-2329), MPDr(620), MP1(II-741), MWL1(741).
  Plaideurs, Les. MP12(VIII-4740), MP8(VI-3695), MP6(V-2386),
  MPDr(638), MP3(II-763), MWL3(763).
Radbertus, Paschasius
  Lord's Body and Blood, The. HAnc(II-1165).
Radcliff, Peter
  Limits of Liberty: Studies of Mill's On Liberty. HEur(II-845).
Radcliffe, Mrs. Ann
  Italian, The. MP12(V-2948), MPCE(II-1083), MP8(IV-2298),
  MP6(III-1468), MPEng(352), MP3(I-521), MWL3(521).
  *Mysteries of Udolpho, The. MP12(VII-4115), MPCE(III-1531),
  MP8(V-3207), MP6(IV-2054), MPEng(552), MP1(II-635),
  MWL1(635).
  *Romance of the Forest, The. MP12(X-5675), MPCE(III-1951),
  MP8(VII-4517), MP6(V-2694), MPEng(748), MPv4(458),
  MP2(II-914), MWL2(914).
Radhakrishnan, Sarvepalli
  Idealist View of Life, An. Ph(II-974).
Radin, Edward D.
  Lizzie Borden. SCL12(VII-4443), SCL7(IV-2730), A62(189).
Rahner, Karl
  On the Theology of Death. RCa(II-1047).
Raine, Kathleen
  Collected Poems. SCL12(II-1370), SCL7(II-803), A58(53).
Rainwater, Lee *and* William L. Yancey
  Moynihan Report and the Politics of Controversy, The.
  HAmer(III-1868).
Rakosi, Carl

Amulet. SCL12(I-290), SCL7(I-167), A69(8).

Raleigh, Sir Walter
Poetry of Raleigh, The. MP12(IX-5118), MP8(VI-4064),
MP4(II-933), MWL4(933).

Ramos Oliveira, Antonio
Politics, Economics, and Men of Modern Spain, 1808-1946. Different
analyses on this title appear in: HEur(II-636; II-728; III-1261).

Ramsay, William M.
Church in the Roman Empire, The. HAnc(II-641).
"Pliny's Report and Trajan's Rescript," in *The Church in the Roman
Empire.* HAnc(II-693).

Ramsaye, Terry
*Million and One Nights: A History of the Modern Motion Picture Through
1925, A.* HAmer(II-1337).

Ramsey, Paul
Basic Christian Ethics. RCh(II-1117).

Ramuz, Charles-Ferdinand
When the Mountain Fell. MP12(XII-7097), MPCE(IV-2491),
MP8(VIII-5612), MP6(VI-3402), MPEur(811), MPv4(587),
MP2(II-1127), MWL2(1127).

Rand, Ayn
Romantic Manifesto, The. SCL12(X-6472), A72(276).

Rand, E. K.
Founders of the Middle Ages. HAnc(II-1021).

Randall, James G.
Lincoln the President, Vol. I: Springfield to Bull Run. HAmer(II-938).
Lincoln the President, Vol II: Bull Run to Gettysburg. HAmer(II-983).

Randall, James G. *and* Richard N. Current
Lincoln the President, Vol. IV: Last Full Measure. SCL12(VII-4389),
SCL7(IV-2686), A55(147), BMA(340).

Randall, John Herman
Aristotle. HAnc(I-365).

Randall, Julia
Adam's Dream. SCL12(I-51), A70(4).
Puritan Carpenter, The. SCL12(IX-6131), SCL7(VI-3753),
A66(256).

Randolph, Alexander
Mail Boat, The. SCL12(VII-4650), SCL7(IV-2828), A54(165).

Rangarajan, L. N.
Commodity Conflict. HWor(III-1208).

Rankin, J. Lee, Earl Warren *and others*
*Report of the President's Commission on the Assassination of President
John F. Kennedy.* SCL12(IX-6354), SCL7(VI-3888), A65(246).

Ranking, G. S. A.
"Life and Works of Rhazes, The," in *Proceedings of the 17th International*

SCL7(VII-4566), A55(252), BMA(540).
Ray, Oakley S.
Drugs, Society and Human Behavior. HWor(II-816).
Read, Evelyn
My Lady Suffolk. SCL12(VIII-5172), SCL7(V-3151), A64(183).
Read, Kenneth E.
High Valley, The. SCL12(V-3431), SCL7(III-2043), A66(127).
Read, Piers Paul
Married Man, A. LA80(II-522).
Polonaise. LA77(II-632).
Reade, Charles
*Cloister and the Hearth, The. MP12(II-993), MPCE(I-363),
MP8(II-770), MP6(I-509), MPEng(112), MP1(I-150),
MWL1(150).
*Peg Woffington. MP12(VIII-4562), MPCE(III-1698),
MP8(V-3553), MP6(IV-2282), MPEng(643), MP1(II-724),
MWL1(724).
Reddaway, W. F.
*Cambridge History of Poland, Vol. II: From Augustus to Pilsudski,
1697-1935, The.* Different analyses on this title appear in: HEur(I-471;
II-889).
Redinger, Ruby V.
George Eliot: The Emergent Self. SCL12(V-2901), A76(98).
Redlich, Fritz
*Molding of American Banking: Men and Ideas, The. History of American
Economy* series. HAmer(I-543).
Reed, Ishmael
Mumbo Jumbo. SCL12(VIII-5139), A73(259).
Shrovetide in Old New Orleans. LA79(II-681).
Rees, David
Korea: The Limited War. HAmer(III-1826).
Rêgo, José Lins do
Dead Fires. MP12(III-1339), MP8(II-1035), MP6(II-678),
MPAm(130), MP3(I-254), MWL3(254).
Reich, Charles
Greening of America, The. SCL12(V-3161), A71(108).
Reid, Forrest
Bracknels, The. MP12(II-619), MPCE(I-223), MP8(I-481),
MP6(I-319), MPEng(60), MPv4(48), MP2(I-113), MWL2(113).
Tom Barber. SCL12(XI-7703), SCL7(VII-4710), A55(269).
Reid, James D.
Telegraph in America: Its Founders, Promoters, and Noted Men, The.
HAmer(II-933).
Reid, Thomas
Essays on the Intellectual Powers of Man and Essays on the Active Powers

of the Human Mind.   Ph(I-538).
Reilly, Robin
  William Pitt the Younger.   LA80(II-873).
Reischauer, Edwin O.
  Japanese, The.   LA78(II-459).
Remarque, Erich Maria
  *All Quiet on the Western Front.   MP12(I-130),   MPCE(I-45),
  MP8(I-102),   MP6(I-63),   MPEur(16),   MPv4(6),   MP2(I-13),
  MWL2(13).
  Black Obelisk, The.   SCL12(II-758),   SCL7(I-433),   A58(36).
Rembar, Charles
  End of Obscenity, The.   SCL12(IV-2239),   SCL7(II-1346),   A69(110).
Remington, Robin Alison
  Warsaw Pact: Case Studies in Communist Conflict Resolution, The.
  HWor(II-717).
Remini, Robert V.
  Andrew Jackson and the Course of American Empire, 1767-1821.
  LA78(I-50).
  Election of Andrew Jackson, The.   HAmer(I-633).
Renan, Ernest
  Life of Jesus, The.   RCh(II-739).
Renard, Maurice
  Docteur Lerne, Le.   SF(II-560).
Renault, Mary
  Bull from the Sea, The.   SCL12(II-959),   SCL7(I-549),   A63(14).
  Fire from Heaven.   SCL12(IV-2601),   A70(132).
  King Must Die, The.   SCL12(VI-4015),   SCL7(IV-2427),
  A59(133),   BMA(284).
  Last of the Wine, The.   MP12(VI-3271),   MP8(IV-2547),
  MP4(I-503),   MWL4(503),   SCL12(VI-4128),   SCL7(IV-2527),
  A57(147),   BMA(298).
Renouvin, Pierre
  Immediate Origins of the War, The.   HEur(III-1343).
Reuther, Victor G.
  Brothers Reuther, The.   LA77(I-124).
Rexroth, Kenneth
  New Poems.   SCL12(VIII-5273),   A75(209).
Reyes, Alfonso
  Visión de Anáhuac.   MP12(XII-6961),   MP8(VIII-5509),
  MP6(VI-3333),   MPNf(318),   MP3(II-1101),   MWL3(1101).
Reymont, Ladislas
  *Peasants, The.   MP12(VIII-4544),   MPCE(III-1690),
  MP8(V-3540),   MP6(IV-2274),   MPEur(566),   MP1(II-720),
  MWL1(720).
Reynolds, Robert L.

Europe Emerges. Different analyses on this title appear in: HAnc(II-1102; III-1305; III-1424).

Rhoads, Edward J. M.
China's Republican Revolution: The Case of Kwangtung, 1895-1913. HWor(I-95).

Rhodes, Frederick L.
Beginnings of Telephony. HAmer(II-1091).

Rhys, Jean
Good Morning, Midnight. SCL12(V-3039), A71(102).

Ribeiro, João Ubaldo
Sergeant Getúlio. LA79(II-672).

Ricciotti, Guiseppe
Julian the Apostate. HAnc(II-891).

Rice, Anne
Interview with the Vampire. LA77(I-384).

Rice, Elmer
Street Scene. MP12(XI-6304), MPCE(IV-2176), MP8(VII-5021), MP6(VI-2999), MPDr(811), MP3(II-1026), MWL3(1026).

Rice, Tamara Talbot
Seljuks in Asia Minor, The. HAnc(III-1254).

Rich, Adrienne
Diving into the Wreck. SCL12(III-1977), A74(94).
Dream of a Common Language: Poems 1974-1977, The. LA79(I-160).
Necessities of Life: Poems, 1962-1965. SCL12(VIII-5237), SCL7(V-3187), A67(237).
Of Woman Born. LA77(II-584).
On Lies, Secrets, and Silence: Selected Prose 1966-1978. LA80(II-622).
Poems: Selected and New. SCL12(IX-5937), A76(245).

Rich, E. E.
Cambridge Economic History, The. HAnc(III-1517).

Rich, Norman
Friedrich von Holstein: Politics and Diplomacy in the Era of Bismarck and Wilhelm II. HWor(I-49).

Richard of St. Victor
Benjamin minor. RCh(I-220).
Benjamin minor and *Benjamin major.* RCa(I-339).

Richards, I. A.
Principles of Literary Criticism. MP12(IX-5334), MP8(VI-4257), MP4(II-1031), MWL4(1031).

Richardson, Dorothy M.
Pilgrimage. MP12(VIII-4696), MP8(VI-3665), MP6(IV-2362), MPEng(674), MP3(II-757), MWL3(757).

Richardson, G. W.
"Actium," in The Journal of Roman Studies. HAnc(I-554).

Richardson, H. Edward

Richter, Werner
  Bismarck.   SCL12(II-739),   SCL7(I-422),   A66(32).
Ridgway, General Matthew B.
  Soldier.   SCL12(X-7067),   SCL7(VI-4337),   A57(247).
Ridpath, Ian
  Worlds Beyond: A Report on the Search for Life in Space.
  HWor(II-832).
Riesenberg, Peter *and* John H. Mundy
  Medieval Town, The.   HAnc(III-1326).
Riesman, David
  Story of Medicine in the Middle Ages, The.   HAnc(III-1480).
Riesman, David *and* Christopher Jenks
  Academic Revolution, The.   HWor(I-517).
Rifkin, Jeremy *and* Ted Howard
  *Who Should Play God? The Artificial Creation of Life and What It Means
  for the Future of the Human Race.*   HWor(III-1326).
Riggs, Lynn
  Green Grow the Lilacs.   MP12(IV-2382),   MPCE(II-868),
  MP8(III-1852),   MP6(II-1163),   MPDr(313),   MP3(I-430),
  MWL3(430).
Rilke, Rainer Maria
  Duino Elegies.   MP12(III-1669),   MP8(II-1296),   MP6(II-838),
  MPPo(69),   MP3(I-307),   MWL3(307).
  Sonnets to Orpheus.   MP12(XI-6175),   MP8(VII-4923),
  MP4(II-1167),   MWL4(1167).
Rimanelli, Giose
  Day of the Lion, The.   SCL12(III-1765),   SCL7(II-1064),   A54(49).
Rimbaud, Arthur
  *Season in Hell, A.   MP12(X-5876),   MP8(VII-4678),
  MP6(V-2800),   MPPo(329),   MP3(II-944),   MWL3(944).
Rist, John M.
  Plotinus: The Road to Reality.   HAnc(II-826).
Ritschl, Albrecht
  Christian Doctrine of Justification and Reconciliation, The.
  RCh(II-758).
Robbe-Grillet, Alain
  Erasers, The.   SCL12(IV-2308),   SCL7(II-1379),   A65(83).
Robbins, Roy M.
  Our Landed Heritage: The Public Domain, 1776-1936.   HAmer(II-774).
Roberts, Chalmers M.
  Nuclear Years: The Arms Race and Arms Control, 1945-1970, The.
  HWor(II-961).
Roberts, Elizabeth Madox
  Great Meadow, The.   MP12(IV-2363),   MPCE(II-863),
  MP8(III-1835),   MP6(II-1155),   MPAm(231),   MPv3(193),

MP6(III-1483), MPAm(306), MPv4(252), MP2(I-506), MWL2(506).

Rodgers, Daniel T.
Work Ethic in Industrial America, 1850-1920, The. LA79(II-904).

Rodgers, William L.
Naval Warfare Under Oars, IV to XVI Centuries. HEur(I-182).

Roethke, Theodore
*Far Field, The. SCL12(IV-2459), SCL7(III-1469), A65(89).
*Poetry of Roethke, The. MP12(IX-5126), MP8(VI-4072), MP4(II-940), MWL4(940).
*Roethke: Collected Poems. SCL12(X-6457), SCL7(VI-3969), A67(290).

Rogers, E. F.
Peter Lombard and the Sacramental System. HAnc(III-1340).

Rogers, Susan, George Houser, Jennifer Davis *and* Herbert Shore
No One Can Stop the Rain. HWor(III-1223).

Rogin, Michael Paul
Fathers and Children. SCL12(IV-2499), A76(90).

Rogow, Arnold A.
James Forrestal. SCL12(VI-3793), SCL7(IV-2285), A65(148).

Rohrbough, Malcolm J.
Land Office Business: The Settlement and Administration of American Public Lands, 1789-1837, The. HAmer(I-585).

Rohwer, J. and H. A. Jacobsen, *eds.*
Decisive Battles of World War II: The German View. Different analyses on this title appear in: HEur(III-1469; III-1475; III-1494).

Rojas, Fernando de
Celestina. MP12(II-865), MPCE(I-320), MP8(I-667), MP6(I-441), MPEur(120), MPv4(70), MP2(I-139), MWL2(139).

Roland, Charles P.
Confederacy, The. HAmer(II-943).

Rolland, Romain
*Jean-Christophe. MP12(V-2988), MPCE(II-1102), MP8(IV-2327), MP6(III-1491), MPEur(404), MP1(I-439), MWL1(439).

Rollin, Betty
First, You Cry. LA77(I-291).

Rolt, C. E.
Dionysius the Areopagite on the Divine Names and the Mystical Theology. HAnc(II-1013).

Rolt, L. T. C.
Aeronauts: A History of Ballooning, 1783-1903, The. HEur(I-498).
James Watt. HEur(I-461).
Mechanicals, The. HEur(II-1103).
Railway Revolution, The. HEur(II-609).

Ross, Earle D.
   *Democracy's College: The Land-Grant Movement in the Formative
   Stage.*   HAmer(II-977).
Ross, Irwin
   Loneliest Campaign: The Truman Victory of 1948, The.
   HAmer(III-1803).
Ross, Ishbel
   First Lady of the South.   SCL12(IV-2645),   SCL7(III-1562),
   A59(89).
Ross, Nancy Wilson
   Return of Lady Brace, The.   SCL12(X-6392),   SCL7(VI-3911),
   A58(212).
Ross, W. David
   Right and the Good, The.   Ph(II-929).
Rossetti, Christina
   Poetry of Christina Rossetti, The.   MP12(VIII-4860),
   MP8(VI-3806),   MP6(V-2424),   MPPo(243),   MP3(II-789),
   MWL3(789).
Rossetti, Dante Gabriel
   Poetry of Dante Gabriel Rossetti, The.   MP12(VIII-4893),
   MP8(VI-3839),   MP6(V-2426),   MPPo(246),   MP3(II-791),
   MWL3(791).
Rossi, A.
   Russo-German Alliance, August, 1939-June, 1941, The.   HEur(III-1438).
Rossiter, Clinton
   Alexander Hamilton and the Constitution.   SCL12(I-191),
   SCL7(I-128),   A65(5).
Rossiter, Frank R.
   Charles Ives and His America.   SCL12(II-1191),   A76(41).
Rossner, Judith
   Attachments.   LA78(I-77).
Rostand, Edmond
   Aiglon, L'.   MP12(VI-3222),   MPCE(II-1194),   MP8(IV-2509),
   MP6(III-1606),   MPDr(438),   MPv4(271),   MP2(I-551),
   MWL2(551).
   Cyrano de Bergerac.   MP12(III-1262),   MPCE(I-464),
   MP8(II-977),   MP6(II-647),   MPDr(194),   MPv3(115),
   MP2(I-210),   MWL2(210).
Rosten, Leo
   Return of H*Y*M*A*N*K*A*P*L*A*N, The.   SCL12(X-6389),
   SCL7(VI-3908),   A60(226).
Rostovtzeff, Mikhail I.
   History of the Ancient World, Vol. II: Rome, A.   HAnc(II-832).
   Social and Economic History of the Hellenistic World, The.
   HAnc(I-414).

Roth, Arthur J.
    Terrible Beauty, A.   SCL12(XI-7482),   SCL7(VII-4559),   A59(231).
Roth, Guenther
    Social Democrats in Imperial Germany, The.   HEur(II-1016).
Roth, Henry
    *Call It Sleep.   MP12(II-744),   MP8(I-577),   MP4(I-102),
    MWL4(102),   SCL12(II-1045),   SCL7(I-599),   A65(28).
Roth, Philip
    Ghost Writer, The.   LA80(I-354).
    *Goodbye, Columbus.   SCL12(V-3051),   SCLs(117).
    *Great American Novel, The.   SCL12(V-3098),   A74(170).
    *Letting Go.   SCL12(VII-4283),   SCL7(IV-2620),   A63(129).
    My Life as a Man.   SCL12(VIII-5183),   A75(201).
    *Our Gang.   SCL12(VIII-5666),   A72(239).
    *Portnoy's Complaint.   SCL12(IX-5971),   A70(242).
    Professor of Desire, The.   LA78(II-669).
    *When She Was Good.   SCL12(XII-8219),   SCL7(VII-5022),
    A68(346).
Rothberg, Abraham
    Heirs of Stalin: Dissidence and the Soviet Regime, 1953-1970, The.
    HWor(II-994).
Rothenberg, Gunther E.
    Art of Warfare in the Age of Napoleon, The.   LA79(I-38).
Rothschild, Emma
    Paradise Lost: The Decline of the Auto-Industrial Age.
    SCL12(IX-5725),   A74(298).
Roubiczek, Paul *and* Joseph Kalmer
    Warrier of God.   HAnc(III-1677).
Rouse, Ruth *and* Stephen Charles Neill, *eds.*
    History of the Ecumenical Movement, 1517-1948, A.   HEur(III-1552).
Rousseau, Jean Jacques
    *Confessions.   MP12(II-1060),   MP8(II-826),   MP6(I-542),
    MPNf(61),   MP3(I-215),   MWL3(215).
    Creed of a Savoyard Priest, The.   RCh(II-605).
    Discourse on the Origin of Inequality.   MP12(III-1522),
    MP8(II-1185),   MP4(I-237),   MWL4(237).
    *Émile.   MP12(III-1755),   MP8(II-1366),   MP6(II-878),
    MPEur(281),   MP3(I-330),   MWL3(330).
    *New Héloïse, The.   MP12(VII-4177),   MPCE(III-1557),
    MP8(V-3256),   MP6(IV-2088),   MPEur(535),   MPv3(367),
    MP2(II-730),   MWL2(730).
    Social Contract, The.   Ph(I-512).
Roussin, André
    Little Hut, The.   SCL12(VII-4415),   SCL7(IV-2708),   A54(153).
Rovere, Richard H.

Arrivals and Departures. LA77(I-62).
"Letter from Washington," in *The New Yorker.* HWor(II-713).
Senator Joe McCarthy. HAmer(III-1819).

Rovit, Earl
Far Cry, A. SCL12(IV-2454), SCL7(II-1463), A68(100).
Player King, The. SCL12(IX-5890), SCL7(V-3598), A66(236).

Rowe, Albert Percival
One Story of Radar. HWor(I-327).

Rowe, Vivian
Great Wall of France, The. HEur(III-1360).

Rowen, Herbert H.
Ambassador Prepares for War, The. HEur(I-346).

Rowley, H. H.
From Joseph to Joshua: Biblical Traditions in the Light of Archaeology. HAnc(I-77).
Growth of the Old Testament, The. HAnc(II-667).

Rowley, William *and* Thomas Middleton
Changeling, The. MP12(II-885), MPCE(I-325), MP8(I-683), MP6(I-451), MPDr(140), MP3(I-169), MWL3(169).

Rowse, A. L.
Churchills, The. SCL12(II-1268), SCL7(II-745), A59(34).
Sir Walter Ralegh. SCL12(X-6997), SCL7(VI-4312), A63(254).

Roy, Jules
Battle of Dienbienphu, The. SCL12(I-559), SCL7(I-330), A66(24).
A different analysis on this title appears in: HEur(III-1582).
War in Algeria, The. SCL12(XII-8103), SCL7(VII-4961), A62(298).

Royce, Josiah
Problem of Christianity, The. RCh(II-878).
World and the Individual, The. Ph(II-739).

Rubin, Louis D., Jr.
Faraway Country, The. SCL12(IV-2467), SCL7(III-1471), A64(80).
Golden Weather, The. SCL12(V-3026), SCL7(III-1805), A62(138).

Rublowsky, John
Stoned Age—A History of Drugs in America, The. HWor(II-818).

Rudd, Robert L.
Pesticides and the Living Landscape. HWor(II-946).

Ruddick, Sara *and* Pamela Daniels, *ed.*
Working It Out. LA78(II-937).

Rudolph, Frederick
American College and University: A History, The. HAmer(I-314).

Rudwick, Elliott M.
W. E. B. DuBois: Propagandist of the Negro Protest. HAmer(III-1388).

Rudy, Willis *and* John S. Brubacher
Higher Education in Transition: A History of American Colleges and

Universities, 1936-1968. HAmer(I-315).

Rufinus of Aquileia
Commentary on the Apostles' Creed, A. RCa(I-169).

Ruiz, Ramón Eduardo
Cuba: The Making of a Revolution. HWor(II-746).

Ruiz de Alarcón, Juan
Truth Suspected. MP12(XI-6740), MPCE(IV-2349),
MP8(VIII-5347), MP6(VI-3225), MPDr(879), MP3(II-1089),
MWL3(1089).

Rukeyser, Muriel
Breaking Open. SCL12(II-906), A74(29).
Collected Poems, The. LA80(I-148).
Waterlily Fire. SCL12(XII-8138), SCL7(VII-4979),
A63(285).

Rulfo, Juan
Pedro Páramo. MP12(VIII-4552), MP8(V-3546), MP4(II-678),
MWL4(678). A different analysis on this title appears in:
SCL12(IX-5792), SCL7(V-3537), A60(186), BMA(425).

Runciman, Steven
"Crusader States, 1243-1291, The," in *History of the Crusades, Vol. II:
The Later Crusades, 1189-1311, A.* HAnc(III-1576).
*History of the Crusades, Vol. I: The First Crusade and the Foundation of
the Kingdom of Jerusalem, A.* HAnc(III-1280).
History of the First Bulgarian Empire, A. HAnc(III-1218).
Medieval Manichee: A Study of the Christian Dualist Heresy, The.
HAnc(III-1444).

Ruskin, John
King of the Golden River, The. MP12(VI-3153), MPCE(II-1166),
MP8(IV-2456), MP6(III-1567), MPEng(407), MPv4(260),
MP2(I-529), MWL2(529).
*Stones of Venice, The. MP12(XI-6262), MP8(VII-4988),
MP4(II-1180), MWL4(1180).

Russ, Joanna
And Chaos Died. SF(I-53).
Female Man, The. SF(II-766).
Picnic on Paradise. SF(IV-1678).

Russel, Robert R.
*Improvement of Communication with the Pacific Coast as an Issue in
American Politics, 1783-1864.* HAmer(II-868).

Russell, Bertrand
Autobiography of Bertrand Russell: 1872-1914, The. SCL12(I-466),
SCL7(I-269), A68(15).
Autobiography of Bertrand Russell: 1914-1944, The. SCL12(I-471),
SCL7(I-273), A69(26).
Autobiography of Bertrand Russell: 1944-1969, The. SCL12(I-476),

A70(45).

Inquiry into Meaning and Truth, An. Ph(II-1052).

Introduction to Mathematical Philosophy. Ph(II-816).

Mysticism and Logic. HWor(I-84).

Nightmares of Eminent Persons. SCL12(VIII-5337), SCL7(V-3253), A55(181).

Our Knowledge of the External World. Ph(II-799).

Russell, Eric Frank

Sinister Barrier. SF(V-2075).

Russell, George William

Poetry of "A.E." MP12(VIII-4795), MP8(VI-3741), MP4(II-709), MWL4(709).

Russell, Harold S.

"Helsinki Declaration: Brobdingnag or Lilliput?, The," in *American Journal of International Law.* HWor(III-1260).

Russell, Ruth B. *and* Jeannette E. Muther

History of the United Nations Charter: The Role of the United States, 1940-1945, A. Different analyses on this title appear in: HEur(III-1509), HAmer(III-1744).

Russell, W. Clark

Wreck of the Grosvenor, The. MP12(XII-7278), MPCE(IV-2554), MP8(VIII-5752), MP6(VI-3496), MPEng(974), MP1(II-1135), MWL1(1135).

Rutherford, Samuel

Lex rex. RCh(I-462).

Rutland, Robert A.

Birth of the Bill of Rights, 1776-1791. HAmer(I-369).

Ordeal of the Constitution: The Antifederalists and the Ratification Struggle of 1787-1788, The. HAmer(I-333).

Rutman, Darrett B.

Winthrop's Boston: A Portrait of a Puritan Town, 1630-1649. HAmer(I-88).

Ruysbroeck, Blessed John

Spiritual Espousals, The. RCa(I-461).

Ryan, Cornelius

Bridge Too Far, A. SCL12(II-923), A75(35).

Last Battle, The. HAmer(III-1750).

Longest Day: June 6, 1944, The. SCL12(VII-4499), SCL7(IV-2768), A60(146).

Ryan, Paul B. *and* Thomas A. Bailey

Hitler vs. Roosevelt: The Undeclared Naval War. LA80(I-404).

Rydberg, Viktor

Last Athenian, The. MP12(VI-3243), MPCE(II-1200), MP8(IV-2528), MP6(III-1613), MPEur(427), MPv4(274), MP2(I-553), MWL2(553).

St. Vincent Millay, Edna
Harp-Weaver and Other Poems, The. MP12(V-2489),
MP8(III-1938), MP6(III-1225), MPPo(122), MP3(I-445),
MWL3(445).
Sainte-Beuve, Charles Augustin
Monday Conversations. MP12(VII-4025), MP8(V-3139),
MP4(I-612), MWL4(612).
Volupté. MP12(XII-6983), MPCE(IV-2445), MP8(VIII-5528),
MP6(VI-3345), MPEur(797), MP3(II-1110), MWL3(1110).
Saint-Exupéry, Antoine de
Night Flight. MP12(VII-4212), MPCE(III-1574), MP8(V-3281),
MP6(IV-2110), MPEur(544), MP3(II-687), MWL3(687).
Wind, Sand and Stars. MP12(XII-7163), MP8(VIII-5665),
MP4(II-1291), MWL4(1291).
Wisdom of the Sands, The. MP12(XII-7189), MP8(VIII-5684),
MP4(II-1294), MWL4(1294).
Saki
Short Stories of Saki, The. MP12(X-6027), MP8(VII-4809),
MP4(II-1148), MWL4(1148).
Unbearable Bassington, The. MP12(XII-6804), MPCE(IV-2377),
MP8(VIII-5391), MP6(VI-3252), MPEng(885), MP1(II-1042),
MWL1(1042).
Salaman, Redcliffe N.
History and Social Influence of the Potato, The. HEur(I-426).
Sale, Kirkpatrick
Power Shift. SCL12(IX-6004), A76(249).
Sale, William
"Dual Vision of the Theogony, *The," in* Arion. HAnc(I-142).
Salgari, Emilio
Meraviglie del duemila, Le. SF(III-1380).
Salibi, Kamel Suleiman
Crossroads to Civil War: Lebanon, 1958-1976. HWor(III-1239).
Salinger, J. D.
Catcher in the Rye, The. SCL12(II-1121), SCLs(58).
Franny and Zooey. MP12(IV-2157), MP8(III-1679),
MP4(I-359), MWL4(359), SCL12(IV-2767), SCL7(III-1651),
A62(127), BMA(195).
Raise High the Roof Beam, Carpenters. SCL12(IX-6238),
SCL7(VI-3821), A64(220).
Salisbury, Harrison E.
900 Days, The. SCL12(VIII-5358), A70(221).
Russia in Revolution, 1900-1930. LA79(II-622).
Soviet Union: The First Fifty Years, The. HEur(III-1621).
War Between Russia and China. HEur(III-1680).
Salmon, J. H. M.

French Wars of Religion, The.   Different analyses on this title appear in:
HEur(I-165; I-206).

Salomone, Arcangelo William
*Italian Democracy in the Making: The Political Scene in the Giolittian Era,
1900-1914.*   HWor(I-141).

Saloutos, Theodore
Farmer Movements in the South, 1865-1933.   HAmer(II-1046).

Salten, Felix
Bambi.   MP12(I-415),   MPCE(I-143),   MP8(I-324),   MP6(I-208),
MPEur(59),   MP1(I-52),   MWL1(52).

Salvador, Tomas
Nave, La.   SF(III-1497).

Salvemini, Gaetano
Fascist Dictatorship in Italy, The.   HEur(III-1321).

Samuels, Ernest
Bernard Berenson: The Making of a Connoisseur.   LA80(I-73).
Henry Adams: The Major Phase.   SCL12(V-3346),   SCL7(III-1993),
A65(124).
Henry Adams: The Middle Years.   SCL12(V-3343),   SCL7(III-1990),
A59(114),   BMA(228). A different analysis on this title appears in:
HAmer(II-1186).

Samuelsson, Kurt
Religion and Economic Action.   HWor(I-41).

Sánchez, Florencio
Gringa, La.   MP12(IV-2401),   MPCE(II-876),   MP8(III-1867),
MP6(II-1175),   MPDr(316),   MPv4(194),   MP2(I-389),
MWL2(389).

Sand, George
Consuelo.   MP12(II-1106),   MPCE(I-396),   MP8(II-865),
MP6(I-566),   MPEur(153),   MP1(I-156),   MWL1(156).
Indiana.   MP12(V-2880),   MPCE(II-1057),   MP8(IV-2245),
MP6(III-1436),   MPEur(400),   MPv3(243),   MP2(I-485),
MWL2(485).

Sandburg, Carl
Abraham Lincoln.   MP12(I-11),   MP8(I-9),   MP6(I-7),   MPNf(1),
MP3(I-2),   MWL3(2).   A different analysis on this title appears in:
SCL12(I-9),   SCL7(I-9),   A54(1),   BMA(1).
Chicago Poems.   MP12(II-918),   MP8(I-706),   MP4(I-124),
MWL4(124).
Letters of Carl Sandburg, The.   SCL12(VI-4225),   SCL7(IV-2578),
A69(193).
People, Yes, The.   MP12(VIII-4593),   MP8(V-3577),
MP6(IV-2303),   MPPo(214),   MP3(II-734),   MWL3(734).
Remembrance Rock.   MP12(IX-5505),   MPCE(III-1883),
MP8(VII-4387),   MP6(V-2613),   MPAm(528),   MPv3(444),

MP2(II-889), MWL2(889).
Sandburg, Helga
Measure My Love. SCL12(VII-4854), SCL7(IV-2954), A60(158).
Wheel of Earth, The. SCL12(XII-8209), SCL7(VII-5016),
A59(274).
Sanders, N. K.
Epic of Gilgamesh, The. HAnc(I-42).
Sanders, Ronald
Lost Tribes and Promised Lands: The Origins of American Racism.
LA79(I-398).
Sandys, John Edwin
History of Classical Scholarship, Vol. I: From the Sixteenth Century B.C.
to the End of the Middle Ages, A. Different analyses on this title
appear in: HAnc(I-356; II-1025; III-1233).
Saner, Reg
Climbing into the Roots. LA77(I-164).
S'añkara,
Crest Jewel of Wisdom. Ph(I-268).
Sansom, William
Blue Skies, Brown Studies. SCL12(II-819), SCL7(I-467), A62(30).
Goodbye. SCL12(V-3048), SCL7(III-1824), A67(131).
Stories of William Sansom, The. SCL12(XI-7259), SCL7(VII-4461),
A64(254).
Santayana, George
Idea of Christ in the Gospels, The. RCh(II-1080).
Last Puritan, The. MP12(VI-3274), MPCE(II-1214),
MP8(IV-2550), MP6(III-1629), MPAm(327), MP1(I-497),
MWL1(497).
Life of Reason, The. Ph(II-761).
Realms of Being. Ph(II-895).
Scepticism and Animal Faith. MP12(X-5831), MP8(VII-4644),
MP6(V-2776), MPNf(273), MP3(II-935), MWL3(935).
Sense of Beauty, The. Ph(II-718).
Santillana, Giorgio de
Crime of Galileo, The. SCL12(III-1615), SCL7(II-947), A55(71). A
different analysis on this title appears in: HEur(I-287).
Saperstein, Alan
Mom Kills Kids and Self. LA80(II-541).
Sappho
Ode to Aphrodite. MP12(VII-4273), MP8(V-3329),
MP6(IV-2139), MPPo(189), MP3(II-694), MWL3(694).
Sargent, Pamela
Cloned Lives. SF(I-402).
Sarkissian, Karekin
Council of Chalcedon and the Armenian Church, The. HAnc(II-966).

Saroyan, William
    Chance Meetings. LA79(I-92).
    *Human Comedy, The. MP12(V-2766), MPCE(II-1017),
    MP8(III-2154), MP6(III-1378), MPAm(288), MP1(I-392),
    MWL1(392).
Sarraute, Nathalie
    Golden Fruits, The. SCL12(V-3009), SCL7(III-1793), A65(112).
    Martereau. SCL12(VII-4790), SCL7(IV-2921), A60(156).
Sarton, George
    Galen of Pergamum. HAnc(II-739).
    *History of Science, Vol. II: Hellenistic Science and Culture in the Last
    Three Centuries B.C., A.* HAnc(I-401).
Sarton, May
    As We Are Now. SCL12(I-404), A74(14).
    Crucial Conversations. SCL12(III-1651), A76(63).
    Grain of Mustard Seed, A. SCL12(V-3061), A72(155).
    World of Light, A. LA77(II-941).
Sartre, Jean-Paul
    Being and Nothingness. Ph(II-1079).
    *Flies, The. MP12(IV-2089), MP8(III-1626), MP4(I-346),
    MWL4(346).
    Life/Situations: Essays Written and Spoken. LA78(II-529).
    Nausea. MP12(VII-4157), MPCE(III-1550), MP8(V-3239),
    MP6(IV-2077), MPEur(532), MPv3(365), MP2(II-726),
    MWL2(726).
    Words, The. SCL12(XII-8395), SCL7(VII-5142), A65(322).
Sassoon, Siegfried
    Memoirs of a Fox-Hunting Man. MP12(VII-3830),
    MPCE(III-1404), MP8(V-3000), MP6(IV-1903), MPEng(494),
    MP1(II-575), MWL1(575).
    Memoirs of an Infantry Officer. MP12(VII-3842), MPCE(III-1409),
    MP8(V-3009), MP6(IV-1910), MPEng(499), MP1(II-579),
    MWL1(579).
Saunders, J. J.
    History of Medieval Islam, A. HAnc(II-1079).
Savage, Thomas
    I Heard My Sister Speak My Name. LA78(I-427).
Sayles, John
    Anarchists' Convention, The. LA80(I-28).
Saywell, John
    Rise of the Parti Québécois 1967-1976, The. HWor(II-822).
Scammon, Richard M.
    Real Majority, The. SCL12(IX-6261), A71(262).
Scarisbrick, J. J.
    Henry VIII. SCL12(V-3350), SCL7(III-1997), A69(148).

MP8(VIII-5659),   MP6(VI-3429),   MPDr(925),   MP1(II-1115),
MWL1(1115).

Schlegel, Friedrich von
Lectures on the Philosophy of Life.   RCa(II-635).

Schleiermacher, Friedrich
Christian Faith, The.   RCh(II-657).
On Religion: Speeches to its Cultured Despisers.   RCh(II-637).

Schlesinger, Arthur M., Jr.
Age of Jackson, The.   HAmer(II-698).
Age of Roosevelt, The. Vol. I.   SCL12(I-153),   SCL7(I-104),   A58(7).
Age of Roosevelt, The. Vol. II.   SCL12(I-157),   SCL7(I-107),
A60(7). A different analysis on this title appears in: HAmer(III-1619).
Age of Roosevelt, The. Vol. III.   SCL12(I-161),   SCL7(I-111),
A61(4).
Bitter Heritage: Vietnam and American Democracy, 1941-1966, The.
HAmer(III-1910).
Imperial Presidency, The.   SCL12(VI-3632),   A74(204).
Thousand Days, A.   SCL12(XI-7578),   SCL7(VII-4626),   A66(313).
A different analysis on this title appears in: HAmer(III-1891).

Schlesinger, Arthur M., Sr.
Colonial Merchants and the American Revolution, 1763-1776, The.
HAmer(I-244).

Schleunes, Karl A.
*Twisted Road to Auschwitz: Nazi Policy Toward German Jews, 1933-1939,
The*.   HWor(I-308).

Schlick, Moritz
Problems of Ethics.   Ph(II-935).

Schmidt, Arno
Gelehrtenrepublik, Die.   SF(II-865).

Schmidt, Dana Adams
Armageddon in the Middle East.   SCL12(I-371),   A75(19).

Schmidt, Harvey *and* Tom Jones
Fantasticks, The.   SCL12(IV-2449),   SCLs(94).

Schmitt, Bernadotte E.
Annexation of Bosnia, 1908-1909, The.   HEur(III-1204).
Coming of the War, 1914, The.   Different analyses on this title appear
in: HEur(III-1246; III-1344).

Schmitz, James H.
Witches of Karres, The.   SF(V-2482).

Schnore, Leo F.
Urban Scene: Human Ecology and Demography, The.
HAmer(III-1813).

Schnürer, Gustav
Church and Culture in the Middle Ages, Vol. I: 350-814.
HAnc(II-1129).

Scholem, Gershom G.
Jewish Gnosticism, Markabah Mysticism, and Talmudic Tradition.
HAnc(III-1562).
Major Trends in Jewish Mysticism. HAnc(III-1561).
Scholes, Walter V. *and* Marie V. Scholes
Foreign Policies of the Taft Administration, The. HAmer(III-1382).
Schonland, Sir Basil
Atomists (1805-1933), The. HWor(I-285).
Schoonover, Lawrence
Spider King, The. SCL12(XI-7174), SCL7(VI-4405), A54(258).
Schopenhauer, Arthur
World as Will and Idea, The. MP12(XII-7259), MP8(VIII-5737),
MP6(VI-3484), MPNf(333), MP3(II-1153), MWL3(1153). A
different analysis on this title appears in: Ph(II-582).
Schorer, Mark
Pieces of Life. LA78(II-657).
Sinclair Lewis. SCL12(X-6980), SCL7(VI-4297), A62(275),
BMA(512).
Schreiber, Herman *and* George Schreiber
Vanished Cities. SCL12(XII-7961), SCL7(VII-4867), A58(252).
Schreiner, Olive
Story of an African Farm, The. MP12(XI-6272), MPCE(IV-2165),
MP8(VII-4997), MP6(VI-2985), MPEur(720), MP1(II-932),
MWL1(932).
Schrier, Arnold
Ireland and the American Emigration, 1850-1900. HEur(II-762).
Schulz, Bruno
Sanatorium Under the Sign of the Hourglass. LA79(II-645).
Street of Crocodiles, The. LA78(II-804).
Schumacher, E. F.
Guide for the Perplexed, A. LA78(I-364).
Schur, Max
Freud. SCL12(IV-2788), A73(177).
Schürer, Emil
History of the Jewish People in the Time of Jesus Christ, The.
HAnc(II-650).
Schuyler, Hamilton
*Roeblings: A Century of Engineers, Bridge-Builders, and Industrialists,
The.* HAmer(II-1064).
Schwartz, Anna J. *and* Milton Friedman
Monetary History of the United States, 1867-1960, A. HAmer(II-1087).
Schwartz, Delmore
Selected Essays of Delmore Schwartz. SCL12(X-6765), A72(291).
Summer Knowledge. SCL12(XI-7330), SCL7(VII-4486), A60(260).
Schwarz-Bart, André

Kenilworth. MP12(VI-3123), MPCE(II-1152), MP8(IV-2434), MP6(III-1552), MPEng(400), MP1(I-469), MWL1(469).
Lady of the Lake, The. MP12(VI-3213), MPCE(II-1191), MP8(IV-2502), MP6(III-1600), MPPo(151), MPv3(279), MP2(I-547), MWL2(547).
Lay of the Last Minstrel, The. MP12(VI-3299), MPCE(II-1225), MP8(IV-2570), MP6(III-1641), MPPo(157), MPv3(283), MP2(I-564), MWL2(564).
Marmion. MP12(VII-3739), MPCE(III-1366), MP8(V-2934), MP6(IV-1856), MPPo(181), MPv3(320), MP2(II-635), MWL2(635).
Old Mortality. MP12(VIII-4334), MPCE(III-1621), MP8(V-3373), MP6(IV-2170), MPEng(598), MP1(II-681), MWL1(681).
Quentin Durward. MP12(IX-5398), MPCE(III-1838), MP8(VI-4307), MP6(V-2559), MPEng(710), MP1(II-795), MWL1(795).
Rob Roy. MP12(X-5638), MPCE(III-1933), MP8(VII-4489), MP6(V-2675), MPEng(733), MP1(II-837), MWL1(837).
St. Ronan's Well. MP12(X-5761), MPCE(IV-1985), MP8(VII-4585), MP6(V-2739), MPEng(768), MP3(II-916), MWL3(916).
Talisman, The. MP12(XI-6387), MPCE(IV-2200), MP8(VII-5087), MP6(VI-3043), MPEng(819), MPv3(506), MP2(II-1009), MWL2(1009).
Waverley. MP12(XII-7052), MPCE(IV-2470), MP8(VIII-5580), MP6(VI-3378), MPEng(937), MP1(II-1094), MWL1(1094).
Woodstock. MP12(XII-7251), MPCE(IV-2545), MP8(VIII-5729), MP6(VI-3477), MPEng(971), MPv3(559), MP2(II-1158), MWL2(1158).
Scott, Winfield Townley
Alpha Omega. SCL12(I-245), A72(4).
Change of Weather. SCL12(II-1180), SCL7(I-680), A65(34).
Scotus, John Duns
De primo principio. RCa(I-423).
Tract Concerning the First Principle, A. Ph(I-329).
Scudéry, Madeleine de
Artamène. MP12(I-322), MPCE(I-116), MP8(I-249), MP6(I-166), MPEur(39), MP3(I-67), MWL3(67).
Scullard, H. H.
Roman Politics 220-150 B.C. HAnc(I-449).
Scipio Africanus: Soldier and Politician. HAnc(I-439).
"Seaborn, Captain Adam"
Symzonia. SF(V-2207).

Seabury, Paul
Wilhelmstrasse: A Study of German Diplomats Under the Nazi Regime, The. HWor(I-379).
Seaman, L. C. B.
From Vienna to Versailles. HEur(II-851).
Seaton, Albert
Russo-German War, 1941-1945, The. HWor(I-452).
Seaver, Henry L.
Great Revolt in Castile, The. HEur(I-74).
Seay, Albert
Music in the Medieval World. HAnc(III-1412).
Seay, James
Let Not Your Hart. SCL12(VI-4199), A71(164).
See, Carolyn
Rest Is Done with Mirrors, The. SCL12(IX-6379), A71(271).
Seebohm, M. E.
Evolution of the English Farm, The. HAnc(II-1171).
Seeley, Sir John Robert
Ecce Homo. RCh(II-747).
Seelye, John
True Adventures of Huckleberry Finn, The. SCL12(XII-7793), A70(313).
Segal, Erich
Love Story. SCL12(VII-4583), A71(189).
Segal, Lore
Lucinella. LA77(I-460).
Seidel, Frederick
Final Solutions. SCL12(IV-2584), SCL7(III-1531), A64(86).
Seidler, Grzegorz Leopold
Political Doctrine of the Mongols, The. HAnc(III-1465).
Seidman, Joel
American Labor from Defense to Reconversion. HWor(II-574).
Selby, Hubert, Jr.
Requiem for a Dream. LA79(II-589).
Sellar, W. Y.
Roman Poets of the Augustan Age: Horace and the Elegiac Poets, The. HAnc(II-576).
Sellars, Roy Wood
Philosophy of Physical Realism, The. Ph(II-980).
Sellers, R. V.
Council of Chalcedon, The. HAnc(II-954).
Semprun, Jorge
Long Voyage, The. SCL12(VII-4494), SCL7(IV-2763), A65(188).
Seneca (Lucius Annaeus Seneca)
Philosophical Treatises and Moral Reflections of Seneca.

Sewall, Richard B.
  Life of Emily Dickinson, The. SCL12(VII-4331), A75(174).
Seward, Desmond
  Eleanor of Aquitaine. LA80(I-277).
  Hundred Years War: The English in France, 1337-1453, The.
  LA79(I-291).
Sexton, Anne
  Anne Sexton: A Self-Portrait in Letters. LA78(I-54).
  Live or Die. SCL12(VII-4426), SCL7(IV-2719), A67(197).
  Love Poems. SCL12(VII-4580), SCL7(IV-2797), A69(212).
  Words for Dr. Y: Uncollected Poems with Three Stories. LA79(II-897).
Seymour, Charles
  Electoral Reform in England and Wales. Different analyses on this title
  appear in: HEur(II-706; II-931; II-1040).
Seymour, Charles, Jr.
  Sculpture in Italy: 1400-1500. HAnc(III-1667).
Seznec, Jean
  *Survival of the Pagan Gods: The Mythological Tradition and Its Place in
  Renaissance Humanism and Art, The.* HAnc(III-1769).
Shaara, Michael
  Killer Angels, The. SCL12(VI-3995), A75(161).
Shachtman, Tom
  Day America Crashed, The. LA80(I-200).
Shaffer, Peter
  Equus. SCL12(IV-2299), A75(89).
  Royal Hunt of the Sun, The. SCL12(X-6521), SCL7(VI-4014),
  A66(275).
Shakespeare, William
  *All's Well That Ends Well. MP12(I-143), MPCE(I-49),
  MP8(I-112), MP6(I-68), MPDr(22), MPv3(10), MP2(I-18),
  MWL2(18).
  *Antony and Cleopatra. MP12(I-258), MPCE(I-91), MP8(I-202),
  MP6(I-131), MPDr(41), MPv3(25), MP2(I-43), MWL2(43).
  *As You Like It. MP12(I-334), MPCE(I-123), MP8(I-257),
  MP6(I-173), MPDr(47), MP1(I-46), MWL1(46).
  *Comedy of Errors, The. MP12(II-1037), MPCE(I-378),
  MP8(II-805), MP6(I-528), MPDr(163), MPv3(83), MP2(I-164),
  MWL2(164).
  *Coriolanus. MP12(II-1116), MPCE(I-398), MP8(II-875),
  MP6(I-571), MPDr(174), MPv3(90), MP2(I-176), MWL2(176).
  *Cymbeline. MP12(III-1255), MPCE(I-462), MP8(II-971),
  MP6(II-645), MPDr(191), MPv3(112), MP2(I-207), MWL2(207).
  *Hamlet. MP12(V-2457), MPCE(II-897), MP8(III-1912),
  MP6(III-1206), MPDr(319), MP1(I-348), MWL1(348).
  *Henry the Eighth. MP12(V-2555), MPCE(II-938),

MWL1(1060).
Winter's Tale, The. MP12(XII-7181), MPCE(IV-2516), MP8(VIII-5678), MP6(VI-3442), MPDr(928), MPv3(554), MP2(II-1146), MWL2(1146).
Shakespeare, William *and* John Fletcher
Two Noble Kinsmen, The. MP12(XII-6775), MPCE(IV-2363), MP8(VIII-5371), MP6(VI-3241), MPDr(889), MPv4(551), MP2(II-1076), MWL2(1076).
Shanks, Bob
Cool Fire, The. LA77(I-180).
Shannon, Claude E. *and* Warren Weaver
Mathematical Theory of Communication, The. HWor(I-5).
Shannon, Fred Albert
Economic History of the United States, Vol. V: The Farmer's Last Frontier: Agriculture, 1860-1897, The. HAmer(II-964).
Organization and Administration of the Union Army, 1861-1865, The. HAmer(II-993).
Shapiro, Karl
Collected Poems 1940-1978. LA79(I-124).
Poetry of Shapiro, The. MP12(IX-5133), MP8(VI-4079), MP4(II-944), MWL4(944).
Shaplen, Robert
Lost Revolution, The. SCL12(VII-4555), SCL7(IV-2787), A66(151).
Sharkey, Robert P.
Money, Class, and Party: An Economic Study of Civil War, and Reconstruction. HAmer(II-987).
Sharlin, Harold I.
Making of the Electrical Age, The. HEur(II-651).
Sharp, Frank Chapman
Ethics. Ph(II-901).
Sharpe, Dores R.
Walter Rauschenbusch. HAmer(II-1197).
Shattuck, Roger
Marcel Proust. SCL12(VII-4763), A75(191).
Shaw, Bob
Orbitsville. SF(IV-1617).
Other Days, Other Eyes. SF(IV-1622).
Shaw, Felicity
Happy Exiles, The. SCL12(V-3240), SCL7(III-1915), A57(105).
Shaw, George Bernard
Back to Methuselah: A Metabiological Pentateuch. MP12(I-412), MP8(I-321), MP6(I-206), MPDr(55), MP3(I-82), MWL3(82). A different analysis on this title appears in: SF(I-120).
Bernard Shaw: Collected Letters, 1874-1897. SCL12(I-655),

HAnc(I-335; I-508).
Sherwood, Robert E.
   Abe Lincoln in Illinois.   MP12(I-4),   MPCE(I-2),   MP8(I-4),
   MP6(I-3),   MPDr(1),   MP1(I-3),   MWL1(3).
   Roosevelt and Hopkins: An Intimate History.   HAmer(III-1634).
Shiel, M. P.
   Purple Cloud, The.   SF(IV-1735).
   Yellow Danger, The.   SF(V-2525).
Shikibu, Lady Murasaki
   Tale of Genji, The.   MP12(XI-6369),   MPCE(IV-2195),
   MP8(VII-5072),   MP6(VI-3031),   MPEur(734),   MPv4(502),
   MP2(II-1006),   MWL2(1006).
Shiras, Wilmar H.
   Children of the Atom.   SF(I-349).
Shirer, William L.
   Collapse of the Third Republic, The.   SCL12(II-1348),   A70(75).
   Rise and Fall of the Third Reich, The.   SCL12(X-6420),
   SCL7(VI-3938),   A61(206),   BMA(477). A different analysis on this
   title appears in: HEur(III-1379).
Shirley, James
   Hyde Park.   MP12(V-2787),   MPCE(II-1027),   MP8(III-2168),
   MP6(III-1391),   MPDr(366),   MP3(I-497),   MWL3(497).
   Traitor, The.   MP12(XI-6643),   MPCE(IV-2307),   MP8(VIII-5277),
   MP6(VI-3178),   MPDr(863),   MP3(II-1077),   MWL3(1077).
Sholokhov, Mikhail
   And Quiet Flows the Don.   MP12(I-202),   MPCE(I-64),
   MP8(I-162),   MP6(I-97),   MPEur(21),   MP1(I-30),   MWL1(30).
   Don Flows Home to the Sea, The.   MP12(III-1585),   MPCE(I-577),
   MP8(II-1234),   MP6(II-796),   MPEur(249),   MPv4(138),
   MP2(I-272),   MWL2(272).
   Harvest on the Don.   SCL12(V-3292),   SCL7(III-1950),   A62(142).
Shore, Herbert, George Houser, Jennifer Davis *and* Susan Rogers
   No One Can Stop the Rain.   HWor(III-1223).
Short, Clarice
   Old One and the Wind: Poems, The.   SCL12(VIII-5520),   A74(282).
Shorthouse, Joseph Henry
   John Inglesant.   MP12(V-3026),   MPCE(II-1119),   MP8(IV-2356),
   MP6(III-1510),   MPEng(376),   MPv3(256),   MP2(I-513),
   MWL2(513).
Shostakovich, Dmitri
   Testimony: The Memoirs of Dmitri Shostakovich.   LA80(II-808).
Shryock, Richard Wallace *and* William Hyland
   Fall of Khrushchev, The.   HWor(II-978).
Shudraka
   Little Clay Cart, The.   MP12(VI-3444),   MPCE(II-1258),

MP8(IV-2696), MP6(III-1702), MPDr(448), MP3(II-586), MWL3(586).

Shulman, Alix Kates
Memoirs of an Ex-Prom Queen. SCL12(VII-4910), A73(251).

Shusky, Ernest
Right to Be Indian, The. HWor(II-869).

Shute, Nevil
On the Beach. SCL12(VIII-5553), SCL7(V-3396), A58(177). A different analysis on this title appears in: SF(IV-1603).
Trustee from the Toolroom. SCL12(XII-7800), SCL7(VII-4777), A61(266).

Shy, John
Toward Lexington: The Role of the British Army in the Coming of the American Revolution. HAmer(I-233).

Sidney, Sir Philip
*Arcadia. MP12(I-293), MPCE(I-106), MP8(I-227), MP6(I-151), MPEng(28), MP3(I-56), MWL3(56).
*Defence of Poesie. MP12(III-1420), MP8(II-1097), MP4(I-206), MWL4(206).
Poetry of Sidney, The. MP12(IX-5136), MP8(VI-4082), MP4(II-947), MWL4(947).

Sidwick, Henry
Methods of Ethics, The. Ph(II-671).

Sieburth, Richard
Instigations: Ezra Pound and Remy de Gourmont. LA80(II-431).

Siegel, Rudolph E.
Galen's System of Physiology and Medicine. HAnc(II-740).

Sienkiewicz, Henryk
Quo Vadis? MP12(IX-5404), MPCE(III-1841), MP8(VI-4310), MP6(V-2562), MPEur(613), MP1(II-797), MWL1(797).
With Fire and Sword. MP12(XII-7195), MPCE(IV-2520), MP8(VIII-5690), MP6(VI-3447), MPEur(822), MPv3(556), MP2(II-1148), MWL2(1148).

Sierra, Gregorio Martínez
Cradle Song. MP12(II-1188), MPCE(I-436), MP8(II-922), MP6(II-607), MPDr(184), MPv4(87), MP2(I-192), MWL2(192).

Sigal, Clancy
Going Away. SCL12(V-3002), SCL7(III-1787), A63(70).
Weekend in Dinlock. SCL12(XII-8175), SCL7(VII-5005), A61(293).

Sigerist, Henry E.
History of Medicine, A. HAnc(I-305).

Sigmund, Paul E.
Overthrow of Allende and the Politics of Chile, 1964-1976, The. LA78(II-630).

Sikes, J. G.
    Peter Abailard.   HAnc(III-1314).
Silk, Leonard
    Economists, The.   LA77(I-251).
Sillanpää, Frans Eemil
    Meek Heritage.   MP12(VII-3804),   MPCE(III-1393),
    MP8(V-2982),   MP6(IV-1890),   MPEur(488),   MPv4(320),
    MP2(II-650),   MWL2(650).
Sillitoe, Alan
    Guzman, Go Home.   SCL12(V-3206),   A70(157).
    *Loneliness of the Long-Distance Runner, The.   SCL12(VII-4458),
    SCL7(IV-2736),   A61(165).
    *Saturday Night and Sunday Morning.   SCL12(X-6629),
    SCL7(VI-4073),   A60(229).
    *Tree on Fire, A.   SCL12(XI-7779),   SCL7(VII-4759),   A69(318).
    Widower's Son, The.   LA78(II-904).
Silone, Ignazio
    *Bread and Wine.   MP12(II-636),   MPCE(I-233),   MP8(I-492),
    MP6(I-327),   MPEur(83),   MP1(I-81),   MWL1(81).
    *Fontamara.   MP12(IV-2104),   MP8(III-1640),   MP4(I-353),
    MWL4(353). A different analysis on this title appears in:
    SCL12(IV-2701),   SCL7(III-1606),   A61(83),   BMA(187).
    Fox and the Camellias, The.   SCL12(IV-2747),   SCL7(III-1642),
    A62(125).
    School for Dictators, The.   SCL12(X-6653),   SCL7(VI-4089),
    A64(228).
    Secret of Luca, The.   SCL12(X-6727),   SCL7(VI-4135),   A59(222).
    *Seed Beneath the Snow, The.   SCL12(X-6741),   SCL7(VI-4144),
    A66(286).
Silsbee, Nathaniel F. *and* Leslie E. Neville
    Jet Propulsion Progress: The Development of Aircraft Gas Turbines.
    HWor(I-358).
Silva, Ruth C.
    Rum, Religion, and Votes: 1928 Re-Examined.   HAmer(III-1569).
Silver, Daniel J.
    Maimonidean Criticism and the Maimonidean Controversy, 1180-1240.
    HAnc(III-1393).
Silverberg, Robert
    Downward to the Earth.   SF(II-591).
    Dying Inside.   SF(II-671).
    Light for the World: Edison and the Power Industry.   HAmer(II-1114).
    Morning of Mankind, The.   HEur(II-823).
    Nightwings.   SF(III-1526).
    Stochastic Man, The.   SF(V-2179).
    Time of Changes, A.   SF(V-2293).

Smith, Gene
When the Cheering Stopped. SCL12(XII-8222), SCL7(VII-5025),
A65(308).
Smith, Goldwin A.
Treaty of Washington, 1871: A Study in Imperial History, The.
HAmer(II-1074).
Smith, Hedrick
Russians, The. LA77(II-694).
Smith, Henry Nash
Mark Twain: A Collection of Critical Essays. Twentieth-Century Views
series. HAmer(II-1149).
Smith, Homer W.
Kamongo. MP12(VI-3115), MP8(IV-2427), MP4(I-486),
MWL4(486).
Smith, James M.
*Freedom's Fetters: The Alien and Sedition Laws and American Civil
Liberties.* HAmer(I-418).
Smith, Jean Edward
Defense of Berlin, The. HEur(III-1626).
Smith, John Chabot
Alger Hiss. LA77(I-38).
Smith, Justin H.
War with Mexico. HAmer(II-821).
Smith, Lee
Fancy Strut. SCL12(IV-2446), A74(124).
Last Day the Dogbushes Bloomed, The. SCL12(VI-4105),
SCL7(IV-2504), A69(185).
Smith, Lillian
Journey, The. SCL12(VI-3919), SCL7(IV-2374), A54(126).
Winner Names the Age, The. LA79(II-879).
Smith, Lucy Margaret
Early History of the Monastery of Cluny, The. HAnc(II-1186).
Smith, Mark
Death of the Detective, The. LA77(I-202).
Smith, Page
John Adams. SCL12(VI-3876), SCL7(IV-2344), A63(112).
New Age Now Begins, A. LA77(II-529).
Smith, Paul H.
Loyalists and Redcoats. HAmer(I-297).
Smith, Pauline
Little Karoo, The. SCL12(VII-4418), SCL7(IV-2711), A60(144).
Smith, R. E.
Failure of the Roman Republic, The. Different analyses on this title
appear in: HAnc(I-484; I-499).
Smith, Stevie

Collected Poems of Stevie Smith, The.   LA77(I-168).
Smith, William Jay
   New & Selected Poems.   SCL12(VIII-5252),   A72(228).
   Streaks of the Tulip, The.   SCL12(XI-7292),   A73(349).
   Tin Can, The.   SCL12(XI-7657),   SCL7(VII-4674),   A67(320).
Smith, W. Eugene *and* Aileen M. Smith
   Minamata.   SCL12(VIII-5003),   A76(225).
Smollett, Tobias
   Humphry Clinker.   MP12(V-2769),   MPCE(II-1018),
   MP8(III-2156),   MP6(III-1380),   MPEng(330),   MP1(I-394),
   MWL1(394).
   Peregrine Pickle.   MP12(VIII-4599),   MPCE(III-1713),
   MP8(V-3582),   MP6(IV-2308),   MPEng(648),   MP1(II-731),
   MWL1(731).
   Roderick Random.   MP12(X-5656),   MPCE(III-1942),
   MP8(VII-4502),   MP6(V-2682),   MPEng(742),   MP1(II-841),
   MWL1(841).
Smyth, Henry DeWolf
   Atomic Energy for Military Purposes.   Different analyses on this title
   appear in: HWor(I-250; I-393).
Snell, Bruno
   Discovery of the Mind: The Greek Origins of European Thought, The.
   HAnc(I-176).
   "Myth and Reality in Greek Tragedy," in The Discovery of the Mind: The
   Greek Origins of European Thought.   HAnc(I-250).
Snell, John L.
   Meaning of Yalta, The.   HEur(III-1504).
Snepp, Frank
   Decent Interval.   HWor(III-1230).
Snodgrass, W. D.
   After Experience.   SCL12(I-96),   SCL7(I-71),   A68(7).
   Heart's Needle.   SCL12(V-3317),   SCL7(III-1970),   A60(88),
   BMA(224).
Snow, C. P.
   Affair, The.   MP12(I-56),   MP8(I-44),   MP4(I-6),   MWL4(6). A
   different analysis on this title appears in: SCL12 (I-76),   SCL7(I-59),
   A61(1),   BMA(11).
   Conscience of the Rich, The.   MP12(II-1091),   MP8(II-853),
   MP4(I-152),   MWL4(152). A different analysis on this title appears in:
   SCL12(III-1549),   SCL7(II-903),   A59(40).
   Corridors of Power.   SCL12(III-1586),   SCL7(II-933),   A65(59).
   Homecoming.   SCL12(V-3500),   SCL7(III-2093),   A57(123).
   Last Things.   SCL12(VI-4142),   A71(161).
   Masters, The.   MP12(VII-3768),   MP8(V-2955),   MP4(I-596),
   MWL4(596).

New Men, The. SCL12(VIII-5267), SCL7(V-3210), A55(172), BMA(388).

Search, The. SCL12(X-6688), SCL7(VI-4113), A60(232), BMA(499).

Strangers and Brothers. SCL12(XI-7277), SCL7(VII-4470), A61(242).

Snyder, Gary

Back Country, The. SCL12(I-513), SCLs(25).

Regarding Wave. SCL12(IX-6311), A72(273).

Turtle Island. SCL12(XII-7821), A75(335).

Söderblom, Nathan

Living God, The. RCh(II-994).

Sohm, Rudolph

Institutes, A Textbook of the History and System of Roman Private Law, The. HAnc(II-1006).

Solberg, Carl

Oil Power. LA77(II-588).

Solmi, Arrigo

Making of Modern Italy, The. HEur(II-926).

Solmsen, Friedrich

"Dialectic Without the Forms," in Aristotle on Dialectic. HAnc(I-351).

Sologub, Fyodor

Petty Demon, The. SCL12(IX-5825), SCL7(V-3550), A63(177).

Solomon, Robert

International Monetary System, 1945-1976: An Insider's View, The. Different analyses on this title appear in: HWor(III-1100; III-1106).

Solovyev, Vladimir

Lectures on Godmanhood. RCh(II-782).

Solzhenitsyn, Aleksandr I.

August 1914. SCL12(I-450), A73(17).

Cancer Ward, The. SCL12(II-1056), SCL7(I-608), A69(61).

First Circle, The. SCL12(IV-2639), SCL7(III-1556), A69(126).

Gulag Archipelago: One, Parts I-II, The. SCL12(V-3195), A75(131).

Gulag Archipelago: Two, Parts III-IV, The. SCL12(V-3199), A76(122).

Gulag Archipelago: Three, Parts V-VII, 1918-1956, The. LA78(I-370).

Love-Girl and the Innocent, The. SCL12(VII-4587), A71(186).

One Day in the Life of Ivan Denisovich. SCL12(VIII-5581), SCL7(V-3418), A64(203).

Somerlott, Robert

Inquisitor's House, The. SCL12(VI-3733), A70(181).

Sontag, Susan

Against Interpretation. SCL12(I-121), SCL7(I-84), A67(5).

Benefactor, The. SCL12(I-637), SCL7(I-365), A64(16).

Death Kit. SCL12(III-1817), SCL7(II-1092), A68(72).

Spenser, Edmund
Faerie Queen, The.   MP12(IV-1953),   MPCE(II-698),
MP8(III-1529),   MP6(II-972),   MPPo(99),   MP1(I-264),
MWL1(264).
Lyric Poetry of Spenser, The.   MP12(VI-3573),   MP8(IV-2804),
MP4(I-581),   MWL4(581).
Mother Hubberd's Tale.   MP12(VII-4078),   MP8(V-3181),
MP4(I-619),   MWL4(619).
Shepheardes Calendar, The.   MP12(X-5972),   MP8(VII-4756),
MP4(II-1114),   MWL4(1114).
Sperber, Manes
Journey Without End.   SCL12(VI-3943),   SCL7(IV-2384),   A54(129).
Sperry, Willard L.
Strangers and Pilgrims.   HAnc(III-1673).
Spielman, John P.
Leopold I of Austria.   LA78(II-518).
Spinka, Matthew
John Hus at the Council of Constance.   HAnc(III-1682).
Spinoza, Benedictus de
Ethics.   MP12(IV-1876),   MP8(III-1473),   MP6(II-931),
MPNf(118),   MP3(I-364),   MWL3(364). A different analysis on this
title appears in: Ph(I-416).
Spinrad, Norman
Bug Jack Barron.   SF(I-265).
Iron Dream, The.   SF(III-1062).
Spitta, Philipp
Johann Sebastian Bach.   HEur(I-382).
Spitz, Jacques
oeil du purgatoire, L'.   SF(IV-1588).
Spooner, F. C.
"Reformation in Difficulties: France, 1519-1559, The," in *Vol. II* of *The
New Cambridge Modern History*.   HAnc(III-1704).
Sprigge, Cecil Jackson Squire
Development of Modern Italy, The.   HWor(I-140).
Sprigge, Elizabeth
Life of Ivy Compton-Burnett, The.   SCL12(VII-4340),   A74(233).
Spring, Howard
These Lovers Fled Away.   SCL12(XI-7526),   SCL7(VII-4577),
A55(256).
Spurgeon, Charles Haddon
John Ploughman's Talks.   RCh(II-755).
Stableford, Brian
Halcyon Drift.   SF(II-936).
Stace, Walter T.
Time and Eternity.   RCh(II-1139).

Stacey, John
  John Wyclif and Reform.   HAnc(III-1643).
Stacton, David
  Dancer in Darkness, A.   SCL12(III-1695),   SCL7(II-997),   A63(32).
  People of the Book.   SCL12(IX-5809),   SCL7(V-3544),   A66(233).
  Segaki.   SCL12(X-6750),   SCL7(VI-4153),   A60(237).
  Sir William.   SCL12(X-7000),   SCL7(VI-4315),   A64(244).
Staël, Madame de
  Considerations on the Principal Events of the French Revolution.
  MP12(II-1100),   MP8(II-859),   MP4(I-155),   MWL4(155).
  Delphine.   MP12(III-1436),   MPCE(I-527),   MP8(II-1110),
  MP6(II-725),   MPEur(224),   MPv4(125),   MP2(I-243),
  MWL2(243).
Stafford, Jean
  Collected Stories of Jean Stafford, The.   SCL12(III-1416),   SCLs(72).
Stafford, William
  Someday, Maybe.   SCL12(XI-7089),   A74(365).
  Stories That Could Be True: New and Collected Poems.   LA78(II-799).
  Traveling Through the Dark.   SCL12(XI-7751),   SCLs(325).
Stahl, William H.
  *Roman Science: Origins, Development, and Influence to the Later Middle
  Ages.*   HAnc(II-656).
Stallman, R. W.
  Stephen Crane.   SCL12(XI-7220),   SCL7(VI-4438),   A69(299). A
  different analysis on this title appears in: HAmer(II-1258).
Stampp, Kenneth M.
  Era of Reconstruction, 1865-1877, The.   SCL12(IV-2302),
  SCL7(II-1373),   A66(87).
Stanford, Ann
  In Mediterranean Air.   LA78(I-439).
Stankiewicz, W. J.
  *Politics and Religion in Seventeenth Century France: A Study of Political
  Ideas from the Monarchomachs to Bayle, as Reflected in the Toleration
  Controversy.*   HEur(I-262).
Stannard, David E.
  Puritan Way of Death, The.   LA78(II-682).
Stansky, Peter *and* William Abrahams
  Unknown Orwell, The.   SCL12(XII-7912),   A73(367).
Stanwood, Edward
  American Tariff Controversies in the Nineteenth Century.
  HAmer(II-1276).
Stapledon, Olaf
  Last and First Men.   SF(III-1140).
  Odd John: A Story Between Jest and Earnest.   SF(IV-1583).
  Sirius: A Fantasy of Love and Discord.   SF(V-2085).

Star Maker. SF(V-2150).

Starkey, Marion L.
Devil in Massachusetts: A Modern Enquiry into the Salem Witch Trials, The. HAmer(I-172).

Starkie, Enid
Flaubert: The Making of the Master. SCL12(IV-2666), A72(151).
Flaubert: The Master. SCL12(IV-2671), SCL7(III-1579), A68(114).

Statius (Publius Papinius Statius)
*Thebais, The. MP12(XI-6469), MP8(VIII-5150), MP6(VI-3085), MPPo(360), MP3(II-1062), MWL3(1062).

Statler, Oliver
Japanese Inn. SCL12(VI-3817), SCL7(IV-2304), A62(165).

Stavenow, Ludvig
"Scandinavia," in The Cambridge Modern History. HEur(III-1168).

Stavrianos, L. S.
Balkans Since 1453, The. Different analyses on this title appear in: HAnc(III-1661), HEur(I-89; I-370; I-476).

Stead, Christina
Little Hotel, The. SCL12(VII-4411), A76(181).
Man Who Loved Children, The. SCL12(VII-4718), SCL7(IV-2865), A66(168).
Miss Herbert. LA77(II-509).
Puzzleheaded Girl, The. SCL12(IX-6142), SCL7(VI-3756), A68(260).

Steck, Francis B.
Jolliet-Marquette Expedition, 1673, The. HAmer(I-149).

Steefel, Lawrence D.
Bismarck, the Hohenzollern Candidacy, and the Origins of the Franco-German War of 1870. Different analyses on this title appear in: HEur(II-952; II-956).

Steegmuller, Francis
Cocteau: A Biography. SCL12(II-1338), A71(42).
Grand Mademoiselle, The. SCL12(V-3064), SCL7(III-1833), A57(90).
"Your Isadora." SCL12(XII-8497), A75(372).

Steele, Sir Richard
*Conscious Lovers, The. MP12(II-1094), MPCE(I-392), MP8(II-856), MP6(I-562), MPDr(171), MPv4(85), MP2(I-174), MWL2(174).
*Funeral, The. MP12(IV-2188), MPCE(II-788), MP8(III-1706), MP6(II-1070), MPDr(286), MPv4(175), MP2(I-350), MWL2(350).

Steele, Sir Richard, Joseph Addison *and* Eustace Budgell
*Sir Roger de Coverley Papers, The. MP12(X-6067), MP8(VII-4840), MP6(V-2887), MPNf(288), MP3(II-988),

MWL3(988).

Stegner, Wallace

All the Little Live Things. SCL12(I-229), SCL7(I-143), A68(11).
*Angle of Repose. SCL12(I-311), A72(7).
Beyond the Hundredth Meridian: John Wesley Powell and the Second Opening of the West. HAmer(II-1107).
Gathering of Zion: The Story of the Mormon Trail, The. HAmer(II-815).
Recapitulation. LA80(II-702).
*Shooting Star, The. SCL12(X-6930), SCL7(VI-4264), A62(272).
Spectator Bird, The. LA77(II-769).
Uneasy Chair: A Biography of Bernard DeVoto, The. SCL12(XII-7884), A75(340).

Steinbeck, John

Acts of King Arthur and His Noble Knights, The. LA77(I-7).
*East of Eden. MP12(III-1689), MPCE(I-620), MP8(II-1313), MP6(II-848), MPAm(163), MP3(I-315), MWL3(315).
*Grapes of Wrath, The. MP12(IV-2344), MPCE(II-835), MP8(III-1824), MP6(II-1146), MPAm(225), MP1(I-324), MWL1(324).
*In Dubious Battle. MP12(V-2850), MPCE(II-1050), MP8(IV-2219), MP6(III-1425), MPAm(293), MPv3(239), MP2(I-478), MWL2(478).
*Of Mice and Men. MP12(VII-4294), MPCE(III-1606), MP8(V-3341), MP6(IV-2149), MPAm(449), MP1(II-672), MWL1(672).
*Sweet Thursday. SCL12(XI-7365), SCL7(VII-4498), A54(264).
Travels with Charley. SCL12(XI-7763), SCL7(VII-4751), A63(270).
*Winter of Our Discontent, The. SCL12(XII-8340), SCL7(VII-5105), A62(306).

Steiner, Bernard C.

Life of Henry Barnard: The First United States Commissioner of Education, 1867-1870. HAmer(II-1033).

Steiner, George

After Babel. SCL12(I-89), A76(1).

Steiner, Jean-François

Treblinka. SCL12(XI-7773), SCL7(VII-4753), A68(337).

Stendhal (Marie-Henri Beyle)

*Charterhouse of Parma, The. MP12(II-895), MPCE(I-328), MP8(I-692), MP6(I-459), MPEur(129), MP1(I-135), MWL1(135).
*Lucien Leuwen. MP12(VI-3547), MPCE(II-1297), MP8(IV-2781), MP6(III-1756), MPEur(458), MPv4(302), MP2(II-606), MWL2(606).
*Red and the Black, The. MP12(IX-5463), MPCE(III-1866),

MWL4(474).
Sentimental Journey, A. MP12(X-5914), MPCE(IV-2042),
MP8(VII-4710), MP6(V-2823), MPEng(784), MP1(II-879),
MWL1(879).
Tristram Shandy. MP12(XI-6712), MPCE(IV-2335),
MP8(VIII-5329), MP6(VI-3212), MPEng(879), MP1(1027),
MWL1(1027).
Stevens, James
Paul Bunyan. MP12(VIII-4537), MPCE(III-1687), MP8(V-3535),
MP6(IV-2270), MPAm(475), MP1(II-717), MWL1(717).
Stevens, Wallace
Collected Poems. SCL12(II-1377), SCL7(II-820), A54(31),
BMA(100).
Harmonium. MP12(V-2480), MP8(III-1931), MP6(III-1220),
MPPo(118), MP3(I-442), MWL3(442).
Letters of Wallace Stevens. SCL12(VI-4276), SCL7(IV-2616),
A67(190).
Opus Posthumous. SCL12(VIII-5630), SCL7(V-3444), A58(182).
Poetry of Stevens, The. MP12(IX-5161), MP8(VI-4107),
MP4(II-962), MWL4(962).
Stevenson, Charles Leslie
Ethics and Language. Ph(II-1089).
Stevenson, Elizabeth
Lafcadio Hearn. SCL12(VI-4073), SCL7(IV-2476), A62(175).
Stevenson, Fanny *and* Robert Louis Stevenson
Our Samoan Adventure. SCL12(VIII-5676), SCL7(V-3475),
A55(196).
Stevenson, Robert Louis
Beach of Falesá, The. MP12(I-456), MPCE(I-160), MP8(I-356),
MP6(I-235), MPEng(45), MP3(I-91), MWL3(91).
Black Arrow, The. MP12(I-552), MPCE(I-202), MP8(I-425),
MP6(I-284), MPEng(54), MP1(I-72), MWL1(72).
Dr. Jekyll and Mr. Hyde. MP12(III-1550), MPCE(I-559),
MP8(II-1208), MP6(II-778), MPEng(162), MP1(I-214),
MWL1(214). A different analysis on this title appears in:
SF(V-2184).
Kidnapped. MP12(VI-3127), MPCE(II-1154), MP8(IV-2436),
MP6(III-1554), MPEng(402), MP1(I-471), MWL1(471).
Master of Ballantrae, The. MP12(VII-3764), MPCE(III-1377),
MP8(V-2952), MP6(IV-1868), MPEng(482), MP1(I-568),
MWL1(568).
Travels with a Donkey. MP12(XI-6659), MPCE(IV-2312),
MP8(VIII-5290), MP6(VI-3186), MPNf(307), MP1(II-1014),
MWL1(1014).
Treasure Island. MP12(XI-6662), MPCE(IV-2313),

Night and Day. LA80(II-586).
**Rosencrantz and Guildenstern Are Dead.* SCL12(X-6502), SCL7(VI-4002), A68(275).
**Travesties.* SCL12(XI-7769), A76(325).
Storey, David
Changing Room, The. SCL12(II-1183), A74(47).
Stourzh, Gerald
Benjamin Franklin and American Foreign Policy. HAmer(I-303).
Stover, John F.
American Railroads. HAmer(I-628).
Life and Decline of the American Railroad, The. HWor(I-522).
Stowe, Harriet Beecher
**Oldtown Folks.* MP12(VIII-4353), MPCE(III-1627), MP8(V-3388), MP6(IV-2179), MPAm(463), MPv4(381), MP2(II-773), MWL2(773).
**Uncle Tom's Cabin.* MP12(XII-6814), MPCE(IV-2381), MP8(VIII-5398), MP6(VI-3258), MPAm(679), MP1(II-1044), MWL1(1044). A different analysis on this title appears in: HAmer(II-862).
Strachey, Lytton
**Eminent Victorians.* MP12(III-1760), MP8(II-1371), MP6(II-882), MPNf(98), MP3(I-335), MWL3(335).
Queen Victoria. MP129IX-5390), MP8(VI-4300), MP4(II-1038), MWL4(1038).
Strack, Hermann L.
Introduction to the Talmud and Midrash. HAnc(II-986).
Strassburg, Gottfried von
Tristan and Isolde. MP12(XI-6705), MPCE(IV-2331), MP8(VIII-5324), MP6(VI-3208), MPPo(362), MP3(II-1083), MWL3(1083).
Strasser, Otto
Hitler and I. HEur(II-1393).
Straub, Peter
Ghost Story. LA80(I-349).
Strauss, David Friedrich
Life of Jesus Critically Examined, The. RCh(II-679).
Strauss, William A. *and* Lawrence M. Baskir
Chance and Circumstance: The Draft, the War and the Vietnam Generation. LA79(I-88).
Strayer, Joseph R.
Western Europe in the Middle Ages: A Short History. HAnc(II-1148).
Streeter, B. H.
Primitive Church, The. HAnc(II-683).
Stremlau, John J.

International Politics of the Nigerian Civil War, 1967-1970, The. HWor(II-1007).

Strindberg, August

Comrades. MP12(II-1047), MPCE(I-379), MP8(II-815), MP6(I-535), MPDr(166), MP3(I-208), MWL3(208).

Dance of Death, The. MP12(III-1283), MPCE(I-472), MP8(II-992), MP6(II-656), MPDr(196), MPv4(101), MP2(I-217), MWL2(217).

*Father, The. MP12(IV-2000), MPCE(II-719), MP8(III-1562), MP6(II-993), MPDr(275), MPv3(167), MP2(I-325), MWL2(325).

Link, The. MP12(VI-3434), MPCE(II-1255), MP8(IV-2689), MP6(III-1697), MPDr(446), MP3(II-581), MWL3(581).

*Miss Julie. MP12(VII-3936), MPCE(III-1448), MP8(V-3077), MP6(IV-1959), MPDr(539), MPv4(332), MP2(II-675), MWL2(675).

*Red Room, The. MP12(IX-5473), MPCE(III-1872), MP8(VI-4360), MP6(V-2596), MPEur(625), MP3(II-868), MWL3(868).

There Are Crimes and Crimes. MP12(XI-6473), MPCE(IV-2233), MP8(VIII-5124), MP6(VI-3087), MPDr(839), MP3(II-1064), MWL3(1064).

Strode, Hudson

Jefferson Davis: American Patriot. SCL12(VI-3835), SCL7(IV-2320), A55(134), BMA(258).

Jefferson Davis: Confederate President. SCL12(VI-3838), SCL7(IV-2323), A60(108), BMA(261).

Jefferson Davis: Private Letters, 1823-1889. SCL12(VI-3841), SCL7(IV-2326), A67(175).

Jefferson Davis: Tragic Hero. SCL12(VI-3845), SCL7(IV-2330), A65(152).

Strong, Augustus Hopkins

Systematic Theology. RCh(II-797).

Strong, L. A. G.

Garden, The. MP12(IV-2200), MPCE(II-793), MP8(III-1715), MP6(II-1075), MPEng(240), MPv4(177), MP2(I-354), MWL2(354).

Strugatsky, Arkady *and* Boris Strugatsky

Far Rainbow. SF(II-756).

Final Circle of Paradise, The. SF(II-776).

Hard to Be a God. SF(II-950).

Nasty Swans, The. SF(III-1488).

Noon: Twenty-Second Century. SF(IV-1548).

Ponedel'nik nachinaetsia v subbotu. SF(IV-1710).

Roadside Picnic. SF(IV-1817).

Second War of the Worlds, The. SF(IV-1879).

MP4(I-544), MWL4(544).
Long March, The. SCL12(VII-4484), SCLs(168).
Set This House on Fire. MP12(X-5919), MP8(VII-4713),
MP4(II-1106), MWL4(1106), SCL12(X-666854), SCL7(VI-4211),
A61(228), BMA(502).
Sophie's Choice. LA80(II-774).
Suarez, Francisco, S. J.
Treatise on Laws. RCa(II-575).
Suckling, Sir John
Poetry of Suckling, The. MP12(IX-5164), MP8(VI-4110),
MP4(II-965), MWL4(965).
Suckow, Ruth
Folks, The. MP12(IV-2094), MP8(III-1631), MP4(I-349),
MWL4(349).
Sudermann, Hermann
Dame Care. MP12(III-1275), MPCE(I-468), MP8(II-986),
MP6(II-651), MPEur(189), MPv4(96), MP2(I-212), MWL2(212).
Song of Songs, The. MP12(XI-6156), MPCE(IV-2121),
MP8(VII-4907), MP6(V-2932), MPEur(706), MP1(II-910),
MWL1(910).
Sue, Eugène
Mysteries of Paris, The. MP12(VIII-4111), MPCE(III-1529),
MP8(V-3204), MP6(IV-2051), MPEur(520), MP1(II-632),
MWL1(632).
Wandering Jew, The. MP12(XII-7010), MPCE(IV-2460),
MP8(VIII-5545), MP6(VI-3359), MPEur(803), MP1(II-1083),
MWL1(1083).
Suetonius (Gaius Suetonius Tranquillus)
Concerning Illustrious Men. MP12(II-1054), MP8(II-820),
MPR(I-148), MWL4(148).
Lives of the Caesars. MP12(VI-3464), MP8(IV-2712),
MP6(IV-1713), MPNf(192), MP3(II-590), MWL3(590).
Suhard, Cardinal Emmanuel
Growth or Decline?: The Church Today. RCa(II-920).
Sukhanov, N. N.
Russian Revolution, 1917, The. SCL12(X-6571), SCL7(VI-4045),
A55(217).
Sullivan, Maurice S.
Jedediah Smith, Trader and Trail Breaker. HAmer(I-622).
Sullivan, Walter
Assault on the Unknown: The International Geophysical Year.
HWor(II-766).
Sulzbach, Walter
German Experience with Social Insurance. HEur(II-1030).
Summers, Hollis

Day After Sunday, The.   SCL12(III-1742),   SCL7(II-1042),   A69(89).
Sumner, B. H.
    Peter the Great and the Emergence of Russia.   HEur(I-365).
    Russia and the Balkans, 1870-1880.   HEur(II-1011).
Sumner, William Graham
    Folkways.   MP12(IV-2097),   MP8(III-1634),   MP4(I-351),
    MWL4(351).
Sundberg, A. C.
    "Towards a Revised History of the New Testament Canon," in Studia
    Evangelica IV: Texte and Untersuchengen.   HAnc(II-770).
Surtees, Robert Smith
    *Handley Cross.   MP12(V-2467),   MPCE(II-901),   MP8(III-1919),
    MP6(III-1210),   MPEng(266),   MP1(I-352),   MWL1(352).
    Hillingdon Hall.   MP12(V-2626),   MPCE(II-962),   MP8(III-2033),
    MP6(III-1297),   MPEng(304),   MPv4(220),   MP2(I-447),
    MWL2(447).
    *Jorrocks' Jaunts and Jollites.   MP12(V-3033),   MPCE(II-1123),
    MP8(IV-2362),   MP6(III-1514),   MPEng(382),   MPv(261),
    MP2(I-518),   MWL2(518).
    Mr. Facey Romford's Hounds.   MP12(VII-3594),   MPCE(III-1456),
    MP8(V-3091),   MP6(IV-1968),   MPEng(519),   MPv4(334),
    MP2(II-679),   MWL2(679).
    Mr. Sponge's Sporting Tour.   MP12(VII-3967),   MPCE(III-1461),
    MP8(V-3102),   MP6(IV-1977),   MPEng(527),   MPv3(347),
    MP2(II-684),   MWL2(684).
Suso, Blessed Henry, O. P.
    Little Book of Eternal Wisdom, The.   RCa(I-458).
Sutch, Richard *and* Roger L. Ransom
    One Kind of Freedom: The Economic Consequences of Emancipation.
    LA78(II-622).
Sutherland, John
    Men of Waterloo.   HEur(II-620).
Sutter, Robert G.
    Chinese Foreign Policy After the Cultural Revolution, 1966-1977.
    LA79(I-108).
Sutton, E. W. *and* Rackham, *eds.*
    Cicero, De Oratore.   HAnc(I-522).
Suzuki, Daisetz T.
    Zen Buddhism.   Ph(II-1115).
Svobida, Lawrence
    Empire of Dust, An.   HAmer(III-1629).
Swados, Harvey
    Celebration.   SCL12(II-1149),   A76(37).
Swanberg, W. A.
    Citizen Hearst.   SCL12(II-1279),   SCL7(II-752),   A62(61). A

different analysis on this title appears in HAmer(II-1245).

Dreiser.   SCL12(III-2073),   SCL7(II-1247),   A66(81).

First Blood: The Story of Fort Sumter.   SCL12(IV-2636),
SCL7(III-1553),   A59(87).

Luce and His Empire.   SCL12(VII-4604),   A73(231).

Norman Thomas.   LA77(II-570).

Pulitzer.   SCL12(IX-6121),   SCL7(VI-3743),   A68(254).

Sickles the Incredible.   SCL12(X-6950),   SCL7(VI-4276),   A57(241).

Swanson, Carl P. *and* Peter L. Webster

Cell, The.   HWor(I-504).

Sward, Keith

Legend of Henry Ford, The.   HAmer(III-1424).

Swarthout, Glendon

Bless the Beasts and Children.   SCL12(II-781),   SCLs(37).

They Came to Cordura.   SCL12(XI-7536),   SCL7(VII-4586),
A59(241).

Swedenborg, Emanuel

Divine Love and Wisdom.   MP12(III-1537),   MP8(II-1197),
MPT(II-768),   MPNf(91),   MP3(I-287),   MWL3(287).

Sweeney, Leo

"Another Interpretation of Enneads," in *Modern Schoolman.*
HAnc(II-825).

"Infinity in Plotinus," in *Gregorianum.*   HAnc(II-825).

Sweet, Paul Robinson

Wilhelm von Humboldt: A Biography, Vol. I: 1767-1808.   LA79(II-868).

Swenson, May

Half Sun Half Sleep.   SCL12(V-3220),   SCL7(III-1903),   A68(130).

Iconographs.   SCL12(VI-3606),   A71(119).

New & Selected Things Taking Place.   LA79(II-472).

To Mix with Time.   SCL2(XI-7687),   SCL7(VII-4703),   A64(271).

Swete, H. B.

Introduction to the Old Testament in Greek, An.   HAnc(I-419).

Swift, Emerson Howland

Hagia Sophia.   HAnc(II-1042).

Swift, Jonathan

Gulliver's Travels.   MP12(IV-2421),   MPCE(II-884),
MP8(III-1883),   MP6(III-1187),   MPEng(254),   MP1(I-341),
MWL1(341).

*Journal to Stella.   MP12(V-3056),   MP8(IV-2383),   MP4(I-476),
MWL4(476).

*Poetry of Swift, The.   MP12(IX-5167),   MP8(VI-4113),
MP4(II-968),   MWL4(968).

*Tale of a Tub, A.   MP12(XI-6366),   MP8(VII-5069),
MPR(II-1201),   MWL4(1201).

Swinburne, Algernon Charles

Still A Dream.   HWor(II-811).
Taine, Hippolyte
  Philosophy of Art.   MP12(VIII-4659),   MP8(V-3634),
  MP6(IV-2340),   MPNf(242),   MP3(II-745),   MWL3(745).
Taine, John
  Before the Dawn.   SF(I-149).
Takamura, Kotaro
  Chieko's Sky.   LA79(I-105).
Tanner, J. R.
  "Revolution of 1688, The" in *English Constitutional Conflicts of the
  Seventeenth Century, 1603-1689.*   HEur(I-362).
Tanzer, Helen H.
  Common People of Pompeii: A Study of the Graffiti, The.
  HAnc(II-662).
Taran, Leonardo
  Parmenides: A Text with Translation, Commentary and Critical Essays.
  HAnc(I-234).
Tarkington, Booth
  *Alice Adams.   MP12(I-104),   MPCE(I-35),   MP8(I-83),
  MP6(I-51),   MPAm(13),   MP1(I-20),   MWL1(20).
  Kate Fennigate.   MP12(VI-3120),   MPCE(II-1151),   MP8(IV-2432),
  MP6(III-1550),   MPAm(320),   MP1(I-467),   MWL1(467).
  *Monsieur Beaucaire.   MP12(VII-4034),   MPCE(III-1495),
  MP8(V-3147),   MP6(IV-2013),   MPAm(425),   MP1(II-616),
  MWL1(616).
  *Seventeen.   MP12(X-5942),   MPCE(IV-2051),   MP8(VII-4732),
  MP6(V-2838),   MPAm(569),   MP1(II-882),   MWL1(882).
Tarle, E. V.
  Napoleon's Invasion of Russia.   HEur(II-587).
Tarn, Sir William W.
  Alexander the Great.   HAnc(I-361).
  "Battle of Actium, The," in *The Journal of Roman Studies.*
  HAnc(I-533).
  Hellenistic Military and Naval Developments.   HAnc(I-359).
Tarn, Sir William W. *and* G. T. Griffith
  Hellenistic Civilization.   HAnc(I-341).
Tasca, Angelo
  Rise of Italian Fascism, The.   HEur(III-1322).
Tasso, Torquato
  *Jerusalem Delivered.   MP12(V-3000),   MPCE(II-1107),
  MP8(IV-2336),   MP6(III-1496),   MPPo(141),   MP1(I-441),
  MWL1(441). A different analysis on this title appears in: RCa(I-548).
Tate, Allen
  Collected Poems, 1919-1976.   LA78(I-188).
  Fathers, The.   MP12(IV-2012),   MP8(III-1568),   MP4(I-324),

MWL4(324),   SCL12(IV-2495),   SCL7(III-1491),   A61(71),
BMA(183).
Memoirs and Opinions.   SCL12(VII-4888),   A76(210).
Poetry of Tate, The.   MP12(IX-5172),   MP8(VI-4118),
MP4(II-972),   MWL4(972).
Swimmers, The.   SCL12(XI-7369),   A72(307).
Tate, James
Absences.   SCL12(I-13),   A73(1).
Viper Jazz.   LA77(II-888).
Tatian
Address of Tatian to the Greeks.   RCh(I-26).
Discourse Against the Greeks, The.   RCa(I-23).
Tatu, Michel
Power in the Kremlin: From Khrushchev to Kosygin.   Different analyses
on this title appear in: HWor(II-909; II-977).
Taubenfeld, Howard J.
Treaty for Antarctica, A.   HWor(II-802).
Taussig, Frank W.
Tariff History of the United States, The.   HAmer(II-1275).
Taylor, Alfred Edward
Faith of a Moralist, The.   RCh(II-954).
Socrates.   HAnc(I-320).
Taylor, A. J. P.
Beaverbrook.   SCL12(I-591),   A73(25).
Bismarck: The Man and the Statesman.   Different analyses on this title
appear in: HEur(II-967; II-971).
Churchill Revised: A Critical Assessment.   HEur(III-1530).
Origins of the Second World War, The.   Different analyses on this title
appear in: HWor(I-202; I-344).
Struggle for Mastery in Europe, 1848-1918, The.   HEur(II-925).
Taylor, Edward
Poetical Works of Edward Taylor, The.   MP12(VIII-4786),
MP8(VI-3732),   MP6(V-2406),   MPPo(225),   MP3(II-771),
MWL3(771).
Taylor, Eleanor Ross
Wilderness of Ladies.   SCL12(XII-8279),   SCL7(VII-5067),
A61(304).
Taylor, Elizabeth
In a Summer Season.   SCL12(VI-3638),   SCL7(III-2172),   A62(155).
Taylor, F. Jay
United States and the Spanish Civil War, 1936-1939, The.
HAmer(III-1663).
Taylor, Harold
Students Without Teachers.   SCL12(XI-7308),   A70(291).
Taylor, Henry

Phenomenon of Man, The. MP12(VIII-4636), MP8(V-3613), MP4(II-683), MWL4(683), SCL12(IX-5831), SCL7(V-3557), A60(189). A different analysis on this title appears in: RCa(II-1017).

Teller, Edward *and* Albert L. Latter
Our Nuclear Future. SCL12(VIII-5673), SCL7(V-3472), A59(198).

Teller, Walter Magnes
Search for Captain Slocum, The. SCL12(X-6691), SCL7(VI-4116), A57(233).

Temperley, Harold W. V.
England and the Near East: The Crimea. HEur(II-814).
Foreign Policy of Canning, 1822-1827: England, the Neo-Holy Alliance, and the New World, The. HEur(II-656).
"Peace of Paris, The" in *The Cambridge History of the British Empire.* HEur(I-453).

Temple, William
Nature, Man and God. RCh(II-999).

Tenn, William
Short Fiction of William Tenn, The. SF(V-2065).

Tennant, Frederick Robert
Philosophical Theology. RCh(II-933).

Tenney, Frank
"Rome and Carthage: The First Punic War," in *Vol. VII* of *The Cambridge Ancient History.* HAnc(I-410).

Tennyson, Alfred, Lord
*Enoch Arden. MP12(III-1787), MPCE(I-651), MP6(II-894), MPPo(75), MP1(I-249), MWL1(249).
*Idyllis of the King, The. MP12(V-2825), MPCE(II-1042), MP8(IV-2199), MP6(III-1410), MPPo(134), MP1(I-417), MWL1(417).
*In Memoriam. MP12(V-2853), MP8(IV-2221), MP4(I-439), MWL4(439).
Poems. MP12(VIII-4777), MP8(VI-3723), MP4(II-702), MWL4(702).
*Princess, The. MP12(IX-5324), MP8(VI-4248), MP4(II-1026), MWL4(1026).

Terence (Publius Terentius Afer)
Andria. MP12(I-212), MPCE(I-68), MP8(I-169), MP6(I-102), MPDr(31), MPv3(17), MP2(I-31), MWL2(31).
Brothers, The. MP12(II-681), MPCE(I-248), MP8(I-528), MP6(I-347), MPDr(112), MP3(I-138), MWL3(138).
Eunich, The. MP12(IV-1891), MPCE(II-670), MP8(III-1485), MP6(II-940), MPDr(256), MPv4(152), MP2(I-302), MWL2(302).
*Phormio. MP12(VIII-4673), MPCE(III-1736), MP8(V-3645), MP6(IV-2349), MPDr(630), MPv3(413), MP2(II-827), MWL2(827).

Self-Tormentor, The. MP12(X-5902), MPCE(IV-2037),
MP8(VII-4701), MP6(V-2815), MPDr(758), MP3(II-956),
MWL3(956).
Teresa of Ávila, Saint
Interior Castle, The. RCa(I-561).
Life of St. Teresa of Ávila, The. RCh(I-392).
Way of Perfection, The. RCa(I-555).
Terkel, Studs
Hard Times. SCL12(V-3267), A71(112).
Working. SCL12(XII-8398), A76(370).
Terra, Helmut de
Humboldt. SCL12(V-3565), SCL7(III-2137), A55(128).
Terrill, Ross
Future of China After Mao, The. Different analyses on this title appear
in: LA79(I-240), HWor(III-1267).
Tertullian
Apology of Tertullian, The. Different analyses on this title appear in:
RCh(I-39), RCa(I-41).
Treatises on Marriage. RCa(I-54).
Tertz, Abram
Makepeace Experiment, The. SCL12(VII-4653), SCL7(IV-2831),
A66(161).
Voice from the Chorus, A. LA77(II-892).
Terzani, Tiziano
Giai Phong!: The Fall and Liberation of Saigon. HWor(III-1246).
Thackeray, William Makepeace
Barry Lyndon. MP12(I-443), MPCE(I-156), MP8(I-345),
MP6(I-226), MPEng(42), MPv3(48), MP2(I-78), MWL2(78).
Henry Esmond. MP12(V-2550), MPCE(II-935), MP8(III-1982),
MP6(III-1259), MPEng(292), MP1(I-361), MWL1(361).
Newcomes, The. MP12(VII-4185), MPCE(III-1561),
MP8(V-3261), MP6(IV-2092), MPEng(567), MP1(II-650),
MWL1(650).
Pendennis. MP12(VIII-4575), MPCE(III-1705), MP8(V-3563),
MP6(IV-2291), MPEng(645), MP1(II-726), MWL1(726).
Vanity Fair. MP12(XII-6875), MPCE(IV-2404),
MP8(VIII-5445), MP6(VI-3287), MPEng(906), MP1(II-1056),
MWL1(1056).
Virginians, The. MP12(XII-6956), MPCE(IV-2437),
MP8(VIII-5506), MP6(VI-3330), MPEng(927), MP1(II-1074),
MWL1(1074).
Thant, U
View from the UN. LA79(II-809).
Tharp, Louise Hall
Three Saints and a Sinner. SCL12(XI-7607), SCL7(VII-4634),

Thomas, Emory M.
   Confederate Nation: 1861-1865, The.   LA80(I-156).
Thomas, Hugh
   Spanish Civil War, The.   SCL12(XI-7157),   SCL7(VI-4391),
   A62(282),   BMA(522). A different analysis on this title appears in:
   HEur(III-1447).
   Suez.   SCL12(XI-7318),   SCL7(VII-4482),   A68(315). A different
   analysis on this title appears in: HEur(III-1592).
Thomas, John I.
   Liberator, The.   SCL12(VII-4294),   SCL7(IV-2631),   A64(157).
Thomas, Lewis
   Lives of a Cell, The.   SCL12(VII-4431),   A75(179).
   Medusa and the Snail: More Notes of a Biology Watcher, The.
   LA80(II-533).
Thomas, Norman
   Ask at the Unicorn.   SCL12(I-407),   SCL7(I-232),   A64(10).
Thomas à Kempis
   Imitation of Christ, The.   MP12(V-2845),   MP8(IV-2215),
   MP6(III-1421),   MPNf(161),   MP3(I-501),   MWL3(501). Different
   analyses on this title appear in: RCh(I-308),   RCa(I-491).
Thompson, Daniel Pierce
   Green Mountain Boys, The.   MP12(IV-2389),   MPCE(II-871),
   MP8(III-1858),   MP6(II-1168),   MPAm(240),   MPv4(190),
   MP2(I-385),   MWL2(385).
Thompson, E. A.
   Visigoths in the Time of Ulfila, The.   HAnc(II-902).
Thompson, E. P.
   William Morris: Romantic to Revolutionary.   LA78(II-913).
Thompson, Francis
   Hound of Heaven, The.   RCa(II-709).
   *Poetry of Thompson, The.   MP12(IX-5177),   MP8(VI-4123),
   MP4(II-974),   MWL4(974).
Thompson, James M.
   Napoleon Bonaparte.   HEur(II-592).
   Robespierre and the French Revolution.   HEur(I-531).
Thompson, James Westfall
   Economic and Social History of the Middle Ages (300-1300), An.
   HAnc(III-1423).
   Feudal Germany.   HAnc(III-1367).
   Wars of Religion in France, 1559-1576, The.   HEur(I-164).
Thompson, J. Eric
   Maya Hieroglyphic Writing: An Introduction.   HAmer(I-7).
Thompson, Leonard *and* Monica Wilson, *eds.*
   Oxford History of South Africa, The.   HWor(I-89).
Thompson, Robert Luther

Lanterns and Lances. SCL12(VI-4097), SCL7(IV-2496), A62(178).
*My Life and Hard Times. MP12(VII-4108), MP8(V-3201),
MP6(IV-2048), MPNf(206), MP3(II-678), MWL3(678).
Years with Ross, The. SCL12(XII-8467), SCL7(VII-5177),
A60(295).
Thurian, Max
Marriage and Celibacy. HAnc(III-1260).
Tiedt, Sidney W.
Role of the Federal Government in Education, The. HAmer(III-1729).
Tierney, Kevin
Darrow: A Biography. LA80(I-188).
Tillich, Paul
Courage to Be, The. Ph(II-1146).
Eternal Now, The. SCL12(IV-2326), SCL7(II-1389), A64(72).
Systematic Theology. Different analyses on this title appear in:
Ph(II-1138), RCh(II-1135).
Tillotson, Geoffrey
View of Victorian Literature, A. LA79(II-814).
Tindal, Matthew
Christianity as Old as the Creation. RCh(II-569).
Tindall, George Brown
Emergence of the New South, 1913-1945, The. SCL12(IV-2209),
SCL7(II-1320), A68(94).
Tiptree, James, Jr.
Short Fiction of James Tiptree, Jr., The. SF(IV-1999).
Tobias, Fritz
Reichstag Fire: Legend and Truth, The. HEur(III-1380).
Tocqueville, Alexis de
Democracy in America. MP12(III-1443), MP8(II-1116),
MP4(I-211), MWL4(211).
Old Regime and the Revolution, The. Different analyses on this title
appear in: HAnc(III-1736), HWor(III-1342).
Todd, Marcus N., E. M. Walker *and* F. E. Adcock
Cambridge Ancient History, Vol. V: Athens, 478-401 B.C.
HAnc(I-244).
Toffler, Alvin
Future Shock. SCL12(IV-2825), A71(82).
Toland, John
Adolf Hitler. LA77(I-17).
Battle: The Story of the Bulge. SCL12(I-553), SCL7(I-323),
A60(22). A different analysis on this title appears in: HEur(III-1498).
But Not in Shame. SCL12(II-1002), SCL7(I-572), A62(39),
BMA(51).
Christianity Not Mysterious. RCh(II-554).
Last Hundred Days, The. HWor(II-580).

Tolkien, J. R. R.
Fellowship of the Ring, The. MP12(IV-2033), MPCE(II-734),
MP8(III-1584), MP4(I-326), MWL4(326).
Return of the King, The. MP12(X-5540), MPCE(III-1891),
MP8(VII-4417), MP4(II-1063), MWL4(1063).
Silmarillion, The. LA78(II-780).
Two Towers, The. MP12(XII-6778), MPCE(IV-2365),
MP8(VIII-5373), MP4(II-1242), MWL4(1242).
Tolles, Frederick B.
*Meeting House and Counting House: The Quaker Merchants of Colonial
Philadelphia, 1682-1763.* HAmer(I-159).
Tolstoi, Alexei
Aelita. SF(I-28).
Tolstoy, Count Leo
Anna Karénina. MP12(I-229), MPCE(I-79), MP8(I-179),
MP6(I-112), MPEur(30), MP1(I-32), MWL1(32).
Childhood, Boyhood, Youth. MP12(II-924), MP8(I-712),
MP4(I-129), MWL4(129).
Cossacks, The. MP12(II-1128), MPCE(I-403), MP8(II-884),
MP6(I-576), MPEur(159), MPv3(95), MP2(I-181), MWL2(181).
Death of Ivan Ilyich, The. MP12(III-1373), MPCE(I-504),
MP8(II-1061), MP6(II-694), MPEur(208), MP3(I-256),
MWL3(256).
Kreutzer Sonata, The. MP12(VI-3192), MPCE(II-1183),
MP8(IV-2485), MP6(III-1591), MPEur(418), MP1(I-481),
MWL1(481).
Power of Darkness, The. MP12(IX-5283), MPCE(III-1799),
MP8(VI-4214), MP6(V-2499), MPDr(655), MP3(II-841),
MWL3(841).
Resurrection. MP12(X-5531), MPCE(III-1887), MP8(VII-4411),
MP6(V-2623), MPEur(634), MP3(II-879), MWL3(879).
Tolstoy's Letters. LA79(II-754).
War and Peace. MP12(XII-7028), MPCE(IV-2463),
MP8(VIII-5561), MP6(VI-3364), MPEur(806), MP1(II-1085),
MWL1(1085).
What I Believe. RCh(II-790).
What Is Art? Ph(II-723).
Tolstoy, Ilya
Tolstoy, My Father. SCL12(XI-7699), A72(325).
Tomlinson, H. M.
Sea and the Jungle, The. MP12(X-5858), MP8(VII-4664),
MP6(V-2790), MPNf(276), MP3(II-942), MWL3(942).
Tomlinson, William W.
North Eastern Railway. HEur(II-661).
Toomer, Jean

MP8(VIII-5568),   MP6(VI-3370),   MPEng(935),   MP1(II-1092),
MWL1(1092).

Trotsky, Leon
*Revolution Betrayed: What Is the Soviet Union and Where Is It Going?,
The.*   HEur(III-1349).

Trowbridge, John Townsend
Cudjo's Cave.   MP12(III-1238),   MPCE(I-455),   MP8(II-959),
MP6(II-636),   MPAm(115),   MPv4(94),   MP2(205),   MWL2(205).

Troyat, Henri
Divided Soul: The Life of Gogol.   SCL12(III-1972),   A74(89).
Pushkin.   SCL12(IX-6138),   A72(262).
Tolstoy.   SCL12(XI-7695),   SCL7(VII-4706),   A69(312).

Troyes, Chrétien de
Cligés.   MP12(II-989),   MPCE(I-362),   MP8(II-766),
MP6(I-506),   MPPo(46),   MP3(I-195),   MWL3(195).

True, Alfred Charles
History of Agricultural Education in the United States, A.
HAmer(II-976).

True, Webster Prentiss
Smithsonian: America's Treasure House, The.   HAmer(II-835).

Truman, Harry S
Memoirs by Harry S Truman, Vol. I: Years of Decision.
SCL12(VII-4880),   SCL7(V-2967),   A55(156). A different analysis on
this title appears in: HAmer(III-1762).
Memoirs by Harry S Truman, Vol. II: Years of Trial and Hope.
SCL12(VII-4884),   SCL7(V-2971),   A57(173). A different analysis on
this title appears in: HAmer(III-1785).

Truman, Margaret
Harry S. Truman.   SCL12(V-3288),   A74(183).

Trumpener, Ulrich
Germany and the Ottoman Empire, 1914-1918.   HWor(I-117).

Tryon, Thomas
Other, The.   SCL12(VIII-5659),   A72(236).

Tryon, W. S.
Parnassus Corner.   SCL12(IX-5739),   SCL7(V-3513),   A64(208).

Tsao Hsueh-chin
Dream of the Red Chamber.   MP12(III-1648),   MPCE(I-605),
MP8(II-1281),   MP6(II-826),   MPEur(263),   MP3(I-302),
MWL3(302). A different analysis on this title appears in:
SCL12(III-2069),   SCL7(II-1243),   A59(65),   BMA(138).

Tseng Tzu *or* Tzu Ssu, Attributed to
Great Learning, The.   Ph(I-212).

Tsuji, Colonel Masanobe
Singapore: The Japanese Version.   SCL12(X-6985),   SCL7(VI-4301),
A62(279).

Tucci, Niccoló
   Before My Time.   SCL12(I-609),   SCL7(I-352),   A63(9).
Tuchman, Barbara W.
   Distant Mirror: The Calamitous 14th Century, A.   LA79(I-151).
   Guns of August, The.   SCL12(V-3202),   SCL7(III-1896),   A63(78).
   Proud Tower, The.   SCL12(IX-6098),   SCL7(VI-3724),   A66(246). A
   different analysis on this title appears in: HEur(III-1194).
   Stilwell and the American Experience in China, 1911-45.
   SCL12(XI-7230),   A72(301).
Tucker, Glenn
   Tecumseh, Vision of Glory.   HAmer(I-500).
   Chickamauga.   SCL12(II-1212),   SCLs(68).
   High Tide at Gettysburg.   SCL12(V-3428),   SCL7(III-2040),
   A59(117).
Tucker, Robert C.
   Soviet Political Mind: Studies in Stalinism and Post-Stalin Change, The.
   HEur(III-1332).
Tucker, Wilson
   Long Loud Silence, The.   SF(III-1238).
   Year of the Quiet Sun, The.   SF(V-2520).
Tugwell, Rexford Guy
   Brains Trust, The.   HAmer(III-1612).
Tuleja, Thaddeus V.
   Statesmen and Admirals: Quest for a Far Eastern Naval Policy.
   HWor(I-371).
Turgenev, Ivan
   *Fathers and Sons.   MP12(IV-2015),   MPCE(II-727),
   MP8(III-1571),   MP6(II-997),   MPEur(296),   MP1(I-273),
   MWL1(273).
   *House of Gentlefolk, A.   MP12(V-2724),   MPCE(II-994),
   MP8(III-2124),   MP6(III-1355),   MPEur(373),   MPv3(233),
   MP2(I-465),   MWL2(465).
   *Month in the Country, A.   MP12(VII-4052),   MPCE(III-1502),
   MP8(V-3161),   MP6(IV-2022),   MPDr(556),   MPv4(353),
   MP2(II-705),   MWL2(705).
   *Smoke.   MP12(X-6105),   MPCE(IV-2101),   MP8(VII-4867),
   MP6(V-2908),   MPEur(691),   MP1(II-897),   MWL1(897).
   *Virgin Soil.   MP12(XII-6944),   MPCE(IV-2431),
   MP8(VIII-5497),   MP6(VI-3323),   MPEur(794),   MP1(II-1069),
   MWL1(1069).
Turgot, Anne Robert Jacques
   Two Discourses on Universal History.   RCa(II-628).
Turley, William S.
   "Vietnam Since Reunification," in *Problems of Communism.*
   HWor(III-1248).

Turnbull, Andrew
    Scott Fitzgerald. SCL12(X-6659), SCL7(VI-4092), A63(234).
Turner, Frederick Jackson
    Frontier in American History, The. MP12(IV-2182), MP8(III-1700),
    MP4(I-366), MWL4(366).
Turner, J. W. Cecil
    Introduction to the Study of Roman Law. HAnc(I-494).
Tutuola, Amos
    Brave African Huntress, The. SCL12(II-890), SCLs(46).
    Palm-Wine Drinkard, The. MP12(VIII-4469), MP8(V-3483),
    MP4(II-668), MWL4(668).
Twain, Mark
    *Connecticut Yankee in King Arthur's Court, A. MP12(II-1083),
    MPCE(I-389), MP8(II-847), MP6(I-557), MPAm(100),
    MP1(I-154), MWL1(154). A different analysis on this title appears in:
    SF(I-428).
    *Huckleberry Finn. MP12(V-2755), MPCE(II-1012),
    MP8(III-2145), MP6(III-1371), MPAm(282), MP1(I-387),
    MWL1(387).
    Letters from the Earth. SCL12(VI-4209), SCL7(IV-2576), A63(120).
    *Life on the Mississippi. MP12(VI-3412), MPCE(II-1244),
    MP8(IV-2673), MP6(III-1687), MPNf(189), MP1(I-504),
    MWL1(504).
    *Prince and the Pauper, The. MP12(IX-5317), MPCE(III-1808),
    MP8(VI-4243), MP6(V-2521), MPAm(506), MPv3(427),
    MP2(II-854), MWL2(854).
    *Roughing It. MP12(X-5722), MPCE(III-1972), MP8(VII-4553),
    MP6(V-2721), MPNf(269), MP1(II-858), MWL1(858).
    *Tom Sawyer. MP12(XI-6604), MPCE(IV-2288),
    MP8(VIII-5250), MP6(VI-3161), MPAm(655), MP1(II-1003),
    MWL1(1003).
Twain, Mark *and* Charles Dudley Warner
    *Gilded Age, The. MP12(IV-2263), MPCE(II-822),
    MP8(III-1759), MP6(II-1107), MPAm(204), MPv3(185),
    MP2(I-368), MWL2(368).
Tyler-Whittle, Michael
    Last Kaiser, The. LA78(II-509).
Tyrrell, George
    Much Abused Letter, A. RCh(II-844).

Udall, Nicholas
    Ralph Roister Doister. MP12(IX-5418), MPCE(III-1846),
    MP8(VI-4322), MP6(V-2569), MPDr(674), MPv3(438),
    MP2(II-876), MWL2(876).
Ulam, Adam Bruno

United States Department of State
  *United States Relations with China: With Special Reference to the Period,
  1944-1949.*   HAmer(III-1766).
University of California Academic Senate (Select Committee on Education)
  Education at Berkeley.   HAmer(II-1914).
Unknown
  Abraham and Isaac.   MP12(I-8),   MPCE(I-4),   MP8(I-7),
  MP6(I-5),   MPDr(4),   MP3(I-1),   MWL3(1).
  Arabian Nights' Entertainments, The (Selections).   MP12(I-281),
  MPCE(I-100),   MP8(I-219),   MP6(I-144),   MPEur(32),
  MPv4(19),   MP2(I-48),   MWL2(48).
  *Aucassin and Nicolette.   MP12(I-356),   MPCE(I-132),
  MP8(I-273),   MP6(I-186),   MPEur(54),   MP1(I-48),   MWL1(48).
  *Beowulf.   MP12(I-500),   MPCE(I-181),   MP8(I-388),
  MP6(I-258),   MPPo(17),   MP1(I-68),   MWL1(68).
  *Bevis of Hampton.   MP12(I-516),   MPCE(I-189),   MP8(I-398),
  MP6(I-267),   MPPo(19),   MP3(I-105),   MWL3(105).
  Cadmus.   MP12(II-725),   MPCE(I-266),   MP8(I-562),
  MP6(I-371),   MPEur(98),   MP1(I-96),   MWL1(96).
  Circle of Chalk, The.   MP12(II-973),   MPCE(I-354),   MP8(II-755),
  MP6(I-497),   MPDr(155),   MP3(I-193),   MWL3(193).
  Cloud of Unknowing, The.   Different analyses on this title appear in:
  RCh(I-288),   RCa(I-466).
  Cupid and Psyche.   MP12(III-1245),   MPCE(I-456),   MP8(II-965),
  MP6(II-639),   MPEur(187),   MP1(I-180),   MWL1(180).
  Didache or *The Teaching of the Twelve Apostles, The.*   Different
  analyses on this title appear in: RCh(I-23),   RCa(I-1.)
  *Epic of Gilgamesh, The.   MP12(III-1796),   MPCE(II-653),
  MP8(II-1400),   MP6(II-900),   MPPo(77),   MP3(I-342),
  MWL3(342).
  Epistle to Diognetus, The.   Different analyses on this title appear in:
  RCh(I-48),   RCa(I-62).
  *Everyman.   MP12(IV-1928),   MPCE(II-690),   MP8(III-1509),
  MP6(II-961),   MPDr(264),   MPv3(161),   MP2(I-314),   MWL2(314).
  Finn Cycle, The.   MP12(IV-2071),   MPCE(II-747),   MP8(III-1612),
  MP6(II-1017),   MPEng(210),   MP3(I-392),   MWL3(392).
  Grettir the Strong.   MP12(IV-2396),   MPCE(II-873),
  MP8(III-1864),   MP6(II-1172),   MPEur(338),   MP1(I-335),
  MWL1(335).
  *Guy of Warwick.   MP12(IV-2433),   MPCE(II-888),
  MP8(III-1892),   MP6(III-1191),   MPPo(115),   MP3(I-439),
  MWL3(439).
  *Havelok the Dane.   MP12(V-2492),   MPCE(II-908),
  MP8(III-1941),   MP6(III-1228),   MPPo(125),   MPv3(205),
  MP2(I-410),   MWL2(410).

MP8(VII-4835), MP6(V-2882), MPPo(340), MPv3(487), MP2(II-969), MWL2(969).

Song of Roland, The. MP12(XI-6150), MPCE(IV-2118), MP8(VII-4904), MP6(V-2929), MPEur(703), MP1(II-907), MWL1(907).

Star of Seville, The. MP12(XI-6242), MPCE(IV-2152), MP8(VII-4975), MP6(VI-2968), MPDr(804), MP3(II-1018), MWL3(1018).

Story of Burnt Njal, The. MP12(XI-6276), MPCE(IV-2166), MP8(VII-5000), MP6(VI-2987), MPEur(723), MPv3(501), MP2(II-997), MWL2(997).

Tao Te Ching. Ph(I-207).

Theologica Germanica. RCh(I-276).

Unknown, but attributed to the Apostle Barnabas
Epistle of Barnabas, The. RCh(I-3).

Unterecker, John
Voyager: A Life of Hart Crane. SCL12(XII-8059), A70(328).

Updike, John
Bech: A Book. SCL12(I-598), A71(21).
Centaur, The. SCL12(II-1153), SCL7(I-662), A64(52).
Coup, The. LA79(I-133).
Couples. SCL12(III-1602), SCL7(II-941), A69(80).
Marry Me. LA77(II-485).
Midpoint and Other Poems. SCL12(VIII-4983), A70(203).
Month of Sundays, A. SCL12(VIII-5065), A76(234).
Museums and Women and Other Stories. SCL12(VIII-5145), A73(262).
Music School, The. SCL12(VIII-5148), SCL7(V-3136), A67(228).
Of the Farm. SCL12(VIII-5493), SCL7(V-3353), A66(206).
Pigeon Feathers. SCL12(IX-5857), SCL7(V-3577), A63(182).
Poorhouse Fair, The. MP12(IX-5244), MP8(VI-4187), MP4(II-1016), MWL4(1016), SCL12(IX-5967), SCL7(V-3653), A60(202), BMA(448). A different analysis on this title appears in: SF(IV-1714).
Problems and Other Stories. LA80(II-697).
Rabbit Redux. SCL12(IX-6211), A72(270).
Rabbit, Run. MP12(IX-5407), MP8(VI-4313), MP4(II-1042), MWL4(1042). A different analysis on this title appears in: SCL12(IX-6215), SCL7(VI-3804), A61(203), BMA(470).
Short Stories of John Updike, The. MP12(X-6014), MP8(VII-4796), MP4(II-1142), MWL4(1142).
Telephone Poles. SCL12(XI-7416), SCL7(VII-4520), A64(257).

Uris, Leon
Trinity. LA77(II-842).

Urofsky, Melvin I.
Big Steel and the Wilson Administration: A Study in Business Government Relations. HAmer(III-1463).

Urquhart, Brian

Hammarskjöld. SCL12(V-3228), A74(179).
Utley, Robert M.
Custer and the Great Controversy: The Origin and Development of a Legend. HAmer(II-1096).

Vacandard, E.
Inquisition: A Critical and Historical Study of the Coercive Power of the Church, The. HAnc(III-1488).
Vailland, Roger
Fête. SCL12(IV-2549), SCL7(III-1508), A62(123).
Law, The. SCL12(VI-4168), SCL7(IV-2553), A59(141).
Vale, Eugene
Thirteenth Apostle, The. SCL12(XI-7555), SCL7(VII-4604), A60(270).
Valency, Maurice
In Praise of Love: An Introduction to the Love-Poetry of the Renaissance. HAnc(III-1299).
Valera, Juan
Pepita Jimenez. MP12(VIII-4595), MPCE(III-1711), MP8(V-3579), MP6(IV-2305), MPEur(584), MPv4(406), MP2(II-813), MWL2(813).
Valéry, Paul
Poetry of Valéry, The. MP12(IX-5184), MP8(VI-4130), MP4(II-981), MWL4(981).
Valmiki,
*Ramayana, The. MP12(IX-5421), MPCE(III-1847), MP8(VI-4324), MP6(V-2571), MPPo(308), MP3(II-861), MWL3(861).
Van Creveld, Martin
Hitler's Strategy 1940-1941: The Balkan Clue. HWor(I-446).
Van Der Post, Laurens
Seed and the Sower, The. SCL12(X-6738), SCL7(VI-4141), A64(231).
Van Der Waerden, B. L.
Science Awakening. HAnc(I-23).
Van Duyn, Mona
Merciful Disguises. SCL12(VII-4938), A74(269).
Van Herck, Paul
Caroline, O Caroline. SF(I-294).
Van Melsen, Andrew G.
From Atomos to Atom. HAnc(I-266).
Van Tine, Warren and Melvyn Dubofsky
John L. Lewis: A Biography. LA78(II-478).
Van Vechten, Carl
Peter Whiffle. MP12(VIII-4629), MPCE(III-1722), MP8(V-3608), MP6(IV-2327), MPAm(481), MP1(II-739), MWL1(739).
Vanbrugh, Sir John
Relapse, The. MP12(IX-5493), MPCE(III-1879), MP8(VI-4377), MP6(V-2606), MPDr(679), MPv4(444), MP2(II-887),

MWL2(887).

Vance, E.
   Reading the Song of Roland.   HAnc(III-1311).
Vance, Jack
   Dragon Masters, The.   SF(II-600).
   Dying Earth, The.   SF(II-665).
   Languages of Pao, The.   SF(III-1135).
   Last Castle, The.   SF(III-1144).
Vandenberg, Arthur H., Jr.
   Private Papers of Senator Vandenberg, The.   HEur(III-1509).
Vandiver, Frank E.
   Black Jack: The Life and Times of John J. Pershing.   LA78(I-96).
   Mighty Stonewall.   SCL12(VIII-4995),   SCL7(V-3036),   A58(161).
Vann, Gerald, O. P.
   Heart of Man, The.   RCa(II-889).
Varende, Jean de la
   Cherish the Sea.   HAnc(III-1506).
Vargas Llosa, Mario
   Captain Pantoja and the Special Service.   LA79(I-75).
   Cubs and Other Stories, The.   LA80(I-165).
   Green House, The.   SCL12(V-3144),   A70(150).
Varley, John
   Ophiuchi Hotline, The.   SF(IV-1608).
Varshavsky, Ilya
   Lavka snovidenyi.   SF(III-1165).
   Solntse zakhodit v Donomage.   SF(V-2113).
Vasiliev, A. A.
   History of the Byzantine Empire, 324-1453.   Different analyses on this
   title appear in: HAnc(II-863; II-890; II-1154; III-1438).
Vaughan, Henry
   *Poetry of Vaughan, The.   MP12(IX-5187),   MP8(VI-4133),
   MP4(II-984),   MWL4(984).
Vazov, Ivan
   Under the Yoke.   MP12(XII-6836),   MPCE(IV-2388),
   MP8(VIII-5417),   MP6(VI-3267),   MPEur(782),   MPv4(561),
   MP2(II-1086),   MWL2(1086).
Veblen, Thorsten
   Theory of the Leisure Class, The.   MP12(XI-6471),
   MP8(VIII-5152),   MP4(II-1213),   MWL4(1213).
Vega, Lope de
   Gardener's Dog, The.   MP12(IV-2203),   MPCE(II-794),
   MP8(III-1718),   MP6(II-1077),   MPDr(289),   MPv3(178),
   MP2(I-356),   MWL2(356).
   *King, the Greatest Alcalde, The.   MP12(VI-3168),   MPCE(II-1171),
   MP8(IV-2469),   MP6(III-1577),   MPDr(421),   MPv3(270),

MPCE(IV-2359),   MP8(VIII-5338),   MP6(VI-3234),   MPEur(771),
MP1(II-1031),   MWL1(1031). A different analysis on this title appears
in: SF(V-2329).
Versfeld, Marthinus
Essay on the Metaphysics of Descartes, An.   HEur(I-297).
Veuillot, Louis
Life of Our Lord Jesus Christ, The.   RCa(II-665).
Vian, Boris
Herbe Rouge, L'.   SF(II-965).
Vickery, Olga W.
Novels of William Faulkner: A Critical Interpretation, The.
HAmer(III-1575).
Vico, Giovanni Battista
New Science, The.   Different analyses on this title appear in:
Ph(I-477),   RCa(II-618).
Vidal, Gore
Best Man, The.   SCL12(I-679),   SCL7(I-386),   A61(19).
Burr: A Novel.   SCL12(II-991),   A74(44).
Julian.   SCL12(VI-3959),   SCL7(IV-2387),   A65(155).
1876.   LA77(I-256).
Vignaux, Paul
Philosophy in the Middle Ages: An Introduction.   HAnc(III-1567).
Vigny, Alfred Victor de
Cinq-Mars.   MP12(II-969),   MPCE(I-353),   MP8(II-752),
MP6(I-494),   MPEur(141),   MPv4(75),   MP2(I-153),   MWL2(153).
Poetry of Vigny, The.   MP12(IX-5191),   MP8(VI-4137),
MP4(II-987),   MWL4(987).
Villari, Pasquale
First Two Centuries of Florentine History, The.   HAnc(III-1305).
Villiers de l'Isle-Adam, Jean Marie
Eve future, L'.   SF(II-735).
Villon, François
Great Testament, The.   MP12(IV-2370),   MP8(III-1841),
MP6(II-1157),   MPPo(113),   MP3(I-426),   MWL3(426).
Lais, Le.   MP12(VI-3226),   MP8(IV-2512),   MP4(I-494),
MWL4(494).
Vincent of Lérins, Saint
Commonitory, The.   Different analyses on this title appear in:
RCh(I-153),   RCa(I-198).
Vinci, Leonardo da
Notebooks of Leonardo da Vinci, The.   MP12(VII-4255),
MP8(V-3314),   MP4(I-633),   MWL4(633).
Vinogradoff, Paul
Roman Law in Medieval Europe.   HAnc(II-1008).
Vinson, John Chalmers

Parchment Peace: The United States Senate and the Washington Conference, 1921-1922, The. HAmer(III-1533).
Vittorini, Elio
Dark and the Light, The. SCL12(III-1703), SCL7(II-1005), A62(90).
Vivante, Arturo
Run to the Waterfall. LA80(II-736).
Vives, Juan Luis
On Education. RCa(I-519).
Voegelin, Eric
Order and History, Vol. III: Plato and Aristotle. HAnc(I-345).
Vogt, A. E. van
Slan. SF(V-2096).
Voyage of the Space Beagle, The. SF(V-2378).
Weapon Shops of Isher, The. SF(V-2442).
World of Null-A, The. SF(V-2501).
Voltaire, François Marie Arouet de
*Candide. MP12(II-759), MPCE(I-278), MP8(I-590), MP6(I-392), MPEur(103), MP1(I-107), MWL1(107).
*Zadig. MP12(XII-7314), MPCE(IV-2572), MP8(VIII-5778), MP6(VI-3518), MPEur(837), MP3(II-1165), MWL3(1165).
*Zaïre. MP12(XII-7318), MPCE(IV-2574), MP8(VIII-5781), MP6(VI-3521), MPDr(955), MP3(II-1168), MWL3(1168).
Von Abele, Rudolph
Cage for Loulou, A. LA79(I-70).
Von Fritz, Kurt
"Reorganization of the Roman Government in 366 B.C. and the So-called Licinio-Sextian Laws, The," in Historia. HAnc(I-394).
Von Hagen, Victor W.
Roads That Led to Rome, The. HAnc(I-376).
Roman Roads. HAnc(I-376).
Von Hefele, Rev. Dr.
Life of Cardinal Ximenes. HAnc(III-1731).
Von Hügel, Friedrich
Reality of God and Religion and Agnosticism, The. HAnc(I-380).
Von Laue, Theodore H.
Sergei Witte and the Industrialization of Russia. HEur(II-1064).
Von Rad, Gerhard
"Form-Critical Problem of the Hexateuch, The," (1938), reprinted in The Problem of the Hexateuch and Other Essays. HAnc(I-99).
Von Simson, Otto
Gothic Cathedral: Origins of Gothic Architecture and the Medieval Concept of Order, The. HAnc(III-1419).

Wakoski, Diane
  Discrepancies and Apparitions.   SCL12(III-1965),   SCL7(II-1183),
  A66(72).
  Inside the Blood Factory.   SCL12(VI-3744),   SCL7(IV-2250),
  A69(169).
  Man Who Shook Hands, The.   LA79(I-414).
Walcott, Derek
  Star-Apple Kingdom, The.   LA80(II-777).
Walker, Alice
  Meridian.   LA77(II-501).
Walker, D. P.
  Spiritual and Demonic Magic from Ficino to Campanella.
  HAnc(III-1726).
Walker, E. M., Marcus N. Todd *and* F. E. Adcock.
  The Cambridge Ancient History, Vol. V: Athens, 478-401 B.C.
  HAnc(I-244).
Walker, Joseph
  River Niger, The.   SCL12(X-6431),   A74(336).
Wallace, Lewis (Lew)
  Ben-Hur: A Tale of the Christ.   MP12(I-491),   MPCE(I-175),
  MP8(I-382),   MP6(I-254),   MPAm(51),   MP1(I-66),   MWL1(66).
Wallace, Lillian Parker
  Papacy and European Diplomacy, 1869-1878, The.   HEur(II-972).
Wallace, R. *and the* Editors of Time-Life Books
  World of Leonardo (1452-1519), The.   HAnc(III-1764).
Wallace, Willard M.
  Sir Walter Raleigh.   HAmer(I-50).
Wallace-Hadrill, D. S.
  Eusebius of Caesarea.   HAnc(II-843).
Wallace-Hadrill, J. M.
  Barbarian West, 400-1000, The.   HAnc(II-1138).
Wallant, Edward Lewis
  Children at the Gate, The.   SCL12(II-1225),   SCL7(I-712),   A65(37).
  Tenants of Moonbloom, The.   MP12(XI-6445),   MP8(VIII-5132),
  MP4(II-1205),   MWL4(1205),   SCL12(XI-7467),   SCL7(VII-4551),
  A64(261).
Waller, Edmund
  *Poetry of Waller, The.   MP12(IX-5194),   MP8(VI-4140),
  MP4(II-989),   MWL4(989).
Waller, George
  Kidnap.   SCL12(VI-3991),   SCL7(IV-2413),   A62(172).
Walpole, Horace
  *Castle of Otranto, The.   MP12(II-829),   MPCE(I-305),
  MP8(I-641),   MP6(I-427),   MPEng(86),   MP1(I-124),   MWL1(124).
  Letters of Walpole, The.   MP12(VI-3368),   MP8(IV-2633),

MP6(III-1663),   MPNf(172),   MP3(I-563),   MWL3(563).
Fortitude.   MP12(IV-2124),   MPCE(II-764),   MP8(III-1655),
MP6(II-1037),   MPEng(222),   MP1(I-286),   MWL1(286).
Fortress, The.   MP12(IV-2128),   MPCE(II-766),   MP8(III-1657),
MP6(II-1039),   MPEng(224),   MP1(I-288),   MWL1(288).
Judith Paris.   MP12(VI-3084),   MPCE(II-1136),   MP8(IV-2405),
MP6(III-1530),   MPEng(394),   MP1(I-457),   MWL1(457).
Rogue Herries.   MP12(X-5661),   MPCE(III-1945),
MP8(VII-4505),   MP6(V-2684),   MPEng(745),   MP1(II-844),
MWL1(844).
Vanessa.   MP12(XII-6871),   MPCE(IV-2402),   MP8(VIII-5442),
MP6(VI-3285),   MPEng(903),   MP1(II-1054),   MWL1(1054).
Walters, F. P.
    History of the League of Nations, A.   HEur(III-1292).
Walters, Raymond, Jr.
    Albert Gallatin.   SCL12(I-180),   SCL7(I-122),   A58(10).
Walton, Izaak
    Compleat Angler, The.   MP12(II-1044),   MP8(II-812),
    MP6(I-532),   MPNf(55),   MP3(I-206),   MWL3(206).
    Lives.   MP12(VI-3461),   MP8(IV-2709),   MP4(I-555),
    MWL4(555).
Walworth, Arthur C.
    Black Ships Off Japan: The Story of Commander Perry's Expedition.
    HAmer(II-886).
    Woodrow Wilson.   SCL12(XII-8388),   SCL7(VII-5139),   A59(280).
Wambaugh, Joseph
    Onion Field, The.   SCL12(VIII-5610),   A74(289).
Ward, A. W.
    "Outbreak of the Thirty Years' War, The," in *The Cambridge Modern
    History.*   HEur(I-253).
    "Peace of Utrecht and the Supplementary Pacifications, The," in *The
    Cambridge Modern History.*   HEur(I-402).
    "Peace of Westphalia, The," in *The Cambridge Modern History.*
    HEur(I-311).
    "Protestant Collapse, 1620-1630, The," in *The Cambridge Modern
    History.*   HEur(I-272).
Ward, Aileen
    John Keats.   SCL12(VI-3889),   SCL7(IV-2348),   A64(143).
Ward, Barbara
    Rich Nations and the Poor Nations, The.   SCL12(X-6403),
    SCL7(VI-3922),   A63(218).
Ward, Barbara *and* René Dubos
    Only One Earth: The Care and Maintenance of a Small Planet.
    HWor(II-1074).
Ward, Harry M.

United Colonies of New England, 1643-1690, The. HAmer(I-111).
Wardman, H. W.
Ernest Renan: A Critical Biography. HEur(II-895).
Warfel, Harry R.
Noah Webster: Schoolmaster to America. HAmer(I-638).
Warfield, Benjamin
Plan of Salvation, The. RCh(II-890).
Warner, Charles Dudley and Mark Twain
*Gilded Age, The. MP12(IV-2263), MPCE(II-822),
MP8(III-1759), MP6(II-1107), MPAm(204), MPv3(185),
MP2(I-368), MWL2(368).
Warner, Oliver
Battle of the Nile, The. HEur(I-540).
Victory. SCL12(XII-7989), SCL7(VII-4887), A59(260),
BMA(577).
Warner, Sylvia Townsend
Flint Anchor, The. SCL12(IV-2679), SCL7(III-1587), A54(77).
Winter in the Air. SCL12(XII-8324), SCL7(VII-5098), A57(284).
Warren, Charles
"New Light on the History of the Federal Judiciary Act of 1789," in
Harvard Law Review. HAmer(I-348).
Supreme Court in United States History, Vol. I: 1789-1821, The.
HAmer(I-441).
Warren, Earl
Memoirs of Earl Warren, The. LA78(II-567).
Warren, Earl, J. Lee Rankin, and others
Report of the President's Commission on the Assassination of President
John F. Kennedy. SCL12(IX-6354), SCL7(VI-3888), A65(246).
Warren, Harris G.
Herbert Hoover and the Great Depression. HAmer(III-1596).
Warren, Robert Penn
*All the King's Men. MP12(I-133), MPCE(I-46), MP8(I-104),
MP6(I-65), MPAm(15), MPv3(8), MP2(I-15), MWL2(15).
Audubon: A Vision. SCL12(I-445), A70(39).
*Band of Angels. SCL12(I-546), SCL7(I-317), A55(17).
*Cave, The. SCL12(II-1145), SCL7(I-658), A60(35).
Flood. SCL12(IV-2686), SCL7(III-1590), A65(99).
Incarnations. SCL12(VI-3694), SCL7(III-2208), A69(167).
Meet Me in the Green Glen. SCL12(VII-4867), A72(219).
*Night Rider. MP12(VII-4218), MP8(V-3286), MP4(I-628),
MWL4(628).
Now and Then: Poems 1976-1978. LA79(II-501).
Poetry of Warren, The. MP12(IX-5197), MP8(VI-4143),
MP4(II-992), MWL4(992).
Promises. SCL12(IX-6087), SCL7(VI-3713), A58(198),

BMA(455).

Segregation. SCL12(X-6753), SCL7(VI-4156), A57(236).

Selected Poems: New and Old 1923-1966. SCL12(X-6817), SCL7(VI-4192), A67(298).

Selected Poems, 1923-1975. LA78(II-753).

*World Enough and Time. MP12(XII-7262), MPCE(IV-2546), MP8(VIII-5740), MP6(VI-3486), MPAm(723), MPv4(600), MP2(II-1160), MWL2(1160).

You, Emperors, and Others. SCL12(XII-8483), SCL7(VII-5189), A61(313).

Warshow, Robert
Immediate Experience: Movies, Comics, Theatre, and Other Aspects of Popular Culture, The. HAmer(III-1505).

Warth, Robert
Joseph Stalin. HEur(III-1569).

Washburn, Mark
Mars at Last. HWor(III-1299).

Washburn, Wilcomb E.
Governor and the Rebel, The. HAmer(I-154).

Wasserman, Dale
Man of La Mancha. SCL12(VII-4709), SCL7(IV-2860), A67(209).

Wassermann, Jacob
World's Illusion, The. MP12(XII-7271), MPCE(IV-2551), MP8(VIII-5746), MP6(VI-3491), MPEur(834), MP1(II-1133), MWL1(1133).

Wast, Hugo
Black Valley. MP12(I-562), MPCE(I-205), MP8(I-434), MP6(I-289), MPAm(63), MP3(I-113), MWL3(113).

Stone Desert. MP12(XI-6259), MPCE(IV-2162), MP8(VII-4985), MP6(VI-2977), MPAm(607), MPv4(495), MP2(II-994), MWL2(994).

Waterhouse, Keith
Billy Liar. SCL12(II-713), SCL7(I-402), A61(24).

Watkins, Oscar D.
History of Penance, A. HAnc(II-764).

Watkins, Vernon
Affinities. SCL12(I-80), SCL7(I-62), A64(1).

Watson, Ian
Embedding, The. SF(II-712).

Watson, J. Steven
Reign of George III, 1760-1815, The. HEur(II-554).

Watson, James D.
Double Helix, The. SCL12(III-2039), SCL7(II-1222), A69(98). A different analysis on this title appears in: HEur(III-1575).

Molecular Biology of the Gene. HEur(III-1576).

Watson, Robert
> *Paper Horse, A.* SCL12(IX-5714), SCL7(V-3504), A63(168).
> *Selected Poems.* SCL12(X-6814), A75(287).

Watt, Richard M.
> *Kings Depart, The. The Tragedy of Germany: Versailles and the German Revolution.* HEur(III-1288).

Watt, W. Montgomery
> *History of Islamic Spain, A.* HAnc(II-1191).

Waugh, Evelyn
> **Brideshead Revisited.* MP12(II-645), MPCE(I-238), MP8(I-498), MP6(I-333), MPEng(68), MP1(I-83), MWL1(83).
> **Decline and Fall.* MP12(III-1404), MPCE(I-517), MP8(II-1085), MP6(II-711), MPEng(145), MPv4(117), MP2(I-235), MWL2(235).
> *Diaries of Evelyn Waugh, The.* LA78(I-258).
> *Edmund Campion.* MP12(III-1705), MPCE(I-624), MP8(II-1326), MP6(II-857), MPNf(93), MP1(I-237), MWL1(237). A different analysis on this title appears in: RCa(II-838).
> *End of the Battle, The.* SCL12(IV-2244), SCL7(II-1351), A62(115), BMA(167).
> **Handful of Dust, A.* MP12(V-2464), MPCE(II-900), MP8(III-1916), MP6(III-1208), MPEng(263), MP1(I-350), MWL1(350).
> *Little Learning, A.* SCL12(VII-4421), SCL7(IV-2714), A65(183).
> *Monsignor Ronald Knox.* SCL12(VIII-5061), SCL7(V-3073), A61(181).
> *Officers and Gentlemen.* SCL12(VIII-5503), SCL7(V-3363), A55(193), BMA(405).
> **Ordeal of Gilbert Pinfold, The.* MP12(VIII-4387), MP8(V-3418), MP4(II-657), MWL4(657).
> **Vile Bodies.* MP12(XII-6918), MPCE(IV-2421), MP8(VIII-5478), MP6(VI-3309), MPEng(921), MPv4(570), MP2(II-1103), MWL2(1103).

Waugh, W. T.
> *"Germany: Charles IV,"* in *Vol. VII* of *The Cambridge Medieval History.* HAnc(III-1636).
> *"Germany: Lewis the Bavarian,"* in *Vol. III* of *The Cambridge Medieval History.* HAnc(III-1622).

Waxman, Meyer
> *History of Jewish Literature, A.* HAnc(III-1335).

Weaver, Warren *and* Claude E. Shannon
> *Mathematical Theory of Communication, The.* HWor(I-5).

Webb, Mary
> *Precious Bane.* MP12(IX-5296), MPCE(III-1803), MP8(VI-4225), MP6(V-2508), MPEng(692), MP1(II-778),

A65(45).

King's War: 1641-1647, The.   SCL12(VI-4039),   SCL7(IV-2448),
A60(124),   BMA(291).

Life of Cromwell, The.   HEur(I-333).

Thirty Years War, The.   Different analyses on this title appear in:
HEur(I-252; I-271; I-291; I-310).

Weesner, Theodore
  Car Thief, The.   SCL12(II-1088),   A73(69).

Weidman, Jerome
  Enemy Camp, The.   SCL12(IV-2264),   SCL7(II-1361),
  A59(71).

Weinbaum, Stanley G.
  Black Flame, The.   SF(I-238).
  Martian Odyssey and Other Science Fiction Tales, A.   SF(III-1353).

Weinberg, Gerhard L.
  *Foreign Policy of Hitler's Germany: Diplomatic Revolution in Europe,
  1933-1936, The.*   Different analyses on this title appear in: HWor(I-346;
  I-352).

Weingartner, Charles *and* Neil Postman
  Teaching as a Subversive Activity.   SCL12(XI-7405),   A70(303).

Weingartner, James J.
  Crossroads of Death: The Story of the Malmédy Massacre and Trial.
  LA80(I-162).

Weinstein, Allen
  Perjury: The Hiss-Chambers Case.   LA79(II-540).

Weintraub, Stanley
  Beardsley.   SCL12(I-566),   SCL7(I-333),   A68(22).
  *London Yankees: Portraits of American Writers and Artists in England,
  1894-1914, The.*   LA80(II-508).

Weisband, Edward *and* Thomas M. Franck
  Resignation in Protest.   SCL12(IX-6371),   A76(265).

Weisberger, Bernard A.
  *They Gathered at the River: The Story of the Great Revivalists and Their
  Impact upon Religion in America.*   HAmer(II-1176).

Weiss, Jan
  Dům o tisíci patrech.   SF(II-644).

Weiss, Peter
  *Persecution and Assassination of Jean-Paul Marat, The.
  SCL12(IX-5818),   SCLs(222).

Weiss, Theodore
  Views & Spectacles: New and Selected Shorter Poems.
  LA80(II-846).

Welch, Adam C.
  Post-Exilic Judaism.   HAnc(I-190).

Welch, James

Winter in the Blood. SCL12(XII-8327), A75(364).
Welles, Orson, Pauline Kael *and* Herman J. Mankiewicz
    Citizen Kane Book, The. SCL12(II-1283), A72(59).
Wells, H. G.
    First Men in the Moon, The. SF(II-782).
    Food of the Gods and How It Came to Earth, The. SF(II-807).
    History of Mr. Polly, The. MP12(V-2640), MPCE(II-967),
    MP8(III-2054), MP6(III-1310), MPEng(310), MPv4(225),
    MP2(I-454), MWL2(454).
    *Invisible Man, The. MP12(V-2918), MPCE(II-1070),
    MP8(IV-2275), MP6(III-1451), MPEng(349), MP1(I-428),
    MWL1(428). A different analysis on this title appears in: SF(III-1057).
    Island of Doctor Moreau, The. SF(III-1079).
    Kipps. MP12(VI-3182), MPCE(II-1178), MP8(IV-2478),
    MP6(III-1585), MPEng(414), MPv4(267), MP2(I-540),
    MWL2(540).
    Men Like Gods. SF(III-1375).
    *Mr. Britling Sees It Through. MP12(VII-3949), MPCE(III-1455),
    MP8(V-3086), MP6(IV-1966), MPEng(516), MP1(II-600),
    MWL1(600).
    Modern Utopia, A. SF(III-1429).
    Shape of Things to Come, The. SF(IV-1902).
    Short Fiction of H. G. Wells, The. SF(IV-1967).
    *Time Machine, The. MP12(XI-6542), MPCE(IV-2263),
    MP8(VIII-5202), MP6(VI-3123), MPEng(844), MP1(II-986),
    MWL1(986). A different analysis on this title appears in: SF(V-2287).
    Tono-Bungay. MP12(XI-6613), MPCE(IV-2293),
    MP8(VIII-5256), MP6(VI-3166), MPEng(867), MP1(II-1006),
    MWL1(1006).
    War in the Air, The. SF(V-2407).
    *War of the Worlds, The. MP12(XII-7035), MPCE(IV-2466),
    MP8(VIII-5566), MP6(VI-3368), MPEng(933), MP1(II-1090),
    MWL1(1090). A different analysis on this title apears in: SF(V-2416).
    When the Sleeper Wakes. SF(V-2459).
Welter, Rush
    Popular Education and Democratic Thought in America.
    HAmer(I-579).
Weltin, E. G.
    Popes Through History, Vol. II: The Ancient Popes, The. Different
    analyses on this title appear in: HAnc(II-821; II-955).
Welty, Eudora
    Bride of the Innisfallen, The. SCL12(II-911), SCL7(I-516),
    A55(35).
    *Delta Wedding. MP12(III-1439), MPCE(I-529), MP8(II-1113),
    MP6(II-727), MPAm(142), MPv4(127), MP2(I-245),

Images of Truth. SCL12(VI-3621), SCL7(III-2165), A63(89).
Pilgrim Hawk, The. MP12(VIII-4693), MP8(VI-3662),
MP4(II-691), MWL4(691). A different analysis on this title appears in:
SCL12(IX-5865), SCL7(V-3581), A68(240).
Wesker, Arnold
Chips with Everything. MP12(II-937), MP8(I-723), MP4(I-132),
MWL4(132).
Wesley, John
Journal of John Wesley, The. RCh(II-581).
Plain Account of Christian Perfection, A. RCh(II-608).
West, Anthony
Heritage. SCL12(V-3386), SCL7(III-2014), A55(118).
West, Jessamyn
Cress Delehanty. SCL12(III-1612), SCL7(II-944), A54(43).
Life I Really Lived, The. LA80(II-491).
Woman Said Yes, The. LA77(II-928).
West, M. L.
Hesiod's Theogony. Edited with *Prolegomena and Commentary.*
HAnc(I-140).
West, Morris L.
Daughter of Silence. SCL12(III-1727), SCL7(II-1027), A62(93).
Devil's Advocate, The. SCL12(III-1920), SCL7(II-1153), A60(57).
Shoes of the Fisherman, The. SCL12(X-6923), SCL7(VI-4261),
A64(238).
West, Nathanael
Complete Works of Nathanael West, The. SCL12(III-1509),
SCL7(II-881), A58(55), BMA(103).
Miss Lonelyhearts. MP12(VII-3941), MPCE(III-1451),
MP8(V-3080), MP6(IV-1961), MPAm(407), MP3(II-664),
MWL3(664).
West, Paul
I'm Expecting to Live Quite Soon. SCL12(VI-3615), A71(122).
West, Rebecca
Birds Fall Down, The. SCL12(II-722), SCL7(I-408), A67(31).
Black Lamb and Grey Falcon. MP12(I-556), MPCE(I-204),
MP8(I-428), MP6(I-287), MPNf(42), MP1(I-75), MWL1(75).
Fountain Overflows, The. SCL12(IV-2734), SCL7(III-1632),
A57(73).
Train of Powder, A. SCL12(XI-7729), SCL7(VII-4732), A55(272).
West, T. F. *and* G. A. Campbell
DDT: And Newer Persistent Insecticides. HWor(I-427).
Westcott, Edward Noyes
David Harum. MP12(III-1331), MPCE(I-490), MP8(II-1027),
MP6(II-674), MPAm(127), MP1(I-192), MWL1(192).
Whale, J. S.

Mass Culture: The Popular Arts in America.   HAmer(III-1503).
White, E. B.
> *Essays of E. B. White.*   LA78(I-295).
> *Letters of E. B. White.*   LA77(I-413).
> *Points of My Compass, The.*   SCL12(IX-5950),   SCL7(V-3647),
> A63(194).
> *Second Tree from the Corner, The.*   SCL12(X-6718),
> SCL7(VI-4126),   A54(246).
White, George S.
> *Memoir of Samuel Slater: The Father of American Manufacturers.*
> HAmer(I-364).
White, H. J.
> *"Vulgate," in A Dictionary of the Bible.*   HAnc(II-912).
White, James
> *Dream Millennium, The.*   SF(II-614).
White, John
> *Birth and Rebirth of Pictorial Space, The.*   HAnc(III-1694).
White, John A.
> *Diplomacy of the Russo-Japanese War, The.*   HEur(III-1150).
White, Leonard D.
> *Republican Era, 1869-1901, The.*   HAmer(II-1133).
White, Leslie A.
> *Science of Culture: A Study of Man and Civilization, The.*   HAnc(I-68).
White, Lynn, Jr.
> *Medieval Technology and Social Change.*   Different analyses on this title
> appear in: HAnc(II-1101; II-1170; III-1512).
White, Patrick
> *Burnt Ones, The.*   SCL12(II-994),   SCL7(I-565),   A65(22).
> *Cockatoos, The.*   SCL12(II-1329),   A76(45).
> *Nation on Trial: America and the War of 1812, A.*   HAmer(I-509).
> *Riders in the Chariot.*   MP12(X-5590),   MP8(VII-4452),
> MP4(II-1069),   MWL4(1069). A different analysis on this title appears
> in: SCL12(X-6411),   SCL7(VI-3930),   A62(246).
> *Tree of Man, The.*   MP12(XI-6676),   MP8(VIII-5301),
> MP4(II-1232),   MWL4(1232),   SCL12(XI-7776),   SCL7(VII-4756),
> A55(278).
White, Patrick
> *Voss.*   SCL12(XII-8046),   SCL7(VII-4926),   A58(258).
White, T. H.
> *Book of Merlyn, The Unpublished Conclusion to* The Once and Future
> King, *The.*   LA78(I-126).
> **Once and Future King, The.*   MP12(VIII-4381),   MP8(V-3412),
> MP4(II-653),   MWL4(653). A different analysis on this title appears in:
> SCL12(VIII-5560),   SCL7(V-3401),   A59(183),   BMA(410).
White, Theodore H.

MP6(V-2913),   MPPo(342), MP1(II-899),   MWL1(899).
Whorton, James
    Before Silent Spring*: Pesticides and Public Health in Pre-DDT America.*
    HWor(II-944).
Whyte, Arthur James
    Evolution of Modern Italy, The.   HEur(II-778).
    Political Life and Letters of Cavour, 1848-1861, The.   Different analyses
    on this title appear in: HEur(II-841; II-872).
Whyte, William H., Jr.
    Organization Man, The.   SCL12(VIII-5649),   SCL7(V-3459),
    A58(185). A different analysis on this title appears in: HWor (I-530).
Whyte-Melville, George J.
    Digby Grand.   MP12(III-1512),   MPCE(I-545),   MP8(II-1176),
    MP6(II-757),   MPEng(157),   MPv3(123),   MP2(I-253),
    MWL2(253).
    Market Harborough.   MP12(VII-3736),   MPCE(III-1365),
    MP8(V-2931),   MP6(IV-1853),   MPEng(475),   MPv4(314),
    MP2(II-632),   MWL2(632).
Wicker, Tom
    Facing the Lions.   SCL12(IV-2402),   A74(120).
    Time to Die, A.   SCL12(XI-7653),   A76(321).
Wickham, Glynne W.
    Early English Stages, 1300-1660.   HAnc(III-1222).
Widegren, George
    Mani and Manichaeism.   HAnc(II-810).
Wiebe, Robert H.
    "Anthracite Strike of 1902: A Record of Confusion, The" in *Mississippi*
    Valley Historical Review.   HAmer(II-1332).
Wieman, Henry Nelson
    Source of Human Good, The.   RCh(II-1084).
Wiener, Philip P.
    Evolution and the Founders of Pragmatism.   HAmer(II-1365).
Wier, Allen
    Blanco.   LA80(I-83).
Wier, Dara
    Blood, Hook & Eye.   LA78(I-112).
Wieruszowski, H.
    Medieval University, The.   HAnc(III-1403).
Wiesel, Elie
    Souls on Fire.   SCL12(XI-7140),   A73(337).
Wigginton, Eliot
    Foxfire Book, The.   SCL12(IV-2754),   A73(174).
Wilbur, Richard
    *Advice to a Prophet.   SCL12(I-69),   SCL7(I-53),   A62(12).
    Mind-Reader, The.   LA77(II-505).

Poetry of Wilbur, The. MP12(IX-5203), MP8(VI-4149), MP4(II-997), MWL4(997).

Responses. LA77(II-679).

Things of This World. SCL12(XI-7546), SCL7(VII-4595), A57(266).

Walking to Sleep. SCL12(XII-8069), A70(331).

Wilde, Oscar

De Profundis. MP12(III-1334), MP8(II-1031), MP4(I-190), MWL4(190).

Importance of Being Earnest, The. MP12(V-2847), MPCE(II-1049), MP8(IV-2217), MP6(III-1423), MPDr(372), MPv3(237), MP2(I-476), MWL2(476).

Lady Windermere's Fan. MP12(VI-3216), MPCE(II-1192), MP8(IV-2505), MP6(III-1602), MPDr(434), MP1(I-488), MWL1(488).

Letters of Oscar Wilde, The. SCL12(VI-4249), SCL7(IV-2600), A63(126), BMA(319).

Picture of Dorian Gray, The. MP12(VIII-4686), MPCE(III-1742), MP8(VI-3656), MP6(IV-2357), MPEng(671), MP1(II-746), MWL1(746).

Poetry of Wilde, The. MP12(IX-5206), MP8(VI-4152), MP4(II-1000), MWL4(1000).

Wilder, Thornton

Bridge of San Luis Rey, The. MP12(II-651), MPCE(I-239), MP8(I-503), MP6(I-337), MPAm(69), MP1(I-86), MWL1(86).

Cabala, The. MP12(II-719), MPCE(I-264), MP8(I-557), MP6(I-367), MPAm(78), MP1(I-94), MWL1(94).

Eighth Day, The. SCL12(IV-2162), SCL7(II-1291), A68(89).

Heaven's My Destination. MP12(V-2528), MPCE(II-926), MP8(III-1967), MP6(III-1249), MPAm(258), MP1(I-357), MWL1(357).

Ides of March, The. MP12(V-2814), MPCE(II-1037), MP8(IV-2190), MP6(III-1406), MPAm(290), MP1(I-413), MWL1(413).

Our Town. MP12(VIII-4443), MPCE(III-1658), MP8(V-3461), MP6(IV-2226), MPDr(597), MP1(II-704), MWL1(704).

Skin of Our Teeth, The. MP12(X-6084), MPCE(IV-2092), MP8(VII-4851), MP6(V-2896), MPDr(786), MP3(II-995), MWL3(995).

Theophilus North. SCL12(XI-7520), A74(391).

Wilhelm, Kate

Killer Thing, The. SF(III-1122).

Where Late the Sweet Birds Sang. SF(V-2469).

Wilken, Robert L.

"Bishop's Maiden, The," in *The Myth of Christian Beginnings*.

HAnc(II-842).

Wilkinson, Maurice
History of the League of Sainte Union, 1576-1595, A.   HEur(I-205).

Wilkinson, Sylvia
Cale.   SCL12(II-1041),   A71(32).
Killing Frost, A.   SCL12(VI-3998),   SCLs(148).
Moss on the North Side.   SCL12(VIII-5094),   SCL7(V-3099),
A67(225).

Wilkinson, J. Harvie, III
From Brown *to* Bakke, *The Supreme Court and School Integration:*
1954-1978.   LA80(I-334).

Willcox, William B.
Portrait of a General: Sir Henry Clinton in the War of Independence.
HAmer(I-296).

Willett, Thomas D.
Floating Exchange Rates and International Monetary Reform.
HWor(III-1108).

William of Ockham
De corpore Christi.   RCh(I-267).
William of Ockham: Selections.   Ph(I-337).

Williams, Charles
All Hallows Eve.   MP12(I-122),   MP8(I-95),   MP4(I-23),
MWL4(23).
Descent into Hell.   MP12(III-1452),   MP8(II-1125),   MP4(I-218),
MWL4(218).

Williams, C. K.
Lies.   SCL12(VII-4301),   A70(184).
With Ignorance.   LA78(II-923).

Williams, Daniel Day
God's Grace and Man's Hope.   RCh(II-1108).

Williams, Emlyn
George.   SCL12(V-2875),   SCL7(III-1715),   A63(65).

Williams, Eric
Capitalism and Slavery.   HEur(II-720).

Williams, Francis
Socialist Britain: Its Background, Its Present, and an Estimate of Its
Future.   HEur(III-1519).

Williams, Joan
Morning and the Evening, The.   SCL12(VIII-5069),   SCL7(V-3077),
A62(209).

Williams, John
Augustus.   SCL12(I-455),   A73(21).

Williams, John A.
Captain Blackman.   SCL12(II-1076),   A73(65).
*Man Who Cried I Am, The.   SCL12(VII-4714),   SCLs(179).

Contours of American History, The.   HWor(II-667).
Williams, William Carlos
   Desert Music and Other Poems, The.   SCL12(III-1891),
   SCL7(II-1131),   A54(52).
   Farmers' Daughters, The.   SCL12(IV-2470),   SCL7(III-1474),
   A62(119).
   Imaginations.   SCL12(VI-3625),   A71(124).
   In the American Grain.   MP12(V-2856),   MP8(IV-2224),
   MP4(I-442),   MWL4(442).
   Paterson.   MP12(VIII-4519),   MP8(V-3521),   MP6(IV-2257),
   MPPo(212),   MP3(II-720),   MWL3(720).
   Paterson Five.   SCL12(IX-5766),   SCL7(V-3520),   A59(201).
   Pictures from Brueghel.   SCL12(IX-5848),   SCL7(V-3573),
   A63(179),   BMA(432).
   Poetry of Williams, The.   MP12(IX-5209),   MP8(VI-4155),
   MP4(II-1002),   MWL4(1002).
Williamson, Harold F. *and* Arnold R. Daum
   American Petroleum Industry: The Age of Illumination, 1859-1899, The.
   HAmer(II-915).
Williamson, Henry
   Salar the Salmon.   MP12(X-5773),   MP8(VII-4595),   MP4(II-1088),
   MWL4(1088).
   Tarka the Otter.   MP12(XI-6411),   MP8(VII-5104),   MP4(II-1203),
   MWL4(1203).
Williamson, Jack
   Humanoids and *"With Folded Hands," The.*   SF(II-981).
   Legion of Time, The.   SF(III-1178).
Williamson, James A.
   *Cabot Voyages and Bristol Discovery Under Henry VII, with the
   Cartography of the Voyages by R. A. Skelton, The.*   HAmer(I-26).
   *Short History of British Expansion: The Modern Empire and
   Commonwealth, A.*   HEur(III-1374).
Willoughby, William R.
   St. Lawrence Waterway: A Study in Politics and Diplomacy, The.
   HWor(II-786).
Wills, Garry
   Inventing America: Jefferson's Declaration of Independence.   LA79(I-322).
   Nixon Agonistes.   HAmer(III-1937).
Willson, D. Harris
   King James VI and I.   HEur(I-228).
Wilmerding, Lucius, Jr.
   Electoral College, The.   HAmer(I-459).
Wilmot, Chester
   Struggle for Europe, The.   Different analyses on this title appear in:
   HEur(III-1479; III-1493; III-1503),   HAmer(III-1722).

Wilson, Angus
 Anglo-Saxon Attitudes. SCL12(I-314), SCL7(I-184), A57(7).
 Death Dance. SCL12(III-1797), A70(98).
 Middle Age of Mrs. Eliot, The. SCL12(VIII-4971),
 SCL7(V-3023), A60(171).
 No Laughing Matter. SCL12(VIII-5380), SCL7(V-3283),
 A68(224).
 Old Men at the Zoo, The. SCL12(VIII-5517), SCL7(V-3373),
 A62(222).
 Strange Ride of Rudyard Kipling, His Life and Works, The.
 LA79(II-717).
Wilson, Arthur M.
 Diderot. SCL12(III-1951), A73(116).
 Diderot: The Testing Years, 1713-1759. HEur(I-429).
Wilson, Charles Marrow *and* W. Robert Nitske
 Rudolf Diesel: Pioneer of the Age of Power. HEur(II-1101).
Wilson, Colin
 Mind Parasites, The. SCL12(VIII-5008), SCL7(V-3039), A68(205).
 A different analysis on this title appears in: SF(III-1401).
 Outsider, The. SCL12(IX-5693), SCL7(V-3487), A57(206).
 Philosopher's Stone, The. SF(IV-1674).
Wilson, Edmund
 Axel's Castle. MP12(I-395), MP8(I-307), MP4(I-60),
 MWL4(60).
 Dead Sea Scrolls, 1947-1969, The. HWor(II-602).
 Letters on Literature and Politics, 1912-1972. LA78(II-522).
 Memoirs of Hecate County. SCL12(VII-4917), SCL7(V-2987),
 A60(162).
 Patriotic Gore. SCL12(IX-5778), SCL7(V-3523), A63(174),
 BMA(422).
 Prelude, A. SCL12(IX-6015), SCL7(V-3672), A68(251).
 Scrolls from the Dead Sea, The. SCL12(X-6667), SCL7(VI-4096),
 A55(220).
 Twenties, The. SCL12(XII-7826), A76(333).
 Upstate: Records and Recollections of Northern New York.
 SCL12(XII-7944), A72(335).
 Window on Russia, A. SCL12(XII-8315), A73(381).
Wilson, Edmund *and* Vladimir Nabokov
 *Nabokov-Wilson Letters: Correspondence Between Vladimir Nabokov and
 Edmund Wilson, 1940-1971, The*. LA80(II-564).
Wilson, Edward O.
 On Human Nature. LA79(II-506).
 Sociobiology: The New Synthesis. HWor(I-220).
Wilson, Erle
 Coorinna. SCL12(III-1576), SCL7(II-923), A54(40).

Wilson, Harriette
  Game of Hearts, The.   SCL12(IV-2840),   SCL7(III-1693),   A55(101).
Wilson, Henry S.
  Imperial Experience in Sub-Saharan Africa Since 1870, The.
  LA78(I-436).
Wilson, John Tuzo
  I.G.Y., the Year of the New Moons.   HWor(II-768).
Wilson, Lanford
  Hot l Baltimore, The.   SCL12(V-3534),   A74(200).
  5th of July.   LA80(I-320).
Wilson, Mitchell
  American Science and Invention, a Pictorial History.   HAmer(II-840).
Wilson, Monica *and* Leonard Thompson, *eds.*
  Oxford History of South Africa, The.   HWor(I-89).
Wilson, Robert Forrest
  *How American Went to War, Vol. VI: Demobilization: Our Industrial and
  Military Demobilization After the Armistice, 1918-1920.*
  HAmer(III-1481).
Wilson, Sloan
  Man in the Gray Flannel Suit, The.   SCL12(VII-4703),
  SCL7(IV-2854),   A55(150).
  What Shall We Wear to This Party?   LA77(II-901).
Wilson, William E.
  Angel and the Serpent: The Story of New Harmony.   HAmer(I-514).
Wilson, W. R.
  Execution of Jesus: A Judicial and Historical Investigation, The.
  HAnc(II-604).
Wiltse, Charles M.
  John C. Calhoun, Vol. I: Nationalist, 1782-1828.   HAmer(I-544).
  John C. Calhoun, Vol. II: Nullifer, 1829-1839.   HAmer(II-706).
Wimsatt, W. K.
  Day of the Leopards.   LA77(I-194).
Wind, Edgar
  Pagan Mysteries in the Renaissance.   HAnc(III-1768).
Windsor, Duke of
  King's Story, A.   HEur(III-1422).
Wingren, Gustaf
  Living Word, The.   RCh(II-1112).
Winslow, Ola E.
  Master Roger Williams.   HAmer(I-100).
Winston, Richard
  Thomas Becket.   SCL12(XI-7570),   SCL7(VII-4619),   A68(328). A
  different analysis on this title appears in: HAnc(III-1378).
Winton, Calhoun
  Captain Steele.   SCL12(II-1083),   SCL7(I-624),   A65(32).

Philippine Islands at the Century's Turn. HAmer(II-1293).
Wolfram von Eschenbach
    Parzival. MP12(VIII-4495), MPCE(III-1673), MP8(V-3503), MP6(IV-2250), MPPo(209), MPv3(405), MP2(II-795), MWL2(795).
Wolfson, Harry A.
    Philo. HAnc(II-613).
    Philosophy of the Church Fathers, The. HAnc(II-759).
Wolpert, Stanley
    New History of India, A. LA78(II-598).
    Nine Hours to Rama. SCL12(VIII-5355), SCL7(V-3267), A63(157).
Womack, John, Jr.
    Zapata and the Mexican Revolution. SCL12(XII-8500), A70(360).
Wongar, B.
    Track to Bralgu, The. LA79(II-768).
Wood, Bryce
    Making of the Good Neighbor Policy, The. HWor(I-264).
Woodbridge, Frederick James E.
    Nature and Mind. Ph(II-1021).
Woodham-Smith, Cecil
    Great Hunger, The. SCL12(V-3113), SCL7(III-1862), A64(115). A different analysis on this title appears in: HEur(II-761).
    Queen Victoria. SCL12(IX-6177), A73(300).
    Reason Why, The. SCL12(IX-6269), SCL7(VI-3840), A54(225).
Woods, John
    Striking the Earth. LA77(II-784).
Woodward, Bob *and* Carl Bernstein
    All the President's Men. SCL12(I-233), A75(15).
    Final Days, The. Different analyses on this title appear in: HWor(III-1134; III-1204).
Woodward, Bob *and* Scott Armstrong
    Brethren: Inside the Supreme Court, The. LA80(I-104).
Woodward, C. Vann
    Battle for Leyte Gulf, The. HAmer (III-1734).
    "Case of the Louisiana Traveler: Plessy *vs.* Ferguson, *The"* in John A. Garraty's *Quarrels That Have Shaped the Constitution.* HAmer(II-1266).
    Reunion and Reaction: The Compromise of 1877 and the End of Reconstruction. HAmer(II-1102).
Woodward, E. L.
    Three Studies in European Conservatism. HEur(II-771).
Woolf, Leonard
    Beginning Again. SCL12(I-616), SCL7(I-359), A65(8).
    Journey Not the Arrival Matters, The. SCL12(VI-3929), A71(156).
Woolf, Virginia

Plain Dealer, The. MP12(VIII-4743), MPCE(III-1766), MP8(VI-3697), MP6(V-2387), MPDr(640), MPv3(418), MP2(II-838), MWL2(838).

Wyckoff, Nicholas E.
Braintree Mission, The. SCL12(II-880), SCL7(I-513), A58(39).

Wycliffe, John
Trialogus. RCh(I-294).

Wyden, Peter
Bay of Pigs: The Untold Story. LA80(I-59).

Wylie, Elinor
Poetry of Elinor Wylie, The. MP12(IX-4925), MP8(VI-3871), MP4(II-798), MWL4(798).
Venetian Glass Nephew, The. MP12(XII-6887), MPCE(IV-2408), MP8(VIII-5454), MP6(VI-3292), MPAm(688), MPv4(566), MP2(II-1096), MWL2(1096).

Wylie, Philip
Disappearance, The. SF(II-543).
Gladiator. SF(II-888).

Wylie, Philip *and* Edwin Balmer
When Worlds Collide and *After Worlds Collide.* SF(V-2463).

Wynd, Oswald
Ginger Tree, The. LA78(I-349).

Wyndham, John
Day of the Triffids, The. SF(I-502).
Midwich Cuckoos, The. SF(III-1391).
Re-Birth. SF(IV-1755).

Wynne-Tyson, Esme *and* John D. Beresford
Riddle of the Tower, The. SF(IV-1780).

Wyss, Johann Rudolf
Swiss Family Robinson, The. MP12(XI-6363), MPCE(IV-2194), MP8(VII-5066), MP6(VI-3028), MPEur(731), MP1(II-943), MWL1(943).

Xenophon
Anabasis, The. MP12(I-196), MP8(I-156), MP6(I-92), MPNf(7), MP3(I-36), MWL3(36).
Cyropaedia. MP12(III-1267), MP8(II-979), MP4(I-174), MWL4(I-174).

Yadin, Yigael
"Finding Bar Kokhba's Despatches: The Exciting Story of an Archaeological Expedition Among the Dead Sea Caves," in *Illustrated London News.* HAnc(II-705).

Yancey, William L. *and* Lee Rainwater